GRAMMAR IN CONTEXT

SANDRA ELBAUM

SECOND EDITION

BOOK I

ITP

Heinle & Heinle Publishers
An International Thomson Publishing Company
Boston, Massachusetts, 02116, USA

The publication of *Grammar in Context,* Second Edition, was directed by members of the Newbury House Publishing Team at Heinle & Heinle:

Erik Gundersen, Editorial Director
John F. McHugh, Market Development Director
Kristin M. Thalheimer, Production Services Coordinator

Also participating in the publication of this program were:

Publisher: Stanley J. Galek
Director of Production: Elizabeth Holthaus
Project Manager/Desktop Pagination: Thompson Steele Production Services
Manufacturing Coordinator: Mary Beth Hennebury
Photo Coordinator: Philippe Heckly
Associate Editor: Ken Pratt
Interior Designer: Sally Steele
Illustrator: Jim Roldan
Photo/video Specialist: Jonathan Stark
Cover Designer: Gina Petti, Rotunda Design

Photo Credits
p. 1 © Henryk T. Kaiser/Photo Network; p. 7 © Werner J. Bertsch; p. 26 Henryk Kaiser/Leo de Wys Inc.; p. 45 © Daemmrich/The Image Works; p. 78 © Michael Newman/PhotoEdit; p. 105 © Melanie Carr/Zephyr Pictures; p. 122 © Paula Lerner/Woodfin Camp & Associates, Inc.; p. 144 Michael Malyszko/Leo de Wys Inc.; p. 172 © Pickerell/The Image Works; p. 193 © Archive Photos; p. 195L UPI/Bettmann; p. 195R AP/Wide World Photos; p. 206 UPI/Bettmann; p. 225 © Therese Frare/The Picture Cube, Inc.; p. 255 © Crews/The Image Works; p. 274 © Richard Hutchings/PhotoEdit; p. 282L Frank Siteman/© Stock Boston; p. 282R © Jean-Claude LeJeune/Stock Boston; p. 290 © Dion Ogust/The Image Works; p. 308 Dean Abramson/© Stock Boston; p. 325 © Claudia Dhimitri/The Picture Cube, Inc.

Heinle & Heinle Publishers is a division of International Thomson Publishing, Inc.

Manufactured in the United States of America

Library of Congress Cataloging-in-Publication Data

Elbaum, Sandra N.
       Grammar in context / Sandra Elbaum.
          p.   cm.
         ISBN 0-8384-4688-4 (bk. 1). —ISBN 0-8384-4689-2 (bk. 2). —ISBN
0-8384-6651-6 (bk. 3)
         1. English language—Grammar—Problems, exercises, etc.
       2. English language—Textbooks for foreign speakers. I. Title.
PE1112.E3641995
428.2'4—dc20

95-49062
CIP

ISBN 0-8384-4688-4

10 9 8 7 6 5 4 3 2 1

IN MEMORY
OF HERMAN ELBAUM

PREFACE

Grammar in Context, Book One is the first part of a three-part grammar series for adult students of English as a Second Language. This series of work-texts is designed for the high beginning to low advanced instructional levels.

As ESL teachers know, presenting English in a meaningful context allows for a better understanding of the grammar point. *Grammar in Context* is unique among grammar texts in its use of culturally rich, informative readings to present and illustrate the target grammar, and to stimulate interest in the topic.

Grammar in Context is organized as follows:

Lesson Focus The lessons begin with an overview and brief explanation of the grammar points covered. The Lesson Focus also includes sentences which illustrate the grammar point(s) being addressed.

Pre-Reading Questions These questions stimulate student interest in the topic of the reading which follows.

Introductory Readings A short reading illustrates each new grammar point in a natural, authentic context. These high-interest readings about cultur-ally rich topics engage the student's attention and help focus on the grammar points. The real-life subject matter provides practical information about American life and customs, stories about famous people and events, and con-temporary issues that are of concern to Americans as well as recently-arrived res-idents. These readings can be used as springboards for lively classroom discus-sions, as well as inspiration for out-of-class activities.

Since *Grammar in Context* is not a reader, the readings are written at a sim-ple, accessible level, for their primary goal is to exemplify the target grammar. The practical vocabulary and idioms that are needed to understand the passage are anticipated and glossed in footnotes or illustrations.

Grammar Boxes and Language Notes This book anticipates difficulties that most students have—for example, count and noncount nouns, contracted verb forms, too *much/many* versus *a lot of*, and question formation. Also, a great deal of attention is given to word order.

The grammar boxes use simple language in grammar explanations, illustrative example sentences, and charts with a clear graphic overview. Because *Grammar in Context* does not rely on a knowledge of linguistic jargon, fine points of grammar are often placed in a footnote so as not to overwhelm students who do not need so much detail.

The Language Notes provide the students with additional information on the functions of language, level of formality/informality, appropriate usage, spelling, and pronunciation. They often include information on the differences between American English and British English.

Exercises There is a great variety of exercise types. The change of pace from one exercise to another reduces boredom in the classroom and offers challenges to different types of language learners as well as language teachers. Exercises include traditional fill-ins, cloze tasks, pair work, editing exercises, and combination exercises which review old material in the context of the new or integrate several subskills from within the lesson. Many of the exercises allow students to personalize their remarks to reflect their own observations about American life, their opinions on cultural matters, and their feelings.

Expansion Activities These activities, grouped at the end of each lesson, allow students to use the grammar points covered in more communicative ways. Expansion Activities include pair work; group discussions; writing; poetry, proverbs, famous quotes and sayings; and outside activities. These activities give subjects for debate and discussion, topics for written reflection, and ideas for further research on the context of the lesson or on a related topic (including suggestions for interviewing Americans and bringing the findings back to share with the class). The poems, proverbs, famous quotes and sayings not only illustrate the grammar items, but also provide an opportunity for a rich cross-cultural interchange.

Because they are progressively more challenging, the Expansion Activities lead away from a mechanical manipulation of grammar toward situations in which students put their recently learned grammatical knowledge to immediate practical use.

The teacher may choose to have students do Expansion Activities after a related grammar point has been thoroughly studied, or may assign them after the lesson has been completed.

Editing Advice Potentially troublesome issues with the grammar points covered in the lesson are presented, showing students common errors, and ways to correct them.

Summary The end-of-lesson summary encapsulates all of the grammar presented in the chapter in a simple graphic format.

Test/Review Each lesson ends with a test/review section that allows both the teacher and the students to evaluate the mastery of concepts. Different formats—editing, fill-ins, and multiple choice questions—are used.

Appendices This book includes appendices that provide useful information in list or chart form. The appendices are cross-referenced throughout the text.

Differences Between the First and Second Editions

There is now a third book in the series. Previous users of this text should note that the new Book One is easier than the original. Users of the former Book One would choose either Book One of the new series for a high beginning class or Book Two of the new series for an intermediate class. The original Book Two corresponds more closely to Book Three of the new series.

In the first edition, Book Two continued where Book One ended. In the new series, grammar points overlap. Since students rarely master a point after only one presentation and practice, there is a repetition at the next level, as well as added complexity. All tenses covered in Book One are also in Book Two. Also included in Books One and Two are singular and plural, pronouns and possessive forms, modals, count and noncount nouns, and comparative and superlative adjectives and adverbs. Included in Books Two and Three are modals, adjective clauses, gerunds, infinitives, and time clauses.

There is a higher degree of contextualization in both the readings and the grammar exercises.

Pre-reading questions have been added to stimulate interest and discussion. New readings contain many topics of a contemporary nature—for example, self-help groups, job rankings and personal ads. Older readings have been updated and extended.

Many of the exercises and exercise types are completely new. Older exercises have been updated and revised. More interactive, task-based activities are included, some to be done in class, asking students to work with a partner or small group. Outside activities encourage students to talk with Americans, note their responses, and report them to the class.

There are more visual aids, illustrations, and charts to support the vocabulary in the readings, and the context of the exercises. Maps of the United States and references to states, major cities, and regions familiarize the students with names they will frequently hear.

Most lessons include editing advice and an error correction or editing exercise. In addtion, a new and comprehensive testing program has been added.

Overall, the new edition of *Grammar in Context* provides thorough coverage of the grammar, a variety of exercise types, and an anticipation of student problems, thereby freeing the teacher from excessive class preparation. By providing grammar practice in the context of relevant and stimulating ideas, the *Grammar in Context* series eases the transition to American life, both linguistically and culturally.

Acknowledgments

I would like to thank my editor at Heinle and Heinle, Erik Gundersen, for his enthusiasm about this new edition, and for his gentle but firm way of pushing me in the direction that I needed to go.

I would also like to show my appreciation to the following teachers who reviewed my books: Kevin McClure, ELS Language Center, San Francisco; Kathi Jordan, Contra Costa College; Laurie Moody, Passaic County CC; Sherry Trechter, George Mason University; Bettye Wheeler, El Paso Community College; Ethel Tiersky, Truman College; Colleen Weldele, Palomar College; Emily Strauss, De Anza College; Peggy Armstrong; Pat Ishill, Union County College; Tay Leslie, ELS Language Centers Central Office; Kiran Razzak, ELS Language Center @ Chapman University; Terry Pruett-Said, Kansas State University.

Thanks to Christine Meyers, Judi Peman, and Merle Weiss for their kindness and understanding in getting me through it all.

And last, but most certainly not least, many thanks to my students at Truman College. They have increased my understanding of my own language and taught me to see life from another point of view. By sharing their insights and life stories, they have enriched my life enormously.

I thought Russians were different from Americans and that was why life in Russia and America were so different. When I came to America, I gradually realized that any national character is nothing but an adaptive social behavior. The more I learned about America, the more I saw that there was no difference between Russians and Americans as individual human beings. I saw a familiar spectrum of personalities, intimate problems, emotions, complexes, virtues, and vices.

American social chemistry was based on the same periodic table as the Russian. Individual atoms of human nature were the same but Russian and American social molecules were arranged differently. The two cultures seemed to contrast as strongly as the lifestyles of birds and fish, although beautiful species could be found among both . . .

The chemistry of society is universal, and history is a record of most unexpected transformations.

(*from* Memoirs of 1984, *by Yuri Tarnopolsky, published by University Press of America, Maryland.*)

CONTENTS

LESSON ONE   1

Lesson Focus	*Be*—Overview	2
	Reading: The United States	2
1.1	Forms and Uses of *Be*	4
1.2	The Subject	5
	Reading: Postcard from Washington, D.C.	7
1.3	Contractions of *Be*	7
1.4	*Be* with Descriptions	9
1.5	*Be* with Nouns	11
1.6	*Be* with Location and Origin	15
1.7	*This, That, These, Those*	17
1.8	Negative Statements with *Be*	18

Expansion Activities	22
Summary of Lesson One	23
Lesson One Test/Review	24

LESSON TWO   26

Lesson Focus	Questions and Answers with *Be*	27
	Reading: Questions about the United States	27
2.1	*Be* in *Yes/No* Questions and Short Answers	28
2.2	Wh- Questions	32
2.3	Questions with *What*	34
2.4	Questions with *How*	36

Expansion Activities	39
Summary of Lesson Two	41
Lesson Two Test/Review	42

LESSON THREE   45

Lesson Focus	Simple Present Tense	46
	Reading: English Spelling	46
3.1	Simple Present Tense—Affirmative Statements	46
3.2	Spelling of the *-S* Form	48
3.3	Simple Present of *Be* and Other Verbs	51
3.4	Negative Statements with the Simple Present Tense	52

3.5   Negative Statements with the Simple Present of *Be* and Other Verbs   55

3.6   *Yes/No* Questions and Short Answers with the Simple Present Tense   57

3.7   Questions with *Be* and Other Verbs   60

3.8   *Or* Questions   63

3.9   *Wh-* Questions with the Simple Present Tense   64

3.10 *Wh-* Questions with *Be* and Other Verbs   69

Expansion Activities   72
Summary of Lesson Three   73
Lesson Three Test/Review   74

LESSON FOUR   78

Lesson Focus   Singular and Plural   79

Reading: Facts About Americans   79

4.1   Regular Plural Nouns   80

4.2   Irregular Plural Nouns   82

4.3   Using the Plural to Make a Generalization   83

Reading: Finding an Apartment   87

4.4   Using *There* + *Be*   88

4.5   Questions with *There*   90

Reading: Calling About an Apartment   96

4.6   Articles and Quantity Words   97

Expansion Activities   100
Summary of Lesson Four   102
Lesson Four Test/Review   103

LESSON FIVE   105

Lesson Focus   Frequency Words and Prepositions of Time   106

Reading: Three Special Days   106

5.1   Frequency Words with the Simple Present Tense   107

5.2   *Yes/No* Questions with Ever   110

5.3   Frequency Expressions and Questions with *How Often*   113

5.4   Prepositions of Time   116

Expansion Activities   117
Summary of Lesson Five   118
Lesson Five Test/Review   119

LESSON SIX   122

Lesson Focus   Possession; Object Pronouns   123
               Reading: Names   123
    6.1   Possessive Form of Nouns   124
    6.2   Possessive Adjectives   126
    6.3   Questions with *Whose*   127
    6.4   Possessive Pronouns   129
    6.5   The Subject and the Object   130
               Reading: More About Names   131
    6.6   Object Pronouns   132
    6.7   Questions About the Subject   137
Expansion Activities   139
Summary of Lesson Six   140
Lesson Six Test/Review   141

LESSON SEVEN   144

Lesson Focus   Present Continuous Tense   145
               Reading: Student Life   145
    7.1   Present Continuous Tense—Forms   146
    7.2   Spelling of the *-ing* Form   148
    7.3   Questions with the Present Continuous Tense   151
               Reading: Observations About Americans   155
    7.4   Contrast of Present Continuous and
          Simple Present   156
    7.5   Nonaction Verbs   160
Expansion Activities   165
Summary of Lesson Seven   167
Lesson Seven Test/Review   168

LESSON EIGHT   172

Lesson Focus   Future Tenses—*Will* and *Be Going To*   173
               Reading: Jobs of the Future   173
    8.1   Forms of *Will* and *Be Going To*   174
    8.2   Questions with *Be Going To* and *Will*   176
    8.3   Future Tense + Time/*If* Clause   178
    8.4   Review and Comparison of Tenses   184
Expansion Activities   187
Lesson Eight Test/Review   189

LESSON NINE   193

Lesson Focus	The Simple Past Tense	194
	Reading: The History of Aviation	194
9.1	Past Tense of *Be*	195
9.2	Questions with *Was/Were*	197
9.3	Simple Past Tense of Regular Verbs	199
	Reading: The Chicago Fire	200
9.4	Spelling and Pronunciation of the Past Tense of Regular Verbs	201
9.5	Simple Past Tense of Irregular Verbs	204
	Reading: John Lennon	206
9.6	Negative Forms of Past Tense Verbs	208
9.7	Questions with Past Tense Verbs	211

Expansion Activities   218
Summary of Lesson Nine   220
Lesson Nine Test/Review   221

LESSON TEN   225

Lesson Focus	Imperatives; Infinitives; Modals	226
	Reading: Change of Address	226
10.1	Using Imperatives	227
10.2	*Let's*	229
	Reading: Traffic Tickets	230
10.3	Verbs Followed by an Infinitive	231
10.4	*It* + *Be* + Adjective + Infinitive	234
10.5	*Be* + Adjective + Infinitive	235
10.6	Modals	236
	Reading: Driving Regulations	237
	Reading: Scene in a Bank	244
10.7	Using Modals for Polite Commands and Requests	244
10.8	Contrasting Modals and Related Words	246

Expansion Activities   248
Summary of Lesson Ten   250
Lesson Ten Test/Review   251

LESSON ELEVEN   255

Lesson Focus	Count and Noncount Nouns; Quantifiers	256
	Reading: A Healthy Diet	256
11.1	Noncount Nouns	257
11.2	Specific Quantities with Nouns	258
11.3	*A Lot of, Much, Many*	260
11.4	*A Few, A Little*	261
11.5	*Some, Any,* and *A*	262
11.6	*Too, Too Many, Too Much, A Lot Of*	267

Expansion Activities   269
Summary of Lesson Eleven   271
Lesson Eleven Test/Review   272

LESSON TWELVE   274

Lesson Focus	Adjectives; Noun Modifiers; Adverbs	275
	Reading: Christmas in the United States	275
12.1	Using Adjectives	276
12.2	Noun Modifiers	278
	Reading: Buying a Used Car	279
12.3	Adverbs of Manner	280
	Reading: The Aging of the American Population	282
12.4	Intensifiers—*Too* vs. *Very*	283
12.5	*Too* and *Enough*	284

Expansion Activities   286
Summary of Lesson Twelve   288
Lesson Twelve Test/Review   289

LESSON THIRTEEN   290

Lesson Focus	Comparatives and Superlatives	291
	Reading: Consumer Decisions	291
13.1	Comparative and Superlative Forms	292
13.2	Comparisons with Adjectives	294
13.3	Comparisons with Adverbs	296
13.4	Comparisons with Nouns	297
	Reading: Facts About America	298
13.5	Superlatives	299

Expansion Activities   302
Summary of Lesson Thirteen   305
Lesson Thirteen Test/Review   306

LESSON FOURTEEN   308

Lesson Focus   Auxiliary Verbs   309
               Reading: Football and Soccer   309
       14.1   Auxiliary Verbs with *Too* and *Either*   310
       14.2   Auxiliary Verbs in Tag Questions   314
       14.3   Answering a Tag Question   318
Expansion Activities   321
Summary of Lesson Fourteen   322
Lesson Fourteen Test/Review   323

LESSON FIFTEEN—VERB REVIEW   325

       15.1   Comparison of Tenses   326
       15.2   Statements and Questions   326
       15.3   Uses of Tenses   327
Expansion Activities   332

Appendix A—The Verb *GET*   335
Appendix B—*MAKE* and *DO*   337
Appendix C—Questions   339
Appendix D—Alphabetical List of Irregular Past Forms   341
Index   343

GRAMMAR
IN CONTEXT

New York City

LESSON ONE

GRAMMAR
Be—Affirmative and Negative
Statements

CONTEXT
The United States
Postcard from Washington, D.C.

LESSON FOCUS *Be*—Affirmative and Negative Statements

Be is an irregular verb. It has three forms in the present: *am, is, are.*

> Canada is north of the United States.
> Mexico isn't north of the United States.

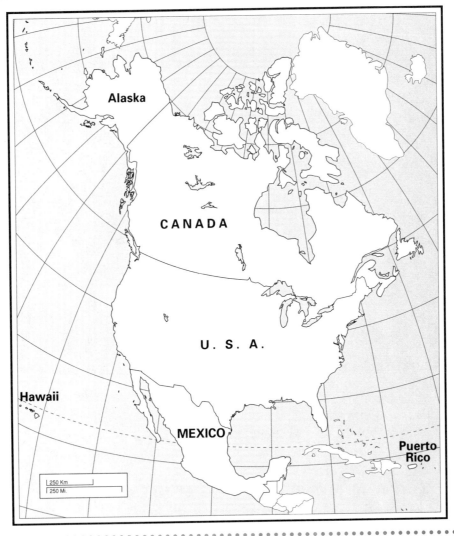

Before you read

1. Look at the map of North America. Find Alaska, Hawaii, and Puerto Rico.
2. Look at the map of the United States. Find the state where you live.

Read the following article. Pay special attention to the forms of the verb *be*.

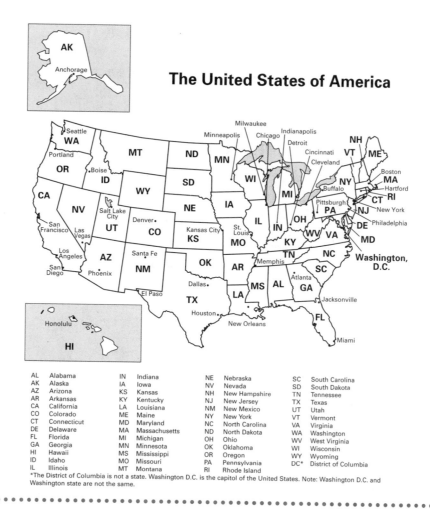

The United States of America

AL	Alabama	IN	Indiana
AK	Alaska	IA	Iowa
AZ	Arizona	KS	Kansas
AR	Arkansas	KY	Kentucky
CA	California	LA	Louisiana
CO	Colorado	ME	Maine
CT	Connecticut	MD	Maryland
DE	Delaware	MA	Massachusetts
FL	Florida	MI	Michigan
GA	Georgia	MN	Minnesota
HI	Hawaii	MS	Mississippi
ID	Idaho	MO	Missouri
IL	Illinois	MT	Montana

NE	Nebraska	SC	South Carolina
NV	Nevada	SD	South Dakota
NH	New Hampshire	TN	Tennessee
NJ	New Jersey	TX	Texas
NM	New Mexico	UT	Utah
NY	New York	VT	Vermont
NC	North Carolina	VA	Virginia
ND	North Dakota	WA	Washington
OH	Ohio	WV	West Virginia
OK	Oklahoma	WI	Wisconsin
OR	Oregon	WY	Wyoming
PA	Pennsylvania	DC*	District of Columbia
RI	Rhode Island		

*The District of Columbia is not a state. Washington D.C. is the capitol of the United States. Note: Washington D.C. and Washington state are not the same.

THE UNITED STATES

The United States **is** a big country. There **are** 50 states in the U.S. Forty-eight states **are** on the mainland. Two states **are** far from the mainland: Alaska and Hawaii. Alaska **is** the largest state. It **is** northwest of the Yukon province of Canada. Hawaii **is** in the Pacific Ocean. This state **is** a group of small islands.

Washington **is** a state. It **is** in the northwest. Washington, D.C. **is** not a state. It **is** a special government district. It **is** on the east coast. It **is** the capital of the U.S. The White House **is** in Washington, D.C. The White House **is** the home of the President.

Most states in the eastern part of the U.S. **are** small. Most states in the West and Southwest **are** large. The biggest city in the U.S. **is** New York. Other big cities **are** Los Angeles, Chicago, Philadelphia, and Boston.

Puerto Rico **is** not a state. It **is** a territory of the U.S. It **is** an island in the Caribbean Sea. Puerto Ricans **are** citizens of the U.S. The languages of Puerto Rico **are** Spanish and English.

1.1 Forms and Uses of *Be*

I	*am*	in New York now.
My father	*is*	in Boston.
He		a mechanic.
My sister		in Puerto Rico.
She		married.
Puerto Rico		an island.
It		small.
We	*are*	students.
You		a teacher.
Puerto Ricans		citizens of the U.S.
Chicago and Boston		cities.
They		big.

Language Notes

We use the verb *be* for the following:

Definition	Puerto Rico *is* an island.	*Description*	Puerto Rico *is* beautiful.
Location	Puerto Rico *is* in the Caribbean Sea.	*Place of origin*	I *am* from Puerto Rico.
		Age	I *am* 25 years old.

EXERCISE 1 Fill in each blank with *is, are,* or *am.*

> EXAMPLE: The U.S. ____*is*____ a big country.

1. Alaska _____ the largest state in the U.S.

2. Alaska and Hawaii _____ far from the mainland.

3. The states in the East _____ small.

4. Puerto Rico _____ an island.

5. Puerto Ricans _____ citizens of the U.S.

6. English _____ the language of the U.S.

7. We _____ in the U.S.

8. I _____ a student in the U.S.

1.2   The Subject

A sentence always has a subject. The subject is usually before the verb.

Subject	*Be*	Complement[1]
Puerto Ricans	are	American citizens.
Puerto Rico	is	an island.
Puerto Rico	is	very small.
Spanish	is	my native language.

The subject pronouns are *I, you, we, they, he, she, it.* The subject pronouns can take the place of the subject noun.

<u>Chicago</u> is very big.
↓
It is in Illinois.

<u>My sister</u> is married.
↓
She is very happy.

<u>My father</u> is at work.
↓
He is busy.

<u>My friend and I</u> are in California.
↓
We are in Los Angeles.[2]

<u>My cousins</u> are in Mexico.
↓
They are in Mexico City.

<u>China and Korea</u> are countries.
↓
They are in Asia.

NOTE: Use *they* for plural people or things.

Language Notes

1. Singular means one. Plural means more than one. A plural noun usually ends in -s.
SINGULAR: The language of the U.S. *is* English.
PLURAL: The language<u>s</u> of Puerto Rico *are* Spanish and English.

2. *You* can be singular or plural.

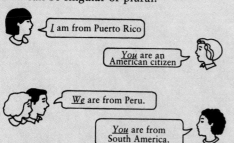

I am from Puerto Rico.

You are an American citizen.

We are from Peru.

You are from South America.

3. Do not use the subject noun and the subject pronoun together.

The President ~~he~~ is in Washington, D.C.
Washington, D.C. ~~it~~ is the capital of the U.S.

4. We use the subject *it* to talk about time and weather.

It is cold today.
It is six o'clock now.

5. The United States (the U.S.) is a singular noun.

The *U.S.* is a big country. *It* is in North America.

NOTE: Always use *the* before United States or U.S.

6. Use the correct word order. Put the subject at the beginning of the sentence.

Cuba is a small country. NOT: Is a small country Cuba.

---

[1]The complement finishes, or completes, the sentence.

[2]Americans often say *L.A.* for Los Angeles.

EXERCISE 2   Fill in each blank with a subject.

EXAMPLE: *Los Angeles*_____ is a big city.

1. _____ is in the East.

2. _____ are citizens of the U.S.

3. _____ is the home of the President.

4. _____ are the languages of Puerto Rico.

5. _____ is the language of the U.S.

6. _____ is a big country.

7. _____ am in the U.S.

8. _____ is warm in July.

EXERCISE 3   Find the mistakes with subjects and the verb *be*, and correct them. Not every sentence has a mistake. If the sentence is correct, write **C**.

EXAMPLES: My daughter ~~she~~ is in California.

California is a state.   *C*

1. Is a nice day.

2. California and Texas are states. Its big.

3. The President he is a busy man.

4. Is very big Texas.

5. You a very nice teacher.

6. You are very nice students.

7. Is warm in Los Angeles.

8. The teacher is from the U.S. You is from Mexico.

9. My cousins they very nice people.

10. We students. You are a teacher.

11. The U.S. are big.

12. Is hot today.

· ·

Before you read

1. Name a place in the U.S. that you want to visit.
2. What is the capital of your country? Is it an interesting city?

Read the following postcard. Pay special attention to the contractions.

POSTCARD FROM WASHINGTON, D.C.

Dear Cousins,

I'm on vacation now. I'm in Washington, D.C. It's the capital of the U.S. It's a beautiful city. This is a picture of the White House. The President lives there, but he's not in Washington now.

My daughter's with me. She's very happy here. We're both happy. The weather's nice now. It's sunny and warm. It's spring, and the trees are beautiful.

How are you? Are you on vacation now? How's the family? I hope you're all fine.

Good bye for now.

Love,

Maria

· ·

1.3   Contractions of *Be*

Full Forms	Contracted Forms
I am	I'm in Washington, D.C.
You are	You're in Mexico.
The President is	The President's in New York now.
He is	He's very busy.
My daughter is	My daughter's with me.
She is	She's very happy.
Washington is	Washington's the capital of the U.S.
It is	It's a beautiful city.
We are	We're very happy.
You are	You're at home.
They are	They're on vacation.

1. We usually say a contraction when we speak. We sometimes write a contraction in informal writing.

2. We can make a contraction with a subject pronoun and *am, is,* and *are.* To make a contraction, we take out the first letter of *am, is,* or *are* and put an apostrophe (') in place of the missing letter. We can also make a contraction with most nouns and *is.*

    New York*'s* big.

    It's in the East.

3. We don't make a contraction with *is* if the noun ends in these sounds: *s, z, sh,* or *ch.*

    The United State*s is* a big country.
    The White Hou*se is* in Washington, D.C.
    Fran*ce is* in Europe.
    New Orlean*s is* a beautiful city.
    Engli*sh is* the language of the U.S.
    Long Bea*ch is* in California.

4. We don't make a contraction with a plural noun and *are.*

    The trees *are* beautiful.

EXERCISE 4   Fill in each blank with the correct form of *be.* Make a contraction whenever possible. Not every sentence can have a contraction.

      EXAMPLE: The United States _____*is*_____ a big country. It ____*'s*____ between Canada and Mexico.

1. Canada and Mexico _____ countries. They _____ in North America.

2. Texas _____ a big state in the U.S. It _____ in the south.

3. The White House _____ in Washington, D.C. It _____ the home of the President. He _____ busy now.

4. Texas and Alaska _____ the biggest states in the U.S.

5. Los Angeles _____ a big city. It _____ in California.

6. Puerto Rico _____ an island. Puerto Ricans _____ American citizens.

7. English _____ the language of the U.S. Spanish and English

    _____ the languages of Puerto Rico. German _____ the

    language of Germany. French _____ the language of France.

8. My daughter and I _____ in Washington, D.C. We _____ happy here.

EXERCISE 5   Fill in each blank. Make a contraction whenever possible. Not every sentence can have a contraction.

I <u>'m</u> a student of English at City College. _____'m happy in the U.S.
                                                                        (1)

My teacher _____ American. His name _____ Charles Madison. Charles
                    (2)   (3)

_____ an experienced teacher. _____'s patient with foreign students.
   (4)   (5)

My class _____ big. _____'s interesting. All the students _____
                (6)   (7)   (8)

immigrants, but we _____ from many different countries. Five students
                           (9)

_____ from Asia. One woman _____ from Poland. _____ from Warsaw,
   (10)   (11)   (12)

the capital of Poland. Many students _____ from Mexico.
                                                (13)

We _____ ready to learn English, but English _____ a difficult
       (14)   (15)

language. I sometimes tell Charles, "You _____ a very kind teacher." Charles
                                                    (16)

says, "_____ all good students, and I _____ happy to teach you English."
           (17)   (18)

1.4 *Be* with Descriptions

Subject	*Be*	*(Very)*	Adjective	Complement
Washington, D.C.,	is		beautiful	in the spring.
My daughter and I	are		interested	in Washington, D.C.
I	am	very	tired.	

Language Notes

1. We use a form of *be* with words that describe the subject. We use adjectives to describe. Descriptive adjectives have no plural form.

New York is *big*. New York and Chicago are *big*.

2. Some words that end with *-ed* or *-ing* are adjectives: mar*ried*; tir*ed*; interest*ing*; bor*ing*.

I'm *worried* about you.
He's *tired*.
She's *bored*.

3. We use a form of *be* with a physical or mental condition.

He's *hungry*.
I'm *thirsty*.
We're *afraid*.
They're *angry*.

EXERCISE 6   Complete each statement with a subject and the correct form of *be*. Write a contraction wherever possible. Make a **true** statement. Use both singular and plural subjects.

> EXAMPLES: <u>*My parents are*</u> _____ **intelligent.**
>
>   <u>*The teacher's very*</u> _____ **patient.**
>
>   <u>*Many people in my country are*</u> **poor.**

1. _____ red.   7. _____ big.

2. _____ expensive.   8. _____ wonderful.

3. _____ cheap.   9. _____ difficult.

4. _____ new.   10. _____ beautiful.

5. _____ rich.   11. _____ famous.

6. _____ lazy.   12. _____ young.

EXERCISE 7   Work with a partner. Write a form of *be* and an adjective to describe each of the following nouns. Report one of your answers to the class.

> EXAMPLES: **This classroom** <u>*is clean.*</u>
>
>   **New York City** <u>*is interesting.*</u>

1. The teacher _____

2. This city _____

3. This college _____

4. Today's weather _____

5. Americans _____

6. American food _____

1.5 *Be* with Nouns

Singular Subject	*Be*	A(*n*)	(Adjective)	Singular Noun
Puerto Rico	is	an		island.
New York	is	a	big	city.

Plural Subject	*Be*		(Adjective)	Plural Noun
They	are			teachers.
We	are		foreign	students.

Language Notes

1. A noun is a person, place, or thing. We use *be* with nouns to classify or define the subject.

   Chicago is *a city*. Illinois is *a state*.

2. We use the article *a* or *an* before a singular noun. We use *an* before a vowel sound. The vowels are *a, e, i, o,* and *u*.

   Spanish is *a* language. Puerto Rico is *an* island.

3. We don't use the article *a* or *an* before a plural noun.

   Chicago and Los Angeles are *cities*.
   Illinois and California are *states*.

4. We can put an adjective before the noun.

   Chicago is a *big* city.

EXERCISE 8   Fill in each blank with a form of *be* and a definition of the subject.

EXAMPLES: California *is a state.*

           Puerto Rico *is an American territory.*

1. Canada _____

2. Alaska _____

3. Blue _____

4. Wednesday _____

5. Christmas _____

6. Saturday and Sunday _____

7. Christmas and Easter _____

    8. White and green _____

    9. January and February _____

   10. California and Illinois _____

EXERCISE 9   Add an adjective to each statement. Be careful to use *a* before a consonant and *an* before a vowel sound.

> EXAMPLE: July 4 is a holiday.
> July 4 is an important holiday.

  1. August is a month.
  2. Cuba is an island.
  3. Burger King is a restaurant.
  4. I'm a student.
  5. Los Angeles and Chicago are cities.
  6. John is a name.

EXERCISE 10   Fill in each blank with the correct form of *be*. Add *a* or *an* for singular nouns only. Don't use an article with plural nouns.

> EXAMPLES: The U.S. *is a* _____ big country.
>
> The U.S. and Canada ___*are*___ big countries.

  1. California _____ state.

  2. San Francisco and Los Angeles _____ cities in California.

  3. Chicago, Los Angeles, and New York _____ big cities.

  4. Puerto Rico _____ island.

  5. Puerto Rico _____ small island.

  6. Puerto Rico and Cuba _____ islands.

  7. Thanksgiving _____ American holiday.

  8. French and Spanish _____ languages.

  9. France and Spain _____ countries.

 10. Coke (Coca-Cola) _____ soft drink.[3]

 11. Coke and 7-Up _____ soft drinks.

---

[3]A *soft drink* has no alcohol.

EXERCISE 11   Work with a partner. Complete each statement. Give a subject and the correct form of *be*. Add *a* or *an* for singular nouns only. Don't use an article with plural nouns. Read some of your sentences to the class.

EXAMPLES: _Russia is a_ _____ big country.

   Canada and Brazil are _____ big countries.

1. _____ nice person.

2. _____ good student.

3. _____ big company.

4. _____ expensive item.

5. _____ nice season.

6. ————————————————American holiday.

7. _____ warm months.

8. _____ small countries.

9. _____ South American countries.

10. _____ big cities.

11. _____ famous people. (NOTE: *people* is plural.)

12. _____ American cars.

EXERCISE 12   Work with a partner. Fill in each blank to talk about your city. Make **true** statements. Remember to add *a* or *an* for a singular noun. Read some of your sentences to the class.

EXAMPLES: _Chez Paul is an_ _____ expensive restaurant in this city.

   January and February are _____ cold months in this city.

1. _____ interesting place.

2. _____ popular tourist attractions.

3. _____ big stores.

4. _____ beautiful month.

5. _____ beautiful park.

6. _____ inexpensive restaurant.

7. _____ wide streets.

8. _____ good college.

9. _____ dangerous area.

10. _____ tall buildings.

EXERCISE 13   Fill in each blank to make a **true** statement about your country. Put in a subject and a form of *be*. Find a partner from another country, if possible, and read your answers to each other. The teacher can fill in the blanks about the U.S. and read his or her answers to you.

EXAMPLES: *American music is* _____ popular in my country.

Politicians are _____ rich in my country.

1. _____ the biggest city in my country.

2. _____ rich.

3. _____ expensive.

4. _____ the language(s) of my country.

5. _____ necessary for a good life.

6. _____ a popular sport.

7. _____ hard to find.

8. _____ very common.

9. _____ a beautiful place.

EXERCISE 14   Work with a partner. Describe a famous person (an actor, a singer, an athlete, a politician). Report your description to the class.

EXAMPLE: **Michael Jordan is tall.**
He's a basketball player.
He's famous.
He's an African American.

1.6 *Be* with Location and Origin

Subject	*Be*	Preposition	Place
I	am	near	the door.
My book	is	on	the floor.
The teacher	is	from	Canada.

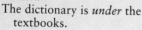
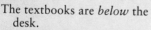
Language Notes

We use prepositions to show location and origin. Study the following prepositions and their meaning.

A. *On*

The book is *on* the table.
The cafeteria is *on* the first floor.

B. *At* shows general area or place:

The students are *at* school.
My brother is *at* home.

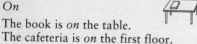

C. *In* shows that something is completely or partially enclosed:

Dallas is *in* Texas.
The wastebasket is *in* the corner.

D. *In front of*

The blackboard is *in front of* the students.

E. *In back of/behind*

The teacher is *in back of* the desk.
The blackboard is *behind* the teacher.

F. *Between*

The empty desk is *between* the two students.

G. *Above/over*

The exit sign is *over* the door.
The clock is *above* the exit sign.

H. *Under/below*

The textbooks are *below* the desk.
The dictionary is *under* the textbooks.

I. *Near/by/close to*

The sharpener is *by* the window.
The bulletin board is *near* the sharpener.
The desk is *close to* the window.

J. *Next to*

The light switch is *next to* the door.

K. *Far from*

Los Angeles is *far from* New York.

L. *Across from*

Room 202 is *across from* Room 203.

M. For addresses, we use *in* for a city, state, or country; *on* for a street; and *at* for an exact address.

The White House is *in* Washington, D.C.
It's *on* Pennsylvania Avenue.
It's *at* 1600 Pennsylvania Avenue.

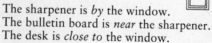

N. We say *in* the East and *on* the East Coast.

New York is *in* the East.
California is *on* the West Coast.

O. We use the present tense of *be* and the preposition *from* to talk about place of origin.

Mario is *from* Brazil. He's *from* Sao Paolo.
Sofia and Alex are *from* Russia. They're *from* Moscow.

NOTE: We can also use *come from* with place of origin. (See Lesson 2.)

I *come from* China. You *come from* Iran.

EXERCISE 15   Use a form of *be* and a preposition to tell the location of these things or people in your classroom or school.

> EXAMPLES: **My dictionary** *is in my backpack.*
>
> **The students** *are in front of the teacher.*

1. This classroom _____

2. The clock _____

3. The teacher _____

4. The wastebasket _____

5. The chalk _____

6. The light switch _____

7. The chalkboard _____

8. I _____

9. My books _____

10. The cafeteria _____

11. The school _____

12. The school library _____

13. We _____

EXERCISE 16   Talk to the student next to you. Find out where he or she is from. Find out the country, the city, the location, and other information. Report to the class.

> EXAMPLES: **Kim is from Korea. He's from Seoul. It's a big city. It's the capital of Korea. It's a beautiful city.**
>
> **Maria's from Spain. She's from Lugo. It's a small town. It's in the northwest corner of Spain. It's near Portugal.**

1.7   *This, That, These, Those*

We can use *this*, *that*, *these*, and *those* to identify objects or people.

	Near	Not Near/Far
Singular	This is my pen.	That is my pen.
Plural	These are my pens.	Those are my pens.

Language Notes

1. After we identify a noun, we can use subject pronouns.

   This is my school. *It's* on Wilson Avenue.
   Those are tall buildings. *They're* downtown.
   That's my cousin. *He's* a good student.

2. Only *that is* can form a contraction in writing: *that's*.

EXERCISE 17   Look at the pictures. Imagine that you are showing a new student the school cafeteria. Point out each part of the cafeteria. Use *this, that, these,* or *those,* and a form of *be* to complete each sentence.

EXAMPLES: *This is* _____ the school cafeteria.

   Those are _____ the clean dishes.

1. _____ the trays.

2. _____ today's special.

3. _____ the napkins.

4. _____ the forks, knives, and spoons.

5. _____ the cashier.

6. _____ the vending machines.

7. _____ the dollar-bill changer.

8. _____ the garbage cans.

9. _____ the no-smoking section.

10. _____ the teachers' section.

1.8 Negative Statements with *Be*

We put *not* after a form of *be* to make a negative statement.

Subject	*Be*	*Not*	Complement
I	am	not	married.
Peter	is	not	from Puerto Rico.
We	are	not	late.

Language Notes

We can make contractions for the negative. There is only one contraction for *I am not*. There are two negative contractions for all the other combinations:

I am not	I'm not	—
you are not	you're not	you aren't
he is not	he's not	he isn't
she is not	she's not	she isn't
it is not	it's not	it isn't
we are not	we're not	we aren't
they are not	they're not	they aren't
Tom is not	Tom's not	Tom isn't

EXERCISE 18 Fill in each blank with a pronoun and a negative verb. Practice using both negative forms.

EXAMPLE: **The classroom is clean and big.**

_It isn't_____ dirty. _It's not_____ small.

1. We're in the classroom.

   _____ in the library. _____ in the cafeteria.

2. Today's a weekday.

   _____ Saturday. _____ Sunday.

3. I'm a student. _____ a teacher.

4. The students are busy.

   _____ lazy. _____ tired.

5. You're on time.

   _____ early. _____ late.

6. My classmates and I are in an English class.

   _____ in the cafeteria. _____ in the library.

7. The teacher's in the classroom.

   _____ in the hall. _____ in the library.

8. This lesson is fine.

   _____ easy. _____ hard.

EXERCISE 19   Fill in each blank with a form of *be* to make a **true** affirmative statement or negative statement about the U.S.

EXAMPLES: The U.S. ___*is*___ in North America.

   The U.S. ___*isn't*___ a small country.

1. Washington, D.C. _____ a state.

2. Washington, D.C. _____ the capital of the U.S. It _____ on the East Coast.

3. The eastern states _____ big.

4. The western states _____ big.

5. The White House _____ in New York.

6. New York _____ a big city.

7. Alaska and Hawaii _____ on the mainland.

8. Puerto Rico _____ a state of the U.S.

9. Puerto Rico and Hawaii _____ islands.

10. Puerto Rico _____ cold in the winter.

EXERCISE 20 Fill in each blank with a form of *be* to make an affirmative statement or negative statement about you, your country, or your hometown. Find a partner from a different country, if possible. Compare answers with your partner.

EXAMPLES: I __'m_____ from the capital city.

          I __'m not__ from a small town.

1. I _____ happy with the government of my country.

2. I _____ from the capital city.

3. My city _____ noisy.

4. American cars _____ common in my country.

5. Teachers _____ strict.[4]

6. Most people _____ rich.

7. Gas _____ cheap.

8. Apartments _____ expensive.

9. Bicycles _____ popular.

10. Public transportation _____ good.

11. My country _____ rich.

12. A college education _____ free.

13. The president (prime minister) _____ a woman.

14. My hometown _____ in the mountains.

15. My hometown _____ very big.

16. It _____ very cold in the winter in my hometown.

[4]A *strict* teacher has a lot of rules.

EXERCISE 21   Use the words in parentheses ( ) to change each sentence into a negative statement.

> **EXAMPLE: My teacher is American. (Canadian)**
>
> _He isn't Canadian._ _____

1. Los Angeles and Chicago are cities. (states)

   _____

2. I'm from Mexico. (the U.S.)

   _____

3. The U.S. is a big country. (Cuba)

   _____

4. Alaska is a big state. (Maryland and Delaware)

   _____

5. We're in class now. (in the library)

   _____

6. You're an English teacher. (a math teacher)

   _____

EXERCISE 22   Fill in each blank with the affirmative or negative of the verb *be* to make a **true** paragraph.

> My name ___*is*___ _____. I _____ from an English-speaking country.
> EXAMPLE   YOUR NAME   (1)
>
> I _____ a student at City College. I _____ in my English class now. The
>   (2)   (3)
>
> class _____ big. My teacher _____ a man. He/She _____ very young.
>   (4)   (5)   (6)
>
> The classroom _____ very nice. It _____ clean. My classmates _____
>   (7)   (8)   (9)
>
> all very young students. We _____ all from the same country. We _____ all
>   (10)   (11)
>
> immigrants. I _____ happy to learn English. English _____ very easy for
>   (12)   (13)
>
> me. It _____ a useful language.
>   (14)

EXPANSION ACTIVITIES

WRITING   Write a paragraph using Exercise 22 as a model. For every negative statement that you write, add an affirmative statement. You may add other information, too.

EXAMPLE:

```
My name is Mohammad. I'm
not from an English-speaking country.
I'm from Iran. I'm not a
student at City College. I'm a
student at Roosevelt University.
I'm in an English class now....
```

PROVERBS   The following proverbs contain a form of the verb *be*. Discuss the meaning of each proverb. Do you have a similar proverb in your language?

Love is blind.

Beauty is only skin deep.

Silence is golden.

POEM   This is a common poem of love or friendship:

Roses are red.
Violets are blue.
Sugar is sweet
And so are you.

Work with a partner. Write your own poem. Read your poem to the class.

OUTSIDE ACTIVITIES   1. Do you have a postcard from your city? Bring it to the class and tell about the picture.

2. Buy a postcard of this city. Write to a friend, giving some information about the picture or about this city. Read your postcard to the class.

SUMMARY OF LESSON ONE

1. Uses of *Be*
   - With a description (adjective):
     > Chicago *is* big.
   - With a classification, definition, or identification of a noun:
     > This *is* Chicago. Chicago *is* a city. It*'s* a big city.
   - With a location:
     > Chicago *is* in Illinois.
   - With a place of origin:
     > The teacher *is* from Chicago.
   - With age:
     > I*'m* 25 (years old).
   - With physical or mental conditions:
     > He*'s* hungry.
     > I*'m* thirsty.
     > She*'s* worried.

2. Subject Pronouns
   > I   we   he/she
   > you   they   it

3. Contractions
   - Subject Pronouns with a Form of *Be:*
     > I*'m*   you*'re*   he*'s*
   - Subject Nouns with *Is:*
     > the teacher*'s*   Tom*'s*   Mary*'s*
   - A Form of *Be* with *Not:*
     > he isn*'t*   you aren*'t*   they aren*'t*

4. *This/That/These/Those*
   > *This* is an English book.
   > *These* are pencils.
   > *That*'s a pen.
   > *Those* are notebooks.

5. Articles *A/An*
   - Use *a/an* before a singular noun to give a definition.
     > Chicago is *a* big city. Puerto Rico is *an* island.
   - Don't use *a/an* before plural nouns.
     > Chicago and New York are big cities.

6. Word Order = Adjective + Noun
   > Chicago is a *big city.*
   > A *good teacher* is popular.

7. Word Order = Noun/Pronoun + *Be* + Adjective
   > Chicago is big.
   > They are happy.

LESSON ONE TEST/REVIEW

Part 1   Write a contraction of the words shown. If it's not possible to make a contraction, put an **X** in the blank.

EXAMPLE: **she is** ___*she's*___   EXAMPLE: **English is** ___*X*___

1. we are _____   5. this is _____

2. you are not _____   6. Los Angeles is _____

3. I am not _____   7. Mary is not _____

4. they are _____   8. he is not _____

Part 2   First read the affirmative statement. Then write a negative statement with the new subject given. Make any necessary changes.

EXAMPLE: **The U.S. is a big country. (Cuba)**

   Cuba isn't a big country. _____

1. Chicago is a big city. (Springfield)

   _____

2. Chicago and Springfield are in Illinois. (Miami)

   _____

3. January is a cold month. (July and August)

   _____

4. We're foreigners. (the teacher)

   _____

5. You're American. (I)

   _____

Part 3   Fill in each blank with the correct preposition.

EXAMPLE: The book is _____on_____ the table.   (Ex.)

1. The exit sign is _____ the door.

2. The wastebasket is _____ the corner.

3. The empty desk is _____ the two students.

4. The chalkboard is _____ the students.

5. The light switch is _____ the door.

6. The White House is _____ Washington, D.C.

7. The White House is _____ Pennsylvania Avenue.

8. The White House is _____ 1600 Pennsylvania Avenue.

(1)   (2)   (3)   (4)   (5)

Part 4   Find the mistakes in the following sentences and correct them. Not every sentence has a mistake. If the sentence is correct, write **C.**

EXAMPLES: My teacher ~~she~~ is very strict.

We aren't bored.   _c_

1. New York and Los Angeles are a big cities.

2. The teacher's not here today.

3. She is'nt in the library.

4. I amn't from Pakistan.

5. The students they are very smart.

6. Alaska and Texas are bigs states.

7. They're not hungry. They aren't thirsty.

8. It's warm today.

9. I'm from Ukraine. My wife from Poland.

10. Is very long this book.

Statue of Liberty

LESSON TWO

GRAMMAR
Questions and Answers
with *Be*

CONTEXT
Questions about the
United States

Lesson Focus   Questions and Answers with *Be*

To ask a question with the verb *be,* we put a form of *be* before the subject.

Is Canada a big country?   Where is Canada?

- -

R
E
A
D
I
N
G

Before you read:

1. What is the biggest city in your country? Is it the capital of your country?
2. Look at the map of the United States on page 3. Where are the small states? Where are the large states?

Read the following questions and answers about the United States. Pay special attention to questions with the verb *be.*

QUESTIONS ABOUT THE UNITED STATES

A. **What is the biggest state in the U.S.?**
B. Alaska is the biggest state in area. However, the population of Alaska is very small. The climate in the winter is very cold.

A. **Where is Alaska?**
B. It isn't near the rest of the states. It's northwest of Canada.

A. **Is Hawaii a state?**
B. Yes, it is.

A. **Where is it?**
B. It is in the Pacific Ocean. It is a group of islands. Hawaii is about 2,400 miles from the west coast of the United States.

A. **What are the biggest cities in the U.S.?**
B. The two biggest cities are Los Angeles and New York City.

A. **Is New York City near Los Angeles?**
B. No, it isn't. New York City is on the East Coast. Los Angeles is on the West Coast. New York City is about 2,800 miles from Los Angeles.

A. We say New York City, but we don't say Los Angeles City. **Why not?**
B. New York is the name of a city and also the name of the state.

A. **Where is Washington?**
B. Washington, D.C., is on the East Coast. It is the capital of the U.S. But there is another Washington. It is Washington state, in the northwest.

A. **Is Puerto Rico a state?**
B. No. It is a territory of the U.S. It is called an "Associated Free State."

A. **Are Puerto Ricans American citizens?**
B. Yes, they are.

2.1 *Be* in *Yes/No* Questions and Short Answers

To ask a *yes/no* question with the verb *be,* we put a form of *be* before the subject. We usually answer a *yes/no* question with a short answer. Compare statements, *yes/no* questions, and short answers with *be.*

Statement	*Yes/No* Question	Short Answer
I am a student.	Am I a good student?	Yes you are.
You are from France	Are you from Paris?	No, I'm not.
He is late.	Is he absent?	No, he isn't.
Kathy is an American.	Is Kathy from Texas?	No, she isn't.
She is married.	Is she happy?	Yes, she is.
It is cold today.	Is it windy?	Yes, it is.
We are here.	Are we late?	No, you aren't.
They are new students.	Are they confused?	Yes, they are.

Language Notes

1. A short answer contains a pronoun.

   Is the teacher here today? Yes, *she* is.
   Are your parents in the U.S.? No, *they* aren't.

2. We don't use a contraction for a short affirmative answer.

   Is Texas a big state? *Yes, it is.* NOT: Yes, it's.

3. We usually end a *yes/no* question with a rising intonation. Listen to your teacher pronounce the statements and questions in the above box.

EXERCISE 1   Look at the map of the U.S. on page 3 and answer these questions.

EXAMPLES: **Is Miami in Florida?**
           Yes, it is.

           Is New York City the capital of the U.S.?
           No, it isn't.

1. Is Texas a big state?
2. Are Puerto Ricans citizens of the U.S.?
3. Is New York City near the Atlantic Ocean?
4. Is Hawaii near Alaska?
5. Is Chicago the capital of Illinois?
6. Is Chicago a big city?
7. Is Puerto Rico an island?

EXERCISE 2   The teacher will ask you some questions. Answer with a **true** short answer. If the answer is negative, you may add more information.

EXAMPLE: **Is your book new?**
          Yes, it is.   OR   **No, it isn't. It's a used book.**

1. Is your country big?
2. Is Spanish your native language?
3. Is English hard for you?
4. Are you from South America?
5. Are you a citizen of the U.S.?
6. Are you married?
7. Are you a lazy student?

8. Is my pronunciation clear to you?
9. Am I a strict teacher?
10. Are all of you from the same country?
11. Are all of you the same age?
12. Are all of you immigrants?
13. Are you tired of my questions?

EXERCISE 3   Ask and answer questions about this school and class with the words given.

EXAMPLE: **school/big**
          A. Is this school big?
          B. Yes, it is.

1. this school/near your house
2. it/near public transportation
3. the cafeteria/on this floor
4. it/open now
5. the library/in this building
6. it/closed now
7. this course/free
8. the textbooks/free

9. the teacher/strict
10. this room/clean
11. it/big
12. the chalkboard/black
13. the chairs/in a circle
14. the windows/open
15. these questions/difficult

EXERCISE 4   Ask and answer questions with the words given. Use the correct form of *be*.

EXAMPLE: **you/a new student**
          A. Are you a new student?
          B. Yes, I am.   OR   **No, I'm not. This is my second semester here.**

1. you/from Asia
2. you/a new student
3. your country/big
4. you/from the capital city
5. you/an immigrant
6. you/happy in the U.S.

7. baseball/popular in your country
8. American cars/popular in your country
9. teachers/strict in your country
10. education/free in your country
11. medical care/free in your country

EXERCISE 5   Ask and answer questions about the U.S. with the words given. If no one knows the answer, ask the teacher.

>   EXAMPLE: movie stars/rich
>   A. Are American movie stars rich?
>   B. Yes, they are. They're very rich.

1. American teachers/rich
2. a high school education/free
3. a college education/free
4. medical care/free
5. doctors/rich
6. blue jeans/popular
7. houses/expensive

8. Americans/friendly
9. English/the official language
10. Japanese cars/popular
11. fast-food restaurants/popular
12. theater tickets/cheap
13. public schools/closed on Christmas

EXERCISE 6   Read each statement. Then write a *yes/no* question about the words in parentheses ( ). Write a short answer.

>   EXAMPLE: **The post office is closed on Sunday. (this school) (yes)**
>
>   *Is this school closed on Sunday? Yes, it is.*

1. July and August are warm months. (January and February) (no)

_____

2. New York is a big city. (Chicago) (yes)

_____

3. California is a big state. (Alaska and Texas) (yes)

_____

4. Coke and Pepsi are soft drinks. (Seven-Up) (yes)

_____

5. Washington, D.C., is in the East. (Washington state) (no)

_____

6. New York is on the East Coast. (California) (no)

_____

7. Chicago isn't a state. (Illinois) (yes)

_____

EXERCISE 7   By going around the room and asking questions, find one person for each of the items below, if possible. Write that person's name in the blank. Then tell the class about something you and another person have in common.

EXAMPLES: **Linda and I are both religious. She's a Catholic, and I'm a Hindu.**

Gabriel and I are both from Africa. He's from Ethiopia, and I'm from Sudan.

1. athletic _____

2. shy _____

3. from Asia _____

4. from Europe _____

5. from Africa _____

6. interested in politics _____

7. a grandparent _____

8. under 20 years old _____

9. lazy _____

10. religious _____

11. (a) Catholic _____

12. hungry _____

13. afraid to speak English _____

14. in love _____

15. an only child[1] _____

16. from the capital of your country _____

17. an American citizen _____

_____

[1]An *only child* has no sisters or brothers.

2.2   Wh- Questions

A *wh-* question asks for information. The question words are *who(m), when, why, what, which, where,* and *how.* To form a *wh-* question, we put the question word first, then a form of *be,* followed by the subject. Compare these statements and questions.

Wh-Word	*Be*	Subject	*Be*	Complement	Short Answer
		Los Angeles	is	a city.	
	Is	Los Angeles		on the West Coast?	Yes, it is.
Where	is	Los Angeles?			
		Sacramento	is	the capital of California.	
	Is	Sacramento		in Southern California?	No, it isn't.
Where	is	Sacramento?			

Study the different question words:

Question Word	Example
Who asks about a person.	Who's your teacher? My teacher is Ms. Weiss. OR Ms. Weiss is my teacher.

What asks about a thing.	What's your name?
	  Linda Tran.
	What's Christmas?
	  It's a holiday.

When asks about time.
  Use *in* for months and years.
  Use *on* for days and dates.
	When is Christmas?
	  It's in December.
	  It's on December 25.

Why asks for a reason.	Why's Mr. Park absent? He's absent because he's sick.

Where asks about a place.
  The answer contains a
  preposition. Review
  prepositions on page 15.
	Where's China?
	  It's in Asia.
	Where are your books?
	  They're on the floor.
	Where are you from?
	  I'm from Hong Kong.

1. In conversation, the *wh-* word + *is* can make a contraction.

   Where's your father?   *How's* the weather now?

   EXCEPTIONS:

   • We can't make a contraction for *which is.*
      Which is your book?

   • There is no contraction of a *wh-* word and *are.*
      Who are they?   Why are they late?

2. We usually end a *wh-* question with a falling intonation. Listen to your teacher say the questions in the box on page 32.

EXERCISE 8   Answer these questions.

   EXAMPLE: **Who's your best friend?**
   David Orlov is my best friend.

   1. Who's your adviser or counselor?
   2. Who's the leader of your country?
   3. Who's your best friend?
   4. Who's absent today? (The answer may be plural.)
   5. Who's near the door? (The answer may be plural.)

EXERCISE 9   Answer these questions.

   EXAMPLE: **Where's Poland?**
   It's in eastern Europe.

   1. Where's Beijing?
   2. Where's Bolivia?
   3. Where's Ethiopia?
   4. Where's Washington, D.C.?
   5. Where are Los Angeles and San Francisco?
   6. Where are Ecuador and Peru?
   7. Where are Nigeria and Cameroon?
   8. Where are Spain and Portugal?
   9. Where are Madrid and Barcelona?

EXERCISE 10   Answer these questions about this classroom and your school. Use the correct preposition. (Your school may not have all of these things.)

> EXAMPLE: **Where's the light switch?**
> **It's next to the door.**

1. Where's the library?
2. Where's the computer lab?
3. Where's the parking lot?
4. Where's the coffee machine?

5. Where's the men's restroom?
6. Where's the women's restroom?
7. Where's the water fountain?
8. Where's the teacher's office?

EXERCISE 11   Answer these questions. Use *in* for months and years. Use *on* for days and dates.

> EXAMPLE: **When's Christmas?**
> **In December**   OR   **On December 25.**

1. When's your birthday?
2. When's spring vacation?
3. When's Christmas vacation?

4. When's Labor Day in your country?
5. When's the last day of this semester?
6. When's spring break?

2.3   Questions with *What*

Study these common questions with *what.*

What (Noun)	*Be*	Complement	Answer
What	is	your name?	My name is Sandy.
What	is	your profession?	I'm a teacher.
What	is	your phone number?	555-3696
What	is	your favorite TV show?	*Sixty Minutes.*
What nationality	is	the teacher?	She's American.
What kind of class	is	this?	It's an English class.
What day	is	today?	It's Friday.
What time	is	it?	It's 4 o'clock.

1. Questions with *what* ask about things.
   What's your major? It's math.
   What's the capital of Texas? It's Austin.

2. Questions with *what* can ask for a definition.
   What is Puerto Rico? It's a territory of the U.S.
   What are Colorado and Nevada? They're states.

3. A noun can follow *what.*
   What color is the American flag? It's red, white, and blue.

EXERCISE 12   Answer these *what* questions.

     EXAMPLE: What's your major?
                 Biology.

1. What's your name?
2. What's your date of birth?
3. What time is it now in your hometown?
4. What nationality is the teacher?
5. What's the capital of your country?
6. What color is the flag of your country?
7. What's your major?
8. What's your favorite TV show?
9. What kind of words are *big, tall, old, new,* and *good*?
10. What kind of names are Charles, Elizabeth, and Andrew?

EXERCISE 13   Answer these *what* questions with a definition. Remember to use the article *a* or *an* before a singular noun.

     EXAMPLES: What's California?
                  It's a state.

                  What are English and French?
                  They're languages.

1. What's Los Angeles?
2. What's Christmas?
3. What's a rose?
4. What's a cat?
5. What are Burger King and McDonald's?
6. What are Spanish and Italian?
7. What are Spain and Italy?
8. What are football and baseball?

2.4   Questions with *How*
• • • • • • • • • •

Study these common questions with *how.*

How	Be	Subject	Answer
How	are	you?	I'm fine.
How	is	the weather?	It's sunny and warm.
How old	is	your brother?	He's 16 (years old).
How tall	are	you?	I'm 5 feet, 3 inches tall.
How big	is	your apartment?	It has four rooms.
How long[2]	is	this course?	It's 10 weeks long.
How long	is	the race?	It's 5 miles long.
How much	is	that painting?	It's $500.

1. *How* can ask about an opinion or a description.

   How's your life in the U.S.? It's difficult, but interesting.

2. *How* can ask about health.

   How's your mother today? She's sick.

3. *How* can ask about the weather.

   How's the weather today? It's cold and windy.

4. Another word[3] can immediately follow *how.*

   How much is that painting? It's $500.
   How tall is your father? He's 5 feet, 8 inches tall.

   NOTE: Americans use feet (') and inches (") for height: 5'8" tall. We say "five feet, eight inches tall" or simply "five-eight."

5. We use the verb *be* to talk about age. It is not usually polite to ask an adult American about his or her age.

EXERCISE 14   Write a question with *how.*

EXAMPLE: *How old is your son?* _____   **My son is 10 years old.**

1. _____   It's sunny and warm in Florida.

2. _____   My brother is 6 feet tall.

3. _____   My parents are fine, thank you.

4. _____   I'm 25 years old.

5. _____   That car is $10,000.

6. _____   This course is six weeks long.

---

[2]*How long* can ask about either time or distance.

[3]These words are adjectives or adverbs.

EXERCISE 15   Fill in each blank to make **true** statements about yourself. Then find a partner from a different country, if possible, and interview your partner by asking questions with the words in parentheses ( ).

> EXAMPLE: I'm from _____*Turkey.*_____ (Where)
>
> > A. I'm from Turkey. Where are you from?
> > B. I'm from Taiwan.

1. My name is _____. (What)

2. I'm from _____. (Where)

3. The president/prime minister of my country is _____. (Who)

4. The president/prime minister of my country is about _____ years old. (How)

5. The flag from my country is _____. (What color)

6. My country is in _____. (Where)
   (continent or region)

7. I'm _____ feet, _____ inches tall. (How tall)

8. I'm _____ today. (How)
   (fine/sick)

9. My birthday is in _____. (When)
   (month)

10. My favorite TV show is _____. (What)

11. My favorite color is _____. (What)

12. My address is _____. (What)

EXERCISE 16   Read each statement. Then write a *wh-* question with the words in parentheses ( ). Answer with a complete sentence.

> EXAMPLE: Miami is in Florida. (Los Angeles)
>
> > _____*Where is Los Angeles? It's in California.*_____

1. Paris is in France. (Washington, D.C.)

_____

2. The capital of England is London. (the capital of the U.S.)

_____

3. Miami and Orlando are in Florida. (Los Angeles and San Francisco)

_____

4. Alaska is a state. (Philadelphia)

_____

5. Canada is in North America. (Peru)

_____

6. Poland is in Europe. (Ethiopia and Nigeria)

_____

7. Korea and Japan are in Asia. (Colombia)

_____

8. The Mexican flag is green, white, and red. (what color/the American flag)

_____

9. Igor and Boris are Russian names. (what kind of names/James and William)

_____

EXERCISE 17   Read the following telephone conversation between Cindy (C) and
Maria (M). Fill in each blank.

C. Hello?

M. Hi, Cindy. This is Maria.

C. Hi, Maria. _How are you?_ _____

M. I'm fine. This is a long-distance call. I'm not home now.

C. Where _____?
                          (1)

M. I'm in Washington, D.C. I'm on vacation. I'm a tourist.

C. _____?
                  (2)

M. Oh, yes. It's very interesting. The White House and the government buildings are here.

C. How _____?
                              (3)

M. It's sunny and warm. The trees and flowers are beautiful now.

C. _____?
                         (4)

M. No, I'm not alone.

C. Who _____?
                              (5)

M. My daughter is with me.

C. _____?
                         (6)

M. She's 12. She's very interested in American government.

C. It's six-thirty in Los Angeles. _____ in
                                                           (7)
Washington.

M. It's nine-thirty.

C. I'm happy to hear from you. Thanks for calling.

M. I'll see you when I get home.

EXPANSION ACTIVITIES

OUTSIDE ACTIVITY
Interview an American (a neighbor, a co-worker, another student or a teacher at this college). Ask him or her these questions:

1. What city are you from?
2. Are your parents or grandparents from another country? Where are they from?
3. Is most of your family in this city?
4. Are you happy with this city? Why or why not?
5. What are your favorite places in this city?

Report this person's answers to the class.

EDITING ADVICE

1. Be careful to use the correct word order.

   New York is very big.

   ~~Is very big New York.~~

   is he
   Where he ~~is~~ from?

2. Use *be* before the complement.

   is
   He ∧ angry.

   am   *old*
   I ~~have~~ 25 years ∧.

   is
   She ~~has~~ hungry.

3. Use *it* before *is* to introduce time or weather.

   It's
   ~~Is~~ ten o'clock.

   It's
   ~~Is~~ very hot today.

4. Don't confuse *your* and *you're*.

   You're
   ~~Your~~ a nice person.

5. Don't confuse *this* and *these*.

   This
   ~~These~~ is my coat.

   These
   ~~This~~ are my shoes.

6. Use an apostrophe ('), not a comma (,) for a contraction. Put the apostrophe in place of the missing letter.

   He's
   ~~He,s~~ late.

   isn't
   She ~~is,nt~~ here today.

7. Use the article *a* before a singular noun.

   a
   New York is ∧ big city.

8. Don't use the article *a* before a plural noun.

   New York and Los Angeles are ~~a~~ big cities.

9. Don't put the article *a* before an adjective with no noun.

   New York is ~~a~~ big.

10. Don't make a contraction after *s, z, sh,* or *ch* sounds.

    Los Angeles is
    ~~Los Angeles's~~ a big city.

11. Don't make an adjective plural.

    Chicago and Boston are big~~s~~.

12. For age, use a number only or number + *years old*.

    old
    He's 12 years ∧.   or   *He's 12.*

13. Don't use a contraction for a short *yes* answer.

    I am.
    Are you from Mexico? Yes, ~~I'm~~.

SUMMARY OF LESSON TWO

1. Statements and Questions with *Be:*

Affirmative	California *is* a state.
Negative	Los Angeles *isn't* a state.
Yes/No Question	*Is* Los Angeles in California?
Short Answer	Yes, it *is*.
Wh- Question	Where *is* Chicago?
Long Answer	It *is* in Illinois.

2. Contractions
   - Pronoun + *Am, Is, Are* (except in a short *yes* answer)

     I'm   she's   we're
   - *Is, Are* + *Not*

     isn't   aren't
   - Question Word + *Is* (except *which is*)

     who's   what's   where's

3. Word Order

   Compare statements and questions:

Wh-Word	*Be*	Subject	*Be*	Complement	Answer
		Boston	is	a big city.	
	Is	Boston		in Maryland?	No, it isn't.
Where	is	Boston?			
		You	are	from Asia?	
	Are	you		from China?	Yes, I am.
What city	are	you	from?		

4. Common Questions with *Be*
   - What's your name? My name is Daniel.
   - What time is it? It's six-thirty.
   - What color is the flag? It's red, white, and blue.

   - What kind of class is this? It's an English class.
   - What's this? It's a pencil sharpener.
   - What's Lisbon? It's a city.

pencil sharpener

   - How are you? I'm fine.
   - How old are you? I'm 24 OR I'm 24 years old.
   - How tall are you? I'm 5'6" tall OR I'm five-six.
   - Where are you from? I'm from Guatemala.

LESSON TWO TEST/REVIEW

Part 1   Find the mistakes and correct them.

> EXAMPLE: A. Where ~~you are~~ *are you* from?
>   B. I'm from Mexico.

A. Are you happy in the U.S.?

B. Yes, I'm. The U.S. is great country!

A. Are you from a big city?

B. Yes. I'm from Mexico City. It's a city very big. These city is a big and beautiful too. But is cold in the winter.

A. Is from Mexico your roommate too?

B. No, he from Taiwan. My roommate is'nt happy. He,s homesick.

A. Why he's homesick?

B. His parents is in Taiwan. He's alone here.

A. How is he old?

B. He's very young. He's only 17 years.

Part 2   Read the conversation between two students, Sofia (S) and Danuta (D). They are talking about their classes and teachers. Fill in the blanks.

D. Hi, Sofia. How's your English class?

S. Hi, Danuta. It 's____ wonderful. I _____ very happy with it.
                                              (1)

D. _____'m in level 3. What level _____ in?
              (2)   (3)

S. I'_____ in level 2.
              (4)

D. My English teacher _____ Ms. Kathy James. _____ a
                                    (5)   (6)

   very good teacher. Who _____?
                                 (7)

S. Mr. Bob Kane is my English teacher. _____ very good, too.
(8)

D. _____ an old man?
(9)

S. No, he _____. He's _____ young man. He
(10)   (11)

_____ about twenty-five years _____. How
(12)   (13)

_____ ?
(14)

D. Ms. James _____ about fifty years old.
(15)

S. How _____ ?
(16)

D. She's about five feet, six inches tall.

S. Is she American?

D. Yes, she _____. She's from New York.
(17)

S. _____ ?
(18)

D. Yes. My class is very big. The students _____ from many
(19)

countries. Ten students _____ from Asia, six students
(20)

_____ from Europe, one student _____ from
(21)   (22)

Africa, and five are _____ Central America. Is your class big?
(23)

S. No, it _____.
(24)

D. Where _____ ?
(25)

S. The students _____ all from the same country. We
(26)

_____ from Russia.
(27)

D. _____ Russian?
     (28)

S. No. Mr. Kane isn't Russian. He's from Canada, but he's _____
                                                                  (29)

American citizen now.

D. _____?
     (30)

S. No. That's not Mr. Kane. That _____ my husband. I
                                    (31)

_____ late! See you later.
     (32)

LESSON THREE

GRAMMAR
Simple Present Tense

CONTEXT
English Spelling

 LESSON FOCUS   Simple Present Tense

We use the simple present tense to talk about general truths and regular activities (habits).

Students have difficulty with English spelling.   We often use our dictionaries.

· ·

R
E
A
D
I
N
G

Before you read:

1. Is spelling easy in your language?
2. Name some words that are hard to spell in English.

Read the following article. Pay special attention to simple present tense verbs.

ENGLISH SPELLING

The English language **has** a difficult spelling system. Students of English as a second language often **complain** about English spelling. One vowel often **has** several pronunciations. For example, the "ou" in the following three words is different: "out," "thought," "through."

Silent letters also **cause** problems. In the word "through," the "gh" is silent. However, in the word "enough," we **pronounce** "gh" like "f." Many people **think** that this **doesn't make** sense.

Some words **sound** the same, but they **have** different spelling and meaning. For example, "know" and "no," "meat" and "meet," "ate" and "eight."

Why **does** English **have** such a difficult system? The answer is simple: We **pronounce** in modern English, but we **continue** to spell in older English.

Even Americans **have** difficulty with spelling. We often **hear** Americans say, "How **do** you **spell** 'receive'?" or "**Does** 'occasion' **have** one **s** and two **c**'s or double **s** and one **c**?" Americans often **need** to use a dictionary to check their spelling.

· ·

3.1   Simple Present Tense—Affirmative Statements

We use the base form when the subject is *I, you, we, they,* or a plural noun.

Subject	Base Form	Complement
I		
You		
We		
They	need	water.
Animals		
Trees		

We use the _-s_ form when the subject is _he, she, it,_ or a singular noun.

Subject	_-S_ Form	Complement
He She It A plant A person	needs	water.

Language Notes

1. We use the _-s_ form with _everyone, everybody, everything, no one, nobody,_ and _nothing._

   Everyone _needs_ water.
   Nobody _knows_ the answer.

2. Three verbs have an irregular _-s_ form:

have—has	I _have_ an American car. She _has_ a Japanese car.
go—goes	I _go_ to a city college. He _goes_ to a state university.
do—does	I _do_ exercises in the morning. She _does_ exercises in the afternoon.

3. We use the simple present tense in the following cases:

   - With general truths, to show that something is consistently true.

     English _has_ a difficult spelling system.
     We _pronounce_ in modern English, but we _spell_ in older English.

   - To show regular activity (a habit) or repeated action.

     I sometimes _use_ my dictionary.
     People often _complain_ about English spelling.

   - To show a place of origin.

     Many English words _come from_ French.
     I _come from_ Hungary.

   NOTE: We can also use _be from_: I'm _from_ Hungary.

EXERCISE I   Fill in each blank with the correct form of the verb.

EXAMPLE: **English** _____ _has_ _____ **a difficult spelling system.**
                            (have/has)

1. "Knife" _____ a silent "k."
          (have/has)

2. Americans _____ difficulty with spelling.
             (have/has)

3. Some words _____ hard to spell.
              (is/are)

4. We _____ one way, but we spell another way.
      (pronounce/ pronounces)

5. A dictionary _____ with spelling.
                  (help/helps)

6. The teacher _____ our spelling.
                  (correct/corrects)

7. A dictionary _____ spelling and meaning.
                  (show/shows)

8. Everybody _____ about English spelling.
            (complain/complains)

3.2   Spelling of the -S Form

The chart below shows the spelling of the -s form. Fill in the last examples.

Rule	Base Form	-S Form
Add s to most verbs to make the -s form.	hope	hopes
	eat	eats
	run	_runs_
	live	_____
When the base form ends in s, z, sh, ch, or x, add es and pronounce an extra syllable /Iz/.	miss	misses
	buzz	buzzes
	wash	_____
	catch	_____
	tax	_____
When the base form ends in a consonant + y, change the y to i and add es.	carry	carries
	worry	worries
	study	_____
	hurry	_____
When the base form ends in a vowel + y, do not change the y.	pay	pays
	obey	obeys
	play	_____
	enjoy	_____

1. We pronounce /s/ if the verb ends in a voice-less sound: /p, t, k, f/. Listen to your teacher pronounce these examples.

hope–hopes   pick–picks
eat–eats   laugh–laughs

2. We pronounce /z/ if the verb ends in a voiced sound. Listen to your teacher pronounce these examples.

live–lives   run–runs
grab–grabs   borrow–borrows
read–reads   sing–sings

3. When the base form ends in *s, z, sh, ch, x, ge, ce,* or *se,* we pronounce an extra syllable /Iz/. Listen to your teacher pronounce these examples.

miss–misses   watch–watches
buzz–buzzes   fix–fixes
wash–washes   dance–dances
change–changes   use–uses

4. These verbs have a change in the vowel sound. Listen to your teacher pronounce these examples.

do /du/–does /dʌz/
say /sei/–says /sɛz/

EXERCISE 2   Write the *-s* form of the following verbs. Say each word out loud.

EXAMPLES: **eat** *eats*

            study *studies*

            watch *watches*

1. try _____

2. play _____

3. have _____

4. go _____

5. worry _____

6. finish _____

7. do _____

8. push _____

9. enjoy _____

10. think _____

11. say _____

12. change _____

13. brush _____

14. obey _____

15. reach _____

16. fix _____

17. work _____

18. raise _____

19. charge _____

20. see _____

EXERCISE 3   Fill in each blank with the -s form of the verb in parentheses ( ). Pay attention to the spelling rules. Then pronounce each sentence.

> EXAMPLE: A teacher _____*tries*_____ to help students learn.
> (try)

1. A pilot _____ an airplane.
   (fly)

2. A dishwasher _____ dishes.
   (wash)

3. A babysitter _____ children.
   (watch)

4. A soldier _____ an officer.
   (obey)

5. A citizen _____ taxes.
   (pay)

6. A mechanic _____ machines.
   (fix)

7. A student _____.
   (study)

8. A student _____ homework.
   (do)

9. A homemaker _____ a home.
   (manage)

10. A secretary _____ a word processor.
    (use)

11. A teacher _____ students.
    (teach)

EXERCISE 4   Find a partner. Tell him or her about your profession or future profession. Tell what someone in this profession does.

> EXAMPLE: I'm a car mechanic. A mechanic tries to find the problem in a car. Then he or she fixes the problem. A mechanic also changes parts, such as tires, oil, and brakes. A mechanic charges for his or her services by the hour.

3.3   Simple Present of *Be* and Other Verbs

Compare *be* and other verbs in affirmative statements:

I'm a student.	You're right.	We're immigrants.
I speak English.	You know the answer.	We come from Laos.
They're kind.	The teacher's American.	He's late.
They help people.	She teaches grammar.	He works hard.

Avoid making these mistakes with the simple present tense.

Wrong: I'm work hard   Wrong: He's comes from Italy.
Wrong: I working hard.   Right: He comes from Italy.
Right: I work hard.   Right: He's from Italy.

EXERCISE 5   A student is comparing himself to his friend. Fill in each blank with the correct form of the underlined verb.

EXAMPLES: My friend and I are very different. I <u>get</u> up at 7 o'clock.

He _____*gets*_____ up at 10.

I<u>'m</u> a good student. He ___*'s*_____ a lazy student.

1. I <u>study</u> every day. He _____ only before a test.

2. I always <u>get</u> A's on my tests. He _____ C's.

3. I <u>have</u> a scholarship. He _____ a government loan.

4. I<u>'m</u> a good student. He _____ an average student.

5. He <u>lives</u> in a dormitory. I _____ in an apartment.

6. He<u>'s</u> from Japan. I _____ from the Philippines.

7. He <u>studies</u> with the radio on. I _____ in a quiet room.

8. He <u>watches</u> a lot of TV. I _____ TV only when I have free time.

3.4 Negative Statements with the Simple Present Tense

We use the base form of the verb for all negative statements.

| I You We They The boys | work. don't work. | He She It My father The telephone | works. doesn't work. |

Language Notes

1. We use *don't* (*do not*) + a base form when the subject is *I, you, we, they,* or a plural noun.

2. We use *doesn't* (*does not*) + a base form when the subject is *he, she, it,* or a singular noun.

3. Compare the affirmative and negative statements below:

   We *say* the "b" in "lumber."
   We *don't say* the "b" in "plumber."

   She *writes* English well.
   She *doesn't write* Spanish well.

4. In American English and British English, the negative of the verb *have* is different. Compare:

   AMERICAN: He doesn't have a dictionary.
   BRITISH: He hasn't a dictionary. (formal)
              OR He hasn't got a dictionary.
              (informal)

EXERCISE 6   Tell if this school has or doesn't have the following.

EXAMPLES: **ESL courses**
             This school has ESL courses.

             classes for children
             It doesn't have classes for children.

1. a library
2. a cafeteria
3. copy machines
4. a parking lot

5. a swimming pool
6. a gym
7. a student newspaper
8. a theater

9. dormitories
10. classes for children
11. _____ [1]
12. _____

---

[1]Where you see a blank space in this book, you can add your own item to the list.

EXERCISE 7   Make an affirmative statement or a negative statement with the words given to state facts about the teacher.

> EXAMPLE: **speak Arabic**
> **The teacher speaks Arabic.**
> OR
> **The teacher doesn't speak Arabic.**

1. talk fast
2. speak English well
3. speak my language
4. give a lot of homework
5. give tests
6. pronounce my name correctly
7. wear glasses
8. wear jeans to class
9. _____
10. _____

EXERCISE 8   Fill in each blank with the negative form of the underlined verb.

> EXAMPLES: **We <u>study</u> English spelling.**
>
> **We** _don't study_ **the history of English.**
>
> **The teacher <u>speaks</u> English in class.**
>
> **He/She** _doesn't speak_ **another language in class.**

1. Americans <u>speak</u> English.

   The people in China _____ English.

2. English <u>uses</u> the Roman alphabet.

   Chinese _____ the Roman alphabet.

3. Spanish <u>has</u> a good spelling system.

   English and French _____ a good spelling system.

4. The word "know" <u>has</u> a silent "k."

   The word "keep" _____ a silent "k."

5. "Know" and "no" <u>sound</u> the same.

   "Know" and "now" _____ the same.

6. We <u>have</u> trouble with English pronunciation.

   The teacher _____ trouble with English pronunciation.

7. We <u>pronounce</u> the "t" in mister."

     We _____ the "t" in "listen."

8. The teacher <u>teaches</u> grammar and pronunciation.

     The teacher _____ the history of the English language.

9. I <u>need</u> a grammar book in this course.

     I _____ a history book.

10. We <u>study</u> American English.

     We _____ British English.

EXERCISE 9   Check (✓) the items that describe you and what you do. Work with a partner. Find out what you and your partner have or don't have in common. Report some of your differences to the class.

     EXAMPLES: __✓__ have children

                  I have two children. Ly doesn't have children.

                  __✓__ like cold weather

                  Ly doesn't like cold weather. He comes from Vietnam.
                  I like cold weather. I come from Moscow.

1. _____ speak Chinese   7. _____ smoke

2. _____ live alone   8. _____ own a car

3. _____ live near school   9. _____ like coffee

4. _____ walk to school   10. _____ like cold weather

5. _____ speak Spanish   11. _____ _____

6. _____ write with my left hand   12. _____ _____

3.5 **Negative Statements with the Simple Present of *Be* and Other Verbs**
• • • • • • • • • • • •

Compare *be* and other verbs in the negative.

I'm not from Mexico.	They're not sure.
I don't speak Spanish.	They don't know the answer.
You aren't sick.	We aren't confused.
You don't need a doctor.	We don't need help.
She isn't hungry.	He's not cold.
She doesn't want dinner.	He doesn't want a sweater.

EXERCISE 10   Check (✓) the items that describe you. Work with a partner. Find out what you and your partner have or don't have in common. Report some of your differences to the class.

EXAMPLES: __✓__ be an immigrant
            **I'm an immigrant. Margarita comes from Puerto Rico.
            She isn't an immigrant. She's a citizen of the U.S.**

            _____ have a computer
            I don't have a computer. Margarita has a computer.

1. _____ be married

2. _____ have children/a child

3. _____ have a computer

4. _____ be an American citizen

5. _____ like this city

6. _____ have a job

7. _____ be a full-time student

8. _____ have a pet[2]

9. _____ be an immigrant

10. _____ be unhappy in the U.S.

11. _____ _____

12. _____ _____

---

[2]A *pet* is an animal that lives in someone's house. Dogs and cats are common pets.

EXERCISE 11   Read each statement. Then make a negative statement with the words in parentheses ( ).

EXAMPLES: English is a European language. (Korean)

Korean isn't a European language.

I speak my language fluently. (English)

I don't speak English fluently.

1. English has a difficult spelling system. (Spanish)

   _____

2. "Ate" and "eight" sound the same. ("hate" and "height")

   _____

3. Spanish is a Romance[3] language. (English)

   _____

4. Colombians speak Spanish. (Brazilians)

   _____

5. Colombia is in South America. (Mexico)

   _____

6. A, E, I, O, and U are vowels. (B, C, D, F, and G)

   _____

7. We pronounce the "b" in "combine." (the "b" in "comb")

   _____

8. I speak English in class. (my native language)

   _____

9. I'm from _____. (the U.S.)
           (your country)

   _____

[3]A *Romance* language comes from Latin. Spanish, Italian, and French are Romance languages.

3.6 ••••••••• *Yes/No* **Questions and Short Answers with the Simple Present Tense**

Yes/no questions in the simple present tense are formed with *do/does.* We use the base form for all *yes/no* questions.

Do/Does	Subject	Verb (Base Form)
Do	I you we they the boys	work?
Does	he she it the phone everyone	

Language Notes

1. We usually answer a *yes/no* question with a short answer.

Short Answer:

YES, + PRONOUN SUBJECT + DO / DOES.

NO, + PRONOUN SUBJECT + DON'T / DOESN'T.

Do Americans speak English? Yes, they do.
Do you speak Polish? No, I don't.
Does the school have a library? Yes, it does.
Does the teacher speak your language? No, she doesn't.

2. Compare affirmative statements, questions, and short answers.

English *has* a difficult spelling system.
Does Spanish *have*[4] a difficult spelling system? No, it doesn't.

You *use* a textbook in class.
Do you *use* a dictionary in class? Yes, we do.

I *speak* my native language well.
Do I *speak* English well? Yes, you do.

The teacher *speaks* English well.
Does the teacher *speak* your language? No, she doesn't.

---

[4]AMERICAN: Does he have a car?

BRITISH: Has he a car?/Has he got a car?

EXERCISE 13   Ask your teacher a question with "Do you . . .?" and the words given. Your teacher will respond with a short answer.

> EXAMPLE: drive to school
>   A. Do you drive to school?
>   B. Yes, I do.   OR   No, I don't.

1. like your job
2. teach in the summer
3. have another job
4. speak another language
5. teach English to Americans
6. know my language
7. like to read students' homework
8. live far from the school
9. have a fax machine
10. have trouble with English spelling
11. _____

EXERCISE 14   Two students are comparing teachers. Fill in each blank to complete this conversation.

A. Do you _____*like*_____ your English class?
              (like)

B. Yes, I _____*do*_____. I _____ a very good teacher. Her
                                   (1 have)
   name is Ms. Lopez.

A. _____ Spanish?
                 (2)

B. No, she doesn't. She comes from the Philippines. She _____
                                                              (3 speak)
   English and Tagalog.

A. My teacher is very good too. But he _____ fast, and sometimes
                                            (4 talk)
   I _____ him. He _____ a lot of
              (5 not/understand)   (6 give)
   homework. _____ a lot of homework?
                          (7)

B. Yes, she does. And she _____ a test once a week.
                                              (8 give)

A. My teacher _____ jeans to class. He's very informal.
                          (9 wear)

_____ jeans to class?
          (10)

B. No, she doesn't. She always wears a dress.

A. My class meets three days a week: Mondays, Wednesdays, and Fridays.

_____ three days a week too?
                    (11)

B. No, it _____ on Tuesdays and Thursdays.
                (12 meet)

EXERCISE 15   Find a partner from a different country, if possible. Tell your partner about differences between classes and teachers in this college and a college in your country. Ask your partner about his or her country.

> EXAMPLES: In my college back home, students stand up when they speak. Do they stand up in your country?
>
> This class has some older people. In my country, only young people study at college. Do older people go to college in your country?

EXERCISE 16   Read each statement. Then write a *yes/no* question about the words in parentheses ( ). Write a short answer.

> EXAMPLES: You know the present tense. (the past tense)
>
> *Do you know the past tense? No, I don't.*
>
> The school has computer classes. (gym classes)
>
> *Does it have gym classes? Yes, it does.*

1. The teacher uses the chalkboard. (a map)

_____

2. You bring your textbook to class. (your dictionary)

_____

3. We need practice with grammar. (with spelling)

_____

4. The teacher speaks English. (another language)

_____

5. I understand the teacher. (you)

_____

6. "Know" has a silent "k." ("knife")

_____

7. The past tense has a lot of irregular verbs. (the present tense)

_____

8. The teacher speaks English fluently. (the students)

_____

3.7   Questions with *Be* and Other Verbs

Compare *be* and other verbs in *yes/no* questions and short answers.

Are you confused?	No, I'm not.	Am I right?	Yes, you are.
Do you need help?	No, I don't.	Do I have the right answer?	Yes, you do.
Are they from Haiti?	Yes, they are.	Is the teacher from your country?	No, he isn't.
Do they speak French?	Yes, they do.	Does the teacher have an accent?	No, he doesn't.

Avoid making these mistakes with short answers to these questions.

Are you hungry?	Wrong: Yes, I do.
	Right: Yes, I *am*.
Do you like movies?	Wrong: Yes, I am.
	Right: Yes, I *do*.

EXERCISE 17   Read each statement. Then write a *yes/no* question about the words in parentheses ( ). Write a short answer.

EXAMPLES: **English is a Germanic language. (Spanish)**

Is Spanish a Germanic language? No, it isn't.

Students of English complain about spelling. (students of Spanish)

Do students of Spanish complain about spelling? No, they don't.

1. Children learn a language easily. (adults)

2. Americans speak English. (Australians) (answer: yes)

3. "Butter" has two "t's." ("later")

4. English spelling is hard. (Spanish spelling) (answer: no)

5. Foreigners make mistakes with English spelling. (Americans) (answer: yes)

6. The "g" in "sign" is silent. (the "g" in "signature") (answer: no)

7. You know American English. (British English)

8. The teacher speaks English well. (you)

9. Some languages use the Roman alphabet. (Spanish) (answer: yes)

10. You're interested in the English language. (American history)

_____

11. Spanish is a Romance language. (Italian) (answer: yes)

_____

EXERCISE 18   Put a check (✓) next to customs from your country. Find a partner from another country, if possible. Tell your partner about customs in your country. Ask your partner if these are customs in his or her country. Tell the class about one custom from your partner's country that surprises you.

EXAMPLE: _____✓_____ **Russians usually take off their shoes before they enter a house.**

1. _____ People take off their shoes before they enter a house.

2. _____ People bow when they say hello.

3. _____ People shake hands when they say hello.

4. _____ People bring a gift when they visit a friend's house.

5. _____ People eat with chopsticks.

6. _____ On the bus, people stand up to let an older person sit down.

7. _____ Women cover their faces.

8. _____ A smoker offers a cigarette to other people.

9. _____ Men open doors for women.

10. _____ Men give flowers to women for their birthdays.

11. _____ People celebrate children's day.

12. _____ High school students wear a uniform.

13. _____ Students stand up when the teacher enters the room.

14. _____ _____

bow

chopsticks

3.8 *Or* Questions

An *or* question gives you a choice of answers.

Do/Does	Subject	Verb	Choice 1	*Or*	Choice 2	Answer
Do	you	study	English	or	French?	I study English.
Does	"better"	have	one T	or	two T's?	It has two T's.

Be	Subject		Choice 1	*Or*	Choice 2	Answer
Is	Washington, D.C		on the East Coast	or	the West Coast?	It's on the East Coast.

Language Notes

The first part of an *or* question has rising intonation; the second part has falling intonation. Listen to your teacher pronounce the questions above.

EXERCISE 19   Find a partner. Ask your partner these questions, using the correct intonation.

> EXAMPLE: **Do you drink coffee or tea in the morning?**
>
> **I drink coffee.**

1. Do you speak English or your native language at home?
2. Do you prefer classical music or popular music?
3. Are you a resident of the U.S. or a visitor?
4. Are you married or single?
5. Do you live in a house, an apartment, or a dormitory?
6. Do you write with your left hand or your right hand?
7. Are you from a big city or a small town?
8. Do you prefer morning classes or evening classes?
9. Is this exercise easy or hard?

3.9   *Wh-* Questions with the Simple Present Tense

When we make *wh-* questions, we use the following word order.

Wh- Word	*Do(n't)* *Does(n't)*	Subject	Verb (Base Form)
Where	do	they	study?
What kind of car	do	you	have?
Why	don't	we	eat?
When	does	the class	begin?
How many sisters	does	he	have?
Why	doesn't	your brother	work?
What	does	complain	mean?

Compare statements and questions with the simple present tense.

Wh- Word	*Don't/Doesn't*	Subject	Verb	Complement	Short Answer
		He	lives	in California.	
	Does	he	live	in San Diego?	No, he doesn't.
Where	does	he	live?		
Why	doesn't	he	live	in Los Angeles?	

When the *wh-* question has a preposition, we use the following word order.

Preposition	*Wh-* Word	*Do/Does*	Subject	Verb (Base Form)	Preposition
With	whom	do	you	live?	
	Who	do	you	live	with?
On	what floor	does	he	live?	
	What floor	does	he	live	on?

1. It is very formal to put the preposition before a question word. In conversation, we often put the preposition at the end of the question. We almost always say: Where do you come *from*?

2. Remember, we can talk about a person's country of origin with *be* or *come*.

Where *are* you from? *I'm* from Poland.
Where *do* you *come* from? I *come* from Poland.

EXERCISE 20   Fill in each blank with the missing word.

EXAMPLE: **Where ____*do*____ you live? I live in Detroit.**

1. Where _____ your brother live? He lives in New York.

2. How _____ children do you have? I have two children.

3. _____ _____ you study? I study in the library.

4. Why _____ you study at home? I don't study at home because it's too noisy.

5. How many languages _____ your teacher _____? He speaks two languages.

6. Where do you _____? I work downtown.

7. _____ do you live _____? I live with my sister.

8. _____ does he come from? He _____ from Thailand.

EXERCISE 21   Ask and answer questions with the words given. First ask a *yes/no* question. Then use the words in parentheses ( ) to ask a *wh-* question, if possible.

EXAMPLE: **live near school (where)**
        A. Do you live near the school?
        B. Yes, I do.
        A. Where do you live?
        B. I live on Green and Main.

1. speak Spanish (what language)
2. need English in your country (why)
3. have American friends (how many)
4. like this city (why)
5. live near the school (where)
6. plan to go back to your country (when or why)
7. live alone (with whom or who . . . with)
8. practice English outside of class (with whom or who . . . with)
9. bring your dictionary to class (why)
10. have an answering machine (why)

EXERCISE 22   Ask the teacher. First, ask the teacher a *yes/no* question. After you get the answer, use the words in parentheses ( ) to ask a *wh-* question, if possible. Your teacher will answer.

> EXAMPLE: teach summer school (why)
> A. Do you teach summer school?
> B. No, I don't.
> A. Why don't you teach summer school?
> B. Because I like to travel in the summer.

1. have an office mate (what/he or she/teach)
2. get paid on the first of the month (when)
3. have a computer (what kind of computer)
4. speak another language (what language)
5. teach summer school (why)
6. work in another school (what other school . . . in)
7. correct the homework in school (where)
8. prefer evening classes (why)
9. drive to school (how . . . get[6] to school)
10. like to teach English (why)
11. come from this city (what city . . . from)
12. have children (how many)
13. _____

EXERCISE 23   Ask and answer questions about another teacher with the words given. First ask a *yes/no* question. Then use the words in parentheses ( ) to ask a *wh-* question, if possible.

> EXAMPLE: speak your language (what languages)
> A. Does your teacher speak your language?
> B. No, he doesn't.
> A. What languages does he speak?
> B. He speaks English and French.

1. give a lot of homework (why)
2. write on the blackboard (when)
3. use a tape recorder in class (why)
4. come to class late (what time)
5. call you by your first name (why)
6. pronounce your name correctly (how)
7. use a textbook (what textbook)
8. wear jeans to class (what)

---

[6]*Get* means arrive.

Language Notes

1. We can use the simple present tense to ask questions about the meaning and spelling of a word.

   How do you say "knife" in Spanish?   "Cuchillo."
   What does "knife" mean?   It means an instrument for cutting.
   How do you spell "knife"?   K-N-I-F-E.

2. *Cost* is a verb. We can use the simple present tense to ask questions about cost.

   How much does a new car *cost*?   It *costs* over $10,000.
   How much do bananas *cost*?   They *cost* 59¢ a pound.

EXERCISE 24   Answer these questions. Practice the *-s* form.

1. How much does postage[7] to your country cost?
2. How much does a phone call to your country cost?
3. What does "postage" mean?
4. What does "10 bucks"[8] mean?
5. How do you spell your last name?
6. How do you spell your first name?
7. How do you say "hello" in your language?
8. How do you say "goodbye" in your language?

EXERCISE 25   Read each statement. Then ask a *wh-* question about the words in parentheses ( ). Answer with a complete sentence.

EXAMPLES: **Mexico has thirty states. (the U.S.)**

   A. *How many states does the U.S. have?*

   B. *It has 50 states.*

   Mexicans speak Spanish. (Americans)

   A. *What language do Americans speak?*

   B. *Americans speak English.*

1. The Mexican President lives in Mexico City. (the American President)

   A. _____

   B. _____

---

[7]*Postage* means the price to mail a letter.

[8]*Buck* is slang for *dollar.*

2. Mexicans speak Spanish. (Canadians)

    A. _____

    B. _____

3. A local phone call costs _____¢. (a stamp)

    A. _____

    B. _____

4. "D.C." means District of Columbia. ("L.A.")

    A. _____

    B. _____

5. You spell "knife" K-N-I-F-E. ("enough")

    A. _____

    B. _____

6. China has more than 1 billion people. (the U.S.) (answer: about 250 million)

    A. _____

    B. _____

7. Chinese people celebrate the New Year in February. (Americans)

    A. _____

    B. _____

8. I don't know the word "large." ("large"/mean)

    A. _____

    B. _____

9. We say "book" in English. ("book" in Spanish) (answer: "libro")

    A. _____

    B. _____

10. The teacher doesn't speak a foreign language in class. (why)

    A. _____

    B. _____

11. Argentina has cold weather in July. (when/the U.S.)

    A. _____

    B. _____

12. Mexicans celebrate Labor Day in May. (Americans) (answer: September)

    A. _____

    B. _____

13. "Fall" means autumn. ("automobile")

    A. _____

    B. _____

14. The school year starts in September. (when/end)

    A. _____

    B. _____

3.10 *Wh-* Questions with *Be* and Other Verbs

Compare *wh-* questions with *be* and other verbs.

Where are they from?	How are they?
What language do they speak?	How do they feel?
Where am I?	Where are we?
What do I need?	Where do we go now?
Who is she?	What's a stamp?
Where does she live?	What does "postage" mean?

EXERCISE 26   Read this conversation between two new students, Ricardo (R) and Alexander (A). Fill in each blank with the missing word.

R. Hi. My name _is_ Ricardo. What _____?
                                                              (1)

A. Alexander.

R. Nice to meet you, Alexander. Where _____?
                                                                   (2)

A. I _____ from Ukraine.
                  (3)

R. What languages _____?
                                          (4)

A. I speak Ukrainian and Russian.

R. _____ a new student?
           (5)

A. Yes, I am. What about you? Where _____ from?
                                                          (6)

R. I _____ from Peru.
            (7)

A. Where _____?
                    (8)

R. It's in South America. We speak Spanish in Peru. I want to learn English and then go back to my country.

A. Why _____ to go back to Peru?
                           (9)

R. Because my father has an export business there, and I want to work with him.

A. What _____?
                       (10)

R. "Export" means to sell your products in another country.

A. Why _____ to know English?
                          (11)

R. I need to know English because we have many American customers.

A. How many languages _____?
                                          (12)

R. My father speaks four languages: English, French, German, and Spanish, of course.

A. Tell me about your English class. _____
                                                                (13)

   your English teacher?

R. Oh, yes. I like her very much.

A. Who _____ your English teacher?
              (14)

R. Barbara Nowak.

A. _____?
                        (15)

R. N-O-W-A-K. It's a Polish name.

A. How many students _____?
                                          (16)

R. It has about 35 students. The classroom is very big.

A. What floor _____?
                        (17)

R. It's on the second floor.

A. When _____ your class _____?
                (18)   (19)

R. It begins at 6 o'clock. I'm late. See you later.

A. _____ "see you later" in Spanish?
                        (20)

R. We say "hasta luego."

EXPANSION ACTIVITIES

DISCUSSION   Find a partner who speaks the same language, if possible. Talk about some differences between your language and English.

   EXAMPLES: In Spanish, we use almost the same alphabet as English. We have some different letters: ll and ñ. Some words sound the same—"casa" and "caza"—but they don't have the same meaning. We don't pronounce the "h" in Spanish words.

       Russian uses a different alphabet. Russian doesn't have so many verb tenses. We sometimes put the verb before the subject in Russian.

WRITING   Write a list of differences between your language and English. Write about the alphabet, grammar, spelling, accent marks, and pronunciation.

GAME   One student comes to the front of the room. He or she thinks of an animal and writes the name of this animal on a piece of paper. The other students try to guess which animal it is by asking questions. The person who guesses the animal is the next to come to the front of the room.

   EXAMPLE: lion

     Does this animal fly? No, it doesn't.

     Does it live in water? No, it doesn't.

     What does it eat? It eats meat.

     Does this animal live in Africa? Yes, it does.

     What color is this animal?

lion

PROVERBS   The following proverbs contain the simple present tense. Discuss the meaning of each proverb. Do you have a similar proverb in your language?

Every cloud has a silver lining.

A stitch in time saves nine.

Practice makes perfect.

stitch

OUTSIDE ACTIVITY   Interview an American. Ask this person to tell you about difficulties he or she has with English spelling. Tell the class what this person said.

SUMMARY OF LESSON THREE

Forms of the Simple Present Tense

1. The simple present has two forms: the base form and the -s form:

I		He	
You		She	
We	eat.	It	eats.
They			
(Plural noun)		(Singular noun)	

2. Simple present tense patterns with the -s form:

Affirmative	The President *lives* in Washington, D.C.
Negative	He *doesn't live* in New York.
Yes/No Question	*Does* he *live* in the White House?
Short Answer	Yes, he *does.*
Wh- Question	Where *does* the Vice President *live*?
Negative Question	Why *doesn't* the Vice President *live* in the White House?

3. Simple present tense patterns with the base form:

Affirmative	We *study* English in class.
Negative	We *don't study* American history in class.
Yes/No Question	*Do* we *study* grammar?
Short Answer	Yes, we *do.*
Wh- Question	Why *do* we *study* grammar?
Negative Question	Why *don't* we *study* history?

4. Present tense patterns with the verb *be:*

Affirmative	The teacher *is* absent.
Negative	She *isn't* here today.
Yes/No Question	*Is* she sick?
Short Answer	No, she *isn't.*
Wh- Question	Where *is* she?
Negative Question	Why *isn't* she here?

Uses of the Simple Present Tense

General truths	**Customs**	**Habits**
English *has* a difficult spelling system.	Japanese people *eat* with chopsticks.	Americans often *complain* about English spelling.
Many English words *have* silent letters.	A lot of Americans *use* credit cards.	They sometimes *spell* a a word wrong.
Americans *speak* English.		
Mexicans *speak* Spanish.		

LESSON THREE TEST/REVIEW

Part 1   Write the *-s* form of the following verbs. Use correct spelling.

EXAMPLE: take _____*takes*_____

1. go _____   5. play _____

2. carry _____   6. study _____

3. mix _____   7. catch _____

4. drink _____   8. say _____

Part 2   Fill in the first blank with the affirmative form of the verb in parentheses ( ). Then write the negative form of this verb.

EXAMPLES: A monkey ___*lives*___ in a warm climate.
                       (live)

It ___*doesn't live*___ in a cold climate.

Brazil ___*is*___ a big country.
              (be)

Haiti ___*isn't*___ a big country.

1. The English language _____ the Roman alphabet.
                                        (use)

   The Chinese language _____ the Roman alphabet.

2. We _____ English in class.
          (speak)

   We _____ our native languages in class.

3. March _____ 31 days.
              (have)

   February _____ 31 days.

4. Mexico and Canada _____ in North America.
                                  (be)

   Colombia and Ecuador _____ in North America.

5. You _____ the "k" in "bank."
      (pronounce)

    You _____ the "k" in "knife."

6. The teacher _____ the English language.
              (teach)

    He/She _____ American history.

7. A green light _____ "go."
           (mean)

    A red light _____ "go."

8. I _____ from another country.
    (come)

    I _____ from the U.S.

9. English _____ hard for me.
        (be)

    My language _____ hard for me.

Part 3   Write a *yes/no* question about the words in parentheses ( ). Write a short answer.

    EXAMPLES: January has 31 days. (February)

           Does February have 31 days? No, it doesn't.

           China is in Asia. (Korea)

           Is Korea in Asia? Yes, it is.

1. "Occasion" has a double "c." ("occupation")

    _____

2. The English language uses the Roman alphabet. (the Russian language) (answer: no)

    _____

3. San Francisco is in California. (Los Angeles) (answer: yes)

    _____

4. McDonald's sells hamburgers. (Burger King) (answer: yes)

_____

5. January and March have 31 days. (April and June) (answer: no)

_____

6. The President lives in the White House. (the Vice President) (answer: no)

_____

7. Americans speak English. (Canadians) (answer: yes)

_____

8. We come to class on time. (the teacher)

_____

9. Canada and Brazil are big countries. (the U.S.)

_____

Part 4   Read each statement. Then write a *wh-* question about the words in parentheses ( ). You don't need to answer.

      EXAMPLES: **February has 28 days. (March)**

            How many days does March have? _____

            Mexico is in North America. (Venezuela)

            Where is Venezuela? _____

1. Mexicans speak Spanish. (Canadians)

_____

2. The U.S. has 50 states. (Mexico)

_____

3. You say "book" in English. (in Polish)

_____

4. The president lives in the White House. (the Vice-President)

_____

5. Thanksgiving is in November. (Christmas)

_____

6. You spell "occasion" O-C-C-A-S-I-O-N. ("tomorrow")

_____

7. "Occupation" means job or profession. ("occasion")

_____

8. English doesn't have a good spelling system. (why)

_____

9. Marek comes from Poland. (you)

_____

LESSON FOUR

GRAMMAR

Singular and Plural
Articles and Quantity Words
There + *Be* + Noun

CONTEXT

Facts About Americans
Finding an Apartment
Calling About an Apartment

Lesson Focus   Singular and Plural

- Nouns can be singular or plural. Plural nouns usually end in -s.

  I have a *brother.*   I have three *sisters.*

  (NOTE: Some nouns have no plural form. These are "noncount" nouns. See Lesson 11 for noncount nouns.)

- We can use the indefinite articles (*a/an*) with singular nouns. We can use quantity words with plural nouns.

  I have *a cousin* in New York.   I have *some cousins* in Boston.
  I have *an aunt* in Miami.   I don't have *any relatives* in Seattle.

- We can introduce a noun with *there* + a form of *be.*

  There's an apple in the refrigerator.   *There are* some peaches on the table.

READING

Before you read:

1. What questions do you have about Americans and American life?
2. What surprises you about life in the U.S.?

Read the following facts and statistics about Americans. Pay special attention to plural nouns.

FACTS ABOUT AMERICANS

1. There are about 258 million **people** in the U.S.
2. The average household has 2.63 **people.**
3. More than 50 percent of American **women** work for pay.
4. Seventy percent of **children** live with two **parents.**
5. One in three **marriages** ends in divorce.
6. The average American lives about seventy-six **years. Women** live longer than **men** (79 years compared with 73 years).
7. Sixty-four percent of American **families** own their **homes.**
8. The average American family moves 14 **times.**
9. Eighty-two percent of **Americans** finish high school.
10. Sixty-two percent of high school **graduates** go to college. More **women** than **men** go to college.

4.1 Regular Plural Nouns

We form the plural of most nouns by adding -*s* at the end of the word. The chart shows regular plural -*s* endings. Fill in the last examples for each spelling.

Word Ending	Example Words	Plural Addition	Plural Addition	Word Ending	Example Words	Plural Addition	Plural Addition
Vowel	bee banana pie name	+ s	bees bananas *pies* _____	Vowel + o	patio radio stereo video	+ s	patios radios _____ _____
Consonant	bed card pin month	+ s	beds cards _____ _____	Consonant + o	mosquito tomato potato hero	+ es	mosquitoes tomatoes _____ _____
s, ss, sh, ch, x, z	church dish box watch class	+ es	churches dishes boxes _____ _____	(Exceptions: photos, pianos, solos, altos, sopranos, autos, avocados)			
				f or fe	knife leaf calf life	f̸ + ves	knives leaves _____ _____
Vowel + y	boy day toy monkey	+ s	boys days _____ _____	(Exceptions: beliefs, chiefs, roofs, chefs)			
Consonant + y	lady story party cherry	ẏ + ies	ladies stories _____ _____				

Language Notes

The regular plural form (with -s) has three pronunciations. Listen to your teacher pronounce these examples.

1. After voiceless sounds /p, t, k, f, θ/, -s sounds like /s/.

lip—lips	cat—cats	rock—rocks
cuff—cuffs	month—months	

2. After voiced sounds /b, d, g, v, ð, m, n, ŋ, l, r/ and all vowels, -s sounds like /z/.

cab—cabs	lid—lids	bag—bags
stove—stoves	lathe—lathes	sum—sums
can—cans	thing—things	bill—bills
car—cars	bee—bees	toe—toes

3. After these sounds /s, z, ʒ, ʃ, ʤ, ʧ/, -es sounds like /ɪz/ and is a separate syllable.

bus—buses	cause—causes
garage—garages	dish—dishes
beach—beaches	bridge—bridges

EXERCISE I   Write the plural form of each noun, then pronounce each plural form.

EXAMPLES: leaf _____ *leaves* _____

toy _____ *toys* _____

1. dish _____
2. country _____
3. half _____
4. book _____
5. boy _____
6. girl _____
7. bench _____
8. box _____
9. table _____
10. stereo _____
11. knife _____
12. story _____
13. sofa _____
14. key _____
15. movie _____
16. bath _____
17. mosquito _____
18. lion _____
19. fly _____
20. cow _____
21. shark _____
22. roach _____
23. fox _____
24. horse _____
25. turkey _____
26. chicken _____
27. wolf _____
28. dog _____
29. squirrel _____
30. pony _____
31. duck _____
32. moth _____

4.2   Irregular Plural Nouns

Some plural nouns are not formed by adding -s.

Language Notes

1. Some nouns have the same singular and plural form.

fish	I have one *fish*.
	He has three *fish*.
sheep	One *sheep* is here.
	Three *sheep* are there.

2. Some nouns change a vowel to make the plural.

man—men	One *man* speaks French.
woman—women	Three *men* speak
mouse—mice	German.
tooth—teeth	One *woman* is tall.
foot—feet	Two *women* are short.
goose—geese	

3. Some nouns have different words for their plural forms.

child—children	One *child* is hungry.
person—people	Two *children* are tired.
(or persons)	One *person* is late.
	Three *people* are absent.

4. Some words only have a plural form.

pajamas	
clothes	Your *clothes* are dirty.
pants	The *pants* are blue.
(eye)glasses	My *glasses* are broken.
slacks	
scissors	

EXERCISE 2   The following nouns have an irregular plural form. Write the plural.

EXAMPLE: man _____*men*_____

1. foot _____

2. woman _____

3. policeman _____

4. child _____

5. fish _____

6. mouse _____

7. sheep _____

8. tooth _____

EXERCISE 3   Use the plural of each noun to ask "How many . . . do you have?" Another student will answer. For a zero answer, say, "I don't have any <plural form>."

EXAMPLE: sister
          A. How many sisters do you have?
          B. I have two sisters.   OR   I don't have any sisters.

1. child	7. telephone
2. brother	8. watch
3. sister	9. television
4. niece	10. radio
5. nephew	11. _____
6. aunt	12. _____

4.3 Using the Plural to Make a Generalization

Study two ways to make generalizations:

No Article	Plural subject	Verb	Complement
	Dogs	are	faithful animals.
	Children	need	love from their parents.
	Immigrants	have to learn	a new language.

Indefinite article	Singular subject	Verb	Complement
A	dog	is	a faithful animal.
A	child	needs	love from his or her parents.
An	immigrant	has to learn	a new language.

Language Notes

1. We often use the plural form of nouns to make generalizations. We say that something is true about all members of a group. We don't use an article with plural nouns to make a generalization.

2. We can also use the singular form of nouns to make generalizations. We use the indefinite article *(a or an)* with singular nouns.

3. After the verb, we usually use the plural form with no article to make a generalization.
    I like *apples.*
    I don't like *peaches.*
    I don't understand American *customs.*

EXERCISE 4   Change the subject from plural to singular. Make other necessary changes. (Both singular and plural give a generalization.)

EXAMPLE: **Immigrants have to learn English.**

An immigrant has to learn English.

1. Adults have a lot of responsibilities.

_____

2. Children like to play.

_____

3. Single parents have a hard job.

_____

4. Women live longer than men.

_____

5. Cars are expensive.

_____

6. Houses cost a lot of money.

_____

EXERCISE 5   Change the subject from singular to plural. Make other necessary changes.
(Both singular and plural give a generalization.)

> EXAMPLE: **An immigrant has many problems.**
>
> _Immigrants have many problems._
> _____

1. A child needs love.

_____

2. An egg has protein.

_____

3. A banana is yellow.

_____

4. A dolphin is intelligent.

_____

dolphin

5. A dolphin doesn't live on land.

_____

6. A mouse is small.

_____

EXERCISE 6   Work with a partner. Use the plural form of the word in parentheses ( ) to make a generalization. Remember, don't use an article with the plural form to make a generalization.

EXAMPLES: (child)

Children like to watch cartoons.

American (highway)

American highways are in good condition.

1. (American)

2. American (child)

3. big (city) in the U.S.

4. (teacher) at this college

5. (student) at this college

6. American (doctor)

7. old (person) in the U.S.

EXERCISE 7   Find a partner from a different country, if possible.[1] Use the noun in parentheses ( ) to give your partner general information about your country. Use the singular
form with an article or the plural form with no article.

EXAMPLE: (woman)
Generally, women don't work outside the home in my country.
OR
Generally, a woman doesn't work outside the home in my country.

1. (person)   5. (house)   9. (_____)

2. old (person)   6. poor (person) 10. (_____)

3. (woman)   7. (car)   11. (_____)

4. (man)   8. (doctor)   12. (_____)

EXERCISE 8   Use the plural form of each noun to tell if you like or don't like the
following:

EXAMPLE: apple
I like apples.   OR   I don't like apples.

1. tomato   6. peach
2. orange   7. radish
3. strawberry   8. pear
4. grape   9. potato
5. banana   10. cherry

peach

radish

pear

EXERCISE 9   Ask "Do you like" + the plural form of the noun. Another student will answer.

EXAMPLES: child
A. Do you like children?
B. Yes, I do.

dog
A. Do you like dogs?
B. No, I don't.

---

[1]If you and your partner are from the same country, see if you agree about your generalizations.

1. cat
2. dog
3. American doctor
4. American car
5. American movie

6. fashion magazine
7. comic book
8. computer game
9. strict teacher
10. _____

comic book

. . . .

R
E
A
D
I
N
G

Before you read:

1. Do you live in a house, an apartment, or a dorm?[2] Do you live alone?
2. Are you happy with the place where you live? Why or why not?

Read the following article. Pay special attention to *there* + *be* followed by singular and plural nouns.

FINDING AN APARTMENT

There are several ways to find an apartment. One way is to look in the newspaper. **There is** an "Apartment for Rent" section in the back of the newspaper. **There are** many ads for apartments. **There are** also ads for houses for rent and houses for sale.

Another way to find an apartment is by looking at the buildings in the neighborhood where you want to live. **There are** often "For Rent" signs on the front of the buildings. **There is** usually a phone number on the sign. You can call and ask for information about the apartment that you are interested in. You can ask:

How much is the rent?
Is heat included?
What floor is the apartment on?
Is there an elevator?
How many bedrooms **are there** in the apartment?
How many closets **are there** in the apartment?
Is the apartment available[3] now?

---

[2]*Dorm* is short for *dormitory,* a building where students live.

[3]*Available* means ready to use now.

If an apartment interests you, you can make an appointment to see it. When you go to see the apartment, you should ask some more questions, such as the following:

Is there a lease?[4] How long is the lease?
Is there a janitor or manager?
Is there a parking space for each tenant? Is it free, or do I have to pay extra?
Are there smoke detectors? (In many places, the law says that the landlord must put a smoke detector in each apartment and in the halls.)
Is there a laundry room in the building? Where is it?

The landlord may ask you a few questions, such as:

How many people **are there** in your family?
Do you have any pets?

You should check over the apartment carefully before you sign the lease. If **there are** some problems, you should talk to the landlord to see if he will take care of them before you move in.

4.4 Using *There + Be*

We use *there + is* to introduce a singular subject into the conversation. We use *there + are* to introduce a plural subject. Observe the types of articles and quantity words that we can use in a statement with *there*.

SINGULAR

There + Is	Singular Word	Singular Noun	Prepositional Phrase
There's	a	janitor	in my building.
There's	one	dryer	in the basement.
There isn't	a	back door	in my apartment.
There's	no	back door	in my apartment.

---

[4]A *lease* is a contract between the owner (landlord or landlady) and the renter (tenant). It tells how much the rent is, how long the tenant can stay in the apartment, and other rules.

PLURAL

There + Are	Plural Word	Plural Noun	Prepositional Phrase
There are	—	numbers	on the doors of the apartment.
There are	several	windows	in the bedroom.
There are	many	Americans	in my building.
There are	some	children	in my building.
There are	two	closets	in the hall.
There aren't	any	shades	on the windows.
There are	no	shades	on the windows.

Language Notes

1. A sentence that begins with *there* often shows a place or a time.

> There is a smoke detector *in the hall.*
> There are apartments available *in May.*

2. If two nouns follow *there,* use a singular verb *(is)* if the first noun is singular. Use a plural verb *(are)* if the first noun is plural.

> There*'s a* closet in the bedroom and two closets in the hall.
> There *are two* closets in the hall and one closet in the bedroom.
> There *is a* washer and a drier in the basement.

3. In conversation, you will sometimes hear *there's* with plural nouns.

> INFORMAL: There's a lot of empty apartments in my building.
> FORMAL: There are a lot of empty apartments in my building.

EXERCISE 10   Use the words given with the patterns in the boxes to make a statement about the place where you live (house or apartment). If you live in a dorm, use Exercise 11 instead.

EXAMPLES: carpet/in the living room
There's a carpet in the living room.
OR
There isn't a carpet in the living room.

trees/in front of the building
There are two trees in front of the building.
OR
There are no trees in front of the building.

1. closet/in the living room
2. blinds/on the windows
3. door/on every room

blinds

4. window/in every room
5. lease
6. porch
7. number/on the door of the apartment
8. roaches/in the kitchen
9. microwave oven/in the kitchen
10. back door
11. fireplace
12. smoke detector

porch

roach

fireplace

EXERCISE 11 Make a statement about your dorm and dorm room with the words given. (If you live in an apartment or house, skip this exercise.)

EXAMPLES: window/in the room
             There's a window in the room.

             curtains/on the window
             There are no curtains on the window.
             There are shades.

shade

1. closet/in the room
2. two beds/in the room
3. private bath/for every room
4. men and women/in the dorm
5. cafeteria/in the dorm

6. snack machines/in the dorm
7. noisy students/in the dorm
8. numbers/on the doors of the room
9. elevator(s)/in the dorm
10. laundry room/in the dorm

4.5 Questions with *There*

Questions and Answers with *There*

Is/Are + There	Noun Phrase	Prepositional Phrase	Short Answer
Is there	a laundry room	in your building?	No, there isn't.
Are there	any cabinets	in the kitchen?	Yes, there are.

Questions with *How Many*

How Many + Noun	*Are There*	Prepositional Phrase	Answer
How many closets	are there	in your apartment?	There are 3.
How many apartments	are there	in your building?	There are 10.

Language Notes

1. We usually use *any* to introduce a plural noun in a *yes/no* question.

2. Do not make a contraction for a short *yes* answer.

Is there an elevator in your building?
Yes, there is. NOT: Yes, there's.

EXERCISE 12   Ask and answer questions with *there* and the words given to find out about another student's apartment and building. (If you live in a dorm, use Exercise 13 instead.)

EXAMPLES: a microwave oven/in your apartment
A. Is there a microwave oven in your apartment?
B. No, there isn't.

closets/in the bedroom
A. Are there any closets in the bedroom?
B. Yes. There's one closet in the bedroom.

1. children/in your building
2. a dishwasher/in the kitchen
3. a yard/in front of your building
4. trees/in front of your building
5. a basement/in the building
6. a laundry room/in the basement
7. a janitor/in the building
8. noisy neighbors/in the building
9. nosy[5] neighbors/in the building
10. an elevator/in the building
11. parking spaces/for the tenants
12. a lot of closets/in the apartment
13. how many apartments/in your building
14. how many parking spaces/in front of your building

---
[5]A *nosy* person is a person who wants to know everyone's business.

EXERCISE 13   Ask and answer questions with *there* and the words given to find out about another student's dorm. (If you live in an apartment or house, skip this exercise.)

> EXAMPLE: a bicycle room/in your dorm
> > A. Is there a bicycle room in your dorm?
> > B. No, there isn't.

1. married students
2. private rooms
3. a bicycle room
4. a computer room
5. an elevator
6. a bulletin board

7. graduate students
8. a quiet place to study
9. an air conditioner/in your room
10. a parking lot/for your dorm
11. how many rooms/in your dorm
12. how many floors/in your dorm

EXERCISE 14   Use the words given to ask the teacher a question about his or her office. Your teacher will answer.

> EXAMPLES: pencil sharpener
> > A. Is there a pencil sharpener in your office?
> > B. No, there isn't.
>
> > books
> > A. Are there any books in your office?
> > B. Yes. There are a lot of books in my office.

1. phone
2. answering machine
3. photos of your family
4. radio
5. copy machine

6. windows
7. calendar
8. bookshelves
9. plants
10. file cabinet

file cabinet

EXERCISE 15   A student is calling about an apartment for rent. Fill in the blanks with *there is, there are, is there, are there,* and other related words to complete this phone conversation between the student (S) and the landlady (L).

S. I'm calling about an apartment for rent on Grover Street.

L. We have two apartments available. _____*There's*_____ a four-room apartment
                                                    Example

on the first floor and a three-room apartment on the fourth floor. Which one are you interested in?

S. I prefer the smaller apartment. _____ an elevator in the
                                                       1

   building?

L. Yes, there is. How many people _____ in your family?
                                                     2

S. It's just for me. I live alone. I'm a student. I need a quiet apartment. Is this a
   quiet building?

L. Oh, yes. _____ no kids in the building.
                            3

S. I have a car. _____ parking spaces?
                                4

L. Yes. _____ 20 spaces in back of the building.
                      5

S. How _____ apartments _____ in the building?
                     6   7

L. _____ 30 apartments.
               8

S. Then _____ enough parking spaces for all the tenants.
                      9

L. Don't worry. Not everyone has a car. Parking is on a first-come, first-served
   basis[6]. And _____ plenty of[7] spaces on the street.
                            10

S. _____ in the building?
              11

L. Yes. There are washers and driers in the basement.

S. How much is the rent?

L. It's $475 a month.

S. When can I see the apartment?

L. How about tomorrow at six o'clock?

S. That'll be fine. Thanks.

---

[6]A *first-come, first-served* basis means that people who arrive first will get something first (parking
spaces, theater tickets, classes at registration).

[7]*Plenty of* means *a lot of.*

1. We use *there* only for the first mention of a noun in a conversation. After we introduce a new noun, we can refer to the noun again with *it*, *they*, or other pronouns.

   There's *an empty apartment* on the first floor. *It's* available now.
   There's *a janitor* in the building. *He's* in the basement now.
   There are a lot of *parking spaces*. *They're* for the tenants.
   There are two *washing machines*. *They're* in the basement.

2. We pronounce *there* and *they're* exactly the same. Listen to your teacher pronounce these examples.

   There are a lot of parking spaces. *They're* for the tenants.

EXERCISE 16 Fill in each blank with *there's, there are, it's* or *they're*.

EXAMPLE: <u>There's</u> a small apartment for rent in my building.

  <u>It's</u> on the fourth floor.

1. _____ two apartments for rent. _____ not on the same floor.

2. _____ a laundry room in the building. _____ in the basement.

3. The parking spaces are in the back of the building. _____ for the tenants with cars.

4. The parking spaces don't cost extra. _____ free for the tenants.

5. The apartment is small. _____ on the fourth floor.

6. The building has 30 apartments. _____ a big building.

7. The student wants to see the apartment. _____ on Grover Street.

8. The building is quiet because _____ no kids in the building.

9. How much is the rent? _____ $475 a month.

10. Is the rent high? No, _____ not high.

EXERCISE 17   Ask a question about this school using *there* and the words given. Another student will answer. If the answer is "yes," ask a question with *where.*

> EXAMPLES: a cafeteria
> A. Is there a cafeteria at this school?
> B. Yes, there is.
> A. Where is it?
> B. It's on the first floor.
>
> lockers
> A. Are there any lockers at this school?
> B. Yes, there are.
> A. Where are they?
> B. They're near the gym.

1. a library
2. vending machines
3. public telephones
4. a computer room
5. a cafeteria
6. a gym
7. a swimming pool

8. tennis courts
9. dormitories
10. a parking lot
11. a bookstore
12. copy machines
13. a student lounge
14. a fax machine

Avoid these common mistakes in sentences which require *there.*

1. Don't confuse *there, they're* and *their.*
   Wrong: Their are two chairs in the living
          room.
   Wrong: They're are two chairs in the living
          room.
   Right: *There are* two chairs in the living
          room.

2. Don't forget to use *there* + *is/are* to introduce
a subject.
   Wrong: Are three students from Haiti in my
          class.
   Wrong: In my class three students from Haiti.
   Right: *There are* three students from Haiti in
          my class.

3. Don't confuse *it* and *there.*
   Wrong: It's a closet in my bedroom.
   Right: *There's* a closet in my bedroom. It's
          not very big.

4. Don't confuse *have* and *there.*
   Wrong: Have a closet in my bedroom.
   Right: *There's* a closet in my bedroom.
   Right: My bedroom *has* a closet.

EXERCISE 18   A woman is showing her new apartment to her friend. Find the mistakes in this conversation and correct them.

A. Let me show you around my new apartment.

B. It's a big apartment.

A. It's big enough for my family. ~~They're~~ *There* are four bedrooms and two bathrooms. Has each bedroom a large closet. Let me show you my kitchen too.

B. Oh. It's a new dishwasher in your kitchen.

A. It's wonderful. You know how I hate to wash dishes.

B. Is there a microwave oven?

A. No, there isn't, unfortunately.

B. Are any washers and dryers for clothes?

A. Oh, yes. They're in the basement. In the laundry room are five washers and five dryers. I never have to wait.

B. There are a lot of people in your building?

A. In my building thirty apartments.

B. Is a janitor in your building?

A. Yes. There's a very good janitor. He keeps the building very clean.

B. I suppose this apartment costs a lot.

A. Well, yes. The rent is high. But I share the apartment with my cousins.

EXERCISE 19   Find a partner and pretend that one of you is looking for an apartment and the other person is the landlady, landlord, or manager. Ask and answer questions about the apartment, the building, parking, laundry, and rent. Write your conversation. Then read it to the class.

. . . .

R
E
A
D
I
N
G

Before you read:

1. Do most people in your country live in apartments or houses? What about your family?
2. Do you prefer to live alone, with a roommate, or with your family? Why?

Read the following phone conversation between a student (S) and the manager (M) of a building. Pay special attention to the definite article *(the)*, the indefinite articles *(a, an)*, and indefinite quantity words *some* and *any*.

CALLING ABOUT AN APARTMENT

S. Hello? I want to speak with **the** landlord. Is he home?

M. I'm **the** manager of **the** building. Can I help you?

S. I need to find **a** new apartment.

M. Where do you live now?

S. I live in **a** big apartment on Wright Street. I have **a** roommate, but he's graduating, and I need **a** smaller apartment. Are there **any** small apartments for rent in your building?

M. There's one.

S. What floor is it on?

M. It's on **the** third floor.

S. Does it have **a** bedroom?

M. No. It's **a** studio apartment. It has **a** living room and **a** kitchen.

S. Is **the** living room big?

M. So-so.

S. Does **the** kitchen have **a** stove and **a** refrigerator?

M. Yes. **The** refrigerator is old, but it works well. **The** stove is pretty new.

S. When can I see **the** apartment?

M. **The** janitor can show it to you tomorrow at 9 a.m.

• •

4.6 Articles and Quantity Words

We use articles and quantity words to introduce nouns in conversations.

	Indefinite	Definite
Singular	*a, an*	*the*
Plural	*some, any*	*the*

1. We use the indefinite article (*a* or *an*) to bring a singular noun into the conversation for the first time. After this noun becomes part of the conversation, we refer to it with *the* or a pronoun (*it, he, she*).

> My apartment has *a living room*, but *the living room* isn't very big.
> There's *a refrigerator* in the kitchen. *The refrigerator* is old, but *it* works well.
> There's *a manager* in the building. *He* shows apartments.

2. We introduce a plural noun with *some, any*, a number, or no article. After a plural noun becomes part of the conversation, we refer to it with *the* or the pronoun *they*.

> There are *three closets* in my apartment. *They're* not very big.
> There aren't *any three-bedroom apartments* in the building. There are *some studio apartments. They* don't have a bedroom.
> There are *washers and dryers* in my building. *They're* in the basement.

3. We use *the* before a noun if it is the only one.

> May I speak to *the landlord* of the building?
> There is a studio apartment on *the third floor.* (There is only one third floor.)

4. We use *the* before a singular or plural noun to refer to specific people or things in our experience. Two tenants who share the experience of living in the same building might have the following conversation:

> A. I need to talk to *the landlord.* Do you know where he is?
> B. He's in *the basement* with *the janitor.*
> A. I need to talk to him about *the washing machines.* They don't work.
> B. I know. *The tenants* are angry.

EXERCISE 20   These are conversations between two students. Fill in each blank with *the, a, an, some,* or *any.*

Conversation 1

A. Is there _____*a*_____ copy machine in our library?
               Example

B. Yes. There are several copy machines in _____ library.
                                         (1)

A. Are _____ copy machines free?
         (2)

B. No. You need to use _____ nickel[8] for _____ copy machines.
                        (3)   (4)

---

[8]*A nickel* is a five-cent coin.

Conversation 2

A. Is there _____ cafeteria at this school?
             (1)

B. Yes, there is.

A. Where's _____ cafeteria?
             (2)

B. It's on _____ first floor.
             (3)

A. Are there _____ snack machines in _____ cafeteria?
              (4)   (5)

B. Yes, there are.

A. I want to buy _____ soft drink.
                  (6)

B. _____ machine is out of order today.
    (7)

Conversation 3

A. Is there _____ bookstore for this college?
             (1)

B. Yes, there is.

A. Where is _____ bookstore?
             (2)

B. It's on Green Street.

A. I need to buy _____ dictionary.
                  (3)

B. Today is _____ holiday. _____ bookstore is closed today.
             (4)   (5)

EXPANSION ACTIVITIES

DISCUSSIONS   In a small group or with the entire class, discuss the following:

1. How do people rent apartments in your hometown? Is rent high? Is heat usually included in the rent? Does the landlord usually live in the building?

2. What are some differences between a typical apartment in this city and a typical apartment in your hometown?

SAYINGS

1. The following sayings use the plural form. Discuss the meaning of each saying. Do you have a similar saying in your language?

   A cat has nine lives.
   A picture is worth a thousand words.

2. The following sayings use *there*. Discuss the meaning of each saying. Do you have a similar saying in your language?

   Where there's a will, there's a way.
   Where there's smoke, there's fire.

WRITING

1. Write a description of a room or place that you like very much. (Review prepositions in Lesson One.)

   ### Example
   My favorite place is my living room. There are many pictures on the walls. There's a picture of my grandparents behind the sofa. There are a lot of pictures of my children on the wall next to the sofa.
   There's a TV set in the corner. Under the TV there is a VCR. There's a box of videocassettes next to the VCR. . . .

2. Write a comparison of your apartment in this city and your apartment or house in your hometown.

   ### Example
   There are many differences between my apartment in Chicago and my apartment in Kiev, Ukraine. In my Kiev apartment, there is a door on every room. In my Chicago apartment, only the bedrooms have doors. In my Kiev apartment, there is a small window inside each large

window. In the winter I can open this small window to get some fresh air. My apartment in Chicago doesn't have this small window. I have to open the whole window to get air. Sometimes the room becomes too cold. . . .

OUTSIDE ACTIVITIES

1. Bring the section of the newspaper that has apartments for rent. Ask your teacher to help you understand the abbreviations.

2. Do you have a picture of your house, apartment, or apartment building in your country? Bring it to class and tell about it.

SUMMARY OF LESSON FOUR

1. Singular and Plural
   Singular means one. Plural means more than one. The plural noun form usually ends with *-s* or *-es*.

   > boy—boys
   > box—boxes
   > story—stories
   > (Exceptions: *men, women, people, children, feet, teeth*)

2. There
   Use *there* to introduce a new noun into the conversation. Do not continue to use *there* for another mention of this noun. Use the definite article or a definite pronoun.

   > *There's* an empty apartment in my building. *It's* big. Are you interested in renting *the* empty apartment?
   > *There are* two washing machines in the basement. *They're* out of order now.
   > *There's* a Chinese man on the first floor. *He* doesn't speak much English.
   > *Are there* any parking spaces? Where are *they*? Are *the* parking spaces for students?

3. Articles
   - To make a generalization:
     Singular   *A dog* has good hearing.
     Plural   *Dogs* have good hearing.
                I like *dogs*.

   - To introduce a new noun into the conversation:
     Singular   I have *a dog*.
     Plural   I have *(some) turtles*.
                I don't have *(any) birds*.

   - To talk about a previously mentioned noun:
     Singular   I have a dog. *The dog* barks when the letter carrier arrives.
     Plural   I have some turtles. I keep *the turtles* in the bathroom.

   - To talk about specific items or people from our experience:
     Singular   *The janitor* cleans the basement once a week.
     Plural   *The tenants* have to take out their own garbage.

   - To talk about the only one:
     The President lives in Washington, D.C.

LESSON FOUR TEST/REVIEW

Part 1   Write the plural form for each noun.

box _boxes_   month _____   child _____

card _____   match _____   desk _____

foot _____   shelf _____   key _____

potato _____   radio _____   story _____

woman _____   mouse _____   bus _____

Part 2   Fill in each blank with *there, is, are, it,* or *they* or a combination of more than one of these words.

A. _Are there_ _____ any museums in Chicago?
        (Example)

B. Yes, _____ a lot of museums in Chicago.
        (1)

A. _____ a history museum in Chicago?
      (2)

B. Yes, _____ is.
      (3)

A. Where _____ the history museum?
        (4)

B. _____ near downtown.
    (5)

A. _____ any mummies in this museum?
    (6)

B. Yes, there are. _____ from Egypt.
        (7)

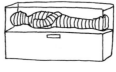

mummy

A. _____ a dinosaur in this museum?
    (8)

B. Yes, there is. _____ on the first floor.
        (9)

A. How many floors _____ in this museum?
        (10)

B. _____ two floors and a basement.
    (11)

dinosaur

A. _____ a parking lot near this museum?
        (12)

B. Yes, _____ , but _____ not very big.
           (13)   (14)

Part 3   Fill in each blank with *the, a, an, some, any,* or *X* for no article.

A. Do you like your apartment?

B. No, I don't.

A. Why not?

B. There are many reasons. First, I don't like _____*the*_____ janitor. He's

   impolite.

A. Anything else?

B. I want to get _____ dog.
                         (1)

A. So?

B. It's not permitted. _____ landlord says that _____
                              (2)   (3)

   dogs make a lot of noise.

A. Can you get _____ cat?
                      (4)

B. Yes, but I don't like _____ cats.
                                (5)

A. Is your building quiet?

B. No. There are _____ children in _____ building.
                        (6)   (7)

   When I try to study, I can hear _____ children in the next
                                            (8)

   apartment. They watch TV all the time.

A. You need to find _____ new apartment.
                           (9)

B. I think you're right.

LESSON FIVE

GRAMMAR
Frequency Words with the
Simple Present Tense
Prepositions of Time

CONTEXT
Three Special Days

Lesson Focus Frequency Words and Prepositions of Time

We use frequency words and prepositions of time with the simple present tense to talk about habits and regular activities or customs. Frequency words, such as *always, usually, never,* tell how often we repeat an activity. Prepositions of time, such as *in, on, at,* tell when the activity takes place.

I *usually* work *on* Saturday.

R E A D I N G

Before you read:

1. What is your favorite holiday? When is it?
2. Do you celebrate Mother's Day in your country? When?
3. Do people send cards for special occasions?

Read the following article. Pay special attention to the frequency words.

THREE SPECIAL DAYS

Valentine's Day is **always** on February 14. On this day, men **often** give flowers or candy to their wives or girlfriends. People **sometimes** send cards, called valentines, to friends and relatives. A valentine **usually** has a red heart and a message of love. Young children **usually** have a party at school and exchange cards.

Another special day is Saint Patrick's Day. It is **always** on March 17. It is really an Irish holiday, but many Americans like Saint Patrick's Day even if they are not Irish. In New York City, there is **always** a parade on St. Patrick's Day. People **often** wear green clothes on this day, and **sometimes** bars serve green beer.

Businesses are **never** closed for Valentine's Day or St. Patrick's Day. People **never** take a day off from work for these days. Schools and government offices are **always** open (except if these days fall on a Sunday).

Another special day is Mother's Day. It is **always** in May, but it isn't **always** on the same date. It is **always** on the second Sunday in May. People **usually** buy presents for their mothers or send special cards. Husbands **often** take their wives out to dinner.

5.1   Frequency Words with the Simple Present Tense

The frequency words are listed in order from the most frequent to the least frequent:

Frequency Word	Frequency	Example
Always	100%	Mother's Day is always in May.
Usually	↑	I usually take my mother out to dinner.
Often		People often wear green on St. Patrick's Day.
Sometimes		Bars sometimes serve green beer.
Rarely/Seldom	↓	We rarely give flowers to children.
Never	0%	Businesses are never closed for Valentine's Day.

Language Notes

1. Frequency words come after the verb *be* but before other main verbs.

Businesses are *never* closed for St. Patrick's Day.

People *never* take the day off from work for St. Patrick's Day.

2. The following words can also come at the beginning of a sentence: *usually*, *often*, and *sometimes*.

Stores are *usually* open on Mother's Day.
Usually stores are open on Mother's Day.

A valentine *often* has a red heart.
Often a valentine has a red heart.

Bars *sometimes* serve green beer on St. Patrick's Day.
Sometimes bars serve green beer on St. Patrick's Day.

EXERCISE 1   Fill in each blank with an appropriate frequency word.

EXAMPLE: Husbands _____*often*_____ **give flowers or candy to their wives.**

1. Valentine's Day is _____ on February 14.

2. People _____ send valentine cards to their friends.

3. A valentine card _____ has a red heart and a message of love.

4. Young children _____ have a Valentine's Day party at school.

5. Saint Patrick's Day is _____ on March 17.

6. In New York City there is _____ a parade on Saint Patrick's Day.

7. Businesses are _____ closed for St. Patrick's Day and Valentine's Day.

8. Mother's Day is _____ in May.

9. Mother's Day is _____ on a Saturday in the U.S.

10. Husbands _____ take their wives out to dinner for Mother's Day.

EXERCISE 2   Add a verb (phrase) to make a **true** statement about people from your country.

EXAMPLE: **people from my country/often**

People from my country often go to the forest on the weekends to pick mushrooms.

1. people from my country/often

_____

2. people from my country/seldom

_____

3. women from my country/usually

_____

4. women from my country/rarely

_____

5. men from my country/usually

_____

6. men from my country/rarely

_____

EXERCISE 3   Add a frequency word to each sentence to make a **true** statement about yourself. Find a partner, and tell your partner about your habits.

EXAMPLE: **I eat fish.**
I usually eat fish on Fridays.
OR
I rarely eat fish.
OR
Usually I eat fish on Fridays.

1. I cook the meals in my house.
2. I stay home on Sundays.
3. I smoke.
4. I read the newspaper in English.
5. I buy a lottery ticket.
6. I'm tired in class.
7. I use my dictionary to check my spelling.

EXERCISE 4   Add a verb phrase to make a **true** statement about yourself.

EXAMPLE: **I/never**

I never go to bed after 11 o'clock.

OR

I'm never in a good mood in the morning.

1. I/never

2. I/always/in the morning

3. I/usually/on Sunday

4. I/often/on the weekend

5. I/seldom

6. I/sometimes/in class

EXERCISE 5   Use the words given below to write a sentence about your impressions of Americans. Discuss your answers in a small group or with the entire class.

   1. Americans/rarely

_____

   2. Americans/often

_____

5.2   *Yes/No* Questions with *Ever*

We use *ever* in a *yes/no* question when we want an answer that has a frequency word.

Do/Does	Subject	*Ever*	Main Verb	Complement	Short Answer
Do	you	ever	celebrate	Mother's Day?	Yes, I always do.
Does	your father	ever	cook	the meals?	No, he never does.

Be	Subject	*Ever*		Complement	Short Answer
Is	Mother's Day	ever		on a Sunday?	Yes, it always is.
Are	you	ever		bored in class?	No, I never am.

1. In a short answer the frequency word comes between the subject and the verb.

2. The verb after *never* is affirmative. We do not put two negatives together.

   Is Mother's Day ever on a Saturday?
   No, it never *is*.

3. We can also give a short *yes* or *no* answer with just the frequency word.

   Do you *ever* buy your mother a present for Mother's Day?
   Yes, *always*.

   Is St. Patrick's Day *ever* on a Sunday?
   Yes, *sometimes*.

EXERCISE 6   Add *ever* to ask these questions. Another student will answer.

EXAMPLES: **Do you eat in a restaurant?**
            A. Do you ever eat in a restaurant?
            B. Yes, I often do.   OR   **Yes, often.**

            Are you bored in class?
            A. Are you ever bored in class?
            B. No, I never am.   OR   **No, never.**

1. Do you use public transportation?
2. Do you drink coffee at night?
3. Do you drink tea in the morning?
4. Do you speak English at home?
5. Do you watch TV at night?
6. Do you rent videos?
7. Are you late to class?
8. Do you ask for directions on the street?
9. Are you homesick?
10. Are you lazy on Saturdays?
11. Does it snow in March?

EXERCISE 7   Add *ever* to these questions to ask about Americans. Another student will answer.

EXAMPLES: **Do Americans eat fast food?**
            A. Do Americans ever eat fast food?
            B. Yes, they sometimes do.

            Are Americans friendly to you?
            A. Are Americans ever friendly to you?
            B. Yes, they usually are.

1. Do Americans eat with chopsticks?
2. Do Americans carry radios?
3. Do Americans say "Have a nice day"?
4. Do Americans kiss when they meet?
5. Do Americans shake hands when they meet?
6. Are Americans impolite to you?
7. Do Americans pronounce your name incorrectly?
8. Do Americans ask you what country you're from?
9. Are Americans curious about your country?

chopsticks

EXERCISE 8   Check (✓) the activities that you usually, often, or always do. Find a partner. Ask "Do you ever . . . ?" with the words given. Write a sentence about your partner. Tell the class something interesting you learned about your partner.

EXAMPLE: ____✓____ jog in the morning

Ana always jogs in the morning in a park near her house.

1. _____ ride a bike in the summer

   _____

2. _____ visit relatives on Sunday

   _____

3. _____ go to sleep before 9 p.m.

   _____

4. _____ (women) wear high heels

   _____

   _____ (men) wear a suit and tie

   _____

5. _____ do exercises

   _____

6. _____ eat meat

   _____

7. _____ drink beer

   _____

8. _____ buy the Sunday newspaper

   _____

9. _____ put sugar in your coffee

   _____

10. _____ take a nap in the afternoon

   _____

11. _____ eat in a restaurant

_____

12. _____ use a fax machine

_____

13. _____ bake bread

_____

14. _____ use cologne or perfume

_____

15. _____ take a bubble bath

_____   bubble bath

16. _____ _____

5.3   Frequency Expressions and Questions with *How Often*

We ask a question with *how often* when we want to know the frequency of an activity.

How Often	Do/Does	Subject	Verb	Complement	Answer
How often	do	you	visit	your mother?	Once a week.
How often	does	the mail	come?		Every day.

Language Notes

1. Expressions that show frequency are these:
   every day (week, month, year)
   every other day (week, month, year)
   from time to time
   once in a while

2. Frequency expressions can come at the beginning of a sentence or at the end of a sentence.

   I learn more about Americans *every day.*
   Every day I learn more about Americans.

   From time to time, I look up words in my dictionary.
   I look up words in my dictionary *from time to time.*

EXERCISE 9   Ask a question with "How often do you . . . ?" and the words given. Another student will answer.

EXAMPLE: get a haircut
A. How often do you get a haircut?
B. I get a haircut every other month.

1. come to class
2. shop for groceries
3. wash your clothes
4. call long distance to your country
5. go out to dinner

6. use public transportation
7. renew your driver's license
8. buy the newspaper
9. buy a lottery ticket

EXERCISE 10   Find a partner. Interview your partner about one of his or her teachers, friends, or relatives. Ask about this person's usual activities.

EXAMPLE: A. What's your math teacher's name?
B. Her name is Kathy Carlson.
A. Does she give a lot of homework?
B. No, she doesn't.
A. What does she usually wear to class?
B. She usually wears a skirt and blouse.
A. Does she ever wear jeans to class?
B. No, she never does.

EXERCISE 11   In a small group or with the entire class, use frequency words to talk about the activities of a famous person (the President, a singer, an actor, etc.).

EXAMPLE: The President of the U.S. often meets with leaders of other countries.

EXERCISE 12   Write a few sentences to complain about a member of your family or another person you know. Use frequency words.

EXAMPLE: *My sister never helps with the housework.*

She always talks on the phone.

She always leaves dirty dishes in the sink.

EXERCISE 13   Find a partner from another country, if possible. Talk about a special holiday in your country. Ask your partner questions about the date of the holiday, food, clothing, preparations, activities, and so on.

> EXAMPLE: A. We celebrate the Lunar New Year.
> B. Do you wear special clothes?
> A. Yes, we do.
> B. What kind of clothes do you wear?

EXERCISE 14   Editing Practice. Read a student's composition about his or her teacher. Find the mistakes with present tense verbs (including spelling) and frequency words. Add the verb *be* where necessary.

My English teacher is Barbara Nowak. She ~~teachs~~ *teaches* grammar and composition at City College. She very nice, but she's very strict. She give a lot of homework, and we take a lot of tests. If I pass the test, I very happy. English's hard for me.

Every day, at the beginning of the class, she takes attendance and we hand in our homework. Then she's explains the grammar. We do exercises in the book. The book have a lot of exercises. Most exercises is easy, but some hard. Sometimes we says the answers out loud, but sometimes we write the answers. Sometimes the teacher askes a student to write the answers on the blackboard.

Everybody like Barbara because she make the class interesting. She brings often songs to class, and we learn the words. Sometimes we watch a movie in class. Always I enjoy her lessons.

After class I sometimes going to her office if I want more help. She very kind and always trys to help me.

Barbara dresses very informally. Sometimes she wear a skirt, but usually she wears jeans. She about 35 years old, but she's looks like a teenager. (In my country, never a teacher wear jeans.)

I very happy with my teacher. She understand the problems of a foreigner because she's also a foreigner. She's comes from Poland, but she speakes English very well. She know it's hard to learn another language.

5.4 Prepositions of Time

We can use prepositions to talk about time.

Preposition	Example
On: days and dates	When do you go to church? 　*On* Sundays. When do Americans celebrate Independence Day? 　*On* July 4.
In: months	When do Americans celebrate Mother's Day? 　*In* May.
In: years	When do Americans vote for President? 　*In* 1996, 2000, 2004, and so on.
At: specific time of day	What time do you eat lunch? 　*At* noon. What time does the class start? 　*At* 8 o'clock.
In the morning *In* the afternoon *In* the evening	When do you work? 　*In* the morning. When do you go to school? 　*In* the evening.
At night	When do you call your family? 　*At* night.
In: seasons	When do we have vacation? 　*In* the summer.
From . . . to: a beginning and ending time	What hours do they work? 　*From* nine *to* five.

EXERCISE 15   Answer these questions. Use the correct preposition.

1. When do you get up in the morning?
2. What time does your English class begin?
3. What days does your English class meet?
4. When is your birthday?
5. What time do you go to bed?
6. When do Americans celebrate Labor Day?
7. When do students in your country have vacation?
8. What is the cheapest time to call long distance?
9. What is the most expensive time to call long distance?
10. When is Valentine's Day?
11. When is Mother's Day in the U.S.?

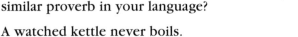

EXPANSION ACTIVITIES

PROVERB   The following proverb contains a frequency word. Discuss the meaning of this proverb. Do you have a similar proverb in your language?

A watched kettle never boils.

WRITING   1. Write about one of your teachers. Describe your teacher and tell about his or her classroom behavior and activities.
2. Write about a holiday in your country. Tell how people celebrate this holiday, or write about how you celebrate your birthday or another special day.

OUTSIDE ACTIVITY   Ask an American to do Exercise 5. See how your answers compare to an American's answers. Report the American's answers to the class.

SUMMARY OF LESSON FIVE

1. Frequency words

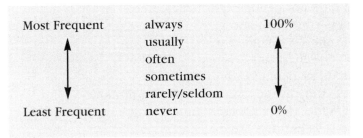

Most Frequent	always	100%
↑	usually	↑
	often	
	sometimes	
↓	rarely/seldom	↓
Least Frequent	never	0%

2. Frequency Questions

   Do you *ever* wear a suit and tie? I seldom do.
   Are you *ever* bored in class? Yes, sometimes.
   How often do you go to the library? About once a month.

3. Frequency words with the simple present tense show regular activities, habits, and customs.

   We *always* have a test at the end of a lesson.
   The teacher *usually* arrives on time.
   People *often* take their mothers out to dinner on Mother's Day.

4. The position of frequency words

Subject	Frequency Word	Verb
I	usually	walk.
I	sometimes	drive.

Subject	*Be*	Frequency Word	Complement
We	are	usually	late.
She	is	sometimes	early.

Frequency Expression	Subject	Verb	Complement	Frequency Expression
Every day	I	watch	TV.	
	I	watch	TV	every day.
Once in a while,	she	eats	fish.	
	She	eats	fish	once in a while.

5. Review prepositions of time on page 116. Review the simple present tense in Lessons 1, 2, and 3.

LESSON FIVE TEST/REVIEW

Part 1   Find the mistakes with frequency words and expressions, and correct them (including mistakes with word order). Not every sentence has a mistake. If the sentence is correct, write **C**.

EXAMPLES: **Do you ever drink coffee?   No, I never ~~don't~~.** *do*

I never eat spaghetti.   *C*

  1. Always I give my mother a present for Mother's Day.

  2. I rarely go downtown.

  3. They never are on time.

  4. It snows seldom in April.

  5. Do you ever take the bus? Yes, rarely.

  6. Are you ever late to class? Yes, always I am.

  7. Do you ever use chopsticks? Yes, I ever do.

  8. What often do you go to the library? I go to the library twice a month.

  9. I once in a while eat in a restaurant.

  10. Every other day she cooks chicken.

Part 2   This is a conversation between two students. Fill in each blank to complete the conversation.

A. Who _____*is*_____ your English teacher?

B. His name _____ David.
    (1)

A. _____ David?
    (2)

B. Yes. I like him very much.

A. _____ he wear a suit to class?
    (3)

B. No, he _____. He always _____ jeans and
    (4)   (5)

running shoes. He dress ____ like a young man.
    (6)

A. _____?
                     (7)

B. He _____ about 60 years old.
          (8)

A. _____ your language?
            (9)

B. No, he doesn't speak Spanish, but he _____ Polish and
                                            (10)

Russian. And English, of course.

A. _____ does your class meet?
          (11)

B. It meets three days a week: Monday, Wednesday, and Friday.

A. My class _____ two days a week: Tuesday and Thursday.
              (12)

B. Tell me about your English teacher.

A. Her name _____ Dr. Misko. She never _____
               (13)   (14)

jeans to class. She _____ wears a dress or suit. She (not)
                         (15)

_____ my language. She only _____ English.
         (16)   (17)

B. Do you like her?

A. Yes, but she _____ a lot of homework and tests.
                (18)

B. _____ does she give a test?
       (19)

A. Once a week. She gives a test every Friday. I (not) _____
                                                     (20)

like tests.

B. My teacher sometimes teaches us American songs. _____
                                                      (21)

your teacher _____ _____ you American songs?
                (22)   (23)

A. No, she never _____.
                                    (24)

B. What book _____?
                                                    (25)

A. My class uses *Grammar in Context.*

B. What _____?
                                    (26)

A. "Context" means the words that help you understand a new word or idea.

B. How _____?
                            (27)

A. C-O-N-T-E-X-T.

Part 3   Fill in the blanks with the correct preposition.

EXAMPLE: **Many people go to church _____*on*_____ Sundays.**

1. We have classes _____ the evening.

2. Valentine's Day is _____ February.

3. Valentine's Day is _____ February 14.

4. A news program begins _____ 6 o'clock.

5. I watch TV _____ night.

6. We have vacation _____ the summer.

7. Many Americans work _____ 9 _____ 5 o'clock.

8. I drink coffee _____ the morning.

9. I study _____ the afternoon.

LESSON SIX

GRAMMAR

Possession
Object Pronouns

CONTEXT

Names
More About Names

Lesson Focus Possession; Object Pronouns

- Nouns have a possessive form. We add an apostrophe + _s_ to most singular nouns. We add an apostrophe to most plural nouns. Compare the possessive nouns in these sentences.

   Marilyn's house is beautiful.   _My parents'_ car is new.

- We can also use possessive adjectives to show possession. Compare these sentences to the ones above.

   Her house is beautiful.   _Their_ car is new.

- We can use object pronouns to substitute for object nouns.

   Do you live near your _parents?_   Yes, I live near _them._

R
E
A
D
I
N
G

Before you read:

1. What is your complete name? What do your friends call you?
2. Do you like your name?

Read the following article. Pay special attention to possessive forms.

NAMES

Americans usually have three names: a first name, a middle name, and a last name (or surname). For example: Marilyn Sue Ellis or Edward David Orleans. Some people use an initial when they sign **their** names: Marilyn S. Ellis, Edward D. Orleans. Not everyone has a middle name.

American women often change **their** last names when they get married. For example, if Marilyn Ellis marries Edward Orleans, her name becomes Marilyn Orleans. Not all women follow this custom. Sometimes a woman keeps **her** maiden name[1] and adds **her husband's** name, with or without a hyphen (-): For example, Marilyn Ellis-Orleans or Marilyn Ellis Orleans. Sometimes a woman does not use **her husband's** name at all. In this case, if the couple has children, they have to decide if **their** children will use **their father's** name, **their mother's** name, or both. A man does not usually change **his** name when he gets married.

Some people use **their mother's** last name as a middle name: John Fitzgerald Kennedy, Franklin Delano Roosevelt.[2]

---

[1] A _maiden name_ is a woman's family name before she gets married.

[2] These are the names of two American presidents.

6.1 Possessive Form of Nouns

Singular	-S Plural	Irregular Plural
Noun + 's	Noun + s'	Noun + 's
Marilyn's husband father's name	parents' house students' desks	children's toys women's dresses

EXAMPLES: I use my *father's* last name.

I don't use my *mother's* last name.

Ted and Mike are *boys'* names.

My *parents'* names are Ethel and Herman.

Marilyn and Sandra are *women's* names.

What are your *children's* names?

Language Notes

1. These irregular plural nouns do not end in *-s*:

   men   women   children   people

   We use *'s* to make the possessive form of these plural nouns.

   Mary and Susan are *women's* names.

2. We can add *'s* or just an apostrophe (') to names that end in *s*. Both forms are correct.

   What is *Charles's* last name?

   or

   What is *Charles'* last name?

3. We use the possessive form for people and other living things.

   My *brother's* name is Joe.
   My *dog's* name is PeeWee.

4. For inanimate (non-living) objects, we usually use "the _____ of _____."

   The door of the classroom is closed.
   Washington College is *the name of my school.*

5. We don't use an article with a possessive noun.

   Wrong: Marilyn's the school has good ESL classes.
   Right: Marilyn's school has good ESL classes.

EXERCISE 1   Fill in each blank with the possessive form of a noun to make a true statement.

EXAMPLE: I use my _____*father's*_____ last name.

1. I use my _____ last name.

2. I don't use my _____ last name.

3. An American married woman often uses her _____ last name.

4. A married woman in my country uses her _____ last name.

5. An American single woman usually uses her _____ last name.

6. An American man rarely uses his _____ last name.

7. John Kennedy used his _____ maiden name as a middle name.

EXERCISE 2   Some of the following sentences can show possession with *'s* or *'*. Rewrite these sentences. Write "no change" for the others.

> EXAMPLES: **The teacher knows the names of the students.**
>
> *The teacher knows the students' names.*
>
> **The door of the classroom is usually closed.**
>
> *No change.*

1. The teacher always corrects the homework of the students.

2. The name of the textbook is *Grammar in Context.*

3. The job of the teacher is to explain the grammar.

4. What are the names of your parents?

5. The color of the book is blue.

6. Do you use the last name of your father?

7. What is the name of your dog?

_____

8. The names of my children are Jason and Jessica.

_____

6.2 Possessive Adjectives

We can use possessive adjectives to show possession. Compare the subject pronouns and the possessive adjectives in the chart.

Subject Pronouns	Possessive Adjectives	Examples
I	my	*I* like *my* name.
you	your	*You*'re a new student. What's *your* name?
he	his	*He* likes *his* name.
she	her	*She* doesn't like *her* name.
it	its	Is *it* your dog? What's *its* name?
we	our	*We* use *our* nicknames.
they	their	*They* are my friends. *Their* last name is Jackson.

Language Notes

1. Be careful not to confuse *his* and *her*.

My *mother* lives in Chicago. *Her* brother lives in Las Vegas.

My *uncle* speaks English well. *His* wife is American.

2. Be careful not to confuse *his* and *he's*. They sound similar.

He's a doctor. *His* wife is a lawyer.

3. Be careful with *your* and *you're*. They sound the same.

You're a good teacher. *Your* pronunciation is clear.

4. Don't use an article with a possessive adjective.

My ~~the~~ brother lives in New York.

The ~~my~~ brother lives in New York.

5. We can use a possessive adjective and a possessive noun together. We can use two (or more) possessive nouns together.

My *sister's* name is Marilyn.
My *sister's husband's* name is Edward.

EXERCISE 3   Fill in the blank with the possessive adjective that relates to the subject.

      EXAMPLE: I like _____*my*_____ teacher.

1. He loves _____ mother.

2. She loves _____ father.

3. A dog loves _____ master.

4. Many American women change _____ names when they get married.

5. Sometimes a woman keeps _____ maiden name and adds _____ husband's name.

6. American men don't usually change _____ names when they get married.

7. Do you use _____ father's last name?

8. I bring _____ book to class.

9. We use _____ books in class.

10. The teacher brings _____ book to class.

11. Some students do _____ homework in the library.

6.3 Questions with *Whose*

Whose + a noun in a question asks about possession.

Whose Noun	*Do/Does*	Subject	Verb?	Answer
Whose name	do	you	use?	I use my father's last name.
Whose pen	does	she	need?	She needs your pen.

We often use *whose* + a noun in a question with *be* to ask about the owner of an object.

Whose Noun	*Be*	*This/That These/Those*	Answer
Whose book	is	that?	It's Bob's book.
Whose glasses	are	those?	They're my glasses.

Language Notes

Don't confuse *whose* with *who's*. They are pronounced the same way.

Whose name do you use?   I use my father's last name.
Who's that man over there?   He's my brother.

EXERCISE 4   Write a question with *whose* and the words given. Answer with the words in parentheses ( ).

EXAMPLES: **wife/that (Robert)**

Whose wife is that? That's Robert's wife.

children/these (Robert)

Whose children are these? These are Robert's children.

1. office/this (the dean)

_____

2. offices/those (the teachers)

_____

3. dictionary/that (the teacher)

_____

4. books/those (the students)

_____

5. car/that (my parents)

_____

6. house/this (my cousins)

_____

7. papers/those (Mr. Ross)

_____

8. diskettes/these (the programmer)

_____

6.4   **Possessive Pronouns**
• • • • • • • • • • • •

Compare the three forms in this table.

Subject Pronouns	Possessive Adjectives	Possessive Pronouns
I	my	mine
you	you	yours
he	his	his
she	her	hers
it	its	—
we	our	ours
they	their	theirs
who	whose	whose

1. A noun never follows a possessive pronoun. Compare the possessive adjective and the possessive pronoun in these sentences.

You don't use your middle initial.	I use _my middle initial._
You don't use your middle initial.	I use _mine._
His name is Robert.	_Her name_ is Patty.
His name is Robert.	_Hers_ is Patty.
This is my book.	_Whose book_ is that?
This is my book.	_Whose_ is that?

2. After a possessive noun, we can omit the noun.

Robert's wife speaks English.	_Peter's wife_ doesn't speak English.
Robert's wife speaks English.	_Peter's_ doesn't.

EXERCISE 5   In each sentence below, replace the underlined words with a possessive pronoun.

> EXAMPLE: Your book is new. My book is old.
>   Your book is new. Mine is old.

1. His name is Charles. Her name is Paula.
2. My car is old. Your car is new.
3. I like my English teacher. Does your brother like his English teacher?
4. I have my dictionary today. Do you have your dictionary?
5. Please let me use your book. I don't have my book today.
6. Whose sweater is this? Whose sweater is that?
7. My parents' apartment is big. Our apartment is small.
8. My teacher comes from Houston. Paula's teacher comes from El Paso.

EXERCISE 6   Find a partner. Compare yourself to your partner. Compare physical characteristics, clothes, family, home, job, car, etc. Report some interesting facts to the class.

> EXAMPLE: My hair is straight. Mark's is curly.
>
>   His eyes are blue. Mine are brown.
>
>   My family lives in this city. Mark's family lives in Rumania.

6.5   The Subject and the Object

In a sentence, the subject (S) comes before the verb (V). An object (O) comes after the verb.

>   S   V   O
>   Bob likes Mary.

We can use pronouns to take the place of subject and object nouns in a sentence.

>   S   V   O   S   V   O
>   Bob likes Mary because she helps him.

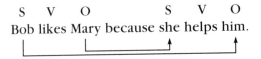

. . . .

R
E
A
D
I
N
G

Before you read

1. What are common American names?
2. What is a very common first name in your country? What is a very common last name in your country?

Read the following conversation. Pay special attention to object pronouns.

MORE ABOUT NAMES

A. I have many questions about American names. Can you answer **them** for me?
B. Of course.
A. Tell **me** about your name.
B. My name is William, but my friends call **me** Bill.
A. Why do they call **you** Bill?
B. Bill is a common nickname for William.
A. Is William your first name?
B. Yes, of course.
A. What's your full name?
B. William Michael Madison.
A. Do you ever use your middle name?
B. I only use **it** for very formal occasions. I sign my name William M. Madison, Jr. (Junior)
A. What does "junior" mean?
B. It means that I have the same name as my father. His name is William Madison, Sr. (senior)
A. What's your wife's name?
B. Anna Marie Simms-Madison. I call **her** Annie.
A. Why does she have two last names?
B. Simms is her father's last name, and Madison is mine. She uses both names with a hyphen (-) between **them.**
A. Do you have any children?
B. Yes. We have a son and a daughter. Our son's name is Richard, but we call **him** Dick. Our daughter's name is Elizabeth, but everybody calls **her** Lizzy.
A. What do your children call **you?**
B. They call **us** Mommy and Daddy, of course.

. . . .

6.6 Object Pronouns

Compare the subject and object forms of the pronouns.

Subject	Object
I	me
you	you
he	him
she	her
it	it
we	us
you	you
they	them*

*NOTE: We use *them* for plural people and things.

Language Notes

1. We can use an object pronoun to substitute for the object noun.

   I have *a middle initial*. I use *it* when I sign my name.
   Richard is my son's name. We call *him* Dick.
   I have *some questions*. Can you answer *them* for me?

2. An object pronoun can follow a preposition.

   I have two last names. I use both *of them*.
   My sister has a son. She always talks *about him.*

EXERCISE 7   Fill in each blank. Substitute the underlined words with an object pronoun.

EXAMPLE: I look like <u>my father</u>, but my brother doesn't look like ____*him.*____

1. <u>My brother's</u> name is William, but we call _____ Bill.

2. <u>I</u> understand the teacher, and the teacher understands _____.

3. I use <u>my dictionary</u> when I write, but I don't use _____ when I speak.

4. I like <u>this city</u>. Do you like _____?

5. I talk to <u>Americans</u>, but I don't always understand _____.

6. We listen to <u>the teacher</u>, and we talk to _____.

7. When <u>we</u> make a mistake, the teacher corrects _____.

8. <u>The President</u> has advisors. They help _____ make decisions.

9. <u>You</u> understand me, and I understand _____.

10. <u>My friends</u> sometimes visit me, and I sometimes visit _____.

EXERCISE 8   Two students are talking. Fill in each blank with an appropriate object pronoun.

A. How do you like Ms. Miller, your new English teacher?

B. I like _____*her*_____, but she gives a lot of homework. This week we have

   to write a composition, and she says we have to type _____.

   $\qquad\qquad\qquad\qquad\qquad\qquad\qquad\qquad\qquad\qquad\qquad\qquad\qquad\qquad$ (1)

   May I borrow your typewriter?

A. I never use _____ any more. I have a word processor. You can

   $\qquad\qquad\qquad$ (2)

   come to my house and use _____, if you like.

   $\qquad\qquad\qquad\qquad\qquad\qquad\qquad\qquad$ (3)

B. But I don't know how.

A. I'll teach _____.

   $\qquad\qquad\qquad$ (4)

B. It's going to be hard. I don't know anything about computers.

A. Don't worry. You just need to know a few basic commands. You can learn

   _____ in less than an hour.

   $\qquad\qquad\quad$ (5)

B. I don't want to bother _____.

   $\qquad\qquad\qquad\qquad\qquad$ (6)

A. You're not bothering _____. I'm glad to help

   $\qquad\qquad\qquad\qquad\qquad$ (7)

   _____. Come to my house tomorrow.

   $\qquad\quad$ (8)

B. Can I bring my brother too? You can teach both of _____ at

   $\qquad\qquad\qquad\qquad\qquad\qquad\qquad\qquad\qquad\qquad\qquad\qquad\qquad$ (9)

   the same time.

A. Do I know your brother?

B. You sit next to _____ in math class.

   $\qquad\qquad\quad$ (10)

A. Do you mean Roberto?

B. Yes. He's my brother.

A. Of course! He looks just like _____. Sure. Bring
                                                    (11)

_____. I'll be happy to teach both of _____
           (12)   (13)

at the same time.

B. Thanks a lot. I'll see _____ tomorrow.
                                   (14)

EXERCISE 9   Fill in each blank with *I, I'm, my, mine,* or *me.*

    EXAMPLE: _____*I'm*_____ a foreign student. _____*I*_____ come from Japan.

        _____*My*_____ roommate's parents live in the U.S., but _____*mine*_____

        live in Japan. _____*My*_____ parents write to _____*me*_____ twice a month.

    1. _____ 20 years old.

    2. _____ parents don't live in the U.S.

    3. _____ study at the University of Wisconsin.

    4. _____ major is engineering.

    5. _____ have a roommate.

    6. _____ roommate's name is Kelly. _____ is Yuki.

    7. _____ roommate helps _____ with my English.

EXERCISE 10   Fill in each blank with *he, he's, his,* or *him.*

    EXAMPLE: I have a good friend. _____*His*_____ name is Paul. _____*He's*_____

        Puerto Rican. _____*He*_____ lives in New York. I like _____*him*_____.

    1. _____ married.

    2. _____ works in an office.

    3. _____ an accountant.

    4. _____ son helps _____ in _____ business.

5. _____ 37 years old. _____ wife is 35.

6. My wife and _____ wife are friends.

7. My wife is a doctor. _____ is a computer programmer.

EXERCISE 11   Fill in each blank with *she, she's, her,* or *hers.*

> **EXAMPLE: I have a friend. _____Her_____ name's Diane. _____She's_____ American.**
>
> _____She_____ **lives in Boston. My native language is Korean.**
>
> _____Hers_____ **is English.**

1. _____ an interesting person.

2. I like _____ very much.

3. _____ married.

4. _____ has two children.

5. My children go to Dewey School. _____ go to King School.

6. _____ a nurse. _____ likes _____ job.

7. _____ husband is a teacher.

EXERCISE 12   Fill in each blank with *they, they're, their, theirs,* or *them.*

> **EXAMPLE: Diane and Richard are my friends. _____They_____ live in Boston.**
>
> _____Their_____ **house is beautiful. _____They're_____ happy. I see _____them_____ on**
>
> **the weekends.**

1. _____ Americans.

2. _____ both work.

3. _____ have two children.

4. _____ children go to public school.

5. My apartment is small. _____ is big.

6. _____ interested in art.

7. I talk to _____ once a week.

EXERCISE 13   Fill in each blank about a cat. Use *it, it's,* or *its*.

EXAMPLE: *It's*   an independent animal.   *It*   always lands on

           its   feet.

1. _____ likes to eat fish.

2. _____ a small animal.

3. _____ fur is soft.

4. _____ catches mice.

5. _____ claws are sharp.

6. _____ a clean animal.

7. Do you see that cat? Yes, I see _____ .

claws

EXERCISE 14   Fill in each blank with *we, we're, our, ours,* or *us*.

EXAMPLE: *We*   study English.   *We're*   foreign students.

     Our   teacher is American. He helps   *us*   .

1. _____ come from different countries.

2. _____ in class now.

3. _____ classroom is comfortable.

4. The teacher asks _____ a lot of questions.

5. The teacher's textbook has the answers. _____ don't have the answers.

6. _____ interested in English.

EXERCISE 15   Fill in each blank with *you, you're, your,* or *yours*.

EXAMPLE: *You're*   a good teacher. Students like   *you*   . My other

teacher's name is hard to pronounce.   *Yours*   is easy to

pronounce.

1. _____ explain the grammar well.

2. We all understand _____ .

3. Our pronunciation is sometimes hard to understand. _____ is clear.

4. _____ a kind teacher.

5. _____ class is very interesting.

6. _____ have a lot of experience with foreign students.

6.7 Questions About the Subject

Compare these statements and related questions.

Wh- Word	Do/Does	Subject	Verb	Complement
When	does	Sarah she	watches watch	TV. TV?
Where	do	My parents your parents	live live?	in Peru.
Who(m)	does	Your sister she	likes like?	someone.
		Someone Who Someone Who	has has needs needs	my book. my book? help. help.

Language Notes

1. Most wh- questions use *do* or *does* and the base form of the verb. *Whom* asks about the object of the sentence. We use *do* or *does* in questions with *whom*.

OBJECT
I see someone.   *Whom* do you see?

Informally, Americans often say *who* instead of *whom*.

Who do you see?

2. *Who* asks about the subject of the sentence. We don't use *do* or *does* with questions about the subject.

SUBJECT
Someone needs help.   *Who* needs help?

3. Notice that we use the -*s* form of the verb to ask a present tense question about the subject. The answer can be singular or plural.

Who *has* a new car?
Jake *has* a new car.
Bill and Ann *have* a new car.

4. We can answer a *who* question with a short answer.

Who needs help?   I *do*.
Who knows the answer?   Marta *does*.
Who is from Ecuador?   Marco *is*.

EXERCISE 16   Talk about some jobs in your house. Ask another student, "Who _____s in your house?" The other student will answer.

EXAMPLES: take out the garbage
           A. Who takes out the garbage in your house?
           B. My brother does.

           vacuum the carpet
           A. Who vacuums the carpets in your house?
           B. Nobody does. We don't have carpets.

vacuum

1. cook the meals
2. make your bed
3. pay the bills
4. wash the dishes
5. shop for groceries
6. wash the clothes
7. vacuum the carpet
8. dust the furniture
9. sweep the floor

dust

sweep

EXERCISE 17   Fill in each blank with *who, whom, who's,* or *whose.*

EXAMPLE: ___*Who*___ speaks Japanese? Yoko does.

1. _____ has the textbook. The teacher does.

2. _____ your English teacher? Bob Marks is.

3. There's a dictionary on the floor. _____ dictionary is it?

4. _____ do you see on the weekends? I see my friends.

EXERCISE 18   Circle the correct word to complete this conversation between two students.

EXAMPLE: (Whose, Who's, Who, Whom) book do you have?

A. (Who, Who's, Whose, Whom) your English teacher?

B. (My, Mine, Me) teacher's name is Charles Flynn.

A. (My, Mine, Me) is Marianne Peters. She's Mr. Flynn's wife.

B. Oh, really? His last name is different from (she, her, hers).

A. Yes. She uses (her, hers, his, he's) father's last name, not her (husband's, husbands', husbands, husband).

B. Do they have children?

A. Yes.

B. (Whose, Who's, Who, Whom) name do they use?

A. (They, They're, Their, Theirs) children use both last names.

B. How do you know so much about (you, you're, your, yours) teacher and (she, she's, her, hers) children?

A. We talk about (we, us, our, ours) names in class. We also talk about American customs. She explains her customs, and we explain (our, ours, us).

B. Mr. Flynn doesn't talk about (her, his, he's, hers) family in class.

A. Do you call (her, his, him, he) "mister"?

B. Of course. (He, He's, His) the teacher. We show respect.

A. But we call Marianne by (her, hers, she) first name. (She, She's, Her) prefers that.

B. I prefer to call (our, us, ours) teachers by (they, they're, their, theirs) last names. That's the way we do it in my country.

A. And in (me, my, mine) too. But (we, we're, us) in the U.S. now. There's an expression: When in Rome, do as the Romans do.

EXPANSION ACTIVITIES

PROVERBS   The following proverbs use possessive forms. Discuss the meaning of each proverb. Do you have a similar proverb in your language?

Man may work from sun to sun, but woman's work is never done.
A fool and his money are soon parted.

DISCUSSION   Discuss naming customs in your country. Do people have a middle name? Do fathers and sons ever have the same name? Tell about your name. Does it mean something?

OUTSIDE ACTIVITY   Ask an American to tell you about his or her name. Tell the class something interesting you learned from this American.

SUMMARY OF LESSON SIX

1. Pronouns and Possessive Forms

Subject Pronoun	Object Pronoun	Possessive Adjective	Possessive Pronoun
I	me	my	mine
you	you	your	yours
he	him	his	his
she	her	her	hers
it	it	its	—
we	us	our	ours
they	them	their	theirs
who	whom	whose	whose

My name is Rosa.
I come from Argentina
The teacher helps *me.*
Your country is small. *Mine* is big.

Their names are Ly and Tran.
They come from Vietnam.
The teacher helps *them.*
Your country is big. *Theirs* is small.

Who has a new car?
With *whom* do you live? (Informal: *Who* do you live with?)
Whose book is that?
This is my dictionary. *Whose* is that?

2. Possessive Nouns
Jack*'s* car is old.
His parents*'* car is new.

The children*'s* toys are on the floor.
What's the name *of our textbook*?

3. Words that Sound Alike
   A. *There, their,* and *they're*
      There are three closets in my apartment.
      Where's the dictionary? It's over *there.*
      My sisters live in Poland. *They're* both married.
      My parents have a car, but I never use *their* car.

   B. *He's* and *his* (The pronunciation is similar but not the same.)
      He's my brother. *His* name is Charles.

   C. *Who's* and *whose*
      Who's that man? He's my brother.   *Whose* coat is this? It's my coat.

   D. *It's* and *its*
      I have a turtle. *It's* very old. *Its* name is Shelly.

   E. *Your* and *you're*
      You're a very intelligent person.   I like *your* ideas.

LESSON SIX TEST/REVIEW

Part 1   Choose the correct word to complete these sentences.

EXAMPLE: Most American women change _____ *c* _____ names when they get married, but not all do.

    a. her   b. hers   c. their   d. theirs

1. I have two _____.

    a. sisters   b. sister's   c. sisters'   d. sister

2. _____ names are Marilyn and Charlotte.

    a. Their   b. Theirs   c. They're   d. They   e. Hers

3. _____ both married.

    a. Their   b. They're   c. They   d. Them   e. There

4. Marilyn uses _____.

    a. the last name her husband
    b. the last name of his husband
    c. her husband's last name
    d. his husband's last name

5. Charlotte uses _____ father's last name.

    a. we   b. our   c. ours   d. us

6. I have one brother. _____ married.

    a. He's   b. His   c. He   d. Him

7. _____ wife is very nice.

    a. Him   b. Her   c. His   d. He's

8. _____ first name is Sandra.

    a. My   b. Mine   c. I'm   d. Me

9. My friends call _____ "Sandy."

    a. me   b. my   c. mine

10. My sister often uses her middle name, but I rarely use _____.

    a. my   b. mine   c. me   d. I'm

11. You have a dog, but I don't know _____ name.

    a. it   b. it's   c. its

12. _____ your teacher?

    a. Whom   b. Who   c. Whose   d. Who's

13. The teacher's name is on _____.
   a. the door of her office
   b. her office's door
   c. the door her office
   d. her the office's door

14. _____
   a. Who's is that office?
   b. Whose is that office?
   c. Who's office is that?
   d. Whose office is that?

15. Her _____ names are Ricky and Eddie.
   a. childs'   b. children's   c. childrens   d. childrens'

16. _____ has the newspaper?
   a. Whom   b. Whose   c. Who   d. Who's

17. Who _____ more time with the test?
   a. need   b. does need   c. needs   d. does needs

Part 2   Two women are talking about names. Fill in each blank with possessive forms and subject and object pronouns. Add apostrophes where necessary.

A. What's your last name?

B. It's Woods.

A. Woods sounds like an American name. But ___*you're*___ Polish, aren't you?

B. Yes, but Americans have trouble pronouncing _____ name, so I use the
                                                                      (1)

   name "Woods."

A. What's _____ real last name?
                  (2)

B. Wodzianicki.

A. My name is hard for Americans too, but _____ like my name, and I don't
                                                             (3)

   want to change _____. I'm proud of it.
                           (4)

B. What's _____ last name?
                  (5)

A. Lopez Hernandez.

B. Why do _____ have two last names?
       (6)

A. I come from Mexico. Mexicans have two last names. Mexicans use both

   parents _____ names.
              (7)

B. What happens when a woman gets married? Does she use _____
                                                              (8)

   parent _____ names and _____ husband _____ name too?
            (9)   (10)   (11)

A. No. When a woman gets married, she usually drops _____
                                                         (12)

   mother _____ name. She adds "of" (in Spanish, "de") and _____
            (13)   (14)

   husband _____ name. My sister is married. _____ name is Maria Lopez
             (15)   (16)

   de Castillo. Lopez is _____ father _____ name and Castillo is her
                            (17)   (18)

   husband _____ name. _____ kids _____ last name is Castillo Lopez.
             (19)   (20)   (21)

B. That's confusing. Everybody in the family has a different last name.

A. It's not confusing for us. You understand your customs, and we understand

   _____.
      (22)

B. Do your sister _____ kids have American first names?
                      (23)

A. My sister gave _____ Spanish names, but _____ friends gave them
                      (24)   (25)

   American names. Her daughter _____ name is Rosa, but _____
                                     (26)   (27)

   friends call her Rose. _____ son _____ name is Eduardo, but
                             (28)   (29)

   _____ friends call _____ Eddie. Ricardo is the youngest one.
      (30)   (31)

   _____ still a baby, but when he goes to school, _____ friends will
      (32)   (33)

   probably call _____ Rick.
                    (34)

LESSON SEVEN

GRAMMAR

Present Continuous Tense

CONTEXT

Student Life
Observations About Americans

Lesson Focus   **Present Continuous Tense**

We use the present tense of *be* + verb + *-ing* to form the present continuous tense. We use the present continuous tense to talk about an action in progress now.

We*'re studying* Lesson Seven now.
The teacher *is explaining* the grammar now.

• •

R
E
A
D
I
N
G

Before you read:

1. What are you studying this semester?
2. How many credit hours are you taking?
3. Besides English, are you learning something new?

Read the following letter. Pay special attention to the present continuous verbs.

STUDENT LIFE

Dear Family,

   I**'m writing** you this letter to tell you about my life at college in the U.S. Many new things **are happening,** and I want to tell you all about my life here.

   First of all, I**'m living** in a dormitory with an American roommate. His name is Ben Kaplan, and he's from California. He**'s majoring** in chemistry. You know, of course, I**'m majoring** in music. Ben and I are very different, but we get along[1] very well. We speak English all the time, and because of him, my English **is improving.** He's not here right now because he**'s studying** for a big test with some friends.

   This semester I**'m taking** five courses (18 credit hours). It's hard, but I**'m getting** good grades. I**'m learning** a new instrument—the guitar. It's a lot of fun for me and not very difficult. I**'m meeting** a lot of new people in my classes, students from all over the world.

   There's one thing I'm not happy about. The food here in the dorm cafeteria is not very good. It's greasy, and I**'m gaining** weight. Ben and I **are thinking** about getting an apartment for next semester. We want to cook for ourselves and have more freedom.

   Thank you for the sweater you sent me. I**'m wearing** it now. It's so cold this week. In fact, it**'s snowing** now. It's so strange to see snow. I**'m looking** out my window. Children **are playing** in the snow. They**'re making** a snowman and **throwing** snowballs.

---

[1]When people *get along well,* they have a good relationship.

I have to finish this letter now. **I'm writing** a term paper² for my music theory class. Please write soon and tell me what **is happening** with all of you.

I hope you are all well.

Love,
Dan

7.1 Present Continuous Tense—Forms

The present continuous tense is: Subject + *be* + verb + *-ing*.

Subject	*Be*	Verb + *-ing*
I	am	studying.
You We They Jim and Sue	are	reading. learning. practicing. writing.
He She It Jim	is	eating. sitting. sleeping. standing.

Language Notes

1. We can make a contraction with the subject pronoun and a form of *be*. Most nouns can also contract with *is*.³

I'm	working.	*He's*	eating.
You're	reading.	*She's*	sitting.
We're	learning.	*It's*	snowing.
They're	practicing.	*Dan's*	writing.

2. To form the negative, we put *not* after the verb *be*. Compare these sentences.

Dan *is writing* a letter. He *isn't writing* a composition.
Children *are playing* in the park. They *aren't playing* inside.

---

²A *term paper* is a paper that students write for class. The student researches a topic. It often takes a student a full semester (or term) to produce this paper.

³See Lesson 1, page 8 for exceptions.

EXERCISE 1 Fill in the missing part of each sentence.

> EXAMPLES: I _'m_____ writing a letter.
>
> I'm look _ing_____ out my window.

1. My roommate and his friend _____ studying.

2. I'm learn_____ to play the guitar.

3. New things _____ happening.

4. I'm meet_____ a lot of new people.

5. I _____ major_____ in music.

6. My roommate is _____ing in chemistry.

7. I'm _____ a sweater now.

8. Children are _____ing snowballs.

Language Notes

1. We can use the present continuous tense to talk about an action that is in progress now, at this moment.

> Dan *is writing* a letter to his family now.
> It's *snowing* now.
> Children *are making* a snowman and *throwing** snowballs.

*NOTE: When the subject is doing two or more things in the present continuous tense, we don't repeat the *be* verb.

2. We can use the present continuous tense to talk about a long-term action that is in progress. (It may not be happening at this exact moment.)

> Dan and his roommate *are gaining* weight.
> Dan *is writing* a term paper this semester.
> He's *majoring* in chemistry.

3. We can use the present continuous tense to describe a state or condition, using the following verbs: *sit, stand, wear, sleep.*

> He's *wearing* a sweater now.
> He's *sitting* near the window.

EXERCISE 2 Answer the following questions with a complete sentence.

> EXAMPLE: What's Dan majoring in?
> He's majoring in music.

1. Why's Dan's English improving?
2. What instrument is he learning to play?
3. How many courses is he taking this semester?
4. Why's Dan unhappy about the food?
5. What are Dan and his roommate thinking about doing?
6. What's Dan wearing now?

7.2 Spelling of the -*ing* Form

The chart below shows the spelling of the -*ing* form. Fill in the last examples.

Rule	Verbs	-*ing* Form
Add -*ing* to most verbs.	eat	eat*ing*
	go	go*ing*
	study	study*ing*
	work	*working*
	worry	_____
For a one-syllable verb that ends in a consonant + vowel + consonant (CVC), double the final consonant and add -*ing*.	p l a n ↓ ↓ ↓ C V C	plan*ning*
	s t o p ↓ ↓ ↓ C V C	stop*ping*
	s i t ↓ ↓ ↓ C V C	sit*ting*
	r u n ↓ ↓ ↓ C V C	_____
	d r a g ↓ ↓ ↓ C V C	_____
Do not double a final *w, x,* or *y.*	show	sho*wing*
	mix	mi*xing*
	stay	sta*ying*
	fix	_____
	pay	_____
For a two-syllable word that ends in CVC, double the final consonant only if the last syllable is stressed.	refér	refer*ring*
	admít	admit*ting*
	begín	begin*ning*
	occúr	_____
	prefér	_____

Rule	Verbs	*-ing* Form
When the last syllable of a two-syllable word is not stressed, do not double the final consonant.	lísten	listen*ing*
	ópen	open*ing*
	óffer	offer*ing*
	vísit	_____
	májor	_____
If the word ends in a consonant + *e*, drop the e before adding *-ing*.	live	liv*ing*
	take	tak*ing*
	write	writ*ing*
	drive	_____
	make	_____

EXERCISE 3   Write the *-ing* form of the verb. (Two-syllable words that end in CVC have accent marks to show which syllable is stressed.)

EXAMPLES: **play** _____*playing*_____

make ____*making*____

1. plan _____

2. ópen _____

3. sit _____

4. begín _____

5. hurry _____

6. háppen _____

7. stay _____

8. grow _____

9. marry _____

10. grab _____

11. write _____

12. fix _____

13. wipe _____

14. carry _____

15. drink _____

16. smoke _____

17. wait _____

18. serve _____

EXERCISE 4   Fill in each blank with the present continuous tense of the verb in parentheses ( ). Use correct spelling.

> EXAMPLE: Dan _is writing_____ a letter.
> _____(write)

1. He _____ in a dorm.
   _____(live)

2. Dan and his roommate _____ weight.
   _____(gain)

3. Dan _____ in chemistry.
   _____(not/major)

4. Children outside _____ a snowman and _____
   _____(make)   _____(throw)

   snowballs.

5. Dan _____ a term paper on music theory.
   _____(write)

6. I _____ in the blanks with the correct verb form.
   ____(fill)

7. My teacher _____ corrections.
   _____(make)

8. We _____ the textbook.
   ____(use)

9. We _____ reading now.
   _____(not/study)

10. We _____ Exercise 4.
    _____(finish)

EXERCISE 5   Make a **true** affirmative statement or negative statement about your activities now with the words given.

> EXAMPLES: **wear a watch**
>   **I'm wearing a watch (now).**
>
>   **drink coffee**
>   **I'm not drinking coffee (now).**

1. sit in the back of the room
2. speak my native language
3. pay attention
4. ask questions
5. learn the present continuous tense
6. look out the window
7. look at the blackboard
8. write a composition
9. use my textbook
10. wear jeans
11. _____
12. _____

EXERCISE 6   Make a **true** affirmative statement or negative statement about yourself with the words given. Talk about a long-term action.

> EXAMPLES: look for a job
> **I'm looking for a job.**
>
> live in a hotel
> **I'm not living in a hotel.**

1. look for a new apartment
2. learn a lot of English
3. gain weight
4. lose weight
5. spend a lot of money
6. save my money
7. write a term paper
8. try to understand American customs
9. meet Americans
10. learn how to drive
11. live in a dorm
12. _____

7.3 Questions with the Present Continuous Tense

Compare statements and questions with the present continuous tense:

Wh- Word	Be	Subject	Be	Verb-ing	Complement	Short Answer
		Dan	is	wearing	a sweater.	
	Is	Dan		wearing	a hat?	No, he isn't.
What	is	Dan		wearing?		
Why	isn't	Dan		wearing	a hat?	
		Who	is	wearing	a hat?	
		Children	are	playing.		
	Are	they		playing	inside?	No, they aren't.
Where	are	they		playing?		
Why	aren't	they		playing	inside?	

Language Notes

When the question is "What ... doing?" we usually answer with a different verb. Compare these questions and answers.

What's he *doing?*	He's *writing* a letter.
What *are* the children *doing?*	They're *playing* in the snow.
What *are* you *doing?*	I'm *studying* verbs.

EXERCISE 7   Use the words given to ask a question about what this class is doing now. Another student will answer.

> EXAMPLE: we/use the textbook now
> A. Are we using the textbook now?
> B. Yes, we are.

1. the teacher/wear a sweater
2. the teacher/write on the blackboard
3. the teacher/erase the blackboard
4. the teacher/sit at the desk
5. the teacher/take attendance
6. the teacher/explain the grammar
7. the teacher/help the students
8. we/practice the present continuous tense
9. we/practice the past tense
10. we/review Lesson 6
11. we/make mistakes
12. what/the teacher/wear
13. where/the teacher/stand or sit
14. what exercise/we/do
15. what/you/think about
16. what/the teacher/do
17. who/wear/jeans

EXERCISE 8   Ask a question about a long-term action with the words given. Another student will answer.

> EXAMPLE: you/study math this semester
> A. Are you studying math this semester?
> B. Yes, I am.

1. you/plan to buy a car
2. you/study biology this semester
3. you/take other courses this semester
4. you/look for a new apartment
5. you/look for a job
6. you/learn about American customs
7. your English/improve
8. your vocabulary/grow
9. the teacher/help you
10. the students/make progress
11. you/learn about other students' countries

EXERCISE 9   Ask and answer questions about Dan's letter.

> EXAMPLE: Dan/lose weight
> A. Is Dan losing weight?
> B. No, he isn't. He's gaining weight.

1. Dan/live in an apartment
2. he/major in art
3. he/study the guitar
4. his roommate/major in chemistry
5. Dan/wear a new sweater
6. what/Dan/major in
7. how many courses/Dan/take
8. _____

EXERCISE 10   Read each sentence. Then ask a *wh-* question about the words in parentheses ( ). Another student will answer.

> EXAMPLE: **We're doing an exercise. (What exercise)**
> A. **What exercise are we doing?**
> B. **We're doing Exercise 10.**

1. We're practicing a tense. (What tense)
2. We're using a textbook. (What kind of book)
3. You're listening to the teacher. (Why)
4. The teacher's helping the students. (Why)
5. I'm answering a question. (Which question)
6. We're practicing questions. (What kind of questions)
7. Your English ability is improving. (Why)
8. Your life is changing. (How)

EXERCISE 11   Read each statement. Then write a question about the words in parentheses ( ). Write an answer. Refer to Dan's letter on page 145 and 146.

> EXAMPLE: **Dan is writing a letter. (to whom)** OR **(who . . . to)**
> A. **Who is he writing to?**   OR   **To whom is he writing?**
> B. **He's writing to his family.**

1. He's learning a new instrument. (what instrument)

   A. _____

   B. _____

2. He's gaining weight. (why)

   A. _____

   B. _____

3. His roommate is studying. (who . . . with) OR (with whom)

   A. _____

   B. _____

4. He's wearing something new. (what)

   A. _____

   B. _____

5. His English is improving. (why)

A. _____

B. _____

6. He's taking courses. (how many courses)

A. _____

B. _____

7. He's meeting new students. (what kind)

A. _____

B. _____

8. Dan and Ben are planning to move. (why)

A. _____

B. _____

EXERCISE 12   Check (✓) the actions that you are doing right now or at this general point in time. Find a partner and ask if he or she is doing these things. Report some interesting information to the class.

EXAMPLES: _✓_ plan to buy a computer

Both Raul and I are planning to buy a computer.

_✓_ learn to drive a car

Maria is learning how to drive. Her husband is teaching her.

1. _____ wear jeans
2. _____ hold a pencil
3. _____ chew gum
4. _____ think about the weekend
5. _____ live in a dorm
6. _____ look for a job
7. _____ plan to take a vacation
8. _____ plan to buy a computer

9. _____ take a computer class this semester
10. _____ get tired
11. _____ gain weight
12. _____ learn about the history of the U.S.
13. _____ learn how to drive
14. _____ _____

• •

R
E
A
D
I
N
G

Before you read:

1. What American behaviors are strange to you?
2. Is your behavior in the U.S. different from your behavior in your country?

Read the following letter. Pay special attention to verbs—simple present and present continuous.

OBSERVATIONS ABOUT AMERICANS

Dear Family,

I**'m sitting** in the school cafeteria now. I**'m writing** this letter between classes. I **see** many strange behaviors and customs around me. You always **ask** me about American customs, so I **think** you probably **want** to know about life in the U.S.

I**'m looking** at a young couple at the next table. The young man and woman **are touching, holding** hands, and even **kissing.** It looks strange because people never **kiss** in public in our country. At another table, a young man and woman **are sitting** with a baby. The man **is feeding** the baby. Men never **feed** the baby in our country. Why **isn't** the woman **feeding** the baby?

Two women **are putting** on make-up. I **think** this is bad public behavior. They**'re** also **smoking.** In our country women never **smoke** in public. These women **are wearing** shorts. In our country women never **wear** shorts.

A group of students **is listening** to the radio. The music is very loud. Their music **is bothering** other people, but they **don't care.** I'm sitting far from them, but I **hear** their music.

A young man **is resting** his feet on another chair. His friend **is eating** a hamburger with his hands. Why **isn't** he **using** a fork and knife?

These kinds of behaviors **look** bad to me. I'**m trying** to understand them, but I'**m having** a hard time. I still **think** many of these actions are rude.[4]

Your son,
Ali

7.4 Contrast of Present Continuous and Simple Present

Compare the simple present and present continuous tenses.

Simple Present	Present Continuous
He sometimes wears a suit.	He's wearing jeans now.
He doesn't usually wear shorts.	He isn't wearing a belt.
Does he ever wear a hat?	Is he wearing a T-shirt?
Yes, he does.	No, he isn't.
When does he wear a hat?	What is he wearing?
Who wears a hat?	Who is wearing a T-shirt?

---

[4]*Rude* means impolite.

Language Notes

1. We use the simple present tense to talk about a general truth, a habitual activity, or a custom.

   The president *lives* in the White House. (general truth)
   We usually *learn* about American life. (habitual activity)
   Americans *eat* hamburgers with their hands. (custom)

2. We use the present continuous for an action that is in progress at this moment, or for a longer action that is in progress at this general time.

   Ali *is writing* a letter to his family now. (at this moment)
   He's *looking* at Americans in the school cafeteria. (at this moment)
   He's *trying* to understand American customs. (at this general time)
   He's *learning* more and more about Americans all the time. (at this general time)

3. When we use *live* in the simple present, we mean that this is a person's home. In the present continuous, it shows a temporary, short-term residence.

   Ali *is living* in a dorm this semester.
   His family *lives* in Jordan.

4. "What do you do (for a living)?" asks about your job. "What are you doing?" asks about your activity at this moment.

   What *does* she *do* for a living?   She's a nurse.
   What *is* she *doing*?   She's *waiting* for the bus.

EXERCISE 13   Look at the pictures. Use the verb in parentheses ( ) to tell what is happening in the picture. Then fill in the blank with the simple present tense to tell about American customs. Then tell about customs in your country.

EXAMPLE: **These men (hug)** _are hugging_

American men seldom _hug_

Russian men sometimes hug.

1. These men (shake) _____ hands.

   Americans often _____ hands.

   _____

2. These women (walk) _____ arm-in-arm.

   American women rarely _____ arm-in-arm.

   _____

3. These people (kiss) _____.

   Americans sometimes _____ in public.

   _____ in public.

4. This man (feed) _____ his baby.

   American fathers sometimes _____ their babies.

   _____

5. This woman (wear) _____ a veil.

   American women never _____ a veil.

   _____

6. These people (bow) _____.

   Americans never _____ when they meet.

   _____

7. These people (eat) _____ with their hands.

   Americans sometimes _____ with their hands.

   _____

8. These women (wear) _____ shorts.

   American women often _____ shorts in the summer.

   _____

EXERCISE 14 Two students meet in the cafeteria and discuss American customs and customs of their country. Fill in each blank with the correct form of the verb in parentheses ( ). Practice the simple present or the present continuous.

A. Hi. What _____*are you doing*_____ here?
            (you/do)

B. I _____ lunch. I always _____ lunch at this time.
       (1 eat)   (2 eat)

   But I _____ American behavior and customs.
         (3 also/observe)

A. What do you mean?

B. Well, look at that man over there. He _____ an earring. It looks
                                          (4 wear)

   so strange. Only women _____ earrings in my country.
                           (5 wear)

A. It *is* strange. And look at that woman. She _____ three earrings
                                               (6 wear)

   in one ear!

B. And she _____ running shoes with a dress. In my country,
            (7 wear)

   people only _____ running shoes for sports activities.
               (8 use)

A. Look at that student over there. He _____ a colored pen to mark
                                       (9 use)

   his textbook. In my country, we never _____ in our textbooks
                                          (10 write)

   because they _____ to the college, not to the students.
                (11 belong)

B. Many college activities are different here. For example, my English

   teacher usually _____ at the desk in class. In my country, the
                   (12 sit)

   teacher always _____ in class. And the students always
                  (13 stand)

   _____ when the teacher _____ the room.
    (14 stand up)   (15 enter)

A. And college students always _____ English or another foreign
                               (16 study)

   language. Here, nobody knows another language. My American roommate

   _____ five courses this semester, but no foreign language.
    (17 take)

B. By the way, how many classes _____ this semester?
                                    (18 you/take)

A. Four. In my country, I usually _____ eight courses a semester,
                                    (19 take)

but my adviser here says I can only take four.

B. I have to go now. My girlfriend _____ for me at the library.
                                    (20 wait)

7.5 Nonaction Verbs

We do not usually use the present continuous tense with certain verbs that are
called nonaction verbs. They describe a state or condition, not an action. We use
the simple present tense, even when we talk about now.

Nonaction Verbs	
believe	own
cost	prefer
have	remember
hear	see
know	seem
like	think
love	understand
need	want

Language Notes

1. Compare the action and nonaction verbs in these sentences.

   Some students *are listening* to the radio. Ali *hears* the music.
   Ali *is looking* at students in the cafeteria. He *sees* some strange behaviors.
   He's *learning* about American customs. He *knows* American customs are different.

2. Some verbs can be used both as action verbs (simple tense or continuous tense) or nonaction verbs
   (simple tense only), depending on their meaning. Study *have* and *think*, and the group of sense-
   perception verbs in the following tables.

Have

Action	Nonaction

In these idiomatic expressions:
  have difficulty
  have problems/trouble
  have a good/bad/hard time
  have a party
  have breakfast/lunch/dinner
    (have = eat)
  have coffee/a Coke/water
    (have = drink)
  have a baby
 	
Example: He's *having* problems now.
	For possession:
	Example: She *has* a bike.
	
	With an illness:
	  have a backache
	  have a cold
	  have a sore throat
	  have a fever
	  have a stomach ache
	  have a toothache
	  have the flu
	Example: He *has* a cold now.

Think

Action	Nonaction
To think about something. Example: Ali *is thinking* about his family now.	To believe, to have an opinion. Example: Ali *thinks* (that) many American behaviors are strange. (This is his opinion.)

Sense Perception Verbs:
look, sound, taste, feel, smell

Action	Nonaction
When these verbs describe an action, they are action verbs. Examples: Ali *is looking* at a woman in shorts. She *is smelling* the milk.	When these verbs describe a state, they are nonaction verbs. Examples: Some American behaviors *look* bad to Ali. The milk *smells* bad.

EXERCISE 15   Fill in each blank with the simple present or the present continuous of the verb in parentheses ( ). Use the simple present for regular activity and with nonaction verbs.

EXAMPLES: Ali _wants_____ to understand American behavior.
                        (want)

                He _is looking_____ at some Americans in the cafeteria now.
                        (look)

1. Ali _____ a letter now.
        (write)

2. He _____ in the school cafeteria now.
        (sit)

3. He _____ a couple with a baby.
        (see)

4. He often _____ to the cafeteria between classes.
            (go)

5. He _____ to his family once a week.
        (write)

6. He _____ that his family _____ to know about
        (think)   (want)

   American customs.

7. He _____ at a young man and woman. They
        (look)

   _____.
        (kiss)

8. This behavior _____ bad in his country.
                    (look)

9. He _____ about American customs now.
        (think)

10. Two women _____ now.
                (smoke)

11. Women in Ali's country never _____ in public.
                                    (smoke)

12. American customs _____ strange to him.
                        (seem)

EXERCISE 16   Read each sentence. Write the negative form of the underlined word, using the word(s) in parentheses ( ).

> EXAMPLES: Ali <u>is looking</u> at Americans. (people from his country)
>
> _He isn't looking at people from his country._
>
> He <u>knows</u> about Arab customs. (American customs)
>
> _He doesn't know about American customs._

1. The father <u>is feeding</u> the baby. (the mother)

_____

2. Ali's <u>sitting</u> in the cafeteria. (in class)

_____

3. He <u>understands</u> Arab customs. (American customs)

_____

4. American men and women sometimes <u>kiss</u> in public. (Arab)

_____

5. Americans <u>use</u> their hands to eat a hamburger. (to eat spaghetti)

_____

6. A man <u>is wearing</u> an earring in one ear. (in both ears)

_____

7. Americans <u>seem</u> strange to him. (Arabs)

_____

8. American men <u>like</u> to take care of the baby. (Ali)

_____

9. American women often <u>wear</u> shorts in the summer. (Moslem women/never)

_____

EXERCISE 17   Read each sentence. Then write a *yes/no* question about the words in parentheses ( ). Write a short answer.

> EXAMPLES: **American women sometimes wear earrings. (American men/ever)**
>
> *Do American men ever wear an earring? Yes, they do.*
>
> **The women are wearing shorts. (the men)**
>
> *Are the men wearing shorts? No, they aren't.*

1. Ali is writing. (his homework)

   _____

2. He's watching people. (American people)

   _____

3. He understands Arab customs. (American customs)

   _____

4. American men wear shorts in the summer. (American women)

   _____

5. The man is eating. (a hot dog)

   _____

EXERCISE 18   Read each statement. Then write a *wh-* question about the words in parentheses ( ). An answer is not necessary.

> EXAMPLES: **A young man is resting his feet on a chair. (why)**
>
> *Why is he resting his feet on a chair?*
>
> **Ali lives in the U.S. (where/his family)**
>
> *Where does his family live?*

1. Ali is writing a letter (to whom) OR (who . . . to)

   _____

2. Ali wants to know about American customs. (why)

   _____

3. Two women are putting on make-up. (where)

_____

4. American men and women touch and kiss in public. (why)

_____

5. Ali writes to his family. (how often)

_____

6. The man isn't using a fork. (why/not)

_____

7. Women don't wear shorts in some countries. (why)

_____

8. Americans often wear blue jeans. (why)

_____

9. "Custom" means tradition or habit. (what/"behavior")

_____

EXPANSION ACTIVITIES

DISCUSSION   In a small group or with the entire class, discuss behaviors that are strange to you. What American behaviors are not polite in your country?

OUTSIDE ACTIVITY   Go to the school cafeteria, student union, or other crowded place. Sit there for a while and look for unusual behaviors. Write down some of the unusual things you see. Report back to the class.

EDITING ADVICE

1. Include *be* with a continuous tense.

    is
    He ∧ working now.

2. Use the *-s* form when the subject is *he, she,* or *it.*

    has   *s*
    He ~~have~~ a new car. He like ∧ to drive.

3. Don't use *be* with a simple present tense verb.

    I'm̶ need a new computer.

4. Use the correct word order in a question.

    are you
    Where ~~you're~~ going?

    don't you
    Why ~~you don't~~ like New York?

5. Use *do* or *does* in a simple present tense question.

    does   *live*
    Where ~~lives~~ your mother ∧ ?

6. Don't use the *-s* form after *does.*

    Where does he take ̶s̶ the bus?

7. Don't use the present continuous with a nonaction verb.

    has
    She ~~is having~~ her own computer.

NOTE: For American English, include *do* or *does* in negatives and questions with the verb *have.*

BRITISH: I *haven't* a car.
AMERICAN: I *don't have* a car.
BRITISH: *Have you* any money?
AMERICAN: *Do you have* any money?

SUMMARY OF LESSON SEVEN

Uses of Tenses

Simple Present Tense	
General truths	Americans speak English.
	Oranges grow in Florida.
Regular activity, habit	I always speak English in class.
	I sometimes eat in the cafeteria.
Customs	Americans shake hands.
	Japanese people bow.
Place of origin	Michael comes from Russia.
	Marek comes from Poland.
With nonaction verbs	She has a new car.
	I like the U.S.
Present Continuous (with action verbs only)	
Now	We're reviewing now.
	I'm looking at page 167 now.
A long action in progress at this general time	Dan is learning how to play the guitar.
A descriptive state	She's wearing shorts.
	He's sitting near the door.
	The teacher's standing.

LESSON SEVEN TEST/REVIEW

Part 1   Find the mistakes in the following sentences and correct them. Not every sentence has a mistake. Change sentences that use British English to American English. If the sentence is correct, write **C.**

EXAMPLES: She's <s>owning</s> a new bike now.
                        owns

I'm not studying math this semester.   *C*

1. Why you aren't listening to me?

2. Usually I'm go home after class.

3. I think that he's having trouble with this lesson.

4. She's thinking about her family now.

5. Does she needs help with her homework?

6. What kind of car do you have?

7. Why he's studying now?

8. Has he any children?

9. He's wearing jeans now.

10. My teacher speak English well.

11. I'm speak my native language at home.

12. The baby sleeping now.

13. When begins summer?

14. Where does your family lives?

Part 2   This is a conversation between two students, Alicia (A) and Teresa (T), who meet in the school library. Fill in each blank with the simple present or the present continuous of the verb in parentheses ( ).

T. Hi, Alicia.

A. Hi, Teresa. What _____*are you doing*_____ here?
                                    (you/do)

T. I _____ for a book on American geography. What about you?
        (1 look)

A. I _____ a book. _____ to go for a cup of coffee?
   (2 return)   (3 you/want)

T. I can't. I _____ for my friend. We _____ on
     (4 wait)   (5 work)

 a geography project together, and we _____ to finish it by
               (6 need)

 next week.

A. _____ your geography class?
  (7 you/like)

T. Yes. I especially _____ the teacher, Bob. He's a handsome young
        (8 like)

 man. He's very casual. He always _____ jeans and a T-shirt to
             (9 wear)

 class. He _____ an earring in one ear.
     (10 have)

A. That _____ very strange to me. I _____ that
    (11 seem)   (12 think)

 teachers in the U.S. are very informal. How _____ the class?
              (13 Bob/teach)

 By lecturing?

T. No. We _____ in small groups, and he _____ us by
    (14 usually/work)   (15 help)

 walking around the classroom.

A. _____ hard tests?
  (16 he/give)

T. No. He _____ in tests.
    (17 not/believe)

A. Why _____ in tests?
   (18 he/not/believe)

T. He _____ that students get too nervous during a test. He
   (19 think)

 _____ it's better to work on projects. This week we
  (20 say)

 _____ on city maps.
  (21 work)

A. That _____ interesting.
   (22 sound)

T. Why _____ me so many questions about my teacher?
   (23 you/ask)

A. I _____ about taking a geography course next semester.
     (24 think)

T. Bob's very popular. Be sure to register early because his classes always

   _____ quickly. Oh. I _____ my friend now. She
        (25 fill)   (26 see)

   _____ toward us. I have to go now.
        (27 walk)

A. Good luck on your project.

T. Thanks. Bye.

Part 3   Fill in each blank with the negative form of the underlined word.

   EXAMPLE: Teresa is in the library. She _____*isn't*_____ at home.

   1. Alicia wants to go for a cup of coffee. Teresa _____ to go for a
      cup of coffee.

   2. Teresa is looking for a book. Alicia _____ for a book.

   3. They are talking about school. They _____ about the news.

   4. They have time to talk now. They _____ time for a cup of coffee.

Part 4   Read each sentence. Then write a *yes/no* question about the words in parentheses ( ). Write a short answer.

   EXAMPLE: Teresa is looking for a book. (a geography book)

   *Is she looking for a geography book? Yes, she is.*_____

   1. Bob likes projects. (tests)

   _____

   2. Alicia has time now. (Teresa)

   _____

   3. They are talking about their classes. (their teachers)

   _____

4. Bob wears jeans to class. (ever/a suit)

_____

Part 5   Read each sentence. Then write a question with the words in parentheses ( ). An answer is not necessary.

EXAMPLE: **Bob is popular. (Why)**

Why is he popular?
_____

1. Bob sounds interesting. (Why)

_____

2. Bob doesn't like tests. (Why)

_____

3. Teresa and her friend are working on a project. (What kind of project)

_____

4. Teresa studies in the library. (How often)

_____

5. Teresa is looking for a book. (What kind)

_____

LESSON EIGHT

GRAMMAR

Future Tenses—*Will* and *Be
Going To*
Review and Comparison of
Tenses

CONTEXT

Jobs of the Future

Lesson Focus **Future Tenses—*Will* and *Be Going To***

We have two ways of talking about the future. We can either use *will* or *be going to* plus a base form to talk about the future.

We *will study* the future tense.
The teacher *is going to explain* the grammar.

R
E
A
D
I
N
G

Before you read:

1. Are you planning a career? (Or are you planning to change careers?) What field are you interested in?
2. What is a good career in your country?

Read the following article. Pay special attention to the future verbs.

JOBS OF THE FUTURE

Some job opportunities are increasing; others are decreasing. In the United States, jobs in the sciences are growing. As a result, we **will need** more biologists to do medical research. Technology is advancing rapidly, so jobs in high technology fields **will grow.** The government predicts that we **will need** more computer analysts. However, many workers **will lose** their jobs as a result of high technology. Factory workers and telephone operators **will have** a hard time finding a job because computers and robots can do their jobs.

There **will be** an increase in service jobs. Some opportunities that **are going to increase** are jobs for legal assistants, physical therapists, computer repairers, and travel agents.

Students who are planning their future careers should look at a government publication called *The Occupational Outlook Handbook.* (You can find this book in the reference section of a library.) This book reports on the job opportunities of the future. It tells what areas **will need** more workers. In areas that are growing, there **will be** a shortage[1] of workers, and it **will not be** difficult to find a job. In areas that are getting smaller, there **are going to be** too many workers and not enough jobs. Another reference book that helps people with their career choice is *The Jobs Rated Almanac.* This book explains how good a job is.

It is important to choose a career that **is going to offer** many jobs in the future.

---

[1]A *shortage* means there isn't enough of something.

8.1 Forms of *Will* and *Be Going To*

There are two ways to form the future tense.

Subject	*Will*	*(Not)*		Verb	Complement
I	will			become	a travel agent.
Some workers	will	not		find	a job.

Subject	*Be*	*(Not)*	*Going to*	Verb	Complement
I	am		going to	study	computer programming.
You	are	not	going to	lose	your job.

Language Notes

1. We use *will* with all persons to form the future tense.

   I *will* find a job.   He *will* find a job.

2. We can make a contraction with the subject pronoun and with *will*.

I will	I'll
You will	You'll
He will	He'll
She will	She'll
It will	It'll
We will	We'll
They will	They'll

   } help you find a job.

3. The negative contraction of *will not* is *won't*.

   Factories *won't* need so many workers.

4. In informal speech, *going to* before another verb often sounds like "gonna." We don't write "gonna." Listen to your teacher's pronunciation of *going to* in the following sentences.

   He's *going to* buy a new car. (He's "gonna" buy a new car.)
   She's *going to* return in² an hour. (She's "gonna" return in an hour.)

   Only *going to* before another verb sounds like "gonna." We don't pronounce "gonna" at the end of a sentence or before a noun.

   He's *going to* study law.

5. We often shorten *going to go* to *going*.

   He's *going to go* to the bookstore. =
   He's *going* to the bookstore.

6. Compare the present and future with *there*.

   There *are* a lot of factory workers today.
   There *will be* a lot of service workers in the future.
   There *are* five advanced classes this semester.
   Next semester there *are going to be* only four advanced classes.

EXERCISE I   Fill in each blank with an appropriate verb in the future tense. Use *will*.

EXAMPLE: Robots _will do_____ the job of today's workers.

1. Many factory workers _____ their jobs.

---

²We often use the preposition *in* with the future to mean *after*.

2. If you look at the *Occupational Outlook Handbook,* you _____ more information about the jobs of the future.

3. In the future, there _____ too many factory workers and not enough jobs.

EXERCISE 2   Fill in each blank with an appropriate verb in the future tense. Use *be going to.*

EXAMPLE: **Many telephone operators** _are going to lose_ _____ their jobs.

1. Jobs for computer analysts _____.

2. Factories _____ more computers and robots in the future.

3. There _____ more service jobs in the future.

Language Notes

1. We use *will* or *be going to* for predictions.

   Job opportunities *are going to* change.
   We *won't* need so many factory workers.
   Factories *are going to* use computers and robots, not workers.
   There *will* be an increase in service jobs.
   There *isn't going to* be an increase in factory jobs.

2. When we have a plan to do something, we usually use *be going to.*

   My brother *is going to* become a biologist. (He already has this plan.)
   On Saturday, I'm *going (to go)* to the library. I'm *going to* look at the *Occupational Outlook Handbook.* (I already have this plan.)

EXERCISE 3   Tell if you have plans to do these things or not. Use *be going to.*

EXAMPLE: **meet a friend after class**
          I'm (not) going to meet a friend after class.

1. get something to eat after class
2. watch TV tonight
3. eat dinner at home tonight
4. go to the library this week
5. go shopping for groceries this week
6. stay home this weekend
7. take a vacation this year
8. move (to a different apartment) this year
9. buy a car this year

EXERCISE 4   Tell if you predict that these things will happen or not in this class. Use *will.*

>   EXAMPLE: **we/finish this lesson today**
>   **We won't finish this lesson today.**

1. the teacher/give a test soon
2. the test/be hard
3. most students/pass the test
4. I/pass the test
5. the teacher/give everyone an A
6. my English/improve

EXERCISE 5   With a partner or in a small group, tell if you predict that these things will happen or not in the next 50 years. Use *will.*

>   EXAMPLE: **people/have more free time**
>   **I think people won't have more free time. They will spend more time at their jobs and less time with their families.**

1. there/another world war
2. the economy of the U.S./get worse
3. people in the U.S./have fewer children
4. Americans/live longer
5. health care/improve
6. cars/use solar energy[3]
7. (add your own prediction) _____

8.2   Questions with *Be Going To* and *Will*

Compare statements and questions with *be going to:*

Wh- Word	*Be*	Subject	*Be*	*Going to*	Verb	Complement	Short Answer
		They	are	going to	leave	soon.	
	Are	they		going to	leave	tomorrow?	No, they aren't.
When	are	they		going to	leave?		
Why	aren't	they		going to	leave?	tomorrow?	
		Who	is	going to	leave?		

---
[3]*Solar energy* comes from the sun.

Compare statements and questions with *will*:

Wh- Word	*Will*	Subject	*Will*	Verb	Complement	Short Answer
		She	will	eat	lunch.	
	Will	she		eat	a sandwich?	Yes, she will.
What	will	she		eat	for lunch?	
Why	won't	she		eat	a salad?	
		Who	will	eat	lunch?	

EXERCISE 6   Ask another student a *yes/no* question with *are you going to* about a later time today. Then ask a *wh-* question with the words in parentheses ( ) whenever possible.

> EXAMPLE: **listen to the radio (when)**
> > **A. Are you going to listen to the radio tonight?**
> > **B. Yes, I am.**
> > **A. When are you going to listen to the radio?**
> > **B. After dinner.**

1. watch TV (what show)
2. listen to the radio (when)
3. read the newspaper (what newspaper)
4. eat dinner (with whom) OR (who . . . with)
5. take a shower (when)
6. go shopping (why)

EXERCISE 7   Ask another student a *yes/no* question with *will* and the words given. Then ask a *wh-* question with the words in parentheses ( ) whenever possible.

> EXAMPLE: **study another English course after this one (which course)**
> > **A. Will you study another English course after this one?**
> > **B. Yes, I will.**
> > **A. Which course will you study?**
> > **B. I'll study level 4.**

1. go back to your country (when) (why)
2. study something new (what)
3. look for a job (when)
4. get an A in this course (what grade)
5. transfer to another school (why) (which school)
6. visit other American cities (which cities)
7. buy a computer (why) (what kind)

8.3 Future Tense + Time/*If* Clause[4]

Notice the verb tenses in the following future sentences:

Time Clause (simple present) When I *find* a job,	**Main Clause (future)** I *won't have* so much free time.
If Clause (simple present) If he *leaves* the country,	**Main Clause (future)** he*'s going to need* a passport.

Main Clause (future) I*'ll go* to the university	**Time Clause (present)** after I *finish* community college.
Main Clause (future) I*'m going to buy* a car	**If Clause (present)** if I *find* a good job.

Language Notes

The above sentences have two clauses. We use the future tense only in the main clause; we use the simple present tense in the time clause/*if* clause.

EXERCISE 8   Complete each statement about the future.

EXAMPLE: **When computers replace workers,** *many people will become unemployed.*

1. If service jobs increase, _____

2. If students don't prepare themselves for the future, _____

   _____

3. When you go to the library, the librarian _____

   _____ books on jobs.

4. If American workers lose their jobs, _____

   _____

---

[4]A *clause* is a group of words that has a subject and a verb. Some sentences have more than one clause.

EXERCISE 9   Complete each statement.

> EXAMPLES: **When this class is over,** *I'll go home.*
>
> **When this class is over,** *I'm going to get something to eat.*

1. When this semester is over, _____

2. When this class is over, _____

3. When I get home today, _____

4. When I graduate (or finish my courses at this school), _____

   _____

5. When I return to my country/become a citizen, _____

6. When I retire, _____

7. When I speak English better, _____

EXERCISE 10   Complete each statement.

> EXAMPLES: **If I drink too much coffee,** *I won't sleep tonight.*
>
> **If I drink too much coffee,** *I'm going to feel nervous.*

1. If I practice English, _____

2. If I don't study, _____

3. If I don't pay my rent, _____

4. If I pass this course, _____

5. If we have a test next week, _____

6. If the teacher is absent tomorrow, _____

7. If I find a good job, _____

EXERCISE 11   On the first day of class, a teacher is explaining the course to the students. Fill in the blanks to complete this conversation between a teacher (T) and his students (S).

T: In this course, you ___*are going to study*___ English grammar. You
                              (study)

   _____ a few short compositions. Tomorrow, I _____
        (1 write)   (2 give)

   you a list of assignments. Do you have any questions about this course?

S: Yes. How many tests _____?
(3 have)

T: You will have 14 tests, one for each lesson in the book. If you're absent from

a test, you can make it up.[5] If you don't make it up, you _____ an
(4 get)

F on that test.

S: _____ us about the tests ahead of time?
(5 tell)

T: Oh, yes. I'll always tell you about a test a few days before.

S: When _____ the midterm exam?
(6 give)

T: I'm going to give you the midterm exam in April.

S: _____very hard?
(7 be)

T: If you _____, it won't be hard.
(8 study)

S: What _____ in this course?
(9 study)

T: You'll study verb tenses, count and noncount nouns, and comparison of
adjectives.

S: _____ everything in this book?
(10 finish)

T: Yes, I think we'll finish everything.

S: _____?
(11 over)

T: The semester will be over[6] in June. Tomorrow I _____ you a
(12 give)

course outline with all this information.

EXERCISE 12   Write a question to ask your teacher about this course.

EXAMPLES: _Will there be a test on this lesson?_   OR   _When will you give us the next test?_

_____?

---

[5]If you are absent on the day of a test, the teacher expects you to take it at a later time.

[6]To *be over* means to be finished.

EXERCISE 13   A young woman (A) is going to leave her country to go to the U.S. Her friend (B) is asking her questions. Fill in each blank to complete this conversation.

A. I'm so happy! I'm going to the U.S.

B. When *are you going to leave* _____?

A. I'm going to leave next month.

B. So soon? _____ anything before you _____?
                    (1 buy)   (2 leave)

A. Yes. I'm going to buy warm clothes for the winter. I hear the winter there is very cold.

B. What city _____?
                     (3 be)

A. I'll be in Ann Arbor, Michigan.

B. Where _____?
                 (4 live)

A. I'm going to live in a dormitory.

B. _____ in the U.S.?
          (5 work)

A. No, I'm not going to work. I have a scholarship. I'm going to study at the University of Michigan.

B. What _____?
               (6 study)

A. I'm going to study to be a computer analyst.

B. When _____ to our country?
               (7 return)

A. I _____ when I _____.
          (8 return)   (9 graduate)

B. When _____?
           (10 you/graduate)

A. In four years.

B. That's a long time! _____?
                           (11 miss)

A. Of course, I'll miss you.

B. _____?
          (12 write)

A. Of course, I'll write to you.

EXERCISE 14   Check (✓) the activities that you plan to do soon. Find a partner. Ask your partner for information about the items he or she checked off. Report something interesting to the class about your partner's plans.

> EXAMPLE: ____✓____ move
> **When are you going to move?**
> **Why are you going to move?**
> **Are your friends going to help you?**
> **Are you going to rent a truck?**
> **Where are you going to move to?**

1. _____ get married

2. _____ go back to my country

3. _____ spend a lot of money

4. _____ write a letter

5. _____ buy something (a computer, a VCR, a TV, an answering machine, etc.)

6. _____ go to a party

7. _____ have a job interview

8. _____ transfer to another college

9. _____ become a citizen

10. _____ eat in a restaurant

11. _____ _____

EXERCISE 15   A young woman is planning to get married. Her friend is asking her questions about her plans. Fill in each blank to complete this conversation.

A. I'm getting married!

B. That's wonderful! Congratulations. _*Are you going to have*_____ a big wedding?

A. No, we're going to have a small wedding. We _____ about
                                                    (1 invite)

    50 people.

B. Where _____?
             (2 be)

A. It'll be at St. Peter's Church. We _____ a reception[7] at a
   (3 have)

   Korean restaurant after the wedding.

B. _____ a wedding dress?
   (4 buy)

A. No, I _____ my sister's dress for the wedding. Then, for the
   (5 use)

   reception, I _____ a traditional Korean dress.
   (6 wear)

B. Where _____ after you get married?
   (7 live)

A. For a few years, we _____ with Kim's parents. When Kim
   (8 live)

   _____ college and _____ a job, we
   (9 finish)   (10 get)

   _____ our own apartment.
   (11 get)

B. You're going to live with your in-laws? I can't believe it.

A. In my country, it's common. My in-laws are very nice. I'm sure it

   _____ a problem. We _____ children
   (12 not/be)   (13 not/have)

   right away.

B. _____ come here for the wedding?
   (14)

A. No, my parents aren't going to come. But a month after the wedding, we

   _____ a trip to Korea, and Kim can meet my parents there.
   (15 take)

B. _____ married?
   (16 get)

A. On May 15. I hope you'll be able to attend. We _____ you an
   (17 send)

   invitation.

B. I _____ glad to attend.
   (18 be)

---

[7]A *reception* is a party.

8.4 **Review and Comparison of Tenses**

Compare the forms of three verb tenses.

Simple Present	Present Continuous	Future
I work.	I'm working.	I will work. I'm going to work.
I don't work.	I'm not working.	I won't work. I'm not going to work.
Do you work? Yes, I do.	Are you working? Yes, I am.	Will you work? Yes, I will. Are you going to work? Yes, I am.
Where do you work?	Where are you working?	Where will you work? Where are you going to work?
Why don't you work?	Why aren't you working?	Why won't you work? Why aren't you going to work?
Who works?	Who is working?	Who will work? Who is going to work?

EXERCISE 16   Read the following letter. Fill in each blank with the simple present, the present continuous, and the future tenses.

Dear Judy,

Please excuse me for not writing sooner. I rarely _____*have*_____ time to sit
                                                        (have)

and write a letter. My husband _____ on his car now, and the baby
                                    (1 work)

_____. So now I _____ a few free moments.
      (2 sleep)   (3 have)

I _____ a student now. I _____ to Kennedy College twice
      (4 be)   (5 go)

a week. The school _____ a few blocks from my house. I usually
                          (6 be)

_____ to school, but sometimes I _____. My mother usually
      (7 walk)   (8 drive)

_____ the baby when I'm in school. This semester I _____
      (9 watch)   (10 study)

English and math. Next semester I _____ a computer course. I
                                                    (11 take)

_____ knowledge about computers _____ me find a good job.
   (12 think)   (13 help)

When the semester _____ over, we _____ to Canada for
                                 (14 be)   (15 go)

vacation. We _____ my husband's sister. She _____ in Montreal.
                        (16 visit)   (17 live)

We _____ Christmas with her family this year. When we _____ to
     (18 spend)   (19 get)

Montreal, I _____ you a postcard.
                (20 send)

Please write and tell me what is happening in your life.

Love,

Barbara

EXERCISE 17   Fill in each blank with the negative form of the underlined verb.

EXAMPLE: **Barbara's a student. She _____ _isn't_ _____ a teacher.**

1. She's <u>writing</u> a letter now. She _____ a composition.

2. Her mother sometimes <u>takes</u> care of her baby. Her father

   _____ care of her baby.

3. They<u>'re going to visit</u> her husband's sister. They _____
   her mother.

4. She <u>goes</u> to Kennedy College. She _____ to Truman College.

5. Barbara and her husband <u>live</u> in the U.S. They _____ in Canada.

6. Her family <u>will go</u> to Montreal. They _____ to Toronto.

EXERCISE 18   Read each statement. Then write a *yes/no* question with the words in
parentheses ( ). Write a short answer, based on the letter.

EXAMPLE: **Barbara's studying English. (math)**

   Is she studying math? Yes, she is. _____

1. The baby's sleeping. (her husband)

   _____

2. She sometimes drives to school. (ever/walk to school)

_____

3. She's going to take a computer course next semester. (a math class)

_____

4. She'll go to Canada. (Montreal)

_____

5. She's going to send Judy a postcard. (a letter)

_____

6. She sometimes writes letters. (write a letter/now)

_____

7. Her sister-in-law lives in Canada. (in Toronto)

_____

EXERCISE 19   Read each statement. Then write a _wh-_ question with the words in parentheses ( ). Write an answer, based on the letter.

EXAMPLE: **She goes to college. (Where)**

A. _Where does she go to college?_ _____

B. _She goes to Kennedy College._ _____

1. Her baby's sleeping. (What/her husband/do)

A. _____

B. _____

2. She's taking two courses this semester. (What courses)

A. _____

B. _____

3. Someone watches her baby. (Who)

A. _____

B. _____

4. She's going to take a course next semester. (What course)

   A. _____

   B. _____

5. They'll go on vacation for Christmas. (Where)

   A. _____

   B. _____

6. Her husband's sister lives in another city. (Where/she)

   A. _____

   B. _____

7. She doesn't usually drive to school. (Why)

   A. _____

   B. _____

EXPANSION ACTIVITIES

PROVERB   The following proverb uses the future tense. Discuss the meaning of the proverb. Do you have a similar proverb in your language?

When the cat's away, the mice will play.

OUTSIDE ACTIVITIES

1. Go to the library. Find the *Occupational Outlook Handbook.* Look for a career that interests you. Find out about the future of this career. Report back to the class.

2. Interview an American about his job. What does this person do at his job? Is he worried about the future of his job? Why? Is he going to retire or change jobs soon?

3. Interview an American about her concerns about the future. What is she worried about? Ask her to tell you about her family, standard of living, the economy, the political situation, etc.

EDITING ADVICE

1. Don't use *be* with a future verb.

   I will ~~be~~ go.

2. You need *be* in a future sentence that has no other verb.

         be
   He will ∧ angry.
          be
   There will ∧ a party soon.

3. Don't combine *will* and *be going to.*

       is
   He ~~will~~ going to leave. *Or He will leave.*

4. Don't use the present tense for a future action.

                         'll
   I'm going home now. I ∧ see you later.

5. Don't use the future tense after *when* or *if.*

   When they ~~will~~ go home, they will watch TV.

6. Use a form of *be* with *going to.*

      is
   He ∧ going to help me.

7. Use *to* after *going.*

           to
   I'm going ∧ study on Saturday.

LESSON EIGHT TEST/REVIEW

Part 1   Fill in each blank with the simple present, the present continuous, or the future tense of the verb in parentheses ( ). Use the affirmative form.

EXAMPLES: We _are filling_ in the blanks now.
                      (fill)

I always _speak_ English with Americans.
                  (speak)

1. We always _____ at the end of each lesson.
                          (review)

2. Now we _____ verb tenses.
                    (review)

3. We always _____ English in class.
                          (speak)

4. The students _____ the answers now.
                            (write)

5. I _____ to improve my English.
            (want)

6. Next week we _____ Lesson Nine.
                          (begin)

7. When we _____ this test, we _____ a break.
                      (finish)   (take)

Part 2   Fill in each blank with the negative form of the underlined verb.

EXAMPLE: It's easy to find a low-paying job. It _isn't_ easy to find a good job.

1. There <u>will be</u> jobs for computer analysts. There _____ a lot of jobs for factory workers.

2. Factory workers <u>are losing</u> their jobs. Computer repairers

   _____ their jobs.

3. The *Occupational Outlook Handbook* <u>explains</u> about the future of many

   occupations in the U.S. It _____ about jobs in other countries.

4. A legal assistant <u>works</u> for a lawyer. A legal assistant

   _____ without a lawyer.

5. Some job opportunities <u>are growing</u>. Jobs for factory workers

   _____.

6. The jobs of the future <u>are going to be</u> different. They _____ the
   same as now.

7. A travel agent <u>has</u> an interesting job. A factory worker _____ an
   interesting job.

8. Technology <u>is</u> a growing field. Manufacturing _____ a growing
   field.

Part 3   Read each statement. Write a *yes/no* question with the words in parentheses ( ).
Write a short answer.

   EXAMPLES: **Doctors make a lot of money. (nurses)**

   Do nurses make a lot of money? No, they don't. _____

   I'm looking for a job. (you)

   Are you looking for a job? Yes, I am. _____

1. I'm studying to be a doctor. (you)

   _____

2. Medicine is a good career. (factory work)

   _____

3. Factory workers will lose their jobs. (computer analysts)

   _____

4. Computer jobs are increasing. (factory jobs)

   _____

5. I'm going to look for a new job. (you)

   _____

6. We'll need more biologists in the future. (more legal assistants)

   _____

7. Job opportunities are going to change. (educational opportunities)

_____

8. A lawyer needs a college education. (a biologist)

_____

Part 4   Read each statement. Then write a *wh-* question with the words in parentheses ( ). No answer is necessary.

EXAMPLES: **Jobs will be different in the future. (why/they)**

Why will they be different?

She works as a pharmacist. (where/she)

Where does she work?

1. I'm looking for a job. (why/you)

_____

2. I'll find a job. (where/you)

_____

3. There won't be many manufacturing jobs. (why)

_____

4. My sister is going to study law. (why/she)

_____

5. The newspaper has job listings. (where/the newspaper)

_____

6. The job listings are in the help-wanted section. (where/the movie listings)

_____

7. I don't have a good job. (why/you)

_____

8. Job opportunities are changing. (why/they)

_____

Part 5   Find the mistakes with future verbs and correct them. Not every sentence has a mistake. If the sentence is correct, write **C**.

EXAMPLES: I ~~will~~ *am* going to buy a newspaper.

If you're too tired to cook, I'll do it.   *C*

1. When you will write your composition?

2. We will be buy a new car soon.

3. Will you going to eat dinner tonight?

4. When he will leave, he will turn off the light.

5. I going to take a vacation soon.

6. Is he going to use the computer?

7. They're going graduate soon.

8. I will happy when I will know more English.

9. I'm going on vacation. I will going to leave next Friday.

10. I'll write you a letter when I arrive.

11. There will a test soon.

12. I'll help you tomorrow.

LESSON NINE

GRAMMAR
The Simple Past Tense

CONTEXT
The History of Aviation
The Chicago Fire
John Lennon

Lesson Focus   The Simple Past Tense

We use the simple past tense to talk about an action that is completely in the past. It usually refers to a specific time in the past.

Some verbs are regular in the past tense and some are irregular; *be* has two forms in the past tense—*was* and *were*.

> World War II *started* in 1939.   It *ended* in 1945.
> Many people *lost* their lives during the war.   It *was* a very tragic time.

We often use a past time expression with the simple past tense.

> My brother got a job *last week*.
> My parents came to America a long time *ago*.[1]

R
E
A
D
I
N
G

Before you read:

1. Do you like to travel by airplane? Why or why not?
2. How long was your trip to the U.S.?

Read the following article. Pay special attention to the past forms of *be*.

THE HISTORY OF AVIATION

The Wright Brothers **were** American inventors. They **were** interested in flight.[2] They invented the first powered airplane. In 1903, their plane **was** in the air for 12 seconds. This **was** a historic moment; it **was** the beginning of aviation.

Charles Lindbergh **was** a person who loved to fly. He **was** born in 1902, one year before the Wright Brothers' historic flight. In 1927, a man offered a $25,000 reward for the first person to fly from New York to Paris nonstop. Lindbergh **was** a pilot for the United States Mail Service at that time. He wanted to win the prize. He became famous because he **was** the first person to fly alone across the Atlantic Ocean. His plane **was** in the air for 33 hours. The distance of the flight **was** 3,600 miles. There **were** thousands of people in New York to welcome him home. He **was** an American hero. He **was** only 25 years old.

Another famous American aviator[3] **was** Amelia Earhart. She **was** the first woman to fly across the Atlantic Ocean alone. She wanted to land in Paris, but her flight **was** difficult and she had to land in Ireland. She **was** thirty-four years old. Americans **were** in love

---

[1]*Ago* means before now.

[2]*Fly* is a verb. *Flight* is the noun form.

[3]*Aviator* means pilot.

with Earhart. In 1937, however, she **was** on a flight around the world when her plane disappeared somewhere in the Pacific Ocean. No one really knows what happened to Earhart.

• •

9.1   Past Tense of *Be*

Amelia Earhart

Charles Lindbergh

The past of *be* uses two forms: *was* and *were*.

I Charles He Amelia She The airplane It	*was*	
		in New York.
We You Thousands of people Amelia and Charles They	*were*	

Language
Notes

1. To make a negative statement, put *not* after *was* or *were*.

> Earhart *was not* alone.
> They *were not* aviators.

You can make a contraction with *was* or *were* and *not*.

> She *wasn't* alone.
> They *weren't* inventors.

2. We use *be* with a classification, a description, a location, a place of origin, with *born*, with *there*.

Classification	Lindbergh was *an aviator*.
Description	Lindbergh was *brave*.
Location	Lindbergh was *in Paris*.
A Place of Origin	Earhart was *from Kansas*.
With *Born*	Earhart was *born* in 1897.
With *There*	*There* were thousands of people in New York to welcome Lindbergh.

EXERCISE 1   Fill in each blank with *was* or *were*.

> EXAMPLE: **Lindbergh and Earhart** ___*were*___ **very famous.**

1. The Wright Brothers _____ the inventors of the airplane.

2. The first airplane _____ in the air for 12 seconds.

3. Lindbergh and Earhart _____ aviators.

4. There _____ thousands of people in New York to welcome Lindbergh home.

5. Earhart _____ the first woman to fly across the Atlantic Ocean.

6. I _____ interested in the story about Earhart and Lindbergh.

7. _____ you surprised that Earhart was a woman?

8. Lindbergh _____ in Paris.

9. We _____ in school last week.

EXERCISE 2   Read each statement. Then write a negative statement with the words in parentheses ( ).

> EXAMPLE: **The Wright Brothers were inventors. (Earhart and Lindbergh)**
>
> *Earhart and Lindbergh weren't inventors.*

1. The train was common transportation in the early 1900s. (the airplane)

_____

2. Earhart was from Kansas. (Lindbergh)

   _____

3. Lindbergh's last flight was successful. (Earhart's)

   _____

4. Lindbergh's plane was in the air for many hours. (the Wright Brothers' first plane)

   _____

5. The Wright Brothers were inventors. (Earhart)

   _____

6. There were a lot of trains 100 years ago. (planes)

   _____

9.2 Questions with *Was/Were*

Compare statements and questions with *was* and *were*.

Wh- Word	*Was/Were*	Subject	*Was/Were*	Complement	Short Answer
		Americans	were	in love with Lindbergh.	
	Were	Americans		in love with Earhart?	Yes, they were.
Why	were	Americans		in love with them?	
		Earhart	wasn't	alone.	
Why	wasn't	she		alone?	
		Someone	was	with Earhart.	
	Who	was		with Earhart?	

EXERCISE 3   Read each statement. Then write a *yes/no* question with the words in parentheses ( ). Give a short answer.

> **EXAMPLE:** **The Wright Brothers were inventors. (Lindbergh)**
>
> _Was Lindbergh an inventor? No, he wasn't._

1. The airplane was an important invention. (the telephone)

   _____

2. Thomas Edison was an inventor. (the Wright Brothers)

_____

3. Amelia Earhart was American. (Lindbergh)

_____

4. Travel by plane is simple now. (75 years ago)

_____

5. There were trains 100 years ago. (airplanes)

_____

6. You are in class today. (yesterday)

_____

7. I was interested in the story about the aviators. (you)

_____

8. I wasn't born in the U.S. (you)

_____

EXERCISE 4   With a partner or in a small group, discuss your answers to these questions.

1. Where were you born?
2. Were you happy or sad when you left your country?
3. Who was with you on your trip to the U.S.?
4. Were you happy or sad when you arrived in the U.S.?
5. What was your first impression of the U.S.?
6. Were you tired when you arrived?
7. Who was at the airport to meet you?
8. How was the weather on the day you arrived?

EXERCISE 5   Read each statement. Then write a *wh-* question with the words in parentheses ( ). Answer the question.

EXAMPLE: **Lindbergh was very famous. (why)**

A. *Why was Lindbergh famous?*

B. *He was one of the first aviators.*

1. Lindbergh was a hero. (why)

    A. _____

    B. _____

2. Lindbergh was American. (what nationality/Earhart)

    A. _____

    B. _____

3. Earhart was thirty-four years old when she crossed the ocean. (Lindbergh)

    A. _____

    B. _____

4. Earhart's last flight wasn't successful. (why)

    A. _____

    B. _____

5. Lindbergh was a famous aviator. (who/the Wright Brothers)

    A. _____

    B. _____

6. Lindbergh was born in 1902. (Earhart) (answer: 1897)

    A. _____

    B. _____

9.3 Simple Past Tense of Regular Verbs

We add *-ed* to the base form to make the simple past tense of regular verbs in affirmative sentences:

Base Form	Past Form
start	started
work	worked
play	played

The past form is the same for all persons.

Subject	Past Form
I	
You	
We	
They	worked.
He	
She	
It	

• •

R
E
A
D
I
N
G

Before you read:

1. Do you know of any big fires, earthquakes, floods, or other natural disasters in your country?
2. What are most houses made of in your country?

Read the following article. Pay special attention to the past tense verbs.

THE CHICAGO FIRE

On October 8, 1871, the Great Chicago Fire **started.** It **rained** much less than usual that year, and everything was dry. No one really knows how the fire **started,** but according to legend,[4] Mrs. O'Leary's cow **kicked** over a lantern in her barn. The fire **traveled** quickly through the wooden buildings of downtown Chicago. Within twenty-four hours, the fire **burned** one third of the city. The fire **destroyed** the downtown area. It **killed** three hundred people and **destroyed** 17,000 buildings. One hundred thousand people were without homes.

lantern

But Chicagoans soon **started** to rebuild[5] their city. The opportunity to rebuild **attracted** some of the best architects from around the nation. The architects **replaced** wood with stone and brick. Chicago is now famous in the U.S. for its great architecture.

---

[4]A *legend* is a story.

[5]A verb after *to* does not use the past form.

9.4 Spelling and Pronunciation of the Past Tense of Regular Verbs

The past form of regular verbs ends in *-ed*. The chart below shows the spelling of the *-ed* form. Fill in the last examples.

Rule	Verbs	-ed Form
Add *-ed* to the base form to make the past tense of most regular verbs.	start	started
	kick	kicked
	burn	*burned*
	rain	
When the base form ends in *e*, add *-d* only.	die	died
	live	lived
	replace	
	move	
When the base form ends in a consonant + *y*, change the *y* to *i* and add *-ed*.	carry	carried
	worry	worried
	study	
	hurry	
When the base form ends in a vowel + *y*, do not change the *y*.	destroy	destroyed
	stay	stayed
	play	
	enjoy	
In a one-syllable word, when the base form ends in consonant-vowel-consonant (CVC), double the final consonant and add *-ed*.	s t o p ↓ ↓ ↓ C V C	stopped
	p l u g ↓ ↓ ↓ C V C	plugged
	grab	
	hug	
Exceptions: Do not double final *w* or *x*.	sew	sewed
	fix	fixed
	show	
	tax	

Rule	Verbs	*-ed* Form
For a two-syllable word, double the final consonant only if the base form ends in consonant-vowel-consonant and the last syllable is stressed.	occúr	occur**red**
	permít	permit**ted**
	refér	_____
	admít	_____
When the last syllable of a two-syllable word is not stressed, do not double the final consonant.	ópen	open**ed**
	háppen	happen**ed**
	lísten	_____
	óffer	_____

Language
Notes

The past tense with *-ed* has three pronunciations. Listen to your teacher's pronunciation.

1. We pronounce a /t/ if the base form ends in a voiceless sound: /p, k, f, θ, s, š, č/.

jump—jumped	kiss—kissed
cook—cooked	wash—washed
cough—coughed	watch—watched

2. We pronounce an extra syllable /Id/ if the base form ends in a /t/ or /d/ sound.

wait—waited	add—added
hate—hated	need—needed
want—wanted	decide—decided

3. We pronounce a /d/ if the base form ends in a voiced sound.

rub—rubbed	name—named
drag—dragged	learn—learned
love—loved	bang—banged
bathe—bathed	call—called
use—used	fear—feared
massage—massaged	free—freed
charge—charged	glue—glued

EXERCISE 6   Write the past tense of these regular verbs. (Accent marks show you where a word is stressed.)

EXAMPLES: learn   *learned*   clap   *clapped*

          love   *loved*   listen   *listened*

1. play _____   6. show _____

2. study _____   7. look _____

3. decide _____   8. stop _____

4. want _____   9. háppen _____

5. like _____   10. carry _____

11. enjoy _____   16. prefér _____

12. drag _____   17. like _____

13. drop _____   18. mix _____

14. start _____   19. admít _____

15. follow _____   20. devélop _____

EXERCISE 7   Fill in each blank with the past tense of the verb in parentheses ( ). Use correct spelling.

> **EXAMPLE: The Chicago fire** _____*started*_____ **in October.**
> (start)

1. The Chicago fire _____ in 1871.
   (occur)

2. A cow _____ over a lantern.
   (kick)

3. The fire _____ quickly.
   (move)

4. The wind _____ the fire.
   (carry)

5. The fire _____ many buildings.
   (destroy)

6. People _____ to escape the fire.
   (try)

7. The fire _____ many people.
   (kill)

8. The fire finally _____.
   (stop)

9. Architects _____ wooden buildings with stone buildings.
   (replace)

EXERCISE 8   Fill in each blank with the correct form of the verb in parentheses ( ). Use correct spelling. Read your answers out loud. Use correct pronunciation.

> **EXAMPLE: Charles Lindbergh** _____*crossed*_____ **the Atlantic Ocean in 1927.**
> (crossed)

1. A rich man _____ $25,000 as a prize.
   (offer)

2. Lindbergh _____ to win the prize.
   (want)

3. Lindbergh _____ for 33 hours.
                    (travel)

4. He _____ in Paris.
          (arrive)

5. He _____ to the U.S.
          (return)

6. Amelia Earhart _____ the Atlantic Ocean in 1932.
                        (cross)

7. She _____ in Ireland.
            (stop)

8. In 1937, she _____ to fly around the world.
                    (decide)

9. She _____ over the Pacific Ocean.
          (disappear)

9.5 Simple Past Tense of Irregular Verbs

An irregular verb is a verb that doesn't use the -ed ending for the past tense. Here is a list of common irregular verbs, grouped according to the type of change. For an alphabetical list of irregular verbs, see Appendix D.

Verbs with No Change	
bet	hurt
cost	let
cut	put
fit	quit
hit	shut

Verbs Ending in -d That Have -t for the Past Form	
bend—bent	send—sent
build—built	spend—spent
lend—lent	

Verbs with a Vowel Change	
feel—felt	bring—brought
keep—kept	buy—bought
leave—left	catch—caught
lose—lost	fight—fought
mean—meant[6]	teach—taught
sleep—slept	think—thought
break—broke	begin—began
choose—chose	drink—drank
freeze—froze	ring—rang
steal—stole	sing—sang
speak—spoke	sink—sank
wake—woke	swim—swam
dig—dug	drive—drove
hang—hung	ride—rode
win—won	shine—shone
	write—wrote
blow—blew	bleed—bled
draw—drew	feed—fed
fly—flew	lead—led
grow—grew	meet—met
know—knew	read—read[7]
throw—threw	
sell—sold	find—found
tell—told	wind—wound
shake—shook	lay—laid
take—took	pay—paid
mistake—mistook	say—said[8]
tear—tore	bite—bit
wear—wore	hide—hid
	light—lit
become—became	fall—fell
come—came	hold—held
eat—ate	

[6]There is a change in the vowel sound. *Meant* rhymes with *sent*.

[7]The past form of *read* is pronounced like the color *red*.

[8]*Said* rhymes with *bed*.

Verbs with a Vowel Change *(continued)*	
give—gave forgive—forgave lie—lay	run—ran sit—sat see—saw
forget—forgot get—got shoot—shot	stand—stood understand—understood
	hear—heard

Miscellaneous Changes	
be—was/were do—did go—went	have—had make—made

. . . .

R
E
A
D
I
N
G

Before you read:

1. What kind of music do you like?
2. What kind of music is popular in your country?

Read the following article. Pay special attention to the past tense of regular and irregular verbs.

— John Lennon

The Beatles

JOHN LENNON

John Lennon **was** a talented musician. He **became** rich and famous. However, when he **was** young, it **seemed** like he was going to be a failure.

John **was** born in Liverpool, England, in 1940 to a working-class family. Soon after he **was** born, his father **abandoned** him. His mother **sent** John to live with her sister when she **left** with a new boyfriend. John **became** the leader of a street gang. He **spent** a lot of time on the streets, where he **stole** things. A teacher once **wrote** on his report card that he **had** no future.

John's mother **lived** not far from him, and she **visited** him from time to time. When John **was** thirteen, his mother **brought** him a guitar when she **came** to see him. She **taught** him how to play a few chords. John **got** together with some classmates and **formed** a rock group. The group **changed** names over the years, but it eventually **became** known as the Beatles.

John and the Beatles **became** popular all over the world in the 1960s. They **were** the most popular musical group for more than a decade. They **got** rich from all the records they sold.

The Beatles greatly **influenced** the music and popular culture of the 1960s and 1970s. They **had** long hair, and young men **started** to grow their hair long to imitate the Beatles.

In 1968, Lennon **married** a Japanese woman, Yoko Ono. In 1970, the Beatles **broke** up, and he **began** to perform with his wife.

On December 8, 1980, Mark Chapman, an unemployed amateur guitarist, **went** to the New York building where Lennon **lived** with his wife and young son. Chapman **waited** outside Lennon's building. When Lennon **came** out, Chapman **fired** several shots and **killed** Lennon. This **was** a great tragedy for Beatles' fans. Lennon's fans **cried** while radio stations **played** music by Lennon and the Beatles.

• •

EXERCISE 9   Fill in each blank with the past form of the verb in parentheses ( ).

> **EXAMPLE:** John Lennon _____*was*_____ born in England.
> (be)

1. His parents _____ him when he was young.
   (leave)

2. He _____ to live with an aunt.
   (go)

3. He _____ a street gang.
   (lead)

4. He _____ things when he was a child.
   (steal)

5. A teacher _____ on his report card that he
   (write)
   _____ no future.
   (have)

6. John's mother _____ to visit him.
   (come)

7. She _____ him a guitar.
   (bring)

8. John Lennon and the Beatles _____ popular all over the world.
                                                          (become)

9. Many young men _____ their hair long to imitate the Beatles.
                              (grow)

10. Lennon _____ and _____ Yoko Ono.
                      (meet)   (marry)

11. The Beatles _____ up.
                              (break)

12. Mark Chapman _____ and _____ Lennon.
                                (shoot)   (kill)

13. Lennon's fans _____ when they _____ of his death.
                                (cry)   (hear)

9.6   Negative Forms of Past Tense Verbs

In a negative statement, we use *didn't* + base form for all verbs, regular or irregular (except *be*). We don't use the past form:

I	
You	
We	worked.
They	didn't work.
He	went.
She	didn't go.
It	

Language Notes

Compare the affirmative and negative sentences below:

The Chicago fire *burned* the area near the lake.
It *didn't burn* the western part of the city.

John Lennon *lived* with his aunt.
He *didn't live* with his mother.

John Lennon's mother *came* to visit him.
His father *didn't come* to visit him.

He *sang* rock music.
He *didn't sing* opera.

EXERCISE 10   Fill in each blank with the negative form of the underlined verb.

EXAMPLE: John Lennon played the guitar. He ____*didn't play*____ the violin.

1. John Lennon <u>lived</u> with his aunt. He _____ with his mother.

2. His mother <u>left</u> with her boyfriend. She _____ with her husband.

3. John <u>spent</u> a lot of time on the streets. He _____ a lot of time in the library.

4. John <u>was</u> a bad student. He _____ a good student.

5. His teacher <u>said</u> bad things about him. She _____ good things.

6. His mother <u>gave</u> him a guitar. His aunt _____ him a guitar.

7. His mother <u>taught</u> him to play a few chords. His aunt _____ him.

8. John <u>became</u> a famous musician. He _____ a criminal.

9. He <u>played</u> with three other musicians. He _____ alone.

10. The Beatles <u>were</u> popular all over the world. They _____ popular just in England.

11. In the 1970s, Lennon <u>performed</u> with his wife. He _____ with the Beatles anymore.

12. Mark Chapman <u>went</u> to New York. He _____ to London.

13. He <u>waited</u> outside Lennon's apartment building. He _____ in the apartment.

14. He <u>had</u> a gun. He _____ a knife.

15. He <u>killed</u> Lennon. He _____ Lennon's wife.

EXERCISE 11   Check (✓) what was true for you before you came to the U.S. Find a partner and compare your list to your partner's list. Report to the class something interesting you learned about your partner.

EXAMPLES: **Marek studied English with a private teacher for three months before he came to the U.S.**

Tran went to Thailand before he came to the U.S. He stayed there for one week.

1. _____ change my money for dollars   4. _____ study English

2. _____ get a passport   5. _____ sell my furniture, my house, etc.

3. _____ apply for a visa

6. ____ say goodbye to my friends

7. ____ buy an English dictionary

8. ____ have a clear idea about life
in the U.S.

9. ____ be afraid about the future

10. ____ go to another country

11. ____ understand English well

12. ____ know a lot of Americans

13. ____ _____

14. ____ _____

EXERCISE 12   Tell if you did or didn't do these things in the past week. Add some information to tell more about each item.

> EXAMPLE: go to the movies
> I went to the movies last weekend with my brother. We saw a great movie.
> OR
> I didn't go to the movies this week. I didn't have time.

1. receive a letter
2. write a letter
3. go to the library
4. do my laundry
5. buy groceries
6. make a long-distance phone call

7. buy a lottery ticket
8. work hard
9. look for a job
10. rent a video
11. _____
12. _____

EXERCISE 13   Tell if these things happened or didn't happen after you arrived in the U.S. If affirmative, tell when.

> EXAMPLE: find an apartment
> I found an apartment two weeks after I arrived in the U.S.
> OR
> I didn't find an apartment right away. I lived with my cousins for two months.

1. find a job
2. register for English classes
3. rent an apartment
4. buy a car

5. get a Social Security card
6. get a driver's license
7. visit a museum
8. _____

9.7 Questions with Past Tense Verbs

Compare statements and questions with the simple past tense:

Wh- Word	*Did*	Subject	Verb	Complement
		The fire	started.	
	Did	the fire	start	in the morning?
When	did	the fire	start?	
		The fire	didn't burn	the whole city.
Why	didn't	the fire	burn	the whole city?
		Lennon's mother	brought	him an instrument.
	Did	she	bring	him a guitar?
Why	did	she	bring	him a guitar?
		Someone	killed	Lennon.
		Who	killed	Lennon?
		A lot of people	died	in the fire.
		How many people	died	in the fire?

1. In all *yes/no* questions, use *did* + the base form for all verbs, regular or irregular (except *be*). Use *did* in a short answer.

   John Lennon *married* Yoko Ono.
   Did he *marry* an American woman? No, he *didn't*.

   John Lennon *became* popular in England.
   Did he *become* popular in the rest of the world? Yes, he *did*.

2. Most *wh*- questions use *did* + the base form.

   The Chicago Fire *started* in October.
   Where *did* the fire *start*?

   Chicagoans *rebuilt* their city.
   When *did* they *rebuild* their city?

   The fire department *didn't put* out the fire immediately.
   Why *didn't* the fire department *put* out the fire immediately?

   Lennon *played* the guitar.
   With whom *did* he *play* the guitar? (formal word order)
   Who *did* he *play* the guitar with? (informal word order)

3. When we ask a *wh*- question about the subject, we use the past form, not the base form.

   Subject Questions:

Who	
What	+ Past Form . . .?
How Many	
Which Noun	

   Something *started* the fire.
   What *started* the fire?

   Someone *gave* Lennon a guitar.
   Who *gave* Lennon a guitar?
   Which relative *gave* Lennon a guitar?

EXERCISE 14   Use these questions to interview a partner about the time when he or she lived in his or her country. Report some interesting information about your partner to the class.

1. Did you study English in your country?
2. Did you live in a big city?
3. Did you live with your parents?
4. Did you know a lot about the U.S.?
5. Were you happy with the political situation?
6. Did you finish high school?
7. Did you own a car?
8. Did you have a job?
9. Did you think about your future?
10. Were you happy?
11. _____

EXERCISE 15   Read each statement. Then write a *yes/no* question with the words in parentheses ( ). Write a short answer. The first word of the answer is given.

EXAMPLE: **John Lennon's father abandoned him. (his mother) (yes)**

Did his mother abandon him? Yes, she did.

1. John Lennon was born in England. (London) (no)

   _____

2. He stole things. (a guitar) (no)

   _____

3. His mother visited him. (his father) (no)

   _____

4. Lennon played music with the Beatles. (with his wife) (yes)

   _____

5. The Beatles were born in England. (John's wife) (no)

   _____

6. The Beatles had long hair in the 1960s. (many young men) (yes)

   _____

7.   Lennon performed with the Beatles. (with his wife) (yes)

_____

8. Lennon lived in New York. (in an apartment) (yes)

_____

9. Mark Chapman went to Lennon's building. (inside the building) (no)

_____

10. Chapman killed Lennon. (Lennon's wife) (no)

_____

EXERCISE 16   Fill in each blank to complete the question and answer.

EXAMPLE: **What did the Wright Brothers invent?**

   They _____*invented*_____ **the airplane.**

1. When did Lindbergh cross the Atlantic Ocean?

   He _____ it in 1927.

2. How long did Lindbergh's trip _____?
   It took 33 hours.

3. Who _____ the airplane?
   The Wright Brothers invented the airplane.

4. Where _____?

   Earhart _____ born in Kansas.

5. How much money _____ Lindbergh win?

   He _____ $25,000.

6. How old _____ Lindbergh when he crossed the ocean?
   He was 25 years old.

7. How many people _____ in the Chicago Fire?
   Three hundred people died in the Chicago Fire.

8. How did the fire _____?
   No one knows how the fire started.

9. When _____?
   Lindbergh was born in 1902.

EXERCISE 17   Read each statement. Then write a question with the words in parentheses ( ). Answer with a complete sentence. (The answers are at the bottom of page 216.)

EXAMPLE: **John Lennon wasn't born in the U.S. (Where)**

Where was he born? _____

He was born in England. _____

1. John Lennon was born in England. (When)

    A. _____

    B. _____

2. His father abandoned him. (When)

    A. _____

    B. _____

3. John didn't live with his mother. (Who . . . with) OR (With whom . . .)

    A. _____

    B. _____

4. His mother went away. (Who . . . with) OR (With whom . . .)

    A. _____

    B. _____

5. A teacher wrote something on his report card. (What)

    A. _____

    B. _____

6. His mother brought him a present. (What)

    A. _____

    B. _____

7. Somebody taught him to play the guitar. (Who)

    A. _____

    B. _____

8. John formed a group. (What kind of)

    A. _____

    B. _____

9. John Lennon became popular. (Where)

    A. _____

    B. _____

10. John married Yoko. (When)

    A. _____

    B. _____

11. The Beatles broke up. (When)

    A. _____

    B. _____

12. John began to perform with his wife. (When)

    A. _____

    B. _____

13. John lived with his wife and son. (Where)

    A. _____

    B. _____

14. Somebody went to John's building on December 8, 1980. (Who)

    A. _____

    B. _____

15. His fans cried. (Why)

    A. _____

    B. _____

EXERCISE 18   Check (✓) and read aloud a statement that is **true** for you. Another student will ask a question with the words in parentheses ( ). Answer the question.

EXAMPLES: __✓__ I did my homework. (where)
              Where did you do your homework?
              I did my homework in the library.

              __✓__ I got married. (when)
              When did you get married?
              I got married six years ago.

1. _____ I graduated from high school. (when)

2. _____ I studied biology. (when)

3. _____ I bought an English dictionary. (where)

4. _____ I left my country. (when)

5. _____ I came to the U.S. (why)

6. _____ I brought my clothes to the U.S. (what else)

7. _____ I rented an apartment. (where)

8. _____ I started to study English. (when)

9. _____ I chose this college. (why)

10. _____ I found my apartment. (when)

11. _____ I needed to learn English. (what else)

12. _____ I got married. (when)

Answers to Exercise 17:

1. In 1940	6. A guitar	11. In 1970
2. Soon after he was born	7. His mother	12. After the Beatles broke up
3. His aunt	8. A rock group	13. In New York
4. With a boyfriend	9. All over the world	14. Mark Chapman
5. He had no future	10. In 1968	15. Because Lennon died

EXERCISE 19 Check (✓) which of these things you did when you were a child. Find a partner and compare your list to your partner's list. Ask your partner about the items he or she checked. Report to the class something interesting you learned about your partner.

1. _____ I attended public school.

2. _____ I enjoyed school.

3. _____ I got good grades in school.

4. _____ I took music lessons.

5. _____ I lived with my grandparents.

6. _____ I got an allowance.[9]

7. _____ I had a pet.

8. _____ I lived on a farm.

9. _____ I played with dolls/played soccer.

10. _____ I studied English.

11. _____ I had a bike.

12. _____ I thought about my future.

13. _____ _____

EXERCISE 20 Fill in each blank in this conversation between two students about their past.

A. I ___*was born*___ in Mexico. I _____ to the U.S. ten years ago.
    (born)   (1 come)

   Where _____ born?
              (2 be)

B. In El Salvador. But my family _____ to Guatemala when I
                                      (3 move)

   _____ 10 years old.
        (4 be)

A. Why _____ to Guatemala?
            (5 move)

B. We _____ afraid to stay in El Salvador.
          (6 be)

A. Why _____ afraid?
            (7 be)

B. Because there _____ a war in El Salvador.
                      (8 be)

A. How long _____ in Guatemala?
                 (9 stay)

B. We stayed there for about five years. Then I _____ to the U.S.
                                                      (10 come)

A. What about your family? _____ to the U.S. with you?
                                (11 come)

_____

[9]An *allowance* is money children get from their parents, usually once a week.

B. No, they _____. I _____ a job,
                     (12 auxiliary)   (13 find)

_____ my money, and _____ them
       (14 save)   (15 bring)

here later.

A. My parents _____ with me either. But my older brother did. I
                      (16 not/come)

_____ to go to school as soon as I _____.
       (17 start)   (18 arrive)

B. Who _____ you while you were in school?
         (19 support)

A. My brother _____.
           (20 auxiliary)

B. I _____ to school right away because I _____ to
       (21 not/go)   (22 have)

work. Then I _____ a grant and _____ to go to
           (23 get)   (24 start)

City College.

A. Why _____ City College?
         (25 choose)

B. I chose it because it has a good ESL program.

A. Me too.

EXPANSION ACTIVITIES

FAMOUS QUOTE   I came, I saw, I conquered.—Julius Caesar

OLD QUESTION   The following old question uses the past tense in a subject question. Do you have this question in your language too?

    Which came first, the chicken or the egg?

OUTSIDE ACTIVITIES   1. Interview an American about a vacation he or she took. Find out where he or she went, with whom, for how long, and other related information.

2. Go to the library to find out about a famous person who interests you. Write a short report about this person's life. (Ideas: Martin Luther King, Jr., John Kennedy, Mohandas Gandhi, Josef Stalin, Anwar Sadat, Benito Juarez, Che Guevara)

DISCUSSIONS

1. In a small group or with the entire class, discuss your first experiences in the U.S. What were your first impressions? What did you do in your first few days in the U.S.?

   EXAMPLE: I lived with my cousins. They helped me find an apartment. I didn't have money to buy furniture. They lent me money. At first I wasn't happy. I didn't go out of the house much. . . .

2. Find a partner to interview. Ask questions about the circumstances that brought him or her to the U.S. and the conditions of his/her life after he/she arrived. Write your conversation. Use Exercise 20 as your model.

   EXAMPLE: A. When did you leave your country?
   B. I left Ethiopia five years ago.
   A. Did you come directly to the U.S.?
   B. No. First I went to Sudan.
   A. Why did you leave Ethiopia?

The Simple Past Tense

1. *Be*

I			We	
He	was in Paris.		You	were in Paris.
She			They	
It				
There was a problem.			There were many problems.	

He *was* in Poland.	They *were* in France.
He *wasn't* in Russia.	They *weren't* in England.
Was he in Hungary?	*Were* they in Paris?
No, he *wasn't.*	No, they *weren't.*
Where *was* he?	When *were* they in France?
Why *wasn't* he in Russia?	Why *weren't* they in Paris?
Who *was* in Russia?	How many people *were* in France?

NOTE: Use *be* with *born.*

Where *were* you born?
I *was* born in India.

2. Other Verbs

Regular Verb (work)	Irregular Verb (buy)
She *worked* on Saturday.	They *bought* a car.
She *didn't work* on Sunday.	They *didn't buy* a motorcycle.
Did she *work* in the morning?	*Did* they *buy* an American car?
Yes, she *did.*	No, they *didn't.*
Where *did* she *work*?	What kind of car *did* they *buy*?
Why *didn't* she *work* on Sunday?	Why *didn't* they *buy* an American car?
Who *worked* on Sunday?	How many people *bought* an American car?

NOTE: The verb after *to* does not use the past form.

She wanted to *leave.*
They had to *work.*

LESSON NINE TEST/REVIEW

Part 1   Find mistakes with past tenses (including mistakes in spelling), and correct them. Not every sentence has a mistake. If the sentence is correct, write **C.**

>   *was*
> EXAMPLE: John Lennon ~~were~~ a good musician.

1. John Lennon born in England.

2. He spended a lot of time on the streets.

3. John didn't liked school.

4. John's mother teached him to play the guitar.

5. He began to play the guitar when he 13 years old.

6. John wanted to be a musician.

7. He enjoied popular music.

8. The Beatles were popular all over the world.

9. He marryed a Japanese woman.

10. He lived in New York with his wife and son.

11. Mark Chapman went to Lennon's house and shoot him.

12. He died at the age of 40.

Part 2   Write the past tense of each verb.

EXAMPLES: **live** _____*lived*_____   **feel** _____*felt*_____

1. eat _____   11. drink _____

2. see _____   12. build _____

3. get _____   13. stop _____

4. sit _____   14. leave _____

5. hit _____   15. buy _____

6. make _____   16. think _____

7. take _____   17. run _____

8. find _____   18. carry _____

9. say _____   19. sell _____

10. read _____   20. stand _____

Part 3   Fill in each blank with the negative form of the underlined verb.

EXAMPLE: Lindbergh <u>worked</u> for the U.S. Mail Service. Earhart

_didn't work_____ for the U.S. Mail Service.

1. There <u>were</u> trains 100 years ago. There _____ any airplanes.

2. Chicago <u>had</u> a big fire. New York _____ a big fire.

3. Charles Lindbergh <u>was</u> an aviator. He _____ a president.

4. The Wright Brothers <u>invented</u> the airplane. They _____ the telephone.

5. Lindbergh <u>went</u> to Paris. Earhart _____ to Paris.

6. Lindbergh <u>came</u> back from his flight. Earhart _____ back from her last flight.

7. John Lennon <u>was</u> born in England. He _____ born in the U.S.

8. Lennon <u>lived</u> with his aunt. He _____ with his mother.

9. He <u>became</u> a musician. He _____ a criminal.

10. The Beatles <u>played</u> popular music. They _____ classical music.

Part 4   Read each statement. Write a *yes/no* question about the words in parentheses ( ). Write a short answer.

EXAMPLE: **Lindbergh crossed the ocean. (Earhart) (yes)**

_Did Earhart cross the ocean? Yes, she did._____

1. Chicago had a big fire. (Miami) (no)

_____

2. Earhart and Lindbergh were aviators. (John Lennon) (no)

_____

3. Lindbergh crossed the Atlantic Ocean. (Earhart) (yes)

_____

4. John Lennon was born in England. (London) (no)

_____

5. His aunt took care of him. (his father) (no)

_____

6. Young people liked the Beatles' musical style. (hair style) (yes)

_____

7. Lennon wrote music. (classical music) (no)

_____

8. He made a lot of records. (a lot of money) (yes)

_____

9. His second wife was from Japan. (his first wife) (no)

_____

10. He spent his last years in the U.S. (in New York) (yes)

_____

Part 5   Write a *wh-* question about the words in parentheses ( ). It is not necessary to answer the questions.

> EXAMPLE: **The Wright Brothers became famous for their first airplane. (why/Lindbergh)**
>
> *Why did Lindbergh become famous?*

1. Earhart was born in 1897. (when/Lindbergh)

_____

2. Thomas Edison invented the phonograph. (what/the Wright Brothers)

_____

3. Thomas Edison invented the phonograph. (who/the airplane)

_____

4. Lindbergh crossed the ocean in 1927. (when/Earhart)

_____

5. Lindbergh got money for his flight. (how much)

_____

6. Earhart wanted to fly around the world. (why)

_____

7. Many people saw Lindbergh in Paris. (how many people)

_____

8. Lennon didn't do well in school. (why)

_____

9. Lennon's parents abandoned him. (why)

_____

10. Lennon lived in New York. (with whom) OR (who . . . with)

_____

LESSON TEN

GRAMMAR

Imperatives
Infinitives
Modals

CONTEXT

Change of Address
Traffic Tickets
Driving Regulations

Lesson Focus   Imperatives; Infinitives; Modals

- We use imperative sentences to make requests, commands, and instructions to other people.

    Stay here.   *Be* good.   *Open* your book.

- The infinitive is *to* + the base form of the verb.

    I want *to leave*.   I need *to go* home.

- We use modal auxiliaries to add certain meanings to verbs.

    I *can* read this paragraph easily.   You *should* help your roommate.

R
E
A
D
I
N
G

Before you read:

1. In your country, did your family move from one place to another, or did you live in the same place for most of your life?
2. If you've ever moved, how did you let your friends know about your move?

Change-of-Address Card

Read the following article. Pay special attention to the imperative forms.

CHANGE OF ADDRESS

If you move to a different address, **inform** the post office. **Ask** the post office for a change-of-address card. **Read** the instructions carefully and **fill out** the form. **Return** this card to the post office.

Sign your name on line 9, but **print** all other information. **Don't write** in the gray areas that say "For Official Use Only." **Include** your old address as well as your new address. **Fill** in the starting date; this is the date when you want the Post Office to start delivering your mail to your new address.

On the other side of the card, **print** the city, state, and zip code of your old address. **Mail** the card to the post office of your old address or **give** it to your letter carrier. **Don't put** a stamp on the card.

On the day of the move, **put** your name on the new mailbox. **Don't leave** your name on the old mailbox. Within a short time, your mail should start to arrive at your new address.

• •

10.1 Using Imperatives

The subject of the imperative is *you,* but we don't include it in the statement.

Don't	Base Form	Complement
	Stay	here.
Don't	go	out.
	Be	on time.
Don't	be	late.

Language Notes

We use the imperative form in the following cases:

1. To give instructions.

   Print the information on the card.
   Don't print on line 9. *Sign* your name.

2. To make a request. *Please* makes the request more polite.

   Please mail this card for me.
   Take this card to the post office for me, *please.*

3. To make a command.

   Don't open my mail!
   Stand at attention!

4. In certain polite conversational expressions.

   Have a nice day (weekend).
   Have a good time.
   Make yourself at home.

5. In some angry expressions.

   Shut up!
   Mind your own business!

EXERCISE 1   Fill in each blank with an appropriate imperative verb (affirmative or negative) to give an instruction.

       EXAMPLE: **If you plan to move,** _fill out_____ **a change-of-address card.**

1. _____ the information on all lines except 9.

2. _____ your name on line 9.

3. _____ the instructions carefully.

4. _____ your old address as well as your new one.

5. _____ the card to the post office of your old address.

6. _____ a stamp on the card.

7. _____ your name on the new mailbox.

8. _____ your name on the old mailbox.

EXERCISE 2   Parents often give their children rules with imperatives. Fill in each blank with an imperative, either affirmative or negative.

       EXAMPLES: _Do_____ **your homework.**

                   _Don't eat_____ **so much candy.**

1. _____ to strangers.

2. _____ after school.

3. _____ before dinner.

4. _____ before you cross the street.

5. _____ your brothers and sisters.

6. _____ with matches.

7. _____ your grandparents.

8. _____ before you go to bed.

EXERCISE 3   Choose one of the activities from the following list (or choose a different one, if you like). Use imperatives to give instructions on how to do the activity.

> EXAMPLE: **how to get from school to your house**
> **Take the number 53 bus north on the corner of Elm Street. Ask the driver for a transfer. Get off at Park Avenue. Cross the street and wait for a number 18 bus.**

1. hang a picture
2. change a tire
3. fry an egg
4. prepare your favorite recipe
5. hem a skirt
6. write a check
7. make a deposit at the bank
8. tune a guitar
9. get a driver's license
10. use a washing machine
11. prepare for a job interview
12. get from school to your house
13. get money from a cash machine (automatic teller)
14. record a TV show on your VCR
15. _____

hem →

10.2 *Let's*

We use *let's* + the base form to make an invitation or suggestion. *Let's* includes the speaker in the invitation. (*Let's* is a contraction of *let* + *us*, but we always use the contracted form.)

Let's	(Not)	Base Form	Complement
Let's		get	married. I love you.
Let's		hurry.	
Let's	not	be	so quick to make a decision.

EXERCISE 4 Fill in each blank with an appropriate verb to complete this conversation.

A. I need a change-of-address card. I'm going to move on Saturday.

B. I need to buy some stamps. Let's _____*go*_____ to the post

office together.

A. I don't have my car. My wife is using it.

B. The post office is not so far. Let's _____.
(1)

A. It looks like rain.

B. No problem. Let's _____ an umbrella.
(2)

A. I need to ask you about good movers.

B. Let's _____ about it now. The post office is going to
(3)

close in 20 minutes.

A. Let's _____. I want to get there before it closes.
(4)

EXERCISE 5 Work with a partner. Write a few suggestions for the teacher or other students in this class. Read your suggestions to the class.

EXAMPLES: *Let's review verb tenses.*

Let's not speak our native languages in class.

1. _____

2. _____

3. _____

EXERCISE 6 Work with a partner. Write a list of command forms that the teacher often uses in class. Read your sentences to the class.

EXAMPLES: *Open your books to page 10.*

Don't come late to class.

1. _____

2. _____

3. _____

Before you read:

1. Did you (or your family) have a car in your country?
2. Are driving rules stricter in the U.S. or in your country?
3. Did you ever get a traffic ticket in this city?

Read the following article. Pay special attention to infinitives.

TRAFFIC TICKETS

A driver can get a ticket for a moving violation or a nonmoving violation. In a moving violation, you break a rule while you are driving your car. Often you have to go to court for a moving violation. A nonmoving violation is not so serious. Parking in a no-parking zone is a nonmoving violation. It is usually not necessary **to go** to court. Usually, you can pay for this ticket by mail. However, if you get a lot of tickets and don't pay them, the city might decide **to put** a "boot" on a tire of your car until you pay these tickets. You can't continue **to drive** your car until you pay all your tickets and the city removes the "boot."

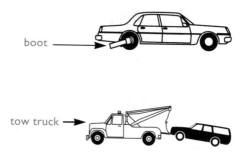

boot

tow truck

If you see a street sign that says "NO PARKING TOW ZONE," do not park in this place. You may not find your car when you return. You will need **to go** to the police station and **pay** the ticket as well as the price of towing. Private businesses often have signs that say "PARKING FOR CUSTOMERS ONLY. VIOLATORS WILL BE TOWED." If you are not a customer and park in this place, your car may not be there when you return. You need **to call** the phone number on the sign to find out where your car is. You will probably have to pay at least $50 to get your car.

No one likes **to get** a ticket or pay for towing. But sometimes people try **to break** the rules.

10.3 Verbs Followed by an Infinitive

We form the infinitive by adding *to* to the base form of a verb.

Subject	Verb	Infinitive	Complement
They	began	to drive	fast.
He	needs	to buy	a new car.
We	try	to obey	the law.

1. We often use an infinitive after the following verbs.

begin	hope	prefer
continue	like	promise
decide	love	start
expect	need	try
forget	plan	want

2. An infinitive never has an ending. It never shows the tense. Only the first verb shows the tense.

> I need *to go* to court next Monday.
> The police officer needed *to see* my license.
> I'm trying *to drive* carefully.
> She doesn't want *to get* a ticket.

3. In an infinitive, we often pronounce *to* like "ta," or, after a <u>d</u> sound or vowel sound, like "da." Listen to your teacher pronounce these sentences.

> Do you like *to dance?*
> I try *to exercise* every day.
> I decided *to leave.*
> I need *to talk* to you.

4. In fast, informal speech, *want to* is often pronounced "wanna." Listen to your teacher pronounce these sentences.

> I *want to* go home. = I "wanna" go home.
> Do you *want to* leave now? = Do you "wanna" leave now?

EXERCISE 7   Ask a question with "Do you want to . . .?" and the words given. Another student will answer. Then ask a *wh-* question with the words in parentheses ( ) whenever possible.

> EXAMPLE: **buy a car (why)**
> **A. Do you want to buy a car?**
> **B. Yes, I do.** OR **No, I don't.**
> **A. Why do you want to buy a car?**
> **B. I don't like public transportation.**

1. take a computer course next semester (why)
2. move (why) (when)
3. return to your country (why) (when)
4. get a job/get another job (what kind of job)
5. become an American citizen (why)
6. transfer to a different school (why)
7. take another English course next semester (which course)
8. learn another language (which language)
9. review the last lesson (why)

EXERCISE 8   Ask a question with the words given in the present tense. Another student will answer.

> EXAMPLE: **like/travel**
> **A. Do you like to travel?**
> **B. Yes, I do.** OR **No, I don't.**

1. expect/pass this course
2. plan/graduate soon
3. plan/transfer to another college
4. like/read

5. like/study grammar
6. try/understand Americans
7. try/learn idioms
8. expect/return to your country

EXERCISE 9   Make a sentence about yourself with the words given. Use an appropriate tense. Find a partner, and compare your sentences to your partner's sentences.

EXAMPLES: **like/eat**

I like to eat pizza.

learn/speak

I learned to speak German when I was a child.

try/find

I'm trying to find a bigger apartment.

1. love/go

_____

2. like/play

_____

3. need/have

_____

4. expect/get

_____

5. want/go

_____

6. plan/buy

_____

7. need/understand

_____

8. not need/have

_____

9. try/learn

_____

10.4 *It + Be* + Adjective + Infinitive

We use an infinitive in this pattern:

It	*Be (Not)*	Adjective	Infinitive Phrase
It	is	important	to know your rights.
It	was	necessary	to clean the apartment.
It	isn't	easy	to learn another language.
It	will be	hard	to find a better job.

We can use an infinitive after the following adjectives:

dangerous	good	possible	expensive
difficult	hard	necessary	impossible
easy	important	fun	

EXERCISE 10 Complete each statement.

EXAMPLE: **It's expensive to own** *a big car.* _____

1. It's important to learn _____

2. It's hard to pronounce _____

3. It's hard to lift _____

4. It's necessary to have _____

5. It's easy to learn _____

6. It's hard to learn _____

7. It isn't important to know _____

EXERCISE 11 Complete each statement with an infinitive phrase.

EXAMPLE: **It's easy** *to ride a bike.* _____

1. It's fun _____

2. It's impossible _____

3. It's possible _____

4. It's necessary _____

5. It's dangerous _____

6. It's hard _____

7. It isn't good _____

8. It isn't necessary _____

10.5 *Be* + Adjective + Infinitive

Some adjectives can be followed by an infinitive in this pattern:

Subject	*Be*	Adjective	Infinitive (Phrase)
I	am	happy	to be here.
You	are	lucky	to have a job.
She	is	ready	to leave.

We can use an infinitive after these adjectives:

afraid	happy	prepared	ready
glad	lucky	proud	sad

EXERCISE 12　Fill in each blank.

EXAMPLE: I'm lucky *to be in the U.S.* _____

1. Americans are lucky _____

2. I'm proud _____

3. I'm happy _____

4. I'm sometimes afraid _____

5. I'm not afraid _____

6. Are the students prepared _____

7. Is the teacher ready _____

10.6 Modals

Modals are auxiliary verbs. A base verb follows a modal.

Subject	Modal	(*Not*)	Main Verb (Base form)
I	can		
You	could		
He	should		go.
She	will	(not)	stay.
It	would		wait.
We	may		
They	might		
	must		

Observe statements and questions with a modal verb.

Wh- Word	Modal	Subject	Modal	Main Verb	Complement	Short Answer
		He	should	study	English.	
	Should	he		study	grammar?	Yes, he should.
What	should	he		study?		
		I	can	take	a pill.	
	Can	I		take	an aspirin?	Yes, you can.
How many aspirins	can	I		take?		
		You	can't	drive	a car.	
Why	can't	you		drive	a car?	
		Someone	should	close	the window.	
		Who	should	close	the window?	

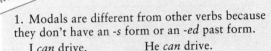

1. Modals are different from other verbs because they don't have an -s form or an -ed past form.

   I *can* drive.   He *can* drive.

2. Modals are different from other verbs because we don't use *to* after a modal.[1] Compare:

   He wants *to leave.*   He likes *to swim.*
   He *must* leave.   He *can* swim.

3. To make a modal negative, we add *not* after the modal verb.

   You *should not* drive.
   He *must not* leave.

4. We often use modals to ask for things in a polite way.

   Would you open the door, please?

---

[1]Exception: *ought to. Ought to* means *should.*

R
E
A
D
I
N
G

Before you read:

1. Do you have a driver's license? When did you get your license?
2. In your country, is there a national driver's license?

Read the following article. Pay special attention to modal verbs.

DRIVING REGULATIONS

In the U.S., driving regulations differ from state to state. There is no national driver's license. If you travel from state to state by car, you **can** use your driver's license in other states. While most laws are the same, there are some differences from state to state. For example, in some states, a driver **must** be 18 years old; in other states, someone who is 16 **can** get a license. In some states, the driver and front seat passenger **must** wear a seat belt, but the backseat passengers don't have to. Almost every state requires car owners to have liability insurance. Some states have stricter laws than others for drunk drivers. You **should** become acquainted with the differences if you plan on interstate driving. If you break a rule, you **might** get a ticket or you **might** have to go to court.

If you move to another state and become a resident there, some states will accept your driver's license from another state. In other states, you **can** use the driver's license from your former state for a few months, but then you **must** take the test in that state and get a new license.

You **can** get more information about driving regulations from the Secretary of State's office in the capital city of the state.

Language Notes

Can

1. We use *can* for ability, possibility, or permission. The negative of *can* is *cannot* or *can't*.
   A. Ability:
      I *can* drive.
   B. Possibility:
      If you drive too fast, you *can* get a ticket.
   C. Permission:
      You *can* park at a meter, but you *can't* park at a bus stop.
      You *can* use your driver's license in another state for a few months.

2. The negative of *can* is *cannot*. The contraction is *can't*.

3. In affirmative statements, we usually pronounce *can* /kIn/. In negative statements, we pronounce *can't* /kænt/. Sometimes it is hard to hear the final *t*, so we must pay attention to the vowel sound to hear the difference. Listen to your teacher pronounce these sentences:

   I *can* go.   I *can* see you.
   I *can't* go.   I *can't* see you.

In a short answer, we pronounce *can* /kaen/.

   Can you help me later?
   Yes, I *can*.

4. We use *can* in the following idiomatic expression:

   I *can't afford* to buy a new car. I don't have enough money to buy a new car.
   I saved my money, and now I *can afford* to take a vacation.

EXERCISE 13   Fill in each blank with *can* or *can't* to tell about your abilities.

EXAMPLES: I ___can___ drive a car.

I ___can't___ fly a plane.

1. I _____ identify traffic signs.
2. I _____ pass a driving test in this state.
3. I _____ drive a car.
4. I _____ drive a truck.

5. I _____ change the oil in a car.
6. I _____ change a tire.
7. I _____ fill up a gas tank.
8. I _____ operate a motorcycle.

EXERCISE 14   Ask a question about a classmate's abilities with the words given. Another student will answer.

EXAMPLE: **speak Spanish**
Can you speak Spanish?
Yes, I can.   OR   **No, I can't.**

1. write with your left hand
2. type sixty words per minute
3. use a word processor
4. play chess

5. ski
6. play the piano
7. speak Arabic
8. bake a cake

chess

EXERCISE 15   Write down one thing that you can do well. By going around the room and asking questions, find another student who has the same talent.

_____

EXERCISE 16   Fill in each blank with *can* or *can't* to show permission or no permission.

EXAMPLE: You ___can't___ park at a bus stop.

1. You _____ park at a parking meter.

2. You _____ park at a fire hydrant.

3. You _____ drive slowly on a highway.

4. You _____ turn right at a red light after stopping.

5. You _____ drive 55 miles per hour on the highway.

6. You _____ drive without a driver's license.

7. You _____ drive without insurance in this state.

8. You _____ drink and drive.

fire hydrant

Language Notes

Should

1. We use *should* to give advice or a warning.
   You *should* be careful when you drive.
   You *shouldn't* drive if you're sleepy.
   It's snowing hard today. She *shouldn't* drive.
   She *should* use public transportation.

2. The negative of *should* is *should not*. The contraction is *shouldn't*.

EXERCISE 17   Fill in each blank with *should* or *shouldn't* to give advice.

   EXAMPLE: You ___should___ be careful when you drive.

   1. Pedestrians[2] _____ wear light-colored clothing at night.

   2. Pedestrians _____ always cross at a corner.

   3. You _____ drive the maximum speed limit on icy roads.

   4. If you drive long distances, you _____ stop and rest frequently.

   5. Passengers _____ wear a seat belt.

   6. You _____ check your motor oil about once a month.

   7. You _____ smoke while filling up your gas tank.

   8. If you drive slowly, you _____ use the left lane.

EXERCISE 18   Tell if children *should* or *shouldn't* do the following.

   EXAMPLE: obey their parents
             Children should obey their parents.

   1. play with matches
   2. study hard
   3. watch adult movies
   4. talk to strangers
   5. go to their parents for advice
   6. play in the street
   7. respect older people

---

[2]A *pedestrian* is a person who is traveling on foot.

EXERCISE 19   Read each statement. Then ask a question with the word in parentheses
( ). Another student will answer.

>   EXAMPLE: **The students should do the homework (why)**
>   **A. Why should they do the homework?**
>   **B. It helps them understand the lesson.**

1. The students should study the lessons. (why)
2. The teacher should take attendance. (when)
3. The students should bring their textbook to class. (what else)
4. I should study modals. (why)
5. We should register for classes early. (why)
6. The teacher should speak clearly. (why)
7. The students shouldn't talk during a test. (why)
8. We shouldn't do the homework in class. (where)
9. The teacher should announce a test ahead of time. (why)

Must

1. We use *must* for laws and rules.

>   You *must* have a license plate on the back of
>   your car.
>   A driver *must* stop at a red light.

2. We use *must not* (*mustn't*) for something that
is against the law or a rule.

>   You *must not* park at a fire hydrant.
>   You *mustn't* pass in a no passing zone.

3. *Must not* and *cannot* have almost the same
meaning.

>   You *must not* park at a fire hydrant. (It's
>   against the law.)
>   You *can't* park at a fire hydrant. (It's not
>   permitted.)

EXERCISE 20   Fill in each blank with *must* or *must not*.

>   EXAMPLES: You _____*must*_____ stop at a red light.
>
>   You _____*must not*_____ drive slowly on the expressway.

1. You _____ pass a driving test if you want a driver's license.

2. You _____ drive when you drink alcohol.

3. If a school bus stops in front of you, you _____ stop.

4. You _____ park at a bus stop.

5. You _____ put money in a parking meter during business hours.

6. You _____ drive over the speed limit.

7. You _____ use your turn signal before you make a turn.

EXERCISE 21   Name something.

> EXAMPLE: **Name something you must have if you want to drive.**
> **You must have a license.**

1. Name something you must have if you want to leave the country.
2. Name something you must not carry onto an airplane.
3. Name something you must not do in the classroom.
4. Name something you must not do during a test.
5. Name something you must not do or have in your apartment.
6. Name something you must do to enter an American university.

Have to or Must

1. *Have to* and *must* both show necessity. Use *must* or *have to* for legal obligations. For personal obligations, *have to* is more common than *must*.

> You *must* have a license if you want to drive.
> You *have to* renew your license every few years.
> I *have to* buy a new car. I'm having problems with my old car.

2. The negative of *have to* is *do not have to*. The contraction is *don't have to*.

3. In the negative, *have to* and *must* have different meanings.

> You *must not* drink and drive. (It is against the law; it's dangerous.)
> You *don't have to* go to court for a parking ticket. You can pay by mail. (It's not necessary to go to court.)

4. In fast speech, *have to* sounds like "hafta"; *has to* sounds like "hasta."

> I "hafta" go.
> He "hasta" go.

EXERCISE 22   Tell if you *have to* or *don't have to* do these things at this school. (Remember: *don't have* to means not necessary.)

> EXAMPLES: **study before a test**
> **I have to study before a test.**
>
> **study in the library**
> **I don't have to study in the library. I can study at home.**

1. wear a suit to school
2. come on time to class
3. stand up to ask a question in class
4. do homework
5. notify the teacher if I'm going to be absent
6. call the teacher "professor"
7. raise my hand to answer
8. take a final exam
9. wear a uniform
10. _____

EXERCISE 23   Ask your teacher what he or she *has to* or *doesn't have to* do.

> EXAMPLE: **work on Saturdays**
>   A. **Do you have to work in Saturdays?**
>   B. **Yes, I do.**   OR   **No, I don't.**

1. take attendance
2. give the students a grade
3. call the students by their last names
4. wear a suit
5. work in the summer
6. have a master's degree
7. work on Saturdays
8. _____

EXERCISE 24   Write four sentences about students and teachers in your country. Tell what they *have to* or *don't have to* do. Use the ideas from the previous exercises. Share your sentences with a small group or with the class.

> EXAMPLE: *In my country, a student has to wear a uniform.* _____

1. _____

2. _____

3. _____

4. _____

Might/May

1. We use *might* or *may* to show possibility (like the word *maybe*). The result is possible but uncertain. Both *may* and *might* have about the same meaning.

> If you park at a bus stop, you *may* get a ticket.
> If you park at a bus stop, a tow truck *might* tow your car away.

2. We do not usually make a contraction for *may not* or *might not.*

> If you don't practice, you *might not* pass the driver's test.

3. If you use *will,* the result is certain. If you use *may* or *might,* the result is not certain.

> The Secretary of State *will* send you a notice when your license is about to[3] expire.
> If you drink and drive, you *might* have an accident.

---
[3]*About to* means *ready to.*

EXERCISE 25   Tell what *may* or *might* happen in the following situations. If you think the result is certain, use *will*.

> EXAMPLES: If you don't put money in a parking meter, *you might get a* *parking ticket.*
>
> If you are absent from tests, *you may not pass the course.*
>
> If I don't pass the tests, *I'll fail the course.*

1. If you drive too fast, _____

2. If you are driving on an icy street, _____

3. If you get a lot of tickets in one year, _____

4. If you move and don't inform the post office, _____

5. If I don't study before a test, _____

6. If I have some free time tonight, _____

7. If I don't lock the door of my house, _____

8. If I eat too much, _____

9. If I buy a lottery ticket, _____

10. If the weather is nice this weekend, _____

EXERCISE 26   Working in a small group, write a list of things a new student or a foreign student *should, must, might,* or *can* do.

> EXAMPLE: **A new student must fill out an application for admission.**
> **A foreign student should speak with the foreign student advisor.**

EXERCISE 27   With a partner, write a few instructions for one of the following situations.

> EXAMPLE: using a microwave oven
> **You shouldn't put anything metal in the microwave.**
> **You can set the power.**
> **You should rotate the dish in the microwave. If you don't, the**
>   **food might not cook evenly.**

1. preparing for the TOEFL[4]
2. registering for this course
3. taking a test in this class
4. preparing for the driver's test in this state

---

[4]The *TOEFL* is the Test of English as a Foreign Language.

teller

R
E
A
D
I
N
G

Before you read:

1. Do you have a checking account?
2. Did you have a checking account in your country?
3. Do most people in your country get paid by cash or by check?

Read the following conversation between a bank teller (T) and a customer (C). Pay special attention to modals used for polite requests.

SCENE IN A BANK

T. **May** I help you?
C. I**'d like to** cash a check.
T. Do you have an account in this bank?
C. Yes, I do. I have a savings account.
T. **Could** you give me your account number, please?
C. Yes. Here it is.
T. **Would** you please sign your name on the back of the check?
C. **Can** I use your pen, please?
T. Of course. How **would you like** your cash?
C. **May** I have my cash in tens and twenties, please?
T. Yes. Here you are. **May** I help you with something else?
C. Yes. I**'d like to** open a checking account.
T. You need to see a bank counselor. **Why don't you** have a seat over there? A bank counselor will be with you shortly.[5]
C. Thank you.

10.7 Using Modals for Polite Commands and Requests

To command someone to do something, we use an imperative.

> *Stand* at attention.
> *Don't* move! You're under arrest!
> *Shut* up!

A command is very strong, and sometimes impolite. We usually tell or ask someone to do something in a more polite way. We can do this by using modal auxiliaries in a question. We can also use *please* to be more polite.

---

[5]*Shortly* means *very soon.*

To request that someone do something:

Command:	*Sign* the check.
Polite Request:	*Would* / *Could* you sign the check, please?

To ask for permission:

Command:	*Give* me your pen.
Polite Form:	*May* / *Can* I use your pen, please?

NOTE: *May* is a little more polite than *can*.

Language Notes

1. A softer way to say *I want* is *I would like* (*I'd like*).

I want to cash a check.
I'd like to cash a check.
How do you want your change?
How *would* you *like* your change?

2. Another way to make a soft request or suggestion is with *Why don't you/we . . .?*

Sit over there.
Why don't you sit over there?
Let's go to the bank.
Why don't we go to the bank?

EXERCISE 28   Read the following conversation between a waiter (W) and a customer (C) in a restaurant. Change the underlined words to make the conversation more polite.

W.   What <u>do you want</u> to order?   *would you like*

C.   <u>I want</u> the roast chicken dinner.

W.   Anything to drink?

C.   Yes. <u>Bring</u> me a glass of wine.

W.   What kind of wine <u>do you want</u>?

C.   <u>Show</u> me the wine list.

W. Here you are, miss. <u>Order</u> the white wine.

C. Fine. You know, it's a little cold at this table. <u>Let me sit</u> at another table.

W. Of course. There's a nice table in the corner. <u>Sit</u> over there.

C. Thanks, and <u>bring</u> me another glass of water.

W. Of course.

10.8 Contrasting Modals and Related Words

Review the meanings of modals and related words.

Ability, Possibility	*Can* you drive a truck? You *can* get a ticket for speeding.
Necessity, Obligation	A driver *must* have a license. I *have to* buy a new car.
Permission	You *can* park at a meter. You *can't* park at a bus stop.
Possibility	I *may* buy a new car soon. I *might* buy a Japanese car.
Advice	You *should* buy a new car. Your old car is in terrible condition.
Permission Request	*May* I borrow your car? *Can* I have the keys, please?
Polite Request	*Would* you teach me to drive? *Could* you show me your new car?
Suggestion	*Why don't you* have a seat? I'll be with you in a few minutes. We both need to go shopping. *Why don't we* go together?
Want	What *would* you *like* to eat? I'd *like* a turkey sandwich.

EXERCISE 29 This is a phone conversation between a woman (W) and her mechanic (M). Fill in each blank with *can, should, may, might, would, could,* or *have to.* (In some cases, more than one answer is possible.)

W. This is Cindy Fine. I'm calling about my car.

M. I ___*can't*___ hear you. _____ you speak louder, please?
    (1)

W. This is Cindy Fine. Is my car ready yet?

M. We're working on it now. We're almost finished.

W. When _____ I pick it up?
    (2)

M. It will be ready by four o'clock.

W. How much will it cost?

M. $375.

W. I don't have that much money right now. _____ I pay by credit card?
    (3)

M. Yes. You _____ use any major credit card.
    (4)

Later, at the mechanic's shop:

M. Your car's ready, ma'am. The engine problem is fixed. But you _____
    (5)
    change your brakes. They're not so good.

W. _____ I do it right away?
    (6)

M. No, you don't have to do it immediately, but you _____ do it within a
    (7)
    month or two. If you don't do it soon, you _____ have an accident.
    (8)

W. How much will it cost to change the brakes?

M. It _____ cost about $100 or it _____ cost about $200, depending on
    (9)   (10)
    whether you need all four brakes or just the front brakes.

W. I _____ like to make an appointment to take care of the brakes next week.
    (11)

    _____ I bring my car in next Monday?
    (12)

M. Yes. Monday is fine. You _____ bring it in early because we get very busy
                                (13)

later in the day.

W. OK. See you Monday morning.

EXPANSION ACTIVITIES

PROVERBS   1. The following proverbs contain modals. Discuss the meaning of each
                 proverb. Do you have a similar proverb in your language?

                 People who live in glass houses shouldn't throw stones.
                 You can lead a horse to water, but you can't make it drink.
                 You can't teach an old dog new tricks.

              2. The following proverbs contain the imperative form. Discuss the mean-
                 ing of each proverb. Do you have a similar proverb in your language?

                 Don't put off until tomorrow what you can do today.
                 Don't look a gift horse in the mouth.
                 Look before you leap.
                 Don't count your chickens before they're hatched.
                 If at first you don't succeed, try, try again.

OUTSIDE   If you have a driver's manual for this state, look for sentences in this book
ACTIVITY   that use modals. If you don't have this book, go to a driver's license test-
              ing facility and pick one up. Or look in the telephone directory, state gov-
              ernment listings, or under Registry of Motor Vehicles, and call to ask for a
              book.

WRITING   Write about differences in traffic, driving regulations, or public trans-
              portation between your hometown and this city.

EDITING ADVICE

1. Don't use *to* after a modal.

    I must ~~to~~ go.

2. Use *to* between verbs.

    They like ^to^ play.

3. Always use the base form after a modal.

    He can swim~~s~~.

4. Use the base form in an infinitive.

    He wants to go~~es~~.

    I wanted to work~~ed~~.

5. Use *it* to introduce an infinitive before + *be* + adjective.

    ^It i^~~Is~~ important to get exercise.

6. Don't put an object between the modal and the main verb.

    She can ~~the lesson understand~~. *understand the lesson.*

SUMMARY OF LESSON TEN

1. Imperatives

   Sit down. *Don't* be late.

2. *Let's*

   Let's go to the movies. *Let's* not be late.

3. Infinitive Patterns

   He wants *to go.*
   It's necessary *to learn* English.
   I'm afraid *to stay.*

4. Meanings of Modals

Modal	Example	Explanation
can	He can swim. An eighteen-year-old can vote. Can I borrow your car?	He has ability to swim. He has permission. I'm asking for permission.
can't	You can't park at a bus stop. I can't help you later. I have to work.	It is not permitted. It is not possible.
should	You should drive slowly when it is raining.	It's a good idea.
may	If you drive too fast, you may get a ticket. May I borrow your car?	Maybe this will happen. I'm asking for permission.
might	If you drive too fast, you might get a ticket.	Maybe this will happen.
must	A driver must have a license. I'm late. I must hurry.	This is the law. It's necessary.
must not	You must not drive without a license.	It's against the law.
will	We will have a test next week.	This is in the future.
would	Would you help me move?	I'm asking a favor.
would like	I'd like to help you.	I want to help you.
could	Could you help me move?	I'm asking a favor.
have to not have to	She has to leave. He doesn't have to wear a suit to work.	It's necessary. It's not necessary.

LESSON TEN TEST/REVIEW

Part 1   Fill in the first blank with *to* or nothing (*X*). Then write a negative form in the second blank.

EXAMPLE: **I'm ready** ____*to*____ **study Lesson 11. I** _*'m not ready to*_____ **study Lesson 12.**

1. I need _____ learn English. I _____ Polish.

2. You must _____ stop at a red light. You _____ on the highway.

3. The teacher expects _____ pass most of the students. She

   _____ all of the students.

4. We want _____ study grammar. We _____ literature.

5. The teacher has _____ give grades. He _____ an A to everyone.

6. We might _____ have time for some questions later. We

   _____ time for a discussion.

7. It's important _____ practice American pronunciation now. It

   _____ British pronunciation.

8. It's easy _____ learn one's native language. It _____ a foreign language.

9. Let's _____ speak English in class. _____ our native languages in class.

10. _____ be here at six o'clock, please. _____ late.

Part 2   Change each sentence to a question.

EXAMPLES: **I'm afraid to drive.**

Why *are you afraid to drive?*

He can help you.

When *can he help me?*

1. You should wear a seat belt.

   Why _____

2. I want to buy a car.

   Where _____

3. He must appear in court.

   When _____

4. She needs to drive to New York.

   When _____

5. You can't park at a bus stop.

   Why _____

6. It's necessary to follow the rules.

   Why _____

7. She has to buy a car.

   Why _____

8. They'd like to see you.

   When _____

Part 3   In the following conversation, find the problems related to modals and infinitives, and correct them.

   A. I have a problem. Can you ~~to~~ help me?

   B. What's your problem?

A. I need appear in court.

B. What I can do for you?

A. You know that my English is not very good. I afraid go to court alone.

B. Why do you have to go to court?

A. I had a traffic accident. I hit another car. Nobody was hurt, but I damaged a car. I wanted pay the other driver, but she decided called the police.

B. What happened after the police came?

A. The police officer wanted to saw my driver's license, but I didn't have it with me.

B. Is necessary have your license with you at all times.

A. I know. That's the reason I must to appear in court.

B. This is very serious. You might lose your license. I'll give you the name of my lawyer. Call him. He's American, but he can our language speak.

A. Thanks.

B. Good luck! And don't to drive without a license again.

A. I won't.

Part 4   This is a conversation between two friends about going to court. Fill in each blank with *can, should, may, might, would, could,* or *have to* and other necessary words. (In some cases, more than one answer is possible.)

> EXAMPLE: A. I _have to_____ go to court a week from Friday. _Can_____
>   you go with me?
>
>   B. Why _do you have to_____ go to court?

A. I got a ticket for speeding.

B. That's terrible. You (not) _____ drive so fast.
                             (1)

A. I know. I _____ lose my driver's license if I get three speeding tickets.
          (2)

B. I'm not just talking about your license. You _____ have an accident.
                                                    (3)

A. You're right. I _____ be more careful. Anyway, _____ go to
                  (4)   (5)

   court with me?

B. Why do you need me?

A. You _____ speak English much better than me.
          (6)

B. Maybe you _____ get a lawyer.
                (7)

A. I _____ like to, but I (not) _____ afford one. So
      (8)   (9)

   _____ you go with me, please?
      (10)

B. When is your court date?

A. A week from Friday.

B. I'm not really sure. I _____ have to work on that Friday.
                            (11)

A. Maybe I can change the date.

B. That's impossible. You (not) _____ change the court date.
                                    (12)

   You _____ appear on your appointed date.
          (13)

A. I don't want to go alone.

B. Why _____ you ask my brother-in-law? He speaks English well. He
          (14)

   _____ help you, if he has the time.
      (15)

A. _____ I have his phone number, please?
      (16)

B. Sure. 123-9876.

LESSON ELEVEN

GRAMMAR

Count and Noncount Nouns
Quantifiers

CONTEXT

A Healthy Diet

Lesson Focus   Count and Noncount Nouns; Quantifiers

* To talk about the definite and indefinite articles and quantity, we need to classify nouns into two groups: count nouns and noncount nouns.

   A **count noun** is something we can count. It has a singular form and a plural form.

one egg	five eggs	one American	a thousand Americans
one book	six books	a child	six children

   A **noncount noun** is something we don't count. It has no plural form.

bread	sugar	cheese
milk	oil	rice

* We use *quantifiers* to tell how much there is of something, when we count or measure.

   I bought *a few* apples   I bought *a lot of* rice.

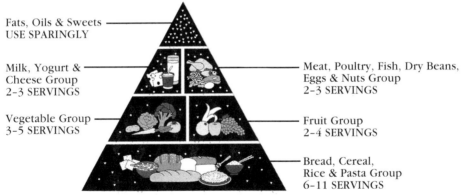

U.S. Department of Agriculture

- -

R
E
A
D
I
N
G

Before you read:

1. What kind of food do you like to eat? What kind of food do you avoid?
2. Do you eat the same kind of food in the U.S. as you did in your country?

Read the following article. Pay special attention to count and noncount nouns.

A HEALTHY DIET

Good **nutrition** is extremely important. Eating the right kinds of **food** can keep you healthy. It is important to get enough **vitamins** and **minerals.**

There are different food **groups.** It is important to eat some **food** from each group daily. The first group includes **bread, cereal, rice,** and **pasta.** You should eat more **foods** from this group than from any other group. The second group includes **vegetables.** The third group includes **fruit.** The fourth group includes **milk, yogurt,** and **cheese.** The fifth group includes **meat, poultry,**[1] **fish, beans, eggs,** and **nuts.**

You should avoid certain **foods.** Foods that contain a lot of **fat, oil,** and **sugar** are not good for you. Also avoid **foods** that are high in **cholesterol.** Cholesterol is a substance found in animal **foods.** A little cholesterol is good for the body, but high levels of cholesterol can be bad for the heart. Red **meat, eggs, cheese,** and **whole milk** contain a lot of cholesterol, and large quantities of these foods are not good for you. Foods from **plants** don't contain any cholesterol. However, palm **oil** and coconut **oil,** which don't contain any cholesterol, can raise the cholesterol level in your **blood.** Doctors recommend that we take in less than 200 **milligrams** of cholesterol a day.

Many Americans are changing their eating habits. They are eating more **chicken, turkey,** and **fish** because these foods have less fat and cholesterol than red meat. They are reading the **labels** on **packages** to determine if a certain kind of food is nutritious.

The chart below shows how many milligrams (mg) of cholesterol there are in certain foods:

Food	Serving Size	Cholesterol (mg)
Ground beef	3 ounces	58
Chicken liver	3 ounces	472
Chicken breast	3 ounces	45
Cod fish	3 ounces	43
Boiled egg	1 (large)	312
Whole milk	1 cup	34
Butter	1 tablespoon	35
Cheese	1 ounce	26

11.1   Noncount Nouns

There are several types of noncount nouns.

Group A: Nouns that have no distinct, separate parts. We look at the whole.		
milk	yogurt	soup
oil	air	bread
water	pork	meat
coffee	cholesterol	butter
tea	paper	poultry

---

[1]*Poultry* includes domestic birds, such as chickens, turkeys, and ducks.

Group B: Nouns that have parts that are too small or insignificant to count.[2]

rice	snow	hair
sugar	sand	grass
salt	corn	

Group C: Nouns that are classes or categories of things. The members of the category are not the same.

money (nickels, dimes, dollars)
food[3] (vegetables, meat, spaghetti)
furniture (chairs, tables, beds)
clothing (sweaters, pants, dresses)
mail (letters, packages, postcards)
fruit[3] (cherries, apples, grapes)
makeup (lipstick, rouge, eye shadow)
homework (compositions, exercises, reading)

Group D: Nouns that are abstractions.

love	advice	happiness
life	knowledge	education
time	nutrition	experience
truth	intelligence	crime
beauty	unemployment	music
luck	patience	art
fun	noise	work
help	information	health

|11.2 Specific Quantities with Nouns

We can put a number before a count noun, but not before a noncount noun. With a noncount noun, we use a unit of measure, which we can count:

Count:		
1 potato	1 apple	1 peach
5 potatoes	7 apples	2 peaches

---

[2] Count and noncount are grammatical terms, but they are not always logical. Rice is very small and is a noncount noun. Beans and peas are also very small but are count nouns.

[3] You sometimes see the plural forms *foods* and *fruits*. For example: *Foods* that contain cholesterol are not good for you. Oranges and lemons are *fruits* that contain vitamin C. *Foods* means *kinds of food*. *Fruits* means *kinds of fruit*.

> Noncount:
>
> a cup of coffee   a jar of coffee
> 5 cups of coffee   5 jars of coffee
>
> a bowl of sugar   a spoon of sugar
> 2 bowls of sugar   2 spoons of sugar

These are some units of measure that we use to count noncount nouns:

a loaf of bread	a piece of fruit
a piece (slice) of bread	a piece of mail
a bottle of wine	a piece (or sheet) of paper
a glass of wine	a piece of advice
a cup of tea	a piece of chalk
a bowl of soup	an ear of corn
a can of soup	a head of lettuce
a roll of film	a bar of soap
a pound of meat	a can of beer
a piece of meat	a six-pack of beer
a gallon of milk	a tube of toothpaste
a quart of milk	a piece of furniture
a glass of milk	a homework assignment

EXERCISE I   Think of a logical measurement for each of these noncount nouns.

  EXAMPLES: **She bought** *five pounds of* _____ **coffee.**

  She drank *two cups of* _____ **coffee.**

1. She ate _____ meat.

2. She bought _____ meat.

3. She bought _____ bread.

4. She ate _____ bread.

5. She bought _____ rice.

6. She ate _____ rice.

7. She bought _____ sugar.

8. She put _____ sugar in her coffee.

9. She bought _____ gas for her car.

10. She put _____ motor oil into her car's engine.

11. She used _____ paper to do her homework.

12. She took _____ film on her vacation.

13. She ate _____ soup.

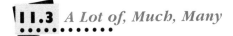

11.3 *A Lot of, Much, Many*

We use *a lot of, much,* and *many* to describe a large quantity of a noun.

	Count (plural)	Noncount
Affirmative	He baked *many* cookies. He baked *a lot of* cookies.	He baked *a lot of* bread.
Negative	He didn't bake *many* cookies. He didn't bake *a lot of* cookies.	He didn't bake *much* bread. He didn't bake *a lot of* bread.
Question	Did he bake *many* cookies? Did he bake *a lot of* cookies? *How many* cookies did he bake?	Did he bake *much* bread? Did he bake *a lot of* bread? *How much* bread did he bake?

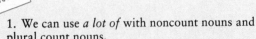

1. We can use *a lot of* with noncount nouns and plural count nouns.

2. We use *many* with plural count nouns only.

3. We use *much* with noncount nouns only. We usually use it with questions and negatives. In affirmative statements, we use *a lot of*.

4. When the noun is omitted, we say *a lot*, not *a lot of*.

> Did he bake *a lot of* bread?
> No, he didn't bake *a lot* because he didn't have time.

EXERCISE 2   Fill in each blank with *much, many,* or *a lot of.*

EXAMPLES: **She doesn't eat** _____*much*_____ **pasta.**

He ate _*a lot of*_____ OR _____*many*_____ **grapes.**

1. I eat _____ cherries.

2. Do you drink _____ alcohol?

3. I drink coffee only about once a week. I don't drink _____ coffee.

4. Asians eat _____ rice.

5. Americans don't eat _____ rice.

6. It is good to eat _____ vegetables.

7. If you eat _____ eggs, you might have a problem with cholesterol.

8. How _____ cholesterol is there in an egg?

9. How _____ calories are there in an egg?

10. How _____ apples did you eat this week?

11. How _____ fruit did you eat this week?

11.4   *A Few, A Little*

We use *a few* with count nouns. We use *a little* with noncount nouns.

I bought *a few* bananas.
I spent *a little* money.

EXERCISE 3   Fill in each blank with *a few* or *a little.*

EXAMPLES: **He has** _*a few*_____ **good friends.**

He has _*a little*_____ **time to help you.**

1. Every day we study _____ grammar.

2. We do _____ exercises in class.

3. The teacher gives _____ homework every day.

4. We do _____ pages in the book each day.

5. _____ students always get an A on the tests.

6. It's important to eat _____ fruit every day.

7. It's important to eat _____ pieces of fruit every day.

8. I receive _____ mail every day.

9. I receive _____ letters every day.

10. I use _____ milk in my coffee.

 **11.5** *Some, Any,* **and** *A*

We can use *some, any,* and *a* before nouns.

	Singular Count	Plural Count	Noncount
Affirmative	I ate *an* apple.	I ate *some* grapes.	I ate *some* rice.
Negative	I didn't eat *an* apple.	I didn't eat *any* grapes.	I didn't eat *any* rice.
Question	Did you eat *an* apple?	Did you eat *any* grapes?	Did you eat *any* rice?

1. We use *a (an)* with singular count nouns only.

2. We use *some* for affirmative statements, with both noncount nouns and plural count nouns.

3. We use *any* for questions and negatives, for both noncount nouns and plural count nouns.[4]

4. To make a negative statement, we can use *a (an)* or *any* with a negative verb, or we can use *no* with an affirmative verb.

Compare:
There isn't *an* elevator in my building.
There's *no* elevator in my building.
I don't have *any* money today.
I have *no* money today.

---

[4]We sometimes use *some* for a question: Do you want *some* fruit?

EXERCISE 4   Fill in each blank with *a, an, some,* or *any.*

EXAMPLE: I ate _____*an*_____ apple.

1. I ate _____ corn.

2. I didn't buy _____ potatoes.

3. Did you eat _____ watermelon?

4. I don't have _____ sugar.

5. There are _____ apples in the refrigerator.

6. Do you want _____ orange?

7. Do you want _____ cherries?

8. I ate _____ banana.

9. I didn't eat _____ strawberries.

watermelon

EXERCISE 5   Take something from your purse, pocket, or book bag. Say, "I have _____ with me." Then ask the person next to you if he or she has this.

EXAMPLES: **I have some keys in my pocket. Do you have any keys in your pocket?**

I have a picture of my daughter in my purse. Do you have any pictures of your family in your purse?

EXERCISE 6   Practice count nouns. Make a statement about people in this class with the words given and an expression of quantity.

EXAMPLE: **Vietnamese student(s)**
There are a few Vietnamese students in this class.
OR
There aren't any Vietnamese students in this class.
OR
There's one Vietnamese student in this class.

1. Polish student(s)
2. Spanish-speaking student(s)
3. American(s)
4. child(ren)
5. woman/women
6. man/men
7. teacher(s)
8. American citizen(s)
9. senior citizen(s)
10. teenager(s)
11. _____
12. _____

EXERCISE 7   Practice noncount nouns. Make a statement with the words given and an expression of quantity.

> EXAMPLES: cholesterol/in liver
> There's a lot of cholesterol in liver.
>
> cholesterol/in an apple
> There's no cholesterol in an apple.

1. cholesterol/in eggs
2. cholesterol/in fruit
3. cholesterol/in red meat
4. fat/in fish
5. fat/in pork

6. sugar/in candy
7. sugar/in a cracker
8. salt/ in a cookie
9. salt/in a potato chip
10. salt/in a soft drink

EXERCISE 8   Practice noncount nouns. Ask a question with *much* and the words given. Use *eat* or *drink*. Another student will answer.

> EXAMPLE: candy
> A. Do you eat much candy?
> B. Yes. I eat a lot of candy.
> OR
> No, not much.
> OR
> No. I don't eat any candy.

Eat
1. rice
2. fish
3. chicken
4. pork
5. bread
6. cheese

Drink
7. beer
8. wine
9. milk
10. tea
11. coffee
12. soda or pop

EXERCISE 9   Ask a question with "Do you have . . ." and the words given. Another student will answer. Practice both count and noncount nouns.

> EXAMPLES: American friends
> A. Do you have any American friends?
> B. Yes. I have many (OR a lot of) American friends.
> OR
> No. I don't have many American friends.
> OR
> No. I don't have any American friends.

free time

A. Do you have any free time?

B. Yes. I have a lot of free time.

   OR

   Yes. I have some free time.

   OR

   No. I don't have any free time

1. money with you now
2. credit cards
3. bread at home
4. bananas at home

5. beer in your refrigerator
6. plants in your apartment
7. _____
8. _____

EXERCISE 10   Fill in each blank. Choose an appropriate word from the words in parentheses ( ).

EXAMPLE: There are _____*many*_____ stores in a big city.
                         (many/much)

1. A small town doesn't have _____ factories.
                                    (many/much)

2. At 8:00 a.m., there is _____ traffic.
                          (much/many/a lot of)

3. At 4:00 a.m., there isn't _____ traffic.
                              (much/many)

4. _____ people have car phones.
   (Any/A little/Some)

5. We don't like homework, but sometimes the teacher gives _____
                                                            (much/a lot of/a lot)

6. The teacher gives _____ homework every day.
                      (some/a/any)

7. Do you need _____ help with this exercise?
               (any/a few)

8. Black coffee doesn't contain _____ calories.
                                 (some/any/no)

9. _____ cholesterol isn't good for you.
   (Many/Much/A lot of)

10. Do you have _____ money with you?
               (any/a)

11. It takes _____ seconds to fill in the blank.
            (a little/a few)

12. There's _____ telephone in the classroom.
           (no/any/no a)

13. There's _____ blackboard in the classroom.
     (a/any)

14. There are _____ public phones in the hall.
     (a/some/any)

15. Is there _____ elevator in your building?
     (a/an/any)

EXERCISE 11   Fill in each blank. Be careful to use a count noun or noncount noun appropriately. Discuss your answers in a small group.

1. I don't own a _____, but I'd like to.

2. I have/don't have _____ time because _____.

3. I don't have _____ in my apartment.

4. There are _____ in my country.

5. I don't eat much _____.

6. In my country, there isn't much _____.

EXERCISE 12   Fill in each blank in this conversation between a husband (H) and wife (W) with a quantity word. (In some cases, more than one answer is possible.)

EXAMPLE: H. **Where were you today? I called you from work ___*many*___ times, but there was no answer.**

W. I went to the supermarket today. I bought _____ things.
                                                (1)

H. What did you buy?

W. There was a special on coffee, so I bought _____ coffee. I didn't buy
                                                  (2)

_____ fruit, because the prices were very high.
  (3)

H. How _____ money did you spend?
        (4)

W. I spent _____ money because of the coffee. I bought 20 5-pound bags. But
            (5)

I saved _____ money because the coffee was so cheap.
        (6)

H. It took you a long time.

W. Yes. The store was very crowded. There were _____ people in the store.
                                                   (7)

And there was _____ traffic at that hour, so it took me _____ time to
              (8)   (9)

drive home.

H. There's not _____ time to cook.
(10)

W. Maybe you can cook today and let me rest?

H. Uh . . . I don't have _____ experience. You do it better. You have
(11)

_____ experience.
(12)

W. Yes. I have _____ because I do it all the time!
(13)

11.6 *Too, Too Many, Too Much, A Lot Of*

too much	+	noncount noun
too many	+	count noun
too	+	adjective or adverb

Language Notes

1. *A lot of* shows a large quantity. *Too much* and *too many* show that the quantity is excessive for a specific purpose.

   I eat *a lot of* fruit.
   If you eat *too much* sugar, you might get cavities in your teeth.
   Last night I had *too many* drinks at the party, and I got drunk.

2. *Too much* and *too many* come before nouns. *Too* comes before adjectives and adverbs.

   I don't eat ice cream. It has *too many* calories. It has *too much* sugar. It is *too* fattening.

3. *Too much* can be at the end of a sentence.
   I need to lose 20 pounds. I weigh *too much*.
   I can't afford a new car because it costs *too much*.

EXERCISE 13   Fill in each blank with *much* or *many,* and complete each statement.

EXAMPLE: **If I drink too ___much___ coffee,** *I won't be able to sleep tonight.*

1. If the teacher gives too _____ homework, _____

2. If I take too _____ classes, _____

3. If I eat too _____ candy, _____

4. If I'm absent too _____ days, _____

5. Too _____ cholesterol _____

EXERCISE 14   Fill in each blank with *too, too much,* or *too many.*

Situation A. Some students are complaining about the school cafeteria. They are giving reasons why they don't want to eat there.

EXAMPLE: It's ____*too*____ noisy.

1. The food is _____ greasy.

2. There are _____ students. I can't find a place to sit.

3. The lines are _____ long.

4. The food is _____ expensive.

5. _____ people are smoking.

6. There's _____ noise.

Situation B. Some students are complaining about their class and school.

1. The classroom is _____ small.

2. There are _____ students in one class.

3. The class periods are _____ short.

4. The teacher gives _____ homework.

5. There are _____ tests.

EXERCISE 15   Write a few sentences to complain about something: your apartment, your roommate, this city, this college, etc. Use *too, too much,* or *too many* in your sentences.

EXAMPLE: **My roommate spends too much time in the bathroom in the morning. He's too messy.**[5]

EXERCISE 16   Fill in the blanks with *too, too much,* or *too many* if a problem is present. Use *a lot of* if no problem is present.[6]

EXAMPLE: **Most people can't afford to buy a Mercedes because it costs**

____*too much*____ **money.**

1. There are _____ noncount nouns in English.

2. "Rice" is a noncount noun because the parts are _____ small to count.

---

[5]A *messy* person does not put his or her things in order.

[6]In some cases, *too much/too many* and *a lot of* are interchangeable.

3. If this class is _____ hard for you, you should go to a lower level.

4. Good students spend _____ time doing their homework.

5. If you spend _____ time watching TV, you won't have time for your homework.

6. It takes _____ time to learn English, but you can do it.

7. Oranges have _____ vitamin C.

8. If you are on a diet, don't eat ice cream. It has _____ calories and _____ fat.

9. Babies drink _____ milk.

10. If you drink _____ beer, you'll get drunk.

EXPANSION ACTIVITIES

DISCUSSION Cross out the phrase that doesn't fit and fill in each blank with an expression of quantity to make a true statement about your country. Find a partner from another country, if possible, and compare your answers.

EXAMPLE: ~~There are~~/There aren't ___*many*___ foreigners in my country.

1. There's/There isn't _____ in my country.

2. There's/There isn't _____ opportunity to make money.

3. People eat/don't eat a lot of _____ because _____.

4. There are/There aren't _____ single mothers.

5. Most people have/don't have _____ education.

6. Parents give/don't give their children _____ advice.

7. People drink/don't drink _____ tea.

8. There are/There aren't _____ foreigners in my country.

OUTSIDE ACTIVITY Bring to class a package of a food or drink you enjoy. Read the label for "Nutrition Facts." Look at calories, grams of fat, cholesterol, sodium, protein, vitamins, and minerals. Do you think this is a nutritious food? Why or why not?

EDITING ADVICE

1. Don't put *a* or *an* before a noncount noun.

   I want to give you ~~an~~ advice.
   (*some* written above *an*)

2. Noncount nouns are always singular.

   My mother gave me ~~many~~ advice~~s~~.
   (*a lot of* written above *many*)

   He received three mail~~s~~ today.
   (*pieces of* inserted before *mail*)

3. Don't use a double negative.

   He doesn't have ~~no~~ time.   OR   *He has no time*
   (*any* written above *no*)

4. Don't use *much* with an affirmative statement.

   Uncommon: There was much rain yesterday.

   Common: There was a lot of rain yesterday.

5. Use *a* or *an*, not *any*, with a singular count noun.

   Do you have ~~any~~ computer?
   (*a* written above *any*)

6. Don't use *a* or *an* before a plural noun.

   She has ✗ blue eyes.

7. Use the plural form for plural count nouns.

   He has a lot of friend~~s~~.
   (*s* inserted)

8. Omit *of* after *a lot* when the noun is omitted.

   In my country, I have a lot of friends, but in the U.S. I don't have
   a lot ~~of~~.

9. Use *of* with a unit of measure.

   I ate three pieces ~~of~~ bread.
   (*of* inserted)

SUMMARY OF LESSON ELEVEN

1. Words that we use before Count and Noncount Nouns

Word	Count (singular) Example: *book*	Count (plural) Example: *books*	Noncount Example: *tea*
a	x		
one	x		
two, three, etc.		x	
some (affirmatives)		x	x
any (negatives and questions)		x	x
a lot of		x	x
much (negatives and questions)			x
many		x	
a little			x
a few		x	
the	x	x	x

2. *Too Much/Too Many/A Lot Of/Too*

   A lot of indicates a large quantity. *Too* indicates that the large quantity causes a problem.

   - *A lot of* + count or noncount noun
       He's a lucky man. He has *a lot of* friends.
       He has *a lot of* free time.
   - *Too much* + noncount noun
       There's *too much* noise in the cafeteria. I can't study there.
   - *Too many* + count noun
       There are *too many* students in the class. I can't find a seat.
   - *Too* + adjective or adverb
       She's *too* young to get a driver's license.
       You came *too* late. The movie is over already.

LESSON ELEVEN TEST/REVIEW

Part 1   Read the following composition. Add an appropriate quantity word or an indefinite article before the noun. In some cases, more than one answer is correct.

I had ____*some*____ problems when I first came to the U.S. First, I didn't have

_____ money. _____ friends of mine lent me _____ money, but I
   (1)   (2)   (3)

didn't feel good about borrowing it.

Second, I couldn't find _____ apartment. I went to see _____
                (4)   (5)

apartments, but I couldn't afford _____ of them. For _____ months, I had
                             (6)   (7)

to live with my uncle's family, but the situation wasn't good.

Third, I started to study English, but soon found _____ job and didn't
                                        (8)

have _____ time to study. As a result, I was failing my course.
       (9)

However, little by little my life started to improve, and I don't need

_____ help from my friends and relatives anymore.
  (10)

Part 2   Fill in each blank with an appropriate measurement of quantity.

EXAMPLE: a _____*cup*_____ of coffee

1. a _____ of wine   6. a _____ of advice

2. a _____ of sugar   7. a _____ of bread

3. a _____ of milk   8. a _____ of paper

4. a _____ of furniture   9. a _____ of meat

5. a homework _____   10. a _____of meicine

Part 3   Find the mistakes with quantity words, and correct them. Not every sentence has a mistake. If the sentence is correct, write **C**.

                                             very

EXAMPLES: She found a good job, and now she is ~~too~~ happy.

           You can be happy if you have a few good friends.   *C*

1. He doesn't have no money with him.

2. He's a lucky man. He has too many friends.

3. There are a lot of tall buildings in a big city. There aren't a lot of in a small town.

4. I don't have much time to help you.

5. A fourteen-year-old person is too much young to get a driver's license.

6. A few students in this class are from Pakistan.

7. I don't have some time to help you.

8. I don't have any car.

9. Did we have many snow last winter?

10. Many people would like to have a lot of money in order to travel.

11. He doesn't have any time to study.

12. I'd like to help you, but I have too many things to do this week. Maybe I can help you next week.

13. She drinks two cups of coffee in the morning.

14. I drink four milks a day.

15. He bought five pounds sugar.

16. How much bananas did you buy?

17. How much money did you spend?

18. This building doesn't have a basement.

19. I have much time to read.

20. She gave me a good advice.

21. The piano is too much heavy. I can't move it.

22. I have a lot of cassette.

23. I don't have much experience with cars.

LESSON TWELVE

GRAMMAR
Adjectives
Noun Modifiers
Adverbs

CONTEXT
Christmas in the United States
Buying a Used Car
The Aging of the American
    Population

Lesson Focus   Adjectives; Noun Modifiers; Adverbs

- An adjective can describe a noun.
  They have a *beautiful* tree.

- A noun can also describe a noun.
  They have a *Christmas* tree.

- An adverb can describe a verb.
  They decorated the tree *beautifully.*

R
E
A
D
I
N
G

Before you read:

1. Does your family celebrate Christmas? How?
2. What is an important religious holiday that you celebrate? How do you celebrate it?

Read the following article. Pay special attention to the description words before nouns.

CHRISTMAS IN THE UNITED STATES

The December holidays are a very **special** time in the United States. It is a **happy** time for children and a **busy** time for adults. It is also a very **religious** time for many people. People from many religions celebrate many **special** occasions in December. Jewish people celebrate Hanukkah. Christian people celebrate Christmas. Christmas is the celebration of the birth of Christ.

Santa Claus

Many people buy a **Christmas** tree. Some people use a **natural** tree. Others use an **artificial** tree. People decorate the tree with **bright** ornaments. They usually put **colorful** lights on the tree.

People buy gifts for their family and friends. They wrap the gifts in **colorful** paper and put them under the tree. Parents often tell their **small** children that Santa Claus brings the gifts. Santa Claus is a **fat, old** man with a **long, white** beard. He wears a **red** suit. He lives at the **North** Pole. Parents tell children that if they are **good,** they will get gifts. Children are very **excited** on Christmas Eve as they wait for Santa to bring the gifts.

Christmas is also a very **commercial** time for **shop** owners. They depend on Christmas for **heavy** business. **Store** windows often have **Christmas** decorations, and TV and magazines have many ads to attract **Christmas** shoppers. Some people complain that Christmas is too **commercial** because people forget about the **religious** meaning of the holiday. People begin to shop for **Christmas** presents after Thanksgiving and are usually very **tired** by the time Christmas arrives. After Christmas, the stores are **full** of people returning gifts.

12.1 Using Adjectives

We can use adjectives before nouns (subjects or objects) or after the verbs *be,* *look, seem,* and other sense-perception verbs.

(Adjective)	Subject	Verb	(Adjective)	Object
Religious	people	celebrate		Christmas.
	I	prefer	a natural	tree.

Subject	Be/Seem/Look	Adjective		
The children	are	happy.		
The tree	looks	beautiful.		

1. We do not make adjectives plural.

   The gift is *expensive.*
   The gifts are *expensive.*

2. Sometimes we put two adjectives before a noun.

   Santa Claus is a *fat, old* man.
   He has a *long, white* beard.

3. We can put *very* before an adjective to make it stronger.

   Some people are *very* religious.

4. Some words that end in *-ed* are adjectives: *married, divorced, excited, worried, finished, located, tired, crowded.*

   Children are *excited* about Christmas.
   Stores are *crowded* before Christmas.

EXERCISE 1   Add an adjective to each of these sentences. Change *a* to *an* if your adjective begins with a vowel sound.

EXAMPLE: Christmas is a ____*religious*____ holiday.

1. Santa Claus is a _____ man.

2. Santa has a _____ beard and wears a _____ suit.

3. We use _____ paper to wrap our gifts.

4. _____ children believe in Santa Claus.

5. Some people use a natural tree. Other people use a _____ tree.

6. Christmas lights are _____.

7. Children are _____ on Christmas.

8. Children believe they will get presents from Santa Claus if they are _____.

Language Notes

1. After an adjective, we can substitute the noun with *one* (singular) or *ones* (plural).

Some people prefer a real Christmas *tree*, but others use an artificial *one*.
Big *children* don't believe in Santa Claus, but small *ones* do.

2. After *this* and *that*, we can substitute *one* for the noun.

This tree is artificial. *That one* is natural.

3. After *these* and *those*, we omit *ones*.

I'm going to wrap *these presents*. You can wrap *those*.

EXERCISE 2   Ask a question of preference with the words given. Follow the example. Use *one* or *ones* to substitute for the noun. Another student will answer.

EXAMPLES: an easy exercise/hard
A. Do you prefer an easy exercise or a hard one?
B. I prefer a hard one.

funny movies/serious
A. Do you prefer funny movies or serious ones?
B. I prefer funny ones.

1. a big city/small
2. an old house/new
3. a cold climate/warm
4. a small car/big
5. a soft mattress/hard
6. green grapes/red
7. red apples/yellow
8. strict teachers/easy
9. noisy children/quiet
10. an artificial Christmas tree/natural

EXERCISE 3   Complete each statement with *one* or *X* for no pronoun.

1. These presents are under the tree.

Those _____ are on the table.

2. This tree is natural.

That _____ is artificial.

3. Those houses have Christmas decorations.

This _____ doesn't have any decorations.

undecorated   decorated

4. These people are Jewish. They celebrate Hanukkah.

5. Those _____ are Christian. They celebrate Christmas.

12.2 Noun Modifiers

An adjective can describe a noun. One noun can also describe another noun.

We see many *Christmas* trees in December.
Shop owners decorate their *store* windows.

Adjective + Noun		Noun + Noun	
tall	tree	Christmas	tree
new	owner	shop	owner
clean	window	store	window
colorful	paper	wrapping	paper

Language Notes

1. An *-ing* form (gerund) can also describe a noun. It shows the purpose of the noun.

   A *shopping* cart is a cart for shopping.
   Wrapping paper is paper for wrapping gifts.
   Running shoes are shoes for running.

2. When two nouns come together, the second noun is more general than the first.

   Wrapping paper is paper.
   A *paper plate* is a plate.

3. Sometimes we write the two nouns separately.

   orange juice   desk lamp   vegetable garden

   Sometimes we write the two nouns as one word.

   flashlight   ashtray   motorcycle

4. The first noun is always singular.

   A tray for ashes is an *ash*tray.
   A store that sells shoes is a *shoe* store.
   A garden of roses is a *rose* garden.

5. Sometimes a possessive form describes a noun. It tells who uses the noun.

   A driver uses a *driver's* license.
   An owner of a VCR uses the *owner's* manual.

6. When a noun describes a noun, the first noun usually receives the greater emphasis in speaking. Listen to your teacher pronounce the following.

   I need a *wínter* coat.
   He works in a *shóe* store.

EXERCISE 4 Fill in each blank by putting the two nouns in the correct order. Remember to take the <u>s</u> off the plural nouns.

EXAMPLES: People need a _____*winter coat*_____ in December.
                              (coat/winter)

We buy groceries in a _____*grocery store.*_____
                                   (groceries/store)

1. A _____ delivers the mail.
      (letters/carrier)

2. We use _____ to wrap presents.
             (wrapping/paper)

3. We use a _____ to paint the walls.
   (brush/paint)

4. If you want to drive, you need a _____.
   (driver's/license)

5. A lot of women like to wear _____.
   (rings/ears)

6. A married woman usually wears a _____ on her left hand.
   (wedding/ring)

7. Please put your garbage in the _____.
   (can/garbage)

8. Many people have a _____ in December and January.
   (Christmas/tree)

9. The college is closed during _____.
   (vacation/Christmas)

• •

R
E
A
D   Before you read:
I
N   1. Do you have a car? Did you buy it new or used? Are you happy with it?
G   2. Do you plan to buy a car soon? What are some important things to look for
        when you buy a used car?

Read the following article. Pay special attention to adverbs of manner.

BUYING A USED CAR

You should be very careful before you buy a used car.

Take the car for a test drive. Check to see if the brakes are working **well.** Take it to the highway and drive it **fast** to see if the engine is running **smoothly** and **quietly.** Drive the car when it is cold to see if it runs **well** with a cold engine.

See the car in the daytime so that you can see the body **clearly.** Check the car **completely,** inside and out. Inspect it **carefully** to see if it was ever in a serious accident.

Notice how many miles the car has. Ask if the owners drove in the city or on the highway. City cars wear out[1] more **quickly** than highway cars. A city-driven car with 50,000 miles is usually in worse shape[2] than a highway-driven car. The brakes and other parts wear out more **quickly.**

It is a good idea to take the car to a mechanic and have it checked over **thoroughly.**[3] It may cost some money to get a mechanic's opinion, but it is better to lose a few hundred dollars than a few thousand dollars. You don't want to spend your money **foolishly.**

• •

———————

[1]When something *wears out,* it gets old little by little as you use it.

[2]*Shape,* in this sentence, means condition.

[3]*Thoroughly* means completely.

12.3 Adverbs of Manner

An **adverb of manner** tells how or in what way the subject does something. It describes the action of the sentence.

The teacher spoke *clearly*.
The students listened *attentively*.

We form most adverbs of manner by putting *-ly* at the end of an adjective.

Adjective	Adverb
smooth	smoothly
quiet	quietly
quick	quickly

Adverbs of manner usually follow the verb phrase.

Subject	Verb Phrase (Verb + Complement)	Adverb
You	should inspect the car	carefully.
You	don't want to spend your money	foolishly.
He	arrived	early.

Language Notes

1. Observe the spelling rules for *-ly* adverbs:
   A. For adjectives that end in *-y*, we change *y* to *i*, then add *-ly*.
   easy/easi*ly*   happy/happi*ly*
   lucky/lucki*ly*
   B. For adjectives that end in *-e*, we keep the *e* and add *-ly*.
   nice/nice*ly*   free/free*ly*
   Exception: true/tru*ly*
   C. For adjectives that end in a consonant + *-le*, we drop the *e* and add *-ly*.
   simple/simp*ly*   comfortable/comfortab*ly*
   double/doub*ly*
2. Some adverbs of manner do not end in *-ly*.
   A. Some adjectives and adverbs have the same form: *fast, late, early, hard*.
   He has a *fast* car. (adjective)
   He drives *fast*. (adverb)

She has a *late* class. (adjective)
She arrived *late* last night. (adverb)
He has a *hard* job. (adjective)
He works *hard*. (adverb)
   B. *Good* is an adjective. *Well* is the adverb form.
   He is a *good* driver.   He drives *well*.

3. *Very* can come before an adjective or adverb. Never put *very* before a verb.
   WRONG: He *very* works hard. He *very* likes his job.[4]
   RIGHT: He works *very hard*. He's *very tired*. He likes his job *very much*.

4. Don't put the adverb between the verb and the complement.
   WRONG: He drove *carefully* the car.
   RIGHT: He drove the car *carefully*.
   WRONG: She *late* came home.
   RIGHT: She came home *late*.

---

[4]In informal conversation, you will hear, *He works really (or real) hard. He really likes his job.*

EXERCISE 5   Fill in each blank with the correct form of the word in parentheses ( ) to give advice about driving.

EXAMPLE: It is important to drive _____*carefully*_____ .
                                          (careful)

1. Don't follow the car in front of you _____.
                                              (close)

2. Make sure your brakes are working _____.
                                            (good)

3. Check your rearview mirror _____.
                                      (frequent)

4. Drive _____ on a curve.
              (slow)

5. Don't use your horn _____.
                            (unnecessary)

6. Don't drive _____ in rain or snow.
                     (fast)

7. If you have an accident, stop _____.
                                       (immediate)

EXERCISE 6   Tell how you do these things.

EXAMPLE: write
          I write a composition carefully and slowly.

1. speak English   6. do your homework
2. speak your native language   7. drive
3. dance   8. sing
4. walk   9. type
5. study   10. work

EXERCISE 7   Name something.

EXAMPLE: Name some things you do well.
          I speak my native language well.
          I swim well.
          I sing well.

1. Name some things you do well.
2. Name some things you don't do well.
3. Name some things you do quickly.
4. Name some things you do slowly.
5. Name something you learned to do easily.

R
E
A
D
I
N
G

Before you read:

1. What are some things you can do to have a longer, healthier life?
2. Who is the oldest member of your family? Is he or she in good health?

Read the following article. Pay special attention to *very, too,* and *enough* used with adjectives and adverbs.

THE AGING OF THE AMERICAN POPULATION

The U.S. population is aging. At the beginning of the twentieth century, only 4% of the population was over 65. Today, 13% is over 65. By the year 2030, we can expect 20%

of the population to be over 65. A person born in the year 1900 could expect to live only 48 years. Today, the life expectancy is about 79 years for women and 73 years for men. The median age today is 33 years old. This means that half the population is over 33, and half is under. By the middle of the twenty-first century, we can expect the median age to be 42. In the past 30 years, the number of people over the age of 85 has multiplied by four. By the middle of the twenty-first century, the over-85 population could be twenty-six times higher than it was in 1990. The future population of America will be **very** different from what it is now.

Why are people living so much longer? First, medical care is much better today. In addition, a lot of people are **very** careful about their personal habits. Many Americans are taking **very** good care of themselves by not smoking, by eating a healthy diet, and by get-

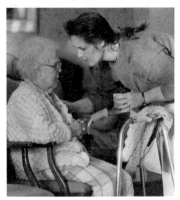

ting **enough** exercise. As a result, many older Americans are healthy **enough** to lead independent and enjoyable lives. Many older people play tennis, travel, and take classes. Some older Americans are **very** active politically; they influence government decisions.

Unfortunately, not all senior citizens[5] are so fortunate. Some seniors are **too** old and **too** sick to take care of themselves. If they live with their children, their children may be **too** busy to give them the care they need. About 5% of seniors spend their last years in a nursing home (22% of those over 85).

---

[5]*Senior citizens,* or *seniors,* is a more polite way to talk about elderly people.

But as a whole, the quality of life for older Americans is **quite** good. According to Robert B. Maxwell, an executive with an association of retired people, "Our society is getting older, but the old are getting younger. The 70 year-old today is more like a person of 50 twenty years ago."[6]

12.4 Intensifiers—*Too* vs. *Very*

Intensifiers (*too* and *very*) modify adjectives and adverbs. We put *too* and *very* in front of the adjective or adverb that we want to intensify.

Language Notes

1. *Very* shows a large degree. It doesn't indicate any problems.

> My grandfather is *very* old. He's in *very* good health.
> The quality of life for older Americans is *very* good.

2. *Too* shows that there is a problem.

> A. Do you want to play tennis?
> B. I'm *too* tired. I just got home from a hard day at work.

3. *Too* + adjective or adverb is often followed by an infinitive.

> My grandmother is *too* sick *to take* care of herself. We had to put her in a nursing home.

4. Compare *very* and *too*.

> My grandmother is *very* old and *very* healthy.
> My grandfather is *too* old to take care of himself. He's in a nursing home.
> Race car drivers drive *very* fast.
> If you drive *too* fast in the city, you'll get a ticket.
> This wine is *very* old. It tastes delicious.
> This bread is *too* old. I can't eat it.

5. We can also put *quite* before an adjective or adverb.

> The quality of life for many older Americans is *quite* good.

EXERCISE 8   Fill in the blanks with *very* or *too*.

EXAMPLES: Basketball players are ___*very*___ tall.

I'm ___*too*___ short to touch the ceiling.

1. In December, it's _____ cold to go swimming outside.

2. June is usually a _____ nice month.

3. Some old people are in _____ good health.

4. Some old people are _____ sick to take care of themselves.

---

[6]Robert B. Maxwell, as quoted in *Lifetrends,* by Jerry Gerber et al. (Stonesong Press, 1989). p. 6.

5. It's _____ important to know English.

6. This textbook is _____ long to finish in three weeks.

7. The President has a _____ important job.

8. The President is _____ busy to answer all his letters.

9. Some Americans speak English _____ fast for me. I can't understand them.

10. I can speak my own language _____ well.

11. When you buy a used car, you should inspect it _____ carefully.

12. A turtle moves _____ slowly.

13. If you drive _____ slowly on the highway, you might get a ticket.

turtle

12.5 *Too* and *Enough*

We use *too* to refer to something excessive. We use *enough* to refer to something sufficient. Compare the word order in sentences with *too* and *enough*.

My father is 65. He's *old enough* to retire.
My mother is 58. She's *too young* to retire.

Too Adjective *Too* Adverb	Adjective *Enough* Adverb *Enough*
too old	old *enough*
too well	well *enough*
too quickly	quickly *enough*

My mother isn't *old enough* to retire.
My father rides a bike every day. He gets *enough* exercise.

Adjective *Enough* Adverb *Enough*	*Enough* Noun
old *enough*	*enough* money
big *enough*	*enough* room
tall *enough*	*enough* time
well *enough*	

EXERCISE 9   Fill in each blank with *too* or *enough* plus the word in parentheses ( ).

EXAMPLES: My son is 12 years old. He's _____*too old*_____ to believe in
                                                    (old)
              Santa Claus.

              My daughter is 18 years old. She's _____*old enough*_____ to get a
                                                                      (old)
              driver's license.

1. I can't read Shakespeare in English. It's _____ for me.
                                                    (hard)

2. My brother is 19 years old. He's _____ to get a driver's license.
                                                (old)

3. My grandfather is 90 years old and in bad health. He's in a nursing home. He's

   _____ to take care of himself.
        (sick)

4. I saved $5000. I want to buy a used car. I think I have _____.
                                                                      (money)

5. I'd like to get a good job, but I don't have _____.
                                                          (experience)

6. She wants to move that piano, but she can't do it alone. She's not

   _____.
        (strong)

7. The piano is _____ for one person to move.
                        (heavy)

8. I work in an office, and I don't get _____.
                                                  (exercise)

EXPANSION ACTIVITIES

DISCUSSIONS   1. In a small group or with the entire class, discuss the situation of older
                      people in your country. Who takes care of them when they are too old
                      or too sick to take care of themselves? How does your family take care
                      of its older members?

                  2. In a small group or with the entire class, discuss Christmas or another
                      important holiday in your country. How do people celebrate this
                      holiday?

WRITING   Describe how you celebrate an important holiday in your country.

EDITING ADVICE

1. Don't make adjectives plural.

   Those are important~~s~~ ideas.

2. Put the specific noun before the general noun.

   He is a ~~driver truck~~. *truck driver*

3. Some adjectives end in *-ed*.

   I'm finish~~^ed~~ with my project.

4. A noun modifier is always singular.

   She is a letter carrier.

5. Put an adjective before the noun.

   He had a ^*very important* meeting ~~very important~~.

6. Use *one(s)* after an adjective to substitute for a noun.

   He wanted a big wedding, and she wanted a small ^*one*.

7. Don't confuse *too* and *very*. *Too* indicates a problem.

   My father is ~~too~~ *very* healthy.

8. Don't confuse *too much* and *too*. *Too much* is followed by a noun. *Too* is followed by an adjective or adverb.

   It's too ~~much~~ hot today. Let's stay inside.

9. Put *enough* after the adjective.

   He's enough ~~old~~ *old* to drive.

10. Don't use *very* before a verb. *Very* is used only with adjectives and adverbs.

He ~~very~~ likes the U.S. *very much.*

11. Put the adverb at the end of the verb phrase.

He ~~late~~ came home. *late*

He opened ~~slowly~~ the door. *slowly*

12. Use an adverb to describe a verb. Use an adjective to describe a noun.

He drives careful. *ly*

That man is very nice~~ly~~.

1. Adjectives and Adverbs:

Adjectives	Adverbs
She has a *beautiful* voice.	She sings *beautifully.*
She is *careful.*	She drives *carefully.*
She has a *late* class.	She arrived *late.*
She is a *good* driver.	She drives *well.*

2. Adjective Modifiers and Noun Modifiers:

Adjective Modifier	Noun Modifier
a tall tree	a Christmas tree
a clean window	a store window
a new store	a shoe store
colorful paper	wrapping paper
warm coats	winter coats
a new license	a driver's license

3. *Very/Too/Enough:*

He's *very* healthy.
He's *too* young to retire. He's only 55.
He's old *enough* to understand life.
He has *enough* money to take a vacation.

LESSON TWELVE TEST/REVIEW

Find and correct the mistakes with adjectives, adverbs, and noun modifiers. Not every sentence has a mistake. If the sentence is correct, write **C.**

EXAMPLES: I had to make a ~~decision very important~~ *very important decision* about her health.

          She drives very carefully.   *C*

1. I took my olds shoes to a shoes repair shop.

2. It's too much cold outside. Let's stay inside today.

3. Basketball players are too tall.

4. I got my license driver's last year.

5. My brother is only 15 years old. He's not enough old to drive.

6. The very rich woman bought an expensive Christmas present for her beautiful daughter.

7. She is only 16 years old. She's too young to get married.

8. I found a wonderful job. I'm too happy.

9. My father is only 50 years old. He is too much young to retire.

10. He speaks English very good.

11. You came home late last night. I was very worry about you.

12. I very like my new apartment.

13. He early woke up this morning.

14. He worked very hard last night.

15. He counted the money very carefully.

16. She opened slowly the door.

LESSON THIRTEEN

GRAMMAR
Comparatives
Superlatives

CONTEXT
Consumer Decisions
Facts About America

Lesson Focus   Comparatives and Superlatives

Adjectives and adverbs have three forms: simple form, comparative form, and superlative form. Compare these sets of adjectives.

	Short Adjectives	Long Adjectives
Simple	A horse is a *big* animal.	She is *intelligent.*
Comparative	An elephant is *bigger than* a horse.	She is *more intelligent than* her sister.
Superlative	A whale is *the biggest* animal in the world.	She is *the most intelligent* person in her family.

• •

R
E
A
D
I
N
G

Before you read:

1. Do you plan to buy something expensive soon? (examples: a TV, a computer, a VCR) What do you plan to buy?
2. Is it easier or harder to make a shopping decision in the U.S. or in your country? Explain.

Read the following article. Pay special attention to comparative forms.

CONSUMER DECISIONS

There are many choices of products to buy. You might be confused when you go to a store and have to decide from such a wide range of choices. You can use consumer magazines to help you make a smart decision.

The March, 1994 issue of *Consumer Reports,* a popular consumer magazine, rated videocassette recorders (VCRs). In comparing the Sony Model SLV-700HF with the Model Sharp VC-H904 in this magazine, you can learn the following:

The Sony VCR is **much more expensive than** the Sharp.
The Sony has a **clearer picture than** the Sharp.
The Sony has a **better** remote control **than** the Sharp. It has a **better** design.
You can program the Sony **more easily than** the Sharp.
You can program the Sony **longer** in advance **than** the Sharp (30 days versus 14 days).
Sony VCRs need **fewer repairs** than Sharp VCRs.
The overall quality of the Sony is **better than** the Sharp.[1]

---

[1]"Videocassette Recorders." Copyright 1994 by Consumers Union of U.S., Inc., Yonkers, NY 10703-1057. Adapted with permission from CONSUMER REPORTS, March 1994. Although this material originally appeared in CONSUMER REPORTS, the selective adaptation and resulting conclusions presented are those of the author(s) and are not sanctioned or endorsed in any way by Consumers Union, the publisher of CONSUMER REPORTS.

When you are in the store, you might want to ask the salesperson questions such as the following, which will help you decide:

1. Which product has a **better** or **longer** warranty?

    Some products have a 90-day warranty for parts and labor. After 90 days, only the parts have a warranty for a year. Look for a product that has a one-year warranty for both parts and labor.

2. Which one has **more** features?

    Decide which features you need. There's no reason to pay for features that you don't need.

3. If I find this product in another store at a **lower** price, will you refund the difference in price?

    Many stores will match the price of another store.

    Consumer magazines help us to be smarter consumers. These magazines can be found in the reference section of a library.

13.1 Comparative and Superlative Forms

The chart below shows comparative and superlative forms. Fill in the last example.

	Simple	Comparative	Superlative
One-syllable adjectives and adverbs	tall	taller	the tallest
	fast	*faster*	*the fastest*
Exceptions:	bored	more bored	the most bored
	tired	more tired	the most tired
Two-syllable adjectives that end in *-y*	easy	easier	the easiest
	happy	happier	the happiest
	pretty	_____	_____
Other two-syllable adjectives	frequent	more frequent	the most frequent
	active	_____	_____
Some two-syllable adjectives have two forms.	simple	simpler	the simplest
		more simple	the most simple
	common	_____	_____
		_____	_____

(Other two-syllable adjectives that have two forms are *handsome, quiet, gentle, narrow, clever, friendly, angry.*)

	Simple	Comparative	Superlative
Adjectives with three or more syllables	important difficult	more important _____	the most important _____
-ly adverbs	quickly brightly	more quickly _____	the most quickly _____
Irregular adjectives and adverbs	good/well	better	the best
	bad/badly	worse	the worst
	far	farther	the farthest
	little	less	the least
	a lot	more	the most

Language Notes

1. For most adjectives and adverbs, we add *-er* to make the comparative form and *-est* to make the superlative form.

    old—older—oldest
    tall—taller—tallest

2. For adjectives that end in *-y*, change *y* to *i* before adding *-er*.

    happy—happier—happiest
    healthy—healthier—healthiest
    sunny—sunnier—sunniest

Remember: Use *more* and *most* for *-ly* adverbs.

    quickly—more quickly—most quickly

3. If the word ends in *-e*, just add *r*.

    nice—nicer—nicest
    fine—finer—finest

4. For one-syllable words that end in consonant-vowel-consonant, we double the final consonant before adding *-er*.

    big—bigger—biggest
    sad—sadder—saddest
    hot—hotter—hottest

Exception: Do not double final *w*.

    new—newer—newest

EXERCISE 1   Give the comparative and superlative forms of the word.

    EXAMPLES: **fat**   *fatter*   *the fattest*

                 important   *more important*   *the most important*

    1. interesting _____ _____

    2. young   _____ _____

    3. beautiful   _____ _____

    4. good   _____ _____

5. common   _____   _____

6. thin   _____   _____

7. carefully   _____   _____

8. pretty   _____   _____

9. bad   _____   _____

10. famous   _____   _____

11. lucky   _____   _____

12. simple   _____   _____

13. high   _____   _____

14. delicious   _____   _____

15. far   _____   _____

16. foolishly   _____   _____

13.2 Comparisons with Adjectives

We use the comparative form to compare two items. We use *than* before the second item we are comparing.

X	Be	Comparative	*than*	Y
The Sharp VCR	is	cheaper	than	the Sony VCR.
The Sony VCR	is	more expensive	than	the Sharp VCR.

1. Omit *than* if the second item of comparison is not included.

> The Sharp VCR is cheaper than the Sony VCR, but the Sony is *better*.

2. *Much* or *a little* can come before a comparative form.

> The Sony is *much* more expensive than the Sharp.
> The picture quality of the Sony is *a little* better.

3. In a question, we use *or* instead of *than*.

> Which is better, the Sony *or* the Sharp?

4. When a pronoun follows *than*, the most correct form is the subject pronoun. Sometimes an auxiliary verb follows.

> She is taller than *he* (is).
> She is older than *I* (am).

Informally, many Americans use the object pronoun after *than*. An auxiliary verb does not follow.

> She is taller than *him*.
> She is older than *me*.

EXERCISE 2   Fill in each blank with the comparative form of the word in parentheses ( ). Add *than* where necessary.

> EXAMPLE: **Warranty A is** <u>*longer than*</u> **warranty B.**
>   (long)

1. The Sony is _____ the Sharp.
                            (good)

2. The Sharp is _____ the Sony.
                            (cheap)

3. The picture quality of the Sharp is _____ the picture quality of the Sony.
                                                (bad)

4. The Sony picture is _____ the Sharp picture.
                                (clear)

5. The Sony is expensive, but the Mitsubishi is _____.
                                                      (expensive)

EXERCISE 3   Compare yourself to another person, or compare two people you know using these adjectives:

> EXAMPLES: **tall**
>   **My father is taller than I am.**   (OR **than me.**)
>
>   **talkative**
>   **My mother is more talkative than my father.**

1. tall
2. educated
3. friendly
4. lazy
5. thin
6. quiet
7. stubborn
8. patient
9. successful
10. strong
11. _____
12. _____

EXERCISE 4   Compare men and women. Give your own opinion. Talk in general terms.

> EXAMPLE: intelligent
> Women are more intelligent than men.
> OR
> Men are more intelligent than women.

1. polite	5. kind	9. romantic
2. strong	6. friendly	10. sensitive
3. tall	7. talkative	11. _____
4. intelligent	8. patient	12. _____

EXERCISE 5   Compare this city to your hometown.

> EXAMPLES: big
> Tokyo is bigger than Boston.
>
> crowded
> Tokyo is more crowded than Boston.

1. crowded	5. beautiful
2. modern	6. interesting
3. big	7. cold in winter
4. noisy	8. _____

13.3 Comparisons with Adverbs

We use adverbs to compare verbs.

X	Verb	Complement	Comparative Adverb	*Than*	Y
I	can program	this VCR	more easily	than	that one.
I	can program	the VCR	better	than	my husband can.

We can also use *more* and *less* to compare verbs.

X	Verb	*More/Less*	*Than*	Y
This VCR	costs	less	than	that one.
I	paid	more	than	you did.

EXERCISE 6   Compare men and women. Give your own opinion. Talk in general terms.

EXAMPLES: work hard
            Men work harder than women.
            OR
            Women work harder than men.

            talk a lot
            Women talk more than men.

1. run fast
2. gossip a lot
3. work hard
4. drive foolishly
5. drive fast
6. spend a lot on clothes

7. take care of children well
8. worry a lot
9. drink a lot (alcohol)
10. live long
11. get old fast
12. _____

13.4 Comparisons with Nouns

We can make comparisons with nouns.

X	Verb	Better Worse More	Noun	Than	Y
The Sony VCR	has	more	features	than	the Sharp.
Which VCR	has	a better	warranty?		

EXERCISE 7   Compare this city to your hometown. Use *better, worse,* or *more.*

EXAMPLES: factories
            Chicago has more factories than Ponce.

            public transportation
            Moscow has better public transportation than Chicago.

1. traffic
2. climate
3. rain
4. crime
5. pollution

6. job opportunities
7. factories
8. tall buildings
9. people
10. _____

EXERCISE 8 Work with a partner or in a small group. Make comparisons with the following words. Give your opinion and reasons.

> EXAMPLE: men/women—have an easy life
>
> In my opinion, men have an easier life than women. Women have to work two jobs—in the office and at home.

1. men/women—have an easy life
2. men/women—live long
3. American women/women in my country—have an easy life
4. American couples/couples in my country—have children
5. married men/single men—are responsible

EXERCISE 9 Work with a partner. Find some differences between the two of you. Then write five sentences that compare you and your partner.

> EXAMPLES: *I'm taller than Anita.*
>
> *Anita is thinner than I am.*

1. _____
2. _____
3. _____
4. _____
5. _____

• •

R
E
A
D
I
N
G

Before you read:

1. What is the biggest city in your country? Do you like this city?
2. In your opinion, what is the most interesting city in your country? Why is it interesting?
3. What cities or regions in your country have the best climate?

Read the following list of facts. Pay special attention to superlative adjectives.

FACTS ABOUT AMERICA

1. **The biggest** city in the U.S. is New York.
2. **The youngest** President was Theodore Roosevelt. He was 42 when he became President. He was President from 1901 to 1909.
3. **The tallest** building is the Sears Tower. It's in Chicago.

4. People in New York pay **the highest** taxes.[2]
5. Hispanics are **the fastest** growing minority in the U.S.
6. Rhode Island is **the smallest** state in area.
7. Alaska is **the largest** state in area, but it has **the smallest** population.
8. California is **the most populated** state.
9. Juneau, Alaska, gets **the most snow.**
10. Phoenix, Arizona, gets **the most sunshine.** Eighty-five percent of the days have sunshine.
11. Juneau gets **the least sunshine.** Thirty-two percent of the days have sunshine.
12. The most expensive homes are in the following areas:

Honolulu, Hawaii	Los Angeles, California
San Francisco, California	Boston, Massachusetts
Orange County, California	New York City, New York

13. **The most common** cause of death for Americans is heart disease.
14. Mount McKinley is **the highest mountain** in the United States (20,320 feet or 6,178 meters). It is in Alaska.

13.5   Superlatives

We use the superlative form to point out the number-one item of a group of three or more items. We use *the* before a superlative, and we usually put a prepositional phrase after it.

X	Verb	*the*	Superlative	Noun	Prepositional Phrase
New York	is	the	biggest	city	in the U.S.
Tokyo	is	the	most populated	city	in the world.

Language Notes

1. We often say "one of the" before a superlative form. Then we use a plural form.

San Francisco is *one of the most beautiful cities* in the U.S.
The Mississippi River is *one of the longest rivers* in the world.

2. When the verb is *be*, there are two possible word orders.

Ivan *is* the youngest student in the class.
The youngest student in the class *is* Ivan.

3. Omit *the* after a possessive form.

My best friend lives in London.
Jack's oldest son got married.

---

[2]This includes income tax, sales tax, gasoline tax, and property tax.

EXERCISE 10   Talk about the number-one person in your family for each of these adjectives.

> EXAMPLES: interesting
> My aunt Rosa is the most interesting person in my family.
>
> tall
> The tallest person in my family is my brother Carlos.

1. intelligent
2. kind
3. handsome/beautiful
4. stubborn
5. lazy
6. tall
7. serious
8. kind
9. strong
10. funny
11. _____
12. _____

EXERCISE 11   Name the person in your family who is the superlative in each of the following activities.

> EXAMPLES: cook well
> My mother cooks the best in the family.
>
> eat a lot
> My brother eats the most in my family.

1. talk a lot
2. drive well
3. walk fast
4. speak English well
5. stay up late
6. get up early
7. speak softly
8. eat a lot
9. spend a lot
10. _____

EXERCISE 12   Write a superlative sentence, giving your opinion about each of the following items. Find a partner. Compare your answers to your partner's answers.

> EXAMPLE: **big problem in my country today**
>
> _The biggest problem in my country today is the civil war._
>
> OR
>
> _The biggest problem in my country today is the economy._

1. good pet

2. bad war

_____

3. bad tragedy in the world or in the U.S.

_____

4. important invention of the twentieth century

_____

5. interesting city in the world

_____

6. big problem in the U.S. today

_____

7. bad job

_____

8. good job

_____

9. hard teacher at this school

_____

EXERCISE 13   Fill in each blank with the comparative or superlative form of the word in parentheses ( ). Include *than* or *the* where necessary.

      EXAMPLES: **August is usually** ____*hotter than*____ **May.**
                                       (hot)

                January is usually ____*the coldest*____ **month of the year.**
                                           (cold)

1. A lion is _____ a dog.
              (big)

2. A whale is _____ animal in the world.
               (big)

3. A dog is _____ a bird.
         (intelligent)

4. A dolphin is one of _____ animals in the world.
   (intelligent)

5. New York is _____ Los Angeles.
   (crowded)

6. Mexico City is one of _____ cities in the world.
   (crowded)

7. New York is a crowded city, but Tokyo is _____
   (crowded)

8. San Francisco is one of _____ cities in the U.S.
   (beautiful)

9. _____ distance between two points is a straight line.
   (short)

10. Line A is _____ line B.
    (short)

EXPANSION ACTIVITIES

DISCUSSIONS   1. Work with a partner from the same country, if possible. Compare American men and men from your country. Compare American women and women from your country. Report some of your ideas to the class.

2. In a small group or with the entire class, discuss how you choose a product when you shop. Talk about inexpensive items like shampoos or toothpaste. Talk about expensive items like televisions and microwave ovens.

PROVERBS   1. The following proverbs contain the comparative form. Discuss the meaning of each proverb. Do you have a similar proverb in your language?

Two heads are better than one.
It's better to give than to receive.
Easier said than done.
Better late than never.
The grass is always greener on the other side of the fence.

2. The following proverbs contain superlative forms. Discuss the meaning of each proverb. Do you have a similar proverb in your language?

The best things in life are free.
Experience is the best teacher.

WRITING

1. Choose one of the topics below to write a comparison:
   a. Compare your present car with your last car.
   b. Compare two cities you know well.
   c. Compare American women and women in your country.
   d. Compare American men and men in your country.
   e. Compare soccer and football.
   f. Compare a word processor and a typewriter.
   g. Compare two pets (a dog and a cat) or two types of dogs.
   h. Compare your life in the U.S. and your life in your country.
   i. Compare the place where you lived in your country with the place where you live now.

2. Write about the biggest problem in the world (or in your country, or in the U.S.) today. Why is this a problem? How can we solve the problem?

OUTSIDE ACTIVITIES

1. Go to the library. Look for a consumer magazine or book that tells about used cars. Look at information about two cars that interest you. Compare the prices and features of these cars. Report something interesting to the class.

2. If you are planning to buy something new soon, find product information in a consumer magazine or book. Use this information to help you make a decision.

3. Interview an American. Get his or her opinion about the superlative of each of the following items. Share your findings with the class.

   Sample Question for an American:

   good car: What do you think is the best car?

   1. good car
   2. famous celebrity
   3. good president in the last 25 years
   4. beautiful city in the U.S.
   5. good university in the U.S.
   6. popular movie at this time
   7. terrible tragedy in American history
   8. big problem in the U.S. today
   9. popular singer in the U.S.

EDITING ADVICE

1. Don't use a comparison word when there is no comparison.

   California is a big~~ger~~ state.

2. Don't use *more* and *-er* together.

   My new car is ~~more~~ better than my old one.

3. Use *than* before the second item in a comparison.

   than
   He is younger ~~that~~ his wife.

4. Use *the* before a superlative form.

   the
   China has ‸ biggest population in the world.

5. Use a plural noun after the phrase "one of the."

   s
   Jim is one of the tallest boy‸ in the class.

6. Use the correct word order.

   drives faster
   She ~~faster drives~~ than her husband.

   more
   I have ‸ responsibilities ~~more~~ than you.

1. Simple, Comparative, and Superlative Forms

   Short words:

   > Chicago is a *big* city.
   > Chicago is *bigger than* Boston.
   > New York is *the biggest* city in the U.S.

   Long words:

   > VCR Model A is *expensive.*
   > VCR Model B is *more expensive* than VCR Model A.
   > VCR Model C is *the most expensive* of the three.

   Comparison with adverbs:

   > Product A works *efficiently.*
   > Product B works *more efficiently* than Product B.
   > Product C works *the most efficiently* of all three.

   Comparison with nouns:

   > He has a *good* accent.
   > He has a *better* accent *than* his sister.
   > He has *the best* accent of anyone in his family.

2. Word Order

   Verb Phrase + Comparative Adverb

   > She *speaks English more fluently* than her husband.

   More + Noun

   > She has *more experience* than her husband.

Part 1   Fill in each blank with the comparative or the superlative of the word in parentheses ( ). Add *the* or *than* if necessary.

EXAMPLES: New York is _____*bigger than*_____ Chicago.
                                            (big)

New York is _____*the biggest*_____ city in the U.S.
                                            (big)

1. Mount Everest is _____ mountain in the world.
                                    (high)

2. A D grade is _____ a C grade.
                            (bad)

3. Johnson is one of _____ last names in the U.S.
                                (common)

4. Tokyo is _____ Miami.
                    (populated)

5. June 21 is _____ day of the year.
                        (long)

6. The teacher speaks English _____ I do.
                                        (well)

7. Lake Superior is _____ lake in the U.S.
                            (large)

8. Children learn a foreign language _____ adults.
                                                (quickly)

9. A lot of people think that Japanese cars are _____ American cars.
                                                        (good)

10. A dog is _____ a cat.
                    (friendly)

11. Women drive _____ men.
                        (carefully)

12. Who is _____ student in this class?
                    (good)

13. The teacher speaks English _____ I do.
                                        (fluently)

14. A dog is intelligent, but a monkey is _____.
                                                    (intelligent)

Part 2   Find the mistakes with comparative and superlative forms, and correct them. Not every sentence has a mistake. If the sentence is correct, write **C.**

EXAMPLES: I am taller *than* my father.

              I am tall, but my father is taller.   *C*

1. Paul is one of the youngest student in this class.

2. I have problems more than you.

3. She is more older than her husband.

4. I'm the most tall person in my family.

5. I earlier woke up than you.

6. My father is more educated my mother.

7. She more fluently speaks English than her mother.

8. She is the most intelligent person in her family.

9. I faster type than you do.

10. New York City is biggest city in the U.S.

LESSON FOURTEEN

GRAMMAR
Auxiliary Verbs

CONTEXT
Football and Soccer

Lesson Focus   **Auxiliary Verbs**

To avoid repetition of the main verb, we use the auxiliary verbs *do/does/did,* modal verbs, and *be.*

I speak French, and the teacher *does* too.
You went to Paris on your vacation, *didn't* you?

R
E
A   **Before you read:**
D
I   1. What's your favorite sport? Do you like to play it or watch it?
N   2. Do you ever watch a football game on TV in the U.S.?
G

Read the following conversation between a student from Ecuador (E) and his American friend (A). Pay special attention to auxiliary verbs.

FOOTBALL AND SOCCER

E. My favorite sport is football. In my country, Ecuador, everyone likes football.
A. I think you mean soccer, **don't** you?
E. In Ecuador we say football, but football means something different for you, **doesn't** it?
A. Yes.
E. What exactly is the difference between football and soccer?
A. Well, for one thing, the ball is different. A soccer ball is round. A football **isn't.** A football player can carry or throw the ball, but a soccer player **can't.**
E. A football team has the same number of players as a soccer team, **doesn't** it?
A. Yes. They both have 11 players, but a football team really has 22 players. There are only 11 players on the field at one time.
E. There are other differences, **aren't there**?
A. Oh, yes. A soccer game lasts ninety minutes, but a football game **doesn't.** A football game lasts sixty minutes.
E. I don't like football very much.
A. I **don't** either.
E. I prefer soccer.
A. I **do** too.
E. That's strange. I thought all Americans love football.
A. Maybe most **do,** but I **don't.**

14.1 Auxiliary Verbs with *Too* and *Either*

Sometimes two statements have the same verb phrase. We can use *and* to combine two sentences with the same verb phrase.

A soccer team *has 11 players.*		A football team *has 11 players.*
A soccer team *has 11 players,*	*and*	a football team *does too.*
Football *isn't popular in Ecuador.*		Baseball *isn't popular in Ecuador.*
Football *isn't popular in Ecuador,*	*and*	baseball *isn't either.*

1. We can use the auxiliary verb (same tense) plus *too* to combine two affirmative sentences in conversation.

    A. A soccer team *has eleven players.*
    B. A football team *does too.*
    A. Football *is popular in the U.S.*
    B. Baseball *is too.*

2. We can use the auxiliary verb (same tense) plus *either* to combine two negative sentences in conversation.

    A. I *don't like football.*
    B. I *don't either.*
    A. I *didn't see the soccer game last night.*
    B. I *didn't either.*
    A. I *can't play tennis very well.*
    B. I *can't either.*

3. In informal speech, Americans often use the forms *me too* and *me neither.*

    A. I like soccer.
    B. *Me too.*
    A. I don't like football.
    B. *Me neither.*

4. When *have* is a main verb, Americans use *do, does,* or *did* as a substitute.

AMERICAN:

    A. I have tickets to a game.
    B. I *do too.*

BRITISH:

    A. I have tickets to the game.
    B. I *have too.*

EXERCISE 1   Terri and David have some things in common. Finish each affirmative statement with an auxiliary verb (the same tense as the main verb) + *too.*

    EXAMPLES: Terri plays volleyball, and David ___*does too.*___

                Terri went to a soccer game last night, and David ___*did too.*___

1. Terri is interested in football, and David _____

2. Terri likes to play tennis, and David _____

3. Terri went bowling last week, and David _____

4. Terri will watch a football game on TV next Sunday, and David _____

5. Terri can play chess, and David _____

EXERCISE 2 Terri and David have some things in common. Finish each negative statement with an auxiliary verb (the same tense) + *either.*

EXAMPLES: Terri doesn't like hockey, and David *doesn't either.*

Terri didn't go to the hockey game, and David *didn't either.*

1. Terri doesn't know how to swim, and David _____

2. Terri can't ski, and David _____

3. Terri won't go to the game next Sunday, and David _____

4. Terri isn't interested in baseball, and David _____

5. Terri didn't play tennis last summer, and David _____

Language Notes

1. We can use the auxiliary verb to make a short opposite statement when the two verb phrases are the same.

A. I like football.
B. I *don't.*
A. I didn't see the soccer game.
B. I *did.*

2. We can use *but* to connect an affirmative statement and a negative statement.

I didn't see the soccer game, *but* my friend *did.*
Football players can carry the ball, *but* soccer players *can't.*

EXERCISE 3 Terri and David are different in some ways. Finish each statement with an auxiliary verb.

EXAMPLES: Terri works downtown, but David _*doesn't.*_

Terri isn't interested in classical music, but David _*is.*_

1. Terri likes to cook, but David _____

2. Terri doesn't play the guitar, but David _____

3. Terri can't speak Russian, but David _____

4. Terri went to Hawaii for vacation, but David _____

5. Terri won't work next Sunday, but David _____

EXERCISE 4   Fill in each blank to compare the U.S. and your country. Use *and . . . too* or *and . . . either* for similarities between the U.S. and your country. Use *but* for differences. Use an auxiliary verb in all cases.

> EXAMPLE: **The U.S. is a big country,** *and Russia is too.* _____
>
> OR
>
> **The U.S. is a big country,** *but Cuba isn't.* _____

1. The U.S. has more than 200 million people, _____

2. The U.S. is in North America, _____

3. The U.S. has a president, _____

4. The U.S. doesn't have a socialist government, _____

5. The U.S. fought in World War II, _____

6. The U.S. was a colony of England, _____

7. Americans like football, _____

8. Americans don't celebrate Labor Day in May, _____

9. American schools are closed on December 25, _____

10. The U.S. has a presidential election every four years, _____

_____

EXERCISE 5   Complete each statement. Then find a partner and compare yourself to your partner by using an auxiliary verb.

> EXAMPLES: **A. I speak** _____ *Chinese.* _____
>
> **B. I do too.** OR **I don't.**
>
> **A. I don't speak** _____ *Spanish.* _____
>
> **B. I don't either.** OR **I do.**

1. I speak _____

2. I don't speak _____

3. I can _____

4. I have _____

5. I don't have _____

6. I'm _____

7. I usually drink _____ every day.

8. I'm going to _____ next week.

9. I come from _____

10. I'm wearing _____ today.

11. I bought _____ last week.

12. I went _____ last week.

13. I don't like _____

14. I brought _____ to the U.S.

15. I don't like to eat _____

16. I can't _____ very well.

17. I should _____ more.

EXERCISE 6   Fill in each blank in the conversation below. Use an auxiliary verb and *too* or *either* when necessary.

A. I'm moving on Saturday. Maybe you and your brother can help me. Are you working on Saturday?

B. My brother is working on Saturday, but I _*'m not*_____. I can help you.

A. I need a van. Do you have one?

B. I don't have one, but my brother _____. I'll ask him if we can use
     (1)
it. Say, why are you moving?

A. There are a couple of reasons. I don't like the apartment, and my wife

_____. She says it's too small for two people.
     (2)

B. How many rooms does your new apartment have?

A. The old apartment has two bedrooms, and the new one _____.
                                                                    (3)

The rooms are much bigger in the new one, and there are more closets. Also,
we'd like to live near the lake.

B. I _____, but apartments there are very expensive.
 (4)

A. We found a nice apartment that isn't so expensive. Also, I'd like to own a dog, but my present landlord doesn't permit pets.

B. Mine doesn't _____. What kind of dog do you plan to get?
 (5)

A. I like big watchdogs. Maybe a German shepherd or a doberman. I don't like small dogs.

B. I _____. They just make a lot of noise.
 (6)

A. So now you know my reasons for moving. Can I count on you for Saturday?

B. Of course you _____.
 (7)

EXERCISE 7   Find a partner. List some things you have in common. List some differences too. Report a few interesting sentences to the class.

EXAMPLE: *Alex plays the violin, and I do too.*

 *Alex is majoring in chemistry, but I'm not.*

 *Alex doesn't have a computer, and I don't either.*

_____

_____

_____

14.2 Auxiliary Verbs in Tag Questions

A tag question is a short question that we put at the end of a statement. Use a tag question to ask if your statement is correct or if the listener agrees with you. Observe the statements and tag questions below:

Statement	Tag Question	Answer
A football team has 11 players,	doesn't it?	Yes, it does.
You can play football,	can't you?	Yes, I can.
Football and soccer aren't the same,	are they?	No, they aren't.
You didn't play soccer last week,	did you?	No, I didn't.

1. Use *be*, a modal verb, or an auxiliary verb in a tag question. Use the same tense as the main verb.

2. An affirmative statement uses a negative tag question. A negative statement uses an affirmative tag question.

3. A tag question always uses a subject pronoun. If the subject is *this* or *that*, use *it* in the tag. If the subject is *these* or *those*, use *they*. If *there* introduces the subject, use *there* in the tag.

> *Your brother* plays soccer, doesn't *he?*
> *This* is a soccer ball, isn't *it?*
> *There* are many differences between soccer and football, aren't *there?*

4. *Am I not?* is a very formal tag. We often say *aren't I?*

> FORMAL: I'm right, *am I not?*
> INFORMAL: I'm right, *aren't I?*

5. Compare the American and British use of the main verb *have*.

> AMERICAN: You have tickets to the game, *don't* you?
> BRITISH: You have tickets to the game, *haven't* you?

EXERCISE 8   Add a tag question. All the statements are affirmative and have an auxiliary verb.

EXAMPLE: **This class is large,** *isn't it?* _____

1. You're a foreign student, _____

2. You can understand English, _____

3. We'll have a test soon, _____

4. We should study, _____

5. There's a library at this school, _____

6. You'd like to improve your English, _____

7. This is an easy lesson, _____

8. I'm asking too many questions, _____

EXERCISE 9   Add a tag question. All the statements are negative and have an auxiliary verb.

EXAMPLE: **You can't speak Italian,** *can you?* _____

1. You aren't an American citizen, _____

2. The teacher can't speak your language, _____

3. We shouldn't talk in the library, _____

4. You weren't absent yesterday, _____

5. There aren't any Japanese students in this class, _____

6. This exercise isn't hard, _____

EXERCISE 10   Add a tag question. All the statements are affirmative and have a main verb.

EXAMPLE: **You have the textbook,** *don't you?* _____

1. English has a lot of irregular verbs, _____

2. You want to speak English well, _____

3. You understood the explanation, _____

4. A soccer team has 11 players, _____

5. They went to a soccer game last week, _____

6. We had a test last week, _____

EXERCISE 11   Add a tag question. All the statements are negative.

EXAMPLE: **We don't have class on Saturday,** *do we?* _____

1. The teacher doesn't pronounce your name correctly, _____

2. Your brother didn't take the last test, _____

3. You didn't bring your dictionary today, _____

4. We don't always have homework, _____

5. I don't have your phone number, _____

6. Your mother doesn't speak English, _____

EXERCISE 12   This is a conversation between two acquaintances, Bob (B) and Sam (S). Sam can't remember where he met Bob.

B. Hi, Sam.

S. Uh, hi. . . .

B. You don't remember me, *do you?* _____

S. You look familiar, but I can't remember your name. We were in the same

    chemistry class last semester, _____
                                            (1)

B. No.

S. Then we probably met in math class, _____
                                            (2)

B. Wrong again. I'm Linda Wilson's brother.

S. Now I remember you. Linda introduced us at a party last summer,

    _____ And your name is Bob, _____
           (3)   (4)

B. That's right.

S. How are you, Bob? You graduated last year, _____
                                                      (5)

B. Yes. And I've got a good job now.

S. You majored in computers, _____
                                   (6)

B. Yes. But I decided to go into real estate.

S. And how's your sister Linda? I never see Linda anymore. She moved back to

    California, _____
                         (7)

B. No. She's still here. But she's married now, and she's expecting a baby.

S. That's wonderful. Give my regards to Linda when you see her. It was great see-
    ing you again, Bob.

EXERCISE 13   A mother (M) is talking to her daughter (D). Fill in the blanks with a tag
question.

M. You didn't get your scholarship, _did you?_____

D. How did you know?

M. Well, you look very disappointed. You can apply again next year,

    _____?
              (1)

D. Yes. But what will I do this year?

M. There are government loans, _____?
(2)

D. Yes.

M. And you don't have to pay them back until you graduate, _____?
(3)

D. No.

M. And your professors will give you letters of recommendation,

_____?
(4)

D. I'm sure they will.

M. So don't worry. Just try to get a loan, and you can apply again next year for a scholarship.

14.3 Answering a Tag Question

When we use a tag question, we expect the listener to agree. When we add a negative tag question, we expect an affirmative answer. When we add an affirmative tag question, we expect a negative anwer. Notice how we answer these tag questions.

Right Information	Agreement
California is in the West, isn't it?	Yes, it is.
New Jersey isn't a big state, is it?	No, it isn't. It's small.

When the listener does not agree with the statement, notice how he answers the tag question.

Wrong Information	Correction
California is in the East, isn't it?	No, it isn't. It's in the West.
California isn't a big state, is it?	Yes, it is. It's very big.

EXERCISE 14   Read a statement to another student, and add a tag question. The other student will tell you if this information is correct or not.

EXAMPLES: **You speak Polish,** _don't you?_ _____

           No, I don't. I speak Ukrainian.

           You aren't from Poland, _are you?_ _____

           No, I'm not. I'm from Ukraine.

           You came to the U.S. two years ago, _didn't you?_ _____

           Yes, I did.

1. You're married, _____

2. You have children, _____

3. You didn't study English in your country, _____

4. You have a car, _____

5. You don't live alone, _____

6. You'll take another English course next semester, _____

7. You won't return to your country, _____

8. You took the last test, _____

9. You have to work on Saturdays, _____

10. The teacher doesn't speak your language, _____

11. You can type, _____

12. This class isn't too hard for you, _____

13. There was a test last Friday, _____

14. You don't speak German, _____

15. I'm asking you a lot of personal questions, _____

EXERCISE 15   Fill in each blank with a tag question and an answer that tells if the information is true or not.

A. You come from Russia, *don't you?*

B. _____ I come from Ukraine.
        (1)

A. They speak Polish in Ukraine, _____
                                     (2)

B. _____ They speak Ukrainian and Russian.
        (3)

A. Ukraine isn't part of Russia, _____
                               (4)

B. _____ Ukraine and Russia are different. They were both part of
        (5)
the former Soviet Union.

A. You come from a big city, _____
                          (6)

B. _____ I come from Kiev. It's the capital of Ukraine.
        (7)

A. Your parents aren't here, _____
                       (8)

B. _____ We came together two years ago. I live with my parents.
        (9)

A. You studied English in your country, _____
                                  (10)

B. _____ I only studied Russian and German. I never studied English
        (11)
there.

A. You're not going to go back to live in your country, _____
                                              (12)

B. _____ I'm an immigrant here. I plan to become an American
        (13)
citizen.

EXPANSION ACTIVITIES

DISCUSSIONS   1. Find a partner. Tell your partner some things that you think you know about him or her and about his or her country. Your partner will tell you if you are right or wrong.

EXAMPLES: **The capital of your country is New Delhi, isn't it?**

Hindus don't eat meat, do they?

You're studying engineering, aren't you?

2. Tell the teacher what you think you know about the U.S. or Americans. The teacher will tell you if you're right or wrong.

EXAMPLES: **Most Americans don't speak a foreign language, do they?**

Alaska is the largest state, isn't it?

WRITING   Choose two sports, religions, countries, people, or stores, and write sentences comparing them.

EXAMPLE: **my mother and my father**

My father speaks English well, but my mother doesn't.

My father isn't an American citizen, and my mother isn't either.

My father was born in 1938, and my mother was too.

SUMMARY OF LESSON FOURTEEN

Uses of Auxiliary Verbs

1. To avoid repetition of the same verb phrase

Affirmative Sentence	*and*	Shortened Affirmative Sentence + *Too*
I *like football*,	and	my friend does *too*.
Football *is* fun,	and	soccer *is too*.

Negative Sentence	*and*	Shortened Negative Sentence + *Either*
I *don't like* baseball,	and	she *doesn't either*.
I *didn't watch* the game,	and	she *didn't either*.

Negative Sentence	*but*	Shortened Affirmative Sentence
I *didn't watch* the game,	but	you *did*.
I *can't go* to the game,	but	you *can*.

Affirmative Sentence	*but*	Shortened Negative Sentence
My brother *likes* baseball,	but	I *don't*.
I *have* tickets to the game,	but	my friend *doesn't*.

2. To form tag questions

Affirmative Sentence	Negative Tag
Soccer *is* fun,	*isn't* it?
You *like* soccer,	*don't* you?

Negative Sentence	Affirmative Tag
He *can't* swim,	*can* he?
She *didn't* go,	*did* she?

LESSON FOURTEEN TEST/REVIEW

Part 1   This is a conversation between two students who meet for the first time. Fill in each blank with an auxiliary verb to complete this conversation. Use *either* or *too* when necessary.

C. Hi. My name is Carlos. I'm a new student.

E. I _am too_____. My name is Elena.

C. I come from Mexico.

E. Oh, really? I _____ . I come from a small town in the northern
   (1)
   part of Mexico.

C. I come from Mexico City. I love big cities.

E. I _____ . I prefer small towns.
   (2)

C. How do you like living here in Los Angeles?

E. I don't like it much, but my sister _____ . She has a good job. But
   (3)
   I _____ . I miss my life back home.
   (4)

C. I love it here. And my family _____ . The climate is similar to the
   (5)
   climate of Mexico City.

E. What about the air quality? Mexico City doesn't have clean air, and Los

   Angeles _____ , so you probably feel right at home.
   (6)

C. Ha! You're right about the air quality, but there are many nice things about
   California. Do you want to get a cup of coffee and continue this conversation?
   I don't have any more classes today.

E. I _____ , but I have to go home. I enjoyed our talk.
   (7)

C. I _____ . Maybe we can continue some other time. Well,
   (8)

   see you in class tomorrow.

Part 2   In this conversation, a new student is trying to find out information about the school and class. Add a tag question.

A. There's a parking lot at the school, _isn't there?_____

B. Yes. It's east of the building.

A. The teacher's American, _____
                                                    (1)

B. Yes, she is.

A. She doesn't give hard tests, _____
                                                    (2)

B. Not too easy, not too hard.

A. We'll have a day off for Christmas, _____
                                                    (3)

B. We'll have a whole week off.

A. We have to write compositions, _____
                                                    (4)

B. A few.

A. And we can't use a dictionary when we write a composition,

_____
            (5)

B. Who told you that? Of course we can. You're very nervous about school,

_____
            (6)

A. Yes, I am. It isn't easy to learn a new language, _____
                                                                    (7)

B. No.

A. And I should ask questions about things I want to know, _____
                                                                            (8)

B. Yes, of course. You don't have any more questions, _____
                                                                    (9)

A. No.

B. Well, I'll see you in the next class. Bye.

LESSON FIFTEEN
VERB REVIEW

15.1 Comparison of Tenses

Compare the four tenses presented in this book.

SIMPLE PRESENT	We usually *study* hard.
PRESENT CONTINUOUS	We *are studying* four tenses now.
SIMPLE PAST	We *studied* the simple past last week.
FUTURE	We *are going to study* Book 2 next semester.
FUTURE	We *will study* Book 2 next semester.

15.2 Statements and Questions

Simple Present	
Base Form	**-S Form**
They *live* in Detroit.	He *lives* in Detroit.
They *don't live* in Lansing.	He *doesn't live* in Lansing.
Do they *live* in the city?	*Does* he *live* in the city?
Yes, they *do.*	Yes, he *does.*
Where *do* they *live?*	Where *does* he *live?*
Why *don't* they *live* in a suburb?	Why *doesn't* he *live* in a suburb?
How many people *live* with them?	Who *lives* with him?

Present Continuous	
They*'re speaking* English now.	She*'s making* dinner.
They *aren't speaking* French.	She *isn't making* lunch.
Are they *speaking* fast?	*Is* she *making* a pie?
Yes, they *are.*	No, she *isn't.*
Why *are* they *speaking* fast?	What *is* she *making?*
Why *aren't* they *speaking* slowly?	Why *isn't* she *making* a pie?
How many people *are speaking?*	Who*'s making* dessert?

Future	
<u>Will</u>	<u>Be Going to</u>
He*'ll buy* a car.	He*'s going to buy* a car.
He *won't buy* a Ford.	He *isn't going to buy* a Ford.
Will he *buy* a Chevy?	*Is* he *going to buy* a Chevy?
No, he *won't.*	No, he *isn't.*
What kind of car *will* he *buy?*	What kind of car *is he going to buy?*
Why *won't* he *buy* a Ford?	Why *isn't* he *going to buy* a Ford?
Who *will buy* a Ford?	Who *is going to buy* a Ford?

Simple Past	
Regular Verb	**Irregular Verb**
He *opened* the door.	She *found* a wallet.
He *didn't open* the window.	She *didn't find* money.
Did he *open* the front door?	*Did* she *find* identification?
Yes, he *did*.	No, she *didn't*.
When *did* he *open* the door?	Where *did* she *find* the wallet?
Why *didn't* he *open* the window?	Why *didn't* she *find* money?
Who *opened* the window?	Who *found* the money?

Be	
Present	**Past**
She*'s* in California.	You *were* late.
She *isn't* in Los Angeles.	You *weren't* on time.
Is she in San Francisco?	*Were* you very late?
No, she *isn't*.	Yes, I *was*.
Where *is* she?	Why *were* you late?
Why *isn't* she in Los Angeles?	Why *weren't* you on time?
Who *is* in Los Angeles?	Who *was* late?

15.3 Uses of the Tenses

Simple Present Tense

1. Use the simple present for habits, customs, regular activities, and facts.

   > Thanksgiving *is* an American holiday.
   > Americans *celebrate* Thanksgiving in November.
   > They usually *eat* turkey on Thanksgiving.
   > The teacher often *tells* us about American holidays in class.

2. Use the simple present for nonaction verbs.

   > We *know* a lot about American customs.
   > We *need* more information about grammar now.

3. In a future sentence, use the simple present in a time clause or *if* clause.

   > When we *finish* this review, we will do an exercise on tenses.
   > If we *don't understand* tenses, the teacher will review them.

Present Continuous Tense

Use the present continuous tense for actions that are happening now or in a present period of time.

> We*'re reviewing* verb tenses now.
> We*'re studying* verbs this week.

EXCEPTIONS: Do not use the continuous tense with nonaction verbs: *have, need, want, know, like, love,* etc.

Future Tense

Use the future tense for actions that will happen at a later time.

> The semester *will end* in June.
> We*'re going to have* a test at the end of the semester.

Do not use the future tense in a time clause or an *if* clause. Use the simple present.

> When the semester *ends,* we*'ll have* a party.

Simple Past Tense

Use the simple past tense to talk about an action that is completely past. It usually refers to a specific past time.

> We *studied* the present tense four weeks ago.
> I *bought* my book at the beginning of the semester.
> John Lennon *died* in 1980.

The Verb *Be*

Use *be* for classification, description, location, origin, with *born,* and with *there.*

> John Lennon *was* a singer.
> He *was* popular.
> He *was* from Liverpool.
> Liverpool *is* in England.
> He *was* born in 1940.
> There *are* many good songs on a Beatles album.

EXERCISE I   Jane, her husband Ed, and their two children are on vacation now. Jane is writing a letter to her friend Rosemary. Fill in the each blank with the correct tense of the verb in parentheses ( ) to complete this letter. Use the simple present, the present continuous, the future, or the simple past.

Dear Rosemary,

We _____*arrived*_____ in Puerto Rico last Monday. Our flight
                (arrive)

_____ smooth and comfortable. We _____ at a
      (1 be)   (2 stay)

beautiful hotel in San Juan this week. It _____ a big swimming pool
                                                  (3 have)

and tennis courts. Ed _____ tennis every morning. I usually
                            (4 play)

_____ late in the morning. In the afternoon, we usually
      (5 sleep)

_____ to the beach or to the pool. The children _____
      (6 go)   (7 love)

to swim. Sometimes I _____ shopping in the early evening. At night
                            (8 go)

we usually _____ at a restaurant. Last night we _____
                (9 eat)   (10 have)

dinner in a lovely Puerto Rican restaurant. The dinner _____
                                                              (11 be)

delicious. Tomorrow we _____ another restaurant.
                              (12 try)

Now I _____ on the beach. I _____ a good suntan.
            (13 sit)   (14 get)

The children _____ in the water. Ed _____ the
                    (15 play)   (16 read)

newspaper in the shade. He always _____ the shade, but I usually
                                          (17 like)

_____ the sun.
      (18 prefer)

Next week we _____ to another island, Saint Thomas. We
                    (19 go)

_____ at 7 o'clock on Friday morning. We _____ there
      (20 leave)   (21 be)

for three days. After that, we _____ home. I _____
                                      (22 return)   (23 call)

you when I _____ home. I _____ you all about our
                    (24 get)   (25 tell)

vacation.

Take care,

Jane

EXERCISE 2   Fill in each blank with the negative form of the underlined verb.

> EXAMPLE: **They <u>ate</u> in a Puerto Rican restaurant. They** _didn't eat_   **in
> a French restaurant.**

1. They <u>went</u> to Puerto Rico. They _____ to Hawaii.

2. They'<u>re staying</u> in a hotel. They _____ with friends.

3. The hotel <u>has</u> tennis courts. It _____ a golf course.

4. They'<u>re</u> at the beach now. They _____ at the hotel.

5. Ed <u>plays</u> tennis every day. Jane _____ tennis.

6. They'<u>ll be</u> home in a few weeks. They _____ home this week.

7. Jane <u>likes</u> the sun. Ed _____ the sun.

8. They'<u>re going</u> to St. Thomas. They _____ to St. John.

9. They'<u>re going to spend</u> three days in St. Thomas. They _____ a
   week there.

EXERCISE 3   Read each statement. Then write a *yes/no* question about the words in
parentheses ( ). Write a short answer.

> EXAMPLE: **Jane went to Puerto Rico. (her husband)**
>
> _Did her husband go to Puerto Rico? Yes, he did._

1. Jane likes to swim. (her husband)

   _____

2. Jane's getting a suntan now. (her husband)

   _____

3. Jane prefers the sun. (her husband)

_____

4. Ed gets up early every day. (Jane)

_____

5. They ate dinner in a restaurant. (in a French restaurant)

_____

6. The hotel has a pool. (tennis courts)

_____

7. The flight was smooth. (comfortable)

_____

8. They'll visit Saint Thomas. (Saint John)

_____

EXERCISE 4   Read each statement. Then write a *wh-* question about the words in parentheses ( ). Answer with a complete sentence.

EXAMPLE: **Ed plays tennis. (when)**

    A. _When does he play tennis?_

    B. _He plays tennis in the morning._

1. They went to Puerto Rico. (how)

    A. _____

    B. _____

2. Ed isn't sitting in the sun. (why)

    A. _____

    B. _____

3. They ate dinner last night. (where)

    A. _____

    B. _____

4. Jane will call Rosemary. (when)

A. _____

B. _____

5. The children are playing now. (where)

A. _____

B. _____

6. They're going to leave on Friday. (what time)

A. _____

B. _____

7. Someone plays tennis every morning. (who)

A. _____

B. _____

8. Jane doesn't go shopping in the morning. (why)

A. _____

B. _____

EXPANSION ACTIVITIES

INTERVIEW Find a partner. Use the words below to ask and answer questions with your partner. Practice the simple present, the present continuous, the future, and the simple past.

EXAMPLES: you/from Asia
A. Are you from Asia?
B. Yes, I am. OR No, I'm not.

where/you/from
A. Where are you from?
B. I'm from Pakistan.

1. when/you/leave your country
2. how/you/come to the U.S.
3. you/come to the U.S. alone
4. where/you/born
5. what language(s)/you speak
6. you/return to your country next year
7. you/have a job now
8. you/have a job in your country
9. how many brothers and sisters/you/have
10. your country/big
11. your country/have a lot of petroleum
12. you/live in an apartment in your country
13. you/study English in your country
14. what/you/study this semester
15. what/you/study next semester
16. you/like this class
17. the teacher/speak your language
18. this class/hard for you
19. who/your teacher last semester
20. who/your teacher next semester
21. _____
22. _____
23. _____

OUTSIDE ACTIVITY Use the words below to interview an American student at this college. Practice the simple present, the present continuous, the future, and the simple past. Report something interesting to the class about this student.

1. you/study another language now (what language)
2. you/live alone (who . . . with)
3. your family/live in this city
4. you/like this city (why/why not)
5. you/go to high school in this city (where)
6. what/your major
7. you/graduate soon (when)
8. what/you do/after/you/graduate
9. you/like to travel (when . . . your last vacation) (where . . . go)
10. you/own a computer (what kind) (when . . . buy it)

11. you/eat in a restaurant/last week (where)
12. you/buy something new/in the near future (what)
13. you/do something interesting/last weekend (what . . . do)
14. you/plan to do something interesting/next weekend (what . . . do)
15. _____
16. _____

Invite the American to interview you. Write down the questions that he or she asks you.

Appendix A

The Verb *GET*

Get has many meanings. Here is a list of the most common ones:

- get something = receive
  I got a letter from my father.

- get + (to) place = arrive
  I got home at six. What time do you get to school?

- get + object + infinitive = persuade
  She got him to wash the dishes.

- get + past participle = become

get acquainted	get used to
get engaged	get dressed
get married	get hurt
get divorced	get drunk
get tired	get bored
get worried	get confused
get lost	get scared
get accustomed to	

  They got married in 1989.

- get + adjective = become

get hungry	get sleepy
get rich	get dark
get nervous	get angry
get well	get old
get upset	get fat

  It gets dark at 6:30.

- get an illness = catch
  While I was traveling, I got malaria.

- get a joke or an idea = understand
  Everybody except Tom laughed at the joke. He didn't get it.
  The boss explained the project to us, but I didn't get it.

- get ahead = advance
  He works very hard because he wants to get ahead in his job.

- get along (well) (with someone) = to have a good relationship
  She doesn't get along with her mother-in-law.
  Do you and your roommate get along well?

•get around to something = find the time to do something
  I wanted to write my brother a letter yesterday, but I didn't get around to it.

•get away = escape
  The police chased the thief, but he got away.

•get away with something = escape punishment
  He cheated on his taxes and got away with it.

•get back = return
  He got back from his vacation last Saturday.

•get back at someone = get revenge
  My brother wants to get back at me for stealing his girlfriend.

•get back to someone = communicate with someone at a later time
  I can't talk to you today. Can I get back to you tomorrow?

•get by = have just enough but nothing more
  On her salary, she's just getting by. She can't afford a car or a vacation.

•get in trouble = be caught and punished for doing something wrong
  They got in trouble for cheating on the test.

•get in(to) = enter a car
  She got in the car and drove away quickly.

•get out (of) = leave a car
  When the taxi arrived at the theater, everyone got out.

•get on = to seat yourself on a bicycle, motorcycle, horse
  She got on the motorcycle and left.

•get on = enter a train, bus, airplane, boat
  She got on the bus and took a seat in the back.

•get off = leave a bicycle, motorcycle, horse, train, bus, airplane
  They will get off the train at the next stop.

•get out of something = escape responsibility
  My boss wants me to help him on Saturday, but I'm going to try to get out of it.

•get over something = recover from an illness or disappointment
  She has the flu this week. I hope she gets over it soon.

•get rid of someone or something = free oneself of someone or something undesirable
  My apartment has roaches, and I can't get rid of them.

•get through (to someone) = to communicate, often by telephone
  She tried to explain the dangers of drugs to her son, but she couldn't get through to him.
  I tried to call her many times, but her line was busy. I couldn't get through.

•get through with something = finish
  I can meet you after I get through with my homework.

•get together = to meet with another person
  I'd like to see you again. When can we get together?

•get up = to arise from bed
  He woke up at 6 o'clock, but he didn't get up until 6:30.

Appendix B

MAKE and *DO*

Some expressions use *make*. Others use *do*.

Make

    make a date/an appointment
    make a plan
    make a decision
    make a telephone call
    make a reservation
    make a meal (breakfast, lunch, dinner)
    make a mistake
    make an effort
    make an improvement
    make a promise
    make money
    make noise
    make the bed

Do

    do (the) homework
    do an exercise
    do the dishes
    do the cleaning, laundry, ironing, washing, etc.
    do the shopping
    do one's best
    do a favor
    do the right/wrong thing
    do a job
    do business
    What do you do for a living? (asks about a job)
    How do you do? (said when you meet someone for the first time)

Appendix C

Questions

1. Statements and Related Questions with a Main Verb.

Wb- Word	Do/Does/Did	Subject	Verb	Complement
		She	watches	TV.
When	does	she	watch	TV?
		My parents	live	in Peru.
Where	do	your parents	live?	
		Your sister	likes	someone.
Who(m)	does	she	like?	
		They	left	early.
Why	did	they	leave	early?
		She	found	some books.
How many books	did	she	find?	
		He	bought	a car.
What kind of car	did	he	buy?	
		She	didn't go	home.
Why	didn't	she	go	home?
		He	doesn't like	tomatoes.
Why	doesn't	he	like	tomatoes?
		Someone	has	my book.
		Who	has	my book?
		Someone	needs	help.
		Who	needs	help?
		Someone	took	my pen.
		Who	took	my pen?
		One teacher	speaks	Spanish.
		Which teacher	speaks	Spanish?
		Some men	have	a car.
		Which men	have	a car?
		Some boys	saw	the movie.
		How many boys	saw	the movie?

2. Statements and Related Questions with the Verb *Be*.

Wh- Word	*Be*	Subject	*Be*	Complement
		She	is	in California.
Where	is	she?		
		They	were	hungry.
Why	were	they		hungry?
		He	isn't	tired.
Why	isn't	he		tired?
		He	was	born in England.
When	was	he		born?
		One student	was	late.
		Who	was	late?
		Which student	was	late?
		Some kids	were	afraid.
		How many kids	were	afraid?
		Which kids	were	afraid?

3. Statements and Related Questions with an Auxiliary (Aux) Verb and a Main Verb.

Wh- Word	Aux	Subject	Aux	Main Verb	Complement
		She	is	running.	
Where	is	she		running?	
		They	will	go	on a vacation.
When	will	they		go	on a vacation?
		He	should	do	something.
What	should	he		do?	
		You	can	take	a pill.
How many pills	can	you		take?	
		You	can't	drive	a car.
Why	can't	you		drive	a car?
		Someone	should	answer	the question.
		Who	should	answer	the question?

Appendix D

Alphabetical List of Irregular Past Forms

Base Form	Past Form	Base Form	Past Form
arise	arose	drink	drank
awake	awoke	drive	drove
be	was/were	eat	ate
bear	bore	fall	fell
beat	beat	feed	fed
become	became	feel	felt
begin	began	fight	fought
bend	bent	find	found
bet	bet	fit	fit
bind	bound	flee	fled
bite	bit	fly	flew
bleed	bled	forbid	forbade
blow	blew	forget	forgot
break	broke	forgive	forgave
breed	bred	freeze	froze
bring	brought	get	got
broadcast	broadcast	give	gave
build	built	go	went
burst	burst	grind	ground
buy	bought	grow	grew
cast	cast	hang	hung[1]
catch	caught	have	had
choose	chose	hear	heard
cling	clung	hide	hid
come	came	hit	hit
cost	cost	hold	held
creep	crept	hurt	hurt
cut	cut	keep	kept
deal	dealt	kneel	knelt
dig	dug	know	knew
do	did	lay	laid
draw	drew	lead	led

---

[1]*Hanged* is used as the past form to refer to punishment by death.

Base Form	Past Form	Base Form	Past Form
leave	left	slit	slit
lend	lent	speak	spoke
let	let	speed	sped
lie	lay	spend	spent
light	lit, lighted	spin	spun
lose	lost	spit	spit
make	made	split	split
mean	meant	spread	spread
meet	met	spring	sprang
mistake	mistook	stand	stood
pay	paid	steal	stole
prove	proved	stick	stuck
put	put	sting	stung
quit	quit	stink	stank
read	read	strike	struck
ride	rode	strive	strove
ring	rang	swear	swore
rise	rose	sweep	swept
run	ran	swim	swam
say	said	swing	swung
see	saw	take	took
seek	sought	teach	taught
sell	sold	tear	tore
send	sent	tell	told
set	set	think	thought
shake	shook	throw	threw
shed	shed	understand	understood
shine	shone	upset	upset
shoot	shot	wake	woke
show	showed	wear	wore
shrink	shrank	weave	wove
shut	shut	weep	wept
sing	sang	win	won
sink	sank	wind	wound
sit	sat	withdraw	withdrew
sleep	slept	wring	wrung
slide	slid	write	wrote

INDEX

A/an, 11, 23, 79, 83, 97-98, 102, 262, 271. *See also* Articles

A few vs. *a little*, 261, 271

A little
   with comparisons, 295
   vs. *a few,* 261, 271

Ability, 237, 246

Adjectives, 275-288
   vs. adverbs, 280
   after *be,* 9, 11, 23
   comparative, 291-295, 305
   definition of, 275
   descriptive, 9, 11, 23
   ending with *-ed,* 9, 276
   after *how,* 36
   followed by infinitives, 234, 235
   ending with *-ing,* 9
   vs. noun modifiers, 275, 278, 288
   possessive, 123, 126, 129, 140
   superlative, 291-293, 299, 305
   with *too* and *very,* 282-283

Abstract nouns, 258

Adverbs, 283, 284, 288
   vs. adjectives, 280
   comparison of, 291, 293, 296, 305
   of frequency, 106, 107
   of manner, 275, 280, 288
   with *too* and *very,* 282-283, 288

Advice, 239, 246

Affirmative statements
   with *be,* 4, 41

   with future, 174
   with modals, 236
   with present continuous, 146, 174
   with same verb phrase, 310
   with simple past tense, 199-200, 208
   with simple present tense, 46-47, 73
   with *there,* 88-89

Ago, 194n

A lot of, 260, 267, 268n, 271

And, 310, 322

Any, 79, 91, 97-98, 102, 262, 262n, 271
   vs. *no,* 262
   vs. *some,* 262, 262n

Apostrophes
   in contractions, 8, 40
   with possession, 123, 124

Articles
   definite, 97-98, 102, 299
   indefinite, 11, 23, 79, 97-98, 102, 262
   omission of, with possessive forms, 124, 126

Auxiliary verbs, 308-324

Base form
   with imperatives, 227
   with *let's,* 229
   with simple past tense, 208, 211, 326
   with simple present tense, 46, 52, 64, 73, 326

Be
  affirmative statements with, 4–5
  with age, 4, 23, 36, 40
  with *born,* 196, 220
  contractions with, 7–8, 18, 23, 28, 41, 196
  with descriptions, 9, 23
  forms of, 2, 4, 195
  with location, 15, 23
  negative statements with, 18, 52, 55, 73, 197
  with nouns, 11, 23
  with origin, 4, 15, 23, 64
  with past tense, 194–196, 220, 327
  with present continuous tense, 145, 146,
      327
  with present tense, 1–25, 51, 73
  questions with, 26–44, 60–73, 197
  short answers with, 60, 73
  with *there,* 79, 87–98, 102
  uses of, 4, 23, 328
  wh- questions with, 32–33, 34, 36, 41, 69, 73
  yes/no questions and short answers with,
      28, 41
Be going to, 173–178, 184, 326
Born, 196, 224, 328
British English, use of *have,* 52, 57n, 166, 310,
    315
But, 311, 322

Can, 237, 240, 245
Clauses
  if, 178
  time, 178
Commands, 226
Comparatives and superlatives, 290–307
  with adjectives, 294–295, 305
  with adverbs, 296, 305
  forms, 292–293
  with nouns, 297, 305
Complement, 5n
Continuous tense, present, 144–171
Contractions
  apostrophes in, 7–8
  with *be,* 7–8, 18, 23, 33, 41, 146

  with *can,* 237
  with *do,* 52
  negative, with *be,* 18, 23
  in short answers, 28
  with *was/were,* 196
  with *will,* 174
Could, 245
Count nouns, 255–273

Definite articles, 97–98, 102, 299
Demonstratives. *See This/that/these/those*
Do, 57, 73
  contractions with, 52
  vs. *make,* 337
  in tag questions, 309
  with *too* and *either,* 309

-ed
  adjectives, 9, 276
  pronunciation of, 201–202
  with regular past tense verbs, 199–202
  spelling of past form with, 201–202
  voiced and voiceless sounds with, 202
Either and *too,* 310, 322
Enough, 284, 288
-er/more, 292–293
-est/most, 292–293
Ever, 110

Frequency words, 106, 107, 118
  in short answers, 110
Future tense, 172–192
  affirmative statements with, 174
  compared with other tenses, 184, 326
  with *if* clause, 178
  negative statements with, 174
  questions with, 176–177
  with *there,* 174

with time clause, 178
uses of, 175, 328

Generalizations with nouns, 83, 102
Get, 335-336
Going to, 173-176
Good vs. *well,* 280, 293

Have
  as action vs. nonaction verb, 161
  British vs. American English, 52, 57n, 166,
    310, 315
  vs. *there,* 95
Have to, 241
Hear vs. *Listen,* 160
How, 32, 36
How many, 91, 211
How often, 113

If clauses, 178, 327, 328
Imperatives, 226, 227, 244
Indefinite articles, 11, 23, 79, 97-98, 102, 262
Infinitives, 226, 231-235
  adjectives before, 234
  verbs followed by, 231-232
Information questions. *See Wh-* questions
-ing
  adjectives, 9
  with present continuous tense, 145, 146
  spelling of, 148-149
Intensifiers, 283
Intonation of questions, 28, 33
Irregular forms. *See also* Irregular verbs
  adverbs, 280
  comparatives and superlatives, 293
  plural nouns, 82
Irregular verbs
  alphabetical list, 341-342
  be, 2, 4, 194, 195

past tense of, 204-206
  -s form of, 47
It
  with infinitives, 234
  vs. *there,* 95
  with time and weather, 5

Less and *more,* 296
Let's, 229
-ly adverbs, 280, 288
  with comparative and superlative, 293

Make vs. *do,* 337
Many vs. *much,* 260, 271
May, 242, 245
Might, 242
Modals, 226, 236-246
  for politeness, 244-245
Modifiers
  adjectives, 275, 276
  gerund, 278
  noun, 275, 278
More, 292-293
  and *less,* 296
Most, 292-293
Much
  with comparisons, 295
  vs. *many,* 260, 271
Must, 240, 241

Necessity, 241, 246
Negative statements
  with *be,* 18, 52, 73
  with future, 174
  with modals, 236
  with *never,* 110
  with present continuous tense, 146
  with same verb phrase, 310
  with simple past tense, 208

with simple present tense, 52, 55, 73
No vs. *not a* or *not any,* 262
Nonaction verbs, 160-161, 327
Noncount nouns, 255-273
Nouns
    abstract, 258
    articles with, 11, 23
    after *be,* 11
    comparisons with, 297, 305
    count vs. noncount, 255-273
    definition of, 11
    as modifiers, 275, 278, 288
    as objects, 130
    plural, 5, 79-83, 88-89, 102, 123, 124
    possession with, 123, 124, 126, 140
    after question words, 34
    as subjects, 5, 130

Objects
    nouns as, 123, 130
    of preposition, 132
    pronouns as, 123, 130, 132, 140
    questions about, 137
    and subjects, 130
One/ones, 277
Or
    with comparatives, 295
    questions with, 63
Origin, *be* with, 4, 15, 23, 64

Participles, present. *See -ing*
Past, simple, 193-224
Past tense, 193-224. *See also* Simple
        past tense
Permission, 237, 245, 246
Plural nouns
    definition of, 5
    generalizations with, 83, 102

irregular forms, 82
    possession with, 123, 124
    vs. singular noun, 79
    spelling of, 80-81
    with *there,* 88-89
Possession, 123-130
    with adjectives, 123, 126, 129, 140
    with nouns, 123, 124, 126, 140
    with pronouns, 123, 129, 140
    with *whose,* 127-128
Possibility, 237, 246
Prepositional phrase after *there,* 88-89, 90-91
Prepositions
    objects after, 132
    of place, 15
    in questions, 64
    of time, 32, 106, 116
    with *wh-* word, 64
Present continuous tense, 144-171, 184, 326
    forms, 146
    -ing with, 145, 146
    negative statements with, 146
    questions with, 151
    vs. simple present tense, 156-157
    uses of, 147, 167, 328
    verbs not used with, 160-161
Present participles. *See -ing*
Present progressive tense. *See* Present
        continuous tense
Present tense, 45-77. *See also* Simple
        present tense
Pronouns
    object, 123, 130, 132, 140
    possessive, 129, 140
    in short answers, 28, 41, 57
    subject, 5, 23, 126, 129, 140
    in tag questions, 315
    after *than,* 295
Pronunciation
    of *-ed* forms, 202
    of *going to,* 174
    of *have to,* 241
    of plural nouns, 81
    of *-s* form of verb, 49
    of *want to,* 232

Quantifiers, 256, 258-259
Quantity words, 79, 88-89, 258-271
Questions
   with *be*, 26-44, 60, 73, 197
   about cost, 67
   about meaning, 67
   with modals, 236
   with prepositions, 64
   with simple past tense, 211
   with simple present tense, 57-73
   about spelling, 67
   about subject, 137, 211
   summary of, 339-340
   tag, 314-315, 322
   with *there*, 90-91
Question words, contractions with, 33, 41
Quite, 283

Regular verbs, past tense of, 199-202, 220

See vs. *look*, 160
Sense perception verbs, 161
-*s* form of verb, 47, 73, 326
   pronunciation of, 49
   in questions, 137
   spelling of, 48
   use of, 47, 73
Short answers,
   with *be*, 28, 41, 60, 73, 197
   contractions in, 28, 91
   with frequency words, 110, 118
   with simple past tense, 211
   with simple present tense, 57, 73
   with *there*, 90-91
Should, 239
Simple past tense, 193-224, 327
   affirmative statements with, 199-200
   with *be*, 194-196, 220
   compared with other tenses, 326-328
   of irregular verb, 204-206

negative statements with, 208
questions with, 211
of regular verbs, 199-202
uses of, 194, 328
Simple present tense, 45-77
   affirmative statements with, 46-47, 73
   with *be*, 1-25
   be vs. other verbs, 51, 55, 60, 69, 73
   compared with other tenses, 184, 326-328
   with frequency words, 107, 118
   negative statements with, 52, 73
   with nonaction verbs, 160-161, 167
   or questions with, 57
   vs. present continuous tense, 156-157, 167
   in time/*if* clauses, 178
   uses of, 46, 73, 167, 327
   wh- questions with, 64, 67, 69, 73
   yes/no questions and short answers with, 57, 60, 73
Singular and plural nouns, 5, 79-89, 102, 256, 271
   possession with, 123, 124
Some/any, 79, 97-98, 102, 262, 262n, 271
Spelling
   of -*ed* form, 202
   -*er* and -*est* form, 293
   of -*ing* form, 148-149
   of -*ly* adverbs, 280
   of plural nouns, 80
   of -*s* form of verb, 48
Statements and questions, 326
Subject pronouns, 5
   contractions with, 8, 23
Subjects, 130
   classification of, 11, 23
   definition of, 5
   and objects, 130, 132
   pronouns as, 5, 23, 126, 129, 140
   questions about, 137, 211
Suggestions, 245, 246
Superlatives and comparatives, 290-307
   with adjectives, 291, 294-295, 299, 305
   forms, 292-293
Tag questions, 314-315, 322
   answers to, 318

Tenses
    comparison of, 184, 325–334
    future, 172–178, 326
    present continuous, 144–171, 326
    simple past, 193–224, 327
    simple present, 45–77, 326
    uses of, 327–328
Than, 295
The, 97–98. *See also* Articles with superlative
    forms, 299
There
    with future tense, 174
    with *is/are,* 79, 87–98, 102
    questions with, 90–91
    there is/there are vs. *it's/they're,* 94, 95
    with *was/were,* 196
Think, as action vs. nonaction verb, 161
This/that/these/those, 17, 23,
    with *one/s,* 277
    tag question after, 315
Time
    with *it,* 5
    prepositions of, 32, 106, 116
Time clauses, 178, 327, 328
To, for infinitive, 226
Too
    vs. *either,* 310, 322
    and *enough,* 284, 288
    vs. *too much/many,* 267, 268n, 271
    vs. *very,* 282–283, 288

Verb phrase, shortened, 310
Verb review, 325–334
Verbs
    auxiliary, 308–324
    followed by infinitive, 231–232
    irregular past tense of, 204–206, 341–342
    nonaction, 160–161
    regular past tense of, 199–202
    sense perception, 161
Verb tense. *See* Tenses

Very, 276, 280
    vs. *too,* 282–283, 288
Voiced and voiceless sounds
    with *-ed,* 202
    with *-s* verb forms, 49
    with *-s* plural forms, 81
Vowels, 11

Weather
    with *it,* 5
    question about, 36
Well vs. *good,* 280
What, 32
    as subject, 211
    noun after, 34
When, 32
    clause with, 178, 327
Where, 32
Which, 32, 211
Who, 32, 137, 140, 211
    vs. *whom,* 137
Whom, 32
    prepositions with, 64
    vs. *who,* 137
Whose, 127–128, 140
Wh- questions
    with *be,* 32–39, 41
    with future, 176–177
    with modals, 236
    with present continuous tense, 151
    with simple past tense, 211
    with simple present tense, 64, 67, 69, 73
    about subject, 137, 211
    summary of, 339–340
    with there, *91*
Wh- word, contractions with, 33, 41
Why, 32
Why don't you/we, 245
Will, 173–178, 326
    contractions with, 173
Word order
    with *be,* 23, 41

with comparatives and superlatives, 305
  in questions, 64
Would, 245

Yes/no questions and short answers
  with *be,* 28, 41
  with *ever,* 110

with future tense, 176–177
with modals, 236
with present continuous tense, 151
with simple past tense, 211
with simple present tense, 57, 73
with *there,* 90
You're vs. *your,* 40

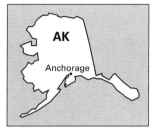

The United States of America

AL	Alabama	IN	Indiana	NE	Nebraska	SC	South Carolina
AK	Alaska	IA	Iowa	NV	Nevada	SD	South Dakota
AZ	Arizona	KS	Kansas	NH	New Hampshire	TN	Tennessee
AR	Arkansas	KY	Kentucky	NJ	New Jersey	TX	Texas
CA	California	LA	Louisiana	NM	New Mexico	UT	Utah
CO	Colorado	ME	Maine	NY	New York	VT	Vermont
CT	Connecticut	MD	Maryland	NC	North Carolina	VA	Virginia
DE	Delaware	MA	Massachusetts	ND	North Dakota	WA	Washington
FL	Florida	MI	Michigan	OH	Ohio	WV	West Virginia
GA	Georgia	MN	Minnesota	OK	Oklahoma	WI	Wisconsin
HI	Hawaii	MS	Mississippi	OR	Oregon	WY	Wyoming
ID	Idaho	MO	Missouri	PA	Pennsylvania	DC*	District of Columbia
IL	Illinois	MT	Montana	RI	Rhode Island		

*The District of Columbia is not a state. Washington D.C. is the capitol of the United States. Note: Washington D.C. and Washington state are not the same.

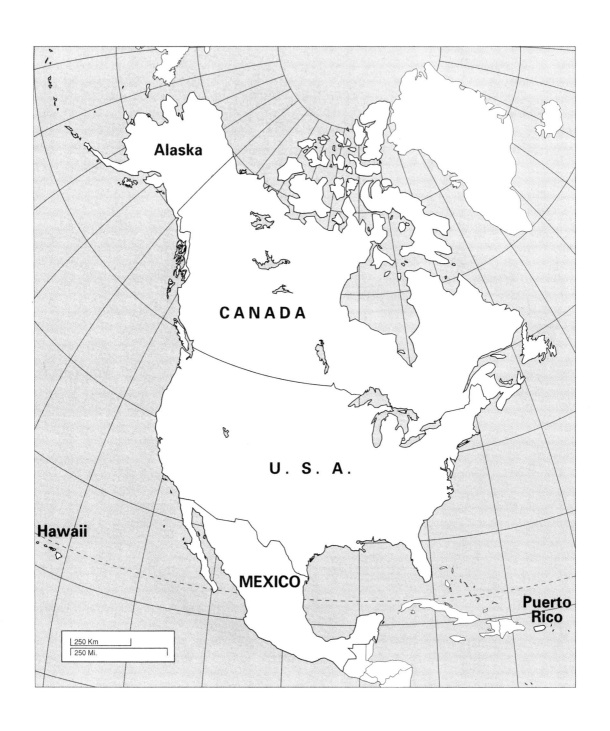

Alaska

CANADA

U. S. A.

Hawaii

MEXICO

Puerto Rico

250 Km
250 Mi.

GRAMMAR
IN CONTEXT

SANDRA ELBAUM

SECOND EDITION

BOOK 2

I(T)P

Heinle & Heinle Publishers
An International Thomson Publishing Company
Boston, Massachusetts, 02116, USA

The publication of *Grammar in Context,* Second Edition, was directed by members of the Newbury House Publishing Team at Heinle & Heinle:

Erik Gundersen, Editorial Director
John F. McHugh, Market Development Director
Kristin M. Thalheimer, Production Services Coordinator

Also participating in the publication of this program were:

Publisher: Stanley J. Galek
Director of Production: Elizabeth Holthaus
Project Manager/Desktop Pagination: Thompson Steele Production Services
Manufacturing Coordinator: Mary Beth Hennebury
Photo Coordinator: Philippe Heckly
Associate Editor: Ken Pratt
Interior Designer: Sally Steele
Illustrator: Jim Roldan
Photo/video Specialist: Jonathan Stark
Cover Designer: Gina Petti, Rotunda Design

Photo Credits
p. 1 © Tony Savino/The Image Works; **p. 2** © Tony Freeman/Photo Edit; **p. 30** © Rick Strange/The Picture Cube; **p. 57** © UPI/Bettman; **p. 77** © Mitchell Klein/Jewell Living Colour; **p. 104** © Anne Dowie/The Picture Cube, Inc.; **p. 131** © UPI/Bettman; **p. 157** © Ulrike Welsch; **p. 179** © Frank Siteman/The Picture Cube; **p. 189** © Emilio Mercado/The Picture Cube, Inc.; **p. 214** © John Nordell/The Picture Cube, Inc.; **p. 232** © Michael Grecco/Stock Boston, Inc.; **p. 261**, Air bag production worker, © N. R. Rowan/Stock Boston, Inc.; **p. 261**, Computer operator, © Bachmann/The Image Works; **p. 261**, Airline pilot, © Laima Druskis/Stock Boston, Inc.; **p. 288** © John Coletti/The Picture Cube, Inc.; **p. 312** © Lynn McLaren/The Picture Cube.

Heinle & Heinle Publishers is a division of International Thomson Publishing, Inc.

Manufactured in the United States of America

Library of Congress Cataloging-in-Publication Data

Elbaum, Sandra N.
        Grammar in context / Sandra Elbaum.
            p.   cm.
        ISBN 0-8384-4688-4 (bk. 1). —ISBN 0-8384-4689-2 (bk. 2). —ISBN
    0-8384-6651-6 (bk. 3)
            1. English language—Grammar—Problems, exercises, etc.
        2. English language—Textbooks for foreign speakers. I. Title.
    PE1112.E3641995
        428.2'4—dc20   95-49062
                                                                            CIP

ISBN 0-8384-4689-2

        10 9 8 7 6 5 4 3 2 1

IN MEMORY
OF MEYER SHISLER
TEACHER, SCHOLAR, AND INSPIRATION

PREFACE

Grammar in Context, Book Two is the second part of a three-part grammar series for adult students of English as a Second Language. This series of work-texts is designed for the high beginning to low advanced instructional levels.

As ESL teachers know, presenting English in a meaningful context allows for a better understanding of the grammar point. *Grammar in Context* is unique among grammar texts in its use of culturally rich, informative readings to present and illustrate the target grammar, and to stimulate interest in the topic.

Grammar in Context is organized as follows:

Lesson Focus The lessons begin with an overview and brief explanation of the grammar points covered. The Lesson Focus also includes sentences which illustrate the grammar point(s) being addressed.

Pre-Reading Questions These questions stimulate student interest in the topic of the reading which follows.

Introductory Readings A short reading illustrates each new grammar point in a natural, authentic context. These high-interest readings about culturally rich topics engage the student's attention and help focus on the grammar points. The real-life subject matter provides practical information about American life and customs, stories about famous people and events, and contemporary issues that are of concern to Americans as well as to recently-arrived residents. These readings can be used as springboards for lively classroom discussions, as well as inspiration for out-of-class activities.

Since *Grammar in Context* is not a reader, the readings are written at a simple, accessible level, for their primary goal is to exemplify the target grammar. The practical vocabulary and idioms that are needed to understand the passage are anticipated and glossed in footnotes or illustrations.

Grammar Boxes and Language Notes This book anticipates difficulties that most students have—for example, count and noncount nouns, contracted verb forms, modal auxiliaries, and question formation. Also, a great deal of attention is given to word order.

The grammar boxes use simple language in grammar explanations, illustrative example sentences, and charts with a clear graphic overview. Because *Grammar in Context* does not rely on a knowledge of linguistic jargon, fine points of grammar are often placed in a footnote so as not to overwhelm students who do not need so much detail.

The Language Notes provide the students with additional information on the functions of language, level of formality/informality, appropriate usage, spelling, and pronunciation. They often include information on the differences between American English and British English.

Exercises   There is a great variety of exercise types. The change of pace from one exercise to another reduces boredom in the classroom and offers challenges to different types of language learners as well as language teachers. Exercises include traditional fill-ins, cloze tasks, pair work, editing exercises, and combination exercises which review previous material in the context of the new or integrate several subskills from within the lesson. Many of the exercises allow students to personalize their remarks to reflect their own observations about American life, their opinions on cultural matters, and their feelings.

Expansion Activities   These activities, grouped at the end of each lesson, allow students to use the grammar points covered in more communicative ways. Expansion Activities include pair work; group discussions; writing; poetry, proverbs, famous quotes and sayings; and outside activities. These activities give subjects for debate and discussion, topics for written reflection, and ideas for further research on the context of the lesson or on a related topic (including suggestions for interviewing Americans and bringing the findings back to share with the class). The poems, proverbs, famous quotes and sayings not only illustrate the grammar items, but also provide an opportunity for a rich cross-cultural interchange.

Because they are progressively more challenging, the Expansion Activities lead away from a mechanical manipulation of grammar toward situations in which students put their recently learned grammatical knowledge to immediate practical use.

The teacher may choose to have students do Expansion Activities after a related grammar point has been thoroughly studied, or may assign them after the lesson has been completed.

Editing Advice   Potentially troublesome issues with the grammar points covered in the lesson are presented, showing students common errors, and ways to correct them.

Summary   The end-of-lesson summary encapsulates all of the grammar presented in the chapter in a simple graphic format.

Test/Review   Each lesson ends with a test/review section that allows both the teacher and the students to evaluate the mastery of concepts. Different formats—editing, fill-ins, and multiple choice questions—are used.

Appendices   This book includes appendices that provide useful information in list or chart form. The appendices are cross-referenced throughout the text.

Differences Between the First and Second Editions

There is now a third book in the series. Previous users of this text should note that the new Book One is easier than the original. Users of the former Book One would choose either Book One of the new series for a high beginning class or Book Two of the new series for an intermediate class. The original Book Two corresponds more closely to Book Three of the new series.

In the first edition, Book Two continued where Book One ended. In the new series, grammar points overlap. Since students rarely master a point after only one presentation and practice, there is a repetition at the next level, as well as added complexity. All tenses covered in Book One are also in Book Two. Also included in Books One and Two are singular and plural, pronouns and possessive forms, modals, count and noncount nouns, and comparative and superlative adjectives and adverbs. Included in Books Two and Three are modals, adjective clauses, gerunds, infinitives, and time clauses.

There is a higher degree of contextualization in both the readings and the grammar exercises.

Pre-reading questions have been added to stimulate interest and discussion. New readings contain many topics of a contemporary nature—for example, self-help groups, job rankings and personal ads. Older readings have been updated and extended.

Many of the exercises and exercise types are completely new. Older exercises have been updated and revised. More interactive, task-based activities are included, some to be done in class, asking students to work with a partner or small group. Outside activities encourage students to talk with Americans, note their responses, and report them to the class.

There are more visual aids, illustrations, and charts to support the vocabulary in the readings, and the context of the exercises. Maps of the United States and references to states, major cities, and regions familiarize the students with names they will frequently hear.

Most lessons include editing advice and an error correction or editing exercise. In addtion, a new and comprehensive testing program has been added.

Overall, the new edition of *Grammar in Context* provides thorough coverage of the grammar, a variety of exercise types, and an anticipation of student problems, thereby freeing the teacher from excessive class preparation. By providing grammar practice in the context of relevant and stimulating ideas, the *Grammar in Context* series eases the transition to American life, both linguistically and culturally.

Acknowledgments

I would like to thank my editor at Heinle and Heinle, Erik Gundersen, for his enthusiasm about this new edition, and for his gentle but firm way of pushing me in the direction that I needed to go.

I would also like to show my appreciation to the following teachers who reviewed my books: Kevin McClure, ELS Language Center, San Francisco; Kathi Jordan, Contra Costa College; Laurie Moody, Passaic County CC; Sherry Trechter, George Mason University; Bettye Wheeler, El Paso Community College; Ethel Tiersky, Truman College; Colleen Weldele, Palomar College; Emily Strauss, De Anza College; Peggy Armstrong; Pat Ishill, Union County College; Tay Leslie, ELS Language Centers Central Office; Kiran Razzak, ELS Language Center @ Chapman University; Terry Pruett-Said, Kansas State University.

Thanks to Christine Meyers, Judi Peman, and Merle Weiss for their kindness and understanding in getting me through it all.

And last, but most certainly not least, many thanks to my students at Truman College. They have increased my understanding of my own language and taught me to see life from another point of view. By sharing their insights and life stories, they have enriched my life enormously.

> *I thought Russians were different from Americans and that was why life in Russia and America were so different. When I came to America, I gradually realized that any national character is nothing but an adaptive social behavior. The more I learned about America, the more I saw that there was no difference between Russians and Americans as individual human beings. I saw a familiar spectrum of personalities, intimate problems, emotions, complexes, virtues, and vices.*
>
> *American social chemistry was based on the same periodic table as the Russian. Individual atoms of human nature were the same but Russian and American social molecules were arranged differently. The two cultures seemed to contrast as strongly as the lifestyles of birds and fish, although beautiful species could be found among both . . .*
>
> *The chemistry of society is universal, and history is a record of most unexpected transformations.*
>
> (from Memoirs of 1984, *by Yuri Tarnopolsky, published by University Press of America, Maryland.*)

C O N T E N T S

LESSON ONE 1

Lesson Focus	The Simple Present Tense—*Be* and Other Verbs; Frequency Verbs	2
	Reading: Disneyland	2
1.1	Forms of *Be*	3
1.2	Negative Statements and Contractions with *Be*	5
1.3	Questions and Short Answers with *Be*	5
1.4	The Simple Present Tense—Forms	8
	Reading: About the United States	8
1.5	Affirmative and Negative Statements with the Simple Present Tense	10
1.6	Questions with the Simple Present Tense	13
1.7	*Wh-* Questions with a Preposition	15
	Reading: Letter About American Customs	17
1.8	Frequency Words	18
1.9	Questions with *Ever*	21
1.10	Frequency Expressions and Questions with *How Often*	22

Expansion Activities	23
Summary of Lesson One	25
Lesson One Test/Review	26

LESSON TWO 30

Lesson Focus	The Present Continuous and Future Tenses	31
	Reading: Observations About Americans— A Letter	31
2.1	The Present Continuous Tense	32
2.2	Contrasting the Simple Present and the Present Continuous	36
2.3	Nonaction Verbs	38
2.4	Questions with the Simple Present and the Present Continuous	41
	Reading: The Aging Population	43
2.6	Future Tense + Time/*If* Clause	47

Expansion Activities	49
Summary of Lesson Two and Comparison of Tenses	52
Lesson Two Test/Review	53

LESSON THREE   57

Lesson Focus	The Simple Past Tense; Habitual Past with *Used To*	58
	Reading: Martin Luther King, Junior	58
3.1	Past of *Be*	59
3.2	Simple Past Tense of Regular Verbs	60
3.3	Simple Past Tense of Irregular Verbs	61
	Reading: Changes in American Life	68
3.4	Habitual Past with *Used To*	52
Expansion Activities		71
Summary of Lesson Three		73
Lesson Three Test/Review		74

LESSON FOUR   77

Lesson Focus	Subjects; Objects; Possessive Forms; Reflexive Pronouns	78
	Reading: An American Wedding	78
4.1	Subject Pronouns and Object Pronouns	79
4.2	Possessive Nouns	80
4.3	Possessive Adjectives	81
4.4	Direct and Indirect Objects	82
4.5	Questions with *Whose*	84
4.6	Possessive Pronouns	85
4.7	Questions About the Subject	88
	Reading: Self-Help	95
4.8	Reflexive Pronouns	95
Expansion Activities		98
Summary of Lesson Four		100
Lesson Four Test/Review		101

LESSON FIVE   104

Lesson Focus	Singular and Plural; Noncount Nouns; Quantity	105
	Reading: Facts About Americans	105
5.1	Singular and Plural Nouns	106
	Reading: Native Americans	110
5.2	Noncount Nouns	111
5.3	*There* + A Form of *Be*	113

5.4 Quantities   114
      Reading: College Tuition   122
Expansion Activities   125
Summary of Lesson Five   127
Lesson Five Test/Review   128

LESSON SIX   131

Lesson Focus The Past Continuous; Time Clauses   132
      Reading: A Foolish Man   132
6.1 Past Continuous Tense   133
6.2 The Simple Past with the Past Continuous   134
      Reading: Albert Einstein   139
6.3 Time Words   140
6.4 Simple Past or Past Continuous
     with Time Clause   142
      Reading: American Education   143
      Reading: Saving for Retirement   145
6.5 Time and *If* Clauses with the Future   146
6.6 Time with Present Participles   148
6.7 More Time Words   149
Expansion Activities   151
Summary of Lesson Six   153
Lesson Six Test/Review   154

LESSON SEVEN   157

Lesson Focus Infinitives; Modals   158
      Reading: An Apartment Lease   158
7.1 Verbs Followed by an Infinitive   159
7.2 Object Before Infinitive   161
7.3 *It* + Adjective + Infinitive   163
7.4 *Be* + Adjective + Infinitive   165
7.5 Modals   166
      Reading: Copyright Law   168
      Reading: American Citizenship   170
7.6 Negatives of Modals   176
      Reading: At a Garage Sale   179
7.7 Using Modals for Politeness   180
Expansion Activities   183
Summary of Lesson Seven   186
Lesson Seven Test/Review   187

LESSON EIGHT   189
• •

Lesson Focus   Present Perfect Tense; Present Perfect
               Continuous Tense   190

               Reading: Alcoholics Anonymous   190

         8.1   The Past Participle   191
         8.2   The Present Perfect Tense   193
         8.3   The Present Perfect: Continuation from
               Past to Present   195
         8.4   The Present Perfect Continuous   199
         8.5   The Present Perfect with Repetition
               Up to the Present   202
         8.6   The Present Perfect: Indefinite Past Time   204

Expansion Activities   208
Summary of Lesson Eight   210
Lesson Eight Test/Review   211

LESSON NINE   214
• •

Lesson Focus   Gerunds   215

               Reading: Smoking   215

         9.1   Gerund as Subject   216
         9.2   Gerund After Verb   217
         9.3   Gerund After Preposition   220
         9.4   Gerund in Adverbial Phrase   223

               Reading: Life Changes   223

         9.5   *Used To* versus *Be Used To*   224

Expansion Activities   226
Summary of Lesson Nine   228
Lesson Nine Test/Review   229

LESSON TEN   232
• •

Lesson Focus   Adjectives; Adverbs; Adjective Clauses   233

               Reading: The Fourth of July   233

        10.1   Adjectives and Noun Modifiers   234
        10.2   Adverbs of Manner   237

               Reading: Social Security   240

        10.3   *Too/Enough*   241

10.4	Adjective Clauses	244
	Reading: Personal Ads	244
10.5	Relative Pronoun as Subject	245
10.6	Relative Pronoun as Object	248
10.7	Whose + Noun as Subject or Object of Adjective Clause	250

Expansion Activities — 253
Summary of Lesson Ten — 257
Lesson Ten Test/Review — 258

LESSON ELEVEN   261

Lesson Focus	Comparatives and Superlatives	262
	Reading: Job Rankings	262
11.1	Comparative and Superlative Forms	263
11.2	Using Superlatives	264
	Reading: Auto Insurance	267
11.3	Comparative Adjectives and Adverbs	268
11.4	Comparison with Nouns	270
	Reading: Generic Drugs	272
11.5	Comparisons with *A . . . As*	272
11.6	Comparing Quantities	274
11.7	*The Same . . . As*	277
11.8	Same or Different	278
11.9	Similarity	279

Expansion Activities — 282
Summary of Lesson Eleven — 285
Lesson Eleven Test/Review — 286

LESSON TWELVE   288

Lesson Focus	Articles; Definite and Indefinite Nouns and Pronouns	289
	Reading: Automatic Teller Machines	289
12.1	Using the Indefinite Article to Classify or Define	290
12.2	Definite and Indefinite Nouns	291
12.3	General and Specific	294
	Reading: Superstitions	298
12.4	Indefinite Pronouns: One, Some, Any	299

	Reading: Language Families	301
12.5	*Another, Other*	302
Expansion Activities		305
Summary of Lesson Twelve		307
Lesson Twelve Test/Review		308

LESSON THIRTEEN   312

Lesson Focus	Review of Verb Tenses; Sentences and Word Order	313
	Reading: Letter of Complaint	314
13.1	The Present Tenses	315
13.2	The Future	317
13.3	Past Tenses	320
13.4	The Present Perfect and Past Perfect Continuous	323
13.5	*Be*	327
13.6	Modals and Infinitives	329
13.7	Review of Questions	331
13.8	Sentences and Word Order	337
Expansion Activities		340

Appendix A—Spelling and Pronunciation	343
Appendix B—Modals	347
Appendix C—The verb *GET*	348
Appendix D—*MAKE* and *DO*	350
Appendix E—Nouns That Can Be Both Count or Noncount	351
Appendix F—Prepositions	352
Appendix G—Phrasal Verbs	353
Appendix H—Direct and Indirect Objects	357
Appendix I—Alphabetical List of Irregular Past Forms	359
Index	361

LESSON ONE

GRAMMAR

The Simple Present Tense—
   Be and Other Verbs
Frequency Words

CONTEXT

Letter from Disneyland
The United States
Letter About American Customs

Lesson Focus   **The Simple Present Tense—*Be* and Other Verbs;**
Frequency Words

• We use the simple present tense to talk about facts and to show regular activities (habits), repeated actions, or customs. The verb *be* is irregular; it has three forms in the simple present tense: *am, is,* and *are.*

• We use frequency words with the simple present to show how often an action happens.

   I *usually* drink coffee in the morning.

R
E
A
D
I
N
G

Before you read:

1. What places would you like to visit in the United States?
2. What is a popular tourist attraction in your country?

Read the following information and letter. Pay special attention to forms of the verb *be.*

DISNEYLAND

Disney parks are tourist attractions. They are big parks with rides, shows, and parades. Children especially like Disney parks. There are Disney parks in California and Florida as well as in France and Japan.

> Dear Cousins,
>
>   I'**m** at Disneyland now. Disneyland **isn't** a city. It'**s** an amusement park in Anaheim, California. It's not far from L.A.[1] It'**s** really for children, but it'**s** fun for adults too.
>
>   I'**m** with my daughter. It'**s** her birthday. She'**s** ten years old now. She'**s** very happy here. We'**re** both happy. Disneyland **is** very crowded because it'**s** so popular. There **are** a lot of people here. The weather **is** nice. It'**s** sunny and warm. This **is** a picture of Mickey Mouse. I'**m** very tired, so I'll say goodbye for now. I hope you'**re** all fine.
>
>   Love,
>   Linda

---

[1]*L.A.* is the abbreviation for Los Angeles.

1.1   Forms of *Be*

In the simple present tense, the verb *be* has three forms: *am, is,* and *are.*

Subject	*Be*	Complement[2]
I	am	at Disneyland.
My daughter She My husband He	is	happy.
Anaheim It	is	a city. in California.
There	is	a picture on the postcard.
We You My friends They	are	in California.
There	are	many children at Disneyland.

We can make a contraction with the subject pronoun and *am, is,* or *are.* We can also make a contraction with most nouns and *is.*

I am	*I'm* at Disneyland.
You are	*You're* my friend.
He is	*He's* late.
She is	*She's* with me.
It is	*It's* four o'clock.
There is	*There's* a picture on the postcard.
We are	*We're* in California.
They are	*They're* at home.
My daughter is	*My daughter's* happy.
California is	*California's* a big state.

---

[2]The *complement* finishes, or completes, the sentence.

Language Notes

1. We don't make a contraction with *is* if the noun ends in these sounds: *s, z, sh,* or *ch.*

   The United State*s is* a big country.
   Thi*s is* a postcard.
   Fran*ce is* in Europe.
   New Orlean*s is* a beautiful city.
   Engli*sh is* the language of the U.S.
   Long Bea*ch is* in California.

2. We don't make a contraction with a noun and *are.*

   There are many children at Disneyland.
   The children are happy.

3. We use a form of *be*

   • with a description (adjective):

   Disneyland is *big.*
   I'm *fine.*
   You're *tired.*
   My daughter is *excited* about Disneyland.

   NOTE: Some words that end in *-ed* are adjectives: *tired, married, worried, interested, bored, excited.*

   • with a noun, to classify or define the subject:

   Disneyland is *a park.*
   California is *a state.*
   Arizona and Texas are *states.*

   • with a location (a prepositional phrase):

   Los Angeles is *in California.*
   I'm *in the classroom.*
   Dallas and El Paso are *in Texas.*

   • with a place of origin:

   Where is your husband *from?*
   He's *from Guatemala.*

   • with age:

   My daughter is *ten years old.* She is *ten.*

   NOT: She is ten years.
   NOT: She has ten years.

   • with physical states. (These words are adjectives in English.)

   She's *hungry.*
   I'm *tired.*
   They're *afraid.*

   NOT: I have hungry.

   • with an indefinite subject introduced by *there.* (See Lesson Five for more about *there.*)

   There are many people at Disneyland.
   There's a picture on the postcard.

   • with time and weather. Use *it* to introduce statements of time and weather.

   When it's *six o'clock* in Los Angeles, it's *nine o'clock* in New York.
   It's *warm* in Los Angeles.

EXERCISE 1 Find and correct the mistakes with *be.* Not every sentence has a mistake. If the sentence is correct, write *C.*

> EXAMPLES: Adults X̶ happy at Disneyland. *(are)*
>
> Disneyland is very crowded.   *C*

1. We're tired. Is very late.

2. It's ten o'clock. My daughter in bed now.

3. My daughter has 10 years.

4. Linda is 35 years.

5. Linda in California now.

6. I have hungry.

7. The weather's nice. Is sunny and warm.

8. She is excited about her trip to California.

9. Los Angeles's in California.

1.2   Negative Statements and Contractions with *Be*

Study these negative contractions with *be*.

I'm not	*	There's not	There isn't
You're not	You aren't	We're not	We aren't
He's not	He isn't	They're not	They aren't
She's not	She isn't	Linda's not	Linda isn't
It's not	It isn't		

*NOTE: There is only one negative contraction for *I am not.*

Compare affirmative and negative statements.

> Linda *is* in California.
> She *isn't* in San Francisco. She*'s not* in San Diego.
>
> They*'re* on vacation.
> They *aren't* at home. They*'re not* at work.
>
> I*'m* happy.
> I*'m not* bored.

1.3   Questions and Short Answers with *Be*

Compare a statement, questions, and a short answer that use *be:*

Wh- Word	*Be*	Subject	*Be*	Complement	Short Answer
		Linda	is	in California.	
	Is	she		in San Diego?	No, she isn't.
Where	is	she?			
Who	is	she		with?	
Why	isn't	she		alone?	

NOTE 1: It is very formal to put the preposition before a question word (With whom is she?). Informally, we put the preposition at the end of the question.

NOTE 2: Most question words can contract with *is*.

> *Where's* Disneyland?
> *What's* your name?

EXCEPTION: *Which is* bigger, Disneyland or Disney World?

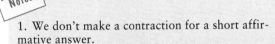

1. We don't make a contraction for a short affirmative answer.

   Is she in California? Yes, *she is.* NOT: Yes, she's.

We can make a contraction with a short negative answer.

   Is she alone? No, *she's not* OR No, *she isn't.*

2. Common questions with *be:*

   What*'s* your name? My name *is* Daniel.
   What time *is* it? It*'s* six-thirty.
   What color *is* the flag? It*'s* red, white, and blue.
   What kind of class *is* this? It*'s* an English class.
   What*'s* this? It*'s* a sharpener.

What*'s* Lisbon? It*'s* a city.
How *are* you? I*'m* fine.
How old *are* you? I*'m* 24 (years old).
How tall *are* you? I*'m* 5'6" tall. OR I*'m* five-six.
Where *are* you from? I*'m* from Guatemala.

EXERCISE 2   Read the following conversation between Alice (who is at Disneyland) and Betty (who is in New York). Find the mistakes and correct them.

B. Hello?

A. Hi. This's Alice.

B. Hi, Alice. How are you? What's new?

A. I'm fine. I amn't at home now. I at Disneyland.

B. What Disneyland? It is a city?

A. No. Is a park in California.

B. What kind of park it is?

A. It's a place to have fun. There a lot of things to do here.

B. Oh, I know. It's a place for children.

A. Well, it's mostly for children, but I happy here too.

B. Are you alone?

A. No, I not. It's my son's birthday. We here for his birthday.

B. How is your son old?

A. He has 13 years now.

B. Your husband with you too?

A. No. Just my son.

B. Why your husband isn't with you?

A. He's in New York. He very busy this week with his work. Anyway, he not

interested in Disneyland.

B. Is ten o'clock in New York. What time it is in California?

A. It's seven in California.

B. How's the weather?

A. Is sunny and warm. Is it warm in New York?

B. No. The weather it's terrible. Is only 50° and rainy. The heat is'nt on in my

apartment, and I very cold now. Your lucky to be in California.

A. Yes, I'm. I'll talk to you next week.

B. Is wonderful to talk to you. I very glad you and your son are happy.

EXERCISE 3   Find a partner from another country, if possible. Interview your partner
with the words given. Tell the class something interesting you learned about your partner
and his country.

> EXAMPLE: **you/a new student**
> **A. Are you a new student?**
> **B. Yes, I am.** OR **No, I'm not. This is my second semester here.**

   1. what country/from
   2. your country/big
   3. what city/from
   4. you/an immigrant
   5. you/happy in the U.S.
   6. what sports/popular in your country
   7. what kind of cars/popular in your country
   8. teachers/strict in your country

9. education/free in your country
10. medical care/free in your country
11. medical care/good in your country
12. gas/cheap in your country
13. schools and businesses/closed on Christmas in your country
14. fast-food[3] restaurants/popular in your country
15. theater tickets/cheap in your country

1.4 The Simple Present Tense—Forms

The simple present has two forms: the base form[4] and the -s form.

I You We They My parents (Plural noun)	work.	He She It My mother (Singular noun)	works.

For a review of the spelling and pronunciation of the -s form, see Appendix A.

READING

Before you read:

1. Does your country have a democratic government? How often is there an election? Do you usually vote?
2. Does your country have a sales tax? How much is it?
3. Is your country divided into states or republics?

Read the following article. Pay special attention to simple present-tense verbs.

ABOUT THE UNITED STATES

The United States **has** a president. The president **lives** in the White House in Washington, D.C. Americans **elect** the president every four years (1996, 2000, 2004, 2008, etc.). The president **leads** the country, but he **doesn't make** the laws. Congress **makes** new laws and sometimes **changes** old laws. Congress **has** two houses: the Senate and the House of Representatives.

---

[3]McDonald's and Burger King are examples of *fast-food* restaurants.

[4]The *base form* can also be called the simple form.

The U.S. **has** 50 states. Each state **sends** two senators to Congress. Each state also **has** representatives in Congress. The number of representatives **depends** on the population of the state. States with a large population, such as New York and California, **have** a large number of representatives. States with a small population, such as Alaska and Wyoming, **have** a small number of representatives. Congress **has** 100 senators (50 times 2) and 435 representatives.

Each state **has** a governor. The governor **lives** in the capital of the state. Each state **has** a congress, also known as the legislature. The congress of each state **makes** the laws of the states. Some laws are different from state to state. For example, the sales tax in California is 7.25%. The sales tax in Hawaii is 4%. Montana and Oregon **don't have** a sales tax at all. The driving age differs from state to state. Some states have a death penalty;[5] others do not. All states now require a person to be at least twenty-one years old to buy or drink alcohol.

All Americans **pay** income tax to the federal government. Most Americans **pay** income tax to the state where they live. However, some states do not need to tax their citizens because they **get** money from other sources. For example, Nevada **gets** a lot of money from gambling. Alaska **gets** money from the oil and gas industry.

Americans like democracy. But no one **likes** to pay taxes. Americans always **complain** about taxes.

• •

Language Notes

1. We use the simple present tense to state a fact.

   The president *lives* in the White House.
   Americans *pay* taxes.
   Congress *makes* the laws.

2. We use the simple present tense to show a regular activity (a habit), a repeated action, or a custom.

   Americans *elect* a president every four years.
   The president sometimes *meets* with foreign leaders.
   Americans *pay* income tax every year.
   Americans always *complain* about taxes.

3. We use the simple present tense to show one's country or city of origin.

   The teacher *comes* from Chicago. I *come* from China.

   • We can also use the verb *be* with place of origin.

   The teacher *is* from Chicago. I'm from China.

   • We do not use *be* and *come* together.

   NOT: I'm come from China.

4. We use the -s form with *everyone, everybody, everything, no one, nobody,* and *nothing.*

   Everyone *knows* the name of the president.
   Nobody *likes* to pay taxes.

---

[5]The *death penalty* means that a criminal can be put to death.

EXERCISE 4   Fill in each blank with the correct form of the verb.

EXAMPLE: The U.S. ____*has*____ 50 states.
(have/has)

1. Americans _____ English.
(speak/speaks)

2. The president _____ in Washington, D.C.
(live/lives)

3. The president and his family _____ in the White House.
(live/lives)

4. Alaska and Hawaii _____ a small population.
(have/has)

5. California _____ a large population.
(have/has)

6. The president _____ for four years.
(serve/serves)

7. Everyone _____ taxes.
(pay/pays)

8. The state of Nevada _____ money from gambling.
(get/gets)

9. We _____ sales tax on the things we buy.
(pay/pays)

10. Sometimes Congress _____ the laws.
(change/changes)

11. A new president usually _____ "I won't raise taxes."
(say/says)

1.5 Affirmative and Negative Statements with the Simple Present Tense

Compare the affirmative and negative statements.

I We You They	work. don't work.
He She It	works. doesn't work.

NOTE: We use the base form in all negative sentences.

EXERCISE 5   Fill in each blank with the negative form of the underlined verb.

EXAMPLES: **The president <u>lives</u> in the White House.**
The vice president *doesn't live* **in the White House.**

Americans <u>vote</u> for president in November.
They *don't vote* **for president in January.**

1. The governor of California <u>lives</u> in Sacramento.

   The governor _____ in Los Angeles.

2. Congress <u>makes</u> the laws.

   The president _____ the laws.

3. England <u>has</u> a royal family.

   The U.S. _____ a royal family.

4. California and New York <u>have</u> a large population.

   Alaska and Wyoming _____ a large population.

5. Americans <u>like</u> democracy.

   They _____ taxes.

6. The number of representatives <u>depends</u> on the population of the state.
   (NOTE: The subject, "number," is a singular noun. It takes a singular verb.)

   The number of senators _____ on the population of the state.

7. The University of Illinois is a state university. It <u>receives</u> money from state taxes.

   The University of Chicago is a private university.

   It _____ money from state taxes.

8. We <u>pay</u> tax when we buy gas.

   We _____ tax when we buy medicine.

9. The president <u>serves</u> for four years.

   He _____ for six years.

royal family

10. The president and his wife <u>live</u> in Washington, D.C.

They _____ in Washington State.

EXERCISE 6   Read each statement. Then write a negative statement using the words in parentheses ( ). Some of these sentences contain the verb *be*.

EXAMPLES: **California has a large population. (Alaska)**

Alaska doesn't have a large population.

Alaska is a big state. (Delaware)

Delaware isn't a big state.

1. The U.S. is a big country. (Japan)

_____

2. Americans like freedom. (taxes)

_____

3. The governor is the leader of the state. (the Senators)

_____

4. The U.S. has a president. (Great Britain)

_____

5. Alaska and Texas are big states. (New Jersey)

_____

6. Washington, D.C., is on the east coast. (Washington state)

_____

7. The people in California pay sales tax. (the people in Alaska)

_____

1.6   Questions with the Simple Present Tense

Compare statements, questions, and short answers that use the simple present tense.

Wh- Word	*Do/Does*	Subject	Verb	Complement	Short Answer
		He	works	on Saturday.	
	Does	he	work	on Sunday?	No, he doesn't.
When	does	he	work?		
Why	doesn't	he	work	on Sunday?	
		They	live	in California.	
	Do	they	live	in Los Angeles?	Yes, they do.
Where	do	they	live?		
Why	don't	they	live	in San Francisco?	

NOTE: We use the base form in questions.[6]

EXERCISE 7   Read each statement. Then write a *yes/no* question about the words in parentheses ( ). Write a short answer.

> **EXAMPLE: Americans like football. (Mexicans) (answer: no)**
>
> *Do Mexicans like football? No, they don't.*

1. California has a large population. (Alaska) (answer: no)

   _____

2. Alaska doesn't have a sales tax. (California) (answer: yes)

   _____

3. England has a royal family. (the U.S.) (answer: no)

   _____

4. U.S. senators work in Washington, D.C. (the president) (answer: yes)

   _____

5. U.S. senators work in Washington, D.C. (U.S. representatives) (answer: yes)

   _____

6. The president doesn't make the laws. (the Congress) (answer: yes)

   _____

---

[6]You will see an exception to this rule in Lesson Four, "Subject Questions."

7. Canada is a big country. (Japan and Korea) (answer: no)

_____

8. Los Angeles and San Francisco are in California. (Miami and Tampa) (answer: no)

_____

9. The Mexican president serves for six years. (the American president) (answer: no)

_____

10. The governor lives in the state capital. (the president) (answer: no)

_____

11. You know about the U.S. (Canada) [Give a true answer about yourself.]

_____

12. Americans speak English. (Canadians) (answer: yes)

_____

EXERCISE 8   Check (✓) the items that describe you. Find a partner. Ask your partner questions with "Do you . . .?" and the words given. Tell the class about an interesting similarity or difference between you and your partner.

EXAMPLES: **Marta and I both speak Spanish.**
            I like cats, but Marta likes dogs.

1. _____ speak Spanish   7. _____ like to wake up early
2. _____ like American movies   8. _____ have a CD player
3. _____ have a car phone   9. _____ like to use computers
4. _____ know the American   10. _____ know a lot about American
         national anthem[7]   history
5. _____ have a pet   11. _____ _____[8]
6. _____ like cats   12. _____ _____

_____

[7]A *national anthem* is the national song of a country.

[8]When you see blank spaces in this book, you can add your own items to the list.

1.7 *Wb-* Questions with a Preposition
•••••••••••

Study the word order of questions that use a preposition:

Preposition	*Wb-* Word	*Do/Does*	Subject	Verb	Preposition
With	whom	do	you	live?	
	Who	do	you	live	with?
On	what floor	does	he	live?	
	What floor	does	he	live	on?
	Where	do	you	come	from?

1. Putting the preposition before a question word is very formal. In conversation, many people put the preposition at the end.

2. We omit *at* in a question about time.
What time does the class begin?
It begins *at* 3 o'clock.

EXERCISE 9   Ask a question using the words given. Then use the words in parentheses ( ) to ask a *wb-* question whenever possible. Another student will answer.

> **EXAMPLE:** **you/eat in the cafeteria (with whom)** OR **(who . . . with)**
> **A. Do you eat in the cafeteria?**
> **B. Yes, I do.**
> **A. Who do you eat with?**   OR   **(With whom do you eat?)**
> **B. I eat with my friends.**

1. you/live alone (with whom) OR (who . . . with)
2. you/go to bed early (what time)
3. the teacher/come to class on time (what time)
4. the teacher/come from this city (where . . . from)
5. you/practice English outside of class (with whom) OR (who . . . with)

1. We use the simple present tense to ask questions about the meaning and spelling of a word.

How do you say "population" in Spanish? "Poblacíon."
What does "population" mean? It means number of people.
How do you spell "population"? P-O-P-U-L-A-T-I-O-N.

2. *Cost* is a verb. We can use the simple present tense to ask questions about cost.

How much *does* a new car *cost*? It *costs* over $10,000.
How much *do* bananas *cost*? They *cost* 59¢ a pound.

EXERCISE 10   Find a partner. Use the words given to ask your partner about his or her country. Report some interesting information to the class.

EXAMPLES: **your country/have/a president**
            A. Does your country have a president?
            B. No, it doesn't. It has a prime minister.

            where/the prime minister/live
            A. Where does the prime minister live?
            B. He lives in the capital.

   1. people in your country/pay tax (how much)
   2. your country/have a president
   3. who/the leader of your country
   4. where/he or she/live
   5. how many states or republics/your country/have
   6. what/the population of your country
   7. what/the capital of your country
   8. you/miss your country (why)
   9. your country/have/a democratic government (what kind of government)
  10. most people/vote in an election (why)
  11. _____

EXERCISE 11   Read each statement. Then write a *wh-* question about the words in parentheses ( ). An answer is not necessary.

EXAMPLE: **Mexico has thirty states. (the U.S.)**

          How many states does the U.S. have?

   1. You spell "government": G-O-V-E-R-N-M-E-N-T. (how/"senator")

      _____

   2. The U.S. doesn't have a royal family. (why)

      _____

   3. The governor lives in the state capital. (where/the president)

      _____

   4. The president lives in Washington, D.C. (where/the governor)

      _____

5. "Population" means number of people. (what/"pollution")

   _____

6. A phone call from a public phone costs ____¢. (how much/a stamp)

   _____

7. California has 52 representatives. (how many/Wyoming)

   _____

8. I don't know the word "election." ("election"/mean)

   _____

9. We say "government" in English and "gobierno" in Spanish. (how/"government" in Italian)

   _____

10. "D.C." means District of Columbia. (what/"L.A.")

   _____

• •

R
E
A   **Before you read:**
D
I   1. Are some American customs strange for you? Which ones?
N   2. When you invite someone to a restaurant in your country, who pays?
G

Read the following letter, from Ludmila in the U.S. to Sophia in Russia. Pay special attention to the frequency words.

LETTER ABOUT AMERICAN CUSTOMS

Dear Sophia,
   I want to tell you about life in the U.S. Some American customs are strange.
   Americans **often** smile when they pass you. Russians don't smile so **often**—only when they are happy about something. Americans think that this smile is pleasant, but for me it isn't sincere. My new American friend Marianne smiles **all the time,** even when she isn't happy. I ask her why, but she says that she doesn't know.
   Another strange thing is this: Americans **often** ask "How are you?" but they don't want an answer. They walk away as soon as they ask this question. Everyone does this. Marianne **usually** asks me this question. If I start to say "I don't feel well," she doesn't hear me and says, "That's nice." Why does she ask this question if she **never** waits for the answer? Russians don't ask this question if they aren't interested in a person's health.

Sometimes Marianne invites me to go to a restaurant. When the check arrives, she **usually** starts to divide the bill in half. Or she says, "Your part is $6.95, and my part is $7.50." In our country, whenever I invite someone to a restaurant, I pay.

Marianne tries to explain American customs to me. She teaches me to behave like an American. If I don't understand something, I ask her, "What does this mean?" and she explains it to me. But life is still strange for me in the U.S.

Please write me soon. How are you? I'm not American. I REALLY want to know the answer.

Your good friend,

Ludmila

1.8 Frequency Words

These are the frequency words in order from the most frequent to the least frequent:

Frequency Word		Example
always	100%	Ludmila always pays when she invites someone to a restaurant.
usually/generally		Marianne usually (generally) divides the bill in half.
often/frequently		Americans often (frequently) ask, "How are you?"
sometimes/occasionally		Marianne sometimes (occasionally) invites me to a restaurant.
rarely/seldom/hardly ever		The people in Russia rarely (seldom) (hardly ever) eat in a restaurant.
never/not ever	0%	Marianne never waits for an answer to her question. She doesn't ever wait for an answer.

EXERCISE 12   Fill in each blank with an appropriate frequency word.

EXAMPLE: **Americans _often_ say, "Have a nice day."**

1. I _____ say, "How are you?" when I meet a friend.

2. I _____ eat in a restaurant.

3. I'm _____ confused about American customs.

4. I _____ smile when I pass someone I know.

5. I _____ shake hands when I get together with a friend.

6. I _____ celebrate my birthday in a restaurant.

7. Americans _____ ask me, "What country are you from?"

8. If I invite a friend to a restaurant, I _____ pay for both of us.

EXERCISE 13   Fill in each blank with an appropriate frequency word. Find a partner from another country, if possible, and compare your answers.

   EXAMPLE: **People in my country** _rarely_ **ask, "How are you?"**

1. Women in my country _____ kiss their friends when they get together.

2. People in my country _____ visit each other without calling first.

3. Men in my country _____ do housework.

4. People in my country _____ work hard.

5. Students in my country _____ stand up when the teacher enters the room.

6. Married women in my country _____ wear a wedding ring.

7. Married men in my country _____ wear a wedding ring.

8. Women in my country _____ wear shorts in the summer.

9. People in my country _____ complain about the political situation.

Language Notes

1. Frequency words come after the verb *be* but before other verbs.

   I'm *often* confused about American customs.

   I *always ask* questions about American customs.

2. The following words can also come at the beginning of a sentence: *usually, generally, often, frequently, sometimes, occasionally.*

   I *usually* eat at home.
   Usually I eat at home.
   We *sometimes* talk about American customs in class.
   Sometimes we talk about American customs in class.
   Americans *often* ask, "How are you?"
   Often Americans ask, "How are you?"

EXERCISE 14   Add a frequency word to each sentence to make a **true** statement about yourself. Find a partner, and tell your partner about your habits.

EXAMPLE: I drink coffee at night.
          I never drink coffee at night.

1. I talk to my neighbors.
2. I pay my rent on time.
3. I'm busy on Saturdays.
4. I receive letters from my friends.
5. I call my family in my country.
6. I travel in the summer.
7. I speak English at home with my family.
8. I eat meat for dinner.

EXERCISE 15   Add a verb (phrase) to make a **true** statement. Share your answers with another student or with the entire class.

EXAMPLE: I/usually

I usually drink coffee in the morning. OR *I'm usually afraid to go out at night.*

1. I/rarely/on Sunday

_____

2. I/usually/on the weekend

_____

3. I/hardly ever

_____

4. I/sometimes/at night

_____

5. people from my country/often

_____

6. people from my country/seldom

_____

7. Americans/sometimes

_____

8. Americans/rarely

   _____

9. women from my country/hardly ever

   _____

10. men from my country/hardly ever

   _____

1.9 Questions with *Ever*

We use *ever* in a *yes/no* question when we want an answer that has a frequency word.

Do/Does	Subject	Ever	Main Verb	Complement	Short Answer
Do	you	ever	eat	in a restaurant?	Yes, I sometimes do.
Does	the teacher	ever	give	surprise tests?	No, he never does.

Be	Subject	Ever	Complement		Short Answer
Are	you	ever	afraid to go out at night?		Yes, I sometimes am.

1. In a short answer the frequency word comes between the subject and the verb.

2. The verb after *never* is affirmative. We do not put two negatives together.

   Do Americans ever bow? No, they *never do.*

3. We can also answer *yes* or *no* with just the frequency word.

   Do you *ever* shake hands when you meet your friends?
   Yes, always.

   Do the students *ever* stand up when the teacher enters the room?
   No, never.

EXERCISE 16   Check (✓) the activities that you usually, often, or always do. Find a partner. Ask questions with "Do you ever . . .?" or "Are you ever . . .?" plus the words given to find out about your partner. Write the frequency of your partner's actions in the blank. Tell the class something interesting you learned about your partner.

EXAMPLE: buy a lottery ticket ___sometimes___

        A. Do you ever buy a lottery ticket?
        B. Yes, I sometimes do.
           Silvia sometimes buys a lottery ticket, but she never wins any money.

1. _____ tell the truth _____

2. _____ sleep with the light on _____

3. _____ watch TV in the morning _____

4. _____ buy a lottery ticket _____

5. _____ smile when you're unhappy _____

6. _____ spend money on foolish things _____

7. _____ drink coffee at night _____

8. _____ afraid to go out at night _____

9. _____ tired while you're in class _____

10. _____ cry at a sad movie _____

11. _____ dream in English _____

12. _____ take off your shoes when you enter your house _____

13. _____ babysit for a member of your family _____

14. _____

1.10 Frequency Expressions and Questions with *How Often*

We ask a question with *how often* when we want to know the frequency of an activity.

How often	Do/Does	Subject	Verb	Complement	Answer
How often	do	you	eat	in a restaurant?	Once a week.
How often	does	your friend	write	to you?	Twice a month.

1. Expressions that show frequency are these:

    every day (week, month, year)
    every other day (week, month, year)
    from time to time OR *once in a while*

Frequency expressions can come at the beginning of a sentence or at the end of a sentence.

   I talk to my friend *every day.*
   Every day I talk to my friend.

   From time to time, I go to the theater.
   I go to the theater *from time to time.*

2. *Whenever* or *when* indicates frequency.
   Whenever I invite someone to a restaurant, I pay.
   Marianne smiles even *when* she's not happy.

EXERCISE 17   Ask a question with "How often do you . . .?" and the words given. Another student will answer.

   EXAMPLE: **eat in a restaurant**
   A. How often do you eat in a restaurant?
   B. I eat in a restaurant once a week.

   1. need to renew your driver's license
   2. shop for groceries
   3. exercise
   4. get a haircut

   5. use your dictionary
   6. water your plants
   7. use public transportation
   8. _____

EXPANSION ACTIVITIES

PROVERBS

1. The following proverbs contain the simple present tense. Discuss the meaning of each proverb. Do you have a similar proverb in your language?

   Haste makes waste.
   Good news travels fast.
   Charity begins at home.

2. The following proverbs contain the verb *be*. Discuss the meaning of each proverb. Do you have a similar proverb in your language?

   Silence is golden.
   Necessity is the mother of invention.
   Beauty is in the eye of the beholder.

OUTSIDE ACTIVITY

Go to the cafeteria. Observe what people are doing. Make note of any behavior that you think is strangs. Talk about your observations with the class.

WRITING   1. Write a letter to a friend telling about your observations about Americans.

2. Write about a famous tourist attraction in your country. Describe this place and tell why it is popular.

EDITING ADVICE

1. Use the -*s* form when the subject is *he, she, it,* or *everyone.*

   My father live*s* in New York.
   Everyone know *s* the answer.

2. Use *doesn't* when the subject is *he, she,* or *it.*

   doesn't
   He ~~don't~~ have a car.

3. Use the base form after *does.*

   He doesn't speak✗ English.
   Where does he live✗?

4. Use *do* or *does* to form the question.

   does
   Where ˄your father work✗

5. Use the correct word order in a question.
   don't you
   Why ~~you don't~~ like your apartment?

6. Don't put an object between *don't* or *doesn't* and the main verb.
   know your friend.
   I don't ~~your friend know.~~

7. Use normal question formation for *spell* and *mean.*
   does "custom" mean?
   What ~~means "custom"~~?
   do you
   How ˄spell "responsible"?

8. Use the correct word order with frequency words.
   sometimes goes
   He goes ~~sometimes~~ to the zoo.
   I never
   ~~Never I~~ eat in a restaurant.
   am never
   I ~~never am~~ late to class.

9. Don't put a frequency phrase between the subject and the verb.

   She ~~all the time~~ talks on the
   all the time
   phone. ˄

10. Don't use *ever* in an affirmative answer.

    Does he ever go to church?
    sometimes
    Yes, ~~ever.~~

SUMMARY OF LESSON ONE

1. Observe the simple present tense with the verb *be*.

    You *are* from California.
    You *are*n't from Massachusetts.
    Are you from Los Angeles? No, I*'m* not.
    Where *are* you from?

    She*'s* late.
    She *is*n't on time.
    Is she here?
    No, she *is*n't.
    Where *is* she?
    Why *is*n't she here?

2. Observe the simple present tense with other verbs.

BASE FORM	-*S* FORM
They *have* a car.	She *speaks* Spanish.
They *don't have* a bike.	She *doesn't speak* Portuguese.
Do they *have* an American car?	*Does* she *speak* English?
Yes, they *do.* OR No, they *don't.*	Yes, she *does.* OR No, she *doesn't.*
What kind of car *do* they *have*?	When *does* she *speak* English?
Why *don't* they *have* a foreign car?	Why *doesn't* she *speak* Portuguese?

3. Frequency words:

    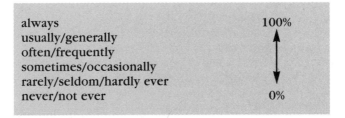

always	100%
usually/generally	
often/frequently	
sometimes/occasionally	
rarely/seldom/hardly ever	
never/not ever	0%

4. Questions with frequency words

    Does he *ever* work at night? Yes, sometimes.
    How often does he work on Saturdays? Once a month.

LESSON ONE TEST/REVIEW

Part 1   Find the mistakes in the following sentences, and correct them. Not every sentence has a mistake. If the sentence is correct, write *C*.

EXAMPLES: **Does your mother speaks Polish?**

Where do they live?   *C*

1. How often does they go shopping?

2. I don't need help.

3. Why you don't answer my question?

4. How many languages speaks your brother?

5. My brother don't like American food.

6. Who does your sister lives with?

7. She doesn't understand your question.

8. She doesn't pizza like.

9. How you spell "occasion"?

10. What means "occasion"?

11. How much costs the textbook?

12. I never am bored in class.

13. I never go out at night.

14. Do you ever rent a video? Yes, often.

15. Does she ever wear jeans? No, ever.

16. Sometimes I don't understand Americans.

17. What often do you get a haircut?

18. She every other day writes a letter.

19. Everyone need love.

Part 2   Fill in each blank with the affirmative form of the verb in parentheses ( ). Then write the negative form of the verb.

EXAMPLE: Ludmila ___*wants*___ to write about strange American customs.
                                (want)

She ___*doesn't want*___ to write about the weather.

1. Marianne _____ Ludmila.
                                (know)
   She _____ Sophia.

2. Americans _____ a lot.
                                (smile)
   Russians _____ a lot.

3. Ludmila _____ in the U.S.
                                (live)
   Sophia _____ in the U.S.

4. Marianne _____ American.
                                (be)
   Ludmila _____ American.

5. You _____ some American customs.
              (understand)
   You _____ all American customs

6. Americans _____ strange for Ludmila.
                                (be)
   Russians _____ strange for Ludmila.

7. I _____ for an answer to "How are you?"
         (wait)
   Americans _____ for an answer.

8. Everyone _____ questions.
                           (ask)
   Ludmila _____ "How are you?" if she's not interested in the answer.

Part 3   Read each statement. Then write a *yes/no* question about the words in parentheses ( ). Write a short answer.

> EXAMPLE: Ludmila lives in the U.S. (Marianne)
>
> _Does Marianne live in the U.S.? Yes, she does._

1. Ludmila speaks Russian. (Sophia) (yes)

   _____

2. Sophia lives in Russia. (Marianne and Ludmila) (no)

   _____

3. Ludmila has an American friend. (Sophia) (no)

   _____

4. The Russian smile is sincere. (the American smile) [Give your own opinion.]

   _____

5. Americans often ask "How are you?" (Russians/ever) (yes/sometimes)

   _____

6. You live in the U.S. (in New York City) [Give a true answer about yourself.]

   _____

7. American customs are strange for Ludmila (for Marianne) (no)

   _____

Part 4   Read each sentence. Then write a *wh-* question about the word in parentheses ( ). An answer is not necessary.

> EXAMPLE: Americans often ask, "How are you?" (why)
>
> _Why do they ask, "How are you?"_

1. You spell "America" A-M-E-R-I-C-A. (Russia)

   _____

2. Ludmila lives in the U.S. (Sophia)

   _____

3. "Pleasant" means nice. ("behave")

   _____

4. You say "How are you?" in English. You say "¿Cómo está Usted?" in Spanish.
   (how/"how are you"/in Russian)

   _____

5. Americans aren't interested in the answer to the question. (why)

   _____

6. Marianne doesn't wait for an answer. (why)

   _____

7. Ludmila writes to Sophia once a week. (Sophia . . . write to Ludmila)

   _____

8. They divide the check in a restaurant. (why)

   _____

9. Ludmila has five Russian friends. (American friends)

   _____

10. You pay for your friends in a restaurant. (why)

    _____

LESSON TWO

GRAMMAR

The Present Continuous
    Tense
The Future Tense

CONTEXT

Observations About
    Americans—A Letter
The Aging Population

Lesson Focus The Present Continuous and Future Tenses

- We use the present continuous tense to talk about an action that is in progress now. We use *am/is/are* + verb *-ing* to form the present continuous tense. Study these sentences:

  We*'re studying* Lesson Two now.   The teacher *is explaining* the grammar now.

- We use the future tense to talk about plans or predictions for the future. We can use *will* or *be going to* + a base form to form the future tense. Study these sentences:

  We *will have* a test soon.   My sister *is going to move* next week.

R
E
A
D
I
N
G

Before you read:

1. Do you like to go to the beach? Why or why not?
2. What kind of summer activities do you enjoy?
3. Do you like to get a suntan? Why or why not?

Read the following letter. Pay special attention to present-continuous tense verbs.

OBSERVATIONS ABOUT AMERICANS—A LETTER

Dear Fatima,

   I'm on my summer break now. I**'m sitting** at the beach now. I**'m watching** Americans and their strange behaviors. I want to describe some of these behaviors to you. I want to know what you think of them.

   Most of the women **are wearing** bathing suits. The men **are looking** at the pretty young women. It looks like the women **are enjoying** the attention. One man **is rubbing** suntan oil onto a woman's back. I'm very shocked by this.

   One man **is playing** Frisbee® with his dog. He**'s throwing** it into the water, and the dog **is running** to catch it. Why **isn't** he **playing** with a friend? Why **is** he **playing** with a dog?

   Some children **are making** a sand castle. The women nearby, probably their mothers, **aren't paying** attention to their children. **They're reading** magazines.

   I**'m sitting** in the shade, but most people **are sitting** in the sun. They**'re trying** to get a suntan. I wonder if they know that the sun is bad for the skin. Why do they want to have dark skin? A lot of people **are listening** to their personal radios or **reading** a book. They **aren't talking** to each other. This doesn't seem like a fun way to be with your friends.

   I**'m learning** a lot about American customs. In fact, I**'m keeping** a diary and **writing** my observations.

   Please write to me soon and let me know what **is happening** back home.

   Your friend,
   Sarah

2.1 The Present Continuous Tense

We use the present continuous tense to talk about an action that is in progress now. Study these forms:

Subject	*Be*	Verb + *-ing*
I	am	studying.
You We They Jim and Sue	are	reading. learning. practicing. writing.
He She It Jim	is	eating. sitting. sleeping. standing.

Compare statements, questions, and short answers using the present continuous tense.

Wh- Word	*Be*	Subject	*Be*	Verb-*ing*	Complement	Short Answer
		Sarah	is	writing	a letter.	
		She	isn't	writing	a composition.	
	Is	she		writing	to her family?	No, she isn't
What	is	she		writing	about?	Her observations.
Why	isn't	she		writing	to her family?	

NOTE: Remember that Americans often put the preposition at the end of the question.

1. When the question is "What . . . doing?" we usually answer with another verb.

   What's Sarah *doing*? She's *writing* a letter.
   What are the men *doing*? They're *looking* at the pretty women.
   What are you *doing*? I'm *studying* verbs.

2. When a subject is doing two or more things, we don't repeat the *be* verb.

   Sarah*'s watching* Americans and *writing* about her impressions.

3. Don't use a contraction for a short *yes* answer.

   Is she writing a letter? Yes, *she is.* (NOT: Yes, she's.)

For a review of the spelling of the *-ing* form of the verb, see Appendix A.

EXERCISE I   Fill in each blank with the correct form of the verb in parentheses ( ). Use the correct spelling.

> EXAMPLE: Sarah _is writing_ a letter.
>   (write)

1. She _____ on the beach.
                    (sit)

2. A man _____ a Frisbee® to a dog.
                       (throw)

3. Why _____ with his dog?
                 (play)

4. Why _____ with his friends?
               (not/play)

5. A man _____ suntan oil on a woman's back.
                      (rub)

6. Some people _____ to their personal radios.
                        (listen)

7. I _____ about American customs.
           (learn)

8. _____ about American customs?
          (you/learn)

9. Where _____?
                (Sarah/sit)

10. Where _____?
              (the children/play)

11. _____ attention to their children? No, they
          (the mothers/pay)

    _____.

12. Why _____ attention to their children?
            (not/the mothers/pay)

Language Notes

We use the present continuous tense for:

1. An action that is in progress now, at this moment.

> A man *is playing* with his dog.
> Some men *are looking* at the pretty young women.
> Sarah*'s writing* about her impressions.

2. A long-term action that is in progress. (It may not be happening at this exact moment.)

> Sarah *is learning* about American customs.
> She*'s keeping* a diary.

3. A description of a temporary state with the following verbs: *sit, stand, wear,* and *sleep.*

> Most of the women *are wearing* bathing suits.
> Sarah*'s sitting* on the beach.

EXERCISE 2   Fill in each blank with an affirmative or negative verb to make a true statement about what is happening now.

EXAMPLES: I _*'m wearing*_ jeans now.
                        (wear)

   The teacher _*isn't writing*_ on the blackboard now.
                           (write)

1. The sun _____ now.
              (shine)
2. It _____ now.
         (rain)
3. I _____ my answers in my book.
        (write)
4. I _____ a pencil to write this exercise.
        (use)
5. We _____ this exercise together.
          (do)
6. The teacher _____ the students with this exercise.
                    (help)
7. The teacher _____ a watch.
                    (wear)
8. I _____ my dictionary now.
        (use)
9. We _____ possessive forms now.
           (practice)
10. I _____ jeans.
         (wear)
11. The teacher _____.
                     (stand)
12. I _____ near the door.
          (sit)

EXERCISE 3   Write three sentences about being a student. Tell what is happening in your life as a student. Share your sentences with the class.

EXAMPLE: I'm taking five courses this semester.
              I'm staying with my sister this semester.
              I'm majoring in math.

You may use these verbs: *learn, study, take courses, stay, live, major, plan.*

1. _____

2. _____

3. _____

EXERCISE 4   Write three sentences to tell which things in your life are changing. Then find a partner and ask your partner if he or she is experiencing the same changes.

> EXAMPLE: **I'm gaining weight. Are you gaining weight?**
> **I'm planning to buy a house. Are you planning to buy a house?**
> **My English pronunciation is improving. Is your pronunciation improving?**

You may use the following verbs: *plan, get (become), learn, grow, gain, lose, improve, think about, change, start.*

1. _____

2. _____

3. _____

EXERCISE 5   Read each statement. Then write a question about the words in parentheses ( ). Write an answer.

> EXAMPLE: **Sarah's writing a letter. (to whom)** OR **(who . . . to)**
>
> *To whom is she writing a letter? (Who is she writing a letter to?)*
>
> *She's writing a letter to her friend.*

1. Sarah is watching Americans. (why)

_____

_____

2. Sarah isn't wearing a bathing suit. (why)

_____

_____

3. Some children are making something. (what)

_____

_____

4. Some men are looking at women. (which women)

_____

_____

5. Sarah is learning about American customs. (how)

_____

_____

6. The mothers aren't paying attention to the children. (why)

_____

_____

7. A dog is running. (why)

_____

_____

8. Sarah isn't sitting in the sun. (why)

_____

_____

2.2 Contrasting the Simple Present and the Present Continuous

Compare the forms of the simple present and the present continuous.

Simple Present	Present Continuous
She sometimes wears a dress.	She's wearing sunglasses now.
She doesn't wear shorts.	She isn't wearing shoes.
Does she ever wear a bathing suit?	Is she wearing a T-shirt?
No, she doesn't.	No, she isn't.
How often does she wear a dress?	What is she wearing?
Why doesn't she ever wear a bathing suit?	Why isn't she wearing shoes?

1. We use the simple present tense for a general truth, a habitual activity, or a custom.

> The president *lives* in the White House. (general truth)
> I usually *study* in the library. (habitual activity)
> Americans often *say*, "Have a nice day." (custom)

2. We use the present continuous tense for an action that is in progress only at this moment, or for a longer action that is in progress at this general time.

> Sarah *is sitting* in the shade now.
> She*'s writing* a letter to a friend.
> She*'s learning* a lot about American customs.

3. *Live* in the simple present shows a person's home. In the present continuous, it shows a temporary, short-term residence.

> Sarah's family *lives* in Iran.
> Sarah *is living* in a dorm this semester.

4. "What do you do (for a living)?" asks about a job. "What are you doing?" asks about an activity now.

> What does she do for a living?
> She's a nurse.
> What is she doing?
> She's waiting for the bus.

EXERCISE 6   The following statements of fact or custom use the simple present tense. Take out the frequency word to tell if these things are happening now to the subject in parentheses ( ). Use the present continuous tense.

> EXAMPLE: **Americans never study the difference between tenses. (we)**
> **We're studying the difference between tenses (now).**

1. Americans often wear blue jeans. (I)
2. American men sometimes wear an earring. [Use the name of a man in this class.]
3. Americans rarely stand in class to answer the teacher's questions. (I)
4. Americans sometimes make a mistake with English grammar. (I)
5. Americans often wear running shoes. (my teacher)
6. American students sometimes study a foreign language. (I)
7. American teachers sometimes sit behind the desk. (my teacher)
8. American students sometimes write in their textbooks. (I)

EXERCISE 7   Read the following statements of fact or custom. Take out the frequency word to write a question about now. Write a short answer.

> EXAMPLE: **The teacher usually corrects the homework.**
>
> *Is the teacher correcting the homework now? No, he isn't.*

1. The teacher often gives tests.

2. The students sometimes ask questions.

_____

3. You sometimes use your dictionary.

_____

4. The teacher often explains the grammar.

_____

5. You usually listen to the teacher.

_____

6. The teacher often uses the blackboard.

_____

7. You sometimes write the answers in your book.

_____

8. The students sometimes make mistakes.

_____

9. The teacher sometimes stands in class.

_____

10. You sometimes use a pencil.

_____

2.3 Nonaction Verbs

We do not usually use the present continuous tense with some verbs. These are called *nonaction* verbs. They describe a state or condition, not an action. We use the simple present tense, even when we talk about now.

Nonaction Verbs				
believe	hear	matter	prefer	think
care	know	mean	remember	understand
cost	like	need	see	want
have	love	own	seem	

1. Compare action and nonaction verbs.

Sarah *is watching* Americans on the beach.   She *sees* some strange behaviors.
She's *learning* about American customs.   She *knows* that American customs are different.
We *are listening* to the teacher now.   We *hear* people outside in the hall.

2. Some verbs can be action verbs (simple tense or continuous tense) or nonaction verbs (simple tense only), depending on their meaning. Study *have* and *think* and the sense perception verbs:

Have

Action	Nonaction

In these idiomatic expressions:
  have difficulty
  have problems/trouble
  have a good/bad/hard time
  have a party
  have breakfast/lunch/dinner
    (have = eat)
  have coffee/a soda/water
    (have = drink)
  have a baby
	For possession:
	  I have a car.
	  She has a bike.
	With an illness:
	  have a backache
	  have a cold
	  have a sore throat
	  have a fever
	  have a stomachache
	  have a toothache
	  have the flu

EXAMPLE: He's having a problem with his car now.	EXAMPLE: He has a fever now.

Think

Action	Nonaction
To think about something.	To believe, to have an opinion.

EXAMPLE: Sarah *is thinking*
  about her friend now.
	EXAMPLE: Sarah *thinks*
	  (that) many American
	  behaviors are strange. (This
	  is her opinion.)

Sense Perception Verbs
look, sound, taste, feel, smell

Action	Nonaction

When these verbs describe an
  action, they are action verbs.
	When these verbs describe a state,
	  they are nonaction verbs.

EXAMPLES:
Sarah *is looking* at women in
  bathing suits.
He *is smelling* the milk.
	EXAMPLES:
	Women in bathing suits *look*
	  strange to Sarah.
	The milk *smells* bad.

EXERCISE 8   Fill in each blank with the simple present or the present continuous form of the verb in parentheses ( ).

EXAMPLES: Most of the women on the beach _____*are wearing*_____ bathing suits.
                        (wear)

Sarah never _____*wears*_____ a bathing suit.
                     (wear)

1. Sarah _____ on the beach now.
           (sit)

2. She usually _____ in the shade because she _____
                    (sit)   (not/like)
   the sun. She _____ the sun is bad for the skin.
                    (think)

3. Sarah _____ much about American customs.
         (not/know)

4. Two people on the beach _____ books. They _____
                                  (read)   (not/talk)
   to each other.

5. Sarah sometimes _____ a book at the beach, but now she
                          (read)
   _____ a letter.
        (write)

6. Two men _____ to a radio. Other people _____ the
              (listen)   (hear)
   loud music, but the men _____.
                                 (not/care)

7. Sarah _____ to describe American customs to her friend.
           (want)

8. Her friend _____ in the U.S.
                  (not/live)

9. Sarah _____ some American customs. She _____ that
           (not/like)   (think)
   women _____ to cover their bodies.
              (need)

10. Men often _____ at pretty women.
                    (look)

11. Some men on the beach _____ women in bathing suits now.
                                 (look)

12. These women _____ strange to Sarah.
                       (look)

2.4 Questions with the Simple Present and the Present Continuous

Compare statements and questions that use the simple present tense.

Wh- Word	*Do/Does/Did*	Subject	Verb	Complement
		She	watches	TV.
When	does	she	watch	TV?
		My parents	speak	English.
What language	do	your parents	speak?	
		Your sister	lives	with someone.
With whom	does	she	live?	
Who	does	she	live	with?
		You	don't like	her.
Why	don't	you	like	her?

Compare statements and questions that use the present continuous tense.

Wh- Word	*Be*	Subject	*Be*	Main Verb	Complement
		She	is	sitting.	
Where	is	she		sitting?	
		You	aren't	listening	to the music.
Why	aren't	you		listening	to the music?

EXERCISE 9   Use the words in parentheses ( ) to write a question. An answer is not necessary.

EXAMPLES: **Sarah is watching Americans. (why)**

Why is she watching Americans?

She wants to describe American behavior. (to whom)

To whom does she want to explain American behavior?

1. She likes to sit on the beach. (when)

_____

2. She doesn't like to sit in the sun. (why)

_____

3. She's very shocked. (why)

_____

4. A man is playing Frisbee®. (with whom) OR (who . . . with)

_____

5. The people on the beach seem strange to Sarah. (why)

_____

6. Many women are wearing bathing suits. (what/Sarah/wear)

_____

7. The sun is bad for the skin. (why)

_____

8. Children are playing. (where)

_____

EXERCISE 10   This is a phone conversation between two friends, Patty (P) and Linda (L). Fill in the blanks with the missing words. Use the simple present or the present continuous tense.

P. Hello?

L. Hi, Patty. This is Linda.

P. Hi, Linda. What _____*are you doing*_____ now?
        (you/do)

L. Not much. _____ to meet for coffee?
                (1 you/want)

P. I can't. I _____. I _____ dinner in the oven now,
            (2 cook)   (3 have)
    and I _____ for it to be finished. What _____ ?
            (4 wait)   (5 you/do)

L. I _____ for a test. But I _____ to take a break now.
        (6 study)   (7 want)
    Besides, I _____ to talk to someone. I usually
                (8 need)
    _____ to my roommate when I _____ a problem,
        (9 talk)   (10 have)
    but she _____ some friends in New York now.
                (11 visit)

P. We can talk while I _____ dinner. It _____ like
                    (12 prepare)   (13 sound)

    something serious _____.
                         (14 happen)

L. My boyfriend and I _____ to get married.
                        (15 plan)

P. That's wonderful! Congratulations!

L. There's one small problem. My parents _____ the idea.
                               (16 not/like)

P. They don't? Why not?

L. Well, as you know, I'm a Christian. And he's a Muslim.

P. That _____.
        (17 not/matter)

L. It _____ to my family. And to his parents too. We
     (18 matter)

    _____ about getting married without telling our parents.
    (19 think)

P. I _____ that's such a good idea.
    (20 not/think)

L. I _____ what else to do.
    (21 not/know)

P. I'll call you later and we can talk more about it. I _____ my
                        (22 hear)

    husband coming in the door, and dinner is almost ready.

L. Thanks for listening. Talk to you later.

• •

R
E
A
D
I
N
G

Before you read:

1. Who is the oldest member of your family? With whom does this person live?
2. What kind of benefits do elderly people in your country get? Do they get a pension? Do they get free medical care?

Read the following article. Pay special attention to the future-tense verbs.

THE AGING POPULATION

The population of the U.S. is aging. People are living longer than ever before. By the middle of the twenty-first century, 76 million Americans **will be** 65 or older, and 13.3 million **will be** over 85. Experts believe that people **will live** longer than they do today. But this doesn't mean they **are going to stay** healthy. The government is afraid of the cost of health care. It **will need** to spend more money for health care for the elderly. This means that taxes **will go** up to cover the costs.

2.5 The Future Tense—*Will* and *Be Going To*

We can use *will* or *be going to* + base form for the future tense.

Subject	*Will*	(*Not*)	Verb	Complement
People	will		live	longer.
We	will	not	need	help.

Subject	*Be*	(*Not*)	*Going to*	Verb	Complement
People	are		going to	live	longer.
We	are	not	going to	need	help.

Compare statements, questions, and short answers using *will*.

Wh- Word	*Will*	Subject	*Will*	Verb	Complement	Short Answer
		She	will	live	with her daughter.	
		She	won't	live	alone.	
	Will	she		live	with her son?	Yes, she will.[1]
						No, she won't.
Where	will	she		live?		
Why	won't	she		live	with her son?	

Compare statements, questions, and short answers with *be going to*.

Wh- Word	*Be*	Subject	*Be* (*Not*)	*Going to*	Verb	Complement	Short Answer
		She	is	going to	live	with her daughter.	
		She	isn't	going to	live	alone.	
	Is	she		going to	live	with her son?	Yes, she is.
							No, she isn't.
Where	is	she		going to	live?		
Why	isn't	she		going to	live	with her son?	

---

[1]Remember, do not make a contraction for a short *yes* answer.

Language Notes

1. Study the contractions with *will*: *I'll, you'll, he'll, she'll, it'll, we'll.*

2. The contraction for *will not* is *won't.*

3. In informal speech, *going to* before another verb often sounds like "gonna." We don't write "gonna." Listen to your teacher's pronunciation of *going to* in the following sentences.

   When's he going to come back?
      (When's he "gonna" come back?)
   He's going to return in[2] an hour.
      (He's "gonna" return in an hour.)

4. Only *going to* before another verb sounds like "gonna." We don't pronounce "gonna" at the end of a sentence or before a noun.

   Where is he going?
   He's going to the bookstore.

5. We often shorten *going to go* to *going.*

   He's *going to go* to the supermarket.
   He's *going* to the supermarket.

6. Compare the present and future using *there.*

   There *is* a grammar test today.
   Tomorrow there *will be* a reading test.
   There *are* five advanced classes this semester.
   Next semester there *are going to be* only four advanced classes.

EXERCISE 11   Fill in each blank with an appropriate verb in the future tense. Use *will*.

   EXAMPLE: **In the future, people** _will live_____ **longer.**

   1. The population of old people _____.

   2. There _____ more older people by the middle of the twenty-first century.

   3. Where _____ you _____ when you are old?

EXERCISE 12   Fill in the blanks with an appropriate verb in the future tense. Use *be going to.*

   EXAMPLE: _Are_____ **your children** _going to take care of_ **you?**

   1. The cost of health care _____.

   2. People _____ higher taxes.

   3. How old _____ you _____ in the year 2050?

---

[2]We use the preposition *in* with the future tense to mean *after.*

Language Notes

In some cases, we can use either *will* or *be going to*. In other cases, it is better to use only one future form. Study the chart and examples below:

	Will	*Be Going To*	Example
Prediction	✓	✓	People *will live* longer. People *are going to live* longer. By 2050, 13 million people *will be* over 85. By 2050, 13 million people *are going to be* over 85.
Expectation	✓	✓	Taxes *will go* up. Taxes *are going to go* up.
Offer	✓		I can't help you now, but I*'ll help* you tomorrow.
Promise	✓		I promise I*'ll give* you the book next week.
Scheduled Event	✓		The movie *will begin* at 8 o'clock.
Plan		✓	My grandfather *is going to move* to Florida. I*'m going to return* to my country next year.

We sometimes use the present continuous tense with a future meaning. We can do this with planned events in the near future. We often use the present continuous tense for a future meaning with verbs of motion.

My grandmother *is moving* into a retirement home on Friday. = She*'s going to move* into a retirement home on Friday.
I*'m helping* her with her move on Friday. = I*'m going to help* her move on Friday.

EXERCISE 13   A foreign student (F) is talking to an American (A) about getting old. Fill in each blank with the correct form of the verb to complete this conversation.

F. How's your grandfather?

A. He's OK. I <u>*'m going to visit*</u> him in his retirement home tomorrow.
                        (visit)

F. How's he doing?

A. He's in great health. Next week he _____ to Hawaii to play golf.
                                              (1 go)

F. How old is he?

A. He _____ 78 next month. Did I tell you? In June, he
           (2 be)

_____ married to a widow he met in the retirement home.
    (3 get)

F. That seems so strange to me. Why _____ that?
                                         (4 he/do)

A. Why not? They like each other, and they want to be together.

F. What _____ when he's no longer able to take care of himself.
              (5 you/do)

A. We never think about it. He's in such great health that we think he

    _____ healthy forever. I think he _____ us all.
              (6 be)   (7 outlive³)

F. But he _____ help as he gets older.
              (8 probably/need)

A. We _____ that bridge when we come to it.⁴ Does your family
              (9 cross)

    have plans for your grandparents as they get older?

F. They _____ with us. In my country, parents always live with the
              (10 live)

    oldest son. My father is the oldest of his sisters and brothers. In our country,
    it's an honor to take care of our parents.

A. I suppose I _____ life in your country. We value
                    (11 never/understand)

    independence in the U.S.

F. When _____ life in the U.S.? We value family.
              (12 I/understand)

2.6   Future Tense + *Time/If* Clause

Notice the verb tenses in the following future sentences:

Time Clause (simple present)	Main Clause (future)
When my parents *are* old,	I'*ll take* care of them.

If Clause (simple present)	Main Clause (future)
If they *need help,*	I'*ll help* them.

---

³To *outlive* means to live longer than other people.

⁴This expression means *We'll worry about that problem when the problem happens, and not before.*

Main Clause (future)	Time Clause (present)
I'*ll cross* that bridge	when I *come* to it.

Main Clause (future)	*If* Clause (present)
I'*m going to leave* early	if the teacher *permits* me.

The sentences in the boxes have two clauses. We use the future tense only in the main clause; we use the simple present tense in the time clause/*if* clause.

EXERCISE 14 Think about a specific time in your near future (when you graduate, when you get married, when you have children, when you find a job, when you return to your country, when you are old). Write three sentences to tell what will happen at that time. Find a partner who is close to your age. Compare your answers to your partner's answers.

EXAMPLE: *When I have children, I won't have as much free time as I do now.*

When I have children, I'll have a lot more responsibilities.

When I have children, my parents will be very happy.

1. _____

2. _____

3. _____

EXERCISE 15 Do you have questions for the teacher about this semester, next semester, his or her life in general? Write three questions to ask the teacher about the near or distant future.

EXAMPLE: *What time are you leaving today?*

When are you going to give us a test?

Are you going to retire soon?

1. _____

2. _____

3. _____

EXERCISE 16   Check (✓) the activities that you plan to do soon. Find a partner. Ask your partner for information about the items he or she checked off. Then report some interesting information about your partner to the class.

>   EXAMPLE: __✓__ move
>   **When are you going to move?**
>   **Why are you moving?**
>   **Are your friends going to help you?**
>   **Are you going to rent a truck?**
>   **Where are you going to move to?**

1. _____ go to the library

2. _____ visit a friend

3. _____ invite guests to my house

4. _____ buy something new

5. _____ take a vacation

6. _____ celebrate a birthday or holiday

7. _____ go to a concert or sporting event

8. _____ transfer to another college

9. _____ move

10. _____

EXPANSION ACTIVITIES

DISCUSSION   Check (✓) your predictions about the future. Find a partner and discuss your predictions. Give reasons for your beliefs. When do you think these things will happen?

1. _____ People are going to have fewer children than they do today.

2. _____ People will live longer.

3. _____ People will have a healthier life.

4. _____ People are going to be happier.

5. _____ People will be lonelier.

6. _____ The government will raise taxes.

7. _____ Everyone is going to have a computer.

8. _____ There will be a cure for cancer and other serious illnesses.

9. _____ Life is going to be easier.

10. _____ Many countries will have a woman president.

11. _____

SAYINGS   The following sayings contain a future verb. Discuss the meaning of each
                     saying. Do you have a similar saying in your language?

                     Ask me no questions, and I'll tell you no lies.
                     Time will tell.
                     When the cat's away, the mice will play.

OUTSIDE   Give the list in Discussion to an American.   Find out his or her predic-
ACTIVITIES   tions. Report to the class something interesting that the American told
                     you.

EDITING ADVICE

1. Always include *be* in a present continuous tense verb.

   She $\overset{is}{\underset{\wedge}{}}$working now.

2. Don't use the present continuous tense with a nonaction verb.

   I ~~am~~ lik$\overset{e}{}$ing your new car.

3. Don't use *be* with another verb for the future.

   I will ~~be~~ go.

4. Include *be* in a future sentence that has no other verb.

   He will $\overset{be}{\underset{\wedge}{}}$angry.

   There will $\overset{be}{\underset{\wedge}{}}$a party soon.

5. Don't combine *will* and *be going to*.

   He will ~~going to~~ leave.   OR *He's going to leave.*

6. Use the future tense with an offer to help.

   The phone's ringing. I$\overset{\prime ll}{\underset{\wedge}{}}$get it.

7. Don't use the future tense after *when* or *if*.

   When they ~~will~~ go home, they will watch TV.

8. Use a form of *be* with *going to*.

   He $\overset{is}{\underset{\wedge}{}}$going to help me.

SUMMARY OF LESSON TWO AND
COMPARISON OF TENSES

Uses of Tenses

Simple Present Tense	
General truths	Americans *value* independence. The United States *has* 50 states.
Regular activity, habit	I always *drink* coffee in the morning. Sometimes I *study* in the library.
Customs	Americans *eat* turkey on Thanksgiving. People *decorate* a tree for Christmas.
Place of Origin	Linda *comes* from Mexico. Maria *comes* from Guatemala.
In a future statement, in a time clause, or in an *if* clause.	When I *get* home, I'll do my homework. If I *pass* this course, I'll go on to the next level.
With nonaction verbs	She *knows* the answer. I *hear* the music.

Present Continuous (with action verbs only)	
Now	We*'re comparing* verb tenses now. I*'m looking* at page 52 now.
A long action in progress at this general time	Sarah *is learning* about American customs. She*'s keeping* a diary in the U.S.
A plan in the near future	I*'m driving* to California next week. My sister *is going* with me.
A descriptive state	She*'s wearing* shorts. She*'s sitting* on the beach.

Future	
A plan	I*'m going to buy* a new car soon.
An expectation	My English *will get* better. It*'s going to rain* tomorrow.
A prediction	You *will marry* a beautiful woman!
A promise	I promise I*'ll work* harder.
An offer to help	I*'ll help* you move on Saturday.

LESSON TWO TEST/REVIEW

Part 1   Find the mistakes with verbs, and correct them. Not every sentence has a mistake. If the sentence is correct, write *C*.

> EXAMPLES: **You can't move this sofa alone. I'll help you.**   *C*
>
> **Where will you ~~be~~ live when you are old?**

1. He sitting near the door.

2. What will you do after you graduate?

3. I'm going to buy a new car soon.

4. He's listening to the radio. He's hearing the news.

5. She going to leave on Friday.

6. I'll going to watch TV tonight.

7. I going to do my homework when I get home.

8. What you going to do tonight?

9. I'm leaving for New York on Friday.

10. There will a test on Friday.

11. I will be study tonight.

12. If you don't eat dinner, you will hungry later.

13. She won't leave her family.

14. If you need something, let me know. I get it for you.

15. Why won't you tell me about your problem?

16. She's looking at the report. She sees the problem.

Part 2   Mary (M) is talking to her friend Sue (S) on the phone. Fill in each blank with
the correct tense and form. Use the simple present, present continuous, and future.

S. Hi, Mary.

M. Hi, Sue. How are you?

S. Fine. What are you doing?

M. I _____*am packing*_____ now. We _____ next Saturday.
         (pack)   (1 move)

S. Oh, really? Why? You _____ such a lovely apartment now.
                              (2 have)

M. Yes, I know we do. But I _____ a baby in four months, so we
                                   (3 have)

_____ a bigger apartment when the baby _____.
     (4 need)   (5 arrive)

S. But your present apartment _____ an extra bedroom.
                                    (6 have)

M. Yes. But my husband _____ to have an extra room for an office. He
                            (7 always/like)

usually _____ a lot of work home. He _____ a place
           (8 bring)   (9 need)

where he can work without noise.

S. Do you need help with your packing?

M. Not really. Bill and I _____ home this week to finish the packing.
                               (10 stay)

And my mother _____ me now too.
                   (11 help)

S. I _____ over next Saturday to help you move.
       (12 come)

M. We _____ professional movers on Saturday. We don't want to
          (13 use)

bother our friends.

S. It's no bother. I _____ to help.
                         (14 want)

M. Thanks. There probably _____ a few things you can help me with
                                (15 be)

on Saturday. I have to go now. I _____ Bill. He _____
                                      (16 hear)   (17 call)

me. He _____ me to help him in the basement. I _____
           (18 want)   (19 call)

you back later.

S.   You don't have to call me back. I _____ you on Saturday. Bye.
(20 see)

Part 3   Fill in each blank with the negative form of the underlined verb.

EXAMPLE: **Mary is busy. Sue** *isn't* _____ **busy.**

1. Sue <u>is talking</u> to Mary. She _____ to her husband.

2. Mary <u>is going to move</u> to a bigger apartment. She _____
   to a house.

3. Mary's husband <u>needs</u> an extra room. He _____ a big
   room.

4. Sue <u>will go</u> to Mary's house on Saturday. She _____
   tomorrow.

Part 4   Write a *yes/no* question about the words in parentheses ( ). Then write a short
answer based on the above conversation.

EXAMPLE: **Sue is busy. (her husband)**

Is her husband busy? Yes, he is.

1. Sue's husband is helping her pack. (her mother)

   _____

2. Her husband works in an office. (at home)

   _____

3. Her present apartment has an extra room for an office. (for the baby)

   _____

4. Professional movers will move the furniture. (her friends)

   _____

5. Mary is staying home this week. (her husband)

   _____

6. Mary's going to have a baby. (Sue)

   _____

Part 5   Write a *wh-* question about the words in parentheses ( ). An answer is not necessary.

> EXAMPLE: **Mary's packing now. (why)**
>
> *Why is Mary packing?*

1. They're going to move to a bigger apartment. (why)

   _____

2. Her husband needs an extra bedroom. (why)

   _____

3. She doesn't want her friends to help her move. (why)

   _____

4. She's going to have a baby soon. (when)

   _____

5. Bill is calling Mary now. (why)

   _____

6. They'll use professional movers. (when)

   _____

Martin Luther King, Jr.

LESSON THREE

GRAMMAR

The Simple Past Tense
Habitual Past with *Used To*

CONTEXT

Martin Luther King, Junior
Changes in American Life

Lesson Focus **The Simple Past Tense; Habitual Past with** *Used To*

- We use the simple past tense to talk about actions that took place in the past and which are finished, and to describe things which were true in the past, but not in the present. Some verbs are regular in the past tense, and use *-ed* to form the past; other verbs are irregular in the past tense.

  I *studied* German in my country. We *saw* a good movie last night.

- *Used to* + a base form shows habitual past actions.

  I *used to have* a dog. Now I have a cat.

R
E
A
D
I
N
G

Before you read:

1. In your country, is there equality for everyone? Is there one group of people that has a harder life than other groups? Which group? What kind of problems do these people have?
2. In your country, who is or was a leader you admire? Why do you admire this person?

Read the following article. Pay special attention to simple past-tense verbs.

MARTIN LUTHER KING, JUNIOR[1]

Martin Luther King, Jr., **was** a great civil rights leader in the U.S. He **fought** for the right of all people to have political, economic, and social equality.

King, an African American,[2] **was** born in Atlanta, Georgia, in 1929. His father **was** a Baptist[3] minister. King **became** a minister, like his father. After he **got** married to Coretta Scott, he and his family **moved** to Alabama, where he **found** a job in a Baptist church.

In many areas of the South, where King **lived,** there **were** segregation laws that **separated** blacks from whites and **gave** them inferior treatment. For example, black people **had** to sit in the back of a city bus and give up their seats to white people who **wanted** them. In public places, blacks **had** to use separate washrooms and drinking fountains. Black children **went** to separate public schools and **got** a lower quality of education. Many restaurant owners **did** not **permit** black people to eat there.

Even from a young age, King **disliked** segregation laws. In 1955 King **led** a bus strike protesting the treatment of African Americans on city buses. One year later, African Americans **won** the right to sit wherever they **wanted** on the bus.

---

[1]When a father and son have the same name, the father uses *senior* (Sr.) after his name; the son puts *junior* (Jr.) after his name.

[2]*African Americans,* whose ancestors came from Africa as slaves, are sometimes called "blacks."

[3]*Baptist* is one kind of Christian religion.

King **moved** back to Atlanta and **organized** many more peaceful protests. He **was** in jail many times as a result of his activities. In 1963 he **led** a peaceful demonstration in Washington, D.C., where he **gave** an emotional speech to the 250,000 people who **attended** this demonstration. He **said:**

"I have a dream. . . . I have a dream that one day . . . the sons of former slaves and the sons of former slave owners will be able to sit down together at the table of brotherhood. I have a dream that my four little children will one day live in a nation where they will not be judged by the color of their skin, but by the content of their character. . . ."

In 1964 Congress **passed** the Civil Rights Act that officially **gave** equality to all Americans. King **won** the Nobel Peace Prize[4] for his work in creating a more just world.

In 1968 in Memphis, Tennessee, a great tragedy **occurred.** A man **killed** King while he was standing on the balcony of a motel. King **was** only 39 years old. As a result of his assassination, there **were** riots in poor black neighborhoods around the country. This **was** an ironic[5] reaction because King **was** a man who **dedicated** his life to peace and brotherhood.

In 1983 Martin Luther King's birthday (January 15) was designated a national holiday.

3.1 Past of *Be*

1. The past of *be* uses two forms: *was* and *were.*

I He She It	was	in Washington, D.C.
We You They	were	
There	was	a demonstration in Washington.
There	were	many people at the demonstration.

---

[4]This is a prize given once a year for great work in literature, science, and world peace.

[5]Something that is *ironic* is opposite from what you expect.

Compare statements, questions, and short answers using *be*.

Wh- Word	*Be*	Subject	*Be*	Complement	Short Answer
		King	was	a minister.	
		He	wasn't	a lawyer.	
	Was	he		a Baptist minister?	Yes, he was.
Where	was	he		in 1963?	
Why	wasn't	he		in the South?	

Language Notes

1. We always use a form of *be* with *born*.
   King *was born* in 1929.
   •We never use *be* with *die*.
   He *died* in 1968.

2. We use *be* with adjectives that end in *-ed* (past participles).

   We were *tired*.   They weren't *bored*.
   She was *excited*.   Why were you *worried*?

EXERCISE I   Fill in each blank with the correct word(s).

> EXAMPLE: **Martin Luther King, Junior, __*was*__ a great American.**

1. Martin Luther King, Junior, _____ born in Georgia.

2. He and his father _____ ministers.

3. There _____ a big demonstration in Washington in 1963.

4. How many people _____ at the demonstration in Washington?

5. Why _____ in jail?

6. Where _____ in 1968 when he was killed? He was in Tennessee.

3.2   Simple Past Tense of Regular Verbs

We add *-ed* to the base form to make the simple past tense of regular verbs in affirmative sentences:

Base Form	Past Form
wait	waited
work	worked
enjoy	enjoyed

The past form is the same for all persons:

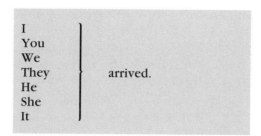

(For a review of the spelling and pronunciation of the *-ed* past form, see Appendix A.)

Use the past form in affirmative statements. Use *did* plus the base form in negatives and questions.[6]

Regular Verb:

Wh- Word	*Did*	Subject	Verb	Complement	Short Answer
		King	liked	equality.	
		He	didn't like	segregation.	
	Did	he	like	peace?	Yes, he did.
Why	did	he	like	equality?	
Why	didn't	he	like	segregation?	

3.3 Simple Past Tense of Irregular Verbs

An irregular verb is a verb that doesn't use *-ed* for the past tense. Here is a list of common irregular verbs, grouped according to the type of change. For an alphabetical list of irregular verbs, see Appendix I.

Verbs with No Change			
bet	fit	put	split
beat	hit	quit	spread
burst	hurt	set	
cost	knit	shut	
cut	let	spit	

---

[6]For an exception to this rule, see Lesson Four, "Questions About the Subject."

Verbs Ending in *-d* That Have *t* for the Past Form		
bend—bent build—built	lend—lent send—sent	spend—spent

Verbs with Vowel Changes			
feel—felt keep—kept leave—left lose—lost	mean—meant* sleep—slept sweep—swept weep—wept	dig—dug hang—hung spin—spun stick—stuck	sting—stung strike—struck swing—swung win—won
awake—awoke break—broke choose—chose freeze—froze	speak—spoke steal—stole wake—woke	begin—began drink—drank forbid—forbade ring—rang shrink—shrank	sing—sang sink—sank spring—sprang swim—swam
bring—brought buy—bought catch—caught	fight—fought teach—taught think—thought	blow—blew draw—drew fly—flew	grow—grew know—knew throw—threw
arise—arose drive—drove ride—rode	rise—rose shine—shone write—wrote	bleed—bled feed—fed flee—fled lead—led	meet—met read—read** speed—sped
sell—sold	tell—told	find—found	wind—wound
mistake—mistook shake—shook	take—took	lay—laid pay—paid	say—said***
swear—swore tear—tore	wear—wore	bite—bit hide—hid	light—lit slide—slid
become—became come—came eat—ate give—gave forgive—forgave lie—lay		fall—fell hold—held run—ran sit—sat see—saw	
forget—forgot get—got	shoot—shot	stand—stood understand—understood	

Miscellaneous Changes	
be—was/were do—did have—had	hear—heard go—went make—made

*There is a change in the vowel sound. *Meant* rhymes with *sent*.
**The past form of *read* is pronounced like the color *red*.
****Said* rhymes with *bed*.

Use the past form in affirmative statements. Use *did* plus the base form in negatives and questions.

Wh- Word	*Did*	Subject	Verb	Complement	Short Answer
		Black children	went	to separate schools.	
		They	didn't go	to school with white children.	
	Did	they	go	to good schools?	No, they didn't.
Where	did	they	go	to school?	
Why	didn't	they	go	to school with white children?	

EXERCISE 2   Fill in each blank with the correct form of the word in parentheses ( ).

EXAMPLE: **Martin Luther King, Junior, __*fought*__ for the rights of all people.**
                                                        (fight)

1. King _____ born in 1929.
                (be)

2. He _____ in 1968.
            (die)

3. He _____ in peace. He _____ in violence.
         (believe)   (not/believe)

4. He _____ equality for everyone. He _____ separation of the
         (want)   (not/want)

   races.

5. He _____ married in 1953.
            (get)

6. In 1963 he _____ a beautiful speech in Washington, D.C.
                    (give)

7. He _____ about his dream for his children.
            (talk)

8. Many people _____ to hear him speak.
                        (go)

9. He _____ an important prize for his work.
            (win)

10. A man _____ and _____ King in Memphis, Tennessee.
              (shoot)   (kill)

EXERCISE 3   Think of a great leader from your country. Write a few sentences about him or her. Find a partner and read your sentences to your partner. Your partner will ask you questions about this person.

_____

_____

_____

EXERCISE 4   A woman wrote a composition about the major events in her life. Fill in each blank with the correct form of the verb in parentheses ( ).

My name is Irina Katz. I ___*was born*___ in 1938 in the former Soviet Union in a
                   (born)

small Ukrainian town. I _____ there until 1941. In 1939 World War II
               (1 live)

_____. In 1941 the German army _____ my country, and my
  (2 start)   (3 invade)

father _____ into the army. My family _____ to leave our city.
      (4 go)   (5 have)

We _____ to Uzbekistan. After the war _____, my family
    (6 go)   (7 end)

_____ to Ukraine, to the city of Lvov. My father _____ back from
  (8 return)   (9 come)

the army as a disabled soldier. In 1989 we _____ permission to leave
                           (10 get)

our country.

There _____ a few circumstances that _____ to our decision
     (11 be)   (12 lead)

to leave our country. First, we _____ that we would have more
                (13 think)

opportunities in the U.S. Second, we _____ to get away from a bad
                  (14 want)

political situation. It _____ not easy to make this decision. My father
          (15 be)

_____ to leave because he _____ sick. However, my married
  (16 not/want)   (17 be)

daughter _____ to the U.S. with her family in 1987. I _____ her
     (18 move)   (19 miss)

very much. In 1988 my father _____, and then we _____ that
             (20 die)   (21 realize)

we _____ no reason to stay. However, it _____ very hard to
    (22 have)   (23 be)

leave behind our way of life, friends, and jobs and go to a place where the future

would be uncertain.

After we _____ Ukraine, we _____ to Vienna, Austria, and
                    (24 leave)   (25 go)
then to Rome, Italy. We _____ permission to come to America, but some
                             (26 get)
of our friends _____ permission.
                 (27 not/receive)

We _____ to Chicago. When I _____ my daughter at the
        (28 come)   (29 see)
airport, we both _____ to cry. I _____ happy to be with my
                    (30 start)   (31 be)
family again.

At first, everything _____ very difficult for me because I
                        (32 be)
_____ English. My children _____ English quickly, and they
(33 not/understand)   (34 learn)
_____ jobs. I _____ to study English at Truman College.
  (35 find)   (36 begin)
Unfortunately, I _____ English when I was in my country. I _____
                   (37 not/study)   (38 study)
German.

Even though it _____ difficult to start a new life, I know we
                   (39 be)
_____ the right decision to come to the U.S.
  (40 make)

EXERCISE 5   Write the negative form of the underlined verb.

EXAMPLE: I <u>lived</u> in a small town as a child. I _*didn't live*_____ in a city.

1. I <u>was</u> born in Ukraine. I _____ in Russia.

2. My father <u>went</u> into the army. My brother _____ into the army.

3. We <u>got</u> permission to leave the country in 1989. We _____ permission to come directly to the U.S.

4. There <u>were</u> a lot of opportunities for our children in the U.S. There

   _____ a lot of opportunities for them in Ukraine.

5. Our oldest daughter <u>moved</u> to the U.S. in 1987. We _____ to the U.S. at that time.

6. My father <u>died</u> in 1988. He _____ during the war.

7. It <u>was</u> hard to leave our country. It _____ easy to leave our friends and jobs behind.

8. We <u>left</u> behind our friends. We _____ a good political situation.

9. We <u>received</u> permission to come to the U.S. Some of our friends

   _____ permission.

10. My children <u>learned</u> English quickly. I _____ English quickly.

11. I <u>studied</u> English in the U.S. Unfortunately, I _____ English in
    Ukraine.

EXERCISE 6 Read each statement. Then write a *yes/no* question about the word in parentheses ( ). Write a short answer.

   EXAMPLE: Irina came to the U.S. (to Los Angeles)

   Did she come to Los Angeles? No, she didn't.

1. Irina was born in 1938. (in Moscow)

   _____

2. She lived in a small town before the war. (after the war)

   _____

3. The German army invaded Poland. (Ukraine)

   _____

4. Her family returned to Ukraine. (to their hometown)

   _____

5. She lived in Lvov until 1989. (her daughter)

   _____

6. It was hard for Irina to leave her family. (her job)

   _____

7. She went to Vienna. (to Rome)

   _____

8. She got permission to come to America. (all her friends)

   _____

9. Her children learned English quickly. (Irina)

   _____

EXERCISE 7   Read each statement. Then write a *wh-* question about the word(s) in parentheses ( ). An answer is not necessary.

> EXAMPLE: **Irina was born in 1938. (where)**
>
> _Where was she born?_

1. She left her town in 1941. (why)

   _____

2. The war began in 1939. (when/the war/end)

   _____

3. The German army invaded her country. (when)

   _____

4. Her family went to Uzbekistan in 1941. (where/after the war)

   _____

5. She wanted to leave her country in the 1980s. (why)

   _____

6. She had several reasons for leaving her country. (how many)

   _____

7. Her father died. (when)

   _____

8. Her future was uncertain in the U.S. (why)

   _____

9. She came to the U.S. in 1989. (when/her daughter)

   _____

10. She saw someone in the Chicago airport. (whom)

    _____

11. She didn't understand English at first. (why)

    _____

EXERCISE 8   Check (✓) the things you did this past week. Find a partner. Get information from your partner about the items checked by using *wh-* questions.

EXAMPLE: ✓ I made a long-distance phone call.

A. I made a long-distance phone call.
B. Who(m) did you call?
A. I called my father in Mexico.
B. How long did you talk?
A. We talked for about 15 minutes.

1. ____ I made a long-distance phone call.
2. ____ I shopped for groceries.
3. ____ I met someone new.
4. ____ I got together with a friend.
5. ____ I wrote a letter.
6. ____ I bought some new clothes.
7. ____ I went to the bank.

8. ____ I read something interesting (a book, an article.)
9. ____ I went to the post office.
10. ____ I did exercises.
11. ____ I got a letter.
12. ____ I went to an interesting place.
13. ____ _____

R
E
A
D
I
N
G

Before you read:

1. In your country, do most women work outside the home? Did your mother work when you were a child?
2. In your country, what is the size of a typical family? Is your family bigger or smaller than the average family?
3. In your country, at what age do people usually get married? (If you're married, at what age did you get married?)

Read the following article. Pay special attention to expressions with *used to*.

CHANGES IN AMERICAN LIFE

American family life is very different from what it was in the past. A typical household **used to** have a father, a mother, and one or two children. Divorce was not very common. Today, however, about 50% of new marriages end in divorce, and many families are headed by single women. The size of the American household dropped from 3.5 people in 1960 to 2.63 people in 1990. People **used to** get married at a younger age than they do now. In 1960 the median marriage age for men was 22.8 and 20.3 for women. In 1990 it rose to 26.3 for men and 24.1 for women. As a result, the number of people living alone is higher than it **used to** be.

Most women **used to** stay home to take care of their children. In 1960 only about 30% of wives worked; in two-parent families today, more than half of wives work. Women generally **used to** work at traditionally "feminine" jobs; they chose to be teachers, nurses, secretaries, and social workers. Women are now entering all professions, not just the traditional ones. However, the average income of women with full-time jobs is about 63% of men's income. In the past, women rarely made more money than their husbands; today 20% of working wives earn more than their husbands.

Most families **used to** live in one place for a long time. Nowadays, the average family moves 14 times, as people relocate for better jobs and housing.

One thing is still the same, though. Wives still complain that they do most of the housework, even when both husband and wife work.

• •

3.4   Habitual Past with *Used To*

Used to + a base form shows a habit or custom that no longer exists.

AFFIRMATIVE: She *used to be* a housewife. Now she's an accountant.
NEGATIVE: She *didn't use to have* a career. Now she has a successful career.
QUESTION: *Did* she *use to stay* home most of the time?

Language Notes

1. *Used to* is not for an action that happened once or a few times.

   When I was a child, my grandfather *used to* read me stories. (This happened many times.)
   When I was a child, my grandfather *bought* me a bicycle. (This happened one time.)

2. We don't pronounce the *d* in *used to*. Therefore, *used to* and *use to* (in negatives and questions) sound the same. Listen to your teacher pronounce these sentences:

   I *used* to live in a small town.
   I didn't *use* to live in a big city.

EXERCISE 9   Tell which of the following you used to do when you were a child.

EXAMPLE: **cry a lot**
         I used to cry a lot.
         OR
         I didn't use to cry a lot.

1. enjoy school
2. obey my parents
3. attend religious school
4. play with dolls
5. play soccer
6. fight with other children
7. draw pictures
8. have a pet
9. tell lies
10. read mystery stories
11. _____
12. _____

EXERCISE 10   Name something. Practice *used to.*

> EXAMPLE: **Name something you used to know when you were in elementary school.**
>
> **I used to know the names of all the presidents (but I don't know them anymore).**

1. Name something you used to do when you were a child.
2. Tell what kind of stories you used to enjoy when you were a child.
3. Name something you used to believe when you were a child.
4. Name something you used to like to eat when you were a child.
5. Tell about some things your parents, grandparents, or teachers used to tell you when you were a child.
6. Tell about some things you used to do when you were in high school.

EXERCISE 11   Read the following composition. We can express some of the underlined verbs in the past tense with *used to.* Which ones?

used to be

When I was a child, I <u>was</u> a tomboy.[7] I <u>was</u> the youngest of three girls. My middle sister and I <u>fought</u> a lot. One time, my father <u>bought</u> me a soccer ball, and I <u>started</u> to play soccer with the boys from next door. My sisters often <u>asked</u> me, "Why don't you play dolls with us?" But I always preferred soccer.

I <u>didn't like</u> school. One time my second-grade teacher <u>hit</u> me, and after that I hated to go to school. I <u>got</u> into fights with the other children. But that <u>changed</u> when I was in the sixth grade. I <u>had</u> a wonderful teacher, and I <u>started</u> to be a good student. At that time, I <u>decided</u> to become a teacher.

EXERCISE 12   Write sentences comparing the way you used to live in your country with the way you live now. Share your sentences with a partner or with the entire class.

> EXAMPLES: *I used to live with my whole family. Now I live alone.*
>
> *I used to work in a restaurant. Now I am a full-time student.*
>
> *I didn't use to speak English at all. Now I speak English pretty well.*

Ideas for sentences:

school   job   hobbies   apartment/house   family life   friends

1. _____

2. _____

----

[7]A *tomboy* is a girl who likes to play like a boy and with boys.

3. _____

4. _____

5. _____

EXPANSION ACTIVITIES

DISCUSSIONS   1. Fill in the blank. Discuss your answers in a small group or with the entire class.

Before I came to the U.S., I used to believe that _____

_____, but now I know it's not true.

2. In a small group or with the entire class, discuss the following:

a. Changes in daily life: Compare how life used to be (20) years ago with how it is now.

b. Fashions: Talk about different styles or fashions in the past.

EXAMPLE: **In the 1960s, men used to wear their hair long.**

WRITING   Choose one of the following topics to write a short composition.

1. Write a paragraph or paragraphs telling about your childhood. Use Exercise 11 as an example.

2. Write a paragraph or paragraphs to tell about changes in your country. Compare how life used to be with how it is now. Use the reading on pages 68–69 as an example.

3. Write a paragraph or paragraphs comparing your life now and your life in your country.

4. If you are married, write a paragraph or paragraphs comparing your life as a married person with your life as a single person.

5. Write about a belief that you used to have that you no longer have. What made you change your mind?

6. Write a short composition about your life. Use the composition in Exercise 4 as your model. Answer the following questions as part of your composition.

a. Where were you born?

b. What was your life like in your country?

c. Why did you decide to leave your country?

d. What happened immediately after you left your country?

e. How was your life in your first few months in the U.S.?

OUTSIDE ACTIVITIES

1. Go to the library. Find information about a world leader who interests you. Tell the class some interesting things this person did.

2. Interview an American. Ask this person to tell you about changes he or she sees in American society. Ask this person to compare how he or she used to live with how he or she lives now. Report some interesting information to the class.

EDITING ADVICE

1. Use *was/were* with *born.*

   was
   He ∧born in Germany.

2. Don't use *was/were* with *die.*

   He ~~was~~ died two years ago.

3. Don't use a past form after *to.*

   leave
   I decided to ~~left~~ early.

   I wanted to go home and watche~~d~~ TV.

4. Don't use *was* or *were* to form a simple past tense.

   went
   He ~~was go~~ home yesterday.

5. Use *there* when a new subject is introduced.

   There w
   ∧~~W~~as a big earthquake in 1906.

6. Use a form of *be* before an adjective.

   were
   They ∧excited about their

   trip to America.

7. Don't use *did* with an adjective. Use *was/were.*

   were
   Why ~~did~~ you afraid?

8. Use the correct word order in a question.

   didn't you
   Why ~~you didn't~~ return?

9. Use *did* + the base form to form a question.

   did
   What kind of car you ∧
   buy
   ~~bought~~?

10. Don't forget the *d* in *used to.*

    She use*d* to live in Miami.

11. Don't add the verb *be* before *used to.*

    I'~~m~~ used to play soccer in my country.

SUMMARY OF LESSON THREE

1. Simple Past Tense

   Be

   > He *was* at work.
   > He *wasn't* at home.
   > *Was* he on time? Yes, he *was.*
   > Where *was* he yesterday?
   > Why *wasn't* he at home?

   Regular Verb

   > She *worked* on Friday.
   > She *didn't work* on Saturday.
   > *Did* she *work* last night?
   > Yes, she *did.*
   > When *did* she *work*?
   > Why *didn't* she *work* on Saturday?

   Irregular Verb

   > He *bought* a new car.
   > He *didn't buy* an American car.
   > *Did* he *buy* a Toyota?
   > Yes, he *did.*
   > Where *did* he *buy* his car?
   > Why *didn't* he *buy* an American car?

2. Habitual Past with *Used To*

   Used to is for habits in the past that no longer exist.

   Most American women *used to* stay home and raise their children. Now at least 50% of American women work.

LESSON THREE TEST/REVIEW

Part 1   Write the past form of the following verbs.

EXAMPLE: **draw** _drew_____

1. eat _____   8. take _____   15. sit _____
2. put _____   9. bring _____   16. go _____
3. give _____   10. talk _____   17. make _____
4. write _____   11. know _____   18. hear _____
5. send _____   12. find _____   19. feel _____
6. listen _____   13. stand _____   20. fall _____
7. read _____   14. leave _____

Part 2   Find the mistakes with past tenses, and correct them. Not every sentence has a mistake. If the sentence is correct, write *C.*

EXAMPLES: She ~~losed~~ *lost* her umbrella.

Did she lose her glove?   *C*

1. My mother borned in Italy.

2. Why you didn't eat breakfast?

3. Did you studied English in your country?

4. When arrived your uncle?

5. Were a lot of people at the airport last night.

6. Why was you late?

7. Did you afraid of the robber?

8. I enjoyed the concert.

9. Last night I read an interesting article.

10. My grandmother was died ten years ago.

11. They decided to drove to New York.

12. I excited about my trip to London last year.

13. What did she do about her problem?

14. Why he wasn't happy?

15. Where you bought your coat?

16. She use to live in Miami.

Part 3   Write a question beginning with the word given. (An answer is not necessary.)

EXAMPLE: **Martin Luther King lived in the South.**

Where *did he live?*

1. King became a minister.

   Why _____

2. King was born in Georgia.

   When _____

3. King didn't like segregation.

   Why _____

4. Black children went to separate schools.

   Why _____

5. Some restaurants didn't permit black people to eat there.

   Why _____

6. King was in jail many times.

   How many times _____

7. King won the Nobel Prize.

   When _____

Part 4   Write two sentences with *used to* comparing your life in your country with your life in the U.S.

    1. _____

    2. _____

Part 5   Which of the following sentences can be expressed with *used to*? Change these sentences. If you can't change the sentence, write *NC* (No Change).

    1. I went to New York one time.

        _____

    2. I lived with my grandparents when I was a child.

        _____

    3. Now I have an American car. Before I had a Japanese car.

        _____

    4. When she was single, she went to a lot of parties.

        _____

    5. We had a picnic last Saturday.

        _____

LESSON FOUR

GRAMMAR

Subjects
Objects
Possessive Forms
Reflexive Pronouns

CONTEXT

An American Wedding
Self-Help

Lesson Focus **Subjects; Objects; Possessive Forms; Reflexive Pronouns**

• The subject comes before the verb. An object can come after the verb.

> S   V   O
> Bob likes Mary.

• We can use pronouns to take the place of subject and object nouns.

> S   V   O   S   V   O
> He likes her because she helps him.

• We can use possessive forms to show ownership or relationship.

> *John's* pencil is in his bag.   *Mine* is in *my* pocket.

• If the subject and the object of a sentence are the same, we use a **reflexive pronoun** for the object. Study these sentences:

> I can help *myself.*   They can feed *themselves.*

veil

bouquet

bride   groom

R
E
A
D
I
N
G

Before you read:

1. Where do people get married in your country?
2. What kind of clothes do the bride and groom wear in your country?
3. At what age do people usually get married in your country?

Read the following article. Pay special attention to object pronouns.

AN AMERICAN WEDDING

At a traditional American wedding, the bride usually wears a white dress. A veil covers her face. She carries a bouquet. When the wedding begins, the groom enters first. Then the bridesmaids and the bride's parents enter. The bride enters last. She enters from the back and walks down the aisle. The bride's father waits for **her,** and the bride walks with

him to the groom's side. During the ceremony, the bride and groom promise to love and respect each other for the rest of their lives. They answer questions about love and respect by saying "I do." Then the groom takes the ring and places **it** on the fourth finger of the bride's left hand. He lifts the veil and kisses **her.** Guests say, "Congratulations!"

There is often a reception, or party, after the ceremony. People eat dinner and drink champagne. Then they dance. The first dance is usually a waltz. The bride and groom usually dance the first dance alone. Then guests join **them.**

Before the bride and groom leave the party, the bride throws her bouquet over her head, and the single women try to catch **it.** It is believed that the woman who catches **it** will be the next one to get married.

When the newlyweds[1] leave the wedding party, friends and relatives sometimes throw rice[2] at **them.**

●●●

4.1 Subject Pronouns and Object Pronouns

Compare the subject pronouns and the object pronouns.

Subject	Object	Examples:		
		S	V	O
I	me	You	love	me.
you	you	I	love	you.
he	him	She	loves	him.
she	her	He	loves	her.
it	it	I	love	it.
we	us	They	love	us.
they	them	We	love	them.

Language Notes

1. We can use an object pronoun directly after the verb.

   The bride wears a veil. The groom lifts *it* to kiss *her.*

2. An object pronoun can follow a preposition.

   The bride walks down the aisle. Her father walks *with her.*

   Friends give gifts to the bride and groom. They throw rice *at them* as they leave the wedding.

3. We use *them* for plural people and things.

   Do you know the bride's parents? Yes, I know *them.*

   Do you like the flowers? Yes, I like *them.*

---

[1]For a short time after they are married, the bride and groom are called *newlyweds.*

[2]The rice is dry and uncooked.

EXERCISE I   Fill in each blank with an object pronoun in place of the underlined word.

EXAMPLE: **The groom doesn't walk down the aisle with the bride.** **Her**

father walks with *her*_____.

1. The bride doesn't enter with the groom. He waits for _____, and

she goes to _____.

2. The groom has a ring. He puts _____ on the bride's hand.

3. The bride wears a veil. The groom lifts _____ to kiss _____.

4. The bride doesn't throw the bouquet to all the women. She throws

_____ to the single women only.

5. The guests don't throw flowers at the bride and groom. They throw

rice at _____.

6. The groom promises to love the bride, and the bride promises to love

_____.

7. The bride and groom receive gifts. They usually open _____ at the reception or at home.

4.2 Possessive Nouns

We can make nouns possessive.

Singular = noun + 's	-S Plural = noun + s'	Irregular Plural = noun + 's
the bride's veil	the bridesmaids' dresses	the men's suits
the groom's tuxedo	the parents' home	the children's clothes
the mother's dress	the guests' gifts	the women's dresses

Examples: The *bride's* dress is white.
The *bridesmaids'* dresses are usually all the same color.
The *women's* dresses are fancy.

1. We can add '_s_ or '_ to names that end in _s_. Both forms are correct.

> Charles's last name is Wilson.
> OR
> Charles' last name is Wilson.

2. We use the possessive form for people and other living things.

> My _brother's_ wife is very nice.
> My _dog's_ name is Pee-Wee.

3. For inanimate objects, we usually use "the _____ of _____."

> _The name of the church_ is Saint Mary's.

4. Don't use an article with a possessive noun.

> WRONG: My brother's _the_ wife is very nice.
> WRONG: _The_ my brother's wife is very nice.
> RIGHT: My brother's wife is very nice.

4.3   Possessive Adjectives

We can use possessive adjectives to show possession. Compare the subject pronouns and the possessive adjectives.

Subject Pronoun	Possessive Adjective	Examples:
I	my	I'm wearing my white dress.
you	your	You're wearing your new dress.
he	his	He's wearing his blue suit.
she	her	She's wearing her new necklace.
it	its	The church has its own reception hall.
we	our	We're attending our cousin's wedding.
they	their	The newlyweds opened their gifts.

1. Be careful with _his_ and _her_.

> _His_ wife is very pretty. (_his_ = the man's)
> _Her_ husband is very handsome. (_her_ = the woman's)

2. Be careful with _his_ and _he's_.

> _He's_ single. _His_ brother is married.

3. Be careful with _its_ and _it's_. They sound the same.

> This college is big. _It's_ a community college.
>   _Its_ library has many books.

4. Be careful with _their_ and _they're_. They sound the same.

> _They're_ married. _Their_ last name is Wilson.

5. Be careful with _your_ and _you're_. They sound the same.

> _You're_ late. _Your_ class started five minutes ago.

6. Don't use an article with a possessive adjective.

> WRONG: My _the_ brother lives in New York.
> WRONG: _The_ my brother lives in New York.
> RIGHT: My brother lives in New York.

7. We can use a possessive adjective and a possessive noun together. We can use two (or more) possessive nouns together.

> My _mother's_ brother lives in Washington, D.C.
> My _sister's_ _husband's_ father is very sick now.

4.4   **Direct and Indirect Objects**

Some sentences have two objects, a direct object (D.O.) and an indirect object (I.O.). For a list of verbs that have two objects, see Appendix G.

Subject	Verb	I.O.	D.O.
I	gave	the newlyweds	a present.
The present	cost	me	$75.

Say and *Tell*

Tell and *say* have the same meaning, but we use them differently. We *say* something. (*Say* has only a direct object.) We *tell* someone something. (*Tell* usually has an indirect object before the direct object.)

He *said* his name.   He *told* me his name.

The teacher *said* the   The teacher *told* us the
    answer.   answer.

1. Uses of *tell*:
   A. We usually follow *tell* with an indirect object.

      The groom told *the bride* his plans.
   B. We use *tell* with an infinitive.

      He told us *to respect* each other.
      They told me *to wait* outside.

C. *Tell* is used in a few expressions without an indirect object:

   tell the truth
   tell a lie
   tell a story
   tell a secret
   tell time
   tell (all) about something

2. Uses of *say*:
   A. We usually use *say* without an indirect object.

      He said his name.
   B. We use *say* with exact quotes.

      The bride and groom *say*, "I do."
      Guests usually *say*, "Congratulations."
   C. We use *say* with *hello* and *goodbye*.

      The newlyweds said *goodbye* to their guests.

EXERCISE 2   Fill in the blanks with the correct form of *say* or *tell*.

      EXAMPLES: **The teacher usually** *says*_____ **hello when he enters the room.**

                  The teacher *told*_____ **the class about the meeting.**

    1. The teacher _____ us her name on the first day of class.

    2. The teacher tries to _____ the students' names correctly.

    3. Don't _____ your classmates the answers during a test.

4. If you know that you're going to be absent, _____ the teacher.

5. Children shouldn't _____ a lie.

6. Some people _____ a prayer before they go to bed.

7. You must _____ the truth in court.

8. I had to _____ goodbye to many friends before I left my country.

9. When you need to interrupt a conversation, you should _____ ,"Excuse me."

10. Some people can't _____ no.

11. He _____ , "Sit down."

12. The teacher _____ us to write a short composition.

EXERCISE 3   Find the mistakes with possessive forms, and correct them. Not every sentence has a mistake. If the sentence is correct, write *C*.

> **Examples: The bride's ~~the~~ parents are very proud.**
> **They are going to get married in their parents' house.   *C***

1. Do you like the bridesmaid's dresses?

2. The groom puts the ring on the brides' left hand.

3. The bride throws his bouquet to the single women.

4. The groom dances with her new wife.

5. When will they open their friends gifts?

6. They're car has a sign that says, "Just married."

7. The groom's friend's often make a party for him before the wedding.

8. Your wedding was very beautiful.

9. She married his best friend's brother.

10. Her husband's mother's friend is wearing a beautiful dress.

11. Do you like your mother-in-law? I don't like mother my husband.

12. The womens' dresses are very elegant.

13. My sister's the wedding will be in March.

14. Your name is different from your husband's name.

4.5 Questions with *Whose*

Whose + a noun asks a question about possession.

> The bride borrowed her wedding dress.
> *Whose dress* did she borrow?
> She borrowed her sister's dress.

Language Notes

1. We often use *whose* to ask about the owner of an object.

> *Whose dictionary* is that? (NOT: Whose is that dictionary?)
> It's the teacher's dictionary.

2. Don't confuse *whose* with *who's*. They sound the same.

> *Who's* that woman?   She's my mother.
> *Whose* flowers are these?   They're the bride's flowers.

EXERCISE 4 Write a question with *whose*. The answer is given.

EXAMPLE: _Whose flowers are these_ ? They're the bride's flowers.

1. _____ ? That's my father's car.

2. _____ ? Those are my brothers' toys.

3. _____ ? I listen to the Beatles' music.

4. _____ ? I'm using my friend's bike.

5. _____ ? I like my mother's cooking.

6. _____ ? The bride borrowed her sister's dress.

4.6   Possessive Pronouns

Compare the subject pronouns, the possessive adjectives, and the possessive pronouns.

Subject Pronoun	Possessive Adjective	Possessive Pronoun
I	my	mine
you	your	yours
he	his	his
she	her	hers
it	its	—
we	our	ours
they	their	theirs
who	whose	whose

Language Notes

1. We can use possessive pronouns to show possession. A noun does not follow a possessive pronoun. Compare possessive adjectives and possessive pronouns.

   You forgot your book today. You can borrow *my book*.
   You forgot your book today. You can borrow *mine*.

My car is old. *Your car* is new.
My car is old. *Yours* is new.

This is my coat. *Whose coat* is that?
This is my coat. *Whose* is that?

2. We can omit the noun after a possessive noun.

   Roberto's wife is in Mexico. *Peter's wife* is here.
   Roberto's wife is in Mexico. *Peter's* is here.

EXERCISE 5   In each sentence below, choose either the possessive pronoun or the possessive adjective.

   EXAMPLE: Can I borrow (your, yours) car?

1. (My, Mine) is in the shop.

2. My sister has a car, but (her, hers) car needs a new battery.

3. My parents have a car. (Their, Theirs) doesn't have air conditioning.

4. My wife and I have a car. (Our, Ours) car is a Chevy.

5. Your car is old. (My, Mine) car is new.

6. My car has a new battery. (Your, Yours) has an old battery.

7. My parents have an American car. (Your, Yours) parents have a Japanese car.

EXERCISE 6   Fill in each blank with *I, I'm, me, my,* or *mine.*

1. _____ a student.

2. _____ live in an apartment near school.

3. _____ apartment is on the first floor.

4. _____ parents often visit _____.

5. They don't have a computer. They use _____.

EXERCISE 7   Fill in each blank with *we, we're, us, our,* or *ours.*

1. _____ classroom is large.

2. _____ study English here.

3. _____ foreign students.

4. The teacher helps _____ learn English.

5. The teacher brings her book, and we bring _____.

EXERCISE 8   Fill in each blank with *you, you're, your,* or *yours.* Pretend you are talking directly to the teacher.

1. _____ the teacher.

2. _____ come from the U.S.

3. My first language is Polish. _____ is English.

4. _____ pronunciation is very good.

5. We see _____ every day.

EXERCISE 9   Fill in each blank with *he, he's, his,* or *him.*

1. I have a brother. _____ name is Paul.

2. _____ married.

3. _____ has four children.

4. My apartment is small. _____ is big.

5. I see _____ the weekends.

EXERCISE 10   Fill in each blank with *she, she's, her,* or *hers.*

1. I have a sister. _____ name is Marilyn.

2. I visit _____ twice a week.

3. _____ lives in a suburb.

4. _____ a teacher. _____ husband is a doctor.

5. My children go to private school. _____ go to public school.

EXERCISE 11   Fill in each blank with *it, it's,* or *its.*

1. A dog is a good pet. _____ a good friend.

2. _____ teeth are sharp.

3. _____ bites when _____ angry.

4. _____ has a good sense of smell.

5. _____ wags _____ tail when _____ happy.

6. Do you like that dog? Yes, I like _____.

EXERCISE 12   Fill in each blank with *they, they're, them, their,* or *theirs.*

1. My parents rent _____ apartment.

2. My apartment is small, but _____ is big.

3. _____ very old now.

4. _____ live in a suburb.

5. I visit _____ on the weekends.

4.7   Questions About the Subject

Wh- questions usually contain the auxiliary verb *do, does,* or *did.* However, when we ask about the subject, we omit the auxiliary verb.

Compare these statements, related questions, and short answers.

Wh- Word	Auxiliary	Subject	Verb	Complement	Short Answer
When	does	The bride she Who	throws throw throws	the bouquet. the bouquet? rice?	The guests do.
Why	did	Some guests they How many guests	gave give gave	money. money? money?	Five guests did.
When	do	Some women they Which women	try try try	to catch the bouquet. to catch the bouquet? to catch the bouquet?	The single women do.

Compare questions that use *who* and *whom.*

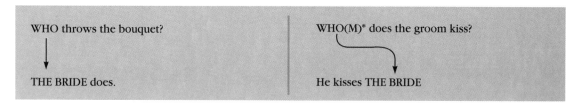

WHO throws the bouquet?

THE BRIDE does.

WHO(M)* does the groom kiss?

He kisses THE BRIDE

*NOTE: *Whom* is the correct way to ask this question. However, many Americans say *who:* Who does the groom kiss?

Compare questions that use *how many.*

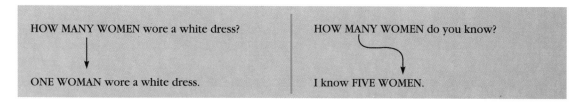

HOW MANY WOMEN wore a white dress?

ONE WOMAN wore a white dress.

HOW MANY WOMEN do you know?

I know FIVE WOMEN.

Compare questions that use *which*.

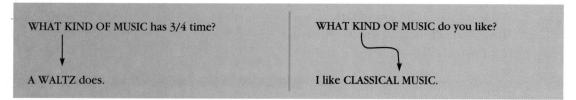

WHICH WOMAN caught the bouquet?

↓

THE BRIDE'S BEST FRIEND caught the bouquet.

WHICH WOMEN did the bride choose for bridesmaids?

She chose HER CLOSE FRIENDS AND RELATIVES.

Compare questions that use *what kind*.

WHAT KIND OF MUSIC has 3/4 time?

↓

A WALTZ does.

WHAT KIND OF MUSIC do you like?

I like CLASSICAL MUSIC.

Compare questions that use *whose*.

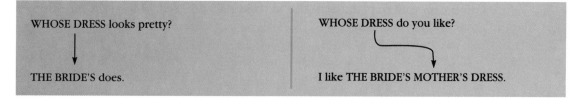

WHOSE DRESS looks pretty?

↓

THE BRIDE'S does.

WHOSE DRESS do you like?

I like THE BRIDE'S MOTHER'S DRESS.

Language Notes

1. We answer a subject question with a subject and *do, does,* or *did.*

Who wears a white dress? The bride *does.*
Who caught the bouquet? The bride's cousin *did.*

2. For the simple present tense, we use the *-s* form of the verb after *who.*

Who *throws* rice? The guests *do.*
How many men *kiss* the bride during the ceremony? One man *does.*

3. *What happens* or *What happened* is a subject question. We usually answer with a different verb.

What happens after the wedding ceremony? There's a dinner.
What happened after your wedding? We went on a honeymoon.[3]

---

[3]The bride and groom often take a trip, or *honeymoon,* after the wedding.

EXERCISE 13   Use the simple present tense of the verb in parentheses ( ) to ask a question about this class. Any student may volunteer an answer.

      EXAMPLES: Who (ride) a bike to school?
                A. Who rides a bike to school?
                B. I do.

                How many students (have) the textbook?
                A. How many students have the textbook?
                B. We all do.

1. Who (explain) the grammar?
2. How many students (speak) Spanish?
3. Who usually (sit) near the door?
4. What usually (happen) after class?
5. Who (want) to repeat this course?
6. Who (need) help with this lesson?
7. _____

EXERCISE 14   Use the simple past tense of the verb in parentheses ( ) to ask a question. Any student may volunteer an answer.

      EXAMPLE: Who (buy) a used textbook?
              A. Who bought a used textbook?
              B. I did.

1. Who (move) last year?
2. Who (find) a job?
3. Who (take) a trip recently?
4. Who (bring) a dictionary to class today?
5. Who (pass) the last test?
6. Which students (come) late today?
7. Which student (arrive) first today?
8. _____

EXERCISE 15   Read each statement. Then write a question about the words in parentheses ( ). No answer is necessary.

EXAMPLE: **Someone leads the bride to the groom. (who)**

Who leads the bride to the groom?

1. Someone drinks champagne. (who)

_____

2. Guests throw rice at the wedding. (who/the bouquet)

_____

3. Two people say "I do." (how many people/"congratulations")

_____

4. The bridesmaids wear matching dresses.[4] (which woman/a white dress)

_____

5. The bride pays for her white dress. (who/the bridesmaids' dresses)

_____

EXERCISE 16   Read each statement. Then write a question about the words in parentheses ( ). Some of the questions are about the subject. Some are not. Write an answer.

EXAMPLES: **The bride wears a white dress. (what/the groom)**

A. _What does the groom wear?_

B. _He wears a tuxedo._

The bride enters last. (who/first)

A. _Who enters first?_

B. _The groom does._

1. Guests throw rice at the bride and groom. (when/throw rice)

A. _____

B. _____

---

[4]*Matching dresses* are all the same style and color.

2. Some women try to catch the bouquet. (which women)

   A. _____

   B. _____

3. The groom puts the ring on the bride's finger. (on which hand) OR (which hand . . . on)

   A. _____

   B. _____

4. The band plays music. (what kind of music)

   A. _____

   B. _____

5. Someone dances with the bride. (who)

   A. _____

   B. _____

6. Guests give presents. (what kind of presents)

   A. _____

   B. _____

7. Some people cry at the wedding. (who)

   A. _____

   B. _____

8. There's a dinner after the ceremony. (what/happen/after the dinner)

   A. _____

   B. _____

EXERCISE 17   In the conversation below, two women are talking about their families. Fill in each blank to complete the question. Some of the questions are about the subject. Some are about the object.

A. How do you have time to work, go to school, and take care of a family?

B. I don't have to do everything myself.

A. Who _____ *helps you* _____?

B. My husband helps me.

A. Who _____?
$\qquad$ (1)

B. Sometimes my husband cooks; sometimes I cook. We take turns.

A. Who _____?
$\qquad$ (2)

B. I usually clean the house.

A. How many _____?
$\qquad$ (3)

B. I have five children.

A. How many _____?
$\qquad$ (4)

B. Three children go to school. The younger ones stay home.

A. How many _____?
$\qquad$ (5)

B. I have one daughter.

A. Do you send them to public school or private school?

B. One of my sons goes to private school.

A. Which _____?
$\qquad$ (6)

B. The oldest does.

A. It's hard to take care of so many children. How do you find the time to go to class?

B. I use a babysitter.

A. I'm looking for a sitter. Who(m) _____.
$\qquad$ (7)

B. I recommend our neighbor, Susan. She's sixteen years old, and she's very good with our children.

A. How many families _____?
                                    (8)

B. I think she works for two families. I'll give you her phone number. If she's not busy, maybe she can work for you too.

A. Thanks. I can use some help.

EXERCISE 18   Fill in each blank with *who, whom, who's,* or *whose.*

1. _____ your English teacher? Cindy Kane is my teacher.

2. _____ do you live with? I live with my sister.

3. _____ has the right answer? I have the right answer.

4. There's no name on this book. _____ is it?

5. _____ parents speak English? My parents do.

EXERCISE 19   Find a partner from another country, if possible. Ask your partner questions about weddings and marriages in his or her country. Tell the class something interesting you learned about your partner's country.

1. Who chooses a husband for a woman?
2. Who pays for the wedding?
3. What happens at the wedding?
4. What happens after the wedding?
5. Do the guests bring gifts to the wedding? What kind of gifts do they give? Where do the bride and groom open the gifts?
6. How many people attend a wedding?
7. Where do people get married?
8. Do people dance at a wedding?
9. Who takes pictures?
10. What color dress does the bride wear?
11. _____
12. _____
13. _____

R
E
A
D
I
N
G
Before you read:

When you have a personal problem, do you prefer to talk about it with a friend, or do you prefer to keep it to yourself?

Read the following article. Pay special attention to reflexive pronouns.

SELF-HELP

Sometimes people have problems that they can't solve by **themselves.** They may go to see a therapist (psychologist, psychiatrist, social worker). Sometimes they join a self-help group. A self-help group is made up of people who share a similar problem. They usually meet once a week and try to help each other deal with their problem. At a typical meeting, each member introduces **himself** or **herself** and has a chance to speak about the problem and how he or she is dealing with it. Members often exchange phone numbers and call each other between meetings to get or give support.

Some groups are for people who are getting divorced. Other groups are for people who are trying to lose weight. Others are for people who have the same illness, such as cancer. There are also groups for family members of people who have an illness. These people may be caretakers of a sick family member.

People in self-help groups want support and understanding from others who share their problem.

4.8   Reflexive Pronouns

If the subject and the object of a sentence are the same, we use a reflexive pronoun for the object.

Subject	Verb	Reflexive Pronoun
I		myself.
You		yourself. (singular)
He		himself.
She	can help	herself.
It		itself.
We		ourselves.
You		yourselves. (plural)
They		themselves.

Compare these sentences.

Is he helping his sister?   Yes. He is helping *her.* (object pronoun)
Whom is he helping now?   He's helping *himself.* (reflexive pronoun)

Language Notes

1. A reflexive pronoun can be a direct object (D.O.), an indirect object (I.O.),[5] or an object of a preposition (O.P.).

> I help *myself*. (D.O.)
> I tell *myself* that I'm okay. (I.O.)
> I talk about *myself*. (O.P.)

2. The expression *(all) by -self* means alone, without any help.

> I can't solve the problem *by myself*. I need help.
> The little girl can tie her shoes *all by herself*.

3. We use reflexive pronouns in a few idiomatic expressions:

> When you are a guest in someone's house and the host wants you to feel comfortable, he may say, "Make *yourself* at home."
> When you are invited to take food at the dinner table, the hostess may say, "Help *yourself*."

4. We can use a reflexive pronoun to emphasize a noun. In this case, it can follow the noun.

> No one in class knows the answer. *The teacher herself* doesn't even know the answer.

EXERCISE 20   Fill in each blank with a reflexive pronoun.

EXAMPLE: I talked about _myself_ at the self-help meeting.

1. She can't solve the problem by _____.

2. They talk about _____ at the meeting.

3. No one can help him. He needs to help _____.

4. You should like _____ more.

5. I promised _____ to lose ten pounds.

6. We often tell _____ that we're too fat.

EXERCISE 21   This is a conversation between two women at lunch. They are discussing weight. Fill in each blank with a reflexive pronoun.

A. Help _____yourself_____ to a piece of cake.

B. I can't. I'm on a diet.

A. But you look so thin.

B. I have to watch _____. I go to an over-eaters group.
                          (1)

A. What goes on at those groups? Do you just talk about food?

---

[5]For more about indirect objects, see Appendix H.

B. Food _____ is not the most important topic. We learn to like
                (2)

   _____ better.
         (3)

A. You mean you don't like _____?
                                   (4)

B. When I'm overweight, I look at _____ and I think I'm ugly. I don't
                                         (5)

   like _____ very much when I'm fat.
             (6)

A. But you're the same person, fat or thin.

B. I know that, but sometimes I don't feel it.

A. Are people in your group successful at losing weight?

B. One woman promised _____ a year ago that she would lose 50
                               (7)

   pounds by January, and she did. We're so proud of her.

A. Every year I tell _____ that I'm going to lose 10 pounds, but it
                         (8)

   never happens. I get very angry at _____.
                                             (9)

B. You have to like_____ whether you're fat or thin. You said so
                         (10)

   _____. You should join our group.
         (11)

A. I don't know if other people can help me. My brother lost 30 pounds, and he

   did it by _____. No one helped him.
                 (12)

B. That's great. But some people can't do it by _____. They need the
                                                        (13)

   help of a group. Why don't you come to our group next Tuesday night?

A. Let me think about it.

EXPANSION ACTIVITIES

PROVERBS   1. The following proverbs contain reflexive pronouns. Discuss the meaning of each proverb. Do you have a similar proverb in your language?

The gods help those that help themselves.
Oh, to see ourselves as others see us.
To thine[6] own self be true. (William Shakespeare)

2. The following proverbs contain possessive forms. Discuss the meaning of each proverb. Do you have a similar proverb in your language?

The way to a man's heart is through his stomach.
A dog's bark is worse than its bite.

DISCUSSIONS   1. In a small group, interview one person who is married. Ask this person questions about his or her wedding.

EXAMPLES: **Where did you get married?**
              How many people did you invite?
              How many people came?
              Where did you go on your honeymoon?

2. According to an American superstition, the bride should wear:

Something old,
Something new,
Something borrowed,
Something blue.

Do you have any superstitions regarding weddings in your country?

3. In a small group or with the entire class, discuss the following:

a. In the U.S., self-help groups can be useful for people who share a problem. Do self-help groups exist in your country? How do people solve their problems?

b. Many Americans are very concerned about weight because American society values thinness. How does the American attitude toward weight compare to attitudes in your country? Are people generally fatter or thinner than Americans?

----

[6]*Thine* is an old form. It means *your*. In modern English, we might say "Be true to yourself."

ACTIVITY   Do you have a video of a wedding in your family? If so, can you bring it to class and tell the class about it? The teacher may have a video of an American wedding to show the class.

WRITING   1. Write about a typical wedding in your country, or describe your own wedding.

2. Write about a problem you once had or have now. Tell what you did (or are doing) to help yourself solve this problem or how others helped you (or are helping you).

SUMMARY OF LESSON FOUR

1. Pronouns and Possessive Forms

Subject Pronoun	Object Pronoun	Possessive Adjective	Possessive Pronoun	Reflexive Pronoun
I	me	my	mine	myself
you	you	your	yours	yourself
he	him	his	his	himself
she	her	her	hers	herself
it	it	its	—	itself
we	us	our	ours	ourselves
you	you	your	yours	yourselves
they	them	their	theirs	themselves
who	whom	whose	whose	—

Examples:

Robert and Lisa are my friends.
They come from Canada.
I like *them.*
My country is small. *Theirs* is big.
Their children are grown.
They live by *themselves.*

Who has a new car?
With *whom* do you live? (INFORMAL:
   Who do you live with?)
Whose book is that?
This is my dictionary. *Whose* is that?

2. Possessive Form of Nouns

Singular Nouns

the boy's name
my father's house
the child's toy
the man's hat
Charles' wife/Charles's wife

Plural Nouns

the boys' names
my parents' house
the children's toys
the men's hats

3. *Say* and *Tell*

He *said* his name.
He *told* me his name.

3. Questions About the Subject

Simple Present:
   Someone knows the answer.
   Who knows the answer?
   How many students know the
      answer?
   Which student knows the answer?
   Which students know the answer?

Simple Past:
   Someone killed Martin Luther
      King, Jr.
   Who killed King?
   Which man killed King?
   What happened to this man?

LESSON FOUR TEST/REVIEW

Part 1   Choose the correct word to complete each sentence.

EXAMPLE: **Do you like** _____ *c* _____ **neighbors?**

a. you   b. you're   c. your   d. yours   e. your's

1. Where do your parents live? _____ live in Colombia.

   a. My   b. Mine   c. Mine's   d. Mines

2. _____ coat is that?

   a. Whose   b. Who's   c. Who   d. Whom

3. _____ is usually white.

   a. The bride's dress   c. The brides' dress
   b. Dress the bride   d. The dress of bride

4. My sister's daughter is 18. _____ son is 16.

   a. His   b. Her   c. Hers   d. Her's

5. What's _____?

   a. the name your son   c. the name your son's
   b. your son's name   d. your the son's name

6. Look at those dogs. Do you see _____?

   a. they   b. its   c. them   d. it's   e. theirs

7. We have your phone number. Do you have _____?

   a. us   b. our   c. ours   d. our's

8. What is _____?

   a. that building name   c. the name of that building
   b. the name that building   d. the name's that building

9. _____

   a. Whose is this sweater?   c. Who's is this sweater?
   b. Whose sweater is this?   d. Who's sweater is this?

10. _____ knows the correct answer?

   a. Who   b. Whom   c. Whose   d. Who's

11. They have my address, but I don't have _____.

   a. their   b. them   c. they're   d. theirs

12. We did it by _____.

   a. self   b. oneself   c. ourself   d. ourselves

13. They can help _____.

   a. theirself   b. theirselves   c. themself   d. themselves

14. I know _____ very well.

   a. myself   b. mineself   c. meself   d. self

15. My teacher speaks Spanish. My _____ teacher doesn't.

   a. husbands   b. husbands'   c. husband's

Part 2   Fill in the blanks with *said* or *told*.

1. She _____, "Excuse me."

2. She _____ them to study.

3. She _____ him the truth.

4. She _____ hello to her neighbor.

5. She _____ the answers.

6. She _____ us about her trip.

7. She _____ an interesting story.

8. She _____ them her name.

Part 3   Complete the question. Some of these questions ask about the subject. Some do not. (The answer is underlined.)

EXAMPLES: What *does the bride wear* _____?

The bride wears a white dress and a veil .

Who *usually cries at the wedding* _____?

 The bride's mother usually cries at the wedding.

1. When _____?

She throws the bouquet <u>at the end of the wedding party</u>.

2. Which women _____?

<u>The single women</u> try to catch the bouquet.

3. On which hand _____?

The groom puts the ring <u>on the bride's left hand</u>.

4. Whom _____?

The groom kisses <u>the bride</u>.

5. Whose _____?

<u>The bride's ring</u> has a diamond.

6. Whose _____?

The bride uses <u>her husband's last name</u>.

7. Who _____?

<u>A professional photographer</u> took pictures at my wedding.

8. Whose _____?

The bride borrowed <u>her sister's dress</u>.

LESSON FIVE

GRAMMAR

Singular and Plural
Count and Noncount Nouns
Quantity

CONTEXT

Facts About Americans
Native Americans
College Tuition

Lesson Focus Singular and Plural; Noncount Nouns; Quantity

- Some nouns have a singular and plural form. These are called count nouns.
  I ate one *apple.* She ate two *apples.*

- Some nouns have no plural form. These are called noncount nouns.
  I ate some *soup.* I drank some *water.*

  We can use *there* to introduce count and noncount nouns.
  There are some apples on the table.
  There's some milk in the refrigerator.

- We can use quantity words with count and noncount nouns.
  I bought *a little* coffee. I bought *a few* bananas.

• •

R
E
A
D
I
N
G

Before you read:

1. What questions do you have about Americans and American life?
2. What surprises you about life in the U.S.?

Read the following facts and statistics about Americans.[1] Pay special attention to plural nouns.

FACTS ABOUT AMERICANS

1. There are about 258 million **people** in the U.S.
2. There are more **women** than **men** in the U.S. (127 million **females** and 121 million **males**).
3. About 12% of **Americans** are African Americans (or **blacks**).
4. The median age in the U.S. is 32.9. Half the population of Americans is older; half is younger.
5. 61% of Americans are **Protestants,** 25% are **Catholics,** and 2% are **Jews.**
6. 14.2% of Americans live below the poverty level.
7. The average household views TV for over seven **hours** a day. **Children** between the **ages** of six and eleven watch TV about 21 hours a week.
8. The most populous **cities** in the U.S. are New York City, Los Angeles, Chicago, Houston, Philadelphia, San Diego, Detroit, Dallas, Phoenix, and San Antonio.
9. The fastest growing group of Americans is the elderly. Since 1960, the number of **people** 85 **years** old and older increased by 232%.
10. There are about 1.9 million **Native Americans** in the U.S. today.

---

[1]These statistics come from the 1990 census.

11. 64% of American **families** own their home. Among Americans between 65 and 69 years old, 81% own a home.
12. 15% of American **teenagers** drop out of high school.[2]

5.1 Singular and Plural Nouns

The chart below shows regular plural endings for nouns. Give the last examples:

Word Ending	Example Noun	Plural Addition	Plural
Vowel	bee banana pie name	+ s	bees bananas _pies_ _____
Consonant	bed card pin month	+ s	beds cards _____ _____
s, ss, sh, ch, x, z	church dish box watch class	+ es	churches dishes boxes _____ _____
Vowel + y	boy day toy monkey	+ s	boys days _____ _____
Consonant + y	lady story party cherry	y + ies	ladies stories _____ _____
Vowel + o	patio radio stereo video	+ s	patios radios _____ _____

_____
[2]*Drop out* of school means to leave before graduating.

Word Ending	Example Noun	Plural Addition	Plural
Consonant + o	mosquito tomato potato hero	+ es	mosquitoes tomatoes _____ _____
(Exceptions: photos, pianos, solos, altos, sopranos, autos, avocados)			
f or fe	knife leaf calf life	*f* + ves	knives leaves _____ _____
(Exceptions: beliefs, chiefs, roofs, cliffs, chefs, sheriffs)			

1. Some singular words end in *-s*: *news, politics, mathematics*.

   The *news* is not good. *Politics* is interesting.

2. Exact numbers use the singular form: *two million, five hundred, six thousand*.

   The U.S. has over *two hundred fifty million* people.

3. Approximate numbers use the plural form: *twenties, thirties, forties*.

   How old is she? She's in her *forties*.

4. Some words use the plural form only: *pajamas, clothes, pants, slacks, (eye) glasses, scissors*.

   My *glasses* are broken. Your *clothes* are dirty.

5. Some nouns have an irregular plural form.

   • In a few cases, the singular and plural form are the same: *fish, sheep, deer*.

   One *sheep* is here. Three *sheep* are there.

   • Some irregular plurals have a vowel change:

   man—men   mouse—mice
   woman—women   tooth—teeth
   foot—feet
   goose—geese

   One *man* speaks French. Three *men* speak German.

   • These two nouns have a different kind of change:

   child—children   person—people[3]

   One *person* is late. Three *people* are absent.

_____

[3]We sometimes say *persons*. *Persons* sounds more formal than *people*.

EXERCISE 1   Write the plural form of each noun.

EXAMPLE: **hour** *hours*

1. American _____   11. butterfly _____

2. family _____   12. man _____

3. leaf _____   13. fish _____

4. child _____   14. wolf _____

5. deer _____   15. donkey _____

6. city _____   16. fox _____

7. language _____   17. country _____

8. cloud _____   18. month _____

9. potato _____   19. goose _____

10. valley _____   20. woman _____

Language Notes

1. We use the plural form to talk about more than one.

   one American   five *Americans*
   a family   ten *families*

2. We can use the plural form with no article for generalizations. We say that something is true of the noun in general.

   Children need love.
   Cows give milk.
   Big *cities* have a lot of crime.

We can also use the singular form with *a* or *an* for generalizations. The meaning is the same.

   A child needs love.
   A cow gives milk.
   A big city has a lot of crime.

3. We use the plural form in the following expression:

   one of the (my, his, etc.) _____
   One of my *friends* lives in Paris.

4. We use a singular noun and verb after *every*.

   Almost every American family *has* a TV.
   Everyone *needs* love and attention.

EXERCISE 2   Find the mistakes with singular and plural nouns, and correct them. In some cases, you need to correct the verb too. Not every sentence has a mistake. If the sentence is correct, write *C*.

> EXAMPLES: Five ~~man~~ *men* left early.
>
> Mathematics ~~are~~ *is* my favorite subject.
>
> I saw two deer in the forest.   *C*

1. She has two childrens.

2. One of her daughter is a doctor.

3. Eleven millions peoples died in the war.

4. The news are on TV at 6 o'clock.

5. His pants is very expensive.

6. Five women in this class speak French.

7. Every students want to pass this course.

8. Math is one of my favorite subject in school.

9. Everyone want to have a good life.

10. Many Americans own a home.

11. Hundreds of people saw the accident.

12. My mother is in her sixties.

· ·

R
E
A
D
I
N
G

Before you read:

1. Who were the original inhabitants of your country?
2. Are there any ethnic groups in your country that have their own language, costumes, food, and traditions?

Read the following article. Pay special attention to count and noncount nouns.

NATIVE AMERICANS

There are about 1.9 million Native **Americans** in the United States today. The Native Americans (sometimes called American **Indians**) are the original **inhabitants** of the United States. There are over 500 **tribes.** Most tribes have a **chief.** Each tribe has its own **language** and **traditions.** However, very few young native Americans speak the language of their **ancestors.**[4]

About one-half of the Indians in the U.S. live on special **land** called **reservations.** This is the land that the U.S. **government** gave to the Indians after taking away their own land. There are 287 reservations in the U.S. Some reservations are very small, having fewer than ten **members** of the tribe. The Navajo reservation, in the Southwest, is the largest with about 100,000 inhabitants.

Some native Americans prefer to live on reservations in order to preserve their traditional way of life. They preserve their **history, music, art, food,** native **costumes,** and appreciation of **nature.** Native American **names** often describe events in nature. Some typical names might be John White Cloud, Mary Running Deer, or William Mountain Snow.

Unemployment and **poverty** have always been problems on reservations. As a result, a lot of Indians left their land to look for **work** in the big **cities.** Lately, some reser-

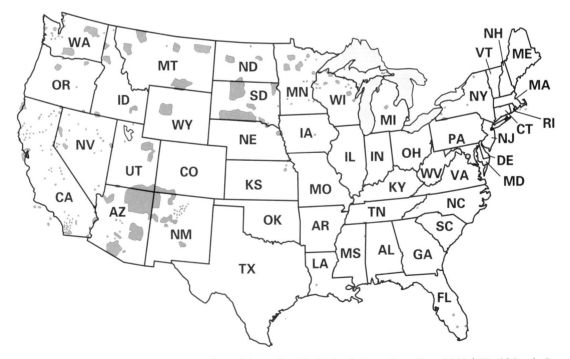

Adapted from the *World Book Encyclopedia.* ©1984 World Book, Inc.

---

[4]*Ancestors* are grandparents, great-grandparents, etc.

vations have been successful in bringing **money** to the reservation by getting into the business of legalized gambling. Some reservations make money with simple bingo **games;** others have large, luxurious **casinos.** A small reservation in Minnesota, with less than 300 members, earned over $500,000 in 1994 from its casino.

• •

5.2   Noncount Nouns
• • • • • • • • • • •

We classify nouns into two groups: count nouns and noncount nouns. A count noun is something we can count. It has a singular form and a plural form (one table—five tables). A noncount noun is something we don't count. It has no plural form. There are several types of noncount nouns.[5]

Group A. Nouns that have no distinct, separate parts. We look at the whole.

milk	wine	bread	electricity
oil	yogurt	meat	lightning
water	pork	butter	thunder
coffee	poultry	paper	cholesterol
tea	soup	air	blood

Group B. Nouns that have parts that are too small or insignificant to count.

rice	hair	sand
sugar	popcorn	corn
salt	snow	grass

Group C. Nouns that are classes or categories of things. The members of the category are not the same.

money or cash (nickels, dimes, dollars)   fruit (cherries, apples, grapes)
food (vegetables, meat, spaghetti)   makeup (lipstick, rouge, eye shadow)
furniture (chairs, tables, beds)   homework (compositions, exercises,
clothing (sweaters, pants, dresses)   reading)
mail (letters, packages, postcards, fliers)   jewelry (necklaces, bracelets, rings)

Group D. Nouns that are abstractions.

love	happiness	nutrition	music	information
life	education	intelligence	art	nature
time	experience	unemployment	work	help
truth	crime	pollution	health	noise
beauty	advice	patience	trouble	energy
luck	knowledge	poverty	fun	

---

[5]Some nouns can be either count or noncount. For a list of these nouns, see Appendix E.

Group E. Subjects of study.

history   grammar   biology
chemistry   geometry   math (mathematics*)

*NOTE: Even though *mathematics* ends with *s*, it is not plural.

Language
Notes

Count and noncount nouns are grammatical terms, but they are not always logical. Rice is very small and is a noncount noun. Beans and peas are also very small but are count nouns.

EXERCISE 3   Go back to the article about Native Americans on pages 110–111. Mark the nouns in the article with *C* for count noun or *NC* for noncount noun.

EXAMPLE: **Native Americans** = *C*
          nature = *NC*

Language
Notes

We can put a number before a count noun, but not before a noncount noun. With a noncount noun, we use a unit of measure, which we can count.

These are some units of measure that we use to count noncount nouns:

a loaf of bread	a piece of meat	an ear of corn
a piece (slice) of bread	a gallon of milk	a head of lettuce
a bottle of wine	a quart of milk	a bar of soap
a glass of wine	a glass of milk	a can of beer
a cup of tea	a piece of fruit	a six-pack of beer
a bowl of soup	a piece of mail	a tube of toothpaste
a can of soup	a piece (or sheet) of paper	a piece of furniture
a roll of film	a piece of advice	a homework assignment
a pound of meat	a piece of chalk	

EXERCISE 4   Fill in each blank with a specific quantity.

EXAMPLE: **I drink** _three glasses of_ **water a day.**

1. You should take _____ film on your vacation.

2. I'm going to buy _____ meat to make dinner for the family.

3. _____ milk is heavy to carry.

4. She drinks _____ coffee every morning.

5. Buy _____ wine for the party.

6. You should eat _____ fruit a day.

5.3 *There* + A Form of *Be*

Use *there* + a form of *be* to introduce a new noun, either count or noncount.

	There	*Be*	Article/ Quantity	Noun	Place/Time
COUNT	There	is	a	reservation	in Wyoming.
	There	are	50	states	in the U.S.
	There	will be	some	rain	tomorrow.
NONCOUNT	There	is	a lot of	unemployment	on the reservation.

Language Notes

1. If two nouns follow *there,* use a singular verb (*is*) if the first noun is singular. Use a plural verb (*are*) if the first noun is plural.

There *is one* Korean student and three Mexican students in this class.
There *are three* Mexican students and one Korean student in this class.

2. In conversation, you will sometimes hear *there's* with plural nouns.

INFORMAL: There*'s* a lot of reservations in California.
FORMAL: There *are* a lot of reservations in California.

3. After we introduce a noun with *there,* we can continue to speak of this noun with a pronoun.

There are over 200 tribes of Native Americans in the U.S. *They* each have their own language.
There is a Navajo reservation in Arizona. *It*'s very big.
There's a Navajo woman in my chemistry class. *She* comes from Arizona.

4. Observe the word order in questions with *there.*

Is there unemployment on some reservations? Yes, there is.
Are there any reservations in California? Yes, there are.
How many Navajo Indians *are there* in Arizona?

EXERCISE 5   Fill in each blank with a time or place.

EXAMPLE: **There was a war** _in my country from 1972 to 1975._

1. There will be a test _____

2. There are a lot of problems _____

3. There's a lot of snow _____

4. There are a lot of people _____

5. There is a lot of crime _____

6. There are a lot of reservations _____

7. There will be a presidential election _____

8. There are a lot of students _____

5.4 Quantities

Study the words that can be used with count and noncount nouns.

Singular Count	Plural Count	Noncount
a tomato	tomatoes	coffee
one tomato	two tomatoes	two cups of coffee
	some tomatoes	some coffee
no tomato	no tomatoes	no coffee
	any tomatoes (with questions and negatives)	any coffee
	a lot of tomatoes	a lot of coffee
	many tomatoes	much coffee (with questions and negatives)
	a few tomatoes	a little coffee
	several tomatoes	
	How many tomatoes?	How much coffee?

Language Notes

Some, Any, A, and _No_

	Singular	Plural Count	Noncount
Affirmative	There's _a_ clock in the kitchen	There are (_some_) windows in the kitchen.	There's (_some_) rice in the kitchen.
Negative	There isn't _a_ clock in the kitchen.	There aren't (_any_) windows in the kitchen.	There isn't (_any_) rice in the kitchen.
	There's _no_ clock in the kitchen.	There are _no_ windows in the kitchen.	There's _no_ rice in the kitchen.
Question	Is there _a_ clock in the kitchen?	Are there (_any_) windows in the kitchen?	Is there (_any_) rice in the kitchen?

1. We use _a_ or _an_ with singular count nouns.[6]

2. We can use _some_ for affirmative statements, with both noncount nouns and plural count nouns. _Some_ can be omitted.

    I have time. I have _some_ time.

3. We can use _any_ for questions and negatives, with both noncount nouns and plural count nouns.[7] _Any_ can be omitted.

4. We can use _no_ with count and noncount nouns. Use an affirmative verb before _no_. Compare:

    There _is no_ time.   There _isn't any_ time.
    There _is no_* answer There _isn't an_ answer to
      to your question.   your question.

*NOTE: Don't use the indefinite article after _no_.

EXERCISE 6   Use _there_ to tell about your hometown. (If you use _no,_ delete the article.) You can add a statement to give more information.

    EXAMPLES: **a mayor**
               There's a mayor in my hometown. He's a young man.

               a subway
               There's no subway in my hometown.

1. a university
2. a subway
3. an English language newspaper
4. an airport
5. a soccer team
6. a river
7. a jail
8. an art museum
9. an English language institute
10. a cemetery
11. _____
12. _____

---

[6]You will sometimes see _any_ with a singular count noun: "Which pen should I use for the test?"
  "You can use any pen." _Any,_ in this case, means whichever you want. It doesn't matter which one.

[7]_Some_ can also be used: "Are there some windows in the room?"

EXERCISE 7   Fill in each blank with *some, any, a, an,* or *no.*

EXAMPLES: I have _some_ money in my pocket.

Do you have _any_ time to help me?

Do you have _a_ new car?

I have _no_ experience as a babysitter.

1. Do you have _____ questions about this exercise?

2. Do you have _____ dictionary with you?

3. Did you have _____ trouble with the homework?

4. If we have _____ extra time, we'll go over the homework.

5. The teacher can't help you now because he has _____ time.

6. I'm confused. I need _____ answer to my question.

7. I have _____ questions about the last lesson. Can you answer them for me?

8. I understand this lesson completely. I have _____ questions.

9. I understand this lesson completely. I don't have _____ questions.

10. I work hard all day and have _____ energy late at night.

EXERCISE 8   Take something from your purse, pocket, book bag, or backpack. Say, "I have _____ with me." Then ask the person next to you if he or she has this. If you're not sure if the item is a count or noncount noun, ask the teacher.

EXAMPLES: I have a comb in my pocket. Do you have a comb in your pocket?

I have some makeup in my purse. Do you have any makeup in your purse?

I have some money from my country in my pocket. Do you have any money from your country?

Language
Notes

A Lot of, Much, Many

Study the use of *a lot of, much,* and *many.*

	Count (plural)	Noncount
Affirmative	He has *many* friends. He has *a lot of* friends.	He has *a lot of* time.
Negative	He doesn't have *many* friends. He doesn't have *a lot of* friends.	He doesn't have *much* time. He doesn't have *a lot of* time.
Question	Does he have *many* friends?	Does he have *much* time?

1. We use *many* with count nouns. We use *much* with noncount nouns. However, we use *much* with questions and negatives only. In affirmative statements, we use *a lot of.*

　Does he have *much* experience with computers?
　Yes. He has *a lot of* experience with IBMs, but he doesn't have *much* experience with Macintosh computers.

2. In conversation, *of* is often pronounced /ə/.

3. When the noun is omitted, we say *a lot,* not *a lot of.*

　Do you get *a lot of* mail?
　No, I don't get *a lot.*

4. In conversation, many people say "lots of" for both noncount and plural count nouns:

　He has *lots of time.* He has *lots of friends.*[8]

EXERCISE 9 Fill in each blank with *much, many,* or *a lot (of).* Avoid *much* in affirmative statements.

EXAMPLES: You don't need <u>*much*</u> **time to do this exercise.**

I have <u>*a lot of (or many)*</u> **friends.**

1. Busy people don't have _____ free time.

2. Was there _____ snow last winter?

3. _____ Americans prefer to live in big cities.

4. There's _____ crime in a big city.

5. There isn't _____ traffic in a small town.

---

[8]Another conversational expression is *plenty of:* "He has plenty of time."

6. There aren't _____ schools in a small town.

7. How _____ coffee do you drink in the morning?

8. I like coffee, but I don't drink _____ because it keeps me awake at night.

9. There are _____ Japanese cars in the U.S.

10. How _____ students in this class come from Korea?

Language Notes

A Few, Several, A Little

1. We use _a few_ or _several_ with count nouns.
   I have _a few questions_.
   I have _several mistakes_ on my composition.

2. We use _a little_ with noncount nouns.
   I need _a little_ help.

EXERCISE 10   Fill in each blank with _a few, several,_ or _a little_.

EXAMPLES: He has _a few_ problems with his car.

He has _a little_ experience as a teacher.

1. Every day we study _____ grammar.

2. We do _____ exercises in class.

3. _____ knowledge can be a dangerous thing.

4. _____ students are absent today.

5. I have _____ cash with me.

6. I have _____ dollars in my pocket.

7. I bought _____ furniture for my apartment.

8. I have _____ chairs in my living room.

9. I had _____ mistakes on my composition.

10. I need _____ help with my composition.

A Few and *(Very) Few, A Little* and *(Very) Little*

1. We can use *few* and *little* without the article *a*. However, the emphasis is on the negative. Compare:

I have *a few* good friends. I'm happy.
I have *few* good friends. I'm lonely.
I have *a little* money. Let's go to the cafeteria and get something to eat.
I have *little* money. I can't buy anything today.

2. To emphasize the negative quantity even more, we often add *very*.

Very few young Native Americans speak the language of their ancestors.
We have *very little* time left today. We won't be able to finish the lesson.

EXERCISE 11   Fill in each blank with *a little, very little, a few,* or *very few*.

EXAMPLES: He has *a little*   extra money. He's going to buy a sandwich.

He has *very little*   extra money. He can't buy anything.

1. I have _____ food in my refrigerator. Let's make dinner at my house.

2. In some countries, people have _____ food, and many people are starving.[9]

3. That worker has _____ experience. He probably can't do that job.

4. That worker has _____ experience. He can probably do that job.

5. I eat _____ meat every day because I want protein in my diet.

6. I want to bake cookies, but I can't because I have _____ sugar in the house.

7. When there is _____ rain, plants can't grow.

8. Tomorrow there may be _____ rain, so you should take an umbrella.

9. Twenty-five years ago, home computers were very rare. _____ people had a home computer.

10. Before I bought my computer, I talked to _____ people about which computer to buy.

11. There are _____ monkeys in the zoo. Let's go to see them.

_____

[9]To *starve* means to suffer or die from not having enough food.

12. There are _____ gray whales in the world. These animals are an endangered species.[10]

13. If you want to study medicine, I can give you a list of _____ good medical schools in the U.S.

14. _____ high schools teach Latin. It is not a very popular language any more.

15. I want to say _____ words about my country. Please listen.

16. My father is a man of _____ words. He rarely talks.

17. English is the main language of _____ countries.

18. Women are still rare as political leaders. _____ countries have a woman president.

EXERCISE 12   Ask a question with *"Are there . . .?"* and the words given about another student's hometown. The other student will answer with an expression of quantity. Practice count nouns.

> EXAMPLE: **museums**
> **A. Are there any museums in your hometown?**
> **B. Yes. There are a lot of (a few, three) museums in my hometown.**
> OR
> **No. There aren't any museums in my hometown.**

1. department stores
2. churches
3. synagogues
4. skyscrapers
5. supermarkets
6. open markets
7. hospitals
8. universities

EXERCISE 13   Ask a question with *"Are there any . . .?"* or *"Are there many . . .?"* and the words given about another student's country. The other student will answer with an expression of quantity. Practice count nouns.

> EXAMPLE: **single mothers**
> **A. Are there many single mothers in your country?**
> **B. There are very few.**

---

[10]An *endangered species* is a type of animal that is becoming more and more rare. The species is in danger of disappearing completely if it is not protected.

1. homeless people
2. working women
3. fast-food restaurants
4. factories

5. American businesses
6. nursing homes
7. rich people
8. _____

EXERCISE 14   Ask a question with *"Is there . . .?"* and the words given about another student's country. The other student will answer with an expression of quantity. Practice noncount nouns.

> EXAMPLE: petroleum/in your country
> A. **Is there much petroleum in your country?**
> B. **Yes. There's a lot of petroleum in my country.**
> OR
> **No. There isn't much petroleum in my country.**
> OR
> **There's very little petroleum in my country.**
> OR
> **There isn't any petroleum in my country.**

In Your Country   In Your Hometown

1. petroleum
2. industry
3. agriculture
4. tourism

5. traffic
6. rain
7. pollution
8. noise

EXERCISE 15   Ask a student a question with *"Do you have . . .?"* and the words given. The other student will answer. Practice both count and noncount nouns.

> EXAMPLES: American friends
> A. **Do you have any American friends?**
> B. **Yes. I have many (or a lot of) American friends.**
> OR
> **No. I don't have many American friends.**
>
> free time
> A. **Do you have a lot of free time?**
> B. **Yes. I have some free time.**
> OR
> **No. I have very little free time.**

1. problems in the U.S.
2. American friends
3. relatives in New York
4. time to relax
5. brothers and sisters (siblings)
6. experience with computers

7. questions about American customs
8. trouble with English pronunciation
9. information about points of interest in this city
10. _____

EXERCISE 16   Fill in each blank with an expression of quantity to make a true statement about your country. Find a partner from another country, if possible, and explain your answers.

EXAMPLE: There's/There isn't _much_ unemployment in my country.

1. There's/There isn't _____ opportunity to make money in my country.

2. There are/There aren't _____ divorced people in my country.

3. There are/There aren't _____ foreigners in my country.

4. There's/There isn't _____ freedom in my country.

5. There are/There aren't _____ American cars in my country.

6. There are/There aren't _____ political problems in my country.

7. There is/There isn't _____ unemployment in my country.

8. There is/There isn't _____ crime in my hometown.

● ●

R
E
A
D
I
N
G

Before you read:

1. Is college tuition expensive in your country? Can most students afford a college education?
2. Can a student get a scholarship or a loan to go to college in your country?

Read the following article. Pay special attention to *too, too much, too many*, and *a lot of.*

COLLEGE[11] TUITION

A college education in the United States costs **a lot of money** these days. College tuition is rising faster than inflation. In 1993 the cost at a public college was $2,256 a year and at a private college, $11,025 a year. **A lot of students** who want to go to college are having difficulty because the tuition is **too high** for them. Students from low-income families might get financial aid. Students from rich families can afford the high tuition. However, students from middle-income families have **too much** money to qualify for

---

[11]Americans often use the words *college* and *university* interchangeably.

financial aid. Middle-income families need to save **a lot of money** for their children's education. Parents often begin to save for their children's education as soon as they are born.

• •

Language Notes

Too, Too Many, Too Much, A Lot of

1. _A lot of_ shows a large quantity. _Too much_ and _too many_ show that the quantity is excessive for a specific purpose.

> A college education costs _a lot of money_.
> I want to get financial aid, but I can't. My family makes _too much money_.

2. _Too much_ and _too many_ come before nouns. _Too_ comes before adjectives and adverbs.

> He can't go to college. The tuition is _too high_. College costs _too much money_. He has _too many expenses_.

3. _Too much_, without a noun, can follow the verb (phrase).

> She can't afford to go to college in another state because it costs _too much_.
> I don't like my neighbor because he talks _too much_.

EXERCISE 17   Fill in each blank after _too_ with _much_ or _many_. Then complete the statement.

> **EXAMPLE:** **If I drink too** _much_ **coffee,** _I won't be able to sleep tonight._

1. If I try to memorize too _____ words, _____

2. If I make too _____ mistakes on my homework, _____

3. If I spend too _____ money on clothes, _____

4. If I drink too _____ alcohol, _____

5. Too _____ coffee _____

6. In my opinion, _____ costs too _____ in the U.S.

EXERCISE 18 Fill in each blank with *too, too much,* or *too many.* A person is complaining about the big city where she lives.

EXAMPLE: This city has _too much_ crime.

1. It's _____ noisy.

2. It's _____ dirty.

3. There are _____ people.

4. There's _____ traffic.

5. There's _____ unemployment.

6. There's _____ pollution.

7. It's _____ big.

8. There are _____ gangs.

9. There are _____ problems.

10. An apartment costs _____.

EXERCISE 19 Fill in each blank with *too much* or *too many* if a problem is present. Use *a lot of* if no problem is present.[12]

EXAMPLE: I'd like to travel to Paris, but I can't because it costs _too much._

1. There are _____ educational opportunities in the U.S.

2. I couldn't call you yesterday because I had _____ work.

3. Healthy people get _____ exercise.

4. Last night, I ate _____ at the party, and I got sick.

5. I can help you move during my vacation because I'll have _____ time.

6. Big cities have _____ cultural events.

7. I can't eat potato chips because they have _____ calories and

   _____ fat.

8. _____ people in the U.S. wear jeans.

9. I can't go to the party because I have _____ things to do this weekend.

---

[12]In some cases, *too much/too many* and *a lot of* are interchangeable.

EXPANSION ACTIVITIES

PROVERBS

1. The following proverbs contain *too*. Discuss the meaning of each proverb. Do you have a similar proverb in your language?

   Too many cooks spoil the broth.
   You can never be too thin or too rich.

2. The following proverbs contain *there*. Discuss the meaning of each proverb. Do you have a similar proverb in your language?

   Where there's a will, there's a way.
   Where there's smoke, there's fire.
   There's no time like the present.

SAYING

The following saying contains an irregular singular form. Discuss the meaning of this saying. Do you have a similar saying in your language?

No news is good news.

OUTSIDE ACTIVITIES

1. Go to the reference desk at the library and ask to see the latest edition of one of the following books:

   Lovejoy's College Guide
   Peterson's Four-Year College Directory

   Look for the names of a few colleges or universities that interest you. Compare tuition costs and any other information you want to know about these colleges. Share this information with the class.

2. Go to the library. Try to find some interesting facts and statistics about your country. Share this information with the class.

WRITING

1. Write about an ethnic minority in your country. Where and how do they live? Use expressions of quantity.
2. Write a paragraph telling about the advantages or disadvantages of living in this city. You may write about pollution, job opportunities, weather, traffic, transportation, and crime. Use expressions of quantity.
3. Write about college education in your country. Who goes to college? Do poor students have the opportunity for a college education? How do students pay for their education?

EDITING ADVICE

1. Don't put *a* or *an* before a non-count noun.

   some OR *a piece of*
   I want to give you ~~an~~ advice.

2. A noncount noun is always singular.

   a lot of
   I have ~~many~~ homework~~s~~ to do.

   pieces of
   She bought three furniture~~s~~.

3. Use a singular noun and verb after *every*.

   Every childr~~en~~ need~~s~~ love.

4. Don't use a double negative.

   any
   He doesn't have ~~no~~ money.
   or He has no money

5. Some plural forms are irregular and don't take *-s*.

   She has two children~~s~~.

6. Use *there* to introduce a noun.

   There
   ~~Are~~ a lot of people in China.

7. Be careful with *there* and *they're*. They sound the same.

   There
   ~~They're~~ are many problems in the world.

8. Use the plural form after *one of*.

   s
   One of my sister~~is~~ a lawyer.

9. Don't use *a* or *an* before a plural noun.

   (some)
   She bought ~~a~~ new socks.

10. Omit *of* after *a lot* when the noun is omitted.

    I have a lot of time, but my brother doesn't have a lot ~~of~~.

11. Include *of* with a unit of measure.

    of
    He bought three rolls film.

12. Use *a little/a few* for a positive meaning. Use *little/few* for a negative meaning.

    He can't help you because
    (very)
    he has ~~a~~ little time.

SUMMARY OF LESSON FIVE

Study the words that we use before count and noncount nouns.

Singular Count	Plural Count	Noncount
one book a book	5 books some/any books many/a lot of books (a) few books several books	5 cups of coffee some/any coffee much/a lot of coffee (a) little coffee

Sentences with *There*

Count

> There's a Vietnamese student in this class.
> There are some Chinese students in this class.

Noncount

> There's some rain in my hometown in the winter.
> How much rain is there in the spring?

Too Much/Too Many/A Lot of/Too

A lot of indicates a large quantity. *Too* indicates that the large quantity causes a problem.

- *A lot of* + count or noncount noun
  She's a healthy woman. She gets a lot of exercise.
  She walks a lot of miles.

- *Too much* + noncount noun
  She doesn't qualify for financial aid because her parents make too much money.

- *Too much* at end of verb phrase
  She can't buy a new car because it costs too much.

- *Too many* + count noun
  There are too many students in the class. The teacher doesn't have time to help everyone.

- *Too* + adjective or adverb
  I'm only 58 years old. I'm too young to retire.
  Slow down. You walk too fast for me.

LESSON FIVE TEST/REVIEW

Part 1   Find the mistakes with singulars, plurals, and quantity words, and correct them. Not every sentence has a mistake. If the sentence is correct, write *C*.

EXAMPLES: How ~~many~~ *much* milk*s* did you drink?

How much time do you have?   *C*

1. He doesn't have no job.

2. One of my friend moved to Montana.

3. I can't go out tonight because I have too much work.

4. Three womens came into the room.

5. I had a lot of friends in my country, but in the U.S. I don't have a lot of.

6. A lot of American own a computer.

7. A person can be happy if he has a few good friends.

8. I have much information about my country.

9. Every workers in the U.S. pays taxes.

10. Are there any mistakes in this sentence?

11. My mother gave me a lot of good advices.

12. You need a luck to win the lottery.

13. Please turn on the air conditioner. It's too much hot in here.

14. I can help you on Saturday because I'll have too much time.

15. Are a lot of students in the cafeteria.

16. A few of my teacher speak English very fast.

17. Did you buy a new furniture for your apartment?

18. Some man are very polite.

19. I have many problems with my landlord.

20. Do you have much time for fun?

21. I have a new dishes in my kitchen.

22. Several students in this class speak French.

23. I have a dog. I don't have any cat.

24. Many people like to travel.

25. He doesn't need any help from you.

26. I have a little time. I can help you.

27. I have a little time. I can't help you.

28. He bought three pounds meat.

29. How much apples did you eat?

30. How many cup of coffees did you drink?

31. They're are four Mexican students in the class.

Part 2   Fill in each blank with an appropriate measurement of quantity.

EXAMPLE: I bought a _loaf_ of bread.

1. I drank a _____ of tea.

2. She bought a _____ of beer.

3. I usually put a _____ of sugar in my coffee.

4. There's a _____ of milk in the refrigerator.

5. I'm going to buy a _____ of furniture for my living room.

6. The teacher gave a long homework _____.

7. My father gave me an important _____ of advice.

8. I took three _____ of film on my vacation.

9. I need a _____ of paper to write my composition.

10. We need to buy a _____ of soap.

Part 3   Read this composition by a Native American. Add an appropriate quantity word or article before the noun—*a, an, some, any, no, (a) little, (a) few, several, much, many, a lot of.* In some cases, more than one answer is correct.

My name is Joseph Falling Snow. I'm _____*a*_____ Native American from a

Sioux[13] reservation in South Dakota. I don't live in South Dakota anymore because

I couldn't find _____ job. There's very _____ work on my reservation.
                            (1)   (2)

There's _____ poverty. My uncle gave me _____ good advice. He told me
              (3)   (4)

to go to Minneapolis to find _____ job. Minneapolis is a big city, so there are
                                        (5)

_____ job opportunities here. It was easy for me to find a job as a carpenter. I
      (6)

had _____ trouble finding a job, even though I don't have _____
          (7)   (8)

education. My skill is more important than my education.

My native language is Lakota, but I only know _____ words in my
                                                              (9)

language. Most of the people on my reservation speak English. _____ older
                                                                                  (10)

people still speak Lakota, but the language is dying out as the older people die.

_____ times a year, I go back to the reservation for a Pow-Wow. This is an
      (11)

Indian celebration. We wear our native costumes and dance our native dances. It

gets very crowded at these times because _____ people from our reservation
                                                          (12)

and nearby reservations attend this celebration. We have _____ fun.
                                                                          (13)

Right now, I don't have _____ money, but I'm trying to save as _____
                                    (14)   (16)

as I can. Someday, when I'm old, I'd like to go back to live on my reservation.

_____
[13]*Sioux* is pronounced /su/.

Albert Einstein

LESSON SIX

GRAMMAR

The Past Continuous Tense
Time Clauses

CONTEXT

A Foolish Man
Albert Einstein
American Education
Saving for Retirement

Lesson Focus The Past Continuous; Time Clauses

- The past continuous tense is *was/were* + verb *-ing.*
  He *was driving* to work.

- We often use the past continuous in a sentence that has two clauses—a main clause and a time clause.[1]
  He *was driving* to work when the accident happened.

- We can use a time clause in present and future sentences too.
  Present: He usually listens to the news *while he drives to work.*
  Future: *When I graduate,* I'll buy a car.

R
E
A
D
I
N
G

Before you read:

1. Did you ever lose something valuable or important? What were you doing or where were you when you lost it?
2. Did you ever do something that was foolish for you and funny for others?

Read the following folk tale. Pay special attention to the simple past and past continuous verbs.

A FOOLISH MAN

One day a man **was walking** to the market with his six donkeys. While he **was walking,** he **got** tired and **decided** to ride on one of the donkeys. While he **was riding,** he **stopped** to count his donkeys and **found** that there were only five. He **got** off and **decided** to look for the sixth donkey. After searching for some time, he **gave up**[2] and **returned** to his donkeys and **counted** them again. This  time he **counted** six. He thought, "Maybe the sixth one **returned** while I **was looking** for it." Again, he **got** on one of the donkeys and **continued** to the market. He counted the animals again and was surprised to find that he had only five. While he **was counting** them, a friend of his passed by and asked him what he **was doing.** "I started out with six donkeys; then I had only five, then six, and now five. I don't know what is happening." His friend said, "You have seven. I will count them for you. One. Two. Three. Four. Five. You are sitting on the sixth. And you, foolish man, are the seventh."

[1]A *clause* is a group of related words that has a subject and a verb.

[2]To *give up* means to stop trying.

6.1 Past Continuous Tense

Past continuous = *was/were* + verb *-ing:*

I He She It	was	
		eating.
We You They	were	

Compare statements, questions, and short answers using the past continuous tense:

Wh- Word	*Be*	Subject	*Be*	*-Ing* Form	Complement	Short Answer
		He	was	eating	lunch.	
		He	wasn't	eating	a sandwich.	
	Was	he		eating	alone?	Yes, he was.
Where	was	he		eating?		
Why	wasn't	he		eating	a sandwich?	
		Who	was	eating	a sandwich?	

Language Notes

1. We use the past continuous to say what was in progress at a specific moment in the past.

   What were you and your family doing *at 10:15 last night*?
   I was watching the news *at 10:15*.
   My parents were sleeping *at that time*.

2. We can use the past continuous to emphasize the length of an action.

   He was working *all morning*.

EXERCISE 1   Tell if the following things were happening in January 1993.

   EXAMPLE: **go to school**
   I was (not) going to school in January 1993.

   1. work
   2. go to school
   3. study English
   4. live in the U.S.
   5. live with my parents

EXERCISE 2   Ask a question with "What were you doing?" at these specific times. Another student will answer.

> EXAMPLE: **at 6 o'clock this morning**
>
> **A. What were you doing at 6 o'clock this morning?**
>
> **B. I was sleeping.**

1. at 10 o'clock last night
2. at 4 o'clock this morning
3. at 5 o'clock yesterday afternoon

4. at this time yesterday
5. at this time last year[3]

6.2   The Simple Past with the Past Continuous

A sentence can have two clauses: a main clause and a time clause.

Main Clause	Time Clause
He was riding his donkey	when he noticed a problem.
A friend passed by	while he was counting his donkeys.

We often use the simple past and the past continuous in the same sentence to show the relationship of a longer past action to a shorter one. There are two ways to show the time relationship of the two verbs:

• We use *when* + the simple past with the shorter action.
• We use *while* + the past continuous with the longer action.[4]

Time Word	Longer Action	Time Word	Shorter Action
	He was riding to the market	when	he noticed a problem.
While	he was riding to the market,		he noticed a problem.
	He was counting his donkeys	when	his friend passed by.
While	he was counting his donkeys,		his friend passed by.

Language
Notes

1. If the time clause precedes the main clause, use a comma.

    I was taking a shower *when the phone rang.*
    When the phone rang, I was taking a shower.

2. In a question with two clauses, only the verb in the main clause is in a question form.

    What *was* the foolish man *doing* when his friend *passed* by?
    Where *were* you *going* when you *had* the accident?

3. We don't use the continuous form with the verb *be,* but it can have a continuous meaning.

    While she *was* at work, her husband called.
    She *was* at work when her husband called.

EXERCISE 3   Decide which of these two verbs has longer action. Fill in the correct tense (simple past or past continuous) of the verb in parentheses ( ) and *when* or *while.*

EXAMPLES: She __*was taking*__ a shower ____*when*____ the telephone ___*rang.*___
            (take)   (ring)

        It ___*started*___ to rain ___*while*___ I _*was walking*_ to school.
               (start)   (walk)

1. _____ the teacher _____ on the blackboard, she _____ the
                            (write)   (drop)

   chalk.

2. He _____ and _____ his arm _____ he _____ a tree.
       (fall)   (break)   (climb)

3. Mary _____ in a department store _____ she _____ her purse.
         (shop)   (lose)

4. I _____ my homework _____ my friend _____ over.
     (do)   (come)

5. She _____ her husband _____ she _____ college.
       (meet)   (attend)

6. _____ I _____ to work, I _____ out of gas.[5]
            (drive)   (run)

7. _____ he _____ at the airport, his friends _____ for him.
           (arrive)   (wait)

8. They _____ dinner _____ someone _____ on the door.
       (eat)   (knock)

9. _____ I _____ a test, my pencil point _____.
          (take)   (break)

10. The baby _____ _____ I _____ to a friend.
        (interrupt)   (talk)

11. I _____ my tooth _____ I _____ a nut.
   (break)   (eat)

---

[5]To *run out of* means to use up everything.

12. I _____ an old friend _____ I _____ in the park.
       (meet)   (walk)

13. She _____ dinner _____ the smoke alarm _____ off.[6]
         (cook)   (go)

14. He _____ the snow _____ he _____ his glove.
       (shovel)   (leave)

15. I _____ a fuse _____ I _____ .
      (blow)   (iron)

16. She _____ _____ the baby _____ to cry.
         (sleep)   (start)

17. She _____ her favorite plate _____ she _____ the dishes.
         (break)   (wash)

EXERCISE 4   Fill in each blank with the simple past or the past continuous of the verb in parentheses ( ) in the following conversations.

Conversation 1, between a wife (W) and husband (H)

W. Look what I found today! Your favorite watch!

H. Where _*did you find*_ it?
              (find)

W. In your top drawer. I _____ away your socks when I _____ it.
                              (1 put)   (2 find)

H. I wonder how it got there.

W. Probably while you _____ something in that drawer, it
                            (3 put)

     _____ off your wrist.
        (4 fall)

Conversation 2, between a wife (W) and husband (H)

H. What happened? I _____ TV when I _____ a loud crash in
                          (1 watch)   (2 hear)
     the kitchen.

W. I _____ to get something off the top shelf when I _____
          (3 try)   (4 drop)
     a vase.

H. Why didn't you ask me to help you?

W. You _____ TV, and I _____ to disturb you.
            (5 watch)   (6 not/want)

_____

[6]When an alarm *goes off*, it starts to sound.

Conversation 3, between a son (S) and mother (M)

S.   I _____ through some old boxes when I _____ this picture
         (1 look)   (2 find)

of you and Dad when you were young. By the way, how _____ you
                                                                              (3 meet)

_____ Dad?

M.   One day I _____ in the park when he _____ me to ask what
                    (4 walk)   (5 stop)

time it was. We _____ to talk, and then he _____ me to go
                          (6 start)   (7 ask)

out with him.

S.   Did you get married right away?

M.   No. At that time, there was a war going on. We _____ for about
                                                                          (8 date)

five months when he _____ drafted.[7] He had to serve in the
                            (9 get)

army. While he _____ in the army, he _____ me a beautiful
                        (10 serve)   (11 write)

letter. He asked me to marry him as soon as he returned from military service.

S.   Did you marry him when he _____ home?
                                            (12 get)

M.   Not right away. When he _____ home, I _____ at the
                                    (13 come)   (14 study)

university, and I wanted to graduate first. We _____ married ten
                                                              (15 get)

days after my graduation.

Language Notes

To describe a past scene, we use the past continuous.

Example 1:
One day a little girl *was walking* through the forest. She *was wearing* a red dress. She *was carrying* a basket of food for her grandmother. A wolf *was following* her. Suddenly the wolf stepped in front of her.

Example 2:
I *was driving* home after work on the expressway. I *was driving* 60 miles an hour. I *was listening* to the radio and *talking* to my friend. We *were* both *wearing* our seatbelts. Suddenly the car in front of me stopped, and I hit it.

---

[7]When a person *gets drafted,* the government chooses him to serve in the military.

EXERCISE 5   Use the past continuous to describe the scene or circumstances that led to the main action of this story. Put the main action in the simple past tense.

I met my wife 15 years ago. We were both students at the university.

We _werelliving_ in the same dormitory, but we didn't know each other. One day
         (live)

she _____ in the library. I _____ at the next table. I _____ my math
       (1 study)   (2 sit)   (3 do)

homework. I _____ on a very difficult problem, and I _____ attention to
            (4 work)   (5 not/pay)

anyone around me. She _____ at the next table.
                      (6 sit)

Suddenly I _____ a soft voice say, "May I borrow your pencil for a
           (7 hear)

moment?" I _____ up and _____ the most beautiful girl in the world.
           (8 look)   (9 see)

We use *was/were going to* + verb to describe a plan that we didn't carry out.

She *was going to buy* a new car, but she lost her job.
I *was going to call* you, but I lost your phone number.

EXERCISE 6   Fill in each blank to tell what prevented a plan from happening.

EXAMPLE: **I was going to call you, but** _I got busy and forgot about it._

1. We were going to have a picnic, but _____

   _____

2. I was going to finish that book last night, but _____

   _____

3. We were going to buy a house, but _____

   _____

4. They were going to leave on vacation on Monday, but _____

   _____

5. She was going to marry her boyfriend, but _____

   _____

6. They were going to drive to Canada, but _____

_____

7. I was going to cook dinner, but _____

_____

Before you read:

1. What kind of a student were you when you were a child?
2. What was your favorite subject in school? What was your worst subject in school?

Read the following article. Pay special attention to words that show time.

ALBERT EINSTEIN

Albert Einstein was born in Germany in 1879. He was one of the greatest geniuses in history.

Some people didn't think Einstein was very smart **when** he was young. He learned slowly; in fact, he didn't start to talk **until** he was three years old. **While** other children played, he sat by himself. His parents thought he was retarded.[8] He was bored in school, and his teachers thought he was a slow learner. He had a poor memory for words, and his high school Greek teacher told him, "You'll never amount to anything."[9]

When Einstein was 11 years old, a young medical student came to eat at his home twice a week. He started to bring books to young Albert on natural science, and Albert started to become interested in the basic forces of the universe.

However, Einstein disliked the discipline of formal German schooling, and he left high school **before** receiving his diploma. He tried to pass the exam to enter the Swiss Polytechnic Institute

$$E = mc^2$$

but failed on his first attempt. However, he passed it on his second try and became a student of mathematics and physics. In 1905, **when** he was only 26 years old, he developed his famous theory of relativity.

In 1933, **while** Einstein was visiting the U.S., Adolf Hitler became chancellor of Germany. Einstein, who was a Jew, found himself in danger. The Nazis took his property, removed him from his job as professor, and took away his citizenship. Germany's loss was

---

[8]The intelligence of a *retarded* person is less than the intelligence of a normal person.

[9]This expression means "You will be a failure."

America's gain. Einstein went to work at the Institute for Advanced Study in Princeton, New Jersey. He lived and worked there **until** he died in 1955.

•••

6.3 Time Words

Time words give information about when the action in a sentence occurs.

when	When I retire, I will move to Florida.
whenever	Whenever I read, I need glasses.
while	While I was reading, the phone rang.
	While I was reading, my brother was watching TV.
until	I'll work until I'm 65 years old.
before	Before she came to the U.S., she lived in Italy.
after	We'll have a test after reviewing this lesson.
for	He studied for two hours.
in	I'll return from my business trip in two weeks.
during	He lived (was living) in France during the war.
by	We will finish this book by the end of the semester.

Language Notes

When, While, Until

1. *Until* shows that one action stops or changes another action.

   Einstein didn't start to talk *until* he was three years old.
   He lived in the U.S. *until* he died.

2. Compare *when* and *until*. In the following examples, *when* means "at that time." *Until* means "before that time."

   When Einstein was at the university, he enjoyed his studies.
   Until Einstein went to the university, he didn't like school.

In the following examples, *when* means "after that time." *Until* means "before that time."

   When he died, people were sad.
   Until he died, he lived in New Jersey.

3. We can use either *when* or *while* with two clauses that happened at about the same time. Both verbs in the sentence have duration.

   While (OR *when*) other children played, Einstein remained silent.
   When (OR *while*) Einstein was in high school, he studied Greek.

4. When an action has no duration, we use *when*, not *while*.

   WRONG: Einstein was upset *while* the Nazis took his home.
   RIGHT: Einstein was upset *when* the Nazis took his home.

EXERCISE 7   Fill in each blank with an appropriate time word: *when, while, after, before, until.* (In some cases, more than one answer is possible.)

> EXAMPLE: _When_   **Einstein was a child, his parents thought he was retarded.**

1. Einstein didn't start to talk _____ he was three years old.

2. In school, he was silent _____ his teachers called on[10] him.

3. Einstein entered the university _____ he passed the college entrance exam.

4. He went to college _____ he came to the U.S.

5. He was 56 years old _____ he came to the U.S.

6. _____ he was in the U.S., the Nazis in Germany took away his citizenship.

7. _____ he lost his home, he decided to live in the U.S.

8. He lived in the U.S. _____ he died.

9. _____ he left high school, he didn't have a diploma.

EXERCISE 8   Add a main clause to complete each statement.

> EXAMPLE: **Before I got to class today, . . .**
>
> **Before I got to class today, I finished all my homework.**

1. While I was in high school, . . .
2. When I finished high school, . . .
3. When I left my country, . . .
4. Until I came to this city/school, . . .
5. When I arrived in the U.S., . . .
6. Before I learned English, . . .

EXERCISE 9   Finish the time expression to complete each statement.

> EXAMPLE: **I stayed in my country until** _a civil war broke out._

1. I decided to come to the U.S. when _____

2. I found my apartment/house after _____

3. I enrolled in this English class after _____

4. I didn't understand English until _____

5. I got married/found a job/bought a car when _____

---

[10]A teacher *calls on* students, or asks them to answer questions in class.

EXERCISE 10   Name something you never . . . until you came to the U.S.

>   EXAMPLE: **Name something you never had.**
>   **I never had a car until I came to the U.S.**

1. Name something you never did.
2. Name something or someone you never heard of.
3. Name something you never saw.
4. Name something you never thought about.

5. Name something you never had.
6. Name something you never ate.
7. Name something you never knew.

6.4   Simple Past or Past Continuous with Time Clauses

Compare these two sentences.

   (A) She *was eating* dinner when he arrived.
   (B) She *ate dinner* when he arrived.

In sentence A, the arrival happened during the time of the dinner.
In sentence B, the person ate dinner after the arrival of another person.

   (A) Einstein *was living* in the U.S. when he died.
   (B) Einstein *lived* in the U.S. when he lost his German citizenship.

In sentence A, his death occurred during the time he was living in the U.S. In sentence B, he started to live in the U.S. after he lost his German citizenship.

Language Notes

  While can connect two past actions that happened during the same period of time. We can use either the simple past or the past continuous in both clauses.

   While other children *played*, Einstein *sat* by himself.
   While Einstein *was visiting* the U.S., the situation in Germany *was getting* worse.

EXERCISE 11   A fable is an old story that teaches us a lesson about life. Fables often use animals to represent people. Here is a fable about an ant and a grasshopper. Fill in each blank with the past or past continuous of the verb in parentheses ( ) to complete this story. In some cases, you may use either tense.

grasshopper   ant

    During the whole summer, the ant ___*was working*___ very hard trying to gather
                                        (work)

the food that she would need for the long, cold winter. While the ant

_____, her neighbor, the grasshopper, _____ a good time. He
   (1 work)   (2 have)

_____ and _____ himself all summer. When winter
   (3 sing)   (4 enjoy)

_____, the ant had plenty of food to eat. However, the grasshopper
  (5 come)

_____ nothing to eat. The grasshopper _____ to the ant's
  (6 have)   (7 go)

house one day to ask for food. The ant _____ a delicious meal when
                                 (8 prepare)

he _____ the grasshopper knock on the door. When she _____
    (9 hear)   (10 open)

the door, the grasshopper _____, "Please give me some food." The ant
                        (11 say)

asked him, "What _____ you _____ all summer while I
                               (12 do)

_____? "The grasshopper _____, "I _____ all summer."
  (13 work)   (14 reply)   (15 sing)

"Then go and dance now," the ant _____ him.
                           (16 tell)

R
E
A
D
I
N
G

Before you read:

1. For how many years do children go to school in your country?
2. Do most people in your country finish high school?

Read the following article. Pay special attention to the time words.

AMERICAN EDUCATION

A basic education in the U.S. is twelve years. Most children start first grade **when** they are about six years old and continue **until** they are about 18 years old. Many children attend kindergarten **before** going to first grade, but this is not a requirement.

Decisions about American education come from the state or local level. Local school districts divide the 12 years of education in different ways. In some school districts, students go directly to high school when they finish elementary school.[11] In other districts, students go to junior high school before they go to high school.

Here are some of the different ways a school district might divide up the twelve years:

8 years—elementary school   8 years—elementary school
4 years—high school   2 years—junior high school[12]
                                     2 years—high school

5 years—elementary school   6 years—elementary school
3 years—junior high school   3 years—junior high school
4 years—high school   3 years—high school

---

[11]*Elementary school* is sometimes called *grammar school* or *grade school.*

[12]*Junior high school* is sometimes called *middle school.*

By law, a student must stay in school **until** he or she is a certain age. The age differs from state to state. It may be as low as thirteen or as high as seventeen.

After high school, some students go to college. It usually takes a full-time student four years to get a college degree—a Bachelor of Arts (B.A.) or a Bachelor of Science (B.S.). Some students continue their education to receive a Master of Arts (M.A.) or a Master of Science (M.S.). The highest degree is the doctorate, or Ph.D. People who get this degree often use the title "Doctor" before their names.

Language Notes

When, While, Until

1. When we are referring to the general present, we use the present tense in both the time clause and the main clause.

    Children *start* high school when they *are* about fourteen.

2. *Whenever* means any time or every time. With the general present, *when* and *whenever* have about the same meaning.

    When I take a test, I feel nervous.
    Whenever I take a test, I feel nervous.

EXERCISE 12   Fill in each blank with an appropriate time word: *before, after, until, when,* or *while.*

> EXAMPLE: **Many children attend kindergarten** *before* **they go to first grade.**

1. Children enter first grade _____ they are about six years old.

2. Some students go directly to high school _____ they finish elementary school.

3. Other students go to junior high school _____ they enter high school.

4. By law, a student in New Mexico must stay in school _____ he or she is seventeen.

5. Some students go to college _____ they finish high school.

6. You get an M.A. _____ you get a Ph.D.

7. You get a diploma _____ you graduate.

8. Some students have a part-time job _____ they are attending college.

EXERCISE 13 Add a main clause to complete each statement. Use the general present.

EXAMPLE: Whenever I take a test, . . .
Whenever I take a test, I feel nervous.

1. Whenever I feel sad or lonely, . . .
2. Whenever I get angry, . . .
3. Whenever I need advice, . . .
4. Whenever I receive a present, . . .
5. Whenever I get a letter from my family, . . .
6. Whenever I'm sick, . . .
7. Whenever the weather is bad, . . .

EXERCISE 14 Finish each sentence with a time clause.

EXAMPLES: I feel nervous . . .
I feel nervous before I take a test.
I feel nervous whenever I have to speak in class.

1. I feel relaxed . . .
2. I get angry . . .
3. I get bored . . .
4. I can't concentrate . . .
5. I'm happy . . .
6. I'm in a bad mood . . .
7. I sometimes daydream[13] . . .
8. Time passes quickly for me . . .

. . . .

R
E
A
D
I
N
G

Before you read:

1. Are you trying to save your money? What are you saving for?
2. Do you have plans for after your retirement?

Read the following article. Pay special attention to time clauses and *if* clauses in future sentences.

SAVING FOR RETIREMENT

If you have a job in the U.S., you probably know that each week your employer deducts money for Social Security. On your check, you may see the letters "FICA." These letters refer to Social Security. **When you retire,** the government will send you a check each month **until you die.** The amount of the check depends on how much money you put into the Social Security system while you were working. However, even people who receive the maximum benefits feel that this amount of money is not enough to live on. For this reason, many people try to save for their retirement.

If you have a job, you should ask your employer if your company offers a tax-sheltered savings plan.[14] With a tax shelter, you can put a certain amount of money away for your retirement and not pay taxes on this money **until you retire.** Let's say you earn $35,000 a

---

[13]To *daydream* means to dream while you are awake. Your mind does not stay in the present moment.

[14]Sometimes a *tax-sheltered savings plan* is called a 401k or a 403b plan.

year and want to save $5000. **If you put this money in a regular savings account,** you must pay taxes on this amount. In addition, you must pay tax on the interest each year. If you put your money into a tax-sheltered account, you do not pay taxes on the $5,000 that you saved. In addition, your interest will continue to grow untaxed **until you retire. When you start to take out your money after retirement,** you will start to pay taxes. **When you retire,** you might be in a lower tax bracket.[15]

Money in a tax-sheltered account should be for retirement only. **If you take your money out of a tax shelter before you retire,** you will have to pay a penalty as well as the tax on the money you take out.

6.5 Time and *If* Clauses with the Future

Notice the tenses in the time or *if* clause.

Main Clause	Time Clause
You *will need* an income	after you *retire.*

If Clause	Main Clause
If you *take* your money out early,	you *will pay* a penalty.

Language Notes

For a future meaning, we use the future tense in the main clause and the simple present tense in the time clause or *if* clause.

EXERCISE 15 This is a conversation between two co-workers. They are talking about retirement. Fill in each blank with the correct form and tense of the verb in parentheses ( ).

A. I hear you're going to retire this year.

B. Yes. Isn't it wonderful? I _____*will be*_____ 65 in September.
   (be)

A. What _____ after you _____?
   (1 you/do)   (2 retire)

---

[15]People pay taxes according to their income. Your income determines what category, or *bracket,* you are in. People with lower incomes pay less tax than people with middle and higher incomes.

B. I'm trying to sell my house now. When I _____ my house, I
   (3 sell)

   _____ to Florida and buy a condo.
   (4 move)

A. What _____ in Florida?
   (5 you/do)

B. I _____ a sailboat and spend most of my time on the water.
   (6 buy)

A. But a sailboat is expensive.

B. When I _____ 65, I _____ to take money out of my
   (7 be)   (8 start)

   tax-sheltered account. Also, I _____ a lot of money when I
   (9 get)

   _____ my house. What _____ when you _____?
   (10 sell)   (11 you/do)   (12 retire)

A. I'm only 45 years old. I have another twenty years until I _____.
   (13 retire)

B. Now is the time to start thinking about retirement. If you _____ your
   (14 save)

   money for the next twenty years, you _____ a comfortable retirement.
   (15 have)

   But if you _____ about it until the time _____ , you
   (16 not/think)   (17 come)

   _____ Social Security checks to live on.
   (18 only/have)

A. I _____ about it when the time _____. I'm too young to
   (19 worry)   (20 come)

   worry about it now.

B. If you _____ until you _____ 65 to think about it, you
   (21 wait)   (22 be)

   _____ a poor, old man. On Monday morning when we
   (23 be)

   _____ at work, I _____ you to a woman who can explain the
   (24 be)   (25 introduce)

   company's tax-shelter plan to you. After you _____ to her, I'm sure
   (26 talk)

   you _____ your mind about when to worry about retirement.
   (27 change)

6.6   Time with Present Participles

When the main clause and the time clause have the same subject, we can delete the subject of the time clause and use a present participle (verb + *-ing*) after the time word:

Main Clause	Time Clause
S V	S V
Some children attend kindergarten	before they go to first grade.
	going

Time Clause ,	Main Clause
S V ,	S V
After Einstein left high school,	Einstein studied mathematics.
leaving	

EXERCISE 16   Change these sentences. Use a present participle after the time word.

EXAMPLE: *After entering the university, Einstein developed his theory.*
~~After Einstein entered the university, he developed his theory.~~

1. Einstein passed an exam before he entered the university.

2. He left high school before he received his diploma.

3. After Einstein developed his theory of relativity, he became famous.

4. He became interested in physics after he received books on science.

5. After he came to the U.S., he got a job at Princeton.

6. Before you begin a test, you should read the instructions carefully.

7. You shouldn't talk to another student while you are taking a test.

8. After children finish kindergarten, they go to first grade.

9. Students in some school districts go to junior high school before they enter high school.

EXERCISE 17   Check (✓) what was true for you before coming to the U.S. Find a partner and compare your list to your partner's list. Discuss any related information.

> EXAMPLE: ___✓___ I studied English
>
>   Student A: I studied English for one year before coming to the U.S.
>   Student B: I didn't study English before coming to the U.S.

1. _____ I studied American history.
2. _____ I studied English.
3. _____ I finished college.
4. _____ I bought new clothes.
5. _____ I had a clear idea about life in the U.S.

6. _____ I was afraid about the future.
7. _____ I read about this city.
8. _____ I had a map of this city.
9. _____ _____

6.7 More Time Words

Study these words that show time.

Use *for* to tell how long.
   He was married *for* ten years. Now he's divorced.
Use *in* to mean after a period of time.
   She finished the test *in* 30 minutes.
Use *during* with an activity.
   I visited Toronto *during* my vacation.
Use *by* to mean "no later than."
   I want you to finish the test *by* 8:30.
Use *ago* to mean before now.
   She got married three years *ago*.

Compare *before* and *ago*.
   She got married *before* she graduated.
   She got married three years *ago*.
Compare *during* and *for*.
   She fell asleep *during* the movie.
   She slept *for* two hours.
Compare *after* and *in*.
   I'll come back *in* an hour.
   I'll come back *after* I finish my homework.
Compare *before* and *by*.
   I have to return my library books *before* I leave on vacation.
   I have to return my library books *by* Friday.

EXERCISE 18 Fill in the blanks with the correct time word: *when, whenever, until, while, before, after, for, during, in, by,* or *ago.* In some cases, more than one answer is possible.

EXAMPLE: **He lived with his parents _until_ he was 19 years old.**

1. _____ he was a child, he lived with his grandparents.

2. _____ several years, he lived with his grandparents.

3. _____ his childhood, he lived with his grandparents.

4. _____ he got married, he lived with his grandparents. Then he found an apartment with his wife.

5. _____ he was ten years old, his grandparents gave him a bike.

6. _____ he was going to elementary school, he lived with his grandparents.

7. She was working for her father _____ she was going to college.

8. She worked for her father _____ her free time.

9. She worked for her father _____ she was single.

10. She worked for her father _____ three years.

11. She worked for her father full time _____ her summer vacation.

12. She worked for her father _____ she got married. Then she quit her job to take care of her husband and children.

13. She worked for her father 12 years _____.

14. _____ her husband needs help in his business, she helps him out.

15. She can't help you now. She's busy. She'll help you _____ an hour.

16. Please finish this exercise _____ 8:30.

17. Please finish this exercise _____ you go home. The teacher wants it today.

18. Please finish this exercise _____ ten minutes.

19. He'll retire _____ two years.

20. He'll retire _____ he's sixty-five years old.

21. He'll work _____ he's sixty-five years old. Then he'll retire.

EXPANSION ACTIVITIES

PROVERBS   The following proverbs contain time clauses. Discuss the meaning of each proverb. Do you have a similar proverb in your language?

Don't count your chickens until they're hatched.
Look before you leap.
I'll cross that bridge when I come (get) to it.
Time passes quickly while you're having fun.

POEM   This short poem contains the simple past and the past continuous. Do you think it's funny? Why?

As[16] I was going up the stair,
I met a man who wasn't there.
He wasn't there again today.
I wish to God he'd go away!

WRITING   1. Write a short fable like the one in Exercise 11.

2. Write a paragraph about the changes that took place after a major historical event in your country or elsewhere in the world.

EXAMPLES: **After the communists took over in Cuba . . .**
After the Khmer Rouge took power in Cambodia . . .
After the coup failed in the former Soviet Union . . .
After the president of my country was assassinated . . .

3. Write about the life of a famous person who interests you.

4. Write about how you met your spouse or how your father and mother met. Use Exercise 5 as a model.

OUTSIDE ACTIVITIES   1. John F. Kennedy, who was president from 1961 to 1963, was killed while he was riding in an open car in Dallas, Texas. Most older people in the United States remember exactly what they were doing or where they were when President Kennedy was shot. Interview an older American. Ask "What were you doing when you heard the news that Kennedy was shot?" Report that person's answer to the class.

2. Is there a famous event in your country that most people remember well? What was it? Ask people from your country what they were doing when this event happened. Report your findings to the class.

---

[16]*As* means *while.*

DISCUSSIONS   1. In a small group or with the entire class, discuss the meaning of the fable in Exercise 11. What do you think this fable teaches us? Do you know anyone like the grasshopper or the ant in this fable?

2. In a small group or with the entire class, discuss these questions about your early education.

   a. Did you like school when you were a child? Why or why not?
   b. Did you like your teachers? Were they strict?

3. In a small group or with the entire class, discuss the educational system in your country. How many years do students go to school? Can they leave school without a diploma? At what age can they leave school? How are the school years divided up? Who goes to college?

4. Most Americans try to save for their retirement. They don't want to depend on their children for support when they are old. How do people in your country prepare financially for retirement? Do elderly parents depend on their children? Does the government help elderly people when they retire?

EDITING ADVICE

1. Don't use the future tense in a time or *if* clause.

   I will call you when I ~~will~~ get home.

2. Put the subject before the verb in all clauses.
   the teacher entered
   When ~~entered the teacher~~, the students stood up.

3. Use *when*, not *while*, if the action has no duration.
   When
   ~~While~~ she spilled the milk, she started to cry.

SUMMARY OF LESSON SIX

1. We use the past continuous tense:

   A. To describe a past action that was in progress at a specific moment:

   He *was sleeping* at 6 o'clock this morning.
   Where *were* you *living* in December 1991?

   B. To emphasize the length or duration of a past action:

   He *was working* all morning.
   I *was studying* for my test all week.

   C. With the past tense, to show the relationship of a longer action to a shorter action:

   He *was sleeping* when the telephone *rang.*
   While she *was eating* lunch in the park, it *started* to rain.
   Martin Luther King, Jr., *was standing* on the balcony of a motel when a man *shot* and *killed* him.

   D. When telling a story, to describe the scene before the main event occurred:

   It *was raining.* Everyone in the house *was sleeping.* Suddenly, we heard a loud noise in the basement.

   E. To show past intentions:

   I *was going to call* you, but I lost your phone number.
   She *was going to cook* dinner, but she didn't have time.

2. Sentences with Time Clauses:

Tense	Main Clause	Time Clause	Sample Sentence
Present	present	present	I *use* glasses when I *read.*
Future	future	present	You *will need* money when you *retire.*
Past	past	past	She *cried* when she *saw* him.

LESSON SIX TEST/REVIEW

Part 1   Find the mistakes in the following sentences, and correct them. Not every sentence has a mistake. If the sentence is correct, write *C*.

> EXAMPLES: We will be happy when he ~~will be~~ *is* here.
>
> While I was walking in the park, I saw my friend. *C*

1. When he will arrive, we will eat dinner.

2. After leaving my country, I went to Thailand.

3. When arrived the teacher, the students had a test.

4. I will graduate until I finish my courses.

5. While she was washing the dishes, she dropped the glass.

6. While she dropped the glass, it broke.

7. He will continue to study English until he becomes fluent.

8. She won't serve dinner until her guests arrive.

9. Einstein lived in the U.S. until he died.

10. They will go home until the movie is over (finished).

11. I'll be back in ten minutes.

12. During three weeks, he was on vacation.

13. Please return your library books by Friday.

14. She found a job three weeks before.

15. He was sick for a week.

16. I ate dinner an hour ago.

17. Einstein was in the U.S. during the Second World War.

18. I was going to call you, but I lost your phone number.

Part 2   Fill in each blank with the simple past or the past continuous of the verb in parentheses ( ).

EXAMPLE: A man __*was walking*__ to the market when he _____*lost*_____ one
                    (walk)   (lose)

   donkey.

1. While the man _____ his donkeys, a friend of his _____ by.
                              (count)   (pass)

2. What _____ at 4 p.m. yesterday afternoon? I tried to call you, but you
            (you/do)

   weren't home.

3. She _____ in Paris when the war _____.
                  (live)   (start)

4. I _____ your necklace while I _____ for my watch.
            (find)   (look)

5. She _____ a house three years ago.
                  (buy)

6. I _____ to buy a new car, but I lost my job and didn't have enough
            (go)

   money.

7. One day, a little girl _____ in the forest. She _____ a basket
                                          (walk)   (carry)

   of food. She _____ to her grandmother's house. Suddenly, a wolf
                          (go)

   _____.
      (appear)

8. He _____ his wife while he _____ in a restaurant.
            (meet)   (work)

Part 3   Fill in each blank with an appropriate time word. Choose *when, whenever, while, until, before,* or *after.*

EXAMPLE: I will continue to work ___*until*___ I am 65 years old. Then I will
                    retire.

1. _____ it snows, there are a lot of traffic accidents.

2. I was walking to my friend's house _____ it started to rain. I was
   glad I had my umbrella with me.

3. _____ I was driving to school, I was listening to the radio.

4. _____ I finished my homework last night, I watched the news
   on TV.

5. I got my visa _____ coming to the U.S.

6. He must stay in his country _____ he gets permission to come to the U.S.

7. _____ he dropped his glasses, they broke.

LESSON SEVEN

GRAMMAR
Infinitives
Modals

CONTEXT
An Apartment Lease
Copyright Law
American Citizenship
At a Garage Sale

Lesson Focus **Infinitives; Modals**

- An infinitive is *to* + the base form of the verb. Many verbs and adjectives are followed by an infinitive.

   I need *to leave.* I want *to go* home.
   It's important *to know* English.

- The modal verbs are *can, could, should, will, would, may, might,* and *must.* These verbs are followed by a base form, not an infinitive.

   I *must* leave. I *should* go home.

• •

R
E
A
D
I
N
G

Before you read:

1. Do you live in an apartment? Do you have a lease? Are you happy with your apartment? Why or why not?
2. Do renters in your country usually have to sign a lease?

Read the following article. Notice that modals are followed by the base form. Some verbs and adjectives are followed by the infinitive.

AN APARTMENT LEASE

Many building owners **want** a tenant (renter) **to sign** a lease. A lease is an agreement between the owner (lessor) and the renter (lessee). A lease states the specific period of time of the rental and the amount of the rent. It also explains the rules that you, the renter, **must follow.** For example, a lease **may say** that you **can't have** a pet or a waterbed. It will probably say when you **have to pay** the rent and what **will happen** if you pay it late. Often there is a fee if you pay your rent after a certain date.

Some landlords[1] (owners) **ask** you **to leave** a security deposit, equal to one or two months' rent. When you move out, the owner **can use** this money to repair any damage that you caused. Before you sign the lease, look the apartment over carefully. If something is already broken, damaged, or dirty, **ask** the landlord **to write** on the lease that the apartment was in this condition when you moved in. If the landlord promises that he will paint the apartment or fix something, **ask** him **to put** his promise in writing too. You **shouldn't** just **take** his word for it.

At the end of your lease, the landlord **can ask** you **to leave,** or he **may offer** you a lease for another year (usually the rent will be higher). When you are **ready to move** out, you **should clean** the apartment thoroughly, making especially sure that the stove, refrigerator, and bathroom are clean. The landlord **can keep** some or all of your deposit for cleaning or repairs. If the landlord **wants to keep** some or all of your deposit, he

------

[1]A *landlord* is a man. A *landlady* is a woman.

must give you a list of the problems and the cost of fixing them. However, he **may not keep** your money for normal wear and tear (the normal use of the apartment). For example, when you walk on your carpet, little by little it **will get** dirtier and older. It is not **necessary** for you **to clean** it after normal use.

A lease is a very complicated legal document. A lawyer **can understand** it, but you probably **won't be able to understand** all of it.

If you don't have a lease, the owner **can ask** you **to leave** at any time. However, usually he **must give** you thirty days' notice.

A lease tells you about your responsibilities. Landlords **must** also **obey** the rules of the city where you live. In some cities, the owner **has to give** you interest on your security deposit. In some cities, an apartment **must have** a smoke detector. You, the renter, **don't have to buy** the smoke detector; the landlord **must put** it in your apartment as well as in the halls. In cold climates, the landlord **must** also **give** you heat during the winter months.

smoke detector

It's **important to know** your rights. You **should check** with the department of housing in your city to find out about the responsibilities of the landlord and the rights and responsibilities of the tenant.

- -

7.1   Verbs Followed by an Infinitive

An infinitive is *to* + the base form of the verb. We can use an infinitive after a verb in this pattern:

Subject	Verb	Infinitive Phrase
I	want	to rent an apartment.
I	need	to sign a lease.
The landlord	wants	to have a deposit.

Language Notes

1. We can use an infinitive after the following verbs:

agree	decide	like	promise
ask	expect	love	refuse
attempt	forget	need	remember
begin	hope	plan	start
continue	learn	prefer	try

2. An infinitive never has a verb ending.

Compare:

He want*s* to leave. NOT: He wants to leave*s*.
I need*ed* to buy bread. NOT: I needed to *bought* bread.
I'm try*ing* to study. NOT: I'm trying to study*ing*.

3. The *to* in infinitives is often pronounced "ta," or, after a *d* sound or vowel sound, "da." Listen to your teacher pronounce these sentences.

I don't *like to live* in an elevator building.
The landlord *promised to paint* the apartment.
Do you *need to sign* a lease?
I'll *try to help* you.

4. In fast, informal speech, *want to* is often pronounced "wanna." Listen to your teacher pronounce these sentences:

I want to go home. = I "wanna" go home.
Do you want to leave now? = Do you "wanna" leave now?

EXERCISE 1   Ask a question with the words given in the present tense. Another student will answer.

EXAMPLE: **like/travel**

       A. Do you like to travel?
       B. Yes, I do.   OR   **No, I don't.**

1. want/learn another language
2. plan/take classes here next semester
3. hope/speak English fluently
4. like/write compositions
5. continue/speak your native language at home
6. try/read novels in English
7. plan/move this year
8. need/own a fax machine
9. expect/return to your country

EXERCISE 2   Write a sentence about yourself, using the words given, in any tense. Share your sentences with the class.

EXAMPLES: **like/eat**

       I like to eat Chinese food.

       try/find

       I'm trying to find a job.

1. like/read

_____

2. not like/eat

_____

3. want/visit

_____

4. decide/go

_____

5. try/learn

_____

6. begin/study

_____

EXERCISE 3   Check (✓) the activities that you like to do. Find a partner and compare your list to your partner's list. Report something interesting about your partner to the class.

EXAMPLE: **Sara likes to play chess with her brother on the weekends.**

1. _____ stay home on the weekends
2. _____ eat in a restaurant
3. _____ get up early
4. _____ talk on the phone

5. _____ play chess
6. _____ dance
7. _____ write letters
8. _____ go to museums
9. _____ _____

chess

7.2   Object Before Infinitive

We can use a noun or object pronoun (_me, you, him, her, it, us, them_) between certain verbs and an infinitive:

Subject	Verb	Object	Infinitive Phrase
I	want	my landlord	to paint my apartment.
I	asked	him	to do it this month.
He	expects	me	to sign a two-year lease.
He	doesn't want	us	to make a lot of noise.

We often use an object after the following verbs:

ask	like	need
expect	love	want

EXERCISE 4   Tell if the teacher wants or doesn't want the students to do the following.

EXAMPLES: do the homework
The teacher wants us to do the homework.

use the textbook during a test
The teacher doesn't want us to use the textbook during a test.

1. talk to another student during a test   4. learn English
2. study before a test   5. speak our native languages in class
3. copy another student's homework   6. improve our pronunciation

EXERCISE 5   Tell if you expect or don't expect the teacher to do the following.

EXAMPLES: give homework
I expect him/her to give homework.

give me private lessons
I don't expect him/her to give me private lessons.

1. correct the homework   6. pass all the students
2. give tests   7. know a lot about my country
3. speak my langauge   8. answer my questions in class
4. help me after class   9. teach us American history
5. come to class on time   10. pronounce my name correctly

EXERCISE 6   Complete each statement. Use an object pronoun with an infinitive.

EXAMPLES: **We have to replace the broken mirror.**

The landlord expects *us to replace the broken mirror.*

I told my landlord, "Paint the apartment."decidedecide
I wanted *him to paint the apartment.*

1. I have to clean my apartment.

My landlady wants _____

2. My landlady has to return my deposit.

   I want _____

3. She said to my family, "Clean the carpet."

   She expected _____

4. You have to sign a lease.

   The landlord expects _____

5. The landlady has to install a smoke detector.

   The tenant wants _____

6. The tenants have to return the keys.

   The landlord expects _____

7. He had to move out by October 1.

   The landlord wanted _____

7.3 *It* + **Adjective** + **Infinitive**

We use an infinitive in this pattern:

It	*Be*	Adjective	Infinitive Phrase
It	is	expensive	to travel.
It	was	important	to read the lease.
It	will be	necessary	to clean the apartment.
It	isn't	hard	to ride a bike.

Language Notes

1. We can use these adjectives in this pattern:

dangerous	good	necessary
difficult	great	possible
easy	hard	sad
expensive	important	wrong
fun	impossible	

2. To make a statement that is true of a specific person or persons, we add *for* + noun or object pronoun:

It	*Be*	Adjective	*For* + Noun/ Pronoun	Infinitive Phrase
It	is	hard	for a foreigner	to understand American customs.
It	is	important	for us	to practice English.
It	isn't	necessary	for you	to clean the carpet.

EXERCISE 7   Complete each statement with an infinitive phrase to talk about apartments. You can add an object, if you like.

> EXAMPLES: It's easy *to clean the refrigerator.*
>
> It's necessary *for me to pay my rent by the fifth of the month.*

1. It's important _____

2. It's impossible _____

3. It's possible _____

4. It's necessary _____

5. It's dangerous _____

6. It isn't good _____

7. _____

EXERCISE 8   Tell if it's important or not important for you to do the following.

> EXAMPLE: **own a house**
> **It's (not) important for me to own a house.**

1. get a college degree
2. find an interesting job
3. have a car
4. speak English well
5. read and write English well
6. study American history
7. become an American citizen
8. _____

EXERCISE 9   Write a sentence with each pair of words below. Read your sentences to the class.

EXAMPLE: **hard/the teacher**

It's hard for the teacher to pronounce the names of some students.

1. important/us (the students)

_____

2. difficult/Americans

_____

3. easy/the teacher

_____

4. necessary/children

_____

5. difficult/a woman

_____

6. difficult/a man

_____

7.4 *Be* + **Adjective** + **Infinitive**

Some adjectives can be followed by an infinitive in this pattern:

Subject	*Be*	Adjective	Infinitive Phrase
I	am	afraid	to go out at night.
You	are	lucky	to be in the U.S.
She	is	ready	to move.

These are some adjectives that can be followed by an infinitive:

afraid	happy	prepared	ready
glad	lucky	proud	sad

EXERCISE 10 Fill in each blank. Compare your answers with another student.

EXAMPLE: **I'm lucky** *to be in the U.S.* _____

1. I was lucky _____

2. I'm proud _____

3. I'm sometimes afraid _____ alone.

4. I'm not afraid _____

5. I'm (not) ready _____

7.5 Modals

The modals are *can, could, should, will, would, may, might,* and *must.* The base form follows a modal.

Compare affirmative statements, negative statements, questions, and short answers using modals.

Wh- Word	Modal	Subject	Modal	Verb	Complement	Short Answer
		He	can	have	a cat in his apartment.	
		He	can't	have	a dog.	
	Can	he		have	a waterbed?	Yes, he can.
What kind of pet	can	he		have?		
Why	can't	he		have	a dog?	
		Who	can	have	a dog?	

1. To make a modal negative, we add *not* after the modal verb. There is no negative contraction for *may not* and *might not*.

> You *shouldn't* drive.
> He *mustn't* leave.
> I *might not* work tomorrow.

2. We don't use an infinitive after a modal.

Compare:

> I need *to leave*.   He wants *to go*.
> I must *leave*.   He can *go*.

3. A modal verb never has an *-s*, *-ed*, or *-ing* ending.

> I *can* go.
> He *can* go.

4. *Have to* is like a modal in meaning. However, grammatically it is like most other verbs.

Compare:

> She *should* go.   He *has to* go.
> She *shouldn't* stay.   He *doesn't have to* stay.
> When *should* she go?   When *does* he *have to* go?

5. We do not use two modals together.

> He *may be able to* get a two-year lease.
> NOT: may can
> I *will have to* move next month.
> NOT: will must

Ability, Possibility

1. We use *can* to show ability, natural or learned.

> I *can* run fast.
> *Can* you speak English well?

2. We use *can* for a possibility.

> A. I'm interested in the apartment for rent in your building.
> B. I *can* show you the apartment at 6 o'clock.

3. The negative of *can* is *cannot*. The contraction is *can't*.

> I *can't* understand my lease, but my lawyer can.

4. Don't use *can* after another modal. Use *be able to*.

> I won't *be able to* help you tonight.
> NOT: won't can

5. We use *can* in the following common expression:

> I *can't afford* a bigger apartment. I don't have enough money.

6. *Can* is usually not stressed in affirmative sentences. Sometimes it is hard to hear the final /t/, so we must pay attention to the vowel sound to hear the difference. Listen to your teacher pronounce:

> I can gó. /kIn/
> I cán't go. /kænt/

In a short answer, we pronounce *can* as /kæn/.

> Can you help me later? /kIn/
> Yes, I can. /kæn/

7. For past ability, use *could* or *was/were able to*.

> I *can* speak English now, but I *couldn't* speak it five years ago.
> I *could* have a dog in my last apartment, but I *can't* have one in my present apartment.
> *Were* you *able* to get your security deposit back? Yes, I was.

EXERCISE 11   Check (✓) the activities that you can do. Find a partner and ask about your partner's abilities. Report something interesting that you learned about your partner to the class.

EXAMPLE: **Maria can knit sweaters and gloves.**

1. _____ speak another language well (besides English and my native language)
2. _____ stand on my head
3. _____ use a word processor
4. _____ change a tire
5. _____ play chess
6. _____ swim
7. _____ jog five miles
8. _____ train a dog
9. _____ knit
10. _____ play a musical instrument
11. _____ _____

to knit

●●

R
E
A
D
I
N
G

Before you read:

1. Look at page iv of this book. Look for the symbol ©.
2. What other information can you find on this page?

Read the following article. Pay special attention to *can, may, be permitted to,* and *be allowed to.*

COPYRIGHT LAW

We often see people at a copy machine copying pages from a book. However, by law, they **are not permitted to** do this. They are violating copyright law. Copyright law is the right of an author, publisher, or composer to exclusive publication of his or her work.

If you look at the copyright page of a book (it follows the title page), you will see the symbol © followed by a date and the following words: "All rights reserved. No part of this book **may** be reproduced, in any form or by any means, without permission in writing from the publisher." This means that you **cannot** copy pages from a book.

If an author wants to use an article, a chapter, a map, or a picture belonging to another author whose work is protected by copyright law, he or she **can** do it only if he or she gets written permission. The author often has to pay for this permission.

Copyright law protects a work until 50 years after the author's death. After this time, we **are allowed to** quote[2] this author without permission.

Unfortunately, when people violate copyright law, the original author receives no money for the work he or she has done.

●●

————
[2]To *quote* means to use someone's exact words.

Permission

1. We use _can, may, be permitted to,_ and _be allowed to_[3] for permission. These words can refer to permission from a legal authority.

	can't	
We	are not permitted to	copy a book.
	are not allowed to	
	may not	

NOTE: Do not use a contraction for _may not._

2. These words can also refer to permission from a person in a superior position.

The child _is not allowed_ to watch TV after 9 p.m. (This is under authority of the parent.)
I'm not permitted to use the company copy machine for personal business. (This is under the authority of one's employer.)
Teacher to student: You _may not_ use your dictionary during the test.
Landlord to tenant: You _cannot_ have a dog in your apartment.

EXERCISE 12 Fill in each blank with an appropriate permission word to talk about what is or isn't permitted at this school.

EXAMPLES: We _aren't allowed to_ smoke in the classroom.

We _can_ leave the room without asking the teacher for permission.

1. We _____ smoke in the cafeteria.

2. Students _____ talk during a test.

3. Students _____ use their dictionaries when they write compositions.

4. Students _____ write a test with a pencil.

5. Students _____ repeat a course a second time.

6. Students _____ sit in any seat they want.

7. Students _____ use their textbooks during a test.

8. Students _____ make a copy of their textbooks.

---

[3]_Permitted_ and _allowed_ are past participles used as adjectives.

EXERCISE 13   Work with a partner. Write questions to ask the teacher about what is permitted in this class, in this school, or during a test. Your teacher will answer.

EXAMPLES: *May we use our textbooks during a test?*

Are we allowed to smoke in the washrooms?

1. _____

2. _____

3. _____

· ·

R
E
A
D
I
N
G

Before you read:

1. Do you plan to become an American citizen? When can you apply for citizenship?
2. If you become a citizen of the U.S., will you have to give up citizenship in your country?

Read the following article. Pay special attention to *must* and *have to.*

AMERICAN CITIZENSHIP

There are certain requirements you **must** meet in order to become a naturalized[4] American citizen:

1. You **must** be at least 18 years old.
2. You **must** be able to speak, read, and write simple English.
3. You **must** pass a test to show that you have a basic knowledge of U.S. government and history. Minor children of parents who become citizens **don't have to** take the test.
4. You **must** be a legal resident for at least five years before you apply.[5]
5. You **must** not support any political group that is disloyal to the U.S.
6. You **must** be a person of good moral character.
7. You **must** submit photos and fingerprints with your application.

fingerprints

---

[4]*Naturalization* is the legal process by which a foreigner becomes a citizen of the United States.

[5]For someone married to an American citizen, the requirement is three years.

8. Finally, you **must** take an oath of allegiance.[6] You **must** state that you will no longer have allegiance to another country and that you will defend the Constitution and laws of the U.S.

These are some questions new citizens sometimes ask:

Q. Do I **have to** vote after I become a citizen?
A. No. You **don't have to** vote.
Q. Do I **have to** give up my citizenship in my native country?
A. It depends on the country you come from. Some countries allow a naturalized American citizen to keep his original citizenship.
Q. Do I **have to** get an American passport?
A. Only if you plan to travel to another country.
Q. Do I **have to** carry my citizenship papers?
A. Legal residents **must** carry their alien card (more commonly known as a "green card") at all times.

Strong Necessity, Obligation

1. We use *must* or *have to* for legal obligations.

   To become a citizen, you *must* (or *have to*) take a citizenship test.

2. For personal obligations, *have to* is more common than *must*. *Must* shows great urgency.

   I can't go to the movies with you. I *have to* study for my citizenship test.
   You *must* leave the building immediately. It's on fire!

3. In fast, informal speech, *have to* is often pronounced "hafta." *Has to* is pronounced "hasta." Listen to your teacher pronounce these sentences:

   I have to move. = I "hafta" move.
   She has to leave. = She "hasta" leave.

4. *Have got to* also shows strong necessity. In fast speech, we often pronounce *have got to* "gotta." We use it mostly in affirmative statements. It is not generally used for questions and negatives.

   I've got to study for a test. = I('ve) gotta study for a test.

EXERCISE 14   What must you do to become an American citizen? (Use *you* in the impersonal sense.) Complete each statement.

EXAMPLE: <u>*You must be able to speak*</u> simple English.

1. _____ a test.

2. _____ a legal resident for five years.

3. _____ three photos and your fingerprints.

---

[6]When you take an *oath of allegiance,* you promise to be a loyal citizen of the United States.

4. _____ at least eighteen years old.

5. _____ an oath of allegiance.

Language Notes

Not Have To versus *Must Not*

1. In an affirmative sentence, *have to* and *must* are very similar, but *must* sounds stronger, more urgent.

    The landlord isn't going to renew my lease. I *must* move.
    I need a bigger apartment. I *have to* move.

2. In negative statements, *must* and *have to* are very different. *Must not* shows prohibition. *Not have to* means not necessary.

    After you become a citizen, you *must not* support an enemy of the U.S. (This is prohibited.)
    You *don't have to* carry your passport with you. (It is not required.)

I *must not* change the locks in my apartment. (This is prohibited.)
My landlady offered me a lease for another year. I *don't have to* move when my lease is up. (This is not necessary. I have a choice.)

3. *Must* has no past form. The past of both *must* and *have to* is *had to*.

    I *had to* take my citizenship test last month.
    I *had to* submit three photos and my fingerprints.

EXERCISE 15   Practice using *must not* for prohibition. (Use *you* in the impersonal sense.)

    EXAMPLE: **Name something you must not do.**
                 You must not steal.

    1. Name something you must not do on the bus.
    2. Name something you mustn't do during a test.
    3. Name something you mustn't do in the library.
    4. Name something you must not do in the classroom.
    5. Name something you mustn't carry onto an airplane.

EXERCISE 16   Tell if you have to or don't have to do the following. For affirmative statements, you can also use *have got to*.

    EXAMPLES: **work on Saturdays**
                I have to work on Saturdays.   OR   **I've got to work on Saturdays.**

                wear a suit to work
                I don't have to wear a suit to work.

    1. speak English every day
    2. use a dictionary to read the newspaper
    3. pay rent on the first of the month
    4. type my homework
    5. work on Saturdays

EXERCISE 17   Fill in each blank with *don't have to* (to show that something is not necessary) or *must not* (to show that something is prohibited).

      EXAMPLES: You _don't have to_ bring your dictionary to class.

              You _must not_ smoke in the classroom.

1. You _____ cheat on a test.

2. You _____ drive through a red light.

3. You _____ speak English perfectly to become an American citizen. It's enough to speak simple English.

4. Resident aliens _____ become American citizens if they don't want to.

5. You _____ steal.

6. People over seventeen years of age _____ attend school. They can leave school if they want.

7. U.S. citizens _____ vote if they don't want to.

8. A U.S. citizen _____ support an enemy of the United States.

9. You _____ marry an American citizen to become a citizen of the U.S.

10. My lease says that I _____ have a dog in my apartment.

EXERCISE 18   Tell if you had to or didn't have to do the following.

      EXAMPLES: **get a visa to come to the U.S.**
              I had to get a visa to come to the U.S.

              pay tuition for this course
              I didn't have to pay tuition for this course.

1. wear a uniform to school when I was a child
2. practice a musical instrument when I was a child
3. serve in the military in my country
4. vote in my country
5. wait a long time to get permission to come to the U.S.

EXERCISE 19 Fill in each blank to make a true statement. Find a partner and compare your answers to your partner's answers.

EXAMPLE: **I've got to** _talk to my counselor_ **after class.**

1. I have to _____ every day.

2. I don't have to _____ on Saturdays.

3. I've got to _____ before a test.

4. When I was a child, I had to _____

5. When I was a child, I didn't have to _____

6. The teacher has to _____

7. The teacher doesn't have to _____

8. I must not _____ in my apartment.

Advice

1. We use _should_ to give advice.
   A. My landlord doesn't provide enough heat in the winter.
   B. You _should_ complain to the city.

2. We use _had better_ to give a warning. Something bad can happen if a person doesn't follow this advice.

   Your stove is very dirty. You_'d better_ clean it if you want your landlady to return your security deposit.

   I have to take my citizenship test next week. I_'d better_ study, or I might fail.

EXERCISE 20 Give advice using _should_.

EXAMPLE: **My landlord is going to raise the rent by 20%.**
          You should move.

1. My next-door neighbors play their stereo loud all the time. I can't sleep at night.
2. My landlady doesn't give us enough heat in the winter.
3. I can't understand my lease.
4. I broke a window in my apartment.
5. My landlord doesn't want to return my security deposit.
6. I have a job interview early tomorrow morning.
7. Some students talk in the library, and other students can't study.

EXERCISE 21   Fill in each blank to complete the statement.

EXAMPLES: You'd better *take an umbrella*_____, or you're going to get wet.

You'd better fill up your gas tank right away, or

*you're going to run out of gas.*_____

1. You'd better _____, or your landlord will keep your deposit.

2. I'd better _____, or I'll lose my job.

3. They'd better _____, or they'll fail this course.

4. He'd better put enough postage on that letter, or _____

5. We'd better hurry, or _____

Language Notes

Possibility

1. We use *will* or *be going to* for certainty about the future. We use *may* or *might* for uncertainty about the future.[7]

My lease *will* expire on April 30.
My landlord *might* raise my rent at that time.
I *may* move. I'm not really sure.

2. We use a simple verb for certainty about the present. We use *may* or *might* for uncertainty about the present.

My brother isn't here today. He *is* sick.
The teacher isn't here today. She *may* be sick.
Her daughter *might* be sick.

3. *May* and *might* are modals. We use them with another verb. *Maybe* is an adverb. It comes at the beginning of the sentence. Compare:

Maybe I will move.
I *might* move.
Maybe he will be late.
He *may* be late.
Maybe he doesn't understand.
He *might* not understand.

4. We don't usually use *may* or *might* in a question about possibility. Instead we ask:

Do you think you will move?
Do you think he will be late?
Do you think he understands?

EXERCISE 22   Fill in each blank with a possibility.

EXAMPLES: If you don't pay your rent on time, *you might have to pay a late fee.*

If I make a lot of noise in my apartment, *the neighbors may complain.*

1. When my lease is up, _____

2. If I don't clean my apartment before I move out, _____

_____

---

[7]*Might* is not a past form of *may*.

3. If a person doesn't graduate from high school, _____

   _____

4. If I don't study for the next test, _____

5. If we don't register for classes early, _____

   _____

6. If I don't pass this course, _____

7.6 Negatives of Modals

Study the meanings of the negatives of modals and related words.

Negative Modal	Meaning	Example
must not	prohibition	You must not steal.
can't	no permission	You can't copy pages from a book without the permission of the publisher. It is not allowed.
had better not	warning	You'd better not park there, or you might get a ticket.
shouldn't	advice; a bad idea	You shouldn't play your music loud in your apartment. It's not good for your neighbors.
not have to	not necessary	An American citizen doesn't have to vote. He or she has a choice.
may not, might not	possibly not	My landlord might not give me a new lease next year. I'm not sure.

EXERCISE 23   Students (S) are asking the teacher (T) questions about the final exam. Fill in each blank with the negative form of an appropriate modal or related word. (In some cases, more than one answer is possible.)

   S. Do I have to sit in a specific seat for the test?

   T. No, you _*don't have to*_. You can choose any seat you want.

   S. Is it OK if I talk to another student during a test?

   T. No. Absolutely not. You _____ talk to another student during a test.

(1)

S. What if I don't understand something on the test? Can I ask another student?

T. You _____ ask another student, or I'll think you're getting an answer. Ask
      (2)
   me if you have a question.

S. What happens if I am late for the test? Will you let me in?

T. Of course I'll let you in. However, if you come late, you _____ have time
                                                                (3)
   to finish the test. My advice is that you _____ come late.
                                               (4)

S. Do I have to bring my own paper for the final test?

T. If you want to, you can. But you _____ bring paper. I'll give you paper if
                                      (5)
   you need it.

S. Must I write the test with a pen?

T. You can use whatever you want. You _____ use a pen.
                                        (6)

S. How long will the test take? The full period?

T. Probably not. You can use the full period, but you _____ need so much
                                                        (7)
   time. Let me give you some advice: if you see an item that is difficult for you,
   go on to the next item. You _____ spend too much time on a difficult item,
                               (8)
   or you won't finish the test.

S. If I finish the test early, do I have to stay in the room?

T. No, you _____ stay. You can leave.
             (9)

EXERCISE 24   Circle a game you like from the list below. Find a partner who also likes
this game. Write a list of some of the rules of this game. Tell what you can, cannot,
should, have to, and must not do. (If you and your partner are from the same country,
you can write about a game from your country.)

chess   tennis   football   poker   other _____
checkers   baseball   soccer   volleyball

EXAMPLE: **checkers**
         You have to move the pieces on a diagonal. You can only move
         in one direction until you get a king. Then you can move in two
         directions.

EXERCISE 25   A student will read one of the following problems out loud to the class, pretending that this is his or her problem. Other students will ask for more information and give advice about this problem.

EXAMPLE: My mother-in-law comes to visit all the time. When she's here, she always criticizes everything we do. I told my wife that I don't want her here, but she says, "It's my mother, and I want her here." What should I do?

A. How long do you think she will stay?
B. She might stay for about two weeks or longer.
C. How does she criticize you? What does she say?
B. She says I shouldn't smoke. It's not good for the children.
D. Well, I agree with her. You shouldn't smoke.
B. My children aren't allowed to watch TV after 8 o'clock. But my mother-in-law lets them watch TV as long as they want.
E. You'd better have a talk with her and tell her your rules.

Problem 1.   My mother is eighty years old, and she lives with us. It's very hard on my family to take care of her. We'd like to put her in a nursing home, where she can get better care. Mother refuses to go. What can we do?

Problem 2.   Last night I was putting my son's socks in his drawer when I found marijuana. He's only 16 years old. I told him that I found his marijuana, and he said, "It's not mine. It belongs to a friend." What should I do?

Problem 3.   My best friend is married. Last week I saw her husband in a restaurant with another woman. They looked very romantic together. Do you think I should tell my friend?

Write your own problem to present to the class. It can be real or imaginary. (Suggestions: a problem with a neighbor, your landlord, a teacher or class, a service you are dissatisfied with)

• •

R
E
A
D
I
N
G

Before you read:

1. People often go to a garage sale or an apartment sale to buy used items. At this kind of sale, people sell things that they don't want or need anymore. Did you ever buy anything at this kind of sale?
2. At a garage sale, it is usually not necessary to pay the asking price. You can bargain[8] with the seller. Can you bargain on prices in your country? In a store? Where?

This is a conversation at a garage sale between a seller (S) and a buyer (B). Read the conversation. Pay special attention to modals and related expressions.

AT A GARAGE SALE

S. I see you're looking at my microwave oven. **May** I help you with it?

B. Yes. I'm interested in buying one. Does it work well?

S. It's only two years old, and it's in perfect working condition. **Would you like** to try it out?

B. Sure. **Could** you plug it in somewhere?

S. I have an outlet right here. **Why don't we** boil a cup of water so you can see how well it works.

outlet

A few minutes later . . .

B. It seems to work well. **Would** you tell me why you're selling it, then?

S. It's too small for our family. We bought a bigger one that can do more things.

B. How much do you want for it?[9]

S. $80.

B. **Will** you take $60?

S. **Can** you wait a minute? I'll ask my wife.

A few minutes later . . .

S. My wife says she'll let you have it for $65.

B. OK. **May** I write you a check?

S. I'm sorry. **I'd rather** have cash.

B. **Would** you hold it for me for an hour? I can go to the supermarket and cash a check.

S. **Could** you leave me a small deposit? Ten dollars, maybe?

B. Yes, I can.

S. Fine. I'll hold it for you, then.

garage sale

• •

---

[8]When a buyer *bargains* with the seller, the buyer makes an offer lower than the asking price and hopes that he or she and the seller will agree on a lower price.

[9]We ask "How much is it?" when the price is fixed. We ask "How much do you want for it?" when the price is negotiable. You can bargain for it.

7.7 Using Modals for Politeness

Modals are often used to make a statement more polite. You have probably heard salespeople say these words to you as a customer:

> May I help you?
> Can I help you?

Observe the use of modals for politeness in the following boxes.

To Ask Permission	
May Can Could	I write you a check?

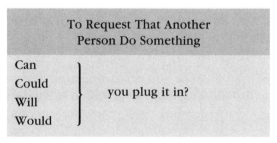

To Request That Another Person Do Something	
Can Could Will Would	you plug it in?

NOTE: *Could* and *would* are softer than *can* and *will.*

To Express a Want or Desire
Would you *like* to try out the microwave oven? Yes, I *would like* to see if it works. *I'd like* a cup of coffee.

To Make a Suggestion
Why don't you go to a cash machine if you need cash? *Why don't we* boil a cup of water to see if the microwave works?

Preference
Would you rather pay with cash or by credit? I'd rather pay by credit (than with cash).

NOTES:

- We use *or* in questions with *would rather.* We use *than* in statements with *would rather.*

- We can use a noun or an infinitive after *prefer.* After *would rather,* we always use the base form of the verb.

I prefer to have cash.	I prefer cash.
I'd rather have cash.	*Not:* I'd rather cash.

EXERCISE 26   Change each request to make it more polite. Practice *may, can, could I?*

      EXAMPLES: **I want to use your phone.**
                    May I use your phone?

                    I want to borrow a quarter.
                    Could I borrow a quarter?

1. I want to help you.   3. I want to leave the room.
2. I want to close the door.   4. I want to write you a check.

EXERCISE 27   Change these commands to make them more polite. Practice *can, could, will, would you?*

      EXAMPLES: **Call the doctor for me.**
                    Would you call the doctor for me?

                    Give me a cup of coffee.
                    Could you give me a cup of coffee, please?

1. Repeat the sentence.   3. Spell your name.
2. Give me your paper.   4. Tell me your phone number.

EXERCISE 28   Make these sentences more polite by using *would like.*

      EXAMPLES: **Do you want some help?**
                    Would you like some help?

1. I want to ask you a question.
2. The teacher wants to speak with you.
3. Do you want to try out the oven?
4. Yes. I want to see if it works.

EXERCISE 29   Make each suggestion more polite by putting it in the form of a negative question.

      EXAMPLES: **Plug it in.**
                    Why don't you plug it in?

                    Let's eat now.
                    Why don't we eat now?

1. Take a sweater.   3. Turn left here.
2. Let's turn off the light.   4. Let's leave early.

EXERCISE 30   Make a statement of preference.

>   EXAMPLE: work indoors/outdoors
>   **I'd rather work indoors than outdoors.**

1. live in the U.S./in my country
2. live in the city/in a suburb
3. get up early/sleep late[10]
4. take a relaxing vacation/an active vacation
5. live in a house/a condo
6. read a story/write a composition

EXERCISE 31   Ask a question with the words given. Another student will answer.

>   EXAMPLE: **eat Chinese food/Italian food**
>
>   **A. Would you rather eat Chinese food or Italian food?**
>   **B. I'd rather eat Italian food.**

1. read fact/fiction
2. watch funny movies/serious movies
3. listen to classical music/popular music
4. visit Europe/Africa
5. own a large luxury car/a small sports car
6. watch a soccer game/take part in a soccer game
7. write a letter/receive a letter
8. _____

EXERCISE 32   This is a conversation between a seller (S) and a buyer (B) at a garage sale. Make this conversation more polite by using modals and other polite expressions in place of the underlined words.

May I help you?
S. <u>What do you want?</u>

B. I'm interested in that lamp. <u>Show it to me</u>. Does it work?

S. I'll go and get a light bulb. <u>Wait a minute</u>.

A few minutes later . . .

B. <u>Plug it in</u>.

S. You see? It works fine.

———————
[10]*Sleep late* means to wake up late in the morning.

B. How much do you want for it?

S. This is one of a pair. I have another one just like it. They're $10 each. I <u>prefer to sell</u> them together.

B. <u>Give them both to me for $15</u>.

S. I'll have to ask my husband. (a few seconds later) My husband says he'll sell them to you for $17.

B. Fine. I'll take them. Will you take a check?

S. I <u>prefer to</u> have cash.

B. I only have five dollars on me.

S. OK. I'll take a check. <u>Show me some identification</u>.

B. Here's my driver's license.

S. That's fine. Write the check to James Kucinski.

B. <u>Spell your name for me</u>.

S. K-U-C-I-N-S-K-I.

EXPANSION ACTIVITIES

PROVERBS   The following proverbs contain modals. Discuss the meaning of each proverb. Do you have a similar proverb in your language?

You can lead a horse to water, but you can't make it drink.
You can't teach an old dog new tricks.
You can't tell (judge) a book by its cover.
People in glass houses shouldn't throw stones.

POEM   This short poem contains *would rather.* Do you think it's funny?

I never saw a purple cow
I never hope to see one.
But I can tell you anyhow
I'd rather see than be one.

WRITING   1. Write a short composition comparing rules in an apartment in this city with rules in an apartment in your hometown or country.
2. Find a partner. With your partner, write a list of instructions on how to register for a course at this college.

3. Write about the differences between this college and a college in your country. Are students allowed to do things here that they can't do in your country?

4. Find out what a student has to do to register for the first time at this college. You may want to visit the registrar's office to interview a worker there. Write a short composition explaining to a new student the steps for admission and registration.

OUTSIDE ACTIVITIES

1. Find out what you must do to get one of the following. Report your information to the class.

   a. a passport (Call or write to the U.S. Department of State.)
   b. a credit card (Get a credit card application from a business.)
   c. a library card (Visit your public library.)
   d. a marriage license (Call the marriage license department of this county.)
   e. a Social Security card (Call or write to the U.S. Social Security Administration.)
   f. a driver's license (Call or write to the Secretary of State of this state, Department of Motor Vehicles.)

2. Call or write to the department of housing in your city. Ask if this department can send you a list of rights and responsibilities of renters and landlords.

3. Look at the Sunday newspaper for notices about garage sales or apartment sales. What kind of items are going to be sold? If you have time, go to a sale. Report about your experience to the class.

DISCUSSIONS

1. Work with a partner from your own country, if possible. Talk about some laws in your country that are different from laws in the United States. Present this information to the class.

EXAMPLE: **Citizens must vote in my country. In the U.S., they don't have to vote.**
People must carry identification papers at all times. In the U.S., people don't have to carry identification papers.
In my country, citizens must not own a gun.

2. Complete each sentence any way you want. Share your answers with a partner, a small group, or the entire class.

   1. _____ years ago I couldn't _____, but I can now.

   2. When I was a child, I could _____, but I can't now.

   3. When I didn't speak English well, I wasn't able to _____

EDITING ADVICE

· ·

1. After a modal, we use the base form. After other verbs, we use the infinitive form.

    I must ~~to~~ study.

    They like *to* swim.

2. After a modal, we use the base form. A base form has no ending or tense.

    He can cook~~s~~.

3. We don't put two modals together. We change the second modal to another form.

    She will ~~must~~ *have to* take the test.

4. An infinitive is *to* + base form.

    I needed to work~~ed~~.

5. After *want* and other similar verbs, we can use an object + infinitive.

    He wants *me to* drive.

6. Every sentence must have a subject. We introduce some infinitives with *it*.

    It ~~i~~s important to learn English.

7. Use *for,* not *to,* before an object.

    It's important *for* ~~to~~ me to find a job.

8. After *for,* use an object pronoun.

    It's important for ~~he~~ *him* to be on time.

SUMMARY OF LESSON SEVEN

1. Summary of Modals and Related Expressions, by Meanings:

Ability, Possibility	*Can* you understand your lease? You *can* ask a lawyer to explain it to you. When I was 12 years old, I *could* run a mile in five minutes. I'll *be able to* help you later.
Necessity, Obligation	The landlord *must* put a smoke detector in the apartment. I've *got to* move next month. I *have to* find a bigger apartment. Last week I *had to* go to court.
Permission	My landlord says I *can't/may not* have a dog in my apartment. We're *not allowed/permitted to* talk during a test.
Possibility	I *might/may* move to New York next year.
Advice	My landlord doesn't provide enough heat. What *should* I do?
Warning	You'*d better* pay your rent on time, or you'll have to pay a late fee.
Preference	I'*d rather* live in a condo than in a house. *Would* you *rather* own or rent?
Want	*Would* you *like* to see my apartment?
Request	It's too hot in here. *Would* *Could* *Can* you open a window? *Will*
Asking permission	*May* *Can* I see your apartment? *Could*

2. Patterns with Infinitives:

He wants *to leave.*
He wants me *to stay.*
It's important *to understand* your rights.
It's necessary for me *to leave* a security deposit.
I'm afraid *to appear* in court.

LESSON SEVEN TEST/REVIEW

Part 1   Find the mistakes with modals and infinitives, and correct them. Not every sentence has a mistake. If the sentence is correct, write *C*.

EXAMPLES: I must ~~to~~ take a citizenship test.

I wanted to help you.   *C*

1. We're not permitted use our books during the test.

2. I can speak English now, but I can't speak it five years ago.

3. It's important to me to know English well.

4. When can she leave?

5. I will can help you tomorrow.

6. It's impossible for I to speak English perfectly.

7. He tried to explained the problem.

8. Is necessary to come to class on time.

9. Did you expect live in the U.S.?

10. They wanted I study.

11. I couldn't understood the lesson.

12. She has to study.

13. He has to worked last night.

14. Is it possible for them to travel?

15. I've got to work tomorrow.

16. It's important for me have a good education.

Part 2 This is a conversation between two friends about moving. Fill in each blank with *can, could, should, may, might, must, would, have to, have got to,* or *be able to.* (In some cases, more than one answer is possible.)

A. I'm moving on Saturday. I ___would___ like to hire movers, but I _____ afford
(1 not)

to. _____ you help me?
(2)

B. I _____ like to help you, but I have a bad back. I went to the doctor last
(3)

week, and she told me that I _____ lift anything heavy for a while. I
(4 not)

_____ help you pack things this week.
(5)

A. Thanks. I don't have enough boxes. I looked for boxes last weekend, but I

_____ find any. _____ you help me find boxes?
(6)   (7)

B. Sure.

A. I have another favor to ask you. _____ I borrow your van?
(8)

B. I'm not really sure. I _____ have to work on Saturday. If I do, I won't
(9)

_____ lend you my van on Saturday. How about Sunday? I _____ work
(10)   (11 not)

on Sunday.

A. I _____ rather move on Saturday. Besides, someone else is moving in to my
(12)

old apartment on Sunday, so I _____ be out by Saturday night.
(13)

B. I'll let you know tomorrow. If I _____ work on Saturday, I won't need my
(14 not)

van. I'll call you on Thursday night to let you know about Saturday.

A. Thanks.

LESSON EIGHT

GRAMMAR

Present Perfect
Present Perfect Continuous

CONTEXT

Alcoholics Anonymous

Lesson Focus **Present Perfect Tense; Present Perfect Continuous Tense**

- We form the present perfect tense with the auxiliary verb *have* or *has* and the past participle. We use the present perfect tense when the action of the sentence is during a period of time that began in the past and includes the present. We also use the present perfect to refer to an action that occurred at an indefinite time in the past.

  I *have studied* English for six months.   They *have visited* us many times.

- We form the present perfect continuous tense with *have* or *has,* plus *been,* and the verb + *-ing*. We use the present perfect continuous tense with actions that began in the past and continue to the present.

  She *has been working* with me for three years.

• •

R
E
A
D
I
N
G

Before you read:

Is alcoholism a problem in your country? How do people try to solve this problem? How do families deal with this problem?

Read the following article. Pay special attention to the present perfect tense verbs.

ALCOHOLICS ANONYMOUS

Alcoholics Anonymous (AA) is an organization that helps alcoholics help themselves. It **has been** in existence since 1935. It was started by two men who found that they could control their drinking problem by getting support from each other. Since 1935, AA groups **have formed** all over the U.S. and in many foreign countries. Many people believe that it is one of the most effective ways of dealing with the problem of alcoholism.

At a typical AA meeting, a member of the group may tell the story of how he or she became an alcoholic and how this behavior **has affected** the lives of the speaker's family. The person may talk about how life **has changed** since he or she started his or her recovery. Each person has a chance to talk about the speaker's story.

Since it started, AA **has been** so successful that many other self-help groups **have started** programs based on the AA model. Today you can find such groups as OA (Overeaters Anonymous), NA (Narcotics Anonymous), ACOA (Adult Children of Alcoholics), and others. Many people **have been** able to quit their addictive[1] or ineffective behavior as a result of these self-help groups.

• •

---

[1]An *addictive behavior* or *addiction* is the inability to stop doing something harmful, such as drinking, smoking, or using drugs.

8.1 The Past Participle

The past participle is a form of the verb. It is not a tense. One use of the past participle is with the auxiliary verb *have* to form the present perfect tense.

My life has *changed.*
I have *been* successful.

In many cases, the past participle and the past form of the verb are the same.

Base Form	Past Form	Past Participle
study	studied	studied
look	looked	looked
leave	left	left
understand	understood	understood
put	put	put

The following verbs have a past participle that is different from the past tense. They are grouped according to the type of change. For an alphabetical listing of irregular past tenses and past participles, see Appendix I.

Base Form	Past Form	Past Participle
become	became	become
come	came	come
run	ran	run
blow	blew	blown
draw	drew	drawn
fly	flew	flown
grow	grew	grown
know	knew	known
throw	threw	thrown
swear	swore	sworn
tear	tore	torn
wear	wore	worn
break	broke	broken
choose	chose	chosen
freeze	froze	frozen
speak	spoke	spoken
steal	stole	stolen

Base Form	Past Form	Past Participle
begin	began	begun
drink	drank	drunk
ring	rang	rung
sing	sang	sung
sink	sank	sunk
swim	swam	swum
arise	arose	arisen
bite	bit	bitten
drive	drove	driven
ride	rode	ridden
rise	rose	risen
write	wrote	written
be	was/were	been
eat	ate	eaten
fall	fell	fallen
forgive	forgave	forgiven
give	gave	given
mistake	mistook	mistaken
see	saw	seen
shake	shook	shaken
take	took	taken

Miscellaneous Changes:

do	did	done
forget	forgot	forgotten
get	got	gotten
go	went	gone
lie	lay	lain
prove	proved	proven (or proved)
show	showed	shown (or showed)

8.2 The Present Perfect Tense

We form the present perfect tense by using the auxiliary verb *have* or *has* + a past participle.

Subject	*Have/Has*	Past Participle	
I You We They	have	worked. eaten. forgotten. understood. spoken.	
He She It	has	left. known. begun.	
There	has	been	a mistake.
There	have	been	some problems.

Compare statements, questions, and short answers using the present perfect.

Wh- Word	*Have*	Subject	*Have*	Main Verb	Complement	Short Answer
		He	has	been	in an AA group.	
		He	hasn't	been	in an NA group.	
	Has	he		been	in the group for long?	Yes, he has.* No, he hasn't.
How long	has	he		been	in the group?	
		Who	has	been	in the group?	

*NOTE: Don't use a contraction for a short *yes* answer.

1. In general, we use the present perfect tense when the action of the sentence is during a period of time that began in the past and includes the present.

> Since 1935, AA groups *have formed* all over the U.S.
> My friend *has been* a member of AA for ten years.
> He *has attended* three meetings this month.

2. We also use the present perfect to refer to an action that occurred at an indefinite time in the past that still has importance to the present situation.

> AA *has helped* my friend a lot.
> Many people *have had* success in AA.

3. We can make contractions with the auxiliary verb and subject pronouns.

I have = I've	He has = He's
You have = You've	She has = She's
We have = We've	It has = It's
They have = They've	There has = There's

4. Be careful not to confuse contractions with *has* and contractions with *is*. The word following the contraction will tell you what the contraction means.

She's leaving. = She *is* leaving.
She's left. = She *has* left.

There's a problem. = There *is* a problem.
There's been a problem. = There *has* been a problem.

EXERCISE 1   This is a conversation between two friends, Ann (A) and Betty (B), who haven't seen each other for a long time. Fill in each blank with the present perfect form of the verb in parentheses ( ).

A. Hi, Betty.

B. Hi, Ann. I _haven't seen_ you for a long time. You look so different.
         (not/seen)

A. Yes. I _____ a lot of weight since we saw each other last.
         (1 lose)

B. Really? How?

A. With my OA group.

B. What's that?

A. It's Overeaters Anonymous. It's a group of people who have a problem with food. It's like AA, but instead of trying to give up alcohol, we try not to overeat. All my life I _____ overweight, and I finally decided to do
                                    (2 be)

something about it.

B. How much weight _____?
                        (3 you/lose)

A. I _____ 20 pounds so far. I want to lose 30 more pounds.
      (4 lose)

B. How long _____ in this group?
      <u>(5 you/be)</u>

A. I started in May. Since then, I _____ to about 15 meetings. It
                                          <u>(6 go)</u>

_____ me a lot. I _____ a lot of people with similar problems,
<u>(7 help)</u>   <u>(8 meet)</u>

and they _____ me support.
              <u>(9 give)</u>

B. I _____ ads on TV about weight-loss clinics.
      <u>(10 see)</u>

A. It's not one of those clinics you see advertised on TV. Those cost a lot of money.
   OA is free.

B. Can I join? I _____ to go on a diet many times, but I just can't do it.
                    <u>(11 try)</u>

A. I go every Thursday night. You can come with me to our next meeting.

8.3 The Present Perfect: Continuation from Past to Present

We use the present perfect tense to show that an action or state started in the past
and continues to the present.

She *has been* in the group since May.

She *has been* in the group for 3 months.

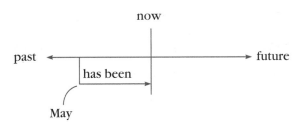

For and Since

1. We use *since* with a time that shows when an event began. We use *for* with the amount of time.

> I have been in the U.S. *since* May.
> I have been in the U.S. *for* five months.

2. In a negative sentence, we can use *for* or *in*.

> I haven't seen you *for* a long time.
> I haven't seen you *in* a long time.

3. *Since* can introduce a clause that shows the start of a continuous action. The verb in the *since* clause is in the simple past tense.

> She has lost 20 pounds *since* she *started* to go to OA meetings.
> She's learned a lot of English *since* she *came* to the U.S.

4. We can ask an information question with "How long . . .?" The answer to this question usually contains *for* or *since*.

> A. *How long* has your brother been in the U.S.?
> B. For ten years.
> A. *How long* has he been a citizen?
> B. Since 1994.

EXERCISE 2   Fill in each blank with the present perfect of the verb in parentheses ( ) to ask a question. Another student will answer with *for* or *since*.

> EXAMPLE: A. How long *have* you (know) *known* the teacher?
> B. I've known the teacher for three months.
>
> OR
>
> I've known the teacher since January.

1. How long _____ you (live) _____ in your apartment?

2. How long _____ you (be) _____ in the U.S.?

3. How long _____ you (study) _____ English?

4. How long _____ we (know) _____ each other?

5. How long _____ you (have) _____ your English dictionary?

The Simple Present versus The Present Perfect

The simple present refers only to the present. The present perfect with *for* or *since* connects the past to the present. Contrast the simple present with the present perfect.

> I *live* in the U.S. now. (simple present)
> I*'ve lived* in the U.S. for six years. (present perfect)

> I*'m* an American citizen now. (simple present)
> I*'ve been* a citizen since January. (present perfect)

EXERCISE 3   The following statements refer to the present only. Show when the action began by changing the tense to the present perfect and adding a phrase with *for* or *since*. Fill in each blank to make a **true** statement about yourself.

> EXAMPLE: I'm interested in _politics_ .
>
> I'm interested in politics. I've been interested in politics since I was in high school.
>
> OR
>
> I've been interested in politics for the past ten years.

1. I'm a college student.
2. Ms./Mr./Dr. _____ is my teacher.
3. I want to learn English.
4. I want to learn (more) about _____
5. I know the teacher.

EXERCISE 4   Read aloud the following present tense questions. Another student will answer. If the answer is *yes,* add a question with "How long have you . . .?"

> EXAMPLE: Do you have a car?
>
> A. Do you have a car?
> B. Yes, I do.
> A. How long have you had your car?
> B. I've had my car for three months.
>
> OR
>
> I've had my car since July.

1. Do you have a driver's license?
2. Do you have a car?
3. Do you have a Social Security card?
4. Do you have a computer?

5. Are you married?
6. Do you want to learn English?
7. Are you interested in American life?

EXERCISE 5   Write a **true** sentence using the present perfect with the word given and *for* or *since.* Share your answers with the class.

> EXAMPLES: **know** _My parents have known each other for over 40 years._
>
> **have** _I've had my car since 1993._

1. have _____

2. be _____

3. want _____

4. know _____

<u>*Always* and *Never*</u>

1. We use the present perfect with *always* to show that an action or state began in the past and continues to the present.

> Ann has *always* wanted to lose weight.
> I've *always* believed in God.

2. We use the present perfect with *never* to show that an action or state has not happened from the past to the present.

> Betty has *never* gone to an OA meeting.
> I've *never* gone to Paris.

3. Notice that *always* and *never* come between the auxiliary verb and the main verb.

EXERCISE 6   Make statements with *always.*

EXAMPLE: **Name something you've always thought about.**
I've always thought about my future.

1. Name something you've always enjoyed.
2. Name a person you've always liked.
3. Name something you've always wanted to do.
4. Name something you've always wanted to have.
5. Name something you've always needed.
6. Name something you've always been interested in.
7. Name something you've always thought about.

EXERCISE 7   Make statements with *never.*

EXAMPLE: **Name a machine you've never used.**
I've never used a fax machine.

1. Name a movie you've never seen.
2. Name a food you've never liked.
3. Name a subject you've never studied.
4. Name a city you've never visited.
5. Name a sport you've never played.

EXERCISE 8   Write four sentences telling about things you've always done (or been). Share your sentences with the class.

EXAMPLES: *I've always cooked the meals in my family.*

　　　　　　　I've always been lazy.

1. _____

2. _____

3. _____

4. _____

EXERCISE 9   Write four sentences telling about things you've never done (or been) but would like to. Share your sentences with the class.

EXAMPLES: *I've never studied photography, but I'd like to.*

　　　　　　　I've never acted in a play, but I'd like to.

1. _____

2. _____

3. _____

4. _____

8.4 The Present Perfect Continuous

Study the formation of the present perfect continuous tense.

Subject	*Have/Has*	*Been*	Verb + *-ing*
She	has	been	working.
I	have	been	studying.
They	have	been	trying.

Compare statements, questions, and short answers using the present perfect continuous.

Wh- Word	Have	Subject	Have	Been	Verb + ing	Complement	Short Answer
		He	has	been	living	in Miami for six months.	
		He	hasn't	been	living	with his parents.	
	Has	he		been	living	alone?	Yes, he has.
How long	has	he		been	living	alone?	
		Who	has	been	living	with him?	

Language Notes

1. We can use either the present perfect or the present perfect continuous tense with actions that began in the past and continue to the present. There is very little difference in meaning.

She *has been living* alone for three months.
She *has lived* alone for three months.

Using the continuous form puts more emphasis on including the present moment.

2. Remember that we do not use a continuous tense with nonaction verbs.

She *has had* a car since she came to the U.S. (NOT: She has been having a car.)

Some nonaction verbs are *like, love, want, need, know,* and *remember.*

EXERCISE 10   The following statements refer to the present only. Include the past by changing to a present perfect continuous statement. Use *for* or *since.* Fill in each blank to make a **true** statement about yourself.

EXAMPLE: **I'm studying** *karate.*
I've been studying karate for six years.

karate

1. I live in _____

_____

2. I work in/as _____.

_____

3. I attend _____ College/University.

_____

4. The teacher is explaining the present perfect tense.

_____

5. The students are practicing the present perfect continuous.

_____

EXERCISE 11   Read aloud each of the following present tense questions. Another student will answer. If the answer is *yes,* add a present perfect continuous question with "How long have you . . .?"

> EXAMPLE: **Do you play a musical instrument?**
> **A. Do you play a musical instrument?**
> **B. Yes. I play the piano.**
> **A. How long have you been playing the piano?**
> **B. I've been playing the piano since I was a child.**

1. Do you drive?   4. Do you wear glasses?
2. Do you work?   5. Do you play a musical instrument?
3. Do you smoke?

EXERCISE 12   Write a **true** sentence using the present perfect continuous with the words given and *for* or *since*. Share your sentences with the class.

> EXAMPLE: **work** *My brother has been working as a waiter for six years.*

1. study English _____

2. work _____

3. live _____

4. _____

EXERCISE 13   Ask the teacher questions with "How long . . .?" and the present perfect continuous of the words given. The teacher will answer your questions.

> EXAMPLES: **speak English**
> **A. How long have you been speaking English?**
> **B. I've been speaking English all[2] my life.**

1. teach English   4. use this book
2. work at this college   5. _____
3. live in this city

_____

[2]Do not use the preposition *for* before *all*.

8.5 The Present Perfect with Repetition Up to the Present

When we talk about the repetition of an action in a time period that includes the present, we can use the present perfect. The present perfect shows that the action can happen again in this time period because the time period is not finished.

I've *made* three phone calls today. (It is possible that I will make more calls today.)

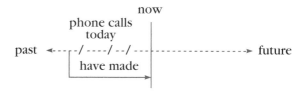

Language Notes

1. We can ask a *yes/no* question about repetition, or a question with "How many/much . . .?"

A. Has the teacher been absent this semester?
B. Yes, she has.
A. *How many times* has she been absent?
B. She's been absent once.
A. Have we had any homework this week?
B. Yes, we have.
A. *How much homework* have we had?
B. We've had two assignments.

2. We sometimes use *so far* or *up to now* or a time expression that includes the present moment (today, this week, this semester, this year).

So far, we have had five tests *this semester.*
I've been absent twice *this semester.*

3. If we use a past time expression, such as *last week*, *last month*, or *yesterday*, we use the past tense. The present is not included. Compare:

I've *gone* to the dentist twice *this year*.
I *went* to the dentist five times *last year*.
She's *driven* her car 200 miles *this month*.
She *drove* her car 500 miles *last month*.

EXERCISE 14   Ask a *yes/no* question with *so far* or *up to now* and the words given. Another student will answer.

> EXAMPLE: **you/come to every class**
> **A. Have you come to every class so far?**
> **B. Yes, I have.**
>   OR
> **B. No, I haven't. I've missed three classes.**

1. we/have any tests
2. this lesson/be difficult
3. the teacher/give a lot of homework
4. you/understand all the explanations
5. you/have any questions about this lesson

EXERCISE 15   Ask a question with "How many . . .?" and the words given. Talk about this month. Another student will answer.

> EXAMPLE: **times/go to the post office**
> **A. How many times have you gone to the post office this month?**
> **B. I've gone to the post office once this month.**
>   OR
> **I haven't gone to the post office at all this month.**

1. letters/write
2. times/eat in a restaurant
3. times/get paid
4. long-distance calls/make
5. books/buy

EXERCISE 16   Write four questions to ask another student or your teacher about repetition from the past to the present. Use *how much* or *how many*. The other person will answer.

> EXAMPLES: *In this city, how many apartments have you lived in?*
>
> *How many English courses have you taken at this college?*

1. _____

2. _____

3. _____

4. _____

8.6   **The Present Perfect: Indefinite Past Time**

We use the present perfect to refer to an action that occurred at an indefinite time in the past that still has importance to the present situation.

Have you ever *gone* to an AA meeting?   Yes, I *have.*

Ever

1. We often ask a present perfect question with ever to find out if something has happened at any time between the past and the present. We put *ever* between the subject and the main verb.

   A. Have you *ever* been on a diet?
   B. Yes, I have.

2. We can answer an *ever* question with a frequency response: *a few times, many times, often, never.*

   A. Have you ever eaten Chinese food?   A. Have you ever driven a truck?
   B. Yes. I've eaten Chinese food *many times.*   B. No. I've *never* driven a truck.

3. We can answer an *ever* question with a specific time. Use the simple past tense with a specific time.

   A. *Have* you ever *been* to Paris?   A. *Have* you ever *taken* a taxi in this city?
   B. Yes. I *was* in Paris *in 1991.*   B. Yes. I *took* a taxi *last week.*

EXERCISE 17   A man (A) is trying to remember where he met a woman (B) whom he sees at a party. Fill in each blank to complete the conversation.

A. You look familiar. _____*Have*_____ we ever _____*met*_____ before?
               (meet)

B. I don't think so.

A. I'm sure I've met you. Have you ever _____ to the University of
                                       (1 go)
   Wisconsin? I was a student there five years ago.

B. No, I _____.
          (2)

A. _____ in Milwaukee?
   (3 ever/live)

B. No, I never _____.
           (4)

A. _____ your picture ever _____ in the newspaper?
        (5 be)

B. No, it never _____.
                    (6)

A. What's your name?

B. Betty Shapiro.

A. Are you related to Michael Shapiro?

B. I _____ of him.
        (7 never/hear)

A. _____ Boone School?
    (8 your children/ever/attend)

B. I don't have any children.

A. _____ at the First National Bank?
        (9 ever/work)

B. Yes! I work there now. I'm a teller.

A. I work there too! I work in the accounting department. So that's where I know you from.

EXERCISE 18   Ask a question with "Have you ever . . .?" and the present perfect tense of the verb in parentheses ( ). Another student will answer. To answer with a specific time, use the past tense. To answer with a frequency response, use the present perfect tense.

> **EXAMPLES:**   **(go) to the zoo**
> **A. Have you ever gone to the zoo?**
> **B. Yes. I've gone there many times.**
>
> **(be) in jail**
> **A. Have you ever been in jail?**
> **B. No. I've never been in jail.**
>
> **(go) to Disneyland**
> **A. Have you ever gone to Disneyland?**
> **B. Yes. I went there last summer.**

1. (work) in a factory
2. (lose) a glove
3. (run) out of gas[3]
4. (fall) out of bed
5. (make) a mistake in English grammar

6. (tell) a lie
7. (eat) raw[4] fish
8. (study) calculus
9. _____
10. _____

---

[3]To *run out of gas* means to use all the gas in your car.

[4]*Raw* fish is not cooked.

EXERCISE 19   Find a partner. Ask your partner a question with "Have you ever . . .?" and the present perfect of the verb in parentheses ( ). If the answer is *yes*, ask for more specific information.

> EXAMPLE: (meet) a famous person
> A. Have you ever met a famous person?
> B. Yes, I have.
> A. Who did you meet?
> B. I met the mayor of my hometown.

1. (meet) a famous person
2. (go) to an art museum
3. (stay) up all night
4. (break) a window
5. (get) locked out[5] of your house or car
6. (see) a French movie
7. (go) to Las Vegas
8. (travel) by ship
9. (be) in love
10. (write) a poem
11. _____
12. _____

EXERCISE 20   Work with a partner. Write five questions with *ever* to ask your teacher. Your teacher will answer.

> EXAMPLES: *Have you ever gotten a ticket for speeding?*
> _____
>
> *Have you ever visited Poland?*
> _____

1. _____
2. _____
3. _____
4. _____
5. _____

EXERCISE 21   Ask a question with *ever* and the words given. Another student will answer.

> EXAMPLE: your country/have a woman president
> A. Has your country ever had a woman president?
> B. Yes, it has. We had a woman president from 1975 to 1979.

1. your country/have a civil war
2. your country's leader/visit the U.S.
3. an American president/visit your country

---

[5]To get *locked out* of your house means that you can't get in because you left the keys inside.

4. your country/have a woman president
5. you/go back to visit your country
6. there/be an earthquake in your hometown

Language Notes

Yet and Already

1. *Yet* and *already* refer to an indefinite time in the near past.

  Have you begun your diet *yet*?
  Yes. I've begun my diet *already*.

2. We use *yet* in a question to ask if an expected activity took place a short time ago. We use *yet* in a negative answer.

  A. Have you lost any weight *yet*?
  B. No, I haven't lost any weight *yet*. OR No, *not yet*.

3. For an affirmative statement, we use *already*.

  I've lost ten pounds *already*. OR I've *already* lost ten pounds.

4. We can answer a *yet* question with the simple past tense and a specific time.

  A. *Have* you *eaten* dinner yet?
  B. Yes. I *ate* dinner about 15 minutes ago.

5. We often use *just* to show that the action happened immediately before the sentence is said.

  We've *just* eaten dinner.
  I've *just* seen that movie.

EXERCISE 22   A mother (M) is trying to give her grown son (S) something to eat. Fill in each blank to complete the conversation.

M. Do you want something to eat? __*Have you eaten*__ yet?
                                        (you/eat)

S. No, thanks. I'm not hungry. I _____ just _____.
                                    (1 eat)

M. Your father _____ his dinner yet. You can eat with him.
                  (2 not/have)

S. I _____ you. I'm not hungry.
       (3 already/tell)

M. Have a little dessert, then. I _____ an apple pie.
                                    (4 just/make)

S. It seems I _____ myself clear yet. I'M NOT HUNGRY!
                (5 not/make)

EXERCISE 23   Ask a student who has recently arrived in this country if he or she has done these things yet.

EXAMPLE: **buy a car**
          A. Have you bought a car yet?
          B. Yes, I have. OR **No, I haven't.**

1. find a job   4. save any money
2. make any American friends   5. buy a car
3. open a bank account   6. write to your family

EXPANSION ACTIVITIES

WRITING   Write a composition about one of the following:

1. How your life has changed
   a. since you came to the U.S.
   b. since you got married
   c. since you had a baby
   d. since you started college
   e. since you graduated from high school

2. How your country has changed since a major event took place (a revo-
   lution, a war, the election of a new president).

Pay careful attention to verb tenses.

DISCUSSION   In a small group or with the entire class, talk about self-help groups. Do
                     you believe that people can improve themselves by getting help from
                     others with a similar problem? What kind of problems can be helped in
                     this way?

OUTSIDE   Use the ideas in Exercises 18 and 19 to interview an American about his
ACTIVITY   or her experiences. Invite the American to interview you. Tell the class
                     something interesting you found out about the American. Tell the class an
                     interesting question that the American asked you.

EDITING ADVICE

1. Don't confuse the *-ing* form and the past participle.

   taking
   She has been ~~taken~~ a test for two hours.

   given
   She has ~~giving~~ him a present.

2. Use the present perfect, not the simple present, to describe an action or state that continues from the past to the present.

   had
   He has a car for 2 years.
   ∧

   have   *ed*
   How long d~~o~~ you work in a factory?
                        ∧

3. Use *for*, not *since*, with the amount of time.

   for
   I've been studying English ~~since~~ three months.

4. Use the simple past, not the present perfect, with a specific past time.

   came
   He has ~~come~~ to the U.S. five months ago.

   did
   When h~~ave~~ you come to the U.S.?

5. Use the simple past, not the present perfect, in a *since* clause.

   came
   He has learned a lot of English since he has ~~come~~ to the U.S.

6. Use correct word order. Put the adverb between the the auxiliary and the main verb.

   never seen
   He has s~~een never~~ a French movie.

   ever gone
   Have you go~~ne ever~~ to France?

7. Use *yet* for negative statements; use *already* for affirmative statements.

   yet
   I haven't eaten dinner a~~lready~~.

SUMMARY OF LESSON EIGHT

1. Compare the Present Perfect and the Simple Past

Present Perfect

A. The action of the sentence began in the past and includes the present:

```
                now
                 |
past  <----- ----+------->  future
```

I've had my car since May.

I've been in the U.S. for ten years.

How long have you known the teacher?

I've always wanted to learn karate.

He has attended several O.A. meetings in the U.S.

She has taken the subway three times this month.

B. The action took place at an indefinite time between the past and the present.

```
                now
                 |
past  <--- ?----+------->  future
```

Have you ever gone to Paris?

I've done the homework already.

Have you visited the art museum yet?

Simple Past

A. The action of the sentence is completely past:

```
                now
                 |
past  <----- ---+---------->  future
```

I bought my car last May.

I was in Thailand for two years before I came to the U.S.

When did you meet the teacher?

When I was a child, I always wanted to ride my bike.

He attended several meetings in his country.

She took the subway four times last month.

B. The action took place at a definite time in the past.

```
                now
                 |
past  <-- X----+------->  future
```

Did you go to Paris in 1990?

I did the homework last night.

Did you visit the art museum last month?

2. Compare the Present Perfect and the Present Perfect Continuous

Present Perfect

A. A continuous action (non-action verbs)

I have had my car for five years.

B. A repeated action

I've gone to two meetings this month.

C. Question with *how many*

How many times have you gone to New York?

Present Perfect Continuous

A. A continuous action (action verbs)

I've been driving a car for 20 years.

B. A nonstop action

I've been losing weight for two months.

C. Question with *how long*

How long has he been living in New York?

LESSON EIGHT TEST/REVIEW

Part 1   Find the mistakes and correct them. Not every sentence has a mistake. If the sentence is correct, write *C*.

> *had*
> EXAMPLES: I have ^ my car for six years.
>   ^
>
>   We've always wanted to learn English.   *C*

1. Since I've come to the U.S., I've been studying English.

2. Have you ever eating Chinese food?

3. How long you've been in the U.S.?

4. Have you gone ever to Canada?

5. I've knew my best friend since I was a child.

6. She's a teacher. She's been a teacher since ten years.

7. I never gone to Mexico.

8. How long time has your father been working as an engineer?

9. Has he ever gone to Paris? Yes, he went to Paris last year.

10. He works in a restaurant. He been working there since 1988.

11. Have you ever study biology?

12. Have they finished the test yet?

13. She's done the homework yet.

14. I've just won the lottery.

Part 2   Fill in each blank with the simple past, the present perfect, or the present perfect continuous of the verb in parentheses ( ).

Conversation 1

A. ___*Have*___ you ever ___*studied*___ word processing?
        (study)

B. Yes. I _____ it in college. And I _____ a word processor at my
            (1 study)   (2 use)

present job for five years. But my job is boring.

A. _____ you ever _____ about changing jobs?

(3 think)

B. Yes. Since I _____ a child, I _____ to be an actor. When I

(4 be)   (5 always/want)

   was in college, I _____ in a few school plays, but since I _____,
                     (6 be)   (7 graduate)

   I _____ time to act.
     (8 not/have)

Conversation 2

A. How long _____ in the U.S.?
            (1 you/be)

B. For about two years.

A. _____ your life _____ a lot since you _____ to the U.S.?
   (2 change)   (3 come)

B. Oh, yes. Before I _____ here, I _____ with my family. Since I
                      (4 come)   (5 live)

   came here, I _____ alone.
                (6 live)

A. _____ in the same apartment?
   (7 always/live)

B. No. I _____ three times so far. And I plan to move again at the end
         (8 move)

   of the year.

A. Do you plan to have a roommate?

B. Yes, but I _____ one yet.
             (9 not/find)

Part 3   Fill in each blank with the simple present, the simple past, the present perfect,
or the present perfect continuous of the verb in parentheses ( ).

Paragraph 1

I _*smoke*_. I _____ since I was 16 years old. I _____ to smoke when
  (smoke)   (1 smoke)   (2 start)

my friends did. I _____ to stop many times, but I _____ successful so far.
                  (3 try)   (4 not/be)

Last month I _____ for five days, but then I _____ again when I got
             (5 quit)   (6 start)

nervous about my job.

Paragraph 2

I _____ to the U.S. when a war _____ out in my country. I _____ in
    (1 come)   (2 break)   (3 live)

the U.S. for five years. At first, everything _____ very hard for me. I
                                                 (4 be)

_____ any English when I _____. But I _____ English for the past
(5 not/know)   (6 arrive)   (7 study)

five years, and now I _____ it pretty well. I _____ my college
                            (8 speak)   (9 not/start)

education yet, but I plan to next semester.

LESSON NINE

GRAMMAR
Gerunds

CONTEXT
Smoking
Life Changes

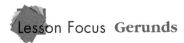Lesson Focus **Gerunds**

- A gerund is formed by putting an *-ing* ending on a verb: *running, swimming, seeing, being.*[1] We can use a gerund as a noun (as a subject, object of a verb, or object of a preposition). Study these sentences:

   Traveling costs a lot of money.

   I enjoy *swimming.*

   She is thinking about *visiting* her cousins.

• •

**R
E
A
D
I
N
G**

Before you read:

1. Do you smoke? How long have you been smoking? Have you ever smoked? Does anyone in your family smoke?
2. Do you know anyone who has been successful in quitting smoking?

Read the following article. Pay special attention to gerunds.

SMOKING

It is a well-known fact that **smoking** is dangerous to your health. Smokers risk **getting** heart disease, cancer, or emphysema (a lung disease). It is believed that 30% of all cancer deaths are related to **smoking.**

Attitudes about **smoking** have changed in recent years. Nonsmokers want smokers to respect their rights. The smoke that is exhaled by smokers can harm others who are near them. As a result, some work places have become "smoke free"; that is, workers cannot smoke in any location at the job. Airlines now prohibit **smoking** on domestic flights, even though some still permit it on international flights. To accommodate nonsmokers, many restaurants permit **smoking** in certain areas only.

Since people have become more aware of the dangers of **smoking,** the percentage of smokers has declined over the years. The percentage of men who smoke dropped from 53% in 1964 to 28% in 1992. The percentage of women who smoke dropped from 32% to 24% during the same time period.

Most smokers are aware of the dangers of **smoking** and would like to break the cigarette habit. However, the average person who tries to quit **smoking** starts again after 17 days. Some people say that the best way to quit is by **going** "cold turkey," that is, by **stopping** completely. Others recommend **going** to special clinics or **undergoing** hypnosis to learn to break the habit little by little. Some doctors recommend **using** a nicotine patch, which is worn like a bandage on the skin. The patch has a success rate of 28%.

Mark Twain, a famous American author, once said, "To cease [quit] **smoking** is the easiest thing I ever did; I ought to[2] know because I've done it a thousand times."

• •

---

[1]Even nonaction verbs like *see* and *be* have a gerund form.

[2]*Ought to* means *should.*

9.1 Gerund as Subject

We can use a gerund or gerund phrase as the subject of the sentence.

Gerund (phrase)	Verb	Complement
Smoking	is	a bad habit.
Quitting this habit	is	often difficult.

Language Notes

1. We form a gerund phrase with the *-ing* form of the verb and other information, such as a prepositional phrase.

   Traveling around the world would be nice.

2. We put *not* in front of a gerund to make it negative.

   Not owning a car in the U.S. is unusual.

3. A gerund subject takes a singular verb.

   Wearing a nicotine patch *helps* some smokers quit.

   Exercising 30 minutes a day *is* good for the heart.

EXERCISE 1   Complete each statement with a gerund (phrase) as the subject.

> EXAMPLE: . . . takes a long time.
>
> **Learning a foreign language takes a long time.**

1. . . . is a healthy activity.
2. . . . is an unhealthy activity.
3. . . . is not permitted in this classroom.
4. . . . is difficult for a foreign student.
5. . . . takes a long time.
6. . . . is not polite.
7. . . . makes me feel good.
8. . . . makes me nervous.
9. . . . scares me.
10. . . . is against the law.

EXERCISE 2   Find a partner. With your partner, write a list of activities that would improve a person's health. Write a list of habits or activities that are not good for a person's health. Read one item from your list to the class.

> EXAMPLES: **Eating a lot of fruits and vegetables can improve a person's health.**
>
> **Living in a big city that has a lot of pollution is bad for a person's health.**

EXERCISE 3   Find a partner. With your partner, write a list of things that a foreign student or immigrant should know about life in the U.S. Use gerunds as subjects. Read one item from your list to the class.

> EXAMPLES: **Getting financial aid is possible for students who can't afford college.**
>
> **Finding a job in your field is not always easy.**

9.2   Gerund After Verb

In Lesson Seven, we saw that some verbs are usually followed by an infinitive (phrase).

Subject	Verb	Infinitive Phrase
They	want	to improve their health.
She	needs	to get more exercise.

Some verbs are commonly followed by a gerund (phrase).

Subject	Verb	Gerund Phrase
Smokers	risk	getting cancer.
Some colleges	forbid	smoking completely.

Language Notes

1. The verbs below can be followed by a gerund:

admit	discuss	mind	put off
appreciate	dislike	miss	quit
avoid	enjoy	permit	recommend
can't help	finish	postpone	risk
consider	keep	practice	suggest

2. *I mind* means that something bothers me. *I don't mind* means that something is OK with me; it doesn't bother me.

> *Do you mind* wearing a suit to work? No, I *don't mind*.

3. *Can't help* means to have no control over something.

> When I see a sad movie, I *can't help* crying.

4. *Go* + gerund is used in many idiomatic expressions:

go boating	go jogging
go bowling	go sailing
go camping	go shopping
go dancing	go sightseeing
go fishing	go skating
go hiking	go skiing
go hunting	go swimming

EXERCISE 4   Make a list of things that you miss from your country. You may use nouns or gerunds. Share your list with a partner.

> EXAMPLE: **I miss the beautiful parks in my hometown.**
> **I miss taking walks by the Black Sea.**

EXERCISE 5   Make a list of suggestions and recommendations for a tourist who is about to visit your country. Read your list to a partner, a small group, or the entire class.

> EXAMPLES: *I recommend taking warm clothes for the winter.*
>
> *You should avoid drinking tap water.*

1. I recommend:

   _____

   _____

   _____

2. You should avoid:

   _____

   _____

   _____

EXERCISE 6   Fill in each blank with an appropriate gerund (or noun) to complete the statement. Share your answers with the class.

> EXAMPLE: **I don't mind** *shopping for food* **, but I do[3] mind** *cooking it.*

1. I usually enjoy _____ during the summer.

2. I don't enjoy _____

3. I don't mind _____, but I do mind _____

4. I appreciate _____ from my friends.

5. I need to practice _____ if I want to improve.

6. I can't help _____ when I walk alone at night.

---

[3]*Do* makes the verb more emphatic. It shows contrast with *don't mind.*

EXERCISE 7   Tell if you like or don't like the following activities. Explain why.

> EXAMPLES: **go shopping**
> **I like to go shopping for clothes because I like to try out new styles.**
>
> **go bowling**
> **I don't like to go bowling because I don't think it is an interesting sport.**

1. go fishing
2. go camping
3. go jogging
4. go swimming
5. go hunting
6. go shopping

1. Some verbs can be followed by either a gerund or an infinitive with almost no difference in meaning.

He started *to smoke* when he was a teenager.
He started *smoking* when he was a teenager.
He continued *to smoke* for three years.
He continued *smoking* for three years.

2. The verbs below can be followed by either a gerund or an infinitive:

attempt	continue	like	start
begin	deserve	love	try
can't stand*	hate	prefer	

*NOTE: *Can't stand* means can't tolerate or hate.

EXAMPLE: I *can't stand* waiting in line.

EXERCISE 8   Complete each statement using either a gerund (phrase) or an infinitive (phrase). Practice both ways.

> EXAMPLES: I started *to learn English four years ago.*
> (learn)
>
> I started *studying French when I was in high school.*
> (study)

1. I started _____ to this school in _____
   (come)

2. I began _____ English _____
   (study)

3. I like _____
   (live)

4. I can't stand _____
   (watch)

5. I like _____
(wear)

6. I hate _____
(wear)

7. I love _____
(eat)

8. I like _____ on TV.
(watch)

9.3 Gerund After Preposition

A gerund can be used as the object of a preposition in these patterns.

Pattern A:

Subject	Verb	Preposition	Gerund Phrase
She	thought	about	moving to New York.
She	plans	on	going to college.

Pattern B:

Subject	Verb	Adjective	Preposition	Gerund Phrase
He	was	successful	in	quitting his smoking habit.
He	was	worried	about	getting cancer.

Language Notes

1. These are some common verb + preposition combinations:

care about	adjust to
complain about	look forward to
dream about	object to
forget about	
talk about	depend on (or upon)
think about	insist on (or upon)
worry about	plan on
believe in	
succeed in	

2. These are some common adjective + preposition combinations:

afraid of	accustomed (or used) to
fond of	
proud of	responsible for
tired of	famous for
concerned about	good at
excited about	
upset about	interested in
worried about	(un)successful in

3. *Look forward to* means to wait for a future event with pleasure.

I *look forward to* seeing my sister next month.

4. *Fond of* means to like very much.

I'm *fond of* gardening.

5. Some expressions contain *to* as a preposition, not as part of an infinitive. Compare:

I like *to travel*. (*To* introduces the infinitive.)
I look forward to *traveling* next summer. (*To* is a preposition and is followed by a gerund.)

6. *Plan, proud,* and *afraid* can also be followed by an infinitive.

I plan *to go.*	I plan *on going.*
I'm afraid *to go* out.	I'm afraid *of going* out.
I'm proud *to be* an American.	I'm proud *of being* an American.

EXERCISE 9 Fill in each blank with a preposition and a gerund (phrase) to make a **true** statement.

EXAMPLE: **I plan** *on going back to my country soon.*

1. I'm (not) afraid _____

2. I'm interested _____

3. I want to succeed _____

4. I'm (not) very good _____

5. I'm accustomed _____

6. I plan _____

EXERCISE 10   Fill in each blank to complete the statement. Compare your experiences in the U.S. with your experiences in your country. Share your answers with a small group or with the entire class.

EXAMPLES: **In the U.S., I'm afraid** _of walking alone at night._

In my country, I was afraid _of not being able to give my children a_ _good future._

1. In the U.S., I'm interested in _____

   In my country, I was interested in _____

2. In the U.S., I'm afraid of _____

   In my country, I was afraid of _____

3. In the U.S., I worry about _____

   In my country, I worried about _____

4. In the U.S., I dream about _____

   In my country, I dreamed about _____

5. In the U.S., I look forward to _____

   In my country, I looked forward to _____

6. In the U.S., I often think about _____

   In my country, I often thought about _____

7. In the U.S., people often complain about _____

   In my country, people often complain about _____

8. In the U.S., families often talk about _____

   In my country, families often talk about _____

9. In the U.S., teenagers are usually interested in _____

   In my country, teenagers are usually interested in _____

10. American students are accustomed to _____

    Students in my country are accustomed to _____

9.4 **Gerund in Adverbial Phrase**
•••••••••••

We can use a gerund in an adverbial phrase that begins with a preposition.

Subject	Verb	Complement	Adverbial Phrase
I	knew	a lot of English	before coming to the U.S.
He	took	the test	without studying.
They	quit	smoking	by using a nicotine patch.

EXERCISE 11   Fill in each blank to complete the sentence.

EXAMPLE: **The best way to improve your vocabulary is by** _reading._

1. The best way to improve your pronunciation is by _____

2. One way to find a job is by _____

3. It is very difficult to find a job without _____

4. The best way to quit smoking is by _____

5. One way to find an apartment is by _____

6. I can't speak English without _____

7. It's impossible to get a driver's license without _____

8. You should read the instructions of a test before _____

••

R
E
A
D
I
N
G

Before you read:

Write a list of four things that are new for you in this country. Include behaviors, food, clothes, living conditions, etc. Read your list to the class or to a partner.

Read the following conversation between an American (A) and a foreign student (F). Notice that *used* is sometimes followed by an infinitive and sometimes followed by a gerund or noun.

LIFE CHANGES

F. My life is so different now.
A. How?
F. For one thing, in India, I **used to live** with my whole family. There were eight people in my house. Here I live alone.

A. Do you like living alone?

F. Well, **I'm not used to it.** There are some things I like. I like my privacy, for example, but it's lonely at times. I can't **get used to eating** dinner by myself. Do you like living alone?

A. I've lived alone since I graduated from high school. So it doesn't bother me. **I'm used to doing** everything for myself.

F. I'm not. When I lived in India, my mother **used to cook, wash the dishes, wash my clothes.** I didn't have to do any of that.

A. What else is different for you?

F. **I'm not used to seeing** romantic behavior between men and women. Here you see men and women holding hands and kissing in public. In movies you see sexual behavior. I can't **get used to it.**

A. I suppose Americans **are** so **used to seeing** these things that we never even think about it.

F. Another difference is in the schools. When I was in India, I **used to stand up** to ask or answer a question in class. Here no one stands up. **I'm used to treating** teachers with more respect.

A. Don't worry. Little by little, you'll **get used to living** in the U.S.

F. I hope so.

● ●

9.5 *Used To* versus *Be Used To*

Used to + base form and *be used to* + gerund/noun have completely different meanings.

Subject	*Used To*	Base Form	Complement
He	used to	live	in India

Subject	*Be Used To*	Gerund/Noun	Complement
He	is used to	treating	teachers with respect.
He	isn't used to	American customs.	

Language Notes

1. *Used to* + base form tells about a past habit or custom. This activity has been discontinued.

   I *used to live* with my whole family, but now I live alone.

   I *used to stand up* to answer a question in class, but now I remain seated.

2. For the negative form, we write *use*, not *used*. The pronunciation for both affirmative and negative sounds the same, however.

   He *used* to study full time.

   He *didn't use* to have a job.

3. *Be used to* + gerund or noun means *be accustomed to.*

   The American student has lived alone since he graduated from high school. He *'s used to living* alone. It's not a problem for him.

   The Indian student *isn't used to washing* his own clothes. He's never done it before.

4. *Get used to* + gerund or noun means *become accustomed to.*

   It's hard to *get used to the customs* of another country.

   I can't *get used to eating* dinner by myself.

EXERCISE 12   Name four things that you had to get used to in the U.S. (These things were strange for you when you arrived.)

> EXAMPLES: I had to get used to *living in a small apartment.*
>
> I had to get used to *American pronunciation.*

1. I had to get used to _____

2. I had to get used to _____

3. I had to get used to _____

4. I had to get used to _____

EXERCISE 13   Answer each question with a complete sentence. Practice *be used to* + gerund or noun.

> EXAMPLE: **What are you used to drinking in the morning?**
> **I'm used to drinking coffee in the morning.**

1. What kind of food are you used to (eating)?
2. What kind of weather are you used to?
3. What time are you used to getting up?
4. What kind of clothes are you used to wearing to class?
5. What kind of things are you used to doing every day?

EXPANSION ACTIVITIES

DISCUSSIONS 1. Fill in each blank and discuss your answers in a small group or with the entire class.

a. Americans are used to _____, but people in my country aren't.

b. People in my country are used to _____, but Americans aren't.

c. If an American goes to live in my country, he or she will have to get used to _____.

2. Are attitudes about smoking the same in your country as in the U.S.? Do restaurants have nonsmoking sections?

OUTSIDE ACTIVITY Interview an American about smoking. Ask these questions:

1. Do you smoke? How long have you smoked?
2. Does other people's smoking bother you?
3. Do you think that restaurants should have a nonsmoking section?
4. Do you think that smoking should be permitted at this college? Why or why not? Where?
5. What is the best way to quit smoking?
6. _____

Report this person's answers about smoking to the class.

WRITING 1. Write about (a) a change you made in your life (like quitting smoking).
OR
(b) a change you would like to make in your life.

2. Write a paragraph beginning with "It has been hard for me to get used to _____ in the U.S."

EDITING ADVICE

· ·

1. Use a gerund after a preposition.

    He read the whole book without ~~use~~ *using* a dictionary.

2. Use a gerund after certain verbs.

    I enjoy ~~to~~ walk*ing* in the park.

    He went ~~to~~ shop*ping* after work.

3. Use the correct preposition.

    She insisted ~~in~~ *on* driving me home.

4. Use a gerund, not a base form, as a subject.

    Finding ~~Find~~ a good job is important.

5. Be careful with *be used to* and *used to*.

    I live alone now. I've lived alone all my life. I *am* used to liv*ing* alone.

SUMMARY OF LESSON NINE

1. We can use a gerund as the subject of the sentence.
   Reading can make you a more educated person.

2. We use a gerund after certain verbs.
   I enjoy *reading* history books.

3. After some verbs, we can use either a gerund or an infinitive for about the same meaning.
   I like *reading* history books.
   I like *to read* history books.

4. We use a gerund in many expressions with *go.*
   She *goes shopping* every Saturday.

5. We use a gerund after a preposition.
   I'm worried *about losing* my job.

6. We use a gerund in an adverbial phrase that begins with a preposition.
   He gave his speech *without reading* it from his paper.

7. *Used to* + base form = a past habit or custom that has been discontinued.
   I *used to smoke* when I was a teenager.

8. *Get used to* + gerund (or noun) = a change in a person's habit
   I can't *get used to living* in a small apartment.

9. *Be used to* + gerund (or noun) = be accustomed to.
   She's from a large family. She*'s used to living* with a lot of people.

(Review Lesson 7 for verbs that are usually followed by an infinitive.)

LESSON NINE TEST/REVIEW

Part 1   Find the mistakes in the following sentences, and correct them. Not every sentence has a mistake. If the sentence is correct, write *C*.

EXAMPLES: **I'm afraid to go~~ing~~ out at night.**

She comes from Laos. She's not used to living in Minneapolis because it's so cold in the winter.   *C*

1. Save your money is important for your future.

2. Do you like to go fish?

3. He found his job by reading the help-wanted section of the newspaper.

4. She used to take the bus every day in her country. Now she has a car and drives.

5. I'm interested in becoming a doctor.

6. She's thinking on spending her vacation in Puerto Rico.

7. I like to walk for exercise, but I don't enjoy to walk in cold weather.

8. Smoking is bad for your health.

9. He wants to quit to smoke.

10. Smokers risk getting cancer.

11. She has always lived in a big city. She's used to living in a big city.

12. I'm afraid of not finding a good job.

Part 2   Fill in each blank with a gerund (phrase) as a subject.

EXAMPLE: ___*Buying a house*_____ **is expensive in the U.S.**

1. _____ is against the law.

2. _____ relaxes me.

3. _____ is a good way to lose weight.

4. _____ makes me feel sad.

Part 3   Fill in each blank with the gerund or infinitive of the verb in parentheses ( ). In some cases, both are possible.

Two friends are talking about smoking.

A. Hi. How's it going?

B. I feel awful.

A. What happened?

B. I quit _____*smoking*_____.
             (smoke)

A. That's wonderful news!

B. I don't feel wonderful. I want _____ a cigarette so much that many
                                        (1 smoke)

   nights I dream about _____ cigarettes. Yesterday I went
                              (2 buy)

   _____, and I almost asked the clerk _____ me a pack of
        (3 shop)   (4 give)

   cigarettes, just out of habit.

A. That's only natural. How long have you been without a cigarette?

B. About two weeks.

A. You know, I used _____ too, but I quit a long time ago.
                   (5 smoke)

B. Really? What made you quit?

A. I like to go _____ every day, but when I smoked, I was always out
               (6 swim)

   of breath. So I decided _____.
                        (7 quit)

B. I've tried _____ many times, but I've never succeeded in
          (8 quit)

   _____ it.
      (9 do)

A. What made you try again?

B. My wife. She says that second-hand smoke is bad for everyone in the

house. I'm especially afraid of _____ the children. My wife agreed
(10 hurt)

_____ my favorite meals if I promised _____ by the end
(11 cook)   (12 stop)

of the month. I went to the doctor, and he gave me a patch to wear. It's still
hard.

A. Well, you're better off, you know. At my job, they don't permit

_____ in the building at all. It's called a "smoke-free work place."
(13 smoke)

B. I suppose more and more work places are becoming "smoke-free." It's probably

a good idea, but it's hard to get used to it. I'm used to _____ a
(14 have)

cigarette whenever I have a cup of coffee.

A. Then stop _____ coffee.
(15 drink)

B. I broke one habit. Don't ask me _____ another. One thing at a time.
(16 break)

Part 4   Fill in each blank with the correct preposition.

EXAMPLE: I care _about_ learning English

1. Let's talk _____ having a party.

2. I plan _____ going to college in New York.

3. She thought _____ getting divorced.

4. He's tired _____ living alone.

5. She looks forward _____ returning to her country.

LESSON TEN

GRAMMAR

Adjectives
Adverbs
Adjective Clauses

CONTEXT

The Fourth of July
Social Security
Personal Ads

Lesson Focus Adjectives; Adverbs; Adjective Clauses

- An adjective describes a noun.
  The Fourth of July is an *American* holiday.

  A noun can also describe a noun.
  The Fourth of July is *Independence* Day.

- An adverb describes a verb phrase.
  We celebrated the holiday *quietly.*

- An adjective clause[1] describes a noun.
  The Fourth of July is a holiday *that children love.*

R
E
A
D
I
N
G

Before you read:

1. Does your country have an Independence Day? How do people celebrate it?
2. For what occasions do people use fireworks in your country?

Read the following article. Pay special attention to adjectives, noun modifiers, and adverbs.

THE FOURTH OF JULY

The Fourth of July is **American Independence Day.** Most people don't have to work on this day. If Independence Day falls on a Monday or Friday, people enjoy a **three-day weekend.**

Americans like to watch **fireworks** on this day. Many cities have a **sky show;** the **fire department** puts on a display of **colorful fireworks,** usually in a **public park.** Sometimes there is a concert, and the band or orchestra plays **patriotic music.**

Youngsters like to buy their own **firecrackers** and other **noise makers.** They like them because they look **bright** and sound **loud.** Sometimes they buy these things **illegally** and get **hurt** from these **dangerous items.** There are many accidents on the Fourth of July. It's better to take children to the **city display,** where the fire department knows how to use fireworks **carefully,** than to let children play with these things **carelessly** with their friends.

---

[1]REMEMBER: A *clause* is a group of related words that contains a subject and a verb.

10.1 Adjectives and Noun Modifiers

An adjective describes a noun. An adjective can come before a noun or after the verb *be*. An adjective can come after sense perception verbs: *look, seem, sound, smell, taste, feel.*

(Adjective)	Subject	Verb	(Adjective)	Object
The public	park	has	a beautiful	show.
A big	band	played	patriotic	music.

Subject	*Be*/Sense Verb	Adjective
The show	is	beautiful.
Firecrackers	sound	loud.
The children	feel	excited.

A noun can describe another noun.

(Noun Modifier)	Subject	Verb	(Noun Modifier)	Object
	I	enjoy	Independence	Day.
The fire	department	has	a sky	show.

1. We do not make adjectives plural.

   a *bright* light   *bright* lights

2. Some *-ed* words are adjectives: *married, divorced, excited, disappointed, worried, finished, located, tired, crowded, frightened.*

   I'm *tired.*
   He's *worried* about the danger of fireworks.
   The children were *frightened* when they heard the loud noise.
   He went to a *crowded* park.

Like other adjectives, these *-ed* words can come before a noun or after *be* or a sense perception verb.

3. An adjective often follows *get*.

   Children can *get hurt* if they play with fireworks.

Get, in the following expressions, means *become*:

   get hurt   get sleepy
   get worried   get thirsty
   get tired   get married
   get hungry   get divorced

4. We can put *very* or *quite* before an adjective.

   The sound was *very* loud.
   Firecrackers can be *quite* dangerous.

5. Conversational words that come before adjectives are *pretty, sort of, kind of,* and *real*.

   The picnic was *kind of* fun.
   We had a *real* nice time.
   She had a *pretty* good time.

6. After an adjective, we can substitute a noun with *one* (singular) or *ones* (plural).

   Do you want a big pizza or a small *one*?
   The first lessons are easy. The last *ones* are hard.

7. When a noun modifies another noun, the second noun is more general than the first.

   A fire *department* is a department.
   A forest *fire* is a fire.
   A department *store* is a store.

The first noun is always singular.

   a three-*day* weekend = a weekend of three day<u>s</u>
   a *book* shelf = a shelf for book<u>s</u>
   a six-*year*-old child = a child who is six year<u>s</u> old

8. Sometimes a gerund describes a noun. It shows the purpose of the noun.

   a *shopping* cart   *running* shoes   a *frying* pan

9. Sometimes a possessive form describes a noun.

   a *bachelor's* degree   a *driver's* license
   an *owner's* manual

10. When a noun describes a noun, the first noun usually receives the greater emphasis in speaking. Listen to your teacher pronounce the following:

   The *fíre department* puts on a show for *Indepéndence Day*.

EXERCISE 1   Fill in each blank by putting the two words in parentheses ( ) in the correct order. Remember to remove the <u>s</u> from plural noun modifiers.

EXAMPLES: **People need a** ___*winter coat*___ **in December.**
                              (coat/winter)

             He bought a _*beautiful car.*_
                           (beautiful/car)

1. In the supermarket, we put our things in a _____
                                                (cart/shopping)

2. I need a _____ to stir my tea.
           (tea/spoon)

3. To fry eggs, you need a _____
                          (pan/frying)

4. A _____ drives a taxi.
      (taxi/driver)

5. The school is closed during _____
                               (vacation/Christmas)

6. She took a _____
               (vacation/very/long)

7. A _____ has a _____
      (factory/worker)   (hard/job)

8. Many _____ use robots.
        (factories/automobiles)

9. _____ buy their _____ at the _____
   (college/students)   (books/text)   (store/books)

10. I had a _____ with my boss.
            (meeting/pretty/long)

EXERCISE 2   Find the mistakes with adjectives and noun modifiers, and correct them.
Not every sentence has a mistake. If the sentence is correct, write *C*.

EXAMPLES: **He bought a car very expensive!**

           **Some students prefer easy teachers. Other students prefer
           strict ones.** *C*

1. He took a two weeks vacation at a beautiful beach.

2. Do you have a driver license?

3. He put the new books on the tall books shelf.

4. I'm too tire to go to a late movie.

5. A truck driver often gets sleepy and has to rest at a truck stop.

6. She has two wonderfuls children and a great husband.

7. He made a long-distance call phone to his favorite uncle.

8. This T-shirt is too small for me. I need a big.

9. This turkey sandwich tastes quite good.

10. A community college has a two-years program.

EXERCISE 3   Work with a partner. Write at least five sentences that contain descriptions
about a specific place at this college: the library, cafeteria, student union, etc. Share
your sentences with the class.

EXAMPLES: **The library has many tall book shelves.**
           The circulation desk is near the exit of the library.
           You can find popular magazines there.

10.2 Adverbs of Manner

An adverb of manner tells how or in what way a person does something. We form most adverbs of manner by putting *-ly* at the end of an adjective.

Adjectives	Adverbs
Some fireworks are *illegal*.	Some people buy them *illegally*.
He is a *careful* driver.	He drives *carefully*.
She seems *sad*.	She said goodbye *sadly*.

Language Notes

1. Study the spelling rules for *-ly* adverbs:
   A. For adjectives that end in *-y*, we change *y* to *i*, then add *-ly*.

   easy/easily   happy/happily   lucky/luckily

   B. For adjectives that end in *-e*, we keep the *e* and add *-ly*.

   nice/nicely   free/freely

   EXCEPTION: true/truly

   C. For adjectives that end in a consonant + *-le*, we drop the *e* and add *-ly*.

   simple/simply   double/doubly
   comfortable/comfortably

2. Some adverbs of manner do not end in *-ly*.
   A. Some adjectives and adverbs have the same form: *fast, late, early, hard*.

   He has a *fast* car. (adjective)
   He drives *fast*. (adverb)

   She has a *late* class. (adjective)
   She arrived *late* last night. (adverb)

   He has a *hard* job. (adjective)
   He works *hard*. (adverb)

   B. *Good* is an adjective. *Well* is the adverb form.

   She has a *good* life.   She lives *well*.

3. Some adjectives end in *-ly*: *lovely, friendly, lively, ugly, lonely*. They have no adverb form. We use an adverbial phrase to describe the action.

   She is a friendly person.
   She behaves *in a friendly manner*.
   He is a lively person.
   He danced *in a lively way*.

4. *Hard* and *hardly* are both adverbs, but they have completely different meanings.

   He worked very *hard*. = He put a lot of effort into his work.
   He *hardly* worked. = He did very little work.

5. *Late* and *lately* are both adverbs, but they have completely different meanings.

   He came home *late*. He missed dinner.
   Lately, he never comes home on time. (*Lately* means "recently.")

6. An *-ly* adverb of manner usually follows the verb phrase.

   The fire department displays fireworks *carefully*.

   Less frequently, we put an *-ly* adverb between the subject and the verb.

   The fire department *carefully* displays fireworks.

   Don't put an *-ly* adverb between the verb and the object.

   He ate the sandwich *quickly*. *Not*: He ate quickly the sandwich.

7. Adverbs of manner that don't end in *-ly* always follow the verb phrase.

   He worked *hard*. *Not*: He hard worked.
   He came home *late*. *Not*: He late came home.

8. *Very* can come before an adjective or adverb. Never put *very* before a verb.

   WRONG: He *very* worked hard. He *very* likes his job.[2]
   RIGHT: He worked *very* hard. He likes his job *very much*.

9. An *-ly* adverb can come before an adjective.

   Her pronunciation is *absolutely* perfect.
   She is *completely* right.

---

[2]In informal conversation, you will hear He worked *really* (or *real*) hard. He *really* likes his job.

EXERCISE 4   Write the adverb form of the word in parentheses ( ). Then check (✓) the activities that you do in this way. Find a partner, and compare your answers with your partner's answers. Report something interesting about your partner to the class.

1. _____ answer every question _____
   (honest)

2. _____ drive _____
   (fast)

3. _____ cook _____
   (good)

4. _____ talk _____
   (constant)

5. _____ work _____
   (hard)

6. _____ study _____
   (hard)

7. _____ speak Spanish _____
   (fluent)

8. _____ type _____
   (fast)

9. _____ type _____
   (accurate)

10. _____ pronounce the English -*th* sound, as in Thursday _____
    (correct)

11. _____ live _____
    (dangerous)

12. _____ love _____
    (passionate)

13. _____ meditate _____
    (quiet)

14. _____ sleep _____
    (sound[3])

15. _____ learned a second language _____
    (easy)

16. _____ lived _____ in my country
    (comfortable)

17. _____ _____

---

[3]When a person sleeps *soundly*, she doesn't wake up easily.

Adjectives versus Adverbs

1. Use an adjective after the following verbs if you are describing a noun, not an action: *smell, taste, sound, look, seem, appear,* and *feel.* Use an adverb if you are describing a verb.

> Jim looks *serious.* (*Serious* describes Jim.)
> Jim is looking at his mistakes *seriously.* (*Seriously* tells how he is looking at his mistakes.)
> The driver appeared *drunk.* (*Drunk* describes the driver.)
> The drunk driver appeared *suddenly.* (*Suddenly* tells how soon the driver appeared.)
> The soup tastes *good.* (*Good* describes the soup.)
> He tasted the soup *slowly.* (*Slowly* tells how he tasted the soup.)

2. Use an adjective, not an adverb, in expressions with *get.*

> He *got angry* when his son took the money.
> He *got sleepy* after drinking a glass of wine.

3. Use the adverb *well* after *be, seem, appear,* and *feel* to talk about health. Use *good* to talk about the quality of a noun.

> He's sick. He doesn't look *well* today.
> The cake looks *good.*

In conversational English, people often use *good* for health.

> He's sick. He doesn't look *good* today.

4. Use the adjective, not the adverb, in the following expression: *as usual.*

> *As usual,* he worked last Saturday.

EXERCISE 5   Fill in each blank with the correct form of the word—adjective or adverb.

Last week I had my first job interview in the U.S. I wanted to do ___*well.*___ A
                                                                        (good)

_____ friend of mine told me about a résumé service. He told me that this
   (1 good)

service helps you prepare your résumé _____. I wanted my résumé to look
                                          (2 careful)

_____. I never wrote a résumé before, so I used this service. I wanted to
 (3 professional)

have a _____ résumé.
          (4 perfect)

A few days before the interview, I worked very _____ to prepare
                                                    (5 hard)

answers to possible questions. The night before the interview, I chose my

clothes _____ and ironed them. I wanted to appear _____. My
          (6 careful)   (7 neat)

friend told me that it's best to look _____ , so I chose my dark-blue
                                         (8 conservative)

suit. I went to bed _____ , as _____ , but I didn't sleep
                       (9 early)   (10 usual)

_____ because I was _____.
  (11 good)   (12 extreme/nervous)

The interview was _____ because I had trouble answering many
                    (13 difficult)

of the questions. The interviewer spoke _____ but she didn't speak
                                    (14 friendly)

_____. I couldn't understand her pronunciation. I could _____
    (15 clear)   (16 hard)

understand some of the questions.

I probably won't get this job. But it was a _____ experience to
                               (17 good)

have this interview. It prepared me _____ for the next interview.
                             (18 good)

EXERCISE 6   In some colleges, students evaluate teachers. Work with a partner and write an evaluation form for teachers at this college or for another profession you are familiar with.

Examples:	**Strongly Agree**	**Agree**	**Disagree**	**Strongly Disagree**

1. **Begins class promptly.**
2. **Treats students with respect.**
3. **Explains assignments clearly.**

• •

R
E
A
D
I
N
G

Before you read:

1. In your country, who usually takes care of older people when they are too old or too sick to take care of themselves?
2. How does your family take care of its older members?
3. Does the government give old people a pension? Is it enough to live on?

Read the following article. Pay special attention to *too* and *enough*.

SOCIAL SECURITY

If you work in the United States, you are probably disappointed when you get your paycheck. Some of your money goes to Social Security (FICA). This money is for retirement. You can start receiving Social Security benefits at 62, but you will be **too young** to get full benefits. You must wait until you are 65. Then you are **old enough** for full benefits. When you apply for benefits, the Social Security office will check to see if you worked **long enough** to get Social Security and Medicare protection. You need to work and contribute for 40 quarters (one year = four quarters) to get benefits. In addition, you must earn **enough money** each quarter for that quarter to count. If you earn **too little,** you don't receive credit for that quarter.

For more information, contact a Social Security office. Look in your local phone book under "Social Security Administration" or "U.S. Government."

10.3 *Too/Enough*

Too can come before an adjective or adverb. *Too* indicates a problem. An infinitive phrase sometimes follows a phrase with *too.*

Subject	Verb	*Too*	Adj/Adv	Infinitive Phrase
My father	is	too	young	to collect Social Security.
I	earned	too	little	to qualify for Social Security.

Enough can come after an adjective or adverb. An infinitive phrase sometimes follows a phrase with *enough.*

Subject	Verb	Adj/Adv	*Enough*	Infinitive Phrase
She	is	old	enough	to retire.
She	worked	long	enough	to get Social Security benefits.

Enough can come before a noun.

Subject	Verb	*Enough*	Noun	
She	earned	enough	money	last year.

Too good to be true shows a positive surprised reaction.
I just won the lottery. It's *too good to be true.*

EXERCISE 7   Read the conversation between a husband (H) and a wife (W). Fill in each blank with *too* or *enough* plus the word in parentheses ( ).

H. I'm tired of my job. Let's retire and go live in Hawaii.

W. But we're only 57 years old. We're _____ *too young* _____ to retire.
                                              (young)

H. I'd like to buy a very big house with a swimming pool.

W. But our house is _____ for us. Besides, we don't have
                                (1 big)

_____ for a bigger house.
      (2 money)

H. And I'd like to travel around the world.

W. But that's _____ .
                      (3 expensive)

H. And I'd like our daughter to go with us.

W. She's 23 years old! She's _____ to make her own decisions.
                                          (4 old)

H. And I'd like to spend the next 50 years on a sailboat.

W. The next 50 years? You're kidding! We don't have _____ . We're
                                                              (5 time)

already 57 years old!

H. I'm just dreaming. You take me _____ .
                                            (6 seriously)

EXERCISE 8   Complete each statement with an infinitive.

EXAMPLES: **I'm too young . . .**
                 I'm too young to get Social Security.

                 I'm not old enough . . .
                 I'm not old enough to retire.

1. I'm not too old . . .   4. I have enough money . . .
2. I'm too young . . .   5. I don't have enough time . . .
3. I'm not tall enough . . .   6. I don't speak English well enough . . .

EXERCISE 9   Use the words given to write questions to ask another student. The other
student will answer.

EXAMPLE: **old enough**

         Are you old enough to retire soon?

1. too busy _____

2. too hard _____

3. enough time _____

4. strong enough _____

5. enough experience _____

Language Notes

Too and *Very*

Don't confuse *very* and *too*. *Too* always indicates a problem in a specific situation. *Very* is a neutral word. COMPARE:

My grandmother is *very old*, but she's in great health.
My brother is 14 years old. He's *too old* to get into the movie theater for half price.
The table is *very heavy*, but I managed to move it.
That piano is *too heavy* for me to move. I need professional movers.

EXERCISE 10   Fill in each blank with *too* or *very*.

EXAMPLES: **My sister is *very*_____ beautiful.**

I'm *too*_____ short to touch the ceiling.

1. My grandfather is in _____ good health. He runs five miles a day.

2. I'm _____ sick to go to work today. I'll just stay in bed.

3. I can't believe I won the lottery. It's _____ good to be true!

4. She won the lottery. She's _____ happy.

5. She should be in an easier English class. This class is _____ hard for her.

6. That meal was delicious. You're a _____ good cook.

7. He is a _____ good person. He always helps his friends and neighbors.

8. My son is only six years old. He's _____ young to stay home alone.

9. Yesterday I saw a _____ beautiful sunset.

10. I can't reach those boxes on that shelf. It's _____ high for me.

 **10.4** Adjective Clauses[4]

An adjective clause is a clause that describes a noun.

	Noun	Adjective Clause
She'd like to marry	a man	who knows how to cook.
She'd like to have	a job	that uses her talents.

Noun	Adjective Clause	
The man	whom she married	doesn't want to have children.
The job	that she has	gives her a lot of satisfaction.

1. An adjective clause is a dependent clause. It is never a sentence.

   NOT: She'd like to marry a man. Who knows how to cook.

2. An adjective comes before a noun. An adjective clause comes after a noun.

   a *helpful* man
   a man *who knows how to cook*

3. Relative pronouns introduce adjective clauses. *Who(m)* is for people, *which* is for things, and *that* is for people or things.

   I want to marry a woman *who/that* loves children.
   I want a job *which/that* uses my talents.

R
E
A
D
I
N
G

Before you read:

1. Are you married? How or where did you meet your spouse?
2. How do single people meet in your country?

Read the following article. Pay special attention to adjective clauses.

PERSONAL ADS

Single people **who are looking for a partner** often use the personal ads in the newspaper. They can advertise for the kind of person **they want to meet,** or they can respond to ads **they find in the newspaper.** An ad usually gives a description of the advertiser and his or her hobbies or interests. The advertiser often lists the characteristics **he or she wants to find in a partner.**

---

[4]An *adjective clause* is sometimes called a *relative clause.*

Look at the ad below:

```
SWM, 35 y.o., 5'8", 165 lbs., enjoys sailing,
swimming, fishing, skiing, wants to meet S/DWF
25-34, under 5'5", N.S., who enjoys sports and
the outdoors. #45112 or Write Box 52.
```

The person **who wrote this ad** is a 35-year-old (y.o.) single white male (SWM). He would like to meet a single or divorced white female (S/DWF) **who is between the ages of 25 and 34.** He wants a woman who **doesn't smoke** (N.S. = nonsmoker).

A woman **who answers this ad** can call a phone number and leave a message for the advertiser. Usually this phone call is to a 900 number and can cost from one to several dollars a minute. Or she can send a letter to a box number. The newspaper will forward the letters to the man **who placed the ad.**

People **who write ads** usually use abbreviations to make their ads shorter and less expensive. These are some common abbreviations:

S = Single	A = Asian
D = Divorced	G = Gay[5]
M = Male	Bi = Bisexual
F = Female	C = Christian
W = White	J = Jewish
H = Hispanic	N.S. = Nonsmoker
B = Black	N.D. = Nondrinker

10.5 Relative Pronoun as Subject

A relative pronoun can be the subject of the adjective clause.

He wants to meet a woman. The woman likes sports.

He wants to meet a woman [who / that] likes sports.

---

[5]*Gay* means homosexual.

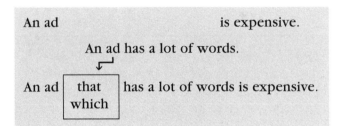

An ad   is expensive.

An ad has a lot of words.

An ad | that / which | has a lot of words is expensive.

Language Notes

1. A present-tense verb in the adjective clause must agree in number with its subject.

The man wants to meet a woman who *likes* sports.

I know a lot of men who *like* sports.

2. Avoid using an adjective clause when a simple adjective is enough.

He doesn't want to meet a *woman who is tall*. BETTER: He doesn't want to meet a *tall woman*.

EXERCISE 11   In each sentence below, underline the adjective clause.

EXAMPLE: People <u>who answer ads</u> have to pay for the service.

1. He wants to meet a woman who doesn't smoke.
2. The man who placed the ad enjoys sports.
3. People who write ads use abbreviations to save space and money.
4. Single people who are looking for a partner sometimes use personal ads.

EXERCISE 12   Complete each statement with an adjective clause. Make sure that the verb in the adjective clause agrees with its subject.

EXAMPLE: I know some women . . .
         I know some women who don't want to have children.

1. (Women) I like men . . .
   (Men) I like women . . .
2. A friend is a person . . .
3. Students like a teacher . . .
4. Teachers like students . . .
5. There are a lot of Americans . . .
6. There are a lot of people in my country . . .
7. I like apartments . . .

EXERCISE 13   Complete each statement with an adjective clause. The subject of the adjective clause is general.

EXAMPLE: People _who have a wonderful family_ are very fortunate.

1.   Women _____ are very popular.

2.   People _____ aren't usually successful.

3.   People _____ have trouble finding a spouse.[6]

4.   Parents _____ are good.

5.   Parents _____ aren't good.

6.   Women _____ have a hard life.

EXERCISE 14   Complete each statement with a verb phrase. The subject contains an adjective clause.

EXAMPLE: **People who leave their countries** *have many new experiences.*

1. People who gossip _____

2. People who can't read or write _____

3. People who have lost their jobs _____

4. People who exercise regularly _____

EXERCISE 15   We often give a definition with an adjective clause. Work with a partner to give a definition of the following words by using an adjective clause.

EXAMPLES: **twins**
           Twins are brothers or sisters who are born at the same time.

           an answering machine
           An answering machine is a device that takes phone messages.

1. a babysitter   4. a verb
2. an immigrant   5. a fax machine
3. an adjective

EXERCISE 16   Write a short definition or description of an object or a person. Read your definition to a small group. The others will try to guess what it is. Continue to add to your definition until someone guesses it.

EXAMPLE: **It is an animal that lives in the water.**
           Is it a fish?
           No, it isn't. It is an animal that needs to come up for air.
           Is it a dolphin?
           Yes, it is.

_____

[6]*Spouse* means husband or wife.

10.6 Relative Pronoun as Object

A relative pronoun can be the object of the adjective clause.

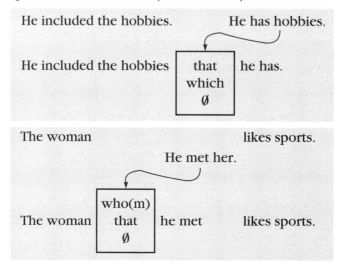

1. The correct relative pronoun for people is *whom.* However, in conversation, *who* is often heard. Or the relative pronoun is omitted completely.

 FORMAL: The woman *whom* he met likes
       sports.
 INFORMAL: The woman *who* he met likes sports.
 INFORMAL: The woman he met likes sports.

2. In an adjective clause, don't repeat the relative pronoun with an object pronoun.

 She is the kind of woman he would like to
  meet ~~her~~.

EXERCISE 17 In each sentence below, underline the adjective clause.

 EXAMPLES: **The man <u>she married</u> works as a computer programmer.**

      Do you know the woman <u>he met</u>?

1. The ad he put in the paper cost him $10.
2. The women whom he met through his ad were all very nice.
3. She's not the kind of person I want to marry.
4. Basketball is a sport he doesn't like.

EXERCISE 18   Complete each statement.

EXAMPLE: **People often want things they** _can't afford._

1. We sometimes don't appreciate the things we _____

2. I tell my problems to people I _____

3. I once had a teacher I _____

4. Americans sometimes say things I _____

5. There are many American customs I _____

6. Do you follow the advice your parents _____

EXERCISE 19   Fill in each blank to complete the adjective clause.

EXAMPLE: **My friend just bought a new car. I don't like the new car**

she bought.

1. I'm going to return the coat _____ last week. It's too small for me.

2. Look at the beautiful sweater that Mary _____ today. I wonder where she bought it.

3. I can't find the card _____ with your phone number on it. Can you give me another one?

4. The movie I _____ last night was terrific. I highly recommend it to you.

5. Could you please return the money you _____ last month?

6. The teacher makes corrections on the students' compositions. The students should read the corrections _____

7. I'm studying American English now. The English _____ in my country was British English.

8. Please speak more slowly. I can't understand a word you

_____

10.7 *Whose* + Noun as Subject or Object of Adjective Clause

Whose is the possessive form of *who. Whose* + noun can be the subject or object of an adjective clause. *Whose* substitutes for *his, her, its, their,* or the possessive form of the noun.

> He doesn't want to marry a divorced woman *whose children are small.* (Her children are small.)
> The man *whose ad she answered* likes sports. (She answered his ad.)

Do not confuse *whose* with *who's. Whose* is a possessive form.
  I met a student *whose* last name is the same as mine. (*whose* = *his*)
  I met a student *who's* from my hometown. (*who's* = *who is*)

EXERCISE 20   Underline the adjective clause.

EXAMPLE: **A student <u>whose score is high</u> can take college courses.**

1. A student whose attendance is bad might fail the course.
2. Students like a teacher whose explanations are clear.
3. The teacher gave an A to the students whose compositions were good.
4. The teacher whose class I took last semester retired.
5. There are some students whose names I can't pronounce.

EXERCISE 21   Use the sentence in parentheses ( ) to form an adjective clause.

EXAMPLES: **The TOEFL is a test for students** *whose native language isn't English.*
            (Their native language isn't English.)

            The man *whose wallet I found and returned* **gave me a reward.**
            (I found and returned his wallet.)

1. Students _____ might be able to get financial aid. (Their family incomes are low.)

2. Parents _____ have a lot of expenses. (Their children are in college.)

3. Parents _____ are usually very proud. (Their children graduate from college.)

4. He wants to meet a woman _____ (Her hobbies are the same as his.)

5. There are some students _____ (I don't remember their names.)

6. The students _____ often ask me questions in our language. (I speak their language.)

7. The teacher _____ went to Japan to teach English. (I took his class last semester.)

8. I bought a used book. The student _____ wrote in all the answers. (I bought his book.)

EXERCISE 22   *Part A:* Some women were asked what kind of man they'd like to marry. Fill in each blank with a response.

> EXAMPLE: **I'd like to marry a man** *whose values are the same as mine.*
> (His values are the same as mine.)

1. I'd like to marry a man _____
   (I can trust him.)

2. I don't want a husband _____
   (He drinks.)

3. I want to marry a man _____
   (He makes a good living.)

4. I'd like to marry a man _____
   (I like his family.)

5. I'd like to marry a man _____
   (He's older than I am.)

6. I'd like to marry a man _____
   (He wants to have children.)

7. (Women: Add your own sentence telling what kind of man you'd like to marry, or what kind of man you married.)

   _____

Part B: Some men were asked what kind of woman they'd like to marry. Fill in each blank with a response.

> EXAMPLE: **I'd like to marry a woman** *who knows how to cook.*
> **(She knows how to cook.)**

1. I'd like to marry a woman _____
   (She has a sense of humor.)

2. I'd like to marry a woman _____
   (I can admire her wisdom.)

3. I'd like to marry a woman _____
   (Her manners are good.)

4. I'd like to marry a woman _____
   (Her mother doesn't interfere.)

5. I'd like to marry a woman _____
   (I have known her for a long time.)

6. I'd like to marry a woman _____
   (She wants to have a lot of kids.)

7. (Men: Add your own sentence telling what kind of woman you'd like to marry, or what kind of woman you married.)

   _____ _____

EXERCISE 23   Complete each statement with an adjective clause. You may use *who, whom, that, which,* or *whose* to introduce the adjective clause. (In some cases, no word is necessary to introduce the adjective clause.)

> EXAMPLES: **I have a neighbor** *whose dog barks all the time.*
>
> **I don't like people** *who tell you one thing and do something else.*

1. I know a man/woman _____

2. I have a TV/VCR/stereo _____

3. My father is/was a person _____

4. My mother is/was a person _____

5. The textbook _____ is called *Grammar in Context.*

6. I would like to buy a car _____

7. I have a neighbor _____

8. I don't like people _____

9. A real friend is a person _____

EXPANSION ACTIVITIES

ACTIVITIES   1. Write a word from your language that has no English translation. It might be the name of a food or a traditional costume. Define the word. Read your definition to a small group or to a partner.

   EXAMPLE: **A *sari* is a typical Indian dress for women. It is made of a cloth that a woman wraps around her. She wraps one end around her waist. She puts the other end over her shoulder.**

2. Bring to class something typical from your country. Demonstrate how to use it.

   EXAMPLE: **a samovar**
   This is a pot that we use in Russia to make tea.

3. Bring to class a newspaper with singles ads. In a group, try to read them with the help of your teacher.

DISCUSSIONS   1. In a small group or with the entire class, discuss what you think of singles ads. Is this a good way to meet a partner? Why or why not?

2. In a small group or with the entire class, talk about your experience with job interviews in the U.S.

3. In a small group or with the entire class, talk about the kind of person who makes a good husband, wife, father, mother, or friend.

PROVERB   The following proverb contains an adjective clause. Discuss the meaning of this proverb. Do you have a similar proverb in your language?

People who live in glass houses shouldn't throw stones.

WRITING   1. Write about the life of older people in your country. What benefits do they get? What problems do they have?

2. Write about how your family takes (took) care of an aging parent or grandparent.

3. Choose one of the following topics and write a paragraph.

   a. I prefer to study English with a teacher who speaks my language.
   b. I prefer to study English with a teacher who doesn't speak my language.

   Give reasons for your preference.

4. Think of a place in this city (a museum, a government office, a park, a shopping center, etc.). Write a brief description of this place.

EXAMPLE: **The Art Museum**

> **The Art Museum is a large building downtown. It has many beautiful paintings by famous artists. I especially like the Impressionists. The museum has marble floors. . . .**

5. Write a paragraph about one of the following places. Use descriptions.

   a. your living room
   b. your hometown (or a specific place in your hometown)
   c. your neighborhood

   Begin your paragraph with a sentence telling your opinion or feeling about this place. (For example, "There is a very beautiful park in my hometown.")

OUTSIDE ACTIVITY

Do you have a job in the United States? If you do, you probably pay Social Security tax. If you want to find out how much you have put into the Social Security system toward your retirement, call 1-800-537-7005 and ask for a Personal Earnings and Benefits Estimate (PEBES) request form. Fill it out and return it. You will get a statement that shows how much you will get if you retire.

EDITING ADVICE   Part 1:

1. Adjectives are always singular.

   I had a two important~~s~~ meetings last week.

2. Certain adjectives end with *-ed*.

   He was tir~~e~~ᵈ after his trip.

3. Put an adjective before the noun.

   She is a ⟨girl⟩ very intelligent↴.

4. Use *one(s)* after an adjective to take the place of a noun.

   He has an old dictionary. She has a new. ∧*one*

5. Put a specific noun before a general noun.

   She made a ~~call~~ phone. *phone call*

6. A noun modifier is always singular.

   She took a three-week~~s~~ vacation.

7. An adverb describes a verb. An adjective describes a noun.

   The teacher speaks English fluent. ∧*ly*

   The teacher looks serious~~ly~~.

8. Put the adverb at the end of the verb phrase.

   He ⟨late⟩ arrived at the meeting↴.

   He opened ⟨carefully⟩ the envelope↴.

9. *Too* indicates a problem. If there is no problem, use *very*.

   Your father is ~~too~~ intelligent. *very*

10. *Too much* is followed by a noun. *Too* is followed by an adjective or adverb.

    She's too ~~much~~ old to take care of herself.

11. Put *enough* after the adjective.

    He's ~~enough old~~ to get married. *old enough*

12. Don't use *very* before a verb.

    He ~~very~~ likes his job. ∧*very much*

13. Don't confuse hard and hardly.

    I'm tired. I worked hard~~ly~~ all day.

EDITING ADVICE   Part 2:

1. Use *who, that,* or *which* to introduce an adjective clause. Don't use *what.*

    who
    I know a woman ~~what~~ has ten cats.

2. If the relative pronoun is the subject, don't omit it.

    who
    I know a man ∧ has been married four times.

3. Use *whose* to substitute for a possessive form.

    whose
    I live next door to a couple ~~their~~ children make a lot of noise.

4. If the relative pronoun is used as the object, don't put an object after the verb of the adjective clause.

    I had to pay for the library book that I lost ~~it~~.

5. Don't use *which* for people.

    that
    The man ~~which~~ bought my car paid me by check.

6. Use subject-verb agreement in all clauses.

    s
    I have a friend who live ∧ in Madrid.

    People who talk ~~s~~ too much bother me.

7. Don't use an adjective clause when a simple adjective is enough.

    I don't like long movies.
    ~~I don't like movies that are long.~~

8. Don't use a comma with an essential adjective clause.[7]

    x
    I don't like to be near people , who smoke.

9. Put a noun before an adjective clause.

    A student
    w
    ~~W~~ho needs help should ask the teacher.

10. Put the adjective clause immediately after the noun it describes.

    The teacher speaks Spanish whose class I am taking.

11. Use correct word order in an adjective clause (subject before verb).

    my father caught
    The fish that ~~caught my father~~ was very big.

---

[7]Some adjective clauses are not essential. A comma separates a nonessential adjective clause from the rest of the sentence. You will find information about nonessential adjective clauses in Book Three.

SUMMARY OF LESSON TEN

Part 1—Adjectives, Adverbs, and Noun Modifiers

1. Adjectives and Adverbs

Adjectives	Adverbs
She has a *beautiful* voice.	She sings *beautifully.*
She has a *late* class.	She arrived *late.*
She is a *good* driver.	She drives *well.*
She looks *serious.*	She looked at the contract *seriously.*
As *usual,* she woke up early.	She *usually* wakes up early.

2. Adjective Modifiers and Noun Modifiers

Adjective Modifier	Noun Modifier
a *good* day	*Independence* Day
old shoes	*running* shoes
a *short* vacation	a *two-week* vacation
a *valid* license	a *driver's* license

3. *Very/Too/Enough*

He's *very* healthy.
He's *too* young to retire. He's only 55.
He's old *enough* to understand life.
He has *enough* money to take a vacation.

Part 2—Adjective Clauses

1. Pronoun as Subject

She likes men *who have self-confidence.*
The man *that arrived late* took a seat in the back.

2. Pronoun as Object

I'd like to meet the man *(who/m) (that) she married.*
The book *(which) (that) I'm reading* is very exciting.

3. *Whose* + Noun as Subject

I have a friend *whose brother lives in Japan.*
The students *whose last names begin with A or B* can register on Friday
   afternoon.

4. *Whose* + Noun as Object

She married a man *whose mother she hates.*
The student *whose dictionary I borrowed* didn't come to class today.

LESSON TEN TEST/REVIEW

Part 1   Find the mistakes with adjectives, noun modifiers, and adverbs in the following sentences, and correct them. Not every sentence has a mistake. If the sentence is correct, write *C*.

EXAMPLES: **When did you get your ~~license~~ driver's? *license***

He gets up early and walks the dog.   *C*

1. Do you know where I can find the shoes department in this store?

2. She doesn't feel well today.

3. The language English is very different from my language.

4. I'm very tire because I worked hard all week.

5. Your answer seems wrongly.

6. My grandfather is too much old to work.

7. I don't like red apples. I like yellows ones.

8. The singer's voice sounds sweet.

9. I wrote carefully my name.

10. She bought a car very expensive.

11. I'm too happy to meet you.

12. He stayed in the library late to finish his class project.

13. She looked beautiful when she got marry.

14. You speak English very fluently.

15. He's not old enough to work.

16. I very like your news shoes.

17. He hardly speaks a word of English.

18. She's going to take her driving test. She looks nervously.

Part 2   Find the mistakes with adjective clauses, and correct them. Not every sentence has a mistake. If the sentence is correct, write *C*.

> EXAMPLES: **Do you know the man ~~whose~~ <u>who's</u> standing in the back of the theater?**
>
> **Could you please return the book I lent you last week?**   *C*

1. The wallet which found my husband has no identification.

2. The coat is too small that I bought last week.

3. I don't know the people that lives next door to me.

4. I have to return the books, that I borrowed from the library.

5. I don't like people what make a lot of noise.

6. I don't like the earrings that you bought them.

7. I have a friend lives in Houston.

8. Who speaks English well doesn't have to take this course.

9. I can't understand a word you are saying.

10. I prefer to have an English teacher which speaks my language.

Part 3   Fill in each blank to complete the adjective clause.

> EXAMPLE: **A. You lost a glove. Is this yours?**
>
> **B. No. The glove** <u>*that I lost*</u> **is brown.**

1. A. My neighbors make a lot of noise. They play their stereo loud every night.

   B. That's too bad. I don't like to have neighbors _____

2. A. I have a new cat. Do you want to see it?

   B. What happened to the other cat _____

   A. It died last month.

3. A. Do you speak French?

   B. Yes, I do. Why?

   A. The teacher is looking for a student _____
   to help her translate a letter.

4. A. Did you meet your boyfriend by answering a singles ad?

   B. No. I didn't like any of the men _____
   from the singles ads.

5. A. Does your last name begin with A?

   B. Yes, it does. Why?

   A. Registration is by alphabetical order. Students _____
   A can register after two o'clock today.

6. A. I heard you got a good price on the house you bought.

   B. Yes. The woman _____ moved to Alaska.

LESSON ELEVEN

GRAMMAR
Superlatives
Comparatives

CONTEXT
Job Rankings
Auto Insurance
Generic Drugs

Lesson Focus **Comparatives and Superlatives**

• Adjectives and adverbs have three forms: simple form, comparative form, and superlative form. Study the forms of short words:

Simple	Chicago is a *big* city.
Comparative	Los Angeles is *bigger than* Chicago.
Superlative	New York is *the biggest city* in the U.S.

• Study the forms of long words:

Simple	A small car is *economical.*
Comparative	A car is *more economical than* a truck.
Superlative	A bicycle is *the most economical* way to travel.

R
E
A
D
I
N
G

Before you read:

1. In your opinion, what is a good job to have in the U.S.?
2. In your opinion, which jobs are very stressful?
3. In your country, what are the best jobs? Who makes the most money?

Read the following article. Pay special attention to superlative forms.

JOB RANKINGS

Money is a popular magazine in the U.S. It gives information about investing money and the changes in the economy. *Money* ranks[1] jobs in the U.S. from **the best** to **the worst.** Look at the 1994 list of jobs on page 266. In comparing the top ten jobs, we see the following:

Computer systems analyst is **the highest** ranking job.
Jobs for computer systems analysts are growing **the most quickly.**
A high school teacher has **the lowest** salary of the top ten jobs.
A physician (doctor) has **the highest** salary.
A physician has **the most prestige.**
A physician has **the most stressful** job.
Pharmacists and computer systems analysts have **the least stressful** jobs.

People who are trying to decide on a career can use **the most recent** list in *Money* magazine to help them make their decision. They should look for jobs that have **the most growth** in the near future. Even **the best paying** job is not good if there will be few openings in the coming years.

---

[1]To *rank* means to put a list of items in order from the most to the least.

11.1 Comparative and Superlative Forms

The chart below shows simple, comparative, and superlative forms. Fill in the last example in each section:

	Simple	Comparative	Superlative
One-syllable adjectives and adverbs	tall	taller	the tallest
	fast	*faster*	*The fastest*
Exceptions	bored	more bored	the most bored
	tired	more tired	the most tired
Two-syllable adjectives that end in *-y*	easy	easier	the easiest
	happy	happier	the happiest
	pretty	_____	_____
Other two-syllable adjectives	frequent	more frequent	the most frequent
	active	more active	_____
Some two-syllable adjectives have two forms.	simple	simpler	the simplest
		more simple	the most simple
	common	commoner	_____
		more common	_____

NOTE: These two-syllable adjectives have two forms: *handsome, quiet, gentle, narrow, clever, friendly, angry.*

	Simple	Comparative	Superlative
Adjectives with three or more syllables	important	more important	the most important
	difficult	more difficult	_____
-ly adverbs	quickly	more quickly	the most quickly
	brightly	_____	_____
Irregular adjectives and adverbs	good/well	better	the best
	bad/badly	worse	the worst
	far	farther/further*	the farthest/furthest
	little	less	the least
	a lot	more	the most

*NOTE: *Farther* is used for distances. *Further* is used for ideas.

(To review spelling rules, see Appendix A.)

EXERCISE 1   Give the comparative and superlative forms of each word.

      EXAMPLES: **fat**   *fatter*   *the fattest*

                    important *more important*   *the most important*

1. interesting   _____   _____

2. young   _____   _____

3. beautiful   _____   _____

4. good   _____   _____

5. common   _____   _____

6. thin   _____   _____

7. carefully   _____   _____

8. pretty   _____   _____

9. bad   _____   _____

10. famous   _____   _____

11. lucky   _____   _____

12. simple   _____   _____

13. high   _____   _____

14. delicious   _____   _____

15. far   _____   _____

16. foolishly   _____   _____

11.2 Using Superlatives

We use the superlative form to point out the number-one item of a group. Use *the* before a superlative.

Subject	Verb	*the* + Superlative Adjective		Noun
A computer systems analyst	has	the	best	job.
A physician	has	the	highest	salary.
What	is	the	most stressful	job?

Subject	Verb	*the*	Superlative Adverb
Jobs for computer systems analysts	are growing	the	most quickly.

Language Notes

1. We often use a prepositional phrase after a superlative form.

What is the worst job *on this list*?
Which is the most interesting job *in the top ten*?

2. We often say "one of the [superlative] [plural noun]."

Electrical engineer is *one of the best jobs* on the list.

3. When the verb is *be*, there are two possible word orders:

Peter *is* the smartest student in the class.
The smartest student in the class *is* Peter.

4. Omit *the* after a possessive form.

My best friend is a lawyer. (NOT: my the best friend)
Finding a job is *Peter's biggest problem.* (NOT: Peter's the biggest problem)

5. An adjective clause with *ever* and the present perfect often completes a superlative statement.

My factory job was the most boring job I *have ever had.*
Leaving her country was the hardest thing she *has ever done.*

EXERCISE 2   Look at the list of jobs on page 266. Use the superlative form to name a job that matches each description. Compare your answers to another student's answers.

EXAMPLE: **interesting**
In my opinion, a psychologist has (one of) the most interesting job(s).

1. interesting
2. dangerous
3. easy
4. tiring
5. dirty
6. boring

EXERCISE 3   Talk about your country. Talk about the superlative of each item.

EXAMPLE: **popular sport**
Soccer is the most popular sport in my country.

1. big city
2. beautiful city
3. important industry
4. popular sport
5. popular car
6. common last name
7. cold month
8. long river

The Money Job Rankings*

Rank	1992 Rank	Occupation	Median annual earnings'	11-Year job growth	Short-term outlook	Job security rating	Prestige rating	Stress & Strain rating	Where the jobs are
1	31	Computer Systems Analyst	$42,700	110%	Excellent	Excellent	Good	Low	Boston, Washington, Silicon Valley
2	3	Physician	148,000	35	Average	Good	Excellent	High	New York, Philadelphia, San Francisco
3	50	Physical Therapist	37,200	88	Excellent	Excellent	Good	Average	Denver, Boston, Seattle
4	13	Electrical Engineer	59,100	24	Good	Excellent	Good	Average	Silicon Valley, Dallas, Boston
5	9	Civil Engineer	55,800	24	Good	Excellent	Good	Average	Houston, Denver, San Francisco
6	7	Pharmacist	47,500	29	Good	Good	Good	Low	Columbus, Pittsburgh, Kansas City
7	29	Psychologist	53,000	48	Average	Average	Good	Average	Boston, San Francisco, New York
8	2	Geologist	50,800	22	Good	Excellent	Good	Average	Houston, Denver, New Orleans
9	15	High School Teacher	32,500	37	Good	Excellent	Good	Average	Dallas, Houston, Atlanta
10	5	School Principal	57,300	23	Average	Good	Good	Average	Dallas, Houston, Atlanta

*Excerpts from the article, "The Money Job Rankings," pp 72-73 (rankings of jobs from 1-100), from the March 1994 issue of *Money*. Reprinted from the March 1994 issue of *Money* by special permission: copyright 1994, Time Inc.

EXERCISE 4   Name the person who is the superlative in your family in each of the following categories.

> EXAMPLE: **work hard**
> **My mother works the hardest in my family.**

1. drive well
2. live far from me
3. speak English confidently
4. spend a lot of money
5. work hard
6. watch a lot of TV
7. worry a lot
8. live well

EXERCISE 5   Fill in each blank. Then find a partner and compare your answers to your partner's answers.

1. _____ is one of the most foolish things I have ever done.

2. _____ is one of the hardest things I have ever done.

3. _____ is one of the most interesting people I have ever met.

EXERCISE 6 Write a superlative sentence giving your opinion about each of the following items. Find a partner. Compare your answers to your partner's answers.

> EXAMPLES: **big problem in my country today**
>
> *The biggest problem in my country today is the civil war.*
>
> **big problem in the U.S. today**
>
> *Crime is one of the biggest problems in the U.S. today.*

1. good way to find a spouse

   _____

2. quick way to learn a language

   _____

3. good thing about living in the U.S.

   _____

4. bad thing about living in the U.S.

   _____

5. terrible world tragedy

   _____

R
E
A
D
I
N
G

Before you read:

1. Do you have auto insurance? How much do you pay
   a year?
2. Do drivers in your country have auto insurance?
   Who pays if a driver damages something or hurts
   someone?

Read the following article. Pay special attention to comparative forms.

AUTO INSURANCE

Do you ever wonder why some people pay **more** for car insurance than others?
Insurance companies calculate your rate (price of your insurance) based on the risk they
take by insuring you. For example, insurance rates for married men are **lower than** for
unmarried men. Statistics show that married men have **fewer** accidents. Insurance rates
for women are **lower than** insurance rates for men. Statistics show that women are **better** drivers **than** men. Rates for teenagers are **higher than** rates for adults. Statistics show

that teenagers have the worst driving records; they drive the fastest and take the most chances.

The cost of insurance also depends on your driving record. If you have several violations on your record, you will pay **more** for insurance. Another factor is the number of miles you drive each year. **The more** you drive, **the more** possibilities there are for accidents. As a result, you pay **more.**

In most states, a driver must have liability insurance. This kind of insurance covers damage to another person or to property. Another kind of insurance protects your own car. This insurance is optional.[2] A **more expensive** car costs **more** to insure **than** a **less expensive** car. Sports cars have the highest rate of theft, and owners of these cars pay the most. The cost of insurance also depends on where you live. Some neighborhoods have **more** crime **than** others; people who live in these areas pay **more.**

When you buy insurance, you choose a deductible amount. If you make a claim,[3] you must pay the deductible amount first, and the insurance company pays the rest. For example, if you have a $250 deductible and you have damage of $1,000, you pay $250 and the insurance company pays $750. **The higher** the deductible, **the lower** your insurance premium[4] is. You can choose a **lower** deductible, but your insurance will cost **more**.

• •

EXERCISE 7   Choose the correct word to complete each statement.

> **EXAMPLE: Insurance rates for teenagers are (<u>higher</u>/lower) than insurance rates for adults.**

1. Married men pay (lower/higher) rates than unmarried men.

2. Women pay (more/less) than men.

3. Women have (more/fewer) accidents than men.

4. The higher the deductible, the (higher/lower) your insurance is.

5. In my opinion, women drive (better/worse) than men.

6. The more you drive, the (more/less) you will pay for insurance.

11.3 Comparative Adjectives and Adverbs

We use the comparative form to compare two items. We use *than* before the second item of comparison.

---

[2]*Optional* means you have a choice. You do not have to buy this insurance if you don't want it.

[3]When you make a *claim,* you are asking your insurance company to pay.

[4]The *premium* is the amount of money you pay for insurance.

Subject	*Be*[5]	Comparative Adjective	*Than*	Noun/Pronoun
Insurance for women	is	cheaper	than	insurance for men.
My car	is	more expensive	than	your car.

Subject	Verb Phrase	Comparative Adverb	*Than*	Noun/Pronoun
Women	drive	more carefully	than	men.
She	learned to drive	more quickly	than	her husband.
I	drive	less	than	you.

Language Notes

1. Omit *than* if the second item of comparison is not included.
    He is tall, but his brother is even *taller*.

2. *Much* or *a little* can come before a comparative form.
    She is *much older* than her husband.
    She is *a little taller* than her husband.

3. In a question, we use *or* instead of *than*.
    Which insurance company is better, yours *or* mine?

4. When a pronoun follows *than*, the most correct form is the subject pronoun. Sometimes an auxiliary verb follows.
    She is taller than *he* (*is*).
    He speaks English better than *I* (*do*).

Informally, many Americans use the object pronoun after *than*. An auxiliary verb does not follow.
    She is taller than *him*.
    He speaks English better than *me*.

5. We can use two comparatives in one sentence to show cause and result.
    The more you drive, *the higher* your insurance premium will be.
    The bigger your car's engine is, *the more* gas it uses.

EXERCISE 8   Compare the people of your country to Americans (in general). Give your own opinion.

EXAMPLE: **tall**
         Americans are taller than Koreans.

1. polite   6. serious
2. friendly   7. wealthy
3. formal   8. educated
4. tall   9. _____
5. thin   10. _____

---

[5]Other linking verbs can be used: "Your car *looks* newer than my car."

EXERCISE 9   Compare the U.S. and your country. Explain your response.

> EXAMPLES: **cars**
> **Cars are cheaper in the U.S. Most people in my country can't afford a car.**
>
> **education**
> **Education is better in my country. Everyone must finish high school.**

1. rent
2. housing
3. cars
4. education
5. medical care
6. food
7. gasoline
8. the government
9. clothes (or fashions)
10. people

EXERCISE 10   Use an adverb to compare the people of your country to Americans (in general). Give your own opinion.

> EXAMPLE: **drive well**
> **Mexicans drive better than Americans.**

1. dress stylishly
2. work hard
3. spend a lot
4. drive well
5. live long
6. worry a little
7. live comfortably
8. _____

 **11.4** **Comparison with Nouns**

We can make comparisons with nouns.

X	Verb	Comparative Word	Noun	*Than*	Y
Women	are	better	drivers	than	men.
Women	have	fewer	accidents	than	men.

We can use *more, less, fewer, better,* or *worse* before nouns.

EXERCISE 11   Compare this college to a college in your country. Use *better, worse, more, less,* or *fewer* before the noun.

EXAMPLE: classroom/spac
         This classroom has more space than a classroom in my country.

1. class/students   4. library/books
2. college/courses   5. college/facilities[6]
3. teachers/experience   6. college/teachers

EXERCISE 12   Work with a partner. Find some differences between the two of you. Then write five sentences that compare you and your partner. Share your answers in a small group or with the whole class.

EXAMPLE: **I'm taller than Alex.**
         Alex is taking more classes than I am.

EXERCISE 13   Fill in the blank with the comparative or superlative form of the word in parentheses ( ). Include *than* or *the* when necessary.

EXAMPLES: **August is usually ___*hotter than*___ May.**
                             (hot)

January is usually ___*the coldest*___ month of the year.
                        (cold)

1. November is _____ December.
                    (short)

2. December 21 is _____ day of the year. It has
                       (short)

   _____ hours of sunlight.
        (few)

3. "Johnson" is one of _____ last names in the U.S.
                            (common)

4. A motorcycle is _____ a car.
                       (economical)

5. _____ way to travel is by bicycle.
      (economical)

6. Baseball is one of _____ sports in the U.S.
                          (popular)

7. Baseball is _____ soccer in the U.S.
                   (popular)

8. _____ time to call long distance is at night or on the weekend.
      (cheap)

9. Paris is far from Los Angeles, but Moscow is even _____.
                                                          (far)

10. Paris is _____ Bucharest, Rumania.
                (beautiful)

---

[6]*Facilities* are things we use, such as a swimming pool, cafeteria, library, exercise room, or student union.

R
E
A
D
I
N
G

Before you read:

1. Is medicine expensive in your country?
2. Do you have to pay for your medicine in the U.S., or do you have medical insurance?

Read the following article. Pay special attention to words that show similarity and difference.

GENERIC DRUGS

When your doctor gives you a prescription for medicine, there are two boxes at the bottom:

❏ may substitute   ❏ may not substitute

If your doctor checks the box "may substitute," this means that the pharmacist may give you a generic drug. A generic drug is equivalent to a name-brand drug. It has **the same active ingredient** and **strength as** a name-brand drug. Generic companies must follow **the same government regulations as** other drug manufacturers. However, generic drugs do not have **the same name as** name-brand drugs. For example, Tylenol® is a brand name. Acetaminophen is the generic, or chemical, name of the drug. Not all drugs have a generic equivalent.

In most cases, a generic drug is **as effective as** its name-brand equivalent. However, it is not **as expensive.** In some cases, it may even be half the price. Why are generic drugs much cheaper than name-brand drugs? Companies that make name-brand drugs spend a lot of money on research before the drug can be sold. The cost of research is part of the price you pay. Generic drug companies don't spend **as much** because they do not conduct research. Their only expenses are in manufacturing and packaging.

11.5 Comparisons with As . . . As

We can show that two things are equal or not in some way by using *as adjective/adverb as.*

Subject	Linking Verb[7]	As	Adjective	As	Noun
Generic medicine	isn't	as	expensive	as	name-brand medicine.
Columbian coffee	tastes	as	good	as	Mexican coffee.

Subject	Verb Phrase	As	Adverb	As	Noun
She	speaks English	as	fluently	as	her husband.
He	doesn't work	as	hard	as	his wife.

[7]Remember: The linking verbs are *be, look, seem, feel, taste, sound, smell.*

Language Notes

1. When we can make a comparison of unequal items, we put the lesser item first.

   A generic drug is not *as expensive as* a name-brand drug. (A name-brand drug is more expensive.)
   Chicago is not *as big as* New York. (New York is bigger.)

2. Omit the second *as* if the second item of comparison is omitted.

   A generic drug may be *as good as* a name-brand drug, but it's not *as expensive.*

mule

3. A very common expression is *as soon as possible*. Some people even say A.S.A.P.

   I'd like to see you *as soon as possible.*
   I'd like to see you *A.S.A.P.*

4. These are some common expressions using *as . . . as.*

   as poor as a church mouse
   as old as the hills
   as quiet as a mouse
   as happy as a lark
   as sick as a dog
   as proud as a peacock
   as gentle as a lamb
   as stubborn as a mule

peacock

EXERCISE 14   Compare yourself to another person. (Or compare two people you know.) Use the following adjectives and *as . . . as.* You may add a comparative statement if there is inequality.

EXAMPLES: **thin**
I'm not as thin as my sister. (She's thinner than I am.)

old
My mother is not as old as my father. (My father is older than my mother.)

1. old	4. patient	7. religious	10. talkative
2. educated	5. lazy	8. friendly	11. _____
3. intelligent	6. tall	9. strong	12. _____

EXERCISE 15   Use the underlined word to compare yourself to the teacher.

EXAMPLES: **speak English <u>well</u>**
I don't speak English as well as the teacher. (The teacher speaks English better than I do.)

speak Spanish <u>well</u>
The teacher doesn't speak Spanish as well as I do. (I speak Spanish better.)

1. arrive to class <u>promptly</u>
2. work <u>hard</u> in class
3. understand American customs <u>well</u>
4. speak <u>quietly</u>
5. speak English <u>fluently</u>
6. understand a foreigner's problems <u>well</u>
7. _____

11.6 Comparing Quantities

We can show that two things are equal or not equal in quantity.

Subject	Verb	*As Many/Much*	Noun	*As*	Noun
She	works	as many	hours	as	her husband.
Milk	doesn't have	as much	fat	as	cream.

Subject	Verb	*As Much As*	Noun
Generic drugs	don't cost	as much as	name-brand drugs.
I	don't drive	as much as	you (do).

EXERCISE 16   Compare men and women (in general). Give your own opinion. Use *as much as.*

EXAMPLES: drink (alcohol)
Women don't drink as much as men. (Men drink more than women.)

show emotion
Men don't show as much emotion as women. (Women show more emotion than men.)

1. earn
2. spend money
3. talk
4. gossip

5. use foul language[8]
6. have responsibilities
7. have freedom
8. _____

EXERCISE 17   Compare this school and another school you attended. Use *as many as.*

EXAMPLE: classrooms
This school doesn't have as many classrooms as King College. (King College has more classrooms.)

1. teachers
2. classrooms

3. floors (or stories)
4. English courses

5. exams
6. students

---

[8]People who use *foul* language use bad, or *dirty,* words.

EXERCISE 18   Part A: Fill in each blank.

1. I drive about _____ miles a week.

2. I'm _____ tall.

3. The highest level of education that I completed is _____ (high school, bachelor's degree, master's degree, doctorate).

4. I work _____ hours a week.

5. I study _____ hours a day.

6. I have had _____ tickets while driving my car.

7. I exercise _____ days a week.

8. I'm taking _____ courses now.
         (number)

9. I have _____ siblings.[9]
         (number)

10. I live _____ miles from this school.
         (number)

Part B: Write statements with the words given and (not) as . . . as or (not) as much/ many as. Find a partner and compare your answers to your partner's answers.

EXAMPLE: drive *I don't drive as much as Lisa.* _____

1. tall _____

2. have education _____

3. work _____

4. study _____

5. drive carefully _____

6. exercise frequently _____

7. take courses _____

8. have siblings _____

9. live far from school _____

EXERCISE 19   Change these statements so that they use *as . . . as.*

_____

[9]*Siblings* are a person's brothers and sisters.

EXAMPLE: **The teacher speaks English more fluently than I (do).**

I don't speak English as fluently as the teacher (does).

1. A car costs more than a motorcycle.

_____

2. Cream has more fat than milk.

_____

3. Women live longer than men.

_____

4. The teacher speaks English better than I do.

_____

5. Chicago has more people than Miami.

_____

6. Tokyo is more crowded than Los Angeles.

_____

EXERCISE 20   Make one or more comparisons for each of the following. Then find a partner. Compare your answers to your partner's answers.

1. an American teenager/a teenager in my country
2. medical care in the U.S./in my country
3. American teachers/teachers in my country
4. learning English in the U.S./learning English in my country

EXERCISE 21   Form a small group (about 3–5 people) with students from different countries, if possible. Make comparisons about your countries. Include a superlative statement.

EXAMPLES: **Cuba is closer to the U.S. than Peru is.**
China has the largest population.
Cuba doesn't have as many resources as China.

If all the students in your class are from the same country, compare cities in your country.

11.7 *The Same . . . As*

We can show that two things are equal or not equal in some way.

PATTERN A					
Subject	Verb	*The Same*	Noun	*As*	Noun/Pronoun
A generic drug	has	the same	ingredients	as	a name-brand drug.
A generic drug	isn't	the same	price	as	a name-brand drug.

PATTERN B			
Subject & Subject	Verb	*The Same*	Noun
A generic drug and a name-brand drug	have	the same	ingredients.
A generic drug and a name-brand drug	aren't	the same	price.

1. We omit *as* in Pattern B.

2. We can make statements of equality with the following nouns: *size, shape, age, price, height, weight, value, length, religion, nationality.*

3. Compare equality with adjectives and nouns:
He is as *tall* as his brother.
He is the same *height* as his brother.
She is as *old* as her husband.
She and her husband are the same *age*.

EXERCISE 22   Talk about two relatives or friends of yours. Compare them using the words given.

EXAMPLE: age
My mother and my father aren't the same age.
OR
My mother isn't the same age as my father. (My father is older than my mother.)

1. age
2. height
3. weight
4. nationality
5. religion
6. (have) level of education

EXERCISE 23   Make a **true** affirmative statement or negative statement with the words given.

      EXAMPLES: the same nationality
                 I'm not the same nationality as the teacher. I'm Colombian, and the teacher's American.

                 the same color
                 My shoes and my purse are the same color. They're both brown.

1. the same color
2. (have) the same value
3. the same size
4. the same shape
5. the same price
6. (speak) the same language

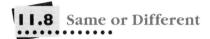
11.8   Same or Different

We can show that two things are equal or not equal.

PATTERN A			
X	Linking Verb	*The Same As/ Different From*	Y
A quarter	is	the same as	twenty-five cents.
A nickel	is	different from	a quarter.

PATTERN B		
X and Y	Linking Verb	*The Same/ Different*
A quarter and twenty-five cents	are	the same.
A nickel and a quarter	are	different.

EXERCISE 24   Tell if the two items are the same or different.

      EXAMPLES: summer, fall
                 Summer and fall are different.

                 fall, autumn
                 Fall is the same as autumn.

1. borrow, lend
2. big, large
3. my book, the teacher's book
4. my last name, my mother's last name
5. 2 + 5, 5 + 2
6. a mile, a kilometer
7. two quarts, a half gallon

 **11.9 Similarity**
• • • • • • • • • • • •

We can show that two things are similar or not in some ways:

PATTERN A				
X	Linking Verb	*Like*	Y	
Beer	is	like	champagne.	They are both alcoholic drinks. They both have carbonation.
Pepsi	looks	like	Coke.	They are both brown.
Regular coffee	tastes	like	decaf.	I can't tell[10] the difference.

PATTERN B		
X and Y	Linking Verb	*Alike*
Beer and wine	are	alike.
Pepsi and Coke	look	alike.
Regular coffee and decaf	taste	alike.

EXERCISE 25   Make a statement with the words given.

> EXAMPLE: **taste/Pepsi/Coke**
> **Pepsi takes like Coke (to me).**
> OR
> **Pepsi and Coke taste alike (to me).**

1. taste/diet cola/Pepsi
2. taste/milk in the U.S./milk in my country
3. sound/British English/American English
4. sound/Asian music/American music
5. feel/polyester/silk
6. smell/cologne/perfume
7. look/salt/sugar
8. taste/salt/sugar
9. (your own comparison)

---

[10]*I can't tell* means "I don't know the difference."

EXERCISE 26   Ask a question with the words given. Use *be like*. Another student will answer.

> EXAMPLE: **you/sister**
> **A. Are you like your sister?**
> **B. Yes. We're alike in many ways. We're both interested in art. We both like to cook.**
> OR
> **I'm not like my sister at all. She's shy, and I'm outgoing.**

1. an English class in the U.S./an English class in your country
2. your house (or apartment) in the U.S./your house (or apartment) in your country
3. the weather in this city/the weather in your hometown
4. food in your country/American food
5. women's clothes in your country/women's clothes in the U.S.
6. a college in your country/a college in the U.S.
7. American teachers/teachers in your country

EXERCISE 27   Work with a partner. Choose one of the categories below, and compare two examples from this category. Use any type of comparative method. Write four sentences. Share your answers with the class.

1. countries	4. teachers	7. types of transportation
2. cars	5. cities	8. schools
3. restaurants	6. animals	9. sports

EXAMPLE: **animals**

> *A dog is different from a cat in many ways.*
>
> *A dog can't jump as high as a cat.*
>
> *A dog is a better pet than a cat, in my opinion.*
>
> *A cat is not as friendly as a dog.*

1. _____

2. _____

3. _____

4. _____

EXERCISE 28   Combination exercise. This is a conversation between two women about marriage and children. Fill in each blank using the word in parentheses ( ) to make a comparative or superlative statement.

A. Do you think it's _____*better*_____ to get married when you're young or wait
                          (good)

until you're in your thirties?

B. If you plan to have children, I think you should get married when

you're young. Women in their thirties don't have _____
                                                        (1 energy)

younger women.

A. But women in their thirties are _____ women in their
                                          (2 mature)

twenties. Also, they're _____.
                              (3 responsible)

B. What do you think is _____ age to get married?
                              (4 good)

A. About 24 for women and 28 for men.

B. Do you think the husband should always be _____ the wife?
                                                    (5 old)

A. In my country, that's the custom. But I don't think it makes sense because

women live _____ men.
                  (6 long)

B. I have three sisters. My _____ sister married a man five years
                                  (7 old)

_____ she is. I don't think it's a problem. My husband and I are
      (8 young)

_____. We're both 27.
      (9 age)

A. Is your husband handsome?

B. I think he's _____ man in the world.
                      (10 handsome)

A. Do you have any children?

B. We have one daughter. She's two years old. Do you want to see her

picture? She looks just[11] like her father. They both have _____

                                                                                        (11 eyes)

and _____, but her hair is not _____ his hair.

                        (12 smile)   (13 curly)

A. She's a beautiful girl.

B. Thank you. Of course, I think she's _____ girl in the world.

                                                                        (14 beautiful)

EXPANSION ACTIVITIES

PROVERBS   1. The following proverbs contain the superlative form. Discuss the
                       meaning of each proverb. Do you have a similar proverb in your
                       language?

                       Honesty is the best policy.
                       It's always darkest before the dawn.

                  2. The following proverbs contain the comparative form. Discuss the
                       meaning of each proverb. Do you have a similar proverb in your
                       language?

                       The bigger they come, the harder they fall.
                       Blood is thicker than water.
                       The pen is mightier[12] than the sword.
                       His bark is worse than his bite.
                       Actions speak louder than words.

sword

SAYINGS   Here are some sayings that use *as . . . as*. Discuss what they mean. Do
                  you have a similar saying in your language?

                  A chain is only as strong as its weakest link.
                  You're only as old as you feel.

DISCUSSIONS   In a small group or with the entire class, discuss one of the following:

                  1. Is the American family like a family in your country? How are they the
                      same? How are they different?
                  2. In what ways are you like your parents? In what ways are you
                      different?

---

[11]*Just*, in this case, means *exactly*.

[12]*Mighty* means strong or powerful.

3. Compare clothing styles in your country and in the U.S.

4. Compare life in the U.S. (in general) with life in your country.

5. Compare your life in the U.S. with your life in your country.

6. Compare the American political system with the political system in your country.

7. From your experience at this school, compare school (teachers, students, classes, etc.) in the U.S. with school in your country.

WRITING

Write a short composition using one of the items from the above discussion.

Additional topics of comparison:

* English grammar and the grammar of your language
* two stores where you shop for groceries
* two friends of yours
* football and soccer (or any two similar sports)
* a word processor and a typewriter
* watching a movie on a VCR and at a movie theater

OUTSIDE ACTIVITIES

1. The next time you go to a drugstore, compare the price of a drug you often buy (such as aspirin) with its generic equivalent. Tell the class about the difference in price.

2. Interview an American. Get his or her opinion about the superlative of each of the following items. Share your findings with the class.

   prestigious job
   beautiful city in the U.S.
   popular TV program
   terrible tragedy in American history
   big problem in the U.S.
   handsome or beautiful actor

3. Go to the reference section of the library. Ask the librarian for the latest edition of the *Occupational Outlook Handbook* or the *Dictionary of Occupational Titles*. Look for a job that interests you. Get some information about this job, and report back to the class.

4. Go to the library. Ask the reference librarian to help you find the most recent listing of *Money* magazine's job rankings. Compare the latest listing with the report from 1994. What are the best jobs today? What changes have taken place in the past few years?

EDITING ADVICE

1. Don't use a comparison word when there is no comparison.

    New York is a bigger city.

2. Don't use *more* and *-er* together.

    He is more older than his teacher.

3. Use *than* before the second item of comparison.

    He is younger ~~that~~ *than* his wife.

4. Use *the* before a superlative form.

    The Nile is *the* longest river in the world.

5. Use a plural noun in the phrase "one of the [superlative] nouns."

    Chicago is one of the biggest ~~city~~ *cities* in the U.S.

6. Use the correct word order.

    She ~~more speaks~~ *speaks more* than her husband.

    I have ~~time more~~ *more time* than you.

7. Use *be like* for similar character. Use *look like* for a physical similarity.

    He ~~is~~ look*s* like his brother. They both have blue eyes and dark hair.

    He is ~~look~~ like his sister. They are both talented musicians.

SUMMARY OF LESSON ELEVEN

1. Simple, Comparative, and Superlative Forms

   Short words

   > California is a *large* state.
   > Texas is *larger* than California.
   > Alaska is the *largest* state in the U.S.

   Long words

   > A small car is *economical.*
   > A motorcycle is *more economical* than a car.
   > A bicycle is the *most economical* way to travel.

2. Other Kinds of Comparisons

   > She looks *as young as* her daughter.
   > She speaks English *as fluently as* her husband.
   > She is *the same age as* her husband.
   > She and her husband are *the same age.*
   > She works *as many hours as* her husband.
   > She doesn't have *as much time as* her husband.
   > She works *as much as* her husband.
   > Her job is *different from* her husband's job.
   > Her job is *the same as* her husband's job.
   > Her job and her husband's job are *the same.*

3. Comparisons with *Like*

   > She*'s like* her mother. (She and her mother *are alike.*) They're both
   >   shy.
   > She *looks like* her sister. They both have blue eyes.
   > Coke *tastes like* Pepsi.
   > Western music doesn't *sound like* Asian music.

LESSON ELEVEN TEST/REVIEW

Part 1 Find the mistakes with comparative and superlative statements, and correct them. Not every sentence has a mistake. If the sentence is correct, write *C*.

EXAMPLES: She ̶i̶s̶ look^s like her sister. They both have curly hair.

A house in the suburbs is much more expensive than a house in the city.   *C*

1. I am the same tall as my brother.

2. New York City is the larger city in the U.S.

3. That man is smarter that his wife.

4. The youngest student in the class has more better grades than you.

5. A big city has crime more than a small town.

6. I have three sons. My oldest son is married.

7. I visited many American cities, and I think that San Francisco is the more beautiful city in the U.S.

8. New York is one of largest city in the world.

9. My uncle is the most intelligent person in my family.

10. She better speaks English than I do.

11. Texas is one of the biggest state in the U.S.

12. He more carefully drives than his wife.

13. Paul is one of the youngest students in this class.

14. She is richer than her best friend, but her friend is happier than.

Part 2 Fill in each blank.

EXAMPLE: Pepsi is ___*the same*___ color ___*as*___ Coke.

1. She's 35 years old. Her husband is 35 years old. She and her husband

   are _____ age.

2. She earns $30,000 a year. Her husband earns $35,000. She doesn't earn

   as _____ her husband.

3. The little girl _____ like her mother. They both have blue eyes and blond hair.

4. My name is Sophia Weiss. My teacher's name is Judy Weiss. We have

    _____ last name.

5. Chinese food is different _____ American food.

6. A dime isn't the same _____ a nickel. A dime is smaller.

7. She is as tall as her husband. They are the same _____

8. I drank Pepsi and Coke, and I don't know which is which. They have

    the same flavor. To me, Pepsi _____ like Coke.

9. She _____ like her husband in many ways. They're both intelligent and hard-working. They both like sports.

10. A. Are you like your mother?

    B. Oh, no. We're not _____ at all! We're completely different.

11. Please finish this test _____ possible!

LESSON TWELVE

GRAMMAR

Articles
Definite and Indefinite
    Nouns and Pronouns

CONTEXT

Automatic Teller Machines
Superstitions
Language Families

Lesson Focus **Articles; Definite and Indefinite Nouns and Pronouns**

- Articles express whether a noun is definite or indefinite. They express whether a noun is specific or general. Sometimes a noun has no article (Ø).

  Do you see *the cat*?   Do you have *a cat*?   *Cats* are independent animals.

- We use definite pronouns (such as *it* or *them*) to substitute for definite nouns. We use indefinite pronouns (*one, some, any*) to substitute for indefinite nouns.

  Do you see *the cat*? Yes, I see *it*.   Do you have *a cat*? Yes, I have *one*.

R E A D I N G

Before you read:

1. Do you have a cash card (ATM card)? How often do you use it?
2. In your country, did you have credit cards? Did you use checks?

Front   Back

Bank Card

Read about automatic teller machines. Pay special attention to nouns with and without articles.

AUTOMATIC TELLER MACHINES

An **automatic teller** is **a machine** that lets you make **a deposit** or take out **cash** from your **bank account.** You use **a plastic card** that looks like **a credit card.** You can get **an ATM card** from **the bank** where you have your **account.** When **the bank** gives you your **card,** it also gives you **a personal identification number** (PIN). You should memorize **the number.** If you lose your **card,** no one can use it without your special **number.**

The bank that gave you your **card** has **a machine.** However, you don't have to use your **card** at this **bank** only. You can use your **ATM card** in many other **banks.** There are also **machines** in other **locations: shopping malls, supermarkets,** and **office buildings,** for example.

Can you use your **card** in every **machine?** No. On **the back** of your **card,** there are **symbols.** You can use your **card** only at **machines** that have these **symbols.**

People use these **cards** for **convenience.** If **the bank** is crowded, you don't have to wait in **a long line.** You save **time.** When **the bank** is closed, you can still get **cash** or make **a deposit.** There are **deposit envelopes** near **the machine.** ATMs are open twenty-four **hours** a **day.**

12.1 Using the Indefinite Article to Classify or Define

We use the indefinite article *a* or *an* to classify or define the subject of the sentence. The verb *be* connects the subject and the definition.

Subject	*Be*	*A/an*	Singular Noun (Phrase)
An ATM	is	a	cash machine.
A teller	is	a	bank worker.

We express the plural with no article.

Subject	*Be*	Plural Noun (Phrase)
California and Oregon	are	states.
Mastercard and Visa	are	credit card companies.

EXERCISE 1   Define the following words.

EXAMPLE: A rose . . . / A rose is a flower.

1. Gold . . .
2. Asia . . .
3. A carrot . . .
4. Canada . . .
5. Chicago . . .
6. English and German . . .
7. Volleyball and basketball . . .
8. An elephant and a giraffe . . .
9. New York and Los Angeles . . .
10. Christmas and Easter . . .

EXERCISE 2   Think of a noun in your language that has no English translation. Tell the class the word and what it is by giving a definition.

EXAMPLE: **borscht**
         In eastern Europe, borscht is a soup we make out of beets.

EXERCISE 3   Think of something from American culture that has no translation in your language. Write a definition. Share your definition with the class.

EXAMPLES: **a Big Mac**
          A Big Mac is a hamburger that is made at McDonald's restaurant.

          Sesame Street
          Sesame Street is a children's program on TV.

12.2   Definite and Indefinite Nouns

We use the indefinite articles *a* and *an* or the quantity words *some* and *any* to introduce a noun into the conversation. We can then refer to this noun with the definite article *the*.

	Singular Count	Plural Count	Noncount
Affirmative	I have an ATM card. I use the card often.	I have some credit cards. The credit cards are in my wallet.	I have some cash. The cash is in my pocket.
Negative	I don't have an ATM card.	I don't have any credit cards.	I don't have any cash.
Question	Do you have an ATM card?	Do you have any credit cards?	Do you have any cash?

Language Notes

1. *There* + a form of *be* can introduce an indefinite noun into the conversation.

> There's *a bank* on the corner of Main and Washington.
> There's *some money* in my checking account.
> There aren't *any coins* in my purse.

There cannot introduce a definite, unique noun.

> WRONG: There's the Statue of Liberty in New York.

2. *Some* and *any* can be omitted before an indefinite noun.

> There's *(some)* money in my checking account.
> I don't have *(any)* cash with me.

3. We use the definite article *the* when the speaker and the listener have the same person(s) or object(s) in mind. In the following cases, the listener knows exactly what the speaker is referring to because:

• The speaker first introduced the noun into the conversation as an indefinite noun.

> The bank gives you *an identification number*. You should memorize *the number*.

> A cash card has *some symbols* on the back. *The symbols* tell you where you can use your card.

I borrowed *some money* from my friend. I'll return *the money* next week.

• The speaker refers to an object that is present.

> Don't take *the money* on the table. It's for the rent.
> *The credit card* on the table expired in May 1995.
> *The cash machines* are out of order.

• There is only one in our experience.

> *The sun* is not very bright in the winter.
> There are many problems in *the world*.
> There are symbols on *the back* of an ATM card. (The card has only one back.)
> I want to talk to *the president* of the bank. (An organization has only one president.)

(continued)

- The speaker and listener share a common experience.

    Students in the same class talk about *the teacher, the textbook, the homework, the blackboard.*
    Where's *the teacher*? I want to give him *the homework.*
    People who live together talk about *the house, the door, the windows,* etc. that they share.
    I closed *the windows* and locked *the door* before I left *the house.*

- The speaker defines or specifies exactly which one.

    I spent *the money that you gave me.*
    I used *the ATM in the supermarket near my house.*

- We often use *the* with certain familiar places and people—*the bank, the zoo, the park, the store, the movies, the beach, the post office, the bus, the train, the doctor*—when we refer to the one that we habitually use.

    I'm going to *the store* after work. Do you need anything?
    The bank is closed. I'll go tomorrow.
    You should make an appointment with *the doctor.*

EXERCISE 4   Fill in each blank with the definite article *the*, the indefinite article *a* or *an*, or quantity words *any* or *some*.

Conversation 1: between two friends

A. Where are you going?

B. To ___*the*___ bank. I want to cash _____ check.
                                                    (1)

A. _____ bank is probably closed now.
    (2)

B. No problem. I have _____ cash card. There's _____ cash machine on
                       (3)   (4)

_____ corner of Wilson and Sheridan.
    (5)

A. I'll go with you. I want to get _____ cash.
                                    (6)

Later, at the cash machine . . .

B. Oh, no. _____ machine is out of order.
           (7)

A. Don't worry. There's _____ cash machine in _____ supermarket near
                         (8)   (9)

my house.

Conversation 2: between two students at the same school

A. Is there _____ cafeteria at this school?
         (1)

B. Yes, there is. It's on _____ first floor of this building.
                        (2)

A. I want to buy _____ cup of coffee.
                (3)

B. You don't have to go to _____ cafeteria. There's _____
                          (4)   (5)

coffee machine on this floor.

A. I only have a one-dollar bill. Do you have _____ change?
                                               (6)

B. There's _____ dollar-bill changer next to _____ coffee machine.
           (7)   (8)

dollar changer

Conversation 3: between two students (A and B) in the same class and, later, the teacher (T)

A. Where's _____ teacher? It's already 7:00.
           (1)

B. Maybe she's absent today.

A. I'll go to _____ English office and ask if anyone knows where she is.
              (2)

B. That's _____ good idea.
          (3)

A few minutes later . . .

A. I talked to _____ secretary in _____ English office. She said that
              (4)   (5)

_____ teacher just called. She's going to be about 15 minutes late. She had
  (6)

_____ problem with her car.
  (7)

Ten minutes later . . .

A. Here's _____ teacher.
          (8)

T. I'm sorry I'm late.

B. Did you fix _____ problem with your car?
              (9)

T. I didn't have time. I left _____ car at home and took _____
                             (10)   (11)

taxi to school.

12.3 General and Specific

Articles (or their absence) tell us if a noun is general or specific, if the statement is true about all members of a group or if it is true of only specific examples.

General	Specific
A credit card is made of plastic.	The credit card is behind the driver's license.
Credit cards are made of plastic.	The credit cards on the table are mine.
Money can't buy happiness.	The money on the table is mine.

Language Notes

1. For a count noun, we use *a* or *an* + a singular form or Ø article + plural form to make a generalization.

2. For a noncount noun, we use Ø article to make a generalization.

3. Do not use *some* or *any* with generalizations. COMPARE:

I ate *some* beef for dinner. (an indefinite quantity)
Beef comes from a cow. (a generalization)
NOT: Some beef comes from a cow.

EXERCISE 5   Decide if the statement is general (true of all examples of the subject) or specific (true of the pictures on this page or of specific objects that everyone in this class can agree on). Fill in the blanks with *a, the,* or Ø article.

EXAMPLES: *The*_____ dog is sleeping.

*A*_____ dog has four legs.

*Ø*_____ elephants have big ears.

*The*_____ elephants are hungry.

*The*_____ sun is bigger than *the*_____ moon.

1. _____ women generally live longer than men.

2. _____ women are talking on the phone.

3. _____ window is broken.

4. _____ window is made of glass.

5. _____ children are playing.

6. _____ children can generally learn a foreign language faster than adults.

7. _____ coffee is hot.

8. _____ coffee contains caffeine.

9. _____ sugar is on the shelf.

10. _____ sugar is sweet.

11. _____ cows give milk.

12. _____ cows are eating grass.

13. _____ salt contains a lot of sodium.

14. _____ salt is in the cabinet.

15. _____ teachers make less money than _____ doctors in the U.S.

16. _____ teacher is trying to teach us about articles now.

EXERCISE 6 Tell if you like the following or not. For count nouns (C), use the plural form. For noncount nouns (NC), use the singular form.

> EXAMPLES: **coffee (NC)**
> **I like coffee.**
>
> **apple (C)**
> **I don't like apples.**

1. tea (NC)
2. corn (NC)
3. peach (C)
4. potato chip (C)
5. milk (NC)
6. orange (C)
7. cookie (C)
8. pizza (NC)
9. potato (C)
10. egg (C)

EXERCISE 7 Fill in each blank with *the, a, an, some, any,* or Ø.

A. Where are you going?

B. I'm going to _____*the*_____ post office. I need to buy _____ stamps.
    (1)

A. I'll go with you. I want to mail _____ package to my parents.
    (2)

B. What's in _____ package?
    (3)

A. _____ shirts for my father, _____ coat for my sister, and _____
     (4)   (5)   (6)

money for my mother.

B. You should never send _____ money by mail.
                               (7)

A. I know. My mother never received _____ money that I sent in my last
                                            (8)

letter. But what can I do? I don't have _____ checking account.
                                        (9)

B. You can buy _____ money order at _____ bank.
               (10)   (11)

A. How much does it cost?

B. Well, if you have _____ account in _____ bank, it's usually free. If not,
                      (12)   (13)

you'll probably have to pay 50¢ or more.

A. What about _____ currency exchange on Wright Street? Do they sell
                    (14)

_____ money orders?
  (15)

B. Yes.

A. Why don't we go there? We can save _____ time. It's on _____ same
                                   (16)   (17)

street as _____ post office.
         (18)

EXERCISE 8   Fill in each blank with *the, a, an, some, any,* or ∅.

A. What would you like for lunch? How about ___*some*___ soup?

B. That sounds good. What are you going to put in _____ soup?
                                           (1)

A. _____ carrots, _____ rice, _____ onion, and _____ pork.
     (2)   (3)   (4)   (5)

B. Can you leave out _____ pork? I'm a Muslim and we don't eat _____
                      (6)   (7)

pork.

A. Why not?

B. _____ pork comes from _____ pig. Muslims believe that _____ pigs
   (8)   (9)   (10)

aren't clean animals.

1. We can use *all, most, many, some, (a) few,* and *(a) little* before general nouns. Before specific nouns, we add *of the*. COMPARE:

All children need love.
All *of the* children[1] in my building are very well-behaved.

Very few Americans speak my language.
Very few *of the* Americans in my math class know where my country is.

Most money in the bank is insured.
I used most *of the* money in my bank account.

2. After *none of the* + plural noun, you will often hear a plural verb in informal speech. However, a singular verb is more correct.

CORRECT: None of the classrooms at this school *has* a telephone.
INFORMAL: None of the classrooms at this school *have* a telephone.

EXERCISE 9   Fill in each blank with *all, most, some,* or *(very) few* to make a general statement about Americans.

EXAMPLE: *Most*   **Americans have a car.**

1. _____ Americans have educational opportunities.

2. _____ Americans have a TV.

3. _____ American families have more than eight children.

4. _____ Americans know where my country is.

5. _____ Americans shake hands when they meet.

6. _____ Americans use credit cards.

7. _____ Americans are natives of America.

8. _____ American citizens can vote.

9. _____ Americans speak my language.

10. _____ Americans are friendly to me.

---

[1]After *all, of* is often omitted: "All the children in my building are very well-behaved."

EXERCISE 10   Fill in each blank with a quantity word to make a **true** statement about specific nouns. (If you use *none*, change the verb to the singular form.)

EXAMPLES: *All of the*_____ students in this class want to learn English.

None of the students _____ in this class come**s** from Australia.

1. _____ students in this class speak Spanish.

2. _____ students brought their books to class today.

3. _____ students are absent today.

4. _____ students want to learn English.

5. _____ students have jobs.

6. _____ students are married.

7. _____ students are going to return to their countries.

8. _____ lessons in this book end with a review.

9. _____ pages in this book have pictures.

10. _____ tests in this class are hard.

. . . .

R
E
A
D
I
N
G

Before you read:

1. What are some superstitions in your country?
2. Are you superstitious? About what?

Read the following article. Pay special attention to *one, some,* and *any.*

SUPERSTITIONS

Do you have any superstitions? You probably have **some.** Some people believe that cats have magical powers and that if a black cat crosses in front of you it will bring bad luck. Some people get upset if they spill salt on the table. They throw **some** over their shoulder to keep away bad luck. Some people believe that it is bad luck to walk under a ladder. Many people will walk around **one** rather than walk under **one.** Some people believe that numbers have special powers: seven

is lucky, and thirteen is unlucky. Many buildings have no thirteenth floor!

People often pass their superstitions on to their children. Did you learn **any** from your parents or grandparents?

● ●

12.4   **Indefinite Pronouns:** *One, Some, Any*

Definite	Singular Count	Plural Count	Noncount
	him her it	them	it
Indefinite	one	some/any	some/any
Definite	I read *the article* about superstitions. Did you read *it*? I have *three cats*. Do you want to see *them*? Do you know *my brother*? Did you see *him*? Don't take *the money* on the table. I need *it*.		
Indefinite	I have *a cat*. Do you have *one*? I have *some* superstitions. Most people have *some*. I need *some money*? Do you have *any*?		

1. We use definite pronouns (*him, her, it, them*) to substitute for definite count nouns. We use *it* to substitute for a definite noncount noun.

2. We use *one* to substitute for an indefinite singular count noun.

3. We use *some* and *any* to substitute for an indefinite plural count noun.

4. We use *some* and *any* to substitute for an indefinite noncount noun.

EXERCISE 11   Tell if you have or don't have the following. Then ask a question with *one*. Another student will answer.

> EXAMPLE: **a car**
>> **A. I don't have a car. Do you have one?**
>> **B. Yes, I do.**   OR   **No, I don't.**

1. a computer	6. a cellular phone
2. a VCR	7. a cat
3. a driver's license	8. a library card
4. a bike	9. a microwave oven
5. a camera	10. an answering machine

EXERCISE 12   Tell if you have or don't have the following. Then ask a question with *any*. Another student will answer.

> EXAMPLE: **American friends**
>> **A. I have some American friends.**
>>> OR
>> **I don't have any American friends. Do you have any?**
>> **B. Yes, I have some.**   OR   **No, I don't have any.**

1. plants in my apartment	5. money with me
2. photos of my family with me	6. beer at home
3. American friends	7. fruit at home
4. questions about this lesson	8. experience with computers

EXERCISE 13   Answer each question. Substitute the underlined words with an indefinite pronoun *(one, some, any)* or a definite pronoun *(it, them)*.

> EXAMPLES: **Do you have a pen with you?**
>> **Yes. I have one.**
>
>> **Are you using your pen now?**
>> **No. I'm not using it now.**

1. Does this school have a library?
2. How often do you use the library?
3. Do you have a dictionary?
4. When do you use your dictionary?
5. Did you buy any textbooks this semester?
6. How much did you pay for your textbooks?
7. Did the teacher give any homework last week?
8. Where did you do the homework?
9. Do you have any American neighbors?

10. Do you know <u>your neighbors</u>?
11. Does this college have <u>a president</u>?
12. Do you know <u>the college president</u>?
13. Did you receive <u>any mail</u> today?
14. What time does your letter carrier deliver <u>your mail</u>?

• •

R
E
A
D
I
N
G

Before you read:

1. Besides your native language and English, do you know another language? Is it similar to your language?
2. Are there any similarities between English and your language? Name a few similarities.

Read the following article. Pay special attention to *other* and *another.*

LANGUAGE FAMILIES

Languages belong to families. Languages in one family have a lot in common with one another. English belongs to the Germanic family of languages. **Another** language in this family is Dutch. **Other** Germanic languages are Swedish, Danish, and German. Even

---

INDO-EUROPEAN LANGUAGES[2]

Germanic	Italic	Hellenic	Slavic	Celtic	Indic	Iranian
Danish	French	Greek	Czech	Irish	Bengali	Persian
Dutch	Italian		Polish	Welsh	Gujarati	Pushtu
English	Portuguese		Russian		Hindi	
German	Rumanian		Slovak		Urdu	
Norwegian	Spanish		Ukranian			
Swedish						

---

[2]This chart is not complete. There are other Indo-European families and languages.

though English is in the Germanic family, many words in English come from French and **other** languages.

Germanic is just one family. There are many **others.** For example, there is the Slavic family. Polish and Russian belong to this family. Can you name **other** ones in this group? **Another** family is the Romance family. Spanish is one language in this group. French, Italian, and Portuguese are **other** languages in this group.

• •

12.5 *Another, Other*

The other + a singular noun is definite. It means the only one remaining.

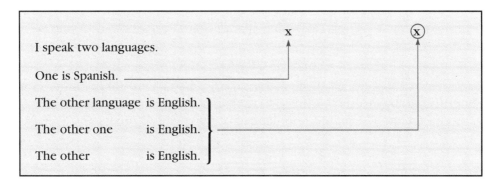

The other + a plural noun is definite. It means all the remaining ones.

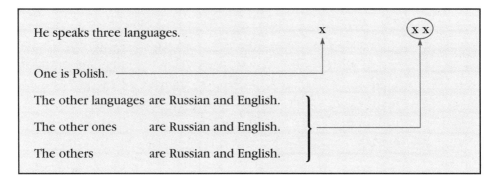

Another + a singular noun is indefinite. It means one of several.

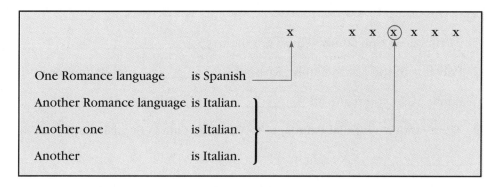

Other + a plural noun is indefinite. It means some, but not all, of the remaining ones.

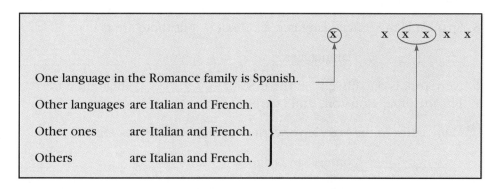

Language Notes

1. When we omit the plural noun or pronoun after *the other*, we use *the others*.

   One student speaks Spanish. The *other* students speak Chinese.

   One student speaks Spanish. The *others* speak Chinese.

2. We omit *the* after a possessive form.

   I'm taking five classes. My math class is easy. *My other* classes are hard.

3. After *some* or *any*, we change *another* to *other*.

   I'm busy now. Can you come *another* time?
                Can you come *some other* time?
                Can you come *any other* time?

EXERCISE 14 Fill in each blank with *the other, another, the others, others,* or *other.*

EXAMPLE: **English is a Germanic language. Swedish is** _another_ **one.**

1. Germanic is one family. There are many _____

2. Polish is in the Slavic family. Russian is _____ language in this

   family. Can you name all _____ in this group?

3. There are two official languages in Canada. One is English, and

   _____ is French.

4. There are more than sixteen languages in India. One is Hindi.

   _____ is Gujerati. _____ languages in India are Tamil
   and Panjabi.

5. Spanish is the official language of Mexico, but there are many

   _____ languages.

6. New York is one big city in the U.S. _____ big cities are
   Philadelphia, Houston, and Detroit.

7. Many cities in the U.S. have warm weather. One city is Miami.

   _____ one is San Diego.

8. Do you know the capital of this state? Do you know _____
   49 capitals?

9. Johnson is a common last name in the U.S. _____ common names
   are Smith, Wilson, and Jones.

10. Some immigrants in the U.S. come from Mexico. _____

    immigrants come from Poland. _____ come from Vietnam.

11. We celebrate two Presidents' birthdays in February. One is Lincoln's

    birthday. _____ is Washington's birthday.

12. There are eight categories of words. Some words are verbs. _____
    are nouns.

13. *Money* is a noncount noun. _____ ones are *love, freedom,* and
    time.

14. A present-tense verb has two forms. One is the base form. _____ is the *-s* form.

15. Some students will get an A in this course. _____ will get a C.

16. If you can't do this exercise today, do it some _____ time.

17. John Lennon had two sons. His first son was by his first wife. His

_____ son was by his second wife.

EXPANSION ACTIVITIES

SAYINGS The following sayings contain *other/another.* Discuss the meaning of these sayings. Do you have a similar saying in your language?

(It goes) in one ear and out the other.
Another day, another dollar.

PROVERBS The following proverbs make generalizations with noncount nouns. Discuss the meaning of each proverb. Do you have a similar proverb in your language?

Love is blind.
Money is the root of all evil.
Beauty is only skin deep.
Blood is thicker than water.

1. Fill in each blank with *all, most, some, a few,* or *very few* to make a general statement about your country. Then find a partner from a different country, if possible, and compare your answers.

    1. _____ people speak English.

    2. _____ children study English in school.

    3. _____ families own a car.

    4. _____ people are Catholic.

    5. _____ people own a computer.

    6. _____ women work outside the home.

    7. _____ married couples have more than five children.

8. _____ people live in an apartment.

9. _____ young men serve in the military.

10. _____ people are happy with the political situation.

11. _____ people have servants.

12. _____ people have a college education.

13. _____ married couples have their own apartment.

14. _____ old people live with their grown children.

2. Some people in the U.S. believe that 13 is an unlucky number. Is there an unlucky number in your country? Talk about the meaning of this number.

OUTSIDE ACTIVITY Interview an American. Ask him or her if he or she has any superstitions. Tell the class about this person's superstitions.

EDITING ADVICE

1. Use *the* after a quantity word when the noun is definite.

   the
   Most of students in my class are from Romania.
        ∧

2. Be careful with *most* and *almost.*

   Most of
   ~~Almost~~ my teachers are very patient.

3. Use a plural count noun after a quantity expression.

   s
   A few of my friend live in Canada.
                 ∧

4. *Another* is always singular.

   Other
   Some teachers are strict. ~~Another~~ teachers are easy.

5. Use an indefinite pronoun to substitute for an indefinite noun.

   one
   I need to borrow a pen. I didn't bring it today.

SUMMARY OF LESSON TWELVE

1. Articles

	Count—Singular	Count—Plural	Noncount
General	*A/An* An orange contains vitamin C.	Ø Article Oranges contain vitamin C. I like oranges.	Ø Article Meat contains cholesterol. I like meat.
Indefinite	*A/An* I ate a cherry.	*Some/Any* I ate (some) cherries. I didn't eat (any) grapes.	*Some/Any* I ate (some) meat. I didn't eat (any) bread.
Specific	*The* The apple on the table is green.	*The* The apples on the table are green.	*The* The meat on the table is fresh.
Classification	*A/An* Boston is a city.	Ø Article Boston and Chicago are cities.	—

2. Other/Another

Definite		Indefinite	
Singular	 the other book my other book the other one the other	 another book some/any other book another one another
Plural	 the other books my other books the other ones the others	 other books some/any other books other ones others

LESSON TWELVE TEST/REVIEW

Part 1   Find the mistakes with articles, quantities, and pronouns, and correct them. Not every sentence has a mistake. If the sentence is correct, write *C*.

> EXAMPLES: She has many friends. One of her friends is a doctor. ~~The other~~ *Another*
> one is a secretary.
>
> Most Americans own a TV.   *C*

1. All of teachers at this college have a master's degree.

2. Some of the animals eat only meat. They are called "carnivores."

3. The students in this class come from many countries. Some of the students are from Poland. Another students are from Hungary.

4. A battery has two terminals. One is positive; another is negative.

5. I'm taking two classes. One is English. The other is math.

6. I lost my dictionary. I need to buy another one.

7. I lost my textbook. I think I lost it in the library.

8. I don't have a computer. Do you have it?

9. Most my teachers have a lot of experience.

10. Cuba is country.

11. Most women want to have children.

12. I have some money with me. Do you have any?

13. Very few of the students in this class have financial aid.

14. I have two brothers. One of my brothers is an engineer. The other my brother is a physical therapist.

15. Almost my friends come from South America.

Part 2   Fill in each blank with *the, a, an, some, any,* or *∅* article.

A. Do you want to come to my house tonight? I rented ___*some*___ movies. We can

make _____ popcorn and watch _____ movies together.
         (1)   (2)

B. Thanks, but I'm going to _____ party. Do you want to go with me?
         (3)

A. Where's it going to be?

B. It's going to be at Michael's apartment.

A. Who's going to be at _____ party?
                              (4)

B. Most of _____ students in my English class will be there. Each student is
              (5)

going to bring _____ food.
                    (6)

A. _____ life in the U.S. is strange. In my country, _____ people don't
       (7)   (8)

have to bring _____ food to a party.
                    (9)

B. That's the way it is in my country, too. But we're in _____ U.S. now. I'm
                                                                (10)

going to bake _____ cake. You can make _____ special dish from your
                    (11)   (12)

country.

A. You know I'm _____ terrible cook.
                      (13)

B. Don't worry. You can buy something. My friend Max is going to buy

_____ crackers and cheese. Why don't you bring _____ beer?
      (14)   (15)

A. But I don't drink _____ beer. I'm _____ Muslim.
                          (16)   (17)

B. Well, you can bring _____ soft drinks.
                            (18)

A. That's _____ good idea. What time does _____ party start?
              (19)   (20)

B. At 8 o'clock.

A. I have to take my brother to _____ airport at 6:30. I don't know if I'll be
                                      (21)

back on time.

B. You don't have to arrive at 8 o'clock exactly. I'll give you _____ address,
                                                                      (22)

and you can arrive any time you want.

Part 3   Fill in each blank with *one, some, any, it,* or *them.*

EXAMPLE: **I have a computer, but my roommate doesn't have** *one.*

1. Do you want to use my bicycle? I won't need _____ this afternoon.

2. I rented two movies. We can watch _____ tonight.

3. My English teacher gives some homework every day, but she doesn't give

    _____ on the weekends.

4. My class has a lot of Mexican students. Does your class have _____

5. I wrote two compositions last week, but I got bad grades because I wrote

    _____ very quickly.

6. I don't have any problems with English, but my roommate has _____

7. I can't remember the teacher's name. Do you remember _____

8. You won't need any paper for the test, but you'll need _____ for the
   composition.

9. I went to the library to find some books in my language, but I couldn't find

    _____

Part 4   Fill in each blank with *other, others, another, the other,* or *the others.*

A. I don't like my apartment.

B. Why not?

A. It's very small. It only has two closets. One is big, but ___*the other*___ is very
   small.

B. That's not very serious. Is that the only problem? Are there

    _____ problems?
         (1)

A. There are many _____
                        (2)

B. Such as?

A. There are a lot of cockroaches.

B. Hmm. That's a real problem. What else?

A. Well, the landlord doesn't provide enough heat in the winter.

B. Did you complain to him?

A. I did, but he says that all _____ tenants are happy.
                                        (3)

B. Why don't you look for _____ apartment?
                                    (4)

A. I have two roommates. One wants to move, but _____ likes it
                                                                (5)

   here.

B. Well, if one wants to stay and _____ two want to move, why don't
                                          (6)

   you move and look for _____ roommate?
                                (7)

LESSON THIRTEEN

GRAMMAR
Review of Verb Tenses
Word Order

CONTEXT
Letter of Complaint

Lesson Focus Review of Verb Tenses; Sentences and Word Order

• We will review the following tenses:

1. The simple present
2. The present continuous
3. The future
4. The simple past
5. The past continuous
6. The present perfect
7. The present perfect continuous

We will also review the verb *be*, simple modal verbs, and infinitives.

For each verb tense, we will practice the following seven patterns:

1. Affirmative *(yes)* statement
2. Negative *(no)* statement
3. *Yes/No* question
4. Short answer
5. *Wh-* question
6. Negative question
7. Subject question

• The basic word order in English sentences is subject–verb–complement. This word order rarely changes, and the position of a word helps us understand its function.

• •

R
E
A
D
I
N
G

Before you read:

Did you ever complain to a company about a product that you bought or a service that you received? Did you receive any satisfaction as a result of your complaint?

The following is a letter of complaint. Read the letter and identify the tense of each verb. Identify the modals and the infinitives too.

LETTER OF COMPLAINT

6761 N. Williams
Chicago, IL 60645

Jackson Movers
1834 W. Howard
Chicago, IL 60626

Dear Mr. Jackson:

I'm **writing** (1) to you to tell you about a problem that **happened** (2) during my move. Two months ago, your movers **moved** (3) me from 7554 N. Oakland to 6761 N. Williams. While they **were carrying** (4) my table upstairs, they **dropped** (5) it and **broke** (6) the corner of the glass top. When I **pointed** (7) it out to them, they **said** (8) that they would speak to the owner about the problem.

I **have been living** (9) in my new apartment for two months already, and so far I **haven't heard** (10) anything from your moving company. I'm **getting** (11) angry because my table **is** (12) still broken. I **want** (13) you **to come** (14) to my house as soon as possible so that you can look at the damage. When you **come** (15) here, you **will see** (16) that the damage is considerable.[1] I **want** (17) you **to take** (18) care of this problem immediately. You **can pay** (19) for the damage or replace the glass top of the table. Please call me when you **receive** (20) this letter so that we can set up an appointment.

I **know** (21) that you **have** (22) insurance. I **have used** (23) your company before, and I **have recommended** (24) your company to many of my friends. However, if you **don't fix** (25) my table, I'll **never use** (26) your company again. In addition, I'll **tell** (27) my friends that you **don't take** (28) responsibility for damage.

Sincerely,

Margaret Walters
Margaret Walters

---

[1]*Considerable* means a great amount.

13.1 The Present Tenses

The Simple Present

The Seven Patterns

With the base form

I *live* in Chicago.
I *don't live* in New York.
Do you *live* on Oakland Street?
No, I *don't.*
Where *do* you *live?*
Why *don't* you *live* on Oakland Street anymore?
How many people live *with* you?

With the -s form

She *has* a problem with her table.
She *doesn't have* a problem with her chair.
Does she *have* a problem with the moving company?
Yes, she *does.*
What kind of problem *does* she *have?*
Why *doesn't* she *have* an answer to her problem?
Who *has* the answer to her problem?

The Present Continuous

The Seven Patterns

Margaret *is writing* a letter.
She *isn't writing* a composition.
Is she *writing* to her friend?
No, she *isn't.*
Why *is* she *writing* a letter?
Why *isn't* she *writing* a composition?
Who *is writing?*

1. We use the simple present tense:
   - With statements of fact
     Margaret *lives* in Chicago.
     Chicago *has* a large population.
   - With statements about regular activity
     Margaret sometimes *writes* letters.
     Jackson Moving Company *moves* people
       every day.
     Whenever Margaret *writes* a letter, she
       uses a word processor.
   - With nonaction verbs
     Margaret *has* a problem with the moving
       company now.
     She *wants* the company to fix her table.
   - In future statements, in an *if* clause, or in a
     time clause
     If you *don't fix* my table, I'm never going
       to use your company again.
     When Mr. Jackson *receives* the letter, will
       he call Margaret?

2. We use the present continuous tense:
   - With actions that are in progress now, at
     this moment
     Margaret *is writing* a letter now.
     We*'re looking* at verbs now.
   - With actions in a period of time that is not
     complete
     This semester we*'re using Grammar in
       Context.*
     This week the teacher *is reviewing* verbs.
   - With a planned activity in the near future
     We*'re having* a test next week.
     I*'m going* to New York on Friday.

3. We do not use a continuous tense with nonaction verbs. The following are usually nonaction verbs: *like, love, want, have, need, see.* See page 38 for a complete list of nonaction verbs.

EXERCISE I   This is a phone conversation between two students. Fill in each blank with the present continuous or the simple present of the verb in parentheses ( ).

A. Hello?

B. Hi. This is Kim.

A. Hi, Kim. What's up?

B. I *am looking* _____ for someone to go to the movies with me. What
        (look)

   _____ now?
      (1 you/do)

A. I _____ for my test.
       (2 study)

B. _____ to go out for a while and take a break?
     (3 you/want)

A. I can't. I _____ to memorize vocabulary words. I have
        (4 try)

   to know 50 words for tomorrow's test.

B. How often _____ a vocabulary test?
       (5 you/have)

A. Once a week.

B. _____ that you have to memorize fifty words a week?
                    (6 you/mean)
A. Yes. Every Friday the teacher _____ a vocabulary test.
                                              (7 give)
B. I _____ that's terrible.
        (8 think)
A. It's not as bad as it _____. Every day I
                                (9 seem)
_____ ten words. Every Thursday, I
        (10 learn)
_____ my list. And every Friday I
        (11 review)
_____ the test. My vocabulary _____
        (12 take)   (13 improve)
a lot this semester.

B. How _____ new words?
            (14 you/learn)
A. I always _____ them on cards with the translation on
                    (15 write)
the back. I _____ my cards whenever I
                    (16 study)
_____ free time. Someone always gives me a practice
        (17 have)
test.

B. Who _____ you a practice test?
            (18 give)
A. My roommate usually does.

13.2 The Future

The Seven Patterns

With *be going to*

> Margaret *is going to tell* her
> friends.
> She *isn't going to use* this
> company again.
> *Is* she *going to send* a letter?
> Yes, she *is.*
> Why *is* she *going to send* a letter?
> Why *isn't* she *going to use* this
> company again?
> Who *is going to use* this company?

With *will*

> Margaret *will tell* her friends.
> She *won't use* this company again.
> *Will* she *send* a letter?
> Yes, she *will.*
> Why *will* she *send* a letter?
> Why *won't* she *use* this company
> again?
> Who *will use* this company?

1. We use *will* or *be going to* for a prediction.

    Will Mr. Jackson *answer* Margaret's letter?
    Is Mr. Jackson *going to answer* Margaret's letter?

2. With something we plan for the future, *be going to* is more common than *will*.

    Margaret *is going to send* a letter to Jackson Movers.

3. With a promise, a threat, or an offer, *will* is more common than *be going to*.

    I can't help you now. I promise I*'ll help* you later.
    If you don't fix my table, I*'ll* never *use* your company again.
    The phone's ringing—I*'ll get* it.

4. With scheduled events, *will* is more common.

    Registration *will begin* on August 20.

5. In an *if* clause or a time clause, we use the simple present tense.

    When you *come* to my house, I *will show* you the problem.
    If Jackson Movers *fixes* her table, she*'ll be* happy.

6. The present continuous can also express near future, especially with verbs of motion.

    I*'m moving* next week.
    We*'re leaving* on Saturday.

EDITING ADVICE

1. Use the *-s* form when the subject is *he*, *she*, *it* or a gerund (verb *+ing*).

    He ~~have~~ *has* a car.

    Buying a house require*s* a lot of money.

2. Don't use the *-s* form after *does*.

    He doesn't ~~has~~ *have* a car.

    Does he live~~s~~ in Philadelphia?

3. Always include *be* in a present continuous tense statement.

    She *is* working now.

4. Don't use the present continuous tense for a nonaction verb.

    I ~~am~~ know~~ing~~ my language very well.

5. Use the simple present, not the future tense, after a time word or *if*.

    When I ~~will~~ get home, I will call you.

    I'll mail the package if I ~~will be~~ *am* at the post office.

6. Don't use *be* with another verb to form the future tense.

    Tomorrow I will ~~be~~ look for a job.

7. Include *be* in a future sentence that has no other verb.

    He will *be* afraid.

8. Use either *will* or *be going to* for the future. Don't combine them.

    She ~~will~~ *is* going to return to her country.
    OR *She will return. . .*

9. Use the future tense with *will* with an offer to help.

    The phone's ringing. I *'ll* get it.

EXERCISE 2   Find the mistakes with present and future verbs, and correct them. Not every sentence has a mistake. If the sentence is correct, write *C*.

> EXAMPLES: **She usually eating a banana every day.**
> (with *s* written above *eating*)
>
> **She will be late for her appointment.**   *C*

1. If you will study here next semester, you will learn a lot.

2. She will be meet her sister after class.

3. Smoking cigarettes is bad for you.

4. This semester I studying English and math.

5. Learning a new language take a long time.

6. They are having a beautiful house.

7. Next week I'm leaving on vacation.

8. You will going to learn a lot of English.

9. Before I will go home today, I will go to the library.

10. Will you angry if I use your car?

11. You can relax. I cook dinner tonight.

12. She needs my help now.

EXERCISE 3   A student is writing a letter to his friend. Fill in the blanks. Use the simple present, the present continuous, or the future of the verb in parentheses ( ) to complete this letter.

> Dear Ali,
>
> I'm in the school library now. I ____*am waiting*____ for my friend to
> _____(wait)
> come and meet me. I _____ you this brief letter while I
> _____(1 write)
>
> _____.
> _____(2 wait)
> This semester I _____ 3 courses—English, biology, and math. I
> _____(3 take)
> _____ biology, but it's hard for me. Next week we
> _____(4 like)

_____our first exam. When my friend _____,
         (5 have)   (6 arrive)

_____ together. He _____ more English than I do.
        (7 study)   (8 know)

Whenever I _____ some English words, he _____
               (9 not/understand)   (10 explain)

them to me in Arabic. Sometimes we _____ at his house, but today
                                           (11 study)

we _____ in the laboratory. He _____ me how to do
       (12 study)   (13 show)

an experiment.

    I _____ my friend now. He _____ toward me. I
           (14 see)   (15 walk)

_____ you later when I _____ more time.
    (16 write)   (17 have)

Your friend,

Hussein

13.3 Past Tenses

The Seven Patterns

With the simple past tense

The movers _broke_ the table.
They _didn't break_ the mirror.
Did they _break_ the glass?
Yes, they _did_.
How _did_ they _break_ the glass?
Why _didn't_ they _break_ the mirror?
Who _broke_ the mirror?

With the past continuous tense

They _were moving_ the table.
They _weren't moving_ the piano.
Were they _moving_ chairs?
Yes, they _were_.
What _were_ they _doing_ when they
   dropped the table?
Why _weren't_ they _moving_ the
   piano?
Who _was moving_ the piano?

1. We use the simple past with a past action of little or no duration.

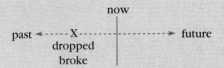

The movers *dropped* the table.
They *broke* the table.

2. We use the simple past for a longer action that is completely past.

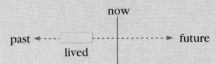

Margaret *lived* on Oakland Street for ten years before she moved.

3. We use the past continuous to show that a continuous past action was in progress at a specific time.

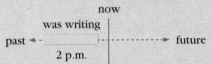

What *was* Margaret *doing* at 2 p.m. yesterday? She *was writing* a letter.

4. We use the past continuous to show the relationship of a longer past action to a shorter one.

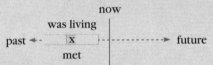

Margaret *was living* on Oakland Street when she *met* her future husband.
While (or When) the movers *were moving* the table into the house, they *dropped* it.

You can use either *while* or *when* with a continuous action or state. With a simple past action, you must use *when*.

5. We can use *while* + the past continuous tense to show that two past actions continued over the same general period of time in the past.

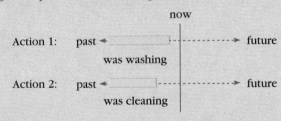

While Margaret *was washing* the floor, her husband *was cleaning* the basement.
NOTE: Sometimes the simple past is used in both clauses.
While Margaret *washed* the floor, her husband *cleaned* the basement.

6. In a question with two clauses, only the verb in the main clause is in a question form.
What *were the movers doing* when they *dropped* the table?

7. Do not use the past continuous with nonaction verbs.

EXERCISE 4   A student wrote a composition about leaving her country and coming to the U.S. Fill in each blank with the simple past or the past continuous of the verb in parentheses ( ).

In 1974, I _____*graduated*_____ from high school in Vietnam and
                     (graduate)

_____ to study at the university. I
     (1 start)

_____ to be a nurse when the government
     (2 study)

_____. I _____ to leave my
     (3 fall)   (4 have)

country. I _____ to Thailand and
           (5 go)

_____ in a refugee camp. While I
     (6 live)

_____ for permission to come to the U.S., I
     (7 wait)

_____ English. Finally, after two years of waiting, I
     (8 study)

_____ permission to come to America. While I
     (9 get)

_____ to the U.S., I _____
     (10 travel)   (11 think)

about all the changes in my life. I _____ nervous and
                 (12 be)

excited about coming to the U.S.

When I _____ in New York, my sponsor
          (13 arrive)

_____ for me. He _____ me to his
     (14 wait)   (15 take)

house. While we _____ to his house, I
          (16 drive)

_____ at the streets of New York. Everything
     (17 look)

_____ strange to me. I _____ of so
     (18 seem)   (19 think)

many different things when, suddenly, my sponsor _____,
                                     (20 say)

"Here we are." At that point, a new life _____ for me.
                                  (21 start)

13.4   The Present Perfect and Present Perfect Continuous

The Seven Patterns

With the present perfect tense	With the present perfect continuous tense
Margaret *has moved.*	Margaret *has been living* on Williams Street for two months.
She *hasn't moved* out of the city.	She *hasn't been living* alone.
Has she *moved* several times?	*Has* she *been living* with her brother?
Yes, she *has.*	No, she *hasn't.*
How many times *has she moved?*	With whom *has* she *been living?*
Why *hasn't* she *moved* out of the city?	Why *hasn't* she *been living* with her brother?
How many people *have moved?*	Who *has been living* with her brother?

Language Notes

1. We use the present perfect continuous:
   With actions that started in the past and continue to the present.

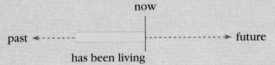

Margaret *has been living* on Williams Street for two months.

NOTE: Do not use the continuous form with nonaction verbs.

2. We use the present perfect:
   • With an action that started in the past and continues to the present.

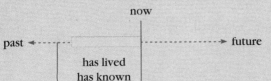

Margaret *has lived* on Williams Street since May.
She *has known* about the problem for a long time.

(continued)

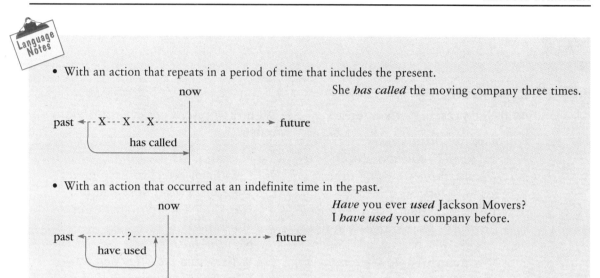

- With an action that repeats in a period of time that includes the present.

She *has called* the moving company three times.

- With an action that occurred at an indefinite time in the past.

Have you ever *used* Jackson Movers?
I *have used* your company before.

EXERCISE 5   Fill in each blank with the simple present, the present continuous, the present perfect, the present perfect continuous, or the simple past of the verb in parentheses ( ).

I _____*work*_____ in a restaurant. I _____ at my present job
            (work)   (1 work)

for about two years. But I don't like it. Recently, I _____ to find a
                                                                         (2 try)

new job. I _____ several interviews lately, but I _____
                (3 have)   (4 not/find)

a good job yet. However, I _____ hope. In my country, I
                              (5 not/lose)

_____ as a bookkeeper, but I can't find this kind of job because I
    (6 work)

_____ enough English yet. Now my brother-in-law and I
  (7 not/learn)

_____ about starting our own business. I _____ to be
    (8 talk)   (9 always/want)

in business for myself.

EDITING ADVICE

1. Don't use *was* or *were* + verb to form the past tense.

         lived
   He was ~~live in~~ Detroit from 1988 to 1995.

2. Use the simple past, not the past continuous, when the action has no duration.

         started
   It was ~~starting to~~ rain a few minutes ago.

         lost
   She was ~~losing~~ her purse yesterday.

3. Use the present perfect or the present perfect continuous for an action that started in the past and continues to the present.

         had
   I have my car for three years.

         has been
   She is living in Chicago since March.

4. Include *have* in a present perfect statement.

         have
   They been working for a long time.

5. Don't confuse a present participle *(-ing)* with a past participle.

         seen
   She has already ~~seeing~~ that movie.

6. Use the base form, not the past form after *did*.

         find
   He didn't ~~found~~ his wallet.

EXERCISE 6   Find the mistakes with past tenses, and correct them. Not every sentence has a mistake. If the sentence is correct, write *C*.

EXAMPLES: **Have you ever ~~being~~ *been* to New York?**

                Last week we went to see a good movie.   *C*

1. I dropped the mirror and it was breaking.

2. She was lived in Pakistan when she was a child.

3. I worked at my present job since January.

4. I been watching you for several minutes.

5. I'm studying English since I came to the U.S.

6. She has had her car for three years.

7. I slept when the telephone rang.

8. He didn't knew the answer.

EXERCISE 7   Fill in each blank with the simple present, present continuous, future, simple past, past continuous, present perfect, or present perfect continuous of the verb in parentheses ( ).

Last week I _____*lost*_____ my job. My co-workers and I
              (lose)

_____ lunch in the company cafeteria when the boss
    (1 eat)

_____ in and told me to go to his office. I _____ him
    (2 come)   (3 follow)

to his office. He _____, "I'm sorry to tell you this, but we have to
              (4 say)

lay off² three workers. You _____ here for only six months, less
                  (5 be)   time

than the other workers. So I _____ to lay you off." I
                    (6 decide)

_____ his office and _____ home. I
    (7 leave)   (8 go)

_____ terrible.
    (9 feel)

---

²To *lay off* a worker means to take away a worker's job because the company doesn't have enough work for everybody. The worker gets laid off.

I _____ for a job now. I _____ the newspaper
    (10 look)   (11 buy)

every day and _____ in the help-wanted section, but I
                    (12 look)

_____ a job yet. Yesterday a friend of mine _____ that
(13 not/find)   (14 suggest)

I see a job counselor. I _____ to see her this morning. While I
                            (15 go)

_____ to see her, I _____ a bulletin board outside her
(16 wait)   (17 notice)

office. I _____ several interesting ads. I _____ down
            (18 see)   (19 write)

some information when she _____ out of her office and
                                (20 come)

_____ herself. She _____ me into her office and
(21 introduce)   (22 take)

_____ me a few phone numbers to call.
(23 give)

    Tomorrow morning, I _____ early. I _____ these
                            (24 start)   (25 call)

numbers to see if I can get an interview. I _____ I can find a job
                                                (26 hope)

soon. I really _____ the money. When I _____ a job, I
                (27 need)   (28 find)

_____ my money in case this ever happens again.
(29 save)

13.5 *Be* • • • • • • • • • • • •

The Seven Patterns

Present	Past
Margaret *is* angry.	The movers *were* careless.
She *isn't* happy.	They *weren't* careful.
Is she angry at Jackson Movers?	*Were* they irresponsible?
Yes, she *is.*	Yes, they *were.*
Why *is* she angry?	Why *were* they irresponsible?
Why *isn't* she satisfied?	Why *weren't* they careful?
How many customers *are* angry?	Who *was* careful?

We use a form of *be*:

- With a description of the subject
  Margaret *is* angry.
  The movers *were* irresponsible.
- With a classification or definition of the subject
  Dallas *is* a city.
  Texas *is* a state.
- With a location
  Dallas *is* in Texas.
  Margaret *wasn't* home yesterday.
- With a place of origin
  She's from New York.
  Where *are* you from?

- With age
  How old *is* Margaret?
  She's 35 years old.
- With *born*
  Where *were* you born?
  I *was* born in Peru.
- With a continuous tense
  Margaret *is* writing a letter.
  The movers *were* moving the table.
- With *there* to show existence
  There's a problem with Margaret's table.
  There *were* four movers at Margaret's house.

EXERCISE 8   Find the mistakes with *be,* and correct them. Not every sentence has a mistake. If the sentence is correct, write *C.*

EXAMPLES: Where you born?
           were
           ∧

           I am studying English.   *C*

1. I waiting for you all morning. Where was you?

2. Where's Chicago? It's in northern Illinois.

3. Have you ever being in California?

4. There are a lot of rain in the spring.

5. Are a lot of poor people in the world.

6. What was they doing when the fire started?

7. How long have you being in the U.S.?

8. We was watching a movie on TV when the phone rang.

9. She talking on the phone now.

10. My sister in Poland now.

13.6 Modals and Infinitives

The Seven Patterns

With modals

Jackson Movers *should fix* the table.

They *shouldn't ignore* the problem.

Should they *fix* the table soon?

Yes, they *should.*

When *should* they *fix* the table?

Why *shouldn't* they *ignore* the problem?

Who *should fix* the table?

With infinitives

She *needs to fix* the table.

She *doesn't need to fix* the chair.

Does she *need to fix* it immediately?

Yes, she *does.*

Why *does* she *need to fix* it?

Why *doesn't* she *need to fix* the chair?

Who *needs to fix* the table?

Language Notes

1. We can use an infinitive after many verbs. We don't use an infinitive after a modal; we use the base form. Compare:

Jackson Movers *needs to fix* Margaret's table.
Jackson Movers *should fix* Margaret's table.
She *tried to reach* them by phone.
She *couldn't reach* them by phone.

2. In some cases, we can put an object between the main verb and the infinitive.

I *want the movers to come* to my house.
I *want them to see* the problem.
They *expect me to show* them the table.

3. We use an infinitive after expressions beginning with *it.*

It's *important* to see the table.
It's *impossible* to fix the glass top.
It's *necessary* for the moving company to have insurance.

4. Some adjectives are followed by an infinitive.

We will be *happy to look* at your table.
I'm *lucky to know* you.

5. We use *to* + base form in the following expressions:

She *has to leave* early.
She's *got to go* home.
They *were able to find* an apartment.

EDITING ADVICE

1. Don't use an infinitive after a modal.

    I must ⨉ talk with you.

2. Use an object pronoun before an infinitive after certain verbs *(want, need, expect)*.

    them to
    She wants ~~they~~ fix the table.

3. Use the base form after *to*.

    She wants to go~~ing~~ home.

4. Use an infinitive after certain adjectives.

    to
    It's important ᶺ understand your rights.

    to
    I'm happy ᶺ meet you.

EXERCISE 9   Find the mistakes with modals and infinitives, and correct them. Not every sentence has a mistake. If the sentence is correct, write *C*.

to
EXAMPLES: I need ᶺ talk to you.

You shouldn't ignore the problem.   *C*

1. You must to help me.

2. I can't using my table.

3. I have to explain the problem to you.

4. Do they have to fix the table?

5. She should call the moving company.

6. She needs to talks with Mr. Jackson.

7. She wants he fix the table.

8. I wanted him paid for the damage.

9. I don't like write letters.

10. She didn't want him to went home.

11. It's important explain the problem.

12. I've got to talk with you.

13. I'm sorry keep you waiting.

14. They want us to help them.

15. He wanted to drove my car.

16. I'm not able help you.

13.7 Review of Questions

Study these statements and related questions with the verb *be*.

Wh- Word	*Be*	Subject	*Be*	Complement
		She	is	in California.
Where	is	she?		
		They	were	hungry.
Why	were	they		hungry?
		He	isn't	tired.
Why	isn't	he		tired?
		He	was	born in England.
When	was	he		born?
		She	is	a teenager.
How old	is	she?		
		She	is	tall.
How tall	is	she?		
		One student	was	late.
Who			was	late?
Which student			was	late?
		Some kids	were	afraid.
How many kids			were	afraid?
Which kids			were	afraid?

Study these statements and related questions with an auxiliary (Aux.) verb and a main verb.

Wh- Word	Aux.	Subject	Aux.	Main Verb	Complement
		She	is	running.	
Where	is	she		running?	
		They	will	go	on a vacation.
When	will	they		go	on a vacation?
		He	should	do	something.
What	should	he		do?	
		You	can	take	a pill.
How many pills	can	you		take?	
		You	can't	drive	a car.
Why	can't	you		drive	a car?
		They	have	lived	in Boston.
How long	have	they	lived		in Boston?
		Someone	should	answer	the question.
		Who	should	answer	the question?
		Some students	have	done	the homework.
		Which students	have	done	the homework?

Study these statements and related questions with a main verb.

Wh- Word	Do/Does/ Did	Subject	Verb	Complement
		She	watches	TV.
When	does	she	watch	TV?
		My parents	live	in Peru.
Where	do	your parents	live?	
		Your sister	likes	someone.
Who(m)	does	she	like?	
		They	left	early.
Why	did	they	leave	early?
		She	found	some books.
How many books	did	she	find?	
		He	bought	a car.
What kind of car	did	he	buy?	
		The car	cost	a lot of money.
How much	did	the car	cost?	
		She	didn't go	home.
Why	didn't	she	go	home?
		He	doesn't like	tomatoes.
Why	doesn't	he	like	tomatoes?

Wb- Word	Do/Does/ Did	Subject	Verb	Complement
How	do	you	spell	"calendar"?
How	do	you	say	"calendar" in French?
What	does	"calendar"	mean?	
		Someone	has	my book.
		Who	has	my book?
		Someone	needs	help.
		Who	needs	help?
		Someone	took	my pen.
		Who	took	my pen?
		One teacher	speaks	Spanish.
		Which teacher	speaks	Spanish?
		Some men	have	a car.
		Which men	have	a car?
		Some boys	saw	the movie.
		How many boys	saw	the movie?
		Something	happened.	
		What	happened?	

EXERCISE 10 Find the mistakes with each question below, and correct them. Not every sentence has a mistake. If the sentence is correct, write *C.*

EXAMPLES: **How long (they) have been living in the U.S.?**

How many times have they gone to Canada? *C*

1. How many people came to the party?

2. Was she buy a new car?

3. Did she drove to the party?

4. When your father came to the U.S.?

5. What was you doing when the accident happened?

6. What were they doing at 7:30 in the morning?

7. When arrived the airplane?

8. Who arrived on the airplane?

9. Why didn't you call me last night?

10. What you were doing when the teacher did arrive?

11. What profession do your husband have?

12. How often he goes for a haircut?

13. What you will do on your vacation?

14. Who know the answer to my question?

15. When will arrive your father from Vietnam?

16. How spell your name?

17. What means "bug"?

18. What language he's speaking now?

19. When will they know the answer?

20. Who has a dictionary?

21. What happened after the accident?

22. Why you can't finish the job?

23. How much does the textbook cost?

24. How you are old?

25. How tall is your father?

EXERCISE 11   Read the letter of complaint to Jackson Movers again. Fill in each blank with the correct form of the verb in parentheses ( ). In some cases, more than one answer is possible.

I _____*am writing*_____ to you to tell you about a problem that _____ during
       (write)   (1 happen)

my move. Two months ago, your movers _____ me from
                                 (2 move)

7554 N. Oakland to 6761 N. Williams. While they _____ my table
                                     (3 carry)

upstairs, they _____ it and _____ the corner of the glass top.
            (4 drop)   (5 break)

When I _____ it out to them, they _____ that they would speak
        (6 point)   (7 say)

to the owner about the problem.

I _____ in my new apartment for two months already, and so far I
   (8 live)

_____ anything from your moving company. I _____ angry
  (9 not/hear)   (10 get)

because my table _____still broken. I _____ you _____
                      (11 be)   (12 want)   (13 come)

to my house as soon as possible so that you can look at the damage. When you

_____ here, you _____ that the damage is considerable. I
  (14 come)   (15 see)

_____ you _____ care of this problem immediately. You
  (16 want)   (17 take)

_____ for the damage or replace the glass top of the table. Please call
  (18 can/pay)

me when you _____ this letter so that we can set up an appointment.
              (19 receive)

I _____ that you _____ insurance. I _____ your
      (20 know)   (21 have)   (22 use)

company before, and I _____ your company to many of my friends.
                (23 recommend)

However, if you _____ my table, I _____ your company again.
            (24 not/fix)   (25 never/use)

In addition, I _____ my friends that you _____ responsibility for
         (26 tell)   (27 not/take)

damage.

Sincerely,

Margaret Walters

EXERCISE 12 Read each statement. Then change the underlined verb to the negative
form to fill in each blank.

    EXAMPLE: **Margaret is writing a letter. She** _isn't writing_ **a letter to a friend.**

1. She's been living in her new apartment for two months. She

    _____ in her apartment for very long.

2. Mr. Jackson will receive an angry letter. He _____
    a letter from a happy customer.

3. The movers broke the glass of her table. They _____
    anything else.

4. Margaret usually writes a letter when she's angry. She

    _____ a letter when she's satisfied with the service.

5. In 1989 Margaret <u>was living</u> on Oakland Street. She _____ on Williams Street.

6. Mr. Jackson <u>needs to fix</u> the glass top. He _____ the rest of the table.

7. She<u>'s going to tell</u> her friends about her problem. She

_____ her friends good things about this company.

8. Jackson Movers <u>can ignore</u> the problem. Margaret _____ the problem.

EXERCISE 13   Read each statement. Then write a question with the words in parentheses ( ). An answer is not necessary.

EXAMPLE: **Margaret is angry. (why)**

Why is she angry?

1. Margaret moved to a new apartment. (when)

_____

2. She lived in her old apartment for ten years. (how long/in her new apartment) (Be careful: The question has a different tense.)

_____

3. She's complaining. (why)

_____

4. Mr. Jackson will receive her letter. (when)

_____

5. She won't use this company again. (why)

_____

6. Someone broke the table. (who)

_____

7. Mr. Jackson should pay Margaret. (how much)

_____

8. Margaret wants him to look at the table. (when)

   _____

9. Mr. Jackson hasn't called her. (why)

   _____

10. Margaret is going to tell someone about her problem. (whom)

    _____

11. Margaret has used this company before. (how many times)

    _____

12. She wants Mr. Jackson to do something. (what)

    _____

13. While the movers were carrying the table, they dropped it.
    (where/they/carry/when/they/drop/it)

    _____

13.8 Sentences and Word Order

- The basic word order in English is almost always Subject + Verb + (Object) for both the main clause and any dependent clause.

  ```
        S      V     O        S    V   O
  After Margaret noticed the problem, she called the company.
  ```

  ```
  S V       S         V  O
  I know that your company has insurance.
  ```

  ```
  S V    O             S      V
  I won't use the company that Margaret used.
  ```

- We can put an adverbial clause or phrase before the subject or after the verb phrase. If the adverbial clause comes before the subject, we usually put a comma before the main clause.

  After she called the company, she wrote a letter.
  She wrote a letter after she called the company.

EDITING ADVICE

1. Every sentence must have a verb.

   　　　　　is
   My teacher ∧ very nice.

2. Every verb must have a subject.[3]

   It is
   ~~Is~~ important to speak English well.

   　　　　　　　　　　　　　　　　　　it
   He didn't understand the lesson because ∧
   was too hard.

   There are
   ~~Are~~ a lot of Asian students at this college.

3. Put the subject before the verb in all
   clauses.

   　　　　　　　　　　the meeting was finished
   The workers left when ~~was finished the
   meeting.~~

   　　　　　　　the teacher said
   Everything that ~~said the teacher~~ is true.

4. An adverbial phrase or clause (time, place,
   reason) can come before the subject or at
   the end of the verb phrase. Do not put a
   phrase between the subject and the verb.

   She (once in a while) takes the bus to
   work.

5. Do not separate the verb from the object.

   She speaks (fluently) English.

6. If a compound subject includes *I*, put *I* at
   the end.

   My brother and I
   ~~I and my brother~~ went to Miami.

7. Do not start with a pronoun and put the
   subject at the end. Start with the subject
   noun.

   Your car is very beautiful.
   ~~It's very beautiful your car~~.

8. Do not repeat the subject with a pronoun.

   My father ~~he~~ works as an engineer.

9. Put the adverb of frequency between the
   subject and simple verb; after the verb *be*;
   between the auxiliary verb and the main
   verb.

   She drinks (never) coffee at night.

   I have gone (never) to Paris.

   She (always) is proud of her son.

10. Don't use a double negative in a sentence.

    　　　　　　　　　any
    She doesn't have ~~no~~ time to study.

    　　　　　　　　　　any
    I didn't understand ~~nothing~~.

---

[3]An imperative sentence omits the subject: Sit down. Listen to me.

EXERCISE 14   Find and correct the mistakes with sentences and word order. Not every sentence has a mistake. If the sentence is correct, write *C*.

>   *she*
> EXAMPLES: **My wife came late because‸couldn't find a parking space.**
>
>   **After the teacher left, the students began to talk.**   *C*

1. I and my sister went to the movies.

2. Before arrived his father, he was very unhappy.

3. She read very quickly the letter.

4. We from time to time go to a baseball game.

5. She is 25 years old.

6. She can't the lesson understand.

7. The class began when the teacher arrived.

8. It's very expensive their house.

9. The car that bought my brother cost $5000.

10. Is very interesting your composition.

11. Are a lot of new books in the library.

12. London a very beautiful city.

13. He didn't go skiing yesterday because was too cold.

14. Every sentence that the student wrote was correct.

15. My wife made dinner when came home from work.

16. Is important to speak English well.

17. I didn't understand nothing the teacher said.

18. I go to bed usually at 11:30.

19. I'm usually tired after work.

20. You should bring always your dictionary to class.

21. I have never met your wife.

22. My wife she is very intelligent.

23. He doesn't have no money for college.

EXPANSION ACTIVITIES

DISCUSSION   Find a partner. Find out as much as you can about your partner and his or her country. Tell the class a few interesting things you learned about your partner.

Sample interview:

A. Where are you from?
B. I'm from Colombia.
A. How long have you been in the U.S.?
B. For two years.
A. Are you married?
B. Yes, I am.
A. How long have you been married?
B. For three years.
A. Is your husband studying English too?
B. No, he isn't. He's working.
A. Are you going to return to your country?
B. Only for vacation. I'm an immigrant.

ACTIVITY   Work with a partner. Write five questions to ask your teacher.

Sample questions and answers:

A. How long have you been teaching English?
B. For ten years.
A. What other languages do you speak?
B. French and Polish.
A. Where did you learn Polish?
B. From my parents. They were born in Poland.

WRITING   1. Use the model letter in this lesson to write your own letter. Complain about a product you bought or a service you used. State what the problem is and how you want the company to help you solve it. Write about a situation that is real for you. If you can't think of a real problem, choose one of the imaginary problems below:

   a. A mechanic fixed your car. You paid $500, but you still have the same problem.
   b. You bought a very expensive shirt. When you washed it, it was ruined. You tried to return it to the store where you bought it, and they told you to write to the manufacturer.

   c. The college where you are studying English has decided to cancel all ESL classes because they want to save money. You are angry. Write to the president of the college.

   d. You gave your landlord a security deposit. You moved out two months ago, and he hasn't returned your money.

2. Write a letter to a company about a product you like. Tell how long you've been using this product and why you like it.

OUTSIDE ACTIVITIES

1. Interview an American about his or her life. Invite the American to interview you too. Report to the class something interesting you learned about this person.

2. Choose a famous person that you are interested in. Choose someone who is still living. Go to the library and find information about this person. Ask the librarian to help you find current information in magazines and newspapers. Write a report on this person. Read your report to the class. Invite the class to ask you questions about this person.

Appendix A

Spelling and Pronunciation

Spelling and Pronunciation of Verb Forms

Spelling of the -*S* Form

The chart below shows the spelling of the -*s* form.

Rule	Verbs	-*S* Form
Add *s* to most verbs to make the -*s* form.	hope eat	hopes eats
When the base form ends in *s, z, sh, ch*, or *x*, add *es* and pronounce an extra syllable, /**Iz**/.	miss buzz wash catch tax	misses buzzes washes catches taxes
When the base form ends in a consonant + *y*, change the *y* to *i* and add *es*.	carry worry	carries worries
When the base form ends in a vowel + *y*, do not change the *y*.	pay obey	pays obeys
Add *es* to *go* and *do*.	go do	goes does

Pronunciation of the -*S* Form

A. We pronounce /**s**/ if the verb ends in a voiceless sound: /**p t k f**/.

    hope—hopes   pick—picks

    eat—eats   laugh—laughs

B. We pronounce /**z**/ if the verb ends in a voiced sound.

    live—lives   read—reads   sing—sings

    grab—grabs   run—runs   borrow—borrows

C. When the base form ends in *s, z, sh, ch, x, se, ge*, or *ce*, we pronounce an extra syllable, /**Iz**/.

    miss—misses   watch—watches   change—changes

    buzz—buzzes   fix—fixes   dance—dances

    wash—washes   use—uses

D. These verbs have a change in the vowel sound.

do /**du**/—does /**d** ʌ **z**/
say /**sei**/—says /**s** ɛ **z**/

Spelling of the -*ing* Form

The chart below shows the spelling of the -*ing* form.

Rule	Verbs	-*ing* Form
Add *ing* to most verbs.	eat go study	eating going studying
For a one-syllable verb that ends in a consonant + vowel + consonant (CVC), double the final consonant and add *ing*.	p l a n | | | C V C	planning
	s t o p | | | C V C	stopping
	s i t | | | C V C	sitting
Do not double final *w, x,* or *y*.	show mix stay	showing mixing staying
For a two-syllable word that ends in CVC, double the final consonant only if the last syllable is stressed.	refér admít begín	referring admitting beginning
When the last syllable of a two-syllable word is not stressed, do not double the final consonant.	lísten ópen óffer	listening opening offering
If the word ends in a consonant + *e,* drop the *e* before adding *ing*.	live take write	living taking writing

Spelling of the Past Tense of Regular Verbs

The chart below shows the spelling of the *-ed* form.

Rule	Verbs	*-ed* Form
Add *ed* to the base form to make the past tense of most regular verbs.	start kick	started kicked
When the base form ends in *e,* add *d* only.	die live	died lived
When the base form ends in a consonant + *y,* change the *y* to *i* and add *ed.*	carry worry	carried worried
When the base form ends in a vowel + *y,* do not change the *y.*	destroy stay	destroyed stayed
For a one-syllable word that ends in a consonant + vowel + consonant (CVC), double the final consonant and add *ed.*	s t o p | | | C V C p l u g | | | C V C	stopped plugged
Do not double final *w* or *x.*	sew fix	sewed fixed
For a two-syllable word that ends in CVC, double the final consonant only if the last syllable is stressed.	occúr permít	occurred permitted
When the last syllable of a two-syllable word is not stressed, do not double the final consonant.	ópen háppen	opened happened

Pronunciation of Past Forms That End in *-ed*

The past tense with *-ed* has three pronunciations. Listen to your teacher's pronunciation.

A. We pronounce a /t/ if the base form ends in a voiceless sound: /p, k, f, s, š, č/.

jump—jumped	cough—coughed	wash—washed
cook—cooked	kiss—kissed	watch—watched

B. We pronounce a /d/ if the base form ends in a voiced sound.

rub—rubbed	charge—charged	bang—banged
drag—dragged	glue—glued	call—called
love—loved	massage—massaged	fear—feared
bathe—bathed	name—named	free—freed
use—used	learn—learned	

C. We pronounce an extra syllable /**Id**/ if the base form ends in a /**t**/ or /**d**/ sound.

wait—waited	want—wanted	need—needed
hate—hated	add—added	decide—decided

Spelling of Short Comparative and Superlative Adjectives and Adverbs

A. For most short adjectives and adverbs, we add –*er* to make the comparative form and –*est* to make the superlative form.

old—older—oldest

tall—taller—tallest

fast—faster—fastest

B. If the word ends in -*e*, just add *r* or *st*.

nice—nicer—nicest

fine—finer—finest

C. For adjectives that end in -*y*, change *y* to *i* before adding *er* or *est*.

happy—happier—happiest

healthy—healthier—healthiest

sunny—sunnier—sunniest

NOTE: Do not add *er* or *est* to an -*ly* adverb.

quickly—more quickly—most quickly

D. For one-syllable words that end in consonant-vowel-consonant, we double the final consonant before adding *er* or *est*.

big—bigger—biggest

sad—sadder—saddest

hot—hotter—hottest

EXCEPTION: Do not double final *w*.

new—newer—newest

Appendix B

Modals

Study the meanings of modals and related expressions. Notice that some modals have more than one meaning.

Modal	Meaning	Example
Must	Legal obligation Urgency Strong necessity	You *must* pay your rent on time. I *must* talk to you right now! You *must* study for the test.
Have to Have got to	Necessity	I *have to* move next month. I'*ve got to* move next month.
Had to	Past necessity	I *had to* go to court last week.
Should	Advice	If you want your landlord to return your deposit, you *should* clean the apartment.
Can	Ability Possibility Permission	A lawyer *can* understand a lease. I *can't* understand it. I *can* help you move on Sunday. The landlord *can* keep your security deposit to pay for repairs.
Could	Past ability	When I was a young, I *could* run ten miles.
Be able to	Present ability Past ability	I *am not able to* understand my lease. I *was able to* mail your package yesterday.
Be allowed/ permitted to	Present permission Past permission	The landlord *is allowed (permitted) to* use your deposit for repair. I *was allowed (permitted) to* paint my last apartment.
May	Permission Possibility	You *may* not have a dog in your apartment. I *may* move to New York next year. I'm not really sure.
Might	Possibility	I *might* move to New York next year. I'm not really sure.

Appendix C

The Verb *GET*

Get has many meanings. Here is a list of the most common ones:

- •get something = receive

  I got a letter from my father.

- •get + (to) place = arrive

  I got home at six. What time do you get to school?

- •get + object + infinitive = persuade

  She got him to wash the dishes.

- •get + past participle = become

  get acquainted   get used to
  get engaged   get dressed
  get married   get hurt
  get divorced   get drunk
  get tired   get bored
  get worried   get confused
  get lost   get scared
  get accustomed to

  They got married in 1989.

- •get + adjective = become

  get hungry   get fat
  get rich   get dark
  get nervous   get angry
  get well   get old
  get upset   It gets dark at 6:30.
  get sleepy

- •get an illness = catch

  While I was traveling, I got malaria.

- •get a joke or an idea = understand

  Everybody except Tom laughed at the joke. He didn't get it.

  The boss explained the project to us, but I didn't get it.

- •get ahead = advance

  He works very hard because he wants to get ahead in his job.

- •get along (well) (with someone) = to have a good relationship

  She doesn't get along with her mother-in-law.

  Do you and your roommate get along well?

•get around to something = find the time to do something

  I wanted to write my brother a letter yesterday, but I didn't get around to it.

•get away = escape

  The police chased the thief, but he got away.

•get away with something = escape punishment

  He cheated on his taxes and got away with it.

•get back = return

  He got back from his vacation last Saturday.

•get back at someone = get revenge

  My brother wants to get back at me for stealing his girlfriend.

•get back to someone = communicate with someone at a later time

  I can't talk to you today. Can I get back to you tomorrow?

•get by = have just enough but nothing more

  On her salary, she's just getting by. She can't afford a car or a vacation.

•get in trouble = be caught and punished for doing something wrong

  They got in trouble for cheating on the test.

•get in(to) = enter a car

  She got in the car and drove away quickly.

•get out (of) = leave a car

  When the taxi arrived at the theater, everyone got out.

•get on = to seat yourself on a bicycle, motorcycle, horse

  She got on the motorcycle and left.

•get on = enter a train, bus, airplane, boat

  She got on the bus and took a seat in the back.

•get off = leave a bicycle, motorcycle, horse, train, bus, airplane

  They will get off the train at the next stop.

•get out of something = escape responsibility

  My boss wants me to help him on Saturday, but I'm going to try to get out of it.

•get over something = recover from an illness or disappointment

  She has the flu this week. I hope she gets over it soon.

•get rid of someone or something = free oneself of someone or something undesirable

  My apartment has roaches, and I can't get rid of them.

•get through (to someone) = to communicate, often by telephone

  She tried to explain the dangers of drugs to her son, but she couldn't get through to him.

  I tried to call her many times, but her line was busy. I couldn't get through.

•get through with something = finish

  I can meet you after I get through with my homework.

•get together = to meet with another person

  I'd like to see you again. When can we get together?

•get up = to arise from bed

  He woke up at 6 o'clock, but he didn't get up until 6:30.

Appendix D

MAKE and *DO*

Some expressions use *make*. Others use *do*.

Make

make an attempt
make a date/an appointment
make a plan
make a decision
make a telephone call
make a reservation
make a meal (breakfast, lunch, dinner)
make a mistake
make an effort
make an improvement
make a promise
make a statement

make a comparison
make a donation
make a discovery
make a reservation
make food (dinner, a salad, a dessert)
make fun of
make noise
make believe
make money
make war
make the bed

Do

do (the) homework
do an exercise
do the dishes
do the cleaning, laundry, ironing,
    washing, etc.
do the shopping
do one's best
do a favor
do the right/wrong thing/
    a foolish thing

do a job
do business
do one's duty
do research
do an experiment
What do you do for a living?
    (asks about a job)
How do you do? (said when you meet
    someone for the first time)

Appendix E

Nouns That Can Be Both Count or Noncount

In the following cases, the same word can be a count or a noncount noun. The meaning is different, however.

Noncount	Count
I spent a lot of *time* on my project.	I go shopping two *times* a month.
I have a lot of *experience* with computers.	I had a lot of interesting *experiences* on my trip to Europe.

In the following cases, there is a small difference in meaning. We see a noncount noun as a whole unit. We see a count noun as something that can be divided into parts:

Noncount	Count
There is a lot of *crime* in a big city.	A lot of *crimes* are never solved.
There is a lot of *opportunity* to make money in the U.S.	There are a lot of job *opportunities* in my field.
She bought a lot of *fruit.*	Oranges and lemons are *fruits* that have a lot of Vitamin C.
I don't have much *food* in my refrigerator.	Milk and butter are *foods* that contain cholesterol.
I have a lot of *trouble* with my car.	He has many *troubles* in his life.

Appendix F

Prepositions

adjust to
agree with
apologize to . . . for
approve of
argue about
believe in
blame . . . for
care about
complain about
concentrate on
consist of
deal with
decide on
depend on

disapprove of
dream about/of
feel like
forget about
forgive . . . for
hear about
hear of
insist on
listen to
look at
look for
look forward to
object to
plan on

prevent . . . from
rely on
speak about
succeed in
suspect . . . of
take care of
talk about
thank . . . for
think about
wait for
warn . . . about
worry about

Adjective + Preposition

accustomed to
afraid of
amazed at/by
angry about
angry at
ashamed of
aware of
bored with/by
capable of
concerned about
different from
excited about
famous for

fond of
glad about
good at
grateful to . . . for
guilty of
happy about
incapable of
interested in
lazy about
mad about
mad at
opposed to
proud of

responsible for
sad about
satisfied with
sick of
sorry about
sorry for
sure of
surprised at
tired of
upset about
used to
worried about

*NOTE: The dots indicate that an object is needed: "He accused the boy of taking the money."

Appendix G

Phrasal Verbs[1]

A phrasal verb consists of a verb and one or two prepositions. Generally, the preposition(s) of the phrasal verb changes the meaning of the verb.

• Some phrasal verbs are separable. A noun or an object pronoun can separate the two parts.

   She *put* the meeting *off.* She *put* it *off* until next week.

• Some phrasal verbs are inseparable. Nothing can come between the two parts.

   She *looked into* the problem.

• Some phrasal verbs are intransitive. This means they have no object.

COMPARE:

   She *brought up* her children well. (transitive)
   Her children *grew up* in the U.S. (intransitive)

Separable Phrasal Verbs

1. With separable phrasal verbs, an object noun may come after a phrasal verb or it may separate the two parts.

She threw away *the letter.*	You can *try out* the computer.
She threw *the letter* away.	You can *try* the computer *out.*

2. If the object is a pronoun, the two parts of a phrasal verb *must* be separated.

   A. Why did she *throw away* the letter?
   B. She *threw* it *away* because it wasn't important.
   A. Should I *fill out* this application?
   B. Yes, please *fill* it *out.*

The following is a list of some common separable phrasal verbs.

   bring up (1) = mention a topic or a question
      The student *brought up* a question about the test.
   bring up (2) = raise children
      It is not easy to *bring* children *up.*
   call off = cancel
      She *called off* the meeting, and everyone went home early.
   call up = telephone
      I *called* you *up* yesterday, but I didn't leave a message.
   do over = repeat a job
      Please *do* your homework *over.* It has a lot of mistakes.

---

[1]Phrasal verbs are often called "two-word verbs."

fill out = complete an application form

 I have to *fill out* an application for a job.

fill up = fill to capacity

 He *filled up* his gas tank before he left on his trip.

give away = give something to another person for free

 The dealer says he is going to *give away* one hundred free cars.

give back = return an object

 You have my dictionary. Please *give* it *back* to me.

hand in/turn in = submit an assignment

 The student *handed* his homework *in* late.

hang up = put something on a hanger or hook

 When she got home, she *hung* her coat *up*.

hold up = delay

 The accident *held up* traffic for hours.

leave out = omit

 On your application, answer every question. Don't *leave* any information *out*.

look over = examine, check

 Please *look over* my composition to see if it has mistakes.

look up = search in a list

 I don't know what that word means. I have to *look* it *up* in the dictionary.

make up (1) = invent a story or lie

 Is that a true story, or did you just *make* it *up*?

make up (2) = do work that one has missed

 If you're absent, you have to *make up* the work when you return to school.

pick out = choose

 We *picked out* a lovely sweater for our mother for Mother's Day.

pick up (1) = lift, take off the floor after something has dropped

 You dropped your pen. *Pick* it *up*.

pick up (2) = meet a person

 I'm going to the airport to *pick up* my uncle.

point out = call attention to

 The teacher *pointed out* our mistakes.

put away = save or store

 A. Where are my tennis shoes?

 B. They're in the closet. I *put* them *away*.

put off = postpone

 We *put off* the meeting until next week.

put on = put clothing on the body

 Here's your sweater. *Put* it *on*. It's cold today.

put out = extinguish

 Put out your cigarette before you enter the classroom.

read over = read to check for accuracy

 I *read over* the composition you wrote, but I didn't find any mistakes.

take (or write) down = make a written note of something

 The bookstore hours are on the door. *Take (Write)* them *down*.

take off = remove clothing from the body

 It's hot in here. I'm going to *take off* my sweater.

talk over = discuss

 We have a problem. We have to *talk* it *over* calmly.

throw away (or out) = put in the garbage

 Please *throw away (out)* those old newspapers.

try on = put on clothing to see if it fits
    When you buy new shoes, you should *try* them *on* to see if they fit.
try out = test
    Before I buy a new car, I like to *try* it *out.*
turn down = lower the volume
    The music is too loud. Will you *turn down* the radio, please?
turn up = raise the volume
    I can't hear the radio. Would you *turn* it *up*?
turn off = switch off the electricity
    Turn off the radio. I'm trying to sleep.
turn on = switch on the electricity
    It's getting dark. *Turn on* the light.
use up = use completely
    A. Where's the coffee?
    B. I'm sorry. I *used* it *up* this morning.

Inseparable Phrasal Verbs—Transitive

The following is a list of some common inseparable phrasal verbs.

call on = ask to recite in class
    Did the teacher *call on* you today?
get over = recover from an illness or disappointment
    It took me five days to *get over* my cold.
go over = review
    We usually *go over* a test in class.
go through = use up; consume completely
    She *went through* all her laundry soap in one week.
look after = take care of
    Who *looks after* your kids while you're in class?
look (or check) into = investigate
    I'm *looking (checking) into* scholarships at American universities.
look like (or take after) = resemble
    Do you *look like* your mother or father?
    I *take after* my father more.
run (or come) across = find by chance (usually things)
    If you *run (come) across* any new words, use your dictionary.
run into = meet by chance (usually people)
    I *ran into* your brother at the library.
wait on = serve
    Some waitresses are very pleasant when they *wait on* you.

Three-Word Phrasal Verbs—Transitive

The following is a list of some common inseparable phrasal verbs that have three parts.
drop out of = leave a school or course without finishing it
    A few students *dropped out of* this course after a few weeks.
get along with = have a good relationship with
    Do you *get along with* your mother-in-law?
get rid of = remove something that is no longer needed
    I want to *get rid of* some of my old clothes. Do you know anyone who wants them?
get through with = finish
    When you *get through with* that novel, can I borrow it?

keep up with = maintain the same pace or level
> You run too fast for me. I can't *keep up with* you.

look forward to = anticipate with pleasure
> She *looks forward to* her brother's arrival.

look (or watch) out for = be careful
> *Look (watch) out for* that car!

make sure of = verify
> I use my dictionary to *make sure of* my spelling.

run out of = exhaust (finish) one's supply
> She *ran out of* sugar when she baked a cake.

take care of = be responsible for
> He has to *take care of* his sick father.

talk back to = answer impolitely
> Some children *talk back to* their teachers.

think (or look) back on = remember
> I often *think (look) back on* my high school years.

Phrasal Verbs—Intransitive

The following is a list of inseparable phrasal verbs. They are intransitive, so are not followed by an object.

come back = return to this place
> After you take a break, please *come back* to class.

come in = enter a house or room
> When you *come in,* close the door behind you.

come over = visit at one's home
> My friends *came over* last Saturday.

drop by = visit without an appointment
> If you're in my neighborhood, *drop by* and say hello.

get up = arise
> What time do you *get up* in the morning?

go back = return to that place
> Will you ever *go back* to your country?

go on (1) = continue to the next
> When you finish this page, *go on* to the next page.

go on (2) = happen
> What's *going on* in the next apartment?

grow up = become an adult
> When she *grows up,* she wants to be an engineer.

keep (or stay) away = remain at a distance
> You should *keep (stay) away* from the dog. It looks angry.

keep on (followed by a gerund) = continue with the same
> It's hard to find a job, but you must *keep on* trying.

pass away = die
> Her grandmother *passed away* last month.

show off = act like you are better than others by displaying what you have
> When he bought a new car, he drove to my house just to *show off.*

show up = arrive
> It snowed hard and no one *showed up* at the meeting.

wake up = come out of sleep
> I *woke up* when the alarm clock rang.

Appendix H

Direct and Indirect Objects

1. The order of direct and indirect objects depends on the verb you use.

        IO   DO
   He told his friend the answer.
         DO   IO
   He explained the answer to his friend.

2. The order of the objects sometimes depends on whether you use a noun or a pronoun object.

     S V IO   DO
   He gave the woman the keys.
     S V DO IO
   He gave them to her.

3. In some cases, the connecting preposition is *to;* in some cases *for.* In some cases, there is no connecting preposition.

     She'll serve lunch *to* her guests.
     She reserved a seat *for* you.
     I asked him a question.

Each of the following groups of words follows a specific pattern of word order and preposition choice.

Group I (Pronouns affect word order.)

Patterns: He gave a present to his wife.
     He gave his wife a present.
     He gave it to his wife.
     He gave her a present.
     He gave it to her.

Verbs:

bring	lend	pass	sell	show	teach
give	offer	pay	send	sing	tell
hand	owed	read	serve	take	write

Group II (Pronouns affect word order.)

Patterns: He bought a car for his daughter.
He bought his daughter a car.
He bought it for his daughter.
He bought her a car.
He bought it for her.

Verbs:

bake	buy	draw	get	make
build	do	find	knit	reserve

Group III (Pronouns don't affect word order.)

Patterns: He explained the problem to his friend.
He explained it to her.

Verbs:

admit	introduce	recommend	say
announce	mention	repeat	speak
describe	prove	report	suggest
explain			

Group IV (Pronouns don't affect word order.)

Patterns: He cashed a check for his friend.
He cashed it for her.

Verbs:

answer	change	design	open	prescribe
cash	close	fix	prepare	pronounce

Group V (Pronouns don't affect word order.)

Patterns: She asked the teacher a question.
She asked him a question.
It took me five minutes to answer the question.

Verbs:

ask	charge	cost	wish	take (with time)

Appendix I

Alphabetical List of Irregular Past Forms

Base Form	Past Form	Past Participle	Base Form	Past Form	Past Participle
be	was/were	been	drive	drove	driven
bear	bore	born/borne	eat	ate	eaten
beat	beat	beaten	fall	fell	fallen
become	became	become	feed	fed	fed
begin	began	begun	feel	felt	felt
bend	bent	bent	fight	fought	fought
bet	bet	bet	find	found	found
bind	bound	bound	fit	fit	fit
bite	bit	bitten	flee	fled	fled
bleed	bled	bled	fly	flew	flown
blow	blew	blown	forbid	forbade	forbidden
break	broke	broken	forget	forgot	forgotten
breed	bred	bred	forgive	forgave	forgiven
bring	brought	brought	freeze	froze	frozen
broadcast	broadcast	broadcast	get	got	gotten
build	built	built	give	gave	given
burst	burst	burst	go	went	gone
buy	bought	bought	grind	ground	ground
cast	cast	cast	grow	grew	grown
catch	caught	caught	hang	hung	hung[1]
choose	chose	chosen	have	had	had
cling	clung	clung	hear	heard	heard
come	came	come	hide	hid	hidden
cost	cost	cost	hit	hit	hit
creep	crept	crept	hold	held	held
cut	cut	cut	hurt	hurt	hurt
deal	dealt	dealt	keep	kept	kept
dig	dug	dug	know	knew	known
do	did	done	lay	laid	laid
draw	drew	drawn	lead	led	led
drink	drank	drunk			

---

[1]*Hanged* is used as the past form to refer to punishment by death.

Base Form	Past Form	Past Participle	Base Form	Past Form	Past Participle
leave	left	left	split	split	split
lend	loaned/lent	loaned/lent	spread	spread	spread
let	let	let	spring	sprang	sprung
lie	lay	lain	stand	stood	stood
light	lit/lighted	lit/lighted	steal	stole	stolen
lose	lost	lost	stick	stuck	stuck
make	made	made	sting	stung	stung
mean	meant	meant	stink	stank	stunk
meet	met	met	strike	struck	struck/stricken
mistake	mistook	mistaken	strive	strove	striven
pay	paid	paid	swear	swore	sworn
prove	proved	proven/proved	sweep	swept	swept
put	put	put	swim	swam	swum
quit	quit	quit	swing	swung	swung
read	read	read	take	took	taken
ride	rode	ridden	teach	taught	taught
ring	rang	rung	tear	tore	torn
rise	rose	risen	tell	told	told
run	ran	run	think	thought	thought
say	said	said	throw	threw	thrown
see	saw	seen	understand	understood	understood
seek	sought	sought	upset	upset	upset
sell	sold	sold	wake	woke	woken
send	sent	sent	wear	wore	worn
set	set	set	weave	wove	woven
shake	shook	shaken	weep	wept	wept
shed	shed	shed	win	won	won
shine	shone	shone	wind	wound	wound
shoot	shot	shot	withdraw	withdrew	withdrawn
show	showed	shown/showed	wring	wrung	wrung
shrink	shrank	shrunk	write	wrote	written
shut	shut	shut			
sing	sang	sung			
sink	sank	sunk			
sit	sat	sat			
sleep	slept	slept			
slide	slid	slid			
slit	slit	slit			
speak	spoke	spoken			
speed	sped	sped			
spend	spent	spent			
spin	spun	spun			
spit	spit	spit			

The past and past participle of some verbs can end in *-ed* or *-t*. Americans generally prefer the *-ed* form:

burn	burned or burnt
dream	dreamed or dreamt
kneel	kneeled or knelt
learn	learned or learnt
spill	spilled or spilt
spoil	spoiled or spoilt

INDEX

A/an, 126
  as indefinite article, 290, 307
  as quantity word, 115–16
Ability/possibility, 167, 186, 347
Abstractions as noncount nouns, 111
Adjective(s), 233, 234–36, 255, 257
  adverbs vs., 239–40
  in *as...as* comparison, 272–73
  comparative, 262, 263–64, 268–70, 346
  followed by infinitive, 158, 163–66
  with *-ly* ending, 237
  past participles as, 169 *n*
  possessive, 81, 100
  simple form, 262
  superlative form, 262, 263–68, 346
  with *too/enough,* 241–42
Adjective clause, 233, 244–53, 257, 265
  with *ever,* 265
  relative pronoun in, 245–49
  as object, 248–49
  as subject, 245–47
  whose + noun as subject or object of,
    250–53, 257
Adverb(s), 233, 255, 257
  adjectives vs., 239–40
  in *as...as* comparison, 272–73
  comparative, 262, 263–64, 268–70, 346
  of manner, 237–40
  simple form, 262
  superlative form, 262, 263–68, 346
  with *too/enough,* 241–42
Adverbial clause, 337
Adverbial phrase, gerund in, 223–24, 228
Advice, 174–75, 176, 186, 347
Affirmative statements
  already in, 207, 209
  have to vs. *must* in, 172
  with present continuous tense, 41
  with present perfect tense, 193

  quantity words in, 115, 117
  with simple past tense, 61
  with simple present tense, 10–12, 13, 41
  with *used to,* 69
  using modals, 166
  using past form of be, 60
After as time word, 140, 149
  with time clause, 144–45
Ago, 149
Alike, 279
All/all of the, 201*n*, 297, 298
 (All) by -self, 96
Almost, 306
A lot of, 117, 123–24, 127
Already
  in affirmative statements, 207, 209
  with present perfect tense, 207
Always
  as frequency word, 18
  with present perfect tense, 198–99
Am, contractions with, 3
Another, 301–5, 306, 307
Any
  as indefinite pronoun, 299–301
  with *other,* 303
  as quantity word, 115–16, 291, 294
Are, contractions with, 3
Articles
  definite, 291–93, 307
  general and specific nouns indicated by,
    289, 294–98, 307
  indefinite, 290, 307
As...as, comparisons with, 272–73
As many/much as, 274–75
As soon as possible (A.S.A.P.), 273
As usual, 239
Auxiliary verbs
  contractions with subject pronouns and,
    194

following *than* and pronoun, 269
have, 191, 193
in *wh-* questions, 88, 332

Base form, 8, 25
    after *did,* 325
    -ed added to, for simple past tense, 60–61
    in infinitive, 159, 185
    after modal, 166, 185
    in negative sentences, 10
    after *used to,* 58, 69–71, 224, 225, 228
    after *will* or *be going to,* 44
Be, 327–28
    adjective after, 234
    + adjective + infinitive, 165–66
    continuous meaning of, 135
    contractions with, 3, 4, 5, 6
    in future sentence, 318
    negative statements with, 5
    past forms of, 59–60, 73, 327
    past continuous, 133–39
    present continuous tense with, 32
    questions with, 5–8, 331
    in sentence of classification or definition,
        290
    short answers with, 5–8
    simple present tense with, 3–5, 25, 327
    superlatives with, 265
    there + form of, 4, 113–14, 127
Be able to
    for ability/possibility, 347
    after modal, 167, 186
Be allowed to, 169–70, 347
Before as time word, 140, 149
    with time clause, 144–45
Be going to, 51, 138
    future tense with, 44–49, 317, 318
Be like, 279, 280, 284
Be permitted to, 169–70, 347
Better/worse, 255
Be used to vs. *used to,* 224–25, 228
By as time word, 140, 149

Can as modal, 166
    for ability/possibility, 167, 186, 347
    for permission, 169–70, 180, 181, 186
    for request, 180, 181, 186
Can't help, 217
Categories as noncount nouns, 111
Cause and result, comparatives to show, 269
Classes as noncount nouns, 111
Classification, indefinite article for, 290, 307
Clause(s)
    if, 47–49, 146–47, 316
    adjective, 233, 244–53, 257, 265
    adverbial, 337
    defined, 233n
    time, 47–49, 132, 134–37, 142–47, 153, 316
Comma
    after adverbial clause preceding subject,
        337
    after time clause preceding main clause,
        135
Comparisons, 262, 263–64, 268–82, 284
    with *as...as,* 272–73
    comparative adjectives and adverbs, 262,
        263–64, 268–70, 346
    comparative and superlative forms, 262,
        263–64, 284, 285, 346
    with nouns, 270–72
    of quantities, 274–76
    with *same/different,* 278
    showing similarity, 279–80
    than in, 267–71
    using *the same...as,* 277–78
Complaint, letter of, 314
Contractions
    with auxiliary verb and subject pronouns,
        194
    with forms of *be,* 3, 4, 5, 6
    negative, 5, 167
    with question words, 6
    with *will,* 45
Could as modal, 166
    for ability/possibility, 347
    for permission, 180, 181, 186
    for request, 180, 181, 186
Count nouns, 105, 106–11, 127
    articles with, 294, 295, 307
    nouns that can be both noncount and,
        351
    quantity words used with, 114, 117

Definite articles, 291-93, 307
Definite nouns, 289, 291-93
  with *the other,* 301, 307
Definite pronouns, 289, 299
Definition, indefinite article for, 290, 307
Desire, expressing, 180
Did. See Do/does/did
Different/same, 278
Direct objects, 82-83, 357-58
  reflexive pronouns as, 96
Do/does/did
  in answer to subject question, 88, 89
  base form after did, 325
  did in simple past tense, 61, 63
  do, expressions with, 350
  do/does in questions with simple present
    tense, 13
  do used for emphasis, 218n
  in *wh-* questions, 88, 332-33
Double negative, 126
During as time word, 140, 149

Enough, 241-42, 255, 257
Equality, comparing, 277, 278
Ever
  adjective clause with, 265
  questions with, 21-22, 204-7
Every, singular form following, 108,
  126
Everybody/everyone/everything, 9

Farther/further, 263
Few/a few/very few, 118-20, 126
  a few of the, 297
Fewer, 255
Fond of, 221
For, 201n
  object pronoun after, 185
  since vs., 196, 197, 200
  as time word, 140, 149, 209
Frequency expressions, 22-23
Frequency words, 2, 18-21, 25
Frequently/often, 18
Further/farther, 263
Future tense, 31, 44-49, 52, 317-20
  + time/if clause, 47-49, 146-47, 316

Generalizations, 108
  articles used with, 294-98, 307
  plural form with no article for, 108
Generally/usually, 18
Gerunds, 215-25
  in adverbial phrase, 223-24, 228
  after *be used to/get used to,* 224, 225, 228
  describing noun, 235
  after preposition, 220-22, 228
  as subject, 216-17, 228
  after verb, 217-20, 228
Get, 348-49
  adjective following, 235, 239
Get used to, 225, 228
Go + gerund, 217, 219, 228
Going/going to go, 45
Good/well, 237, 239

Habitual past, 58, 69-71, 73
Had better, for advice, 174-75
Had to, 172, 347
Hard/hardly, 237, 255
Hardly ever/rarely/seldom, 18
Has
  contractions with, 194
Have got to, 171, 186, 347
Have/has
  contractions with *has,* 194
  have as action vs. nonaction verb, 39
  have as auxiliary verb, 191, 193
  in present perfect continuous tense,
    199-201
  in present perfect tense, 193-99, 325
Have to
  compared to modal, 167
  not have to vs. *must not,* 172-73
  for obligation/necessity, 171, 186, 347
His/her, 81
How many/much, 88, 202, 203
How often, questions with, 22-23

Idiomatic expressions
  go + gerund in, 217, 219
  reflexive pronouns in, 96
If clause, 47-49, 146-47, 316
Imperative sentence, 338n

In as time word, 140, 149

Indefinite articles, 290, 307

Indefinite nouns, 289, 291-93

   with *another/other,* 303, 307

Indefinite pronouns, 289, 297, 298-301

Indirect objects, 82-83, 357-58

   reflexive pronouns as, 96

Infinitives, 158, 159-66, 185, 186, 329-31

   with *it* + adjective, 163-65

   object before, 161-63

   after *too/enough,* 241-42

   verbs followed by, 158, 159-61, 217, 219-20

-ing form

   for gerunds, 215-25

   in past continuous tense, 133-39

   in present continuous tense, 32-38

   in present perfect continuous tense,

     199-201

   spelling of, 344

Intransitive phrasal verbs, 356

Irregular adjectives and adverbs, comparative

     and superlative forms of, 263

Irregular plural nouns, 107

Irregular verbs, 61-69, 73, 359-60

Is, contractions with, 3, 4, 194

Its/it's, 81

It with infinitives, 163-65, 185

Just, 282*n*

   with present perfect tense, 207

Kind of, 235

Late/lately, 237

Less/more, 255

Letter of complaint, 314

Like, comparisons with, 279, 280, 285

Linking verbs, 272*n*

Little/a little/very little, 118-20, 126

   before comparative form, 269

   a little of the, 297

Look forward to, 221

Look like, 284

Lots of, 117

Make, expressions with, 350

Manner, adverbs of, 237-40

Many, 117, 297

Many of the, 297

May as modal, 166

   for permission, 180, 181, 186, 347

   for possibility, 175-76, 186

Maybe, 175

Measure, units of, 112, 126. See also Quantity

   words

Might as modal, 166

   for possibility, 175-76, 186, 347

Mind, 217, 218

Modals, 158, 166-83, 329-31, 347

   base form after, 166, 185

   negatives of, 167, 176-79

   for politeness, 180-83

More/-er, 263, 284

More/less, 255

Most/-est, 263, 264-68

Most/most of the, 297, 306

Much, 117

   before comparative form, 269

Must as modal, 166

   for obligation/necessity, 171, 186, 347

Must not vs. *not have to,* 172-73

Necessity/obligation, 171, 186, 347

Negative, double, 126

Negative contractions, 5, 167

Negative question, 181

Negatives of modals, 167, 176-79

Negative statements

   with *be,* 5

   past form, 60

   must not vs. *not have to* in, 172-73

   with present continuous tense, 41

   with present perfect tense, 193

   quantity words in, 115, 117

   with simple past tense, 61

   with simple present tense, 10-12, 41

   with *use to,* 69

   using modals, 166

   yet in, 209

Never/not ever, 18

   with present perfect tense, 198-99

No as quantity word, 115-16

Nonaction verbs, 38-40, 200, 316

Noncount nouns, 105, 111-13, 126, 127

articles with, 294, 295, 307
nouns that can be both count and, 351
quantity words used with, 114, 117
None of the, 297, 298
No one/nobody/nothing, 9
Not ever, 18
Not have to vs. *must not,* 172-73
Not in front of gerund, 216
Noun(s)
  comparisons with, 270-72
  count, 114, 117, 127, 294, 295, 307, 351
  definite, 289, 291-93, 301, 307
  general vs. specific, articles indicating,
    294-98, 307
  gerunds as. *See* Gerunds
  indefinite, 289, 291-93, 303, 307
  noncount, 105, 111-13, 114, 117, 126, 127,
    294, 295, 307, 351
  plural, 105, 106-11
  possessive, 80-81, 100
  reflexive pronouns to emphasize, 96
  singular, 105, 106-11
Noun modifiers, 234, 235-36, 255, 257
Numbers, singular and plural form, 107

Object(s), 78
  direct, 82-83, 96, 357-58
  indirect, 82-83, 96, 357-58
  before infinitive, 161-63
  of preposition, gerund as, 220-22
  reflexive pronouns for, 95-97
  relative pronouns as, 248-49
  whose + noun as, 250-53, 257
Object pronouns, 79-80, 100, 185
Obligation/necessity, 171, 186, 347
Occasionally/sometimes, 18
Often/frequently, 18
One(s), 235
  after adjective to replace noun, 255
  as indefinite pronoun, 299-301
One of, plural form after, 126
Other, 301-5, 307

Participles. *See* Past participle; Present participle
Past continuous tense, 132, 133-40, 153,
  320-22
  with simple past tense, 134-39
  with time clauses, 142-46
Past participle, 191-92
  as adjective, 169*n*
  of irregular verbs, 359-60
  in present perfect tense, 193-99
Past tense. *See* Simple past tense
Past time
  indefinite, present perfect for, 204-7
  with simple past tense, 202
Permission, 169-70, 176, 186, 347
  asking, 180, 181, 186
Phrasal verbs, 353-56
  inseparable, 355
  intransitive, 356
  separable, 353-55
  three-word, 355-56
  transitive, 355-56
Plenty of, 117n
Plural nouns, 105, 106-11
Politeness, modals for, 180-83
Possessive forms, 78
  describing noun, 235
  possessive adjectives, 81, 100
  possessive nouns, 80-81, 100
  possessive pronoun, 85-87, 100
  whose, 84, 89, 250-53, 257
Possibility, 167, 175-76, 186, 347
Preference, 180, 182, 186
Preposition(s), 352
  gerund after, 220-22, 228
  in adverbial phrase, 223-24
  object pronoun following, 79
  before question word, 5
  wh- questions with, 15-18
Prepositional phrase after superlative form,
  265
Present continuous tense, 31, 32-38, 41, 52,
  315-17, 318
  with future meaning, 46, 318
  questions with, 41-44
  simple present in contrast to, 36-38
Present participle, 148-49
Present perfect continuous tense, 190,
  199-201, 323-27
  present perfect tense in contrast to, 210
Present perfect tense, 190, 193-99, 323-27

for indefinite past time, 204-7
present perfect continuous tense in contrast to, 210
with repetition up to the present, 202-3
to show continuation from past to present, 195-99
simple past tense in contrast to, 210
simple present tense in contrast to, 196
Present tense. *See* Simple present tense
Pretty, 235
Prohibition, 172-73, 176
Pronoun(s), 78
   definite, 289, 299
   following *than,* 269
   indefinite, 289, 297, 298-301
   object, 79-80, 100, 185
   possessive, 85-87, 100
   reflexive, 78, 95-97, 100
   relative, 244, 245-49
   subject, 79-80, 100, 194
Pronunciation
   of *going to,* 45
   of *to* in infinitives, 160
   of *used to,* 69
   of verb forms, 343-46

Quantities, 114-24
   comparing, 274-76
Quantity words, 105, 291, 294, 306
Question(s)
   with *be,* 5-8, 331
   with *ever,* 21-22, 204-7
   with frequency words, 25
   how many/much, 88, 202, 203
   with *how often,* 22-23
   negative, 181
   with present continuous tense, 41-44
   with present perfect tense, 193, 204-7
   quantity words in, 115, 117
   review of, 331-34
   with simple past tense, 61
   with simple present tense, 13-14, 41-44
   about subject, 88-95, 100
   with *there,* 113
   with two clauses, 135
   with *use to,* 69

using modals, 166
wh-, 15-18, 41-44, 88, 331-33
with *whose,* 84, 89
yes/no, 21-22, 202, 203
Quite before adjective, 235

Rarely/seldom/hardly ever, 18
Real, 235
Really, 237n
Reflexive pronoun, 78, 95-97, 100
Regular verbs, simple past tense of, 60-61, 73
   spelling of, 345
Relative clause. *See* Adjective clause
Relative pronouns
   to introduce adjective clauses, 244
   as object, 248-49
   as subject, 245-47
Request, polite, 180, 181, 186

Same/different, 278
Say/tell, 82-83, 100
Seldom/rarely/hardly ever, 18
Sense perception verbs, 39
   adjective after, 234
Several, 118
-*s* form of simple present tense, 8, 9, 25
   pronunciation of, 343-44
   spelling of, 343
Short answers
   with *be,* 5-8
   past form, 60
   with present perfect tense, 193
   with simple present tense, 13
   using modals, 166
Should as modal, 166
   for advice, 174-75, 186, 347
Similarity, 279-80
Simple past tense, 58, 73, 209, 320-22, 325
   of irregular verbs, 61-69, 73
   with past continuous tense, 134-39
   past time expression with, 202
   present perfect tense in contrast to, 210
   of regular verbs, 60-61, 73
   with time clauses, 142-46
Simple present tense, 2-18, 52, 315-17, 318.
   See also Be

affirmative and negative statements with,
    10–12, 13, 41
forms of, 8–10, 25
nonaction verbs used in, 38–40
present continuous tense in contrast to,
    36–38
present perfect tense in contrast to, 196
questions with, 13–14, 41–44
in time clause or *if* clause, 146
Since
    for vs., 196, 197, 200
    simple past tense with, 209
Singular nouns, 105, 106–11
So far/up to now, 202, 203
Some
    as indefinite pronoun, 299–301
    with *other,* 303
    as quantity word, 115–16, 291, 294, 297
Sometimes/occasionally, 18
Sort of, 235
Spelling of verb forms
    -ing *form,* 344
    past tense of regular verbs, 345
    -s *form,* 343
Subject(s), 78
    gerund as, 216–17, 228
    questions about, 88–95, 100
    relative pronouns as, 245–47
    whose + *noun as,* 250–53, 257
Subject pronouns, 79–80, 100
    contractions with auxiliary verbs and,
        194
Subjects of study as noncount nouns, 112
Suggestion, polite, 180
Superlatives, 262, 263–68, 284, 285
    spelling of, 346
    using, 264–68

Tell/say, 82–83, 100
Tense(s)
    future, 31, 44–49, 52, 317–20
    past continuous, 132, 133–40, 153,
        320–22
    present continuous, 31, 32–38, 41–44, 46,
        52, 315–17, 318
    present perfect, 190, 193–99, 202–7, 210,
        323–27
    present perfect continuous, 190, 199–201,
        210, 323–27
    simple past, 58, 60–69, 73, 134–39,
        142–46, 202, 209, 210, 320–22, 325
    simple present, 2–18, 52, 315–17, 318
Than *in comparisons,* 267–71
That *in adjective clause,* 244, 245, 246
The
    as definite article, 291–93, 307
    after quantity word, 306
    before superlative, 264–68, 284
Their/they're, *81*
The other, *301, 307*
There
    + *form of be,* 4, 113–14, 127
    to introduce count and noncount nouns,
        105
    to introduce indefinite noun, 291
    in present vs. future tense, 45
    questions with, 113
The same...as, *comparisons using,* 277–78
They're/their, *81*
Think *as action vs. nonaction verb,* 39
Three-word phrasal verbs, 355–56
Time, questions about, 15
Time clause, 132, 134–37, 142–47, 153, 316
    future tense with, 47–49, 146–47
    simple past or past continuous with,
        142–46
Time words, 140–42, 149, 209
    present participle after, 148–49
To
    for infinitives, 158, 159
    as preposition, 221
Too, *123–24, 127, 241–42, 255, 257*
    very *vs.,* 243
Too many/too much, *123–24, 127, 255*
Transitive phrasal verbs, 355–56
Two-word verbs. See *Phrasal verbs*

Units of measure
    of *with,* 126. See also*Quantity words*
    to count noncount nouns, 112
Until *as time word,* 140–42
    with time clause, 142–46

Up to now/so far, *202, 203*
Used to, *58, 68-71, 73*
    be used to *vs., 224-25, 228*
Usually/generally, *18*

Verbs
    auxiliary, 88, 191, 193, 194, 269, 332
    followed by infinitive, 158, 159-61, 217,
        219-20
    gerund after, 217-20, 228
    -ing forms of, 32-38, 133-39, 199-201,
        344
    irregular, 61-69, 73, 359-60
    linking, 272n
    modal, 158, 166-83, 185, 329-31, 347
    nonaction, 38-40, 200, 316
    phrasal, 353-56
    regular, 60-61, 73, 345
    sense perception, 39, 234
    singular, with gerund subject, 216
    spelling and pronunciation of, 343-46
Verb tenses. See *Tense(s)*
Very, *255, 257*
    before adjective or adverb, 235, 237
    too *vs., 243*
Very few, *119-20*
Very little, *119-20*

Want, expressing, 180, 186
Warning, 176, 186
Well/good, *237, 239*
What happens/what happened, *89*
What kind, *questions using, 89*
When
    to indicate frequency, 23
    with past continuous tense, 321
    with time clause, 134, 142-46
    as time word, 140-42
Whenever, *23, 140, 144*
Which
    in adjective clause, 244, 246
    questions using, 89
While
    connecting two past actions, 142
    with past continuous tense, 321
    with time clause, 134, 142-46

    as time word, 140-42
Who *in adjective clause, 244, 245*
Whose
    + noun as subject or object of adjective
        clause, 250-53, 257
    questions with, 84, 89
    who's *vs., 84, 250*
Who/whom, *248, 252-53*
    questions using, 88
Wh- *questions, 331-33*
    with preposition, 15-18
    with present continuous tense, 41-44
    with simple present tense, 41-44
    about subject, 88
Why *for suggestion, 180*
Will
    future tense with, 44-49, 317, 318
    as modal, 166
    for request, 180, 181, 186
Word order
    for adverbs, 209
    in comparisons, 284
    with direct and indirect objects, 357-58
    of questions using preposition, 15
    in sentences, 313, 337-39
Worse/better, *255*
Would *as modal, 166*
    for request, 180, 181, 186
Would like, *180, 181, 186*
Would rather, *180, 182, 186*

Yes/no *questions*
    ever *in, 21-22*
    with present perfect, 202, 203
Yet, *209*
    with present perfect tense, 207
Your/you're, *81*

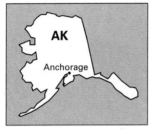

The United States of America

AL	Alabama	IN	Indiana	NE	Nebraska	SC	South Carolina
AK	Alaska	IA	Iowa	NV	Nevada	SD	South Dakota
AZ	Arizona	KS	Kansas	NH	New Hampshire	TN	Tennessee
AR	Arkansas	KY	Kentucky	NJ	New Jersey	TX	Texas
CA	California	LA	Louisiana	NM	New Mexico	UT	Utah
CO	Colorado	ME	Maine	NY	New York	VT	Vermont
CT	Connecticut	MD	Maryland	NC	North Carolina	VA	Virginia
DE	Delaware	MA	Massachusetts	ND	North Dakota	WA	Washington
FL	Florida	MI	Michigan	OH	Ohio	WV	West Virginia
GA	Georgia	MN	Minnesota	OK	Oklahoma	WI	Wisconsin
HI	Hawaii	MS	Mississippi	OR	Oregon	WY	Wyoming
ID	Idaho	MO	Missouri	PA	Pennsylvania	DC*	District of Columbia
IL	Illinois	MT	Montana	RI	Rhode Island		

*The District of Columbia is not a state. Washington D.C. is the capitol of the United States. Note: Washington D.C. and Washington state are not the same.

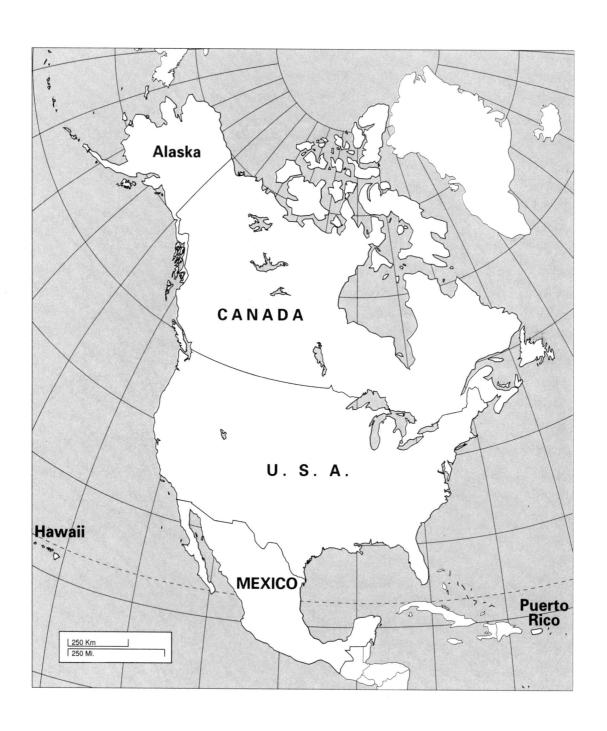

Alaska

CANADA

U. S. A.

Hawaii

MEXICO

Puerto
Rico

250 Km
250 Mi.